FEDERAL INCOME TAX

A STUDENT'S GUIDE
TO THE
INTERNAL REVENUE CODE

FIFTH EDITION

By

DOUGLAS A. KAHN
Paul G. Kauper Professor of Law
University of Michigan

JEFFREY H. KAHN
Associate Professor of Law
Santa Clara University

FOUNDATION PRESS

NEW YORK, NEW YORK

2005

THOMSON
—————*—————TM
WEST

© 1990, 1992, 1994, FOUNDATION PRESS
© 1999 DOUGLAS A. KAHN
© 2005 By FOUNDATION PRESS
        395 Hudson Street
        New York, NY 10014
        Phone Toll Free 1–877–888–1330
        Fax (212) 367–6799
        fdpress.com

Printed in the United States of America

ISBN 1–58778–887–X

TEXT IS PRINTED ON 10% POST CONSUMER RECYCLED PAPER

To Gladys

"Age cannot wither her, nor custom stale her infinite variety."
—William Shakespeare, *Anthony and Cleopatra*

*

PREFACE

Although this edition adds a co-author with a familiar last name, the goals and basic structure of the book have not changed from previous editions. This book was written to meet the needs of the tax student who wishes to have a text to supplement the casebook or problem sets that are utilized in the student's course. It is designed to serve two functions.

One function is to provide an overview of the federal income tax laws so that the reader has a blueprint of the structure of the federal income tax system and accordingly is better able to see the role that specific provisions play in that scheme. To determine the meaning and scope of a specific statutory provision, it is useful to examine the provision in the context of the role that it plays in the overarching tax scheme. The authors believe that his book will be helpful to the reader's determination of how specific Code provisions fit within the Code's structure and will be a valuable aid to interpretation.

Another major function of the book is to set forth concise, lucid explanations of the major principles of income taxation and important specific income tax statutory provisions. If a text were written that discussed in detail all (or most) of the current income tax Code provisions, it would consist of a great many volumes. This single volume does not provide that type of coverage. Instead, the book focuses on the major principles of income taxation and examines these statutory provisions that the authors selected as of importance to tax students. Many of the statutory provisions that are included in this text are examined in detail. Others are described briefly, and the text merely explains the general manner in which they operate. In some instances, the authors have examined and critiqued the likely policy justifications for a statutory provision or for a common law tax doctrine.

Examples or illustrations of statutory provisions are provided throughout the book in order to help the reader understand how they apply in various factual contexts. The extensive use of factual illustrations is a key feature of this book.

The authors wish to give special thanks to Christina Johnson, an administrative assistant at Santa Clara University School of Law, and Diane Liang, a third year student at Santa Clara University School of Law, for their help in preparing the publication of this book.

This book is up to date as of April 1, 2005.

DOUGLAS A. KAHN
Paul G. Kauper Professor of Law
University of Michigan Law School

JEFFREY H. KAHN
Associate Professor of Law
Santa Clara University School of Law

April 20, 2005

*

TABLE OF CONTENTS

*

FEDERAL INCOME TAX

A STUDENT'S GUIDE
TO THE
INTERNAL REVENUE CODE

*

CHAPTER ONE

INTRODUCTION

§ **1.0000.** **HISTORY.** The federal income tax was first adopted in the United States during the Civil War to meet the need for additional revenue. Both the North and the South adopted an income tax. The North's income tax was repealed shortly after the war, and the government of the South was dissolved.

In 1894, a federal income tax was again adopted by Congress. This tax was at a flat rate of two percent, but individual taxpayers (as contrasted to corporations) were granted a $4,000 exemption (in 2003, the current value of that amount was approximately $85,000). The validity of the tax was attacked on several grounds, including the assertion that an income tax is a direct tax and that the 1894 Act violated Article I, Section 9, Clause 4 of the Constitution since this "direct tax" was not apportioned among the states in proportion to population. The meaning and scope of the reference in the Constitution to a "direct tax" remain uncertain.

In the first decision in *Pollock v. Farmers' Loan & Trust Co.*, 157 U.S. 429 (1895), the Supreme Court held six to two that a tax on rental income from realty was invalid as a direct tax that was not properly apportioned among the states. The Court also held, for a different reason, that a tax on municipal bond interest was unconstitutional. This latter holding was expressly overruled by the Court in *State of South Carolina v. Baker*, 485 U.S. 505 (1988). Because the first opinion in *Pollock* left many vital questions unanswered, the parties sought and were granted a rehearing. In the second *Pollock* opinion [158 U.S. 601 (1895)], the Court held five to four that a tax on income from realty or personalty was invalid as a direct tax. The Court further held that taxes on such income were integral elements of the revenue act which could not be separated from the other parts of the act and so the entire act was struck down.

In 1909, Congress adopted an income tax on the income of corporations. This tax was held to be valid by the Supreme Court in *Flint v. Stone Tracy Co.*, 220 U.S. 107 (1911) on the ground that it was a tax on the privilege of doing business and not a direct tax that had to be apportioned by state population.

At the same time that Congress passed the 1909 corporate tax, it proposed a constitutional amendment which was ratified by the states on February 25, 1913 as the Sixteenth Amendment. That amendment provides:

> The Congress shall have power to lay and collect taxes on incomes from whatever source derived, without apportionment among the several states, and without regard to any census or enumeration.

Since ratification of the Sixteenth Amendment, courts have sustained the federal income tax laws against most constitutionally-based objections.

The United States tax laws are administered by the Internal Revenue Service (sometimes referred to herein as the "Service"), which is part of the Treasury Department and is headed by the Commissioner of Internal Revenue (referred to as the "Commissioner").

REVENUE ACTS

Shortly after the ratification of the Sixteenth Amendment, Congress passed the Revenue Act of 1913, which constituted an integrated federal income tax law. The 1913 Act imposed a normal tax of one percent (subject to certain exemptions) and a surtax of one percent to six percent on net income over $20,000, depending on the amount of the taxpayer's net income. By its terms, the 1913 Act was effective for only a number of years after which it would lapse unless extended or unless a new revenue act was adopted. From 1913 to 1939, Congress passed revenue acts every two to three years, and each of those acts constituted a complete body of federal income tax law. The enactment of a new body of tax laws every few years proved to be inefficient, especially since many of the provisions of the expired acts were readopted in the new acts. In 1939, Congress codified the then existing tax laws as the Internal Revenue Code of 1939.

INTERNAL REVENUE CODE

With the adoption of the 1939 Code, a tax law remains in effect until repealed or amended. Amendments, additions, or deletions to provisions of the Code are made by Congressional action; typically, Congress will amend a number of provisions within a single act rather than separately pass numerous acts changing individual sections of the Code. The acts amending provisions of the Code carry a variety of titles. Many are called "Revenue Acts" such as the Revenue Act of 1948 and the Revenue Act of 1978. Thus, a citation to a "Revenue Act" dated before 1939 refers to the entire body of federal tax law for that time; however, a "Revenue Act" subsequent to 1939 constitutes only a number of amendments to the Code. Examples of other names given to acts amending the Code are "Technical Amendments Act," "Tax Reduction and Simplification Act," "Taxpayer Relief Act," and "Jobs and Growth Tax Relief Reconciliation Act." The title "Tax Reform Act" is especially popular because it clearly designates the statutory changes as desirable; it is difficult to oppose a change labeled a "reform."

In 1954, Congress repealed the 1939 Code and adopted the Internal Revenue Code of 1954 in its place. The 1954 Code made substantive changes, but principally it was adopted to reorganize the Code into a more rational structure. The 1954 Code has been substantially altered over the years by Congressional amendments. Until 1986, the title of the Code continued to be the "Internal Revenue Code of 1954." The Tax Reform Act of 1986 changed the title of the Code to the "Internal Revenue Code of 1986." References herein to the "IRC" followed by a number are references to sections of the 1986 Code as amended at the time of this writing.

§ 1.1000. RATE STRUCTURE. The federal income tax is imposed on taxable income rather than on gross receipts or gross income. In general, taxable income is equal to gross income less certain deductions.

For the years prior to 1988, the federal income tax was a graduated or progressive tax system (i.e., the rate structure was set so that the more dollars that a taxpayer earned in a taxable year, the higher was his rate of tax). The Tax Reform Act of 1986 (1986 TRA) adopted a somewhat different graduated rate structure. Under a graduated or progressive tax structure, the tax rates increase in brackets so that while an additional dollar earned by a taxpayer may be taxed at a higher rate than the dollar earned just before it, the additional dollar earned will not increase the taxpayer's tax on the dollars previously earned.

The tax rate schedule that applies to an individual depends upon that individual's filing status—i.e., the status under which the individual filed a federal income tax return for that year. For example, separate tax rate schedules apply to: (1), a married couple who jointly file a return; (2), a married individual who files a separate return; (3), (4), and (5), an unmarried individual who files a return as a "surviving spouse," a "head of household," or as an individual who is in neither of the above two categories. Different tax schedules are provided for each of the filing status categories listed above. A far more steeply progressive tax schedule is applied to estates and trusts. IRC § 1(c). For convenience, in setting forth illustrations or examples of the application of the rate structure, we will use the rates applicable to a married couple who file a joint return.

The current tax rate schedule was established by the Jobs and Growth Tax Relief Reconciliation Act of 2003. As noted in § **1.1100**, the dollar amounts that comprise each tax bracket are adjusted each year to reflect increases in the cost-of-living. IRC § 1(f). The following schedule sets forth the nominal tax rate schedule for a taxable year beginning in 2005 for married taxpayers who file a joint return.

Taxable Income	Tax Rate
Up to $14,600	10%
Over $14,600 but not over $59,400	15%
Over $59,400 but not over $119,950	25%
Over $119,950 but not over $182,800	28%
Over $182,800 but not over $326,450	33%
Over $326,450	35%

Tax rates can be viewed from several perspectives, each of which is designated by a specific term. The schedule above shows the tax rates that are applied to the dollar amounts in each tax bracket. The highest tax rate that is applied to any of a taxpayer's taxable income is referred to as the taxpayer's "marginal rate." For example, if a married TP filing a joint return had taxable income of $119,951 in 2005, that TP's marginal rate for that year is 28%. The quotient obtained from dividing a TP's tax liability for a given year by the taxpayer's income for that year is referred to as the TP's "average rate"—i.e., the percentage of the TP's income that is payable as income tax. In calculating the average rate, the "income" that is used sometimes is the TP's "taxable income" and sometimes is the TP's "adjusted gross income" (See § **1.6310** for the meaning of those terms). For some purposes it is important to know a TP's marginal rate; and, for others, the average rate is important.

While the *nominal* maximum marginal rate for post–2002 years is 35%, the *effective* marginal rate can be somewhat larger. There are several tax provisions that, when an individual's income exceeds a specified figure, reduce the amount of certain deductions that an individual otherwise would be allowed. A reduction of an individual's allowable deductions because he earned additional income is equivalent to increasing the marginal tax rate on those additional dollars of income, and so the actual maximum marginal rate can exceed 35%. Examples of deductions that are reduced or eliminated when a taxpayer's income rises above a specified amount are: the deduction for personal exemptions (see § **4.2000** et seq.), the reduction of "miscellaneous itemized deductions" (see IRC § 67), the reduction required by IRC § 68 for most itemized deductions, and the floors provided for medical expense deductions (IRC § 213(a)) and for personal casualty and theft losses (IRC § 165(h)(2)(A)).

Another aspect of the current tax rates is that the Code establishes a maximum marginal tax rate that can apply to an individual's net capital gains. IRC § 1(h). The meaning of "capital gains," and "net capital gains," and the tax treatment of capital gains are described in Chapter Eighteen. For example, for the year 2005, the net capital gain of a TP, otherwise having a 35% marginal tax rate, may be taxed at a rate of only 15%—a very substantial savings in tax liability. As a consequence of an amendment adopted in 1997, there are several different tax rates applicable to different categories of capital gains. While much of the complexity engendered by the 1997 Act was removed by simplifying and liberalizing amendments adopted in 1998, there are still different rates for specified categories of capital gains. As a consequence of the tax bill adopted in 2001, certain dividends, although not treated as capital gains, may also qualify for the 15% rate.

§ 1.1100. **Indexing for Inflation.** The taxable income figures that delineate each tax bracket will be increased annually to reflect increases in the cost-of-living. IRC § 1(f). In other words, the tax brackets are indexed for inflation. Before indexing was adopted, the tax rate structure was subject to "bracket creep." That is, inflation would reduce the purchasing power of the dollar figures that delineated each tax bracket, and consequently, over a period of years, a taxpayer who earned more dollars because of inflation, but who earned the same (or even less) purchasing power as in prior years, would have a larger portion of his income taken from him as taxes. So, tax rates effectively were increased without Congress' passing any legislation. Indexing for inflation has eliminated that problem.

§ 1.1200. **Retroactive Increase in Tax.** A change in the tax law that results in an increase in the amount of a taxpayer's tax liability can be made retroactive without violating the Constitution. *Reed v. United States*, 743 F.2d 481 (7th Cir. 1984). See also *United States v. Hemme*, 476 U.S. 558 (1986).

§ 1.2000. SOURCES OF THE TAX LAW.

§ 1.2100. **The Internal Revenue Code.** The most important source, of course, is the statutes which are contained in the Internal Revenue Code of 1986. Taxation is primarily a statutory subject, and one of the purposes of a course in that subject is to develop skills in statutory construction. A statute must be read with extreme care. Each word must be considered and weighed; even punctuation must be taken into account.

In construing a tax statute, it is helpful to examine the table of contents to the Internal Revenue Code and note where the section in question is listed. The organizational structure of the Internal Revenue Code may provide guidance to the construction of specific statutory language. In some circumstances, even the heading to a section may influence its construction. E.g., *House Jr. v. Commissioner*, 453 F.2d 982 (5th Cir. 1972).

§ 1.2110. Amendments. As previously noted, from time to time Congress adds new sections to the Internal Revenue Code, deletes some sections, and amends others. Typically, a number of these changes are combined in one statutory act (e.g., the Tax Reform Act of 1969, the Tax Reform Act of 1976, the Revenue Act of 1978, the Economic Recovery Tax Act of 1981, and the Tax Reform Act of 1986).

§ 1.2120. Legislative History. The legislative history of the statutes included in the Code provide an important guide to their construction. Since 1939, the Committee Reports for each Act usually can be found in a volume of the Cumulative Bulletin [see **§ 1.2300**] for the year in question. The Committee Reports for Acts adopted prior to 1939 are collected in one volume of the 1939 Cumulative Bulletin. In addition to the Reports, the Committee Hearings, the congressional debates and other historical material can be useful, but the Committee Reports will usually prove to be the major useful source. For a number of years now, the staff of the Joint Committee on Taxation has published an explanation of most tax acts after their adoption. The explanations published by the Joint Committee Staff are sometimes referred to as the "Blue Book." Blue Books have been cited by courts and by the Commissioner as authoritative guides to the construction of the statutes discussed therein. *Miller v. United States*, 65 F.3d 687 (8th Cir. 1995); *Holiday Village Shopping Center v. United States*, 773 F.2d 276 (Fed. Cir. 1985); and PLR 8550022. See also *Redlark v. Commissioner*, 141 F.3d 936 (9th Cir. 1998), reversing, 106 T.C. 31 (1996), in which the Ninth Circuit said, "While such post-enactment explanations cannot properly be described as 'legislative history,' they are at least instructive as to the reasonableness of an agency's interpretation of a facially ambiguous statute." The Supreme Court has characterized the Blue Book as a "compelling contemporary indication" of the meaning of a statutory provision. *FPC v. Memphis Light, Gas & Water Dir.*, 411 U.S. 458, 472 (1973).

§ 1.2200. Treasury Department Regulations. After the Internal Revenue Code, the most important primary source of tax law is the Regulations promulgated by the Treasury Department. Most Regulations are descriptive in form, often including examples to illustrate the operation of the statutory provision. Because of the increased activity of Congress in passing tax legislation on a virtually annual basis, the burden on Treasury to promulgate Regulations has led to the use of a question and answer format in some instances. Such Regulations are sometimes referred to as "Q and A Regulations."

Regulations can be divided into three separate types: interpretative, legislative and procedural. See *Dunn v. Commissioner*, 615 F.2d 578 (2d Cir. 1980). The most common form is the interpretative Regulation, which, as the name implies, construes and explains the statutes located in the Code. See IRC § 7805. Interpretative Regulations "clarify ambiguous terms in the statute or explain how a provision operates." *Snowa v. Commissioner*, 123 F.3d 190 (4th Cir. 1997). A second category is that of "legislative Regulations." Certain statutes expressly delegate to the Secretary of Treasury the task of resolving by "legislative Regulation" certain important matters that were omitted from the statute, and some statutes delegate the task of establishing the procedure for making an election authorized by the statute. E.g., IRC § 453(d)(2). The Supreme Court stated that "if Congress has explicitly left a gap for the agency to fill, there is an express delegation of authority to the agency to elucidate a specific provision of the statute by regulation." *Chevron U.S.A. v. Natural Res. Def. Council*, 467 U.S. 837, 843–844 (1984). That type of regulation is legislative. *Redlark v. Commissioner*, 141 F.3d 936 (9th Cir. 1998). For a discussion of the distinction between legislative and interpretative Regulations, see Asimow, *Public Participation in the Adoption of Temporary Tax Regulations*, 44 The Tax Lawyer 343, 350–361 (1991). A procedural Regulation, which may also be either legislative or interpretative, deals with such matters as the time, place and manner of making elections, filing forms or statements, seeking administrative review of proposals, etc.

The Regulations for a specific statute are easily located. Since 1954, the income tax Regulations have the prefix "1" and the number following the prefix is the number of the section of the Code under consideration. For example, a student seeking to examine a Regulation construing IRC § 105, would look at Regulation § 1.105–1. The "–1" indicates that the Regulation is the first in order promulgated under IRC § 105. The Regulations following Reg. § 1.105–1 are: §§ 1.105–2, 1.105–3, etc.

§ 1.2210.   Validity of Regulations. Legislative Regulations are given "controlling weight unless they are arbitrary, capricious, or manifestly contrary to the statute." *National Muffler Dealers Ass'n v. United States*, 440 U.S. 472, 476 (1979); *Chevron U.S.A v. Natural Resources Defense Counsel, Inc.,* 467 U.S. 837 (1984). "Only if the code has a meaning that is clear, unambiguous and in conflict with a regulation does a court have the authority to reject the Commissioner's reasoned interpretation and invalidate the regulation." *Redlark v. Commissioner*, 141 F.3d 936 (9th Cir. 1998). While interpretive Regulations are entitled to great weight, an interpretive Regulation may be held invalid by a court when it is inconsistent with the statutory language or when there is no statutory language to support the regulatory provision. When a statute may reasonably be construed to have any one of several alternative meanings, the selection of one such meaning in the Regulations will be conclusive even if one or more of the alternative constructions were preferable. *Atl. Mut. Ins. Co. v. Commissioner*, 523 U.S. 382, 389 (1998); *Chevron U.S.A. v. Natural Resources Defense Counsel, Inc., supra*; *Fulman v. United States*, 434 U.S. 528 (1978). A court will invalidate a Regulation only if its construction is "unreasonable and inconsistent with the language, history and purpose of the statute." *Estate of Bullard v. Commissioner*, 87 T.C. 261 (1986) (reviewed by the court). See also *National Muffler Dealers Ass'n v. United States*, 440 U.S. 472, 476–477 (1979); *Chevron U.S.A. v. Natural Resources Defense Counsel, Inc., supra*. Even when a Regulation presents an unreasonable construction of a statute, it is doubtful that the Internal Revenue Service can repudiate its own Regulation retroactively (i.e., a taxpayer can generally act in reliance that the Service will accept the validity of a Regulation). But see the concurring opinion of Justice Scalia in *United States v. Burke*, 504 U.S. 229, 246 (1992), in which Justice Scalia said that an agency cannot be bound by its own regulation if that regulation is "contrary to law."

It is more difficult for a taxpayer to invalidate a legislative Regulation than an interpretative Regulation, but both types are given great weight. See *United States v. Vogel Fertilizer Co.*, 455 U.S. 16 (1982). Some of the criteria employed in determining whether a Regulation is valid are discussed in the Supreme

Court's decision in *Rowan Cos., Inc. v. United States*, 452 U.S. 247 (1981).

When a tax statute is readopted in essentially the same terms, a court may assume that Congress approved of the regulations that had interpreted the prior statutory provision. See *United States v. Correll*, 389 U.S. 299, 305–306 (1967); *Cottage Savings Ass'n v. Commissioner*, 499 U.S. 554 (1991).

§ 1.2220. Retroactive Application. Unless the Regulation states otherwise, a Regulation operates retroactively. *Pollack v. Commissioner*, 47 T.C. 92, 110 (1966), aff'd 392 F.2d 409 (5th Cir. 1968). Treasury is authorized by IRC § 7805(b) to prescribe the extent to which a Regulation will not have retroactive application.

§ 1.2230. Proposed and Temporary Regulations. Before final Regulations are promulgated, Treasury issues Proposed Regulations to inform the public of the position that the Treasury plans to take in its Final Regulations. The Proposed Regulations often are promulgated prior to Treasury's holding hearings or receiving comments from interested parties. In addition to Proposed Regulations, because of the quantity of tax legislation and the need for guidance by the public, Treasury often promulgates Temporary Regulations, which remain effective until replaced by the Final Regulations. Temporary Regulations issued after November 20, 1988, will expire within three years of issuance, and any Temporary Regulation issued after that date must also be issued simultaneously as a Proposed Regulation. IRC § 7805(e). Typically, there will be no hearings or comments prior to the promulgation of Temporary Regulations. Public comments on Temporary Regulations are invited before they become Final Regulations. For a criticism of the current practice of issuing Temporary Regulations without first obtaining public comments, see Asimow, *Public Participation in the Adoption of Temporary Tax Regulations*, 44 The Tax Lawyer 343 (1991).

§ 1.2231. Significance of Proposed Regulations. The courts have held that Proposed Regulations are not entitled to receive the deference that is granted to Final Regulations. E.g., *Mearkle v. Commissioner*, 838 F.2d 880 (7th Cir. 1988). The Tax Court has held in several decisions that Proposed Regulations "carry no more weight than a position advanced on brief by the" Commissioner. *Zinniel v. Commissioner*, 89 T.C. 357, 369 (1987); *F.W. Woolworth v. Commissioner*, 54

T.C. 1233, 1265–1266 (1970). However, even the Tax Court has said that Proposed Regulations "are not a complete nullity," and do give a "warning of things to come." *Butka v. Commissioner*, 91 T.C. 110, 130 (1988), aff'd 886 F.2d 442 (D.C. Cir. 1989). See also, *Estate of Howard v. Commissioner*, 910 F.2d 633 (9th Cir. 1990).

§ 1.2232. **Significance of Temporary Regulations.** Temporary Regulations are given the same deference and weight that is granted to Final Regulations. *Nissho Iwai American Corp. v. Commissioner*, 89 T.C. 765–776 (1987); *Truck & Equipment Corp. v. Commissioner*, 98 T.C. 141, 149 (1992); *Redlark v. Commissioner*, 141 F.3d 936 (9th Cir. 1998); *Miller v. United States*, 65 F.3d 687 (8th Cir. 1995).

§ 1.2300. **Revenue Rulings.** In addition to the Regulations, the Service publishes rulings indicating its interpretation of the tax law and its application of the tax laws to factual circumstances. Since 1954, these rulings have been published as "Revenue Rulings" which are cited as "Rev. Rul." Some Revenue Rulings are published as "Revenue Procedures" cited as "Rev. Proc." The Service also publishes "Notices" which are equivalent to Rulings. The rulings and notices are published in a Bulletin called the "Internal Revenue Bulletin," cited as "I.R.B." The Internal Revenue Bulletins are published weekly; so 52 Bulletins are published each year (except that in 1993, as a cost cutting measure, the Service announced that it would publish only two Bulletins a month for the four months of June through September of that year). In any event, the Bulletins are accumulated semiannually in a bound volume called the "Cumulative Bulletin." The Revenue Rulings are numbered by the year in which they are promulgated and by the order in which they were considered. Thus, Rev. Rul. 2000–11 refers to a ruling prepared in the year 2000 which has been numbered "11" (prior to 2000, only the last two digits of the year were used, e.g., Rev. Rul. 99–4). The Cumulative Bulletins (Cum. Bull. or C.B.) are also cited by the year involved. For example, 1958–2 Cum. Bull. 150 refers to page 150 of the second volume of the Cumulative Bulletin published in the year 1958. Accordingly, Rev. Rul. 70–11 is cited: Rev. Rul. 70–11, 1970–1 Cum. Bull. 229. Notices are numbered in the same manner as is employed for rulings; an example of a typical citation for a notice is: Notice 90–43, 1990–2 Cum. Bull. 336. If a citation is to an I.R.B. because, for example, the Bulletin has not yet been incorporated into a Cumulative Bulletin, the citation will give the date, number, and page of the I.R.B. For example, Ann. 93–82, 1993–22 I.R.B. 31 refers to the Announcement number 82 published in 1993 at page 31 of I.R.B. number 22.

In the interest of brevity, this text omits citations to Cum. Bulls. and I.R.B.'s and merely cites the Rev. Rul., Rev. Proc., or other item without directing the reader to the volume in which it is contained. The identity of the correct volume can be readily determined.

§ **1.2310. Acquiescences.** The Commissioner also publishes an acquiescence or nonacquiescence in certain (but not all) issues which the government lost in civil litigation. Prior to 1991, the Commissioner issued an acquiescence or nonacquiescence only with respect to Tax Court cases that were not decided by a Memorandum decision. Since 1991, the Commissioner has expanded the scope of its acquiescence/nonacquiescence policy to other civil tax cases, including Memorandum Decisions of the Tax Court, District Court, Court of Federal Claims decisions, and decisions of the Circuit Courts of Appeals. See 2003–1 Cum. Bull. xxi. An acquiescence (Acq.) or nonacquiescence (Nonacq.) is equivalent to a Rev. Rul. and is given about the same weight. The acquiescences and nonacquiescences are first published in the I.R.B. and then are accumulated and published in a Cumulative Bulletin.

§ **1.2320. Information Releases.** The Commissioner occasionally issues what amounts to a press release which is referred to as an "information release" (IR) and is published in the I.R.B. but not in the Cum. Bull. The Commissioner also issues, for informational purposes, General Litigation Bulletins which describe the decisions made in cases that involve related issues.

§ **1.2330. Internal Memoranda.** As a consequence of a circuit court decision made under the Freedom of Information Act, the Commissioner is required to make available to the public most of the internal memoranda prepared by its staff. See *Taxation With Representation Fund v. IRS*, 646 F.2d 666 (D.C. Cir. 1981). The internal memoranda involved were General Counsel Memorandum (GCM), Actions on Decision (AOD), and Technical Memoranda (TM).

There are also documents known as Field Service Advice memoranda (FSAs) and Chief Counsel Advice memoranda (CCAs) that the National Office of the IRS issues to agents in local offices throughout the country. These advisory memoranda are required by statute to be made available to the public. IRC § 6110(a), (b)(1)(A), (i).

§ 1.2340. Significance. Rev. Ruls., Acq. and Nonacq. are indicative of the viewpoint of the Service, but they are not entitled to great weight. The Service is not obligated to follow its published rulings or its long-standing administrative construction of the tax law, and they may be repudiated by the Service or by a court. E.g., *Dickman v. Commissioner*, 465 U.S. 330 (1984) where the Supreme Court stated: "It is well established that the Commissioner may change an earlier interpretation of the law, even if such a change is made retroactive in effect . . . This rule applies even though a taxpayer may have relied to his detriment upon the Commissioner's prior position." See also, *Dixon v. United States*, 381 U.S. 68, 72–75 (1965); and *Automobile Club of Michigan v. Commissioner*, 353 U.S. 180, 183–184 (1957). However, there is a question whether the government is barred from asserting a position in litigation that is at odds with a position taken in a published ruling that has not been withdrawn or modified. The Tax Court holds that the government is not permitted to make a contention in litigation that is contrary to a published ruling *unless* the IRS first withdraws or modifies the ruling. *Phillips v. Commissioner*, 88 T.C. 529, 534 (1987) (reviewed by the court), rev'd on an unrelated issue, 851 F.2d 1492 (C.A.D.C., 1988); *Rauenhorst v. Commissioner*, 119 T.C. 157, 169–173 (2002). It appears that the withdrawal or modification can be made effective retroactively.

The Tax Court has stated on numerous occasions that a revenue ruling "is simply the contention of one of the parties to the litigation and is entitled to no greater weight." E.g., *Estate of Lang v. Commissioner*, 64 T.C. 404 (1975). See also *Beyer v. Commissioner*, 92 T.C. 1304, 1311 (1989). However, a number of circuit courts of appeals have not accepted the Tax Court's relegation of rulings to the scrap pile (except for the Tax Court's policy of preventing the government from contradicting its published rulings in litigation without first withdrawing or modifying them). While most appellate courts give little weight to rulings, even they have attached some significance to them; and some appellate courts give considerable deference to rulings. For example, the Ninth Circuit stated that it would give weight to an established revenue ruling of long standing that fell within the Commissioner's "authority to implement the congressional mandate in some reasonable manner." *Estate of Lang v. Commissioner*, 613 F.2d 770 (9th Cir. 1980). In *Ricards v. United States*, 683 F.2d 1219 (9th Cir. 1981), the Ninth Circuit stated that while revenue rulings do "not have the force and effect of law," they "do constitute a body of experience and informed judgment to which courts may properly resort for guidance." See also *Bob Jones University v. United States*, 461 U.S. 574 (1983); *Oetting v. United States*, 712 F.2d 358 (8th Cir. 1983). The Fifth Circuit said, "the Tax Court has long been fighting a losing battle with the various courts of appeals over the proper deference to which revenue rulings are due ... they are clearly less binding on the courts than treasury regulations or code provisions, but probably ... more so than the mere legal conclusions of the parties." *Estate of McLendon v. Commissioner*, 135 F.3d 1017 (5th Cir. 1998). However, in a footnote to a subsequent portion of the Fifth Circuit's opinion, the court said that "the position of the Tax Court [on this issue] is not without some merit." *McLendon v. Commissioner, supra*, f.n. 12. Also, in *Davis v. United States*, 495 U.S. 472 (1990), the Supreme Court stated: "Although the Service's interpretive rulings do not have the force and effect of regulations [citation omitted], we give an agency's interpretations and practices considerable weight where they involve the contemporaneous construction of a statute and where they have been in long use." The Sixth Circuit went even further and said, "revenue rulings 'are entitled to great deference and have been said to have the force of legal precedents unless unreasonable or inconsistent with the provisions of the Internal Revenue Code.'" *The Progressive Corporation and Subsidiaries v. U.S.*, 970 F.2d 188, 194 (6th Cir. 1992).

In any event, it can be valuable for a taxpayer to know the current position of the Service on an issue.

§ 1.3000. LETTER RULINGS.

§ 1.3000. **LETTER RULINGS.** If, before embarking on a transaction, a taxpayer wishes to know the position the Service will take as to the tax consequences of that transaction, the taxpayer may request the Commissioner to rule in advance on that issue. The request for a ruling is made by sending a formal letter to the Commissioner according to procedures laid down by the Service. See Rev. Proc. 2004–1. The Service will not rule on certain questions (e.g., it generally will not rule on a question if it requires the resolution of a factual issue). One important limitation is that the Service ordinarily will not issue a "comfort" ruling—that is, absent extraordinary circumstances, it will not rule "with respect to an issue that is clearly and adequately addressed by statute, regulations, decisions of a court, tax treaties, revenue rulings or revenue procedures." Rev. Proc. 2004–7 (Sec. 3.02(6)). Also, the Service will not rule on a "frivolous" issue. Rev. Proc. 2004–1 (Sec. 6.09).

If the Service is willing to rule, it does so in the form of a letter to the taxpayer answering his question, and this letter is sometimes called a "letter ruling" or a "private letter ruling." As a matter of its practice, the Service will abide by its letter ruling but only as to the very taxpayer who formally requested the ruling, only if the taxpayer accurately stated all of the relevant facts in his request for the ruling, and only if the law is not changed after the ruling has been given. Rev. Proc. 2004–1 (Sec. 11). Except for certain information, including company name, which must be deleted, the Service must disclose its letter rulings to the public. IRC § 6110. In this book, a letter ruling is cited as "PLR" or "Private Letter Ruling" followed by the number of that ruling. You will often see a letter ruling cited as "PLR" (i.e., "private letter ruling") even though there is very little privacy accorded to the ruling. Some of the letter rulings are deemed to be of such general interest that they are studied further by the Service and eventually serve as the basis for a published revenue ruling.

Upon receiving a request from a field office, the National Office of the Service will give advice or guidance to the field office in the form of an internal memorandum. Rev. Proc. 2004–2. The advice will relate to technical and procedural questions and to the interpretation and proper application of the tax law. These advice memorandums are called "Technical Advice Memorandums" or "TAMs." The TAMs, in form and substance, are similar to Private Letter Rulings.

Both Private Letter Rulings and TAMs are identified by a nine-digit number, the first four digits of which designate the year in which it was promulgated (prior to 1999, only the last two digits of the year were used), the next two digits of which designate the week of that year in which it was promulgated, and the last three digits of which merely identify that PLR or TAM. For example, PLR 200038006 is a Private Letter Ruling that was promulgated in the 38th week of the year 2000, and is designated by the number 006.

While IRC § 6110(k)(3) prohibits the use of letter rulings as precedents, the courts have occasionally referred to letter rulings as evidence of the interpretative position held by the Service during the period of time in which the rulings were in effect. E.g., *Rowan Cos, Inc. v. United States*,

452 U.S. 247, n. 17 (1981). In general, PLRs, TAMs, and other written determinations of the IRS must be open to the public. IRC § 6110(a).

§ 1.3100. User Fees for Seeking a Ruling. Prior to 1988, the Service did not impose a charge for providing letter rulings or other statements of its views on issues posed by a taxpayer. That is no longer true. Since February 1, 1988, a taxpayer is required to pay a fee to the Service for requests for rulings, opinion letters, determination letters, and for similar requests. While this provision briefly expired on September 30, 1990, it was reinstated as of December 5, 1990. The current fee schedule is set forth in Rev. Proc. 2004–1 (Appendix A). The fees range from a low of $45 to a high of $6,000 (although a request for an advanced pricing agreement can cost as much as $25,000). The amount charged as a fee is determined by the category of the subject matter of the request. The fee is payable in advance and typically is not refundable unless the Service refuses to rule on the issues.

§ 1.3200. Transactional Tax Risk Insurance. Insurance companies offer to insure that a TP will obtain a desired tax consequence for a proposed transaction. Rather than to seek to obtain a ruling from the Service, a TP can purchase insurance to cover the risk of adverse tax consequences. The insurer will have its panel of tax experts screen a request for insurance coverage to evaluate the likelihood of the TP's prevailing on the issue and to determine whether the insurer should issue the policy. Kenneth A. Geary, "New Opportunities for Tax Lawyers: Insuring Tax Transactions," 104 Tax Notes 26 (July 5, 2004).

§ 1.4000. TAX LITIGATION. Tax disputes can be litigated in any one of three courts at the choice of the taxpayer. He may select the Tax Court (previously known as the "Board of Tax Appeals"), a United States District Court, or the United States Court of Federal Claims. The Tax Court is authorized to have 19 active judges, who are appointed for a 15–year term, plus senior judges and special trial judges. To bring suit in a District Court or the United States Court of Federal Claims, the taxpayer must first pay the entire amount of his tax deficiency and then claim a refund from the Service. IRC § 7422(a); *Flora v. United States*, 357 U.S. 63 (1958), aff'd on rehearing, 362 U.S. 145 (1960). If any interest or penalty is owing on the deficiency, it is unsettled whether they must also be paid before a refund suit can be brought. The taxpayer can petition for a redetermination of his tax deficiency in the Tax Court without first paying the deficiency. An appeal from the Tax Court or the District Court can be taken to a United States Court of

Appeals for the appropriate circuit, and from there the losing party can seek certiorari to the United States Supreme Court. An appeal from the United States Court of Federal Claims can be taken to the United States Court of Appeals for the Federal Circuit. Further review can be obtained only by certiorari to the Supreme Court.

While the Tax Court is located in Washington, D.C., its judges hold court in numerous cities throughout the United States.

§ 1.4100. Review of Tax Court Decisions by the Entire Court. A Tax Court decision typically is made by a single Tax Court judge. However, the Chief Judge of the Tax Court has the authority to have a proposed decision of a judge reviewed by all of the active members of the Court. When a decision has been so reviewed, all of the active judges vote, and the decision is referred to as "reviewed by the court."

In an interview, a former Chief Judge of the Tax Court said that a decision of a single judge generally is selected by a Chief Judge for review by the entire court if: (1) it proposed to invalidate a regulation; (2) it conflicts with an opinion of a circuit court of appeals; or (3) it would reverse the effect of a prior Tax Court decision or opinion. Daily Tax Report (DTR) No. 128 at p. G–2 (July 2, 1992).

§ 1.4200. Memorandum Decisions of the Tax Court. Tax Court opinions typically are published in an official reporter called the "United States Tax Court Reports" and cited as "T.C." The Chief Judge of the Tax Court can designate a judge's opinion as a "Memorandum Opinion," and those opinions are not published in the official publication. Memorandum Opinions are published by two unofficial publications that are readily available to the general public. At one time, Tax Court judges pretended to ignore Memorandum Opinions and would not cite them. That practice was changed, and Tax Court judges now do cite to Memorandum Opinions. However, a former Chief Judge of the Tax Court stated that Tax Court judges do not treat Memorandum Opinions as precedents to which stare decisis applies. Daily Tax Reports (DTR) No. 128 at p. G–2 (July 2, 1992).

§ 1.4300. Board of Tax Appeals (BTA). Originally, the Tax Court was knows as the United States Board of Tax Appeals, and its decisions were cited as "BTA."

§ 1.4400. Burden of Proof. "Burden of proof" refers only to factual issues. Prior to the adoption of the Internal Revenue Service

Restructuring and Reform Act of 1998, the burden of proof in tax cases, regardless of the forum in which the case was tried, was on the taxpayer. There were some exceptions in which the burden was placed on the government for certain issues, but there were only a few statutory provisions for which that was true.

There are a few statutory provisions in which the burden of proof that the taxpayer must carry is heavier than the usual one. E.g., IRC § 533(a) requires a corporation to prove by "a preponderance of the evidence" that it did not have a tax avoidance purpose even though it had allowed its earnings to accumulate beyond its reasonable needs. While the 1998 Act significantly changed the general rules on burden of proof, it does not alter the burden that is placed on a party by a specific statutory provision (such as the provision mentioned above in IRC § 533(a)). IRC § 7491(a)(3).

The 1998 Act added IRC § 7491 to the Code. This provision places the burden of proof in any tax case on the government if certain conditions are satisfied. The taxpayer must first introduce credible evidence with respect to a factual issue that is relevant to the taxpayer's liability for an income or transfer tax. The burden of proof then shifts to the government on that factual issue provided that the taxpayer has complied with applicable statutory requirements to substantiate certain expenditures (e.g., charitable gifts and travel and entertainment expenses) and provided that the taxpayer has maintained records required by the Code and has cooperated with reasonable requests of the government for witnesses, information, documents, meetings, and interviews. IRC § 7491(a). According to the legislative history, one element of the requirement of cooperating with the government is that the taxpayer must have exhausted all administrative remedies (including appeal rights within the Service), but the exhaustion of remedies requirement does not require the taxpayer to agree to an extension of the statutory period of limitations. As to corporations, partnerships, and trusts, they can avail themselves of this provision only if they satisfy certain net worth requirements (generally, the entity's net worth cannot exceed $7 million) and the entity cannot have more than 500 employees. IRC § 7491(a)(2)(C). As to each of the conditions required for shifting the burden of proof to the government, the taxpayer has the burden of proving that he has satisfied those conditions.

The government also has the burden of production with respect to the liability of an *individual* for a penalty, or an addition to tax, or any additional amount imposed by the Code. IRC § 7491(c). Also, in certain circumstances where the government raised a new issue late in the proceedings, the burden of proof shifted to the government; that principle may still be applicable when the 1998 Act's amendment does not apply to shift the burden to the government because one of its conditions was not satisfied.

While the burden of proof applies only to factual issues, once the Commissioner has assessed a tax, the Commissioner's construction of a statute is entitled to a "legal presumption of correctness." *U.S. v. Fior D'Italia, Inc.*, 536 U.S. 238 (2002). It is doubtful that the presumption of correctness is given much weight by the courts.

§ 1.4500. **Recovery of Litigating Costs.** In certain (but not all) circumstances, a taxpayer who prevails in litigation against the government can recover administrative and litigating costs from the government. This can include attorney fees, but there is a ceiling on the hourly rate that can be recovered. The 1998 Act raised the ceiling on the hourly rate for attorney fees and generally liberalized the provision for cost recovery.

§ 1.5000. **CHECKLIST OF ISSUES.** In analyzing a tax problem, the following checklist of questions may be helpful in spotting relevant issues:

Does an item constitute income?

Does an item constitute a loss?

Is the income or loss realized?

To whom was the income or loss realized?

When was the income or loss realized?

Was the income or loss "recognized" and, if so, when?

How is the income or loss characterized (e.g., capital gain or loss, section 1231 gain or loss, or ordinary income or loss)?

If a loss was recognized, is it deductible?

What items constitute tax deductions?

Are such tax deductions allowed?

When are such tax deductions allowed?

How is a tax deduction to be characterized (e.g., as an ordinary deduction or as a capital loss)?

Is a tax deduction an itemized or nonitemized deduction?

Is a tax deduction a "miscellaneous itemized deduction?"

What surtaxes are applicable?

What credits may be deducted from the tax bill (e.g., dependent care credit)?

§ 1.6000. ACCOUNTING FOR TAX PURPOSES.

§ 1.6100. Accounting Period. Income and deductions for tax purposes are determined for a taxable accounting period. Income and deductions are determined on an annual basis. See § **1.6400.**

§ 1.6110. Election Period. The taxable period is usually a calendar year, but a taxpayer may be permitted to elect to report his income for a fiscal year which ends on the last day of any calendar month.

§ 1.6120. Short Year. A taxable year may be a period less than 12 months; for example, where a taxpayer dies prior to the close of his regular taxable year. IRC §§ 441(b) and 443(a).

§ 1.6130. Variable Year. In certain circumstances, a taxable year may be a period which varies between 52 and 53 weeks. IRC § 441(f).

§ 1.6200. Method of Accounting. The period in which a taxpayer reports income or loss may depend upon the method of accounting used. If, as to one or more items, the method of accounting used by a taxpayer (TP) does not "clearly reflect income," the TP can be required to report that item in a manner that does clearly reflect income. IRC § 446(b). See, e.g., *Ford Motor Co. v. Commissioner*, 71 F.3d 209 (6th Cir. 1995).

§ 1.6210. Cash Receipts and Disbursements Method. The standard method of tax reporting for individuals is based upon cash receipts. Under the cash receipts and disbursements method, income is reported when cash or its equivalent is actually or constructively received by the taxpayer and expenses are generally deducted when actually paid. Treas. Reg. § 1.451–1. Certain corporate taxpayers are not permitted to use the cash receipts and disbursements method. The cash method also is prohibited to certain partnerships that have at least one partner that is a corporation, and tax shelter enterprises cannot use the cash method. IRC § 448. Even for individual taxpayers, a taxpayer usually cannot use the cash method if his business consists of the sale of inventories. IRC § 471(a); Treas. Reg. § 1.446–1(c)(2)(i).

For convenience, the word "taxpayer" sometimes is abbreviated as "TP" in this text. There are a few circumstances in which the

Code requires a TP, even a TP who otherwise utilizes the cash method, to report certain types of income on what amounts to the accrual method. For example, if a corporate bond or other debt instrument is issued for a discount price (i.e., a price that is less than the principal of the debt (such as the face amount of a bond)), the amount of the discount may be treated as "original issue discount." If so, the discount may have to be reported as income of the bondholder (or noteholder) over the term of the debt instrument even if payment will not be received in that year. IRC § 1272. Original issue discount is discussed at §§ **5.5000–5.5400.**

§ **1.6211. Constructive Receipt.** If a cash method taxpayer has an unqualified vested right to receive immediate payment, the taxpayer cannot escape the recognition of income therefrom by deferring the time that payment is to be made or by otherwise turning his back on the income. Such income is recognized at the time that the taxpayer has the right to immediate payment, and the doctrine which causes that recognition of income is called "constructive receipt." Treas. Reg. § 1.451–2. However, if a cash method taxpayer agrees to the deferral of payment *before his right to the payment has been earned*, the taxpayer will not recognize income until the date on which the deferred payment or payments are to be made. *Robinson v. Commissioner*, 44 T.C. 20 (1965). Similarly, an agreement to defer receipt of an income payment prior to the date on which the right to the payment becomes unconditional generally will not trigger the constructive receipt doctrine, and such income usually will not be recognized until the deferred payment is due. *Martin v. Commissioner*, 96 T.C. 814 (1991).

If a taxpayer's control of the receipt of property is subject to substantial limitations or restrictions, the taxpayer will not be treated as having constructively received the property. Treas. Reg. § 1.451–2(a).

§ **1.6212. Economic Benefit.** A cash method employee will recognize income on the employer's creation for the employee of a vested right to deferred compensation even though the employee will not receive the amount of the deferred compensation until some years later. Income will be recognized at the time that the employee's rights are established if the employee's interest has an ascertainable fair market value and if it provides the employee with an economic benefit that is the equivalent of the receipt of cash. See *Sproull v. Commissioner*, 16 T.C. 244 (1951), aff'd 194 F.2d 541 (6th Cir. 1952); *Goldsmith v. United States*, 586 F.2d 810 (Ct. Cl. 1978). This principle is referred to as the "economic benefit" doctrine. A common circumstance in which this doctrine is applied occurs when an employer creates an obligation to provide an annuity for an employee to begin at a later date when the employee retires, and the employer funds its obligation so that the present value of employee's right to an annuity at a future date can be determined. See *United States v. Drescher*, § **2.1581–3.** While the economic benefit doctrine continues to be important, the provisions of IRC § 83, which deal with an employee's or independent contractor's receipt of property or an interest in property as compensation for services, have preempted most of the subject matter of that doctrine. IRC § 83 is discussed at §§ **2.1572–2.1572–4.**

§ **1.6220.** **Accrual Method.** Under the accrual method, income or deductions are "realized" when the taxpayer's right to receive payment or his obligation to make a payment becomes fixed and the amount is determinable with reasonable accuracy. The test for the proper date for the accrual of an expense is the "all events" test—i.e., the earliest date on which all of the events have occurred that determine the fact of liability and permit the determination of the amount of such liability with reasonable accuracy. See *Charles Schwab Corp. And Subsidiaries v. Commissioner,* 107 T.C. 282, 291–296 (1996), aff'd 161 F.3d 1231 (9th Cir. 1998). In certain circumstances described in IRC § 461(f), the payment of a contested liability will accrue that liability even though the taxpayer continues to contest it. Under IRC § 461(h), subject to certain exceptions, a liability with respect to an item will not accrue under the "all events" test any earlier than the date on which economic performance with respect to that item occurs. Moreover, even if the "all events" test is satisfied, an accrual method TP will be denied a deduction if its allowance would contravene the requirement of IRC § 446(b) that a TP's reporting method must "clearly reflect income." See, e.g., *Ford Motor Co. v. Commissioner*, 71 F.3d 209 (6th Cir. 1995).

§ **1.6230.** **Other Methods.** Various accounting methods may be developed to meet the special demands of a particular business. For example, income from most construction, building, manufacturing, or installation contracts that are not completed within the taxable year in which the contract was made (i.e., so-called "long-term contracts") must be reported on the percentage-of-completion method. IRC § 460. Generally, in the absence of a specific requirement, the Service will permit reporting based upon any fair, good-faith accounting method.

§ 1.6300.   Computation of Tax.

§ 1.6310.   Method of Computation. The method of tax computation for an individual may be described as follows:

(a) Determine taxpayer's *gross income*.

(b) Subtract those *deductions* (referred to as nonitemized deductions) that are listed in IRC § 62(a) in order to determine taxpayer's *adjusted gross income* (hereinafter AGI). [Note that the Code does establish a *few* nonitemized deductions that are not listed in IRC § 62. E.g., IRC § 71(f)(1)(B)].

(c) Subtract from AGI the taxpayer's exemption deductions (explained in Chapter Four) and subtract the greater of the taxpayer's itemized deductions or the taxpayer's standard deduction (explained in Chapter Three).

(d) Apply tax rates to determine the normal tax. *Note:* Tax rates change in stages so that not every dollar of income is taxed at the same rate.

(e) Subtract *tax credits* and add *surtaxes* to arrive at bill or refund. *Note:* In some instances, a tax credit is deducted before adding any applicable surtax; in some instances, a tax credit is deducted afterwards, depending upon the credit and surtax involved. Unless the surtax is computed as a percentage of the tax bill (and no present surtax is so computed), it makes no difference whether the credit is deducted before or after adding the surtax.

§ 1.6320.   Illustration of Computation.

$50,200.00	(Gross Income for the Calendar Year 2003)
–$3,500.00	(IRC § 62(a) Deductions)
$46,700.00	(AGI)
–$10,500.00	(Exemptions plus Itemized Deductions)
$36,200.00	(Taxable Income)
$36,200.00	(Taxable Income)
$4,730.00	(Tax) [Tax on $36,200 taxable income using the tax rates applicable to married taxpayers filing a joint return]
$4,730.00	(Tax)
–$300.00	(Credits)
$4,473.00	(Total Tax Bill)

§ **1.6330.** **Civil Penalties.** There are a large number of circumstances in which civil penalties are imposed on a taxpayer either for failing to comply with a requirement (such as: failing to file a return or a required statement or failing to pay all of a tax that is due) or for providing misleading information. Several of the most important of these civil penalties are discussed below.

§ **1.6331.** **Accuracy–Related Penalty.** Section 6662 of the Code imposes a penalty for the underpayment of a tax required to be shown on a return if the underpayment is attributable to one of five circumstances described in that provision. This penalty does not apply to any portion of an underpayment for which a fraud penalty (see § **1.6332**) is imposed. IRC § 6662(b). An "underpayment" is the excess of the proper amount of tax that is owing over the amount shown to be owing on the return. IRC § 6664(a). The underpayment is reduced by the amount of the unreported tax that was previously assessed or paid and is increased by any rebates to the taxpayer. There are three exceptions to the accuracy-related penalty: the reasonable cause exception, the substantial authority exception, and the adequate disclosure exception. These three are described below.

Reasonable Cause. No penalty will be imposed on any portion of an underpayment if there was reasonable cause for the taxpayer's position and the taxpayer acted in good faith. IRC § 6664(c)(1).

Substantial Authority. As noted below, an underpayment that is attributable to a taxpayer's substantial "understatement" of the tax that is owing will trigger a penalty. However an understatement will not include any item for which there is or was substantial authority for the treatment accorded by the taxpayer. IRC § 6662(d)(2)(B)(i). In other words, such an item is treated, for purposes of determining a penalty, as if the item were correctly reported on the return. Treas. Reg. § 1.6662–4(d)(1). The substantial authority exception does not apply to the extent that the underpayment is attributable to a tax shelter. IRC § 6662(d)(2)(C)(i). A "tax shelter" is an entity or investment plan or arrangement of which a significant purpose is the avoidance or evasion of federal income tax. IRC § 6662(d)(2)(C)(ii).

The substantial authority standard is an objective standard that requires an analysis of the existing law and an application of the law to the applicable facts. The subjective belief of the taxpayer is irrelevant to the availability of this exception. The types of authorities that can be utilized in determining whether substantial authority exists represent a wide variety of sources, including: proposed and temporary regulations, letter rulings, the Blue Book, legislative histories, and, of course, the Code, final regulations, and cases. Treas. Reg. § 1.6662–4(d)(3). While letter rulings are barred from being treated as precedents, they can be used to satisfy the substantial authority exception. All of the relevant authorities must be considered, and there is substantial authority only if "the weight of the authorities supporting the treatment is substantial in relation to the weight of the authorities supporting contrary treatment.... There may be substantial authority for more than one position with respect to the same item." Treas. Reg. § 1.6662–4(d)(3). Even if there are no interpretive authorities on point, a "position that is supported only by a well-reasoned construction of the applicable statutory provision" will constitute substantial authority. *Ibid*.

If the question of whether there was substantial authority turns on a resolution of conflicting evidence, the TP will be deemed to have had substantial authority unless the evidence is such that the government could have obtained a reversal of a decision in favor of the TP on the basis that such a decision would be "clearly erroneous." *Osteen v. Commissioner*, 62 F.3d 356, 359 (11th Cir. 1995); *Streber v. Commissioner*, 138 F.3d 216 (5th Cir. 1998). A decision is "clearly erroneous" if a court is left with a definite and firm conviction that a mistake has been made. *Chamberlain v. Commissioner*, 66 F.3d 729, 732 (5th Cir. 1995); and *Streber v. Commissioner*, *supra*.

Adequate Disclosure and Reasonable Basis. That portion of an understatement that is attributable to an item with respect to which the relevant facts affecting its tax treatment are adequately disclosed in the return or in a statement attached to the return and for which there is a reasonable basis for the taxpayer's treatment is treated as properly reported and therefore is not subject to a penalty. IRC § 6662(d)(2)(B)(ii). The adequate disclosure and reasonable basis exception does not apply to tax shelter items. IRC § 6662(d)(2)(C)(i). The "reasonable basis" standard is a significantly higher standard than merely not being "patently improper." Prop. Reg. § 1.6662–3(b)(3). The reasonable basis standard is *not* satisfied by a so-called "return position" that is merely arguable or merely a colorable claim.

A *corporate* TP cannot use the adequate disclosure and reasonable basis exception for its tax treatment of an item attributable to multiple party financing if the treatment does not clearly reflect the corporation's income. § 6662(d)(2)(B).

The penalty imposed by IRC § 6662 is 20% of the amount of underpayment that is attributable to a circumstance that is one of the five listed in that provision. For example, if a taxpayer has an underpayment for a taxable year and if part of that underpayment is due to the taxpayer's negligence and part is due to a non-negligent error, the penalty will be 20% of the amount of the underpayment that is attributable to the taxpayer's negligence. IRC § 6662(b). If an underpayment is attributable to a "gross" valuation misstatement, which term is defined below as it applies to most income tax property valuations, the penalty will be 40% of the portion of the underpayment that is attributable to that inaccurate valuation. IRC § 6662(h).

The five circumstances to which, subject to the three exceptions discussed above, the accuracy-related penalty applies are:

(1) *Negligence or disregard of rules or regulations.* The term "negligence" refers to a failure to make a reasonable effort to comply with the Code or to take ordinary and reasonable care in preparing a tax return. Negligence can arise from the failure to keep adequate books or records or to substantiate items properly. The term "disregard" includes any careless, reckless, or intentional disregard of rules or regulations. IRC § 6662(c). If a position taken by a taxpayer is contrary to a regulation, the taxpayer's position must also represent a good faith challenge to the regulation.

(2) *Any substantial understatement of income tax.* An understatement of income tax for a taxable year is substantial if it

exceeds the greater of: (i) 10% of the proper income tax for that year, or (ii) $5,000 ($10,000 for most corporations who also are subject to a maximum floor of $10,000,000). IRC § 6662(d)(1). An "understatement" is the excess of the proper amount that is required to be shown on the return over the amount actually shown on the return (less rebates). IRC § 6662(d)(2).

(3) *Any income tax substantial valuation misstatement.* As to property valuation, a misstatement on a return is substantial if the value or basis of any property that is claimed on the return is twice (or more than twice) the actual value or basis of that property. A typical example of a misstatement of value is an overvaluation of property contributed to a charity. No penalty is imposed, however, unless the underpayment for that year that is attributable to substantial valuation misstatements exceeds $5,000 ($10,000 for most corporations). IRC § 6662(e). As noted above, if there is a gross valuation misstatement, the penalty imposed is 40% of the underpayment attributable thereto—in other words, the penalty on that portion of an underpayment is doubled. As to the income tax substantial valuation misstatement, the misstatement is gross if the value or basis of the property as reported on the return is quadruple or more of the actual value or basis of the property. IRC § 6662(h).

(4) *Any substantial overstatement of pension liabilities.*

(5) *Any estate or gift tax substantial valuation understatement.*

The Code imposes additional reporting requirements and penalties for transactions connected to a tax shelter.

§ 1.6332.   Fraud Penalty. If any part of an underpayment is due to fraud, the penalty will be equal to 75% of that amount of the underpayment that is due to fraud. If the Service succeeds in proving that any portion of an underpayment is attributable to fraud, then all of the underpayment will be deemed attributable to fraud except for the portion of the underpayment that the taxpayer can prove is not due to fraud—i.e., the burden of proof shifts to the taxpayer once the government establishes fraud. IRC § 6663.

§ 1.6333.   Failure to File Return. If a taxpayer fails to file an income tax return on the required date and if the failure is not due to reasonable cause, a penalty will be imposed equal to

5% of the tax due for each month (or part thereof) that the return is not filed. The total penalty cannot exceed 25% of the tax due—i.e., the penalty applies only to the first five months of neglect to file. If the failure to file is attributable to fraud, the 5% monthly penalty is raised to 15%, and the maximum penalty is increased from 25% to 75%. There is a minimum penalty of the lesser of $100 or 100% of the tax due if the return is not filed within 60 days of the due date. IRC § 6651(a), (f). If no tax is due, there is no civil penalty for a failure to file. A willful failure to file a return is subject to a criminal penalty [IRC § 7203], but if no tax is due, it is unlikely that the Service will prosecute. The penalty for a failure to file a return is the exclusive civil penalty for that failure; neither the accuracy-related penalty nor the fraud penalty can apply to an underpayment due to a failure to file, but once the return is filed late, the accuracy-related penalty or the fraud penalty can apply to any underpayment attributable to an understatement in the late return. Treas. Reg. § 1.6662–2(a).

§ 1.6334. Failure to Pay Tax. If a taxpayer fails to make a timely payment of an income tax that is shown to be owing on a tax return filed by the taxpayer, a penalty is imposed in the amount of .5% of any unpaid tax for each month (or fraction thereof) in which an amount is unpaid. The penalties that can be imposed under this provision cannot exceed 25% in the aggregate. A similar penalty is applied if the taxpayer fails to pay within 10 days after notice and demand for payment any tax that is not shown on a return but which is due and owing. In certain circumstances, the monthly penalty will be 1%, instead of .5%. IRC § 6651(a)(2),(3), (d). The penalties will not apply if there is reasonable cause for the delay.

§ 1.6335. Other Penalties. The Code contains a great many civil penalties in addition to the several described above. For example, a taxpayer who files a frivolous income tax return is required to pay a $500 penalty in addition to any other penalties that might apply. IRC § 6702. Some of these penalties are severe, and some are relatively minor. Some of the penalties described above are applied more stringently, and are subject to more restricted exceptions, when a transaction is connected to a tax shelter.

§ 1.6336. Suspension of Penalty. A 1998 amendment provides that the imposition of certain penalties and additions to tax on an *individual* TP are suspended if the Service fails within a specified period to provide the individual with notice of the basis for the individual's liability and the amount thereof. IRC § 6404(g). This provision does not apply if the individual did not file a timely tax return for the year in question.

§ 1.6340. Criminal Penalties. When a taxpayer's failure to do a required act is willful or when fraud is involved, criminal penalties may apply. For example, if a person willfully attempts to evade or defeat any tax imposed by the Code, that person may be guilty of a felony which is punishable by a fine of up to $100,000 ($500,000 for a corporation) and by imprisonment for up to five years. IRC § 7201. If a person willfully fails to file a return, pay a tax, or keep or supply required information, that person may be guilty of a misdemeanor, which is punishable by a fine of up to $25,000 and by imprisonment of up to one year. IRC § 7203. The Code contains a number of criminal tax provisions.

§ 1.6350. Interest on Underpayments and Overpayments. In the event that a taxpayer fails to make a timely payment of the correct amount of tax that is due, interest is charged on the underpayment from the date that payment was due. IRC § 6601. If the taxpayer pays the government more than the required tax, the government is required to pay interest on the overpayment from the date thereof. IRC § 6611. As a consequence of a 1998 amendment, the interest rate for noncorporate taxpayers is the same for both overpayments and underpayments.

For noncorporate taxpayers, the rate of interest payable by the government on an overpayment and the rate of interest payable by a noncorporate taxpayer on an underpayment is equal to the "Federal short-term rate" plus three percentage points. IRC § 6621(a). The Federal short-term rate is the average market yield (during a calendar month) of marketable obligations of the United States that have remaining periods to maturity of three years or less. IRC § 1274(d)(1)(C). The Federal short-term rate is adjusted quarterly (the rate determined in the first month of a calendar quarter becomes the rate for the *following* calendar quarter), and so interest rates can change each quarter during a period in which an overpayment or underpayment is outstanding. IRC § 6621(b).

An individual taxpayer's liability for interest is suspended in the same manner as applies to penalties when the Service fails to provide timely notice to him as described in **§ 1.6336.** IRC § 6404(g).

§ 1.6360. Interest on Penalties. Interest does accumulate on a taxpayer's obligation to pay a penalty. For most penalties, interest commences on the date that a notice and demand for payment is made, and no interest is payable if the penalty is paid within ten days of the notice and demand. § 6601(e)(2)(A). However, for certain penalties, interest commences on the date on which the return for the taxable year in question was required to be filed. § 6601(e)(2)(B). The penalties for which interest commences with the due date of the return include: the fraud penalty, the accuracy-related penalty, and the penalty for failure to file a return. For suspension of an individual's liability for interest, see **§ 1.6350.**

§ 1.6400. Annual Accounting. Income tax liability is determined for annual periods according to the facts as they existed at that time. This annual reporting requirement, based on the facts known at that time, is necessary because of the administrative difficulties that a more open-ended approach would engender. See, *e.g.*, *Burnet v. Sanford & Brooks*, 282 U.S. 359, 365 (1931). If a return was properly filed on the basis of facts and estimates available at that time, the TP cannot change the tax liability by filing an amended return after the filing deadline for the original periods has passed unless the Commissioner accepts the amended return. The acceptance of the amended return is subject to the Commissioner's discretion. *Cameron v. Commissioner*, 105 T.C. 380, 386–387 (1995), aff'd *sub nom. Broadaway v. Commissioner*, 111 F.3d 593 (8th Cir. 1997).

§ 1.7000. CONCEPT OF INCOME. The tax system is based upon the concept of "income." The Sixteenth Amendment grants Congress the authority to "lay and collect taxes on incomes, from whatever source derived, without apportionment among the several states and without regard to any census or enumeration." The reference to "incomes" in the Sixteenth Amendment has been construed to refer to gross income as distinguished from gross receipts or taxable income.

§ 1.7100. Gross Income Generally. The general definition of gross income is set forth in IRC § 61 which provides that: "Except as otherwise provided in this subtitle, gross income means all income from whatever source derived...."

§ 1.7110.   Less Cost-of-Goods Sold. Gross income is equal to gross receipts less the cost-of-goods sold. For example, X sold a radio to Y for $50. X had paid $30 for the radio and $3 of his advertising and sales personnel expenses were attributable to the sale of the radio. X has gross receipts of $50, but his gross income is only $20. X had a net income of $17 after deducting his selling costs; the costs attributable to selling the radio are not deducted in determining gross income. However, in certain cases (such as the sale of stock), commissions and brokerage fees paid on a specific sale will reduce the amount realized by the taxpayer on the sale and thus will reduce the taxpayer's gross income. See **§§ 16.1530–16.1540.**

§ 1.7120.   Statutory Interpretation. The statutory language of IRC § 61 provides only very broad guidelines for determining income. The statute, however, is supplemented by extensive regulations. In addition, part II of subchapter B lists items which are specifically included in gross income while part III of subchapter B lists items which are specifically excluded from gross income.

§ 1.7130.   Rule-of-Thumb Test: Increase in Net Worth. There is no single criterion for determining what is income for tax purposes, but it may be helpful to think of gross income as an increase in net worth. Gross income may arise from the receipt of money, services, property, or any other benefit having financial value. One popular definition of income is that income equals the amount of wealth accumulated plus the value of the personal consumption enjoyed by a taxpayer during a taxable year. This is called the Haig–Simons definition.

§ 1.7200.   Realization of Income or Loss. A basic principle in tax law is that gain is not included in a taxpayer's gross income until the gain is "realized." The word *realized* is a term of art that refers to a significant event that represents the severance of gain from the property that produced the gain. Realization also is required before a loss incurred by a taxpayer can be taken into account. In general, realization of gain or loss occurs when property either is converted into cash or is exchanged for other property differing materially either in kind or in extent. Treas. Reg. § 1.1001–1(a). The difference in exchanged properties need not be great to be treated as "material." See, e.g., *Cottage Savings Ass'n v. Commissioner*, 499 U.S. 554 (1991). As noted below, there are only a few exceptions to the principle that realization is a prerequisite to inclusion in income.

§ 1.7210. Illustration. In Year One, *X* purchased stock for $100. By December, Year Two, the stock rose in value to $200. *X* enjoyed an economic (paper) gain on his stock in Year Two, but the gain was not realized in that year. In Year Three, *X* sold the stock for $500 cash; $100 of the $500 constitutes a return to *X* of the capital he had invested in the stock, and the remaining $400 is a realized gain which is included in *X*'s gross income. The sale of the stock severed the gain from the capital stock which produced that gain. The result would be the same if in Year Three *X* transferred his stock to *Y* in exchange for stock of a different corporation owned by *Y* and having a fair market value of $500.

§ 1.7220. Constitutional Limitation. The landmark case of *Eisner v. Macomber*, 252 U.S. 189 (1920) indicated that as a constitutional matter a gain *must* be realized by a taxpayer before it can be taxed by the government. Although there is now substantial doubt as to the continuing vitality of that decision, the substance of the opinion has been incorporated in general policy not to tax gain before it has been realized. However, there are exceptions to that policy, and so realization is not required in a few circumstances. See, e.g., the requirement in IRC § 1272 that the so-called "original issue discount" of certain debt instruments be accrued daily as interest income to the holder of the debt instrument even though it is not realized. The general rule is that realization will be required, and the few exceptions to that general rule rest on compelling policy considerations.

§ 1.7300. The Concept of Basis. *Basis* is another vital term of art in tax law. It represents a concept of fundamental importance which must be fully mastered in any tax course.

§ 1.7310. Definition. A taxpayer's basis in property is his investment in that property for tax purposes. Basis is the maximum amount a taxpayer can receive in payment for an asset *without* realizing a gain.

§ 1.7320. Use of Basis. The concept of basis is most frequently used in determining the amount of gain or loss realized on the sale, exchange, or other disposition of an asset. Basis may also be used for other purposes such as the determination of the amount of depreciation that is allowable for an asset used in a trade or business.

§ 1.7321. Illustration 1. *X* purchased unimproved land in Year One for $10,000 cash and made no improvements. In

Year Three, the land had a value of $10,000 and X sold the land for $10,000 cash. Since X had a basis of $10,000 in the land, the $10,000 payment received by him in Year Three was a return of his capital, and X will not realize either a gain or a loss on the sale.

§ 1.7322. Illustration 2. X purchased unimproved land for $10,000 cash and made no improvements. Three years later, the land had a value of $8,000, and X sold the land for $8,000. X realized a loss of $2,000 on the sale since his investment in the land was $2,000 greater than the amount he realized on the sale. Whether X will be allowed a deduction for this loss depends upon statutory rules to be discussed later in this book.

§ 1.7323. Illustration 3. X purchased unimproved land for $10,000 cash and made no improvements. Three years later, the land had a value of $14,000, and X transferred the land to Y in exchange for stocks having a fair market value of $14,000. Thus, X received property having a value of $14,000 in exchange for land in which X had a basis of $10,000. Therefore, X realized a gain of $4,000 on the exchange.

§ 1.7330. Determination of Basis. There are several distinct methods of determining basis. Each method has application in special tax contexts.

§ 1.7331. Cost Basis. In most circumstances, a taxpayer's initial basis in an asset will be equal to the actual amount of his investment (i.e., his cost). Thus, where a taxpayer pays $500 cash for an automobile, his basis in the automobile is $500. If he subsequently sells the automobile for $600, he realizes a gain of $100 (amount received less the cost basis). If a taxpayer owns unimproved land with a basis of $10,000 and a fair market value of $15,000, and he exchanges the land for corporate stock having a value of $15,000, he will realize a gain of $5,000 on the exchange. Moreover, he will have a basis of $15,000 in the stock he received since that amount represents his cost investment in the stock. The basis of property acquired in exchange for services performed by the taxpayer is equal to the fair market value of the property on the date of acquisition. See § 2.1530–2.1531. The basis of property purchased subject to an encumbrance is determined in the manner stated at § **16.1520** and § **16.2200.**

If a taxpayer exchanges one item of property in kind (Item A) for another item of property (Item B) and if the exchange constitutes a taxable transaction, the Court of Claims held that the taxpayer's basis in Item B is equal to the fair market value of Item B at the time of the exchange. *Philadelphia Park Amusement Co. v. United States*, 126 F.Supp. 184 (Ct. Cl. 1954). [Note that the Court of Claims subsequently was absorbed into the United States Court of Appeals for the Federal Circuit.] Thus, the critical element for determining the basis of property acquired in an arm's length exchange (as contrasted to a purchase for cash) is the fair market value of the *acquired* property; the value of the transferred property is not utilized.

§ 1.7332. Transferred Basis. In some circumstances, a taxpayer's initial basis in an asset will be established by reference to someone else's basis (i.e., the basis of one person in an asset may be transferred to another who takes legal possession of the asset). For example, subject to an adjustment for gift taxes paid, the donee of a gift has the same basis in the donated property that the donor had. IRC § 1015. Property, the basis of which is determined in whole or in part by reference to the basis that a transferor had in that property, is referred to as "transferred basis property." IRC § 7701(a)(43).

§ 1.7333. Exchanged Basis. In some circumstances, a taxpayer's basis in one asset may be transferred (in whole or in part) to another asset of the taxpayer. The asset to which basis is transferred is referred to as "exchanged basis property." IRC § 7701(a)(44).

§ 1.7333–1. Illustration. *X* owns all 100 outstanding shares of stock of Win All, Inc. Win All, Inc. declares a stock dividend of 100 shares of its stock to *X*. *X* realizes no gain on receiving the stock dividend [IRC § 305], but his basis in his original 100 shares of stock will be reallocated among the 200 shares of stock he holds after the stock dividend was distributed. IRC § 307. The new 100 shares of stock that *X* received is exchanged basis property.

§ 1.7334. Substituted Basis Property. Transferred basis properties [§ 1.7332] and exchanged basis properties [§ 1.7333] are collectively referred to as "substituted basis property." IRC § 7701(a)(42).

§ **1.7335. Constructive Basis.** In some circumstances, a taxpayer's basis in an asset is determined without regard to the amount invested in the asset by the taxpayer or by anyone else. For example, where a taxpayer acquires property from a decedent by inheritance or in some similar manner, the taxpayer's basis usually will equal the fair market value of the asset at the decedent's death. IRC § 1014.

§ **1.7336. Adjusted Basis.** A taxpayer's initial basis in an asset will be adjusted upward or downward to reflect subsequent events having tax significance. The basis of an asset at any given time is referred to as the *adjusted basis* of the asset. It is the adjusted basis of an asset that is used to determine the amount of a taxpayer's gain or loss for tax purposes on the sale or disposition of the asset.

§ **1.7336–1. Capital Improvement.** An upward adjustment of basis will be necessary when a taxpayer makes a capital improvement to an asset. Thus, if a taxpayer invests $5,000 in landscaping realty with an initial basis of $10,000, his basis for tax purposes is adjusted to $15,000.

§ **1.7336–2. Recapture of Investment.** A downward adjustment to basis will be made when a taxpayer *recaptures* part of his investment or when a taxpayer becomes entitled to a tax benefit which is dependent upon his basis in the asset. Examples of such a benefit include a depreciation deduction and a partial loss caused by a casualty.

§ **1.7336–2A. Illustration.** In Year One, X purchased a truck for $5,000 which he used in his business. X properly took a depreciation deduction of $1,000 on his tax return for Year One on account of his use of the truck, and accordingly his basis in the truck is reduced by $1,000. Then, on January 1, Year Two, X's truck was damaged when a tree limb fell on it. The *value* of X's truck before the accident was $3,600 and its value immediately afterwards was $3,400. Because of this casualty loss, X is entitled to a tax deduction of $200 and X's adjusted basis must be reduced by the corresponding amount. Thus, immediately after the casualty, X's adjusted basis in the truck is $3,800 (i.e., $4,000 basis minus the $200 casualty loss).

§ 1.7336–3. Mortgages and Liens. The effect that mortgages and liens on property have on a taxpayer's basis in the property, as well as the effect that the transfer or receipt of property subject to a lien has on the amount of gain or loss recognized on an exchange, are discussed at **§§ 16.1510–16.1520** and **§ 16.2200**.

§ 1.7400. The Concept of Recognition. *Recognition* is another term of art in tax law. As noted above, a gain or loss or other income to a taxpayer will not be taken into account for tax purposes until the gain, loss, or income is realized. However, even realized gain or loss will not be included in the computation of taxable income unless the realized gain, loss, or other income item is also *recognized*. Thus, realization is essential to taxability but not sufficient. The concept of recognition refines the question of when and how a particular gain or loss is to be taxed. Problems of recognition relate to specific tax law provisions governing certain transactions. *In the absence of a special nonrecognition provision, income is recognized and taxable in the year that it is realized.* IRC § 1001(c). A "nonrecognition transaction" is a disposition of property in which gain or loss is not recognized in whole or in part. IRC § 7701(a)(45).

§ 1.7410. Effect of Nonrecognition. A nonrecognition provision in the tax laws differs from a provision excluding an item of income from tax in that the latter *excludes* the item from *all* tax consequences while a nonrecognition provision typically only *defers* the tax consequences to a later date. It is useful to distinguish the concept of "nonrecognition" from the concept of "exclusion," but the reader should be aware that the term "nonrecognition" frequently is used to refer to exclusions as well as to tax-deferral provisions. See, e.g., IRC § 7701(a)(45).

§ 1.7420. Adjustment of Basis. Tax deferral through a nonrecognition provision typically is accomplished by making an adjustment to a taxpayer's basis in the property involved. The operation of several of these nonrecognition provisions will be examined in more detail later, but a few illustrations may be helpful.

§ 1.7421. Illustration 1. *X* has a basis of $10,000 in Blackacre (unimproved land) which he holds for investment and which has a value of $25,000. *X* transfers Blackacre to *Y* in exchange for Whiteacre having a value of $25,000. *X* also holds Whiteacre (unimproved land) for investment. *X recognizes* no taxable gain on the exchange of land even though he *realizes* a gain of $15,000. IRC § 1031. *X*'s basis in Whiteacre, however, will not equal his cost (the $25,000 value of Blackacre transferred by him). Since $15,000 of *X*'s cost investment in Whiteacre is attributable to the appreciated value of Blackacre in excess of his basis, and since *X* did not recognize the gain from that appreciation, *X* cannot include that $15,000 of appreciation in his basis in Whiteacre. Accordingly, IRC § 1031(d) provides that *X*'s basis in Whiteacre is $10,000—the same as it was in Blackacre. If, two years later, *X* sells Whiteacre for $25,000, he would *recognize* a gain of $15,000 ($25,000 amount realized minus $10,000 basis). Thus, in effect, the $15,000 gain realized by *X* on the exchange of Blackacre is deferred in recognition until *X* sells Whiteacre. Note that Whiteacre is exchanged basis property in *X*'s hands. § **1.7333.**

§ **1.7422. Illustration 2.** If, in § **1.7421**, *X* had sold Whiteacre for $20,000, he would recognize a gain of $10,000 ($20,000 amount realized minus $10,000 basis). At first blush, it would appear that $5,000 of the gain realized by *X* in the exchange of Blackacre would then have no tax consequences whatsoever, but this is not so. If the $15,000 gain *realized* by *X* on the exchange of Blackacre had been *recognized*, *X* would have had a basis of $25,000 in Whiteacre; and then, when *X* sold Whiteacre for $20,000 he would have recognized a *loss* of $5,000 ($25,000 basis minus $20,000 amount realized). Thus, *X* would have had a net effect of a $10,000 gain (a $15,000 gain on the exchange of land minus a $5,000 loss on the sale of Whiteacre). The deferral of the gain on Blackacre ultimately resulted in the same tax effect to *X*; namely, a $10,000 gain on the entire transaction when he sold Whiteacre.

§ **1.7423. Illustration 3.** If, in § **1.7421**, *X* had had a basis of $30,000 in Blackacre, he would have *realized* a $5,000 loss on the exchange for Whiteacre ($30,000 basis minus $25,000 received) but this loss would not be *recognized* because of IRC § 1031. Instead, the tax consequences of the transaction are deferred, and *X*'s basis in Whiteacre would become $30,000. If *X* later sold Whiteacre for $25,000, he would *recognize* a loss of $5,000 at that time.

§ **1.8000. IMPUTED INCOME FROM PROPERTY OR SERVICES.** A taxpayer's personal enjoyment of property that he owns provides him with the benefit of the use of that property. However, the benefit thus derived by the taxpayer from the use of his own property is not included in his gross income. Similarly, a taxpayer's performance of services for his own benefit (or for that of his immediate family) will benefit him by the value of those services, but such self-created benefits are excluded from gross income. Some examples of imputed income that are excluded from gross income are given below.

§ **1.8100. Home Ownership.** *X* has $40,000 which she has invested at a ten percent rate of return. *X* wishes to reside in a house currently owned by *Y*. *Y* offers to sell the house to *X* for $40,000 or to rent it to *X* at an annual rental of $4,000. If *X* elects to rent the house, she can continue to collect $4,000 income on her investment; yet since that income is subject to tax, *X* cannot satisfy the full amount of the rent solely by paying over the after-tax income from her investment. *X* must make up the difference between the $4,000 income and the tax thereon from her capital or from other income sources. If, instead, *X* withdraws her $40,000 investment and purchases the house for cash, she will enjoy the benefit (or "income") of the $40,000 investment in her use of the house. Since *X*'s use of the house does not increase her gross income, she can enjoy the benefit of living in the house by utilizing the "income" from the $40,000 that she invested in the house. If *X* decides to rent the house from *Y*, the income from her $40,000 investment will not be sufficient to pay the rent because that income is included in her gross income.

§ **1.8200. Improvements.** A taxpayer purchases wood worth $50 and uses it to construct a cabinet having a value of $460. While the taxpayer has converted his services into $410 of value of property and thus has increased his net worth, none of the value added by his services is included in his gross income. Of course, the taxpayer's basis in the cabinet is equal to his cost of $50.

§ **1.8300. Services.** *B* shaves his face each morning. A barber would charge *B* $10 for that service. *B* does not recognize gross income from the value of the service he performed for himself.

§ **1.9000. SIGNIFICANCE OF STATE LAW AND FORM OF TRANSACTION.**

§ **1.9100. State Law.** The rights and interests of persons in property typically are determined by local law; federal law rarely deals with such rights and interests. Federal tax law, therefore, looks to the applicable state law to determine the interests, rights, powers, duties and liability of parties, but the tax consequences of possessing those rights, powers, etc. are determined by federal law. *Morgan v. Commissioner*, 309 U.S. 78 (1940). For example, whether a husband is obligated to make a payment to his divorced wife and the circumstances in which such obligation is terminated are determined by state law; whether payments having the characteristics established by state law are deductible as "alimony" for tax purposes is determined by federal tax law. In determining whether such payments qualify as "alimony" as that term is used in IRC §§ 71 and 215(a), it is irrelevant whether the payments are characterized as "alimony" for state law purposes.

§ 1.9200. Substance Versus Form. When a transaction or a series of steps to a transaction have no economic significance and are designed solely to obtain favorable tax consequences, the tax law will recharacterize the transactions (or the steps) so as to reflect the economic substance of what was accomplished without regard to economically meaningless transactions or steps. See, §§ **1.9300**, **19.4121.**

§ 1.9300. Economic Substance. The economic substance doctrine dictates that a transaction which has no independent non-tax purpose will be disregarded for tax purposes. The economic substance doctrine is discussed at § **5.9100.**

§ 1.9A000. ESTOPPEL OF THE COMMISSIONER. While, in theory, equitable estoppel can be applied to prevent the Commissioner from asserting a position or imposing a tax, the courts are loathe to estop the Service and will do so only in rare circumstances. *Bennett v. Commissioner*, 935 F.2d 1285 (4th Cir. 1991) (unpublished opinion). In the absence of compelling features, "the policy in favor of efficient collection of the public revenues outweighs the policy of the estoppel doctrine in its usual context." *Schuster v. Commissioner*, 312 F.2d 311, 317 (9th Cir. 1962). A necessary, but not sufficient, element to the successful imposition of the estoppel doctrine against the Commissioner is that the taxpayer must establish that conduct of a government agent or entity reasonably induced detrimental reliance by a private party. *Bennett v. Commissioner, supra.*

CHAPTER TWO

GROSS INCOME

§ 2.0000. **ITEMS INCLUDED IN AND EXCLUDED FROM GROSS INCOME.** The code and the regulations devote substantial attention to the various forms that gross income may take. They list and describe many items that are to be included in and excluded from gross income.

§ 2.1000. **ITEMS INCLUDED IN GROSS INCOME.** A taxpayer may realize a taxable gain in a great number of ways. Some forms of gross income are rather subtle. Over the years, the code and regulations have been modified to close loopholes and to prevent artificial tax avoidance transactions. Remember that the underlying policy of gross income determinations is to see that a taxpayer pays a proportional share of his yearly financial gains (in the broadest sense) as taxes.

§ 2.1100. **Borrowed Funds.** If a taxpayer borrows $1,000 from a bank, his assets are increased by that amount; but since the taxpayer's liabilities also are increased by $1,000, there is no increase in the taxpayer's net worth. Even though the loan provides the taxpayer with ready cash, it would be poor tax policy to tax the taxpayer on the borrowed funds since they do not reflect an increase in his wealth. It also would be poor economic policy to discourage the obtaining of loans by taxing the debtor on the amount borrowed; at the very least, if loans were taxed, the debtor would have to be granted a deduction for repayments, which would unduly complicate the administration of the tax. While there is no statutory provision for exclusion, the courts and the Service uniformly have excluded borrowed funds from the debtor's gross income. See, e.g., *Commissioner v. Tufts*, 461 U.S. 300, 307 (1983). This exclusion is part of the common law of taxation.

§ 2.1110. **Deposits.** It has been settled for some time that a transferee of a deposit will not recognize income therefrom if the function of the deposit is to secure that the depositor will not damage the transferee's property during the term of a lease or other contractual period or to secure the performance by the depositor of some contractually required act. However, until a few years ago, the Commissioner maintained that a "deposit" is included in the gross income of a transferee upon receipt if it secures the performance of a contractually required act (such as a payment for services or goods) that would constitute gross income to the transferee when performed. The Commissioner did not treat such transfers as a "deposit" but rather treated them as advance payments for goods or services. This matter was resolved by the Supreme Court in its decision in *Commissioner v. Indianapolis Power & Light Co.*, 493 U.S. 203 (1990), in which the Court rejected the Commissioner's position. The Court held that the critical issue is whether the transferred funds constitute security for the performance of an act, or whether the transferred funds constitute a prepayment for goods or services to be received by the "depositor" at some future date. While the former is not income to the transferee, a prepayment (or advance payment) is included in the transferee's gross income upon receipt. While this is not always an easy distinction to make, the Supreme Court provided helpful guidelines in *Indianapolis Power*.

In *Indianapolis Power*, the taxpayer was an electrical company (a utility) that required customers who failed to meet certain credit standards to deposit funds with the taxpayer (the transferee). About 5% of the taxpayer's customers were required to make that deposit. For some of the years involved, the taxpayer paid no interest to the depositor for the first six months and then paid interest at a 3% rate. After a change of its practice, there were several years in which the taxpayer paid no interest for the first twelve months of a deposit and then paid the depositor interest at a 6% rate. The deposited funds were commingled with the taxpayer's own funds. The depositor was entitled to a return of the deposited funds upon satisfying any one of the following conditions: (1) the depositor subsequently satisfies a credit test, (2) the depositor makes timely payments either for nine consecutive months or ten out of twelve consecutive months, or (3) the depositor discontinues the use of the utility's electricity. The depositor was not obligated to purchase any electricity from the utility. When entitled to a refund of a deposit, the depositor could choose either to have the refund paid in cash or by check, or the depositor could elect to have the refund applied to future bills from the utility. If the depositor defaulted on the payment of a utility bill when the deposit was still in the hands of the taxpayer, the taxpayer had the right to use the deposit to pay the defaulted amount. Any deposit that was left unclaimed for seven years escheated to the State.

The Court held that the deposits that the taxpayer received are not included in the taxpayer's gross income. The Court acknowledged that the deposit gave an economic benefit to the taxpayer since the taxpayer had the use of the deposited funds at less than market interest rates. But, the Court held that a transferee's economic benefit is not sufficient to characterize a transfer as an advance payment. To be so characterized, the transferee must have "complete dominion" over the transferred funds—i.e., the transferee must have some guarantee that it will be allowed to keep the funds.

The taxpayer in *Indianapolis Power* paid no interest at all for some months of its use of the funds, and thereafter its interest payments were substantially below market rates. But, the benefit that the taxpayer obtained thereby was the opportunity to use the deposited funds to produce income at a higher rate than the interest payable on the deposit. The Court deemed that opportunity comparable to what occurs in a typical loan setting—i.e., the borrower is able to produce more income with the borrowed funds than his interest payments. So, the Court held that the tax characterization of the transaction is not determined by the fact that the transferee obtains an economic benefit. The Court also held that the taxpayer's commingling of the deposited funds with its own did not affect the characterization of the deposit; borrowed funds typically are commingled with the borrower's own funds.

The Court stressed that, while a prepayment can secure the payor's performance just as a deposit does, a prepayment does more than that. "It protects against the risk that the purchaser will back out of a deal before the seller performs." When a transfer is a prepayment, the transferee is assured that so long as it fulfills its part of the bargain, the transferred funds are its to keep. In the case of the utility, the taxpayer could not retain the transferred funds permanently unless the depositor used its electricity (which the depositor was not required to do) and either elected to have the taxpayer apply the deposited funds in payment therefor or defaulted on payment so that the taxpayer was entitled to apply the deposit in payment of the defaulted amount. In *Indianapolis Power*, the Court stated:

> The individual who makes an advance payment retains no right to insist upon the return of the funds; so long as the recipient fulfills the terms of the bargain, the money is its to keep. The customer who submits a deposit to the utility, like

> the lender in the previous hypothetical, retains the right to insist upon repayment in cash; he may *choose* to apply the money to the purchase of electricity, but he assumes no obligation to do so, and the utility therefore acquires no unfettered "dominion" over the money at the time of receipt. [Emphasis in original.]

For a criticism of the Supreme Court's decision, see Klein, *Tailor to the Emperor with No Clothes: The Supreme Court's Tax Rules for Deposits and Advance Payments*, 41 UCLA L. Rev. 1685 (1994).

When funds are borrowed at below market interest rates, there usually will be tax consequences to both the borrower and the lender, but not in all such cases. See §§ **2.1540–2.1547**, and **5.4200.** The tax provision that imposes tax consequences on below market interest rate loans (IRC § 7872) was adopted in 1984, and the taxable years involved in the *Indianapolis Power* cases preceded that date. Under current law, the deposits that were the subject of that case would constitute a "compensation-related loan" within the meaning of IRC § 7872(c)(1)(B)—i.e., the bargain element in the utility's cost of receiving the economic benefit of the loan would constitute partial consideration for the service that the utility provides to the depositors.

The Proposed Regulations treat a deposit as a loan to the transferee unless the beneficial enjoyment derived from the deposited funds are retained by the transferor—for example, when the deposited funds are required to be held in escrow and *all* of the interest earned from the escrowed funds is payable to the transferor, the deposit will not be treated as a loan to the transferee. Prop. Reg. § 1.7872–2(b)(1)(iii). Under the facts that occurred in *Indianapolis Power*, the deposit in that case would constitute a loan to the transferee.

Therefore, if the facts of *Indianapolis Power* had occurred after the adoption of IRC § 7872, Prop. Reg. § 1.7872–2(b)(1) would apply IRC § 7872 to the utility company and to the depositors for the period during which the interest rate payable to the depositors (if any) was below a standardized rate of interest called the "applicable Federal rate." However, § 7872(c)(3) provides a *de minimis* exception under which that Code provision does not apply on any day on which the balance of the outstanding loans between the borrower and the lender does not exceed $10,000, provided that tax avoidance was not a principal purpose of the interest arrangement. It is highly unlikely that any of a utility's depositors would deposit more than that amount, and so IRC § 7872 usually will cause no tax consequences in such cases. But, in commercial settings in which a deposit of a large sum is made or in which a substantial amount of loans between the parties is outstanding, IRC § 7872 may impose tax consequences.

It is noteworthy that the Supreme Court's decision in *Indianapolis Power* has been applied to more than deposits. Property or funds are not received under a claim of right, and therefore are not included in the recipient's gross income, if the property or funds are subject to a substantial restriction on their disposition or use. The same exclusion applies if there is a fixed obligation to return the property or funds. See *Florida Progress Corp. v. Commissioner*, 114 T.C. 587 (2000); *Houston Industries Inc. v. U.S.*, 125 F.3d 1442, 1444–45 (Fed. Cir. 1997).

§ 2.1120.   Prepayments. The general rule is that the receipt of an advanced payment for services or property must be included in income at the time of receipt. See Treas. Reg. § 1.61–8(b). This rule is subject to certain specialized exceptions. See Rev. Proc. 2004–34.

§ 2.1200.   Discharge of Indebtedness. A creditor's discharge of a debtor's pecuniary obligation for less than the full amount that is due increases the debtor's net worth (or decreases the amount of his insolvency).

§ 2.1210.   Income to Debtor. In its decision in *United States v. Kirby Lumber Co.*, 284 U.S. 1 (1931), the Supreme Court established that the forgiveness or discharge of a debt can constitute income to the debtor. Prior to that decision, it was doubtful that a discharge of a debt could cause the debtor to realize income. The Supreme Court's decision is codified in § 61(a)(12), which expressly includes in gross income the amount of a taxpayer's discharge of indebtedness. A discharge or a forgiveness of a debt refers to a creditor's cancellation of all or a portion of a debt without receiving adequate consideration. Several terms are used interchangeably to refer to the elimination or reduction of a debt for inadequate consideration—namely, it is referred to as: (1) discharge of indebtedness, (2) forgiveness of indebtedness or (3) cancellation of indebtedness.

For purposes of IRC § 108 (the principal statutory provision that deals with discharge of indebtedness income), a "debt" refers to an indebtedness for which the taxpayer is liable or which constitutes an encumbrance on property that the taxpayer holds. IRC § 108(d)(1). Should that statutory definition also be utilized in cases involving the application of a common law rule of discharge of indebtedness income as codified in IRC § 61(a)(12)? See *Zarin v. Commissioner*, **§ 2.1297–4**, in which the Third Circuit, while dividing 2–1 on that issue, held that the definition of debt in IRC § 108(d)(1) also applies to IRC § 61(a)(12).

After the *Kirby Lumber* decision, the courts began to define the circumstances when a discharge of a debt will constitute income and when it will not. Thus, initially, the rules for determining income in this area were court-made, i.e., they were common law rules rather than statutory ones.

If certain entities forgive $600 or more of debt, the entity is required to file a return setting forth information about the discharge. The entity must also send information about the discharge (and the information filed on the return) to the debtor. IRC § 6050P.

    § 2.1211. Statutory Rules. In 1939, Congress passed the antecedent of IRC § 108, which was substantially modified in later years especially as a result of the amendments adopted as part of the Bankruptcy Tax Act of 1980 and of the 1986 Tax Reform Act (TRA). Prior to the 1980 amendments, the exclusive function of IRC § 108 was to permit a debtor who *realized* income from a discharge of indebtedness to elect not to *recognize* that income in certain circumstances. If the election were made, the nonrecognition of income was balanced by adjustments required by IRC § 1017 to the basis of property held by the debtor [for the meaning of "basis," see **§ 1.7300**]. The 1980 amendments substantially expanded the scope of IRC § 108 so that much (but not all) of what had been treated as unrealized income under the common law rules for a discharge of indebtedness was removed from the common law rules and subjected to special treatment in IRC § 108 itself. The 1980 amendments continued the prior law's authorization for a taxpayer to elect nonrecognition of realized income in certain circumstances, but this election was terminated by the 1986 TRA. Thus, after 1986, income realized from a discharge of a debt will be recognized or not according to statutory or common law directions; with one minor exception for certain "qualified real property business indebtedness" [see

§ **2.1240**], the taxpayer is not granted an election to prevent recognition.

Under the current state of the law, the determination of the income tax consequences of a discharge of indebtedness is determined to a greater extent by statutory rules than was previously so. However, there are a number of common law rules concerning discharge of indebtedness that were not codified or altered by the 1980 and 1986 amendments, and it appears that those common law rules continue to operate. So, those common law rules are equally as important as the statutory provision. Even where statutory rules apply, it is helpful in construing the statute to know the common law rules that were codified or altered by the statute. The discussion below will indicate whether the rules in question are statutory or common law principles.

§ **2.1212. Distinguish Realization from Recognition and Exclusion from Nonrecognition.** In analyzing a discharge of indebtedness, the student should first determine whether income is *realized*. If so, the student should then determine whether the income is recognized. If an item of realized income is not recognized, the student should then consider whether the item is excluded from income or whether it is nonrecognized under some type of deferral arrangement. The meaning of "realization," "recognition," and "exclusion" are discussed at §§ **1.7200–1.7210**, and §§ **1.7400–1.7423**. While it is not essential to make these distinctions, to do so should enhance the student's comprehension of the principles involved.

§ **2.1212–1. Illustration 1: Satisfaction at Less than Face Amount.** X loans $8,000 to Y who is not engaged in a farming business. Because of Y's subsequent financial difficulties, X accepts $6,000 in full satisfaction of Y's $8,000 debt even though Y is solvent. Y *realizes* income of $2,000 (the amount of debt that was forgiven by X). Since the 1986 TRA repealed the provisions of IRC § 108 that would permit a debtor to elect nonrecognition of discharge of indebtedness income in certain cases, Y will recognize the entire $2,000 of realized income.

§ **2.1212–2. Illustration 2: Redemption of Bonds.** Win All, Inc. issued $1,000 face amount bonds for which it received $1,000 per bond. One year later, Win All purchased its own bonds on the open market for $950 per bond. At the time of purchase, Win All was solvent. Win All realized and recognized income of $50 per bond since that amount of its debt was, in effect, discharged.

§ 2.1212–3. Illustration 3: Expiration of Period of Limitations. *X* loaned $10,000 to *Y*, who is not engaged in a farming business, in a bona fide transaction. Four years later, the statute of limitations for *X*'s collection of the loan expired. The expiration of the limitations period provides *Y* with a valid defense to any claim that *X* might make for the repayment of the loan. The date on which a liability is terminated turns on the factual issue as to when the debtor no longer intends to pay the debt and the creditor can no longer reasonably expect payment. *Bear Mfg. Co. v. United States*, 430 F.2d 152 (7th Cir. 1970). The expiration of the statute of limitations does not necessarily terminate a debt since the debtor may nevertheless intend to repay it. In the absence of evidence that the debtor intends to repay, however, the expiration of the limitations period will constitute a discharge of the debt. See *Estate of Bankhead v. Commissioner*, 60 T.C. 535 (1973). In the instant case, the expiration of the statute of limitations likely will be treated as a discharge of the $10,000 debt, and the rules governing discharge of indebtedness are applicable.

§ 2.1212–4. Illustration 4: Prepayment of Mortgage Debt at a Discount. *X* owned a personal residence which had a value of $125,000 and was subject to a mortgage debt, the outstanding balance of which was $45,000. *X* was solvent. The mortgage debt was owed to the Friendly National Bank. *X* had purchased the property 10 years earlier from *Y*, and so the mortgage debt was not a purchase money mortgage. The Bank offered to cancel the mortgage debt for a payment of $30,000. *X* accepted the Bank's offer and paid $30,000 to the Bank in full satisfaction of the debt. *X* will recognize gross income of $15,000 because the cancellation of the debt at a discount constitutes a discharge of indebtedness of that amount. *Michaels v. Commissioner*, 87 T.C. 1412 (1986).

§ 2.1213. Acquisition of Debt by Person Related to the Debtor. Section 108(e)(4), which was added to the Code in

1980, treats an acquisition of a debt by a person who is related to the debtor as an acquisition by the debtor himself, and so the acquisition can give rise to discharge of indebtedness income if the price paid is less than the amount owing on the debt. The statute defines who are related persons for this purpose. For example: (1) the spouse, children, grandchildren, and parents of an individual (as well as spouses of the individual's children and grandchildren) are related to that individual [IRC § 108(e)(4)(B)]; (2) an individual and a corporation more than 50% of the value of whose stock is owned by that individual are related; and (3) a grantor or beneficiary of a trust is related to the fiduciary of that trust. The foregoing is only a short list of related persons. Section 108(e)(4) does not apply if the related party acquires the debt *from* a person who also is related to the debtor.

Presumably, the purpose of this provision is to prevent a debtor from circumventing the discharge of indebtedness rule by having the debt acquired by a person who is closely related to the debtor. While, in such a case, the debtor remains liable for the repayment of the entire debt, the amount of "repayment" that is in excess of the amount paid by the related person to purchase the debt in substance may represent a gift to the related person or a contribution to its capital.

The problem is that although the debtor is treated as if he acquired the debt, the debt still is outstanding in the hands of the related party. How is the outstanding debt to be treated? What treatment is to be accorded to the debtor's subsequent actual satisfaction of the debt? If the related party sells the debt to an unrelated third person, how is that sale to be treated? These and other questions have been answered by Treasury in the regulation that it promulgated under IRC § 108 on December 28, 1992. While the treatment accorded by the regulation differs from the treatment suggested in the legislative history to the 1980 Act, the regulation adheres to the current treatment of original issue discount, which was omitted from the legislative history's treatment of this item. It would seem that the regulation's validity will be sustained.

§ 2.1214. Spurious Discharge of a Debt. As noted above, a discharge of a debt occurs only to the extent that the debt is canceled for inadequate consideration. If adequate consideration is given for the cancellation, the debt is satisfied (as contrasted to forgiven). A "spurious" discharge of indebtedness is a cancellation of a debt that appears superficially to be a discharge but in fact is made for valuable consideration. For example, if a debt were canceled in consideration of services performed for the creditor by the debtor or in payment for property acquired by the creditor from the debtor, the cancellation of the debt would not constitute a discharge covered by IRC § 108 or by the common law rules governing discharge of indebtedness. Instead, the cancellation constitutes consideration paid for the services or the property received by the creditor—i.e., the debt was satisfied. The amount of such cancelled debt will constitute an amount realized by the debtor for the sale of services or property. See § **2.1252.**

In some cases, a debt may be canceled in part as consideration for value received by the creditor and in part as a discharge of a portion of the debt. Only the latter portion of the canceled debt is covered by IRC § 108 and by the previously mentioned common law rules.

§ **2.1215.   Student Loans.** The discharge of *certain* student loans will not cause the debtor to recognize gross income if the discharge is pursuant to a provision in the loan agreement that all or a portion of the debt would be canceled if the student worked for a specified period of time in certain professions for any of a broad class of employers. IRC § 108(f). To qualify, the purpose of the loan must be to assist the student in attending a qualified educational institution, and the lender must be an entity that is one of those listed in IRC § 108(f)(2). The repayment of a taxpayer's student loans under the National Health Service Corps (NHSC) Loan Program (or under a similar state program) because the taxpayer provided medical services in a specified geographic area is excluded from the taxpayer's gross income. IRC § 108(f)(4).

§ **2.1216.   Modification of the Terms of a Debt Instrument.** If the amount of principal required by a debt instrument to be paid to a creditor is reduced, then the reduction *may* cause discharge of indebtedness income to the debtor. But, regardless of whether the amount of principal that is payable is altered, what if other terms of the debt instrument are changed? For example, what if the interest rate or the maturity date is changed? Changes that do not lower the amount of principal payable by the debtor will not cause discharge of indebtedness income, but they may cause other tax consequences.

Treas. Reg. § 1.1001–1(a) states that an exchange of one item of property for another that differs *materially*, either in kind or in extent, will trigger realization of gain or loss. In *Cottage Savings Ass'n v. Commissioner*, 499 U.S. 554 (1991), the Supreme Court sustained the validity of that regulation and adopted a very broad construction as to what constitutes a *material* difference in exchanged properties. In *Cottage Savings*, a taxpayer was permitted to realize and recognize a loss on what amounted to an exchange of participating interests in 252 residential mortgages for participating interests in 305 different residential mortgages. While the mortgages were secured by different properties and had different obligors, they were economically equivalent interests. The Supreme Court held that to constitute materially different properties, it was necessary only that the exchanged properties "embody legally distinct entitlements." The Court held that the differences in obligors and security for the two sets of mortgages were sufficient to satisfy that requirement.

In Treas. Reg. § 1.1001–3, expanding on the *Cottage Savings* decision, Treasury maintains that a substantial modification of a debt instrument represents an exchange of the old instrument for a new debt instrument and can trigger realization and recognition of a gain or loss. With one exception, a "modification" refers to any alteration of a legal right or obligation of the issuer or the holder of the debt instrument. Treas. Reg. § 1.1001–3(c). With some exceptions, a change of rights or obligations that occurs by reason of the terms of the debt instrument itself will not constitute a modification. *Ibid.* A modification will not result in there being a constructive exchange of debt instruments unless the modification is "substantial," and the regulation provides guidance as to what constitutes a "substantial" change. See also, PLR 9819043 for examples of changes that were not deemed substantial. The regulation is discussed at §§ **16.1700**, **16.1720** *infra*.

§ 2.1220. Lost Deduction. If a debtor would have been allowed an income tax deduction had the debtor paid a debt which instead was discharged (and so was never paid), the discharge of the debt is excluded from the debtor's income by IRC § 108(e)(2).

This exclusion from income was added by the 1980 amendments to IRC § 108, and it constitutes a true exclusion in that there is no adjustment of basis or other tax attributes because of it.

§ 2.1221. **Rationale.** When a debtor recognizes income from the discharge of a debt, the substance of the transaction is that the debtor received from the creditor property equal to the amount discharged and then returned that property to the creditor in payment of the debt. Thus, while the debtor should recognize income from the value received from the creditor, the debtor should be permitted a deduction to the extent that the payment of the debt would be deductible. If the payment of the debt would be fully deductible, the amount of the constructive deduction equals the income recognized by virtue of the discharge of the debt; and, so far as the debtor is concerned, the income and deduction from the transaction is a wash. For that reason, the Code excludes the discharge of deductible debts from the debtor's income and thereby reflects the fact that the debtor does not have any net income from the transaction.

§ 2.1230. **Insolvency of Debtor.** Prior to the 1980 amendments to IRC § 108, a debtor realized no income from the discharge of a debt if the debtor was insolvent immediately after the debt was discharged. Originally, this was a common law rule, but the current version is a statutory replacement of the common law. In this context, a person is insolvent if the total of his outstanding liabilities exceed the total value of his assets. In determining insolvency, there is authority that assets of the taxpayer that are exempted by state (or federal) law from the claims of creditors (e.g., a homestead may be exempt) are not taken into account. *Hunt v. Commissioner*, 58 T.C.M. 965 (1989). In *Hunt*, the Tax Court ignored the exempted assets because those assets were not "freed" as a consequence of the discharge of a debt. For the treatment of nonrecourse debts in determining a debtor's solvency, see § **2.1231–2**, *infra*.

If a debtor was insolvent before the debt was discharged but became solvent as a consequence of that discharge, under the common law rule, the debtor would realize income only to the extent of his solvency. *Lakeland Grocery Co. v. Commissioner*, 36 B.T.A. 289 (1937). As noted below, that treatment continues to apply under the statutory replacement.

Under the common law (but not under current statutory law), no adjustment was made to the tax attributes of the debtor when a discharged debt was excluded from income because of insolvency. The common law rules were supplanted by the 1980 amendments of IRC § 108 and IRC § 1017 which were expanded to deal with the discharge of the debts of a bankrupt or insolvent debtor. IRC § 108(e)(1). Some of those statutory rules are described below.

§ 2.1231. **Nonrecognition of Income.** If a debt is discharged in a bankruptcy proceeding or if the debtor is insolvent when the discharge occurs, the amount discharged is excluded from the debtor's income by IRC § 108(a)(1)(A) and (B). If the debt was not discharged in a bankruptcy proceeding and if the debtor was insolvent before the discharge took place but becomes solvent by virtue of it, the debtor will recognize income to the extent of his solvency immediately after the discharge of the debt, provided that no other exception to income recognition is applicable. IRC § 108(a)(3) accomplishes that result by limiting the amount of discharge of a debt that is not recognized because of the insolvency exception to the amount by which the debtor was insolvent immediately prior to the discharge.

The statute adopts the same meaning of insolvency as was used in the common law rule—namely, the excess of a debtor's liabilities over the fair market value of his assets. IRC § 108(d)(3). In order to include contingent liabilities, such as guarantees, a taxpayer must show, by a preponderance of the evidence, that he will be called upon to pay the contingent obligation. *Merkel v. Commissioner*, 192 F.3d 844 (9th Cir. 1999), *affirming* 109 T.C. 463 (1997). For this purpose, it is an all or nothing proposition. If the taxpayer can carry the burden, he may count the entire face value of the liability in the IRC § 108(a)(3) formula. If not, the contingent obligation is not counted as a liability of the taxpayer.

The statutory rules depart from the common law approach by requiring that the amount of discharged debt that was excluded from the debtor's income because of his insolvency or bankruptcy causes adjustments to favorable tax attributes of the debtor. The adjustments will reduce positive tax attributes of the debtor in the manner described at § **2.1232**–§ **2.1232–8**, *infra*. This treatment of requiring adjustments transforms the common law insolvency exception, which was a true exclusion from income, into a nonrecognition provision.

§ 2.1231–1. Reason for the Insolvency Exception.
When a taxpayer is insolvent, a creditor may agree to
discharge all or part of a debt in order to permit the
taxpayer to obtain a "fresh start." A creditor might be
motivated to do that in the hope of obtaining additional
business from the debtor if the latter recovers and becomes
successful, or the creditor may simply be able to obtain a
greater return from a voluntary arrangement than he could
obtain by imposing involuntary bankruptcy on the debtor.
The purpose of the insolvency exception is to preserve a
debtor's "fresh start" by relieving him of the burden of
taxation that otherwise would be imposed on the discharge
of his debt. H.R. Rep. No. 833, 96th Cong., 2d Sess. 7, 9
(1980); S. Rep. No. 1035, 96th Cong., 2d Sess. 8, 10 (1980).
The imposition of a tax burden on the canceled debt of an
insolvent debtor would simply increase the debtor's insolvency and therefore deter creditors from agreeing to debt
reduction arrangements. However, to the extent that the
discharge of a debt renders the debtor solvent, the debtor
has assets available to pay the tax on an equal amount of
debt that was forgiven; and so, Congress has taxed the
amount of discharged debt that increases a debtor's solvency.

Instead of taxing the amount of discharged debt that increases a debtor's solvency, Congress could have chosen to
tax the entire amount of the discharged debt, subject to the
limitation that the tax imposed cannot exceed the amount
by which the debtor became solvent. One can only speculate as to why that approach was not adopted. It would be
somewhat more difficult to administer than the current
treatment. Also, Congress may have wished to allow the
debtor to remain solvent after payment of taxes since the
motivation for a creditor to forgive some of the debt may
have been to provide some solvency for the debtor, which
solvency may be necessary to provide the debtor with a
reasonable prospect of building a successful business.

§ 2.1231–2. Nonrecourse Debts. A nonrecourse debt is
an indebtedness which is secured by property of the debtor,
but for which the debtor has no personal obligation (i.e., if
the debtor defaults, the creditor can collect only by levying
on the security and cannot require any payments from the

debtor). For the purposes of the discharge of indebtedness rules, a nonrecourse debt that is secured by a taxpayer's property is treated as a debt of the taxpayer. IRC § 108(d)(1)(B). The discharge of a nonrecourse debt can cause recognition of discharge of indebtedness income, and this is so even when the amount of the nonrecourse debt exceeds the value of the property securing it. Rev. Rul. 91–31.

In determining whether and to what extent a debtor is insolvent, should the amount by which a nonrecourse debt exceeds the fair market value of the property that secures that debt (hereinafter, that portion of a nonrecourse debt is sometimes referred to as the "excess nonrecourse debt") be treated as a liability of the debtor? Since the creditor cannot collect the excess nonrecourse debt unless its security increases in value, that portion of the debt has no effect on the debtor's solvency and generally is ignored by the Commissioner in determining the extent to which a debtor is solvent or insolvent. However, if all or a portion of the excess nonrecourse debt itself is discharged, it would contravene the policy of the insolvency exception to ignore, in determining the extent of the debtor's insolvency, the amount of the liability that was discharged. Accordingly, the Commissioner has ruled that the excess of a nonrecourse debt over the fair market value of the security generally is ignored in determining the debtor's solvency; but if all or a portion of the nonrecourse debt itself is discharged, the amount of such excess nonrecourse debt that is discharged will be counted as a liability of the debtor. Rev. Rul. 92–53.

§ 2.1231–3. Illustration 1: Insolvent Before and After Discharge. *A* had assets with an aggregate value of $100,000, and *A*'s liabilities (none of which were nonrecourse debts) totalled $142,000. One of *A*'s creditors agreed to accept a $10,000 payment to cancel $50,000 of *A*'s liability. *A* was insolvent both before and after the discharge took place; after the discharge, *A* had assets of $90,000 and liabilities of $92,000. Although $40,000 of *A*'s liabilities was discharged, thus triggering realization of $40,000 of income, *A* did not *recognize* any income. IRC § 108(a). Some of *A*'s tax attributes may be reduced as a

consequence of that nonrecognition of income. See
§ 2.1232 et. seq.

§ 2.1231–4. Illustration 2: Solvent After Discharge.

The same facts as those stated in **Illustration 1** except
that $60,000 of *A*'s liability was canceled for the $10,000
payment. As a consequence of the discharge, *A* realized
income of $50,000, but he recognized income only to the
extent that he became solvent. After the discharge, *A* had
assets of $90,000 and liabilities of $82,000, and so he
became solvent to the extent of $8,000. Therefore, *A* recog-
nized income of $8,000. The remaining $42,000 of discharged debt does not cause income recognition, but can
cause a reduction of tax attributes.

Stating it differently and in accord with statutory language,
the amount of discharged debt ($50,000) that is not recog-
nized as income cannot exceed the amount by which *A* was
insolvent before the discharge took place ($42,000). So,
$42,000 of the discharged debt is not recognized as income,
and $8,000 is recognized.

§ 2.1231–5. Illustration 3: Nonrecourse Debt that is Secured by Property with a Greater Value than the Amount of the Debt.

B owns a building with a fair
market value of $300,000. The building is subject to a
mortgage in the amount of $250,000, and *B* has no personal
liability to repay that mortgage debt (i.e., the mortgage
debt is a nonrecourse debt). The meaning of "recourse
debts" and "nonrecourse debts" is set forth in
§ 16.1500A. None of *B*'s debts are purchase-money debts.
B owns other assets with a value of $80,000, and *B* is
personally liable for debts (i.e., recourse debts) totalling
$200,000. A creditor of *B* cancels $62,000 of *B*'s recourse
debt for a payment of $12,000, and that constitutes a
discharge of $50,000 of debt. Since the amount of *B*'s
nonrecourse debt is less than the value of its security, it is
treated as a liability for purposes of determining *B*'s insolvency. Therefore, immediately before the discharge, *B* was
insolvent in the amount of $70,000. None of the discharged
debt of $50,000 is included in *B*'s income, but it can reduce
his tax attributes.

§ 2.1231–6. Illustration 4: Nonrecourse Debt that is Greater in Amount than the Property Securing It.

The same facts as those stated in **Illustration 3** except
that: (1) the amount of the nonrecourse debt that is se-

cured by the building is $450,000, and (2) the value of *B*'s other assets (i.e., assets other than the building) is $180,000. To the extent that the nonrecourse debt exceeds the $300,000 value of the building (it exceeds that value by $150,000), it is not treated as a liability of *B* for purposes of applying the insolvency exception. So, before the $50,000 discharge of *B*'s recourse debt took place, *B* had assets valued at $480,000, and his liabilities totalled $500,000 ($200,000 recourse debts and only $300,000 of the nonrecourse debt is counted as a liability). Since *B* was insolvent in the amount of $20,000 prior to the discharge of $50,000 of his recourse debts, $20,000 of that discharge is not included in his income, and only the remaining $30,000 constitutes recognized income.

§ 2.1231–7. Illustration 5. Discharge of Nonrecourse Debt. The same facts as those stated in **Illustration 4** except that, in addition to the discharge of $50,000 of *B*'s recourse debts and on the same date, the creditor of the nonrecourse debt forgave $150,000 of that debt. Consequently, after that discharge of $150,000 of the nonrecourse debt, the outstanding balance of the nonrecourse debt ($300,000) equalled the fair market value of the building that secured it. The entire amount of the nonrecourse debt that was discharged was the portion of the debt that exceeded the value of the building that secured it. If the excess of the nonrecourse debt over the value of the security were not treated as a liability of *B*, the discharge of that amount would cause *B* to recognize income of $150,000 in addition to the $30,000 of income that *B* recognized because of the discharge of $50,000 of recourse debts. [If the $150,000 excess nonrecourse debt is ignored in determining *B*'s insolvency, *B* would have been insolvent in the amount of only $20,000 prior to the discharge of $200,000 of debts ($50,000 recourse debts and $150,000 nonrecourse debts), and so *B* would recognize $180,000 of income from those discharges. But after the discharges were completed, *B* would have only $30,000 excess of asset value over his liabilities with which to pay the tax on that income—i.e., the total value of his assets would be $468,000, and the total amount of his liabilities would be $438,000.] Clearly, to include $180,000 in *B*'s income would contravene the Congressional policy to limit the amount of income recognized to the amount of net asset value that is available to pay the income tax. To prevent that from occurring, the Commissioner ruled in Rev. Rul. 92–53 that the amount of excess nonrecourse debt that is discharged is treated as a liability of the debtor. Accordingly, since the entire $150,000 excess nonrecourse debt was discharged, that entire amount is treated as a liability of *B*. The amount of *B*'s insolvency prior to the discharges, therefore, was $170,000; and so that amount of the $200,000 discharged debts is not recognized as income. Only the remaining $30,000 of discharged debts is recognized as income.

§ 2.1232. Reduction of Tax Attributes. After the taxable income of the debtor for the year of discharge is determined [IRC § 108(b)(4)(A)], the amount of discharged debt that is excluded from the debtor's income because of insolvency or bankruptcy causes the following reductions of the debtor's tax attributes in the order indicated (subject to an election of the debtor, described in **§ 2.1232–8**, to reduce his basis in depreciable property and in realty held for sale to customers in the ordinary course of business in lieu of the adjustments to other favorable tax attributes):

§ 2.1232–1. Net Operating Loss. The meaning of "net operating loss" and the operation of the rules for carrying forward that loss and deducting it in other taxable years are described briefly in **§§ 13.6000–13.6300**. The debtor's net operating loss for the taxable year and any net operating loss carryover to that taxable year are reduced dollar for dollar for the amount of discharged debt that was so excluded from income. IRC § 108(b)(1), (2)(A), (3)(A). An adjustment is made first to any loss incurred in the taxable year and then any remaining adjustments are applied to carryover losses incurred in prior years in the order of years in which they were incurred. IRC § 108(b)(4)(B).

§ 2.1232–2. General Business Credits. General business tax credits and credit carryovers to the taxable year (allowable under IRC § 38) are reduced on a ratio of 33 1/3 cents for each $1 of discharged debt that was excluded from income and was not applied as an adjustment to the debtor's net operating losses as indicated in § **2.1232–1.** IRC § 108(b)(2)(B), (3)(B).

§ **2.1232–3. Minimum Tax Credit.** The minimum tax credit allowable under IRC § 53(b) is reduced on the ratio of 33⅓ cents for each $1 of discharged debt that was excluded from income and that did not cause a reduction of the tax attributes listed above. IRC § 108(b)(2)(C), (3)(B). The minimum tax credit is discussed at § **15.5000.**

§ **2.1232–4. Capital Loss.** The debtor's capital loss for the taxable year and any capital loss carryover to such year is reduced dollar for dollar by any remainder of the discharged debt that was excluded from income. IRC § 108(b)(2)(D).

§ **2.1232–5. Basis of Property.** The next tax attribute to be reduced (dollar for dollar) is the basis of property held by the debtor at the beginning of the taxable year following the year of discharge. IRC §§ 108(b)(2)(E), § 1017(a). If a taxpayer has more than one type of property, the ordering in which basis reduction will take place is described in Treas. Reg. § 1.1017–1. Subject to those ordering rules, the property whose basis is to be reduced includes all of the debtor's property (except for certain "exempt property" of an individual [IRC §§ 108(d)(10), 1017(c)]); it is *not* limited to depreciable property or to realty held for sale to customers. However, when a discharge occurs while the taxpayer is insolvent or in a Title 11 case, IRC § 1017(b)(2) provides a special rule for the reduction of basis pursuant to IRC § 108(b)(2)(E); namely, the amount of reduction of basis cannot exceed the difference between the aggregate bases of the properties held by the debtor immediately after the discharge over the aggregate of the debtor's liabilities at that time. For the tax treatment of the subsequent disposition of property whose basis was reduced pursuant to IRC § 1017 see Chapter Nineteen, and see §§ **19.3200, 19.3231.**

§ **2.1232–6. Passive Activity Loss and Credit Carryovers.** The carryover under IRC § 469(b) of an unused passive activity loss or credit is the next tax attribute to be reduced. IRC § 108(b)(2)(F). The carryover of such losses is reduced dollar for dollar for any remainder of the excluded discharged debt, but the carryover of a passive activity credit is reduced on a ratio of 33⅓ cents for each dollar of remaining excluded discharged debt. IRC § 108(b)(3).

§ 2.1232–7. Foreign Tax Credit. Finally, any remaining amount of the discharged debt will reduce the debtor's foreign tax credit [IRC § 27] for the taxable year and the foreign tax credit carryover to that taxable year. IRC § 108(b)(2)(G). This adjustment is made on the ratio of 33 1/3 cents for each $1 of remaining discharged debt. IRC § 108(b)(3)(B).

§ 2.1232–8. Election to Prevent Reduction of Net Operating Loss, Capital Loss, Credits and Credit Carryovers. In lieu of all or any portion of the adjustments to be made to the debtor's tax attributes, as described in §§ **2.1232–2.1232–7**, the debtor can elect instead to have reduced (dollar for dollar) the basis of depreciable property held by the debtor at the beginning of the taxable year following the year of discharge. IRC § 108(b)(5). If this election is made, the reduction in basis is not limited to the difference between the aggregate bases and the aggregate liabilities of the properties held by the debtor immediately after discharge. IRC § 1017(b)(2). The debtor is permitted to elect to treat as depreciable property certain realty which is held by the debtor for sale to customers in the ordinary course of the debtor's trade or business. IRC § 1017(b)(3)(E). To the extent that the discharged debt reduces the debtor's basis in his depreciable property, that amount of the discharged debt will not affect the other tax attributes of the debtor. IRC § 108(b)(5)(C). For the tax treatment of the subsequent disposition of property whose basis has been reduced pursuant to IRC § 1017, see Chapter Nineteen.

§ 2.1233. Exclusion Versus Nonrecognition. As noted in § 2.1231, the statutory exclusion from income of discharged debts of an insolvent or bankrupt debtor actually is a nonrecognition provision because of the adjustments that are required to be made to certain favorable tax attributes of the debtor. However, if the amount of the tax attributes of the debtor that can be reduced are less than the discharged debt, the debtor can nevertheless exclude all of the discharged debt from his income. To the extent that the amount of the discharged debt causes no adverse tax consequence to the debtor, the exclusion of that portion of the debt from the debtor's income constitutes a true exclusion as contrasted to a nonrecognition provision.

§ 2.1240. Qualified Farm Indebtedness and Qualified Real Property Business Indebtedness. A taxpayer does not recognize income from the discharge of a debt that constitutes "qualified farm indebtedness." IRC § 108(a)(1)(C). A "qualified farm indebtedness" is a debt that was incurred directly in connection with the taxpayer's operation of a farming business and which satisfies certain conditions specified in IRC § 108(g). For this nonrecognition provision to apply, the creditor who discharges the debt must be either: (1) a Federal, State, or local government or agency or instrumentality thereof, or (2) a "qualified person" as that term is defined in IRC § 46(c)(8)(D)(iv). The amount of such discharged debt for which nonrecognition is granted cannot exceed the sum of the "adjusted tax attributes" of the taxpayer, as defined in IRC § 108(g)(3)(B), and the adjusted bases of "qualified property" held by the taxpayer at the beginning of the next taxable year. IRC § 108(g)(3). "Qualified property" is any property that is used or held for use in a trade or business or for the production of income. IRC § 108(g)(3)(C). To the extent that income from a discharge of a qualified farm indebtedness is not recognized, the taxpayer's tax attributes will be reduced in the identical manner that is described in **§§ 2.1232–2.1232–8** for the reduction of tax attributes due to nonrecognition granted for insolvency or bankruptcy. IRC § 108(b).

A taxpayer (other than a C corporation) also can elect not to recognize income from the discharge of so-called "qualified real property business indebtedness." IRC § 108(a)(1)(D). Qualified real property business indebtedness refers to debt that was assumed or incurred by the taxpayer in connection with real property used in a trade or business and that is secured by that real property and that meets certain other requirements. If the debt was incurred or assumed after 1992, it must have been incurred or assumed to acquire, construct, reconstruct or substantially improve the realty. The term does not include qualified farm indebtedness, and the exclusion from income applies only if the taxpayer elects it. The amount excluded from income will reduce the basis of depreciable real property of the taxpayer. IRC § 108(c)(1). No other tax attributes are reduced.

The amount of discharge of qualified real property business indebtedness that can be excluded from income is limited to the excess of the principal amount of the debt (immediately before the discharge) over the fair market value of the realty that secures that debt (which value is reduced by any other qualified real property business indebtedness secured by that realty). IRC § 108(c)(2)(A). Thus, this provision is applicable only to the extent that the principal of a debt is greater than the value of the realty securing it. In addition, the amount excluded from income cannot exceed the aggregate basis of the taxpayer in certain depreciable real property as determined immediately before the discharge. IRC § 108(c)(2)(B).

To the extent that the taxpayer is insolvent, the insolvency exclusion takes precedence over both the qualified farm exclusion and the qualified real property business exclusion. IRC § 108(a)(2)(B).

§ 2.1250. Purchase–Money Debt Reduction. If the purchaser of property incurs a debt *to the seller* arising from the purchase of that property, a subsequent discharge of all or a portion of that debt which otherwise would have caused the debtor to realize income will not cause income to the debtor. Instead, the reduction of the debt will be treated as a reduction of the purchase price of the property and thus will reduce the purchaser's basis in that property. IRC § 108(e)(5). This statutory provision is essentially a codification of the previously existing common law rule. This treatment of a discharge of a purchase-money debt does not apply to a discharge that takes place in a bankruptcy proceeding or when the debtor is insolvent; in those cases, the normal treatment of bankruptcy and insolvency discharges is applicable. IRC § 108(e)(5)(B).

When property is purchased with the proceeds of a nonrecourse loan that was borrowed from a person other than the seller and is secured by the acquired property, a subsequent discharge of all or part of that nonrecourse debt (which does not involve a transfer of the property) will cause discharge of indebtedness income to the taxpayer unless one of the statutory exceptions (such as insolvency) is applicable. Since the debt is not owed to the seller, § 108(e)(5) is inapplicable. See Rev. Rul. 91–31; *Preslar v. Commissioner*, 167 F.3d 1323 (10th Cir. 1999). A debtor can have discharge of indebtedness income even if the amount of the nonrecourse debt that is discharged exceeds the fair market value of the property securing it. *Ibid.* However, to the extent that the debt qualifies for the nonrecognition election for qualified real property business indebtedness, the taxpayer can elect to reduce the basis of the property instead of recognizing that amount of income. See § **2.1240.** For the extent to which a nonrecourse debt is treated as a liability for the purpose of applying the insolvency exception, see §§ **2.1231–1** and **2.1231–5** to **2.1231–7,** *supra.*

§ **2.1251.** **Illustration 1: Genuine Discharge.** *X* sells an apartment building to *Y* for $1,000,000. *Y* pays *X* $200,000 cash and assumes an outstanding first mortgage of $650,000. *Y* gives *X* his personal note for the $150,000 difference and secures the debt with a second mortgage on the building. Subsequently, a dispute arises between *Y* and *X* as to certain representations made by *X* as to the quality of the wiring in the building. In settlement of that dispute, *X* cancels $20,000 of *Y*'s personal obligation to him, thereby reducing *Y*'s debt to $130,000. At the time of the discharge, *Y* was solvent. The cancellation of part of *Y*'s debt constitutes a reduction of the purchase price for the building and does not constitute income to *Y*.

§ **2.1252.** **Illustration 2: Spurious Discharge.** The same facts apply as in § **2.1251** except that there was no dispute concerning the representations that *X* made. Instead, *X* canceled $20,000 of *Y*'s debt to compensate *Y* for personal services that *Y* had performed for *X*. The cancellation of $20,000 of *Y*'s debt is a spurious discharge and is not covered by IRC § 108. The meaning of "spurious discharge" is set forth in § **2.1214.** The cancellation of the debt will constitute income to *Y* as compensation for personal services.

§ **2.1260.** **Discharge As a Gift.** A discharge of a debt might constitute a gift and thus be exempted from income under IRC § 102. The initial response of the Supreme Court was to treat a debt cancellation as a gift where a creditor collected the maximum amount that appeared feasible. *Helvering v. American Dental Co.,* 318 U.S. 322 (1943). However, the Court changed its position and subsequently held that a discharge of a debt under such circumstances will yield gross income to the debtor. *Commissioner v. Jacobson,* 336 U.S. 28 (1949). Consequently, a discharge of a debt in a normal commercial setting is no longer likely to be treated as a nontaxable gift. Where the discharge is not in a commercial setting, as in the cancellation of a debt owed by one member of a family to another, the discharge may be construed as a gift. For the definition of "gift" for income tax purposes, see §§ **2.4220–2.4226.**

§ **2.1270.   Contribution to a Corporation's Capital.** A person's contribution to a corporation of which the person is a shareholder may constitute a contribution to the capital of the corporation and as such is excluded from the corporation's income by IRC § 118. This exclusion of such contributions is similar in some respects to the exclusion of gifts from the income of a donee by IRC § 102. Just as a discharge of indebtedness that constitutes a gift typically is excluded from the debtor's income, so one might expect the same treatment for a discharge of a corporation's debt to its shareholder where the discharge constitutes a contribution by the shareholder to the capital of the corporation. In many circumstances, such a discharge of a corporation's indebtedness will not cause income to the corporation. A difficulty arises, however, where a corporation which reports its income on the accrual method has accrued and deducted an obligation to a cash method shareholder who has not included that item in his income because of his method of accounting (e.g., where a corporation has deducted accrued but unpaid salary to a cash method shareholder-employee). If the shareholder subsequently discharges the corporation's debt, there would be a windfall to the taxpayers unless either the corporation is required to recognize income (under a tax benefit concept described in § **2.1280**) or the shareholder is required to recognize income because of having essentially utilized his previously unpaid claim against the corporation as a contribution to the corporation's capital and thus derived an economic benefit from his claim. The Tax Court held, however, that neither the corporation nor the shareholder recognized income in such circumstance, and the Fifth Circuit affirmed the Tax Court's decision as to the corporation (the Government's having failed to appeal the decision concerning the shareholder). *Putoma Corp. v. Commissioner*, 66 T.C. 652 (1976), aff'd 601 F.2d 734 (5th Cir. 1979); see § **20.2300.** The Congressional response to this problem is described in §§ **2.1271–2.1272.**

§ **2.1271.   Statutory Treatment.** Congress addressed this problem when it amended IRC § 108 in 1980. In effect, IRC § 108(e)(6) provides that a shareholder's discharge of a corporation's debt will not be excluded from the corporation's income under IRC § 118 to the extent that the debt exceeds the shareholder's basis therein. Thus, to the extent that the shareholder has not taken the debt into income or otherwise obtained a basis therein, the corporation will have a discharge of indebtedness which typically will be included in its gross income if it is solvent. Of course, if the corporation reports on the cash method so that it had not previously taken a deduction for the debt, and if a deduction would be allowable to the corporation on payment of the debt, the discharge of the debt will *not* cause the corporation to recognize income because of the exclusion in IRC § 108(e)(2).

§ 2.1272. Corporation's Satisfaction of Debt With Its Own Stock. When a corporation issues its own stock to a creditor in satisfaction of a debt, the corporation is treated as having satisfied the debt by the payment of an amount of cash equal to the fair market value of its stock. IRC § 108(e)(8). So, the corporation will have discharge of indebtedness income to the extent of the difference between the principal amount of the debt and the value of the corporation's stock. However, if the distribution to the creditor is made in connection with a Title 11 case (i.e., a bankruptcy case), the debtor corporation will not recognize income because of the exception in IRC § 108(a)(1)(A). Similarly, even if the distribution is not made in connection with a Title 11 case, if the debtor corporation is insolvent, it will not recognize discharge of indebtedness income to the extent of its insolvency. IRC § 108(a)(1)(B), (3). See **§ 2.1231.** Of course, certain favorable tax attributes of the debtor corporation will be reduced by IRC § 108(b) to the extent that the corporation's discharge of indebtedness income is not recognized.

The same rules as those described above apply to a partnership's transfer of a capital or profits interest in the partnership to a creditor in satisfaction of a debt. IRC § 108(e)(8). The partnership will have discharge of indebtedness income to the extent that the amount of the debt exceeds the fair market value of the interest that was transferred to the creditor.

If a corporation's debt is held by its shareholders in the same proportion as the corporation's stock is held, and if the stock distributed in cancellation of that debt is distributed pro rata to the corporation's shareholders, there is a question whether IRC § 108(e)(8) will apply. The authors believe that, in such a case, the distribution should be treated as a stock dividend coupled with a cancellation of the corporation's debt. If so, the stock dividend usually will be excluded from the shareholder's income by IRC § 305, and the cancellation of the corporation's debt will be determined by IRC § 108(e)(6). See **§ 2.1271.**

A debt instrument of a corporation may be exchanged for stock of the same corporation pursuant to a conversion provision or to a recapitalization. There is a question whether IRC § 108(e)(8) will apply to such an exchange.

§ 2.1280.   Tax Benefit Rule. When an accrual method taxpayer is allowed a deduction for an accrued but unpaid expense, the subsequent discharge of that debt may cause the taxpayer to recognize income under the tax benefit doctrine [see **§ 2.3000**] even though the discharge would not otherwise have caused the debtor to recognize income because of the transactional view [see **§ 2.1290**]. However, if the taxpayer had not derived a tax benefit from all or part of the deduction previously allowed him, then all or a portion of the discharged debt will be excluded from the taxpayer's gross income under IRC § 111. See Rev. Rul. 67–200. If the discharge of the taxpayer's debt was gratuitous, there may be no income to the debtor even though the tax benefit rule would otherwise have caused the taxpayer to recognize income from the recovery of the debt. Compare *Putoma Corp.* in **§ 2.1270** excluding a gratuitous cancellation from income, with Rev. Rul. 76–316, where the Commissioner held that the tax benefit rule caused the debtor to recognize income even though the discharge was gratuitous. As noted in **§ 2.1271**, in 1980 Congress dealt with this problem as it arises in connection with contributions to a corporation's capital. In so doing, Congress indicated in the legislative history to the 1980 amendments that it was acting in response to the *Putoma* decision which involved a contribution to capital. While a similar problem can arise where a cash method creditor makes a gift by discharging the deductible obligation of an accrual method debtor, Congress did not expressly deal with that problem. It remains to be seen whether the courts will extend the policy evidenced by IRC § 108(e)(6) to gifts despite the failure of Congress to so provide.

§ 2.1290.   Transactional View. In determining whether the amount of a discharged debt will be included in gross income, the courts should examine the entire transaction commencing with the creation of the debt, and the debtor will not be deemed to realize income unless it is apparent that the entire transaction resulted in a gain to him. This view is sometimes referred to as the "transactional view" or the "transactional approach." The courts have not uniformly embraced the transactional approach. Some courts have severely limited its application; but the authors believe that the better view, which has been adopted in a number of court decisions, is to apply the transactional rule liberally. There is little justification for placing a tax cost on what in effect is merely a renegotiation of the terms of a prior agreement. The transactional view permits parties to alter the terms of a prior agreement without incurring a tax cost unless the alteration constitutes a recovery of a previously enjoyed tax benefit.

The application of the transactional approach to prevent realization of discharge of indebtedness income should not require that there be an actual renegotiation of the terms of a contract. It should be sufficient that the consequences of the reduction of a debt be the same as those that would follow from a renegotiation of terms. Unless a discharged debt had previously provided the debtor with some tax benefit such as a tax deduction or an exclusion from gross income of an item that otherwise would have been included in income, the reduction or elimination of that debt merely places the debtor and creditor in the same position that they could have occupied at the time that the debt was created without changing the tax position of either party. For example, if in Year One, G contractually obligates herself to make a gift of $10,000 to her nephew, N, to be delivered to N in Year Four, and if in Year Four, N agrees to accept $6,000 in satisfaction of G's obligation, the position of G and N in Year Four is the same as it would have been if G had obligated herself in Year One to make a gift of only $6,000 to N. There is no reason to tax G differently from what she would have been taxed if she had originally committed to make a gift of $6,000. Since the incurrence of G's liability had no tax consequence, the reduction of that liability should not cause a tax liability. See § **2.1295** for a discussion of the authors' view of the rationale for the transactional approach. Note that the transactional approach applies only to a genuine discharge of indebtedness; it does not apply to a spurious discharge of a debt, as described in § **2.1214**.

§ **2.1291. Illustration 1: Charitable Pledges.** X pledged to donate $1,000 to the Salvation Army, and under local law his pledge was a binding legal obligation. No deduction is allowed to an individual for making a charitable contribution

until actual *payment* of the contribution is made. IRC
§ 170(a)(1). *X* later reneged, and the Salvation Army agreed to
accept $600 in full satisfaction of his pledge. The $400 debt of
X that was forgiven by the Army is not income to *X* since the
net effect was merely to reduce the charitable gift made by *X*
from $1,000 to $600, and the $400 forgiveness represents no
true gain for *X*.

Moreover, IRC § 108(e)(2) may provide relief in this situation,
even if the transactional view is not applied, if the $400
payment to the charity would have resulted in a charitable
deduction under IRC § 170. If so, since a charitable deduction
is one of the itemized deductions that are subject to reduction
by IRC § 68, there could be a question as to whether the § 68
limitation is to be taken into account in applying § 108(e)(2),
and, if so, how much of that § 68 reduction would be attributable to the charitable contribution. The application of the
transactional view makes those questions moot.

§ 2.1292. Illustration 2: Cost of Inventory. *X* purchased
1,000 pairs of shoes from a company in England on credit for
2,000 pounds sterling; at the time of purchase, a pound eq-
ualed $3 in American currency. At the time *X* paid the English
company, the pound had been devalued to $2 in American
currency, allowing *X* to satisfy his contemplated $6,000 debt
for $4,000. The $2,000 "saving" to *X* in dollars has been
treated as income to *X* on the theory that *X* gained that
amount on the transaction. Note that there is some judicial
support for the contention that the entire "transaction" must
be examined and that *X* may not be taxed unless the net effect
of the purchase *and* sale of the shoes by *X* resulted in a gain.
Thus, if *X* had sold the shoes at a loss, the amount of the loss
must be deducted from the gain realized on the pound transaction. See *English Shoes Ltd. v. Commissioner*, 229 F.2d 957
(2d Cir. 1956). It would appear that in *English Shoes* the court
misconstrued the transactional approach. If a transactional
approach were applied to the above facts, the effect of the
devaluation would be to reduce *X*'s basis in his inventory,
thereby increasing his gain or decreasing his loss on the sale of
the shoes. The application of the transactional approach
should not depend upon whether *X* incurred a loss on the
transaction. One consequence of the courts' failure to establish
a conceptual structure for determining whether a forgiven

debt constitutes gross income to a debtor is that some of the decisions in this area are irreconcilable.

§ 2.1292–1. **Severability of Credit.** In § 2.1292, the applicability of the transactional rule depends entirely upon whether the credit element of X's purchase is severable from the purchase of the shoes or whether credit was such an integral part of the purchase that the reduction of the dollar amount of X's debt should be treated as a reduction of the cost of purchasing the shoes. In the authors' view, the debt is so interwoven with the purchase of the shoes that the two are not severable for this purpose.

In Rev. Rul. 78–281, the taxpayer borrowed from a bank foreign currency which the taxpayer used to purchase a machine which it rented to a foreign customer. The foreign currency was devalued before the taxpayer repaid the debt. The Commissioner ruled that the debt was severable from the purchase of the machine and so the taxpayer's basis in the machine was the dollar value of the foreign currency it paid for the machine as of the date of purchase. The taxpayer will recognize ordinary gain or loss on each installment payment to the bank in repayment of the loan. This circumstance differs from that involved in *English Shoes* in that the bank that loaned taxpayer the foreign currency had no connection with the seller or with the purchase transaction. See §§ **2.1293** and **2.1293–1.**

§ 2.1293. **Illustration 3: Payment from Third Party as Reduction of Purchase Price.** In a case that did not involve a discharge of indebtedness, the Tax Court adopted a position that is similar to the transactional approach. In *Freedom Newspapers, Inc. v. Commissioner*, 36 T.C.M. 1755 (1977), the court treated the receipt of a cash payment from a third party as a reduction of the purchase price paid for a newspaper. The taxpayer (a corporation) had been induced by a broker to purchase four newspapers, including one which the taxpayer did not want, by the broker's promise to resell the unwanted newspaper or, if the broker failed to resell it, to pay $100,000 to the taxpayer. The broker failed to resell the unwanted newspaper and therefore was required to pay $100,000 to the taxpayer. This payment was made more than two years after the taxpayer had purchased the four newspapers. Holding that the broker's guaranty was intimately tied to the purchase of the newspaper, the court treated the guaranty and the purchase of the newspaper as an integrated transaction. The Tax Court held that the $100,000 that the taxpayer received from the broker constituted a reduction of the price it paid for the unwanted newspaper and did not constitute income to the taxpayer but rather reduced its basis in that newspaper.

Since the broker's promise induced the taxpayer to purchase the newspapers, perhaps the contractual arrangement between the broker and the taxpayer can be said to be so integrally connected to the sale that the payment to the taxpayer can be viewed as a reduction of the purchase price. In the authors' view, that analysis stretches the transactional approach beyond its proper boundary and the more proper analysis is described in *Preslar v. Commissioner*, 167 F.3d 1323 (10th Cir. 1999). However, the same result can be reached by a different route. Indeed, the Tax Court itself adopted an alternative holding that the $100,000 payment to the taxpayer should be characterized as a return of capital under the *Arrowsmith* doctrine that a later payment or receipt is to be characterized according to earlier events to which the payment or receipt is intimately related. See § **18.4420**, for a discussion of the Supreme Court's 1952 decision in *Arrowsmith* from which the doctrine of correlating the characterization of a payment or receipt with prior transactions sprung. Rather than rely on a transactional view or on the *Arrowsmith* doctrine, the broker's payment pursuant to its guaranty can be viewed as similar to a damage or insurance payment and should be given the same tax treatment—i.e., such a payment is treated as a return of the property owner's capital and merely reduces its basis in the property in question. In this regard, consider the discussion below of the Commissioner's treatment of the discharge of a debt owed to a third party when the loan was made in connection with the purchase of property.

§ 2.1293–1. Third Party's Discharge of Debt as Reduction of Purchase Price.
A somewhat similar circumstance to the one that arose in *Freedom Newspapers* is the discharge of a portion of a nonrecourse debt that represents a loan that was made previously by a financial institution to permit the debtor to purchase realty from an unrelated party and which debt is secured by the purchased property.

The typical reason that a financial institution will discharge a portion of such a debt is that the value of the property securing the debt has fallen below the balance of the nonrecourse debt that is outstanding. The discharge of the debt cannot qualify under IRC § 108(e)(5) as a purchase price adjustment because the debt is not owed to the seller of the property. But can the discharge be excluded from the debtor's income under the common law transactional approach? In Rev. Rul. 92–99, the Commissioner rejected those cases that permitted such a discharge to be treated as a reduction of purchase price, and the Commissioner ruled that the discharge of the debt constituted income to the debtor. Surprisingly, however, the Commissioner did state in that ruling:

> The Service will, however, treat a debt reduction in third-party lender cases as a purchase price adjustment to the extent that the debt reduction by the third party is based on an infirmity that clearly relates back to the original sale (e.g., the *seller's* inducement of a higher purchase price by misrepresentation of a material fact or by fraud).... No other debt reduction by a third party lender will be treated as a purchase price reduction. [Emphasis added.]

The concession made by the Commissioner in Rev. Rul. 92–99 appears to be unwarranted and overly generous. It is difficult to understand why a misrepresentation or fraud by the *seller* should change the characterization of a discharge of debt by a third party. A possible justification for the Commissioner's position may be that the third party would not cancel part of the debt because of the seller's fraud or misrepresentation unless the third party itself had been involved in the seller's original effort to sell the property to the taxpayer. The authors are not persuaded by that approach. The third party's reduction of the nonrecourse debt is attributable to the reality that it cannot collect that amount because the security from which collection must be made is inadequate. It seems unlikely that the third party's decision to discharge the debt rests on whether the discovery that the value of the security is inadequate is caused by a revelation of the seller's fraud rather than on a decline in the real estate market. But, even if the third party's decision to reduce the debt were to rest on the seller's misrepresentations, that does not appear to tie the loan and the sale together so that the reduction of one can be said to change the price of the other. Only if the third party and the seller had acted in concert so that they were joint venturers should the loan and the sale be tied together as an integrated transaction.

In *Preslar v. Commissioner*, 167 F.3d 1323 (10th Cir. 1999), the court stated that the purchase price reduction exclusion applies only to direct agreements between purchasers and sellers. Modifications by third parties alone will be treated under the normal discharge of indebtedness rules. Note, however, that certain third party debt reductions may qualify for exclusion treatment under IRC § 108(a)(1)(C) and (D). See § **2.1240.**

§ 2.1294. Overview of Transactional Approach. In the authors' view, the reason for the judicial confusion concerning the application of the transactional approach is that the Supreme Court's opinion in the landmark decision to include discharge of indebtedness in the debtor's income (*Kirby Lumber*, see § **2.1210**) rested on an erroneous rationale. The Supreme Court in *Kirby Lumber* emphasized that a reduction in a debtor's obligations increases his net worth, and this net worth approach has engendered confusion. While virtually every discharge of indebtedness will increase the debtor's net worth (except possibly for an insolvent debtor), it is obvious that many such discharges should not cause the realization of income, and thus the courts and Congress have struggled with the task of segregating those discharges that should be included in income from those that should not. The following rationale for the discharge of indebtedness rule which has been suggested by several commentators is more realistic than the net worth approach.

§ 2.1295. Suggested Rationale. When a person borrows money, he is not required to recognize income because his increase in assets is offset by a liability. Since it is assumed that he will satisfy the debt, the borrower recognizes no income by borrowing the funds. However, if it subsequently becomes clear that the debtor will not satisfy the debt, there no longer is a bar to including in income the amount previously borrowed by the debtor. Thus, when a debt is discharged, the realization of income should not be attributed to the increase in the debtor's net worth at that time but rather should be viewed as a removal of a bar to including a prior increase in the debtor's assets in his income. If a debt is not attributable to an increase in the debtor's assets or to the enjoyment of some tax benefit by him, there is little reason to treat the discharge of that debt as income to the debtor. It should be emphasized that the foregoing rationale is a theory of the authors and perhaps of a few commentators; it has not been adopted by any court. Note, however, that this rationale is consistent with the Supreme Court's treatment of an analogous problem concerning the application of the tax benefit rule in *Hillsboro National Bank v. Commissioner*, 460 U.S. 370 (1983).

§ 2.1296. Effect of 1980 Amendment of IRC § 108. As noted above, in 1980, Congress made significant modifications to IRC § 108 some of which codified many of the common law rules concerning what constitutes a discharge of indebtedness. Except for the special treatment of the discharge of a purchase-money debt (see **§ 2.1250**), the amendments did not deal with the applicability of the transactional approach. One might question whether Congress intended the provisions of IRC § 108 to be exclusive and so intended to repudiate common law rules that were not expressly codified. The authors believe that no such repudiation was intended and that the transactional approach is still alive and well. Note that when Congress wished to make an aspect of IRC § 108 exclusive, it did so expressly. For example, in IRC § 108(e)(1) Congress provided that there is no insolvency exception other than the insolvency provisions that are made in IRC § 108 itself. Also, in Rev. Rul. 92–99, the Commissioner noted that the common law transactional rule continues to apply, although the Commissioner did not refer to it as the "transactional" rule or approach.

§ 2.1297. Discharge of an Unenforceable Debt. The decision of a majority of the Tax Court and the reversal of that decision by a divided Third Circuit in *Zarin v. Commissioner*, 92 T.C. 1084 (1989), rev'd 916 F.2d 110 (3d Cir. 1990) are worthy of careful examination. *Zarin* involved the cancellation of gambling debts that were unenforceable under state law from the date that they were incurred by the taxpayer. In an 11–8 decision, the Tax Court held that the taxpayer recognized gross income to the extent that the gambling debt was canceled without consideration. In a 2–1 decision, the Third Circuit reversed and held the taxpayer did not recognize any income. In view of the significance of this decision, the basic facts of *Zarin* are set forth below.

§ 2.1297–1. The Facts of the *Zarin* case.

The taxpayer in *Zarin* was a compulsive gambler. A considerable amount of taxpayer's gambling took place at a casino in a hotel (hereinafter referred to as "the Hotel") in Atlantic City. In 1978, taxpayer was given a line of credit of $10,000 at the Hotel. Within a year and a half, taxpayer's line of credit was increased to $200,000 even though the Hotel made no additional investigation of his credit worthiness.

Gambling at the Hotel's casino was done with chips provided by that casino. The chips could not be used outside of the casino for any purpose. Taxpayer's line of credit permitted him to obtain chips from the casino with which to gamble. Taxpayer obtained the chips by signing negotiable drafts commonly called "markers." The markers were held by the Hotel for a period of some 90 days after which they were redeemed by taxpayer who gave the Hotel his personal check in the same amount.

In 1979, the New Jersey Casino Control Commission ordered the Hotel to cease and desist giving credit in excess of the properly approved credit limit, and all undeposited checks were ordered to be treated as credit provided to a patron. The complaints of credit abuse that led to the cease and desist order included 100 instances of abuse in providing excessive credit to taxpayer and a gambling companion. In violation of that order, the Hotel subsequently substantially increased the credit that taxpayer could draw upon to purchase chips.

By January, 1980, taxpayer was gambling daily at the Hotel's casino for 12 to 16 hours per day. Taxpayer mostly played craps, and he was betting up to $15,000 on a roll. Taxpayer's gambling attracted other patrons of the casino to his table and induced many of them to increase the size of their bets. For that reason, taxpayer was a valued patron of the Hotel's casino.

In April, 1980, for the acquisition of chips, taxpayer delivered his personal checks and markers to the Hotel's casino in the aggregate amount of $3,435,000; those checks and markers were returned to the Hotel as having been drawn against insufficient funds. Under New Jersey law, gambling debts are enforceable only if certain conditions are satisfied. The Hotel sued taxpayer for the unsatisfied amount, and the taxpayer asserted a number of affirmative defenses. The suit was settled by taxpayer's paying the Hotel $500,000 in cancellation of the $3,435,000 debt. A majority of the Tax Court held that taxpayer thereby had discharge of indebtedness income in the amount of the difference of $2,935,000.

One of the issues in *Zarin* was whether the gambling debts that taxpayer incurred were enforceable. The excessive credit granted by the Hotel to taxpayer in contravention of a cease and desist order made the enforceability of those debts highly questionable. Because of the procedural framework in which the case arose, the Commissioner was held to have the burden of proof on that issue. Since the Commissioner could not meet its burden of proof, taxpayer's gambling debts were deemed by the Tax Court and by the Third Circuit to be unenforceable at the time that they were incurred. The majority of the Tax Court held, and a majority of the Third Circuit disagreed, that the unenforceability of taxpayer's debts was irrelevant to the question of whether he had recognized gross income from the discharge of a portion of those debts.

§ 2.1297–2. Harsh Result In The Tax Court. The result reached by the Tax Court's majority is extremely harsh. The taxpayer's debt to the Hotel represented gambling losses that he had incurred. The majority of the Tax Court took the position that taxpayer's gambling losses were incurred in a different taxable year from the year in which the debt was canceled, and gambling losses can be deducted only from gambling winnings of the same taxable year. See Treas. Reg. § 1.165–10.

§ 2.1297–3. Application of Transactional Approach. If the court had adopted a transactional approach, the taxpayer would have prevailed. The taxpayer did not purchase chips as an item of property. The chips were merely the tokens that were used to measure the amount of a patron's gambling winnings or losses. Indeed, the Tax Court's majority itself stated in their opinion that the chips were not property that the taxpayer purchased but rather represented the "opportunity to gamble." The taxpayer's gambling can be viewed as a service provided by the Hotel, and the credit provided to taxpayer was therefore provided by the same person (the Hotel) that was providing the service which was the exclusive object to which the credit could be applied. On a transactional approach, the settlement of taxpayer's debt for a lesser figure can be viewed as a reduction of the cost of the gambling service or as a reduction of taxpayer's gambling losses. In other words, the credit accorded taxpayer was so inextricably attached to the gambling activity that the cancellation of part of that debt cannot properly be treated as an event isolated from the gambling itself.

One court decision did not apply this approach. In *Rood v. Commissioner*, RIA T.C. Memo ¶ 96,248, *affirmed*, 122 F.3d 1078 (11th Cir. 1997), the Tax Court held the cancellation of a gambling debt to be income to a taxpayer where the debt was not disputed.

§ 2.1297–4. The Third Circuit's Decision. In a 2–1 decision, the Third Circuit reversed the Tax Court and held that the taxpayer did not recognize income. *Zarin v. Commissioner*, 916 F.2d 110 (1990). The court rested its reversal on two independent grounds.

The court noted that § 108(d)(1) defines the term "indebtedness" of a taxpayer as an indebtedness either: (1) for which the taxpayer is liable, or (2) subject to which the taxpayer holds property. While that provision expressly states that the definition applies only for purposes of that section, a majority of the Third Circuit held that § 108 is merely an elaboration of the general rule of inclusion in gross income that is set forth in § 61(a)(12), and so the majority held that the definition adopted in § 108(d)(1) was equally applicable for purposes of § 61(a)(12). [Judge Stapleton disagreed with the majority on this issue among others.] The majority agreed with the Tax Court's determination that taxpayer's "debt" was unenforceable from the date that it was created, and so the court concluded that the taxpayer was never liable therefor. The majority also held that since the gambling chips did not constitute property but rather were "nothing more than an accounting mechanism, or evidence of a debt, to facilitate gambling," taxpayer did not hold property subject to an indebtedness. Consequently, neither of the alternative definitions provided by § 108(d)(1) was satisfied. The taxpayer's "debt" did not constitute an "indebtedness" within the meaning of either § 108 or § 61(a)(12), and so the reduction of that "debt" did not cause discharge of indebtedness income.

This first ground on which the Third Circuit rested is highly questionable. If cash or property is acquired in a transaction that would otherwise be taxable to the recipient, it is the existence of an offsetting debt that prevents the recognition of income. If an unenforceable "debt" of a taxpayer is not treated as a debt for discharge of indebtedness purposes, it should not constitute a debt for purposes of preventing income recognition from the taxpayer's receipt of property. In such cases, the receipt of property should not be included in the recipient's income so long as the recipient acts in a manner that indicates his intention to pay the "debt." Once the facts indicate that the recipient does not intend to repay the debt, then the value of the property received earlier should be included in his gross income. Whether the inclusion of that item in income is the result of the discharge of indebtedness doctrine or of a comparable doctrine is of little moment (unless the taxpayer is insolvent or falls within one of the other exceptions to the recognition of discharge of indebtedness income). The proper test for determining whether the taxpayer recognized income when the "debt" was settled is whether the canceled "debt" had prevented the taxpayer's recognition of income in a previous year—i.e., whether it represented property that the taxpayer had received.

As an alternative ground for its decision for the taxpayer, the majority held that the settlement of a disputed or contested liability does not cause discharge of indebtedness income. In light of the dispute as to whether the casino could enforce the taxpayer's debt, the court treated the *amount* of liability as being in dispute so that the settlement at a lower figure than demanded did not cause the taxpayer to recognize income. The court's decision on this point might be seen as an application of the transactional approach which the authors proposed in **§ 2.1297–3.** The court's analysis of a hypothetical circumstance that the court propounded to illustrate the operation of the contested liability rule appears to be an attempt to adopt a transactional approach. The court stated that if a taxpayer (*F*) borrowed $10,000, then refused in good faith to repay, and if the debt was settled for $7,000, "the transaction would be treated as if the initial loan was $7,000" and *F* would recognize no income. While the hypothetical was poorly chosen, it does appear that the rule that the court had in mind is encompassed by a transactional approach.

If the court's disputed or contested liability rule is taken literally, it is of doubtful validity. The problem with that approach is the same as that noted above with the court's assertion that the cancellation of an unenforceable debt does not cause income recognition. The proper question to ask is whether the "debt" that was eliminated by the settlement had prevented the taxpayer's recognition of income in a prior year.

A better explanation of the correct approach is set out in *Preslar v. Commissioner*, 167 F.3d 1323 (10th Cir. 1999). In *Preslar*, the court noted that the problem with the *Zarin* approach is that it treated liquidated and unliquidated debt alike. The court held that in order for the contested liability doctrine to apply, the amount of the original debt must be unliquidated. That is, the IRS must be "unaware of the exact consideration initially exchanged in a transaction."

§ 2.1300. Compensatory Damages. Income in the form of damages resulting from litigation (pursuant to a court judgment or a private settlement) calls into play special tax rules concerning compensatory damages. Note however that punitive damages are includable in gross income. *O'Gilvie v. United States*, 519 U.S. 79 (1996); *General American Investors Co. v. Commissioner*, 348 U.S. 434 (1955); and *Commissioner v. Glenshaw Glass Co.*, 348 U.S. 426 (1955). See also, IRC § 104(a)(2). For example, two-thirds of the amount received under a treble damage award (e.g., for an antitrust claim) will constitute gross income to the recipient.

The tax treatment of compensatory damages must be divided into two categories—damages for harming or destroying property and damages for personal injuries suffered by an individual. The paragraph below briefly summarizes the current treatment of damages, and subsequent sections expand on this topic.

Damages for harming or destroying property will constitute realized income to the recipient to the extent that the amount of such damages exceeds the recipient's adjusted basis in the damaged or destroyed property. The realized income will be recognized (and therefore taxable) unless some or all of the damages are reinvested in property that permits the recipient to elect nonrecognition under IRC § 1033. See **§ 17.4000** et seq. To the extent that such damages do not exceed the TP's adjusted basis, they will be included in a gross income only to the extent (if any) that the TP had previously been allowed a deduction for the loss, which deduction benefitted the TP by reducing his tax liability.

Damages received for a *physical* injury to one's person are excluded from income by IRC § 104(a)(2). Damages received for a nonphysical injury to one's person generally are treated as income.

§ 2.1310. Damage to Tangible Property. Unless the tax benefit rule (which rule is explained at **§ 2.3000** et seq.) applies, compensation received by a taxpayer for damage caused to the taxpayer's property will be included in gross income only to the extent that the amount of the compensation exceeds the taxpayer's basis in the damaged property. This is true regardless of whether the payor of the compensation is the person who caused the damage or is an insurer. Under the tax benefit rule, the compensation will also be included in taxpayer's gross income to the extent that the taxpayer previously claimed a deduction for the damage to that property and obtained a tax benefit from that deduction (i.e., the deduction resulted in a reduction of the taxpayer's tax liability).

§ 2.1311. Deduction Illustration. X negligently collided with a car in which Y had a basis of $3,000. The car had a value of $2,500 before the collision and $1,500 after the collision. As a consequence of the collision, an antique vase which Y was transporting in his car was broken beyond repair. Y had a basis of $500 in the vase, which had a value of $1,200 prior to the accident. Because of limitations in IRC § 165, no tax deduction was allowable to Y for the casualty loss he incurred. Neither the car nor the vase was used by Y in his business. X paid Y $1,000 compensation for the damage to Y's car, and $1,200 compensation for having destroyed Y's vase. Y did not recognize any gain from the $1,000 damages paid on the car since the payment was less than his basis for the car. Y's basis for his car will be reduced by the amount recovered as damages (i.e., $1,000) to $2,000. However, Y will realize a gain of $700 ($1,200 compensation minus $500 basis) on the damages paid for the broken vase. This gain will be *recognized* unless a statutory provision for nonrecognition is applicable, such as IRC § 1033. See § **17.4000** et seq. The remaining $1,500 of recovery is excluded from income as a recovery of capital, Y's basis in the vase is reduced to zero, and his basis in the car is reduced to $2,000.

§ **2.1312.   Illustration 2.** The same facts as those stated in **Illustration 1**, except that a portion of the casualty loss that Y incurred was deductible. As explained in Chapter 7, for tax purposes, the amount of loss that Y sustained as a result of the collision is $1,500 (i.e, the difference between the values of each item before and after the collision but limited to the amount of the TP's basis in the item). At the time that TP filed his tax return for the year of the collision, there was no reasonable prospect that he would be reimbursed for any of the loss. [Note that a TP cannot take a deduction for a casualty loss so long as he has a reasonable prospect of being reimbursed.   § **7.2510.**] Because   of   limitations   in   IRC § 165(h)(1), (2) on the amount that can be deducted for a casualty loss, TP was allowed a deduction of only $250 for the loss that he sustained. TP claimed a $250 deduction and obtained a tax benefit thereby. As stated in **Illustration 1,** in a subsequent year, X did obtain a recovery from Y of $2,200 for the loss he incurred. As noted in **Illustration 1**, $700 of that recovery is income to Y because the $1,200 he received for the destruction of the vase exceeded his basis by that amount. Of the remaining $1,500 of Y's recovery, $250 is gross income to Y under the tax benefit rule (see § **2.3000** *et seq.*). The remaining $1,250 of Y's recovery is excluded from income but reduces his basis in the items.

§ **2.1313.   Illustration 3.** The same facts as those stated in **Illustration 1**, except that Y's car was used in his business. Nevertheless, because of a prospect of obtaining reimbursement, no deduction was allowable to Y for the loss he incurred, and he did not claim a deduction. Prior to receiving the payment from X, Y expended $900 in repairing the car, and Y claimed and was allowed a business expense deduction for that expense. The amount of the recovery that is included in Y's gross income is $700—the same amount that was included in **Illustration 1** and for the same reason. The deduction that Y

obtained for repairing the car has no effect on the tax treatment of the damages he received. The damage payment was not a reimbursement of the repairs he made, but rather was compensation for the loss he suffered when his property was damaged. The tax benefit rule does not apply. The amount expended for repairs can be used as an indicator of the amount of loss that the TP suffered from the casualty, but the payment received from X is for the property loss itself and not a reimbursement of the amount expended on repairs.

It should be noted that the IRS has stated that the cost incurred in repairing a damaged item for which a casualty loss was allowable (which loss reduced the TP's basis in the damaged item under IRC § 1016(a)(1)) is "in the nature of a replacement of the part of the property that was damaged," and therefore such a repair cost must be capitalized (i.e., added to the TP's basis) rather than deducted. Rev. Rul. 71–161. The Service's ruling on this issue is suspect and was questioned by a District Court in dictum in *Waldrip v. United States*, 48 AFTR2d 81–6031, fn.5 (N.D. Ga. 1981). The authors do not believe that the position adopted by the IRS in that ruling is valid, and so the repair in this **Illustration** should be treated as a deductible item.

§ 2.1314. Recovery Not Required by Law. While early statements of the IRS as to the exclusion of compensatory recoveries indicated that a recipient must have had a legal right to the recovery to qualify for the exclusion [GCM 38032], the Service later repudiated its earlier stance. GCM 39228 (1983), GCM 39480 (1986), and GCM 39558 (1986). The General Counsel Memorandums dealt with the question of whether a receipt that was not obtained by legal right could be treated as compensation (or a prospect of compensation) that would prevent the deduction of a loss that was the source of the "compensatory" payment. The Service concluded that, for such treatment, compensatory payments need not be legally required to be made. A reasonable extension of that conclusion is that such receipts can qualify as compensatory payments for purposes of excluding them from income as well.

Accordingly, it appears that the current view of the Service is that there need only be a significant nexus between the loss and the payment for the latter to be treated as compensatory.

There is no requirement that the recipient have had an enforceable right to the funds. It would seem to be sufficient if the purpose of the payment was to redress a harm that the payor had caused, regardless of whether the payor had a legal obligation to make that payment.

Of course a compensatory payment must be distinguished from a gift, which is the product of detached and disinterested generosity. For example, if a payment is made because the payor feels a moral responsibility to mitigate the loss that his actions caused another, that would not be a gift, but would be a compensatory payment. To the extent that a payment is treated as a gift, then the entire amount of the gift is excluded from the payee's income by IRC § 102.

§ 2.1315.   Recovery of Lost Dollars. If X's error or wrongful action causes a loss of money to Y, if the loss is not deductible by Y, and if X reimburses Y for all or part of the dollars lost, will the reimbursement constitute gross income to Y? Just as damages received for injuries to property are excluded from income to the extent of the recipient's basis in the property, so are recoveries of lost dollars. They are treated as returns of capital and are not taxable. *Clark v. Commissioner*, 40 BTA 333 (1939), Acq.; *Concord Instruments Corp. v. Commissioner*, 67 T.C.M. 3036 (1994); Rev. Rul. 57–47.

§ 2.1316.   Illustration 4. X, a lawyer, gave bad advice to a client and caused the client to pay $20,000 more in federal income tax then the client actually owed. By the time that the error was discovered, the statute of limitation for amending the tax return had expired, and so the client could not obtain a refund of his $20,000 overpayment. X then paid the client $20,000 to replace the $20,000 that the client had lost to the government because of X's error. The $20,000 that the client received from X is not included in the client's gross income. It is a recovery of capital. See, *Clark v. Commissioner, supra.*

What if X's error did not rise to the level of malpractice and X had no legal obligation to compensate the client? The result to the client should be the same—i.e., the payment should be exempt from tax. There are several reasons why X might wish to make that payment even if X had no legal obligation to do so. X might feel a moral responsibility for the loss and wish to make it right. X might have a selfish, business motive to make the payment to mute any criticism of his work that might circulate if the loss were left unabated. Such motives are not detached and disinterested generosity, so the payment would not be a gift. However, the nexus between the payment and X's role in causing the loss makes it a compensatory payment. Accordingly, the replacement of dollars lost is equivalent to the replacement of basis lost through the destruction of property and is excluded from the client's income.

If X were legally liable for the $20,000 that the client paid to the IRS, and if X's insurance carrier paid $20,000 to the client to replace the lost dollars, the client would not have any income from the receipt of that payment. *Concord Instruments Corp. v. Commissioner, supra.*

§ 2.1317. Illustration 5. Z, a CPA firm, negligently caused Client to fail to take action necessary to qualify Client as a "regulated investment company" and thereby qualify for favorable tax treatment. Because of that error, Client became liable for higher income taxes than it otherwise would have incurred, and Client incurred penalties and interest on its tax liability. Z's insurance carrier reimbursed Client for the additional federal income tax Client incurred plus the associated penalties and interest that Client had to pay. Initially, relying on the *Clark* decision, the IRS ruled (in a Letter Ruling) that the payments received by Client were not income to it. Six years later, in 1997, the IRS revoked the earlier Letter Ruling and ruled that the payments are included in Client's gross income. PLR 9743034 and PLR 9743035. The Service distinguished the instant situation from *Clark* on the basis that in *Clark* and related precedents, the advisor's error caused the TP to pay the government a larger amount then the TP actually owed. In contrast, in the instant problem, the TP actually did owe the taxes that were collected and the interest and penalties for not paying it. The error was in failing to have Client take action that would have precluded those taxes; but, since the action was not taken, Client did owe the money in question. The Service then cited Treas. Reg. § 1.61–14(a) for the proposition that one person's payment of the income tax liability of another is income to the other unless excluded by law. The Service concluded that the payments received by Client from the insurance carrier were income to the Client.

The Commissioner gave a similar ruling in PLR 9833007. Under the facts of that ruling, after winning a state lottery, the taxpayer consulted attorneys for tax preparation advice. The attorneys failed to advise taxpayer to pay the state income tax on his winning in the year in which he received the prize so that he could deduct that tax from his winnings in computing his federal income tax. This failure caused taxpayer to incur a higher federal income tax liability, and taxpayer sought indemnification from the attorneys' malpractice insurer. The Commissioner ruled that any indemnification the taxpayer obtained will be included in his gross income.

In the view of the authors, the position taken by the Service in the 1997 and 1998 Letter Rulings is wrong and cannot be sustained. See *Concord Instruments Corp. v. Commissioner*, 67 T.C.M. 3036 (1994). As to the 1997 rulings, regardless of whether the Client actually owed the taxes, Z's negligence caused the client to pay out a greater amount of taxes and associated costs than it otherwise would have incurred, and the payment that Client received was compensation for the loss that it suffered from that negligence. The compensatory replacement of lost dollars should be excluded from income. Of course, by not taking the action needed to qualify as a "regulated investment company," Client may have benefitted in some manner, such as saving some costs. But, that only goes to the question of the amount of damage that Z caused and to the correct amount of compensatory payment that should be made. It should have no effect on the question of the taxability of Client's receipt of the compensatory payment. Similarly, an indemnification of the taxpayer in the 1998 ruling for the negligence of the attorneys in failing to advise taxpayer of a tax minimization step constitutes damages for lost capital in the form of a higher tax liability than was necessary.

§ 2.1320. Damage Caused to Intangible Property. Intangible assets (e.g., goodwill, trademarks, copyrights) may be damaged by tortious conduct. Compensatory damages relating to such assets will consist of gross income only to the extent that the compensation exceeds the taxpayer's basis in the asset.

§ 2.1321. Damage to Goodwill. An unfair trade practice or a defamatory statement concerning the quality of a product or service of a business may cause damage to the "goodwill" of the business, for which the injured party may collect damages.

"Goodwill" is an intangible asset that represents the potential that a business possesses to attract customers for its products or services. Following the general rule, compensation for damage to a taxpayer's goodwill constitutes gross income to the extent that the compensation exceeds the taxpayer's basis in his goodwill.

§ 2.1321–1. **Determining Basis in Goodwill.** In many instances, a taxpayer will not have a basis in his goodwill. As a consequence, the entire compensatory payment will be included in his gross income. A taxpayer usually will have a basis in his goodwill only when he has purchased the goodwill of another business. For example, if *X* purchased a going business from *Y*, he will typically purchase the goodwill of that business. Thus, a part of the purchase price will be allocated to goodwill. *X* will have an adjusted basis in the goodwill equal to the allocated part of the purchase price less amortization deductions previously allowed or allowable under IRC § 197.

§ 2.1322. **Reimbursement for Lost Profits.** Reimbursement for profits lost by a taxpayer due to some wrongful action by another will constitute gross income. There is no offset for basis. The distinction between compensation for damages inflicted on a taxpayer's goodwill and compensation for lost profits is nebulous at best, inasmuch as the value of goodwill relates directly to its income producing quality. The trend in the cases is to favor the taxpayer by finding that compensation was paid for damages caused to the taxpayer's goodwill. This is so even though the value of the goodwill is determined by referring to the loss of profits suffered. *Raytheon Production Corp. v. Commissioner*, 144 F.2d 110 (1st Cir. 1944). But see *Bresler v. Commissioner*, 65 T.C. 182 (1975) where the court held that a large portion of an antitrust settlement was for lost profits rather than for damage to goodwill. The court held in *Bresler* that the taxpayer had the burden of proving that the corporation had suffered damage to its goodwill or that the settlement included a specific amount for damaged goodwill. The court would not accept the taxpayer's contention that the settlement should be allocated according to the types of damage requested by the taxpayer in the complaint. Only a relatively small amount of the settlement was treated as damages for goodwill. See also § **2.1321** and § **2.1321–1.**

A plausible distinction that might be employed is to treat compensation received for depriving the taxpayer of the profit that the taxpayer would have earned under a specific contract as a substitute for that lost profit and so taxed as ordinary income. On the other hand, compensation received for damage done to a broad range of the taxpayer's business (which thereby reduced the taxpayer's future profits from that portion of the business) should be characterized as a compensatory payment for the damage to the taxpayer's goodwill.

§ 2.1322–1.   Illustration 1. *ABC*, Inc. collected $100,000 compensatory damages from *XYZ*, Inc. for federal antitrust violations committed by the latter. The compensatory damages were measured by the amount of profits that *ABC* lost because of the unlawful activity of *XYZ*. It has been determined in many such cases that the lost profits are used only to measure the extent of the damage done to *ABC*'s goodwill. If *ABC* had a basis of $60,000 in its goodwill, it will realize income of $40,000 ($100,000 damages less $60,000 basis). Note that IRC § 186 may provide some tax relief for *ABC* if the injury suffered by *ABC* as a consequence of the antitrust violation resulted in *ABC*'s having a net operating loss during the period in which such injuries were sustained (i.e., *ABC* may be permitted to reduce the amount of income it recognized from the receipt of the award for damages by the amount of such net operating losses that were not previously deducted).

§ 2.1322–2.   Illustration 2. *X* breached a contract with *Y*. *Y* recovered $5,000 damages for profits lost because of *X*'s breach. The $5,000 damage payment will be included in *Y*'s gross income and will be fully taxable.

§ 2.1322–3.   Illustration 3. *Z* filed a complaint with the National Labor Relations Board against a union for causing *Z*'s employer to fire him. *Z* recovered damages for lost wages. While such damages typically will not constitute wages for social security tax or unemployment tax purposes since they were not paid by or on behalf of *Z*'s employer, they do constitute gross income to *Z* for income tax purposes. Rev. Rul. 75–64. The damage payment relates entirely to lost earnings (equivalent to lost business profits) and thus will be treated as gross income.

§ 2.1323. Characterization of Insurance Proceeds. The tax treatment of insurance proceeds collected upon the suffering of a loss may turn upon the nature of the risk that is insured. If the insurance proceeds are paid to compensate a taxpayer for property loss or damage, the proceeds will not be taxable to the extent of the taxpayer's basis in that property, and the taxpayer's basis will be reduced accordingly. Any excess insurance proceeds will be treated as income to the taxpayer, although the taxpayer may be permitted to elect nonrecognition under IRC § 1033 if he reinvests the insurance proceeds in qualified property within the statutory period. See **§ 17.4000** and following. However, in *Marshall Foods, Inc. v. United States*, 393 F.Supp. 1097 (D.Minn. 1974), aff'd per curiam, 36 AFTR2d 75–5095 (8th Cir. 1975), the courts held that insurance proceeds received by a taxpayer after a fire had damaged his business were paid to compensate the taxpayer for a loss of income due to an interruption of his business, and therefore all the proceeds were deemed to be income to the taxpayer. In other words, the court held that the proceeds were payable to compensate the taxpayer for lost profits rather than as compensation for property damage. See also, Treas. Reg. § 1.1033(a)–2(c)(8).

In *Johnson v. Commissioner*, 66 T.C. 897 (1976), aff'd per curiam by a divided court, 574 F.2d 189 (4th Cir. 1978), the courts denied a loss deduction to a taxpayer who had liquidated his partnership business for less than his basis because the taxpayer had received life insurance proceeds from a policy insuring his partner's life and the court deemed the insurance to be compensation for the loss of value of the business due to the partner's death. The Tax Court held that, while the taxpayer realized a loss on the liquidation of the partnership, he was reimbursed for that loss by his receipt of the insurance proceeds, and so no deduction is allowable under IRC § 165(a).

While the result reached in *Johnson* has pragmatic appeal, the decision is questionable. The authors doubt the wisdom of adopting a policy that requires an examination of the motive for acquiring insurance on the life of an employee or owner of a business as a condition to allowing a deduction for a business loss that is sustained after the insured's death. Despite *Johnson*, there has been no subsequent movement by the courts or the Service in that direction. For example, if a corporation purchases insurance on the life of a key employee, it is unlikely that the corporation will be denied a deduction for operating losses incurred after the employee's death on the ground that it was compensated for those losses through its receipt of the insurance proceeds. The typical reason for purchasing such insurance is to protect the employer from the decline in revenue or rise in costs that will occur when the key employee departs, and the *Johnson* rationale would deny a deduction for losses incurred in those circumstances. If the corporation did not incur losses after the employee's death but merely incurred a reduction in its revenue, the *Johnson* doctrine would not apply; and so, even if the *Johnson* approach were adopted, the receipt of the insurance proceeds would have no tax consequence. It is questionable whether the result should be different when losses are incurred.

If a corporation did not incur losses after the insured employee's death but did incur increased expenses because of the loss of the employee's expertise, it is unlikely that a deduction will be denied for those additional business expenses. While the statutory provision for deducting a loss expressly provides in IRC § 165(a) that no deduction will be allowed for a loss that is compensated by insurance, no similar provision is included in IRC § 162 (the business expense deduction provision). However, if a business expense were reimbursed, either the expense would not be deductible or the reimbursement would be included in income. So, the tax status of such additional business costs is not much different from the status of business losses. The same question will control the tax issue—namely, whether the receipt of the life insurance proceeds constitutes a reimbursement of the additional expenses or losses that were incurred after the insured's death.

As yet, *Johnson* has been cited by only one other court decision, which distinguished the case. Therefore, its approach has not been adopted and there is no sign of a trend in that direction. Perhaps, *Johnson* will remain an isolated and eccentric case.

§ 2.1323–1. Illustration. *B* owned a boat in which he had a basis of $10,000, and which had a value of $11,000. *B* had a casualty insurance policy on the boat. The boat was damaged by a fire, and *B* collected $2,000 from his insurer to compensate for the damage to his boat. No deduction was allowable for *B*'s loss since *B* was compensated. *B* did not recognize gross income on collecting the $2,000 insurance payment, but his basis in the boat was reduced to $8,000. If the boat had been completely destroyed by the fire and *B* had collected $11,000 from his insurer, *B* would have realized a gain of $1,000; but if within a specified period of time he replaced the boat at a cost of more than $10,000, *B* could elect not to recognize all or part of the $1,000 gain under IRC § 1033. See § **17.4000** et seq.

§ 2.1330.   Damages Received on Account of Personal Injuries. Damages received as compensation for a personal physical injury caused by tortious conduct is exempt from taxation, except for the recovery of previously deducted items. "The amount of any damages (other than punitive damages) received (whether by suit or agreement and whether as lump sums or periodic payments) on account of personal physical injuries or physical sickness ..." are excluded from gross income. IRC § 104(a)(2). The personal injuries to which the statute refers are expressly limited to physical injuries. For example, while emotional harm and loss of reputation are personal injuries, they do not qualify as physical injuries. However, damages received for emotional distress are excluded from income to the extent that the amount of such damages does not exceed the nondeducted medical expenses attributable to that distress. IRC § 104(a). Treas. Reg. § 1.104–1(c) defines the statutory reference to "damages ... received" as an amount received "through prosecution of a legal suit or action based upon tort or tort type rights, or through a settlement agreement entered into in lieu of such prosecution."

The scope of the IRC § 104(a)(2) exclusion from income is very broad. Once that provision applies, even amounts compensating for lost wages are excludable from gross income. Rev. Rul. 85–97.

In addition to the exclusion of such damages, amounts received under a workers' compensation act as compensation for personal injuries or sickness are excluded from gross income. IRC § 104(a)(1). The exclusion also applies to payments that are deemed similar in nature to worker's compensation. See PLR 200016012 where the Service excluded disability payments made to injured police officers.

When interest is paid to a taxpayer on an award for compensatory damages, the interest represents compensation for the use of the taxpayer's money; it is not compensation for the injury that the taxpayer suffered. The taxpayer must include the interest payment in gross income. *Aames v. Commissioner*, 94 T.C. 189 (1990). One might question whether prejudgment interest (i.e., interest for a period prior to the entry of a judgment) on an award for a physical injury should be excluded by IRC § 104(a)(2) as being part of the plaintiff's loss from the physical injury. The courts have held that prejudgment interest is taxable and is not excluded from gross income by IRC § 104. *Rozpad v. Commissioner*, 154 F.3d 1 (1st Cir. 1998); *Brabson v. United States*, 73 F.3d 1040 (10th Cir. 1996). Taxation is also imposed on payments similar to interest. For example, in *Francisco v. U.S.*, 267 F.3d 303 (3rd Cir. 2001), the court held that a portion of a settlement was for "delay damages" which were similar to prejudgment interest and therefore taxable to the taxpayer.

In *Rozpad*, the plaintiffs had obtained a judgment for a personal injury which included an award for prejudgment interest. During the appeal period, plaintiffs settled with defendants for a smaller amount than the judgment. The settlement was for a specified amount, which was stipulated to be without interest or costs. The First Circuit noted that when there is no indication of the amount of interest reflected in a judgment for or settlement of a physical injury claim, the courts will exclude the entire amount rather than speculate on the portion of the award or settlement that represents interest. But, when the amount of interest can be determined on a reasonable basis, it will be taxed. The court deemed the percentage of the trial judgment that interest constituted as a reasonable allocation, and so the court applied the same percentage to plaintiffs' settlement. See § **2.1335**. The portions of the settlement that the court found to be interest was held to be taxable.

§ **2.1331. Tort–Type Claims.** As the quotation in § **2.1330** from a regulation reflects, IRC § 104(a)(2) excludes from gross income certain damages obtained pursuant to tort or tort type rights. No exclusion is provided for amounts received pursuant to contract type rights. While it often is easy to distinguish torts from contract type rights, there are a number of circumstances in which that distinction is cloudy. In such cases, the courts had difficulty determining whether the exclusion is applicable. However, as a consequence of the 1996 amendment that limits the § 104(a)(2) exclusion to *physical* injuries, there is no longer likely to be any need to distinguish between tort and contract type claims since physical injuries will raise tort issues. The one possible exception is the exclusion of damages for emotional distress that does not exceed medical care expenses. In that latter circumstance, an issue might arise as to whether the claim for damages for emotional stress is a tort type claim. The standards for classifying a claim as tort type are set forth in the Supreme Court's 1992 decision in *United States v. Burke*, 504 U.S. 229.

§ 2.1332. Physical and Nonphysical Personal Injuries. An amendment to IRC § 104, which was adopted as part of the Small Business Job Protection Act of 1996, limited the § 104(a)(2) exclusion from income to damages that are based on a claim that is attributable to a physical injury. See the penultimate sentence of IRC § 104(a). The statute explicitly states that "emotional distress" does not constitute a physical injury, and the House Report to the 1996 Act states that "the term emotional distress includes physical symptoms (e.g. insomnia, headaches, stomach disorders) which may result from such emotional distress." H. Rept. 104–586, p. 144, fn24 (104th Cong. 2d Sess. 1996). The statute does permit the exclusion of damages received on a claim for emotional distress to the extent that the amount of the damages do not exceed the amount of medical expenses attributable to that emotional distress that were not previously deducted. The requirement that the medical expenses not have been previously deducted is not stated in the statute, but is a consequence of the tax benefit rule. See § **2.3000** *et seq.*

Thus, if a TP has no physical injury within the meaning of the statute, damages received for a personal injury will be taxable except for the medical expense provision described above. Even if there are physical manifestations of a nonphysical personal injury, damages will be taxable. However, if the TP did suffer a physical injury, *any damages* that are based on a claim attributable to that physical injury are excluded from gross income. As previously noted, damages provided to compensate for lost wages or other income are excluded from gross income if the source of the claim is a physical injury. Moreover, damages for emotional distress and for consequences of that distress are excluded from income if the distress itself is the product of a physical injury. H. Rept. 104–586, p. 144 (104th Cong. 2d Sess. 1996).

The key to the exclusion is that there has been a physical injury and that the damages received are attributable to that injury. The physical injury need not have occurred to the recipient of the damages. For example, the House Report states that damages received for the loss of consortium due to a physical injury to the TP's spouse are excluded from gross income by IRC § 104(a)(2). H. Rept. 104–586, p. 144 (104th Cong. 2d Sess. 1996). The IRS followed the House Report in an asbestos case in PLR 200121031.

When a TP incurs only a very minor physical injury, but suffers substantial emotional distress, questions are likely to arise as to whether damages for that injury are excluded by the statute. If the TP suffered a physical injury, will all damages arising out of the events in which the physical injury occurred be excluded? In the authors' view, for damages to be excluded, the injury being compensated must be a consequence of the physical injury. See *Commissioner v. Schleier*, 515 U.S. 323 (1995). *Schleier* held that damages for violation of the Age Discrimination in Employment Act of 1967 were not excluded by the pre–1996 version of IRC § 104(a)(2). While damages for all claims based on discrimination were made taxable by the 1996 amendment to IRC § 104(a)(2), and that amendment resolves the issue decided in *Schleier*, the Supreme Court's analysis is likely to influence the construction of the 1996 version of the statute. In *Schleier*, the Court held that damages must be attributable to a personal injury to be excluded from income—that is, the personal injury itself must be a source of the injury, it is not sufficient that the same acts that caused the personal injury also caused other injuries. It seems likely that the same approach will be applied to the requirement that the damages be attributable to a physical injury.

In PLR 200041022, the IRS provided some guidance to this issue. The facts of the ruling are that A was employed by C. C began sexually harassing A. Two dates are particularly important for purposes of the ruling. During the initial period, C physically touched A but did not leave any bodily harm (e.g., cuts, bruises, etc.). Next, C assaulted A causing A to experience extreme pain (described by the ruling as the "First Pain Incident"). After that incident, A began to experience physical ailments, but doctors could find anything wrong with her. At a later date, C again assaulted A, cutting and biting her (described by the ruling as the "First Physical Injury"). After A filed suit against C, A and C agreed to a settlement. The issue requested by the taxpayer was whether the settlement proceeds were excluded under IRC § 104(a)(2).

The IRS ruled that any damages allocable to events prior to the First Pain Incident were not received on account of a physical injury and therefore should be included in the taxpayer's income. Any damages allocable to events beginning with the First Physical Injury were excluded from the taxpayer's gross income under IRC § 104(a)(2). However, the IRS refused to rule on damages allocable to events after the First Pain Incident (but before the First Physical Injury). The IRS stated that since the perception of pain is a factual matter, it could not rule whether the damages were excluded. This suggests that a physical mark is not required in order to qualify for the exclusion under IRC § 104(a)(2). The Service also refused to rule on the proper allocation of the damages between the events and also between compensatory and punitive damages.

§ 2.1332–1. Illustration 1. *R* was an employee of *X* Corporation. *T* was *R*'s supervisor. Over the course of several years, *T* made lewd and improper statements to *R* and suggested that she would advance more rapidly in the company if she were to agree to a sexual relationship with him. *R* rejected these proposals. On one occasion, after *R* had again said "no" and turned to leave the room, *T* pinched her derriere. The pinch was hard enough to leave a bruise, but the bruise was minor and disappeared within a few days. Having had more than she could stand, *R* then sued *X* for allowing sexual harassment to take place. The suit was settled by *X*'s paying *R* $1,000,000 in damages. Will all or any part of those damages be excluded from *R*'s gross income by IRC § 104(a)(2)? The answer to this is not yet settled. In the authors' view, the damages should be apportioned, and only damages directly attributable to the pinch should be excluded. While the pinch was one item in a pattern of harassment conduct, it was the only act that caused a physical injury. Most of *R*'s recovery is attributable to the emotional distress and humiliation that she suffered independently of the physical intrusion. To the extent that *R* recovered damages for emotional distress arising from the pinch itself, those damages would be excluded.

The division of damages in such cases will be difficult to make, but not impossible, and equally difficult divisions have been required to be made in other areas of this same tax law. See § 2.1335. If such an allocation is not required, then there are likely to be claims of some physical harm in many cases otherwise resting on emotional harm. An alternative or supplementary approach is to disregard minor physical injuries as de minimis.

§ 2.1332–2. Illustration 2. *G* is employed by *Z*. *Z* touches *G*'s breast, but does not bruise or otherwise injure *G*. Does that touching constitute a physical injury within the meaning of the statute? It would seem that the real harm suffered by *G* is essentially the same as that suffered by victims of discrimination or defamation, the damages from which are clearly taxable under the current version of IRC § 104(a)(2). The source of *G*'s injury is a physical act, but her injury is the distress and humiliation of being treated in such a demeaning fashion. It does not appear to be a *physical injury*. It remains to be seen how the IRS and the courts will deal with this issue. Even after PLR 200041022, it is by no means clear how it will be resolved.

§ 2.1332–3. Illustration 3. While attempting to cross a street, *N* is struck by an automobile and seriously injured. One of *N*'s legs had to be amputated, and *N* had permanent brain damage because of the injuries he suffered. *N* was unable to work for some months after his accident, and the work that he could do paid much less than he was earning before the accident. As a consequence of the accident, *N* became fearful of automobiles and had nightmares about his accident. His emotional distress caused him to have headaches. The insurance company for the driver of the car settled *N*'s claim for damages by paying *N* $5,000,000 as compensation for his injuries. The settlement allocated the damage payment among the following injuries: (1) Wages lost while *N* was unable to work, (2) Reduction of future income that *N* will suffer because of his injuries, (3) Reimbursement of *N*'s medical expenses, (4) Estimated future medical expenses that *N* will incur as a consequence of his injuries, (5) Emotional distress that *N* suffered, (6) Pain and suffering that *N* has had, and (7) Pain and suffering that N will likely have in the future because of the injuries. All of the $5,000,000 damages that N received is excluded from his gross income by IRC § 104(a)(2). The only exception is that the damages allocated to medical expenses will be taxable to the extent that N previously took a tax deduction for those expenses.

§ 2.1333. Damages for Victims of Discrimination or Defamation. Prior to the 1996 amendment, damages for personal defamation were excluded from gross income, and damages for defamation of business reputation sometimes was. The treatment of damages for violation of statutes prohibiting employment discrimination was mixed. Damages for some types of discrimination were excluded while others were taxed. The determining factor was the type of remedy that the anti-discrimination provision provided. The 1996 amendment changed all that. Discrimination and defamation do not constitute physical injuries, even though the emotional distress that the victim suffers can lead to physical harm. The House Report on the 1996 amendment expressly states that, "the exclusion from gross income does not apply to any damages received . . . based on a claim of employment discrimination or injury to reputation accompanied by a claim of emotional distress." H. Rept. 104–586, p. 144 (104th Cong. 2d Sess. 1996).

§ 2.1334. Punitive Damages. Prior to the 1996 amendment, there was considerable litigation over the question of whether punitive damages received in connection with a claim for compensatory damages for a personal injury were excluded from gross income by IRC § 104(a)(2). Over the years, the Commissioner changed his position several times, and court decisions were mixed. In a 1989 amendment to IRC § 104(a), Congress made clear that punitive damages awarded when there was no physical injury was taxable, but Congress did not then address the question of whether punitive damages are excluded when there is a physical injury. The 1996 amendment resolved all doubts by making all punitive damages taxable, with one exception. The single exception applies to wrongful death damages in those states in which only punitive damages are permitted to be awarded for a wrongful death. In such a case, the punitive wrongful death award is excluded from income. The apparent reason for this exception is that the punitive award in such cases is a substitute for and in lieu

of compensatory payments. This exception applies only if the
state law providing only punitive damages for wrongful death
was in effect on September 13, 1995. IRC § 104(c).

The legislative history to the 1996 amendment makes clear
that it operates prospectively only and is not intended to effect
the construction of IRC § 104 for years prior to the effective
date of the amendment. How should punitive damages be
treated if received before the amendment was effective? The
confusion as to the pre–1996 treatment of punitive damages
was resolved by the Supreme Court in *O'Gilvie v. United
States*, 519 U.S. 79 (1996), in which the Court held that
punitive damages are included in gross income. Consequently,
regardless of when received, except for certain wrongful death
damages, punitive damages are included in gross income.

**§ 2.1335.   Allocation of Damages Between Punitive and
Compensatory Elements.** When a judgment is granted to a
plaintiff in a suit in which punitive damages were sought for a
physical injury, the court's verdict typically will state what
amount of the award is compensatory damages and what
amount is punitive; only the latter amount will be included in
the plaintiff's gross income. When there has been no allocation
by a court, a determination must be made as to the amount (if
any) of damages that were received by a taxpayer that constitute punitive damages. The allocation between compensatory
and punitive damages is a question of fact on which the
taxpayer usually has the burden of proof. *Miller v. Commissioner*, 65 T.C.M. 1884 (1993), on remand from the Fourth
Circuit's decision in *Commissioner v. Miller*, 914 F.2d 586 (4th
Cir. 1990). Factors to be considered in making that allocation
include: the allegations made in the complaint, the defenses
asserted, and the background of the litigation. The intent of
the payor (if that can be determined) is a critical factor. *Miller
v. Commissioner*, *supra*, and cases cited therein.

If the parties settle their dispute by a payment of damages, the
Commissioner may accept as determinative a reasonable allocation made in the settlement agreement of the amount of the
damages that is compensatory and the amount that is punitive. See *Matray v. Commissioner*, 56 T.C.M. 1107 (1989). If no
allocation is made in a settlement agreement, the payment
often will be allocated between compensatory and punitive

damages in the same ratio as those damages were requested in
the plaintiff's complaint. Rev. Rul. 85–98. But see *Bresler v.
Commissioner*, [at § **2.1322**] where the Tax Court rejected the
contention that the antitrust settlement there involved should
be allocated between lost profits and damaged goodwill according to the damages requested in the plaintiff's complaint. Also
see *Francisco v. U.S.*, 267 F.3d 303 (3d Cir. 2001), where the
allocation of "delay damages" to a lump sum settlement,
which was executed after a jury verdict and while the case was
on appeal, was made in the same proportion as was the delay
damages in the jury's verdict.

In *Commissioner v. Miller*, 914 F.2d 586 (4th Cir. 1990), the
court remanded the case to the Tax Court to determine the
proper allocation between compensatory and punitive damages
of a lump sum settlement of two suits against the same party
that was made after a jury verdict was issued in one of the
plaintiff's suits. In *Miller*, the Fourth Circuit suggested several
alternative methods of allocation which might be adopted, and
the court indicated that an allocation agreed to by the parties
to the suit might be accepted by the Tax Court. On remand,
the Tax Court allocated the settlement between punitive and
compensatory damages on the same ratio that the jury applied
in the verdict of the first case (which case was included in the
lump sum settlement). *Miller v. Commissioner*, 65 T.C.M.
1884 (1993).

A reasonable allocation of damages that is made by a settlement agreement of the parties generally will be adopted by the
courts to the extent that the "agreement is entered into by the
parties in an adversarial context at arms' length and in good
faith" *Robinson v. Commissioner*, 102 T.C. 116 (1994); aff'd on
that issue and rev'd on an unrelated issue, 70 F.3d 34 (5th Cir.
1995). The difficulty with that principle is that a defendant
rarely has anything at stake in the manner in which a damage
payment is to be allocated among the various claims that the
plaintiff made. The allocation can affect the plaintiff's tax
liability, but it often will have little or no effect on the
defendant. So, the defendant might use the allocation issue as
a bargaining chip to reduce the amount of damages payable,
but it is difficult to see how an allocation can be "adversarial
and at arms' length" when only one of the parties has anything at stake in the outcome. Nevertheless, courts and the
IRS are likely to accept an allocation by the parties provided

that the allocation is reasonable. There is considerable subjectivity in determining the proper allocation, and so a reasonable amount will lie within a wide range of permissible allocations. If an allocation made by the parties falls within that reasonable range, it likely will be accepted by the courts and by the Service. But, if the parties overreach and make an allocation that eliminates obviously significant items claimed by the plaintiff, the entire allocation will be ignored by the courts, who will then make their own determination of how the damages are to be allocated. See e.g., *Robinson v. Commissioner, supra*; *Rozpad v. Commissioner*, § **2.1330**; *Delaney v. Commissioner*, 99 F.3d 20 (1st Cir. 1996); *Bagley v. Commissioner*, 121 F.3d 393 (8th Cir. 1997).

In the *Robinson* case, cited above, the Tax Court declined to accept an allocation that was made in the judgement of a state court that resolved the issue in dispute. The Tax Court found that the state court judge had merely accepted the allocation given to the judge by the plaintiff (with no objection from the defendant) and had not made an independent determination. Applying the *Bosch* rule (referring to the rule established by the Supreme Court in *Commissioner v. Estate of Bosch*, 387 U.S. 456 (1967)), the Tax Court treated the state court's judgment as merely a datum to be weighed in determining the allocation (as contrasted to treating it as a binding determination). After weighing the state court's allocation, the Tax Court decided to make its own determination. Perhaps it is relevant to the Tax Court's decision in *Robinson* that the state court allocated 95% of the damages to items that were excluded from the plaintiff's income even though the plaintiff had substantial claims for items an award for which would have been taxable to the plaintiff. The Fifth Circuit affirmed this aspect of the Tax Court's decision. 70 F.3d 34. See also, the similar treatment of taxpayers' efforts to avoid taxation on prejudgment interest that had been awarded in a judgement by subsequently settling the judgement for an undifferentiated lump sum. *Rozpad v. Commissioner, supra*, and *Delaney v. Commissioner, supra*.

§ **2.1336. Allocation of Lump Sum Award or Settlement Into Its Likely Component Parts.** In *Niles v. United States*, 710 F.2d 1391 (9th Cir. 1983), the taxpayer had received a jury award of $4,025,000 for personal injury. The defendant had appealed on the contention that the award was excessive. In successfully defending the amount of the award on appeal, the taxpayer had presented a detailed hypothetical itemization of the amounts that might have made up the award, and the taxpayer's itemization allocated $1,588,176 to future medical expenses. The Commissioner contended that the taxpayer could not claim a medical expense deduction for medical expenses incurred after the award was made until the aggregate of such expenses exceeded $1,588,176 (the amount of the award that the taxpayer allocated to future medical expenses in defending the size of the award). The Ninth Circuit held that no allocation is to be made where the award is a lump sum, and therefore the taxpayer's expenses are deductible. The court reasoned that the taxpayer's itemization was not evidence of what the jury intended to allocate for the taxpayer's future medical expenses and thus any allocation would be too speculative. Note that this decision is contrary to the Commissioner's holding in Rev. Rul. 79–427. In that ruling the Commissioner stated that it was proper to allocate some portion of the award to future medical expenses and that medical expenses may be deducted under IRC § 213 only to the extent they exceed the allocated amount. See also Rev. Rul. 75–230, holding that a portion of a lump sum settlement of a negligence suit was attributable to medical expenses that the taxpayer had previously deducted and so was included in taxpayer's income. See § **2.1334.** Also, note Rev. Rul. 75–232, denying a deduction for medical expenses to the extent that a prior settlement of a personal injury suit specifically allocated a portion of the amount paid to future medical expenses.

In cases where a taxpayer has multiple claims, the damages for some of which would be excluded from gross income and for some of which would be included in gross income, a determination must be made as to the source of the damages collected by the taxpayer. If the award of damages was made by a third party (e.g., a judge or a jury in a state court case), the Service is not obliged to accept that allocation but usually will do so unless the taxpayer essentially dictated the allocations with no input from an adverse party. See *Robinson v. Commissioner*, 70 F.3d 34 (5th Cir. 1995). If the allocation was dictated by the taxpayer because the other party had no interest in the manner in which a sum was allocated and the state court simply accepted the uncontested allocation, the Service and the courts will make their own determination of the proper allocation. *Ibid.*

§ 2.1337. Liquidated Damages. Some statutes provide for liquidated damages in cases involving a violation of certain rights or requirements. The legislative purpose for allowing liquidated damages sometimes is to provide compensation for injuries that are difficult to measure or to prove and sometimes is to punish the wrongdoer and to deter violations. In some cases, both purposes may exist. If a liquidated damage provision is compensatory for a personal physical injury, then the receipt of such damage should be excluded from income under IRC § 104(a)(2). If, instead, the purpose of a liquidated damage provision is punitive, it will be included in gross income. The determination of whether the function of a liquidated damage provision is compensatory or punitive can be difficult to make. The problem becomes even more difficult when (as is often the case) a liquidated damage provision serves both a compensatory and a punitive function. In that circumstance, should an allocation be made or should the liquidated damage be classified according to the principal purpose that it serves?

In several pre–1996 cases involving nonphysical injuries, the Tax Court held that the liquidated damages provided by the Age Discrimination in Employment Act (ADEA) when the violation of the Act is willful was not punitive, *Downey v. Commissioner (Downey I)*, 97 T.C. 150 (1991) (reviewed by the court); and *Downey v. Commissioner (Downey II)*, 100 T.C. 634 (1993) (reviewed by the court). The Supreme Court held in an unrelated case that the liquidated damages in that Act are punitive. *Commissioner v. Schleier*, 515 U.S. 323 (1995). Since discrimination damages were made taxable by the 1996 amendment, it no longer matters that ADEA liquidated damages are punitive.

In the authors' view, if a liquidated damage is provided only when the tortfeasor's wrongful action was willful or egregious, it should be characterized as a punitive provision for tax purposes and dealt with accordingly. Unlike the case of the tort of malicious prosecution where malice is an element of *liability*, in the case of liquidated damages, the extent of the tortfeasor's bad behavior serves as the standard for the *amount* of damages to be awarded. In any event, the condition of willfulness or egregious behavior would seem to prevent the damage provision from being received "on account of" a personal injury as required by IRC § 104(a)(2). Moreover, in the post–1996 era, the issue is not likely to arise since liquidated damages will not often occur when there is a physical injury.

§ 2.1340. Rationale for Exclusion. There is no definitive statement as to the reason for excluding physical personal injury damages from income. Before Congress enacted the exclusion, there were administrative and judicial determinations excluding the receipt of certain damages from income, and Congress codified that treatment when it adopted the antecedent to § 104(a)(2) in 1919. Neither Congress nor the courts have provided an explanation of the justification for the exclusion.

There have been suggestions from time to time as to the purpose of the exclusion. One suggestion is that the exclusion was adopted in order to reduce the size of damage awards. If damages were taxed to a plaintiff, a jury might increase the size of the award in order to increase the plaintiff's after-tax receipt to an amount that satisfies the jury's notion of fair compensation. However, it is highly unlikely that that consideration played a significant part in formulating the exclusion. If a damage award is properly classified as income, there is little reason to exclude it from income in order to reduce the burden on a tortfeasor. If the focus of Congress were on the size of damage awards, a more likely concern would be the tax consequence to a victim for recognizing a large amount of income in one taxable year due to the progressive rate structure of the income tax. A bunching of income could occur in such cases if the damages are paid in one lump sum. The cure for bunching is to provide income averaging for the receipt of such sums so that the victim can utilize lower tax rates for a larger portion of the damage award. An exemption of the entire amount of the award for such a purpose would be overkill and is not likely to have been the justification for the adoption of the rule. The rationale for the rule is likely to lie elsewhere.

The damages received by a victim because of a personal injury constitute an involuntary conversion of part of the victim's person. For example, if a victim recovers compensatory damages for the loss of an arm in an automobile accident, the measure of the amount of damages is a rough valuation of the personal and financial benefits that the victim could have enjoyed if he had retained the arm. In addition, the damages may compensate for pain and suffering and for out of pocket expenses incurred as a consequence of the injury. While an individual may use his arm to earn income, the arm is part of the individual's person as contrasted to items that the individual owns as property. So, the peculiar aspects of a damage award for a physical personal injury are the involuntariness of the conversion to cash and the personal, noncommercial nature of the item that was damaged. The taxation of an award for such a loss may conform to economic tax theory, but it would be harsh and grossly insensitive to the plight of a victim.

If a person's property is involuntarily converted, the victim usually can prevent the recognition of any gain realized on the conversion by reinvesting the proceeds in property that is similar or related in service or use to the converted property. IRC § 1033. There is no truly comparable means of reinvesting the proceeds received because of a personal injury. Since there is no effective device for deferring the income realized upon the receipt of damages for a personal injury, and since there are humanitarian reasons to feel concern for the plight of the victim, some form of tax relief is desirable. There is still a question whether the exclusion from income of the entire amount of such damages is too generous, but, to date, there has been no movement to substitute a different and less magnanimous provision.

§ 2.1341.   Rationale for the Exclusion of Back Pay. As previously noted, the amount of damages for a physical injury that represent compensation for back pay is excluded from the recipient's gross income. Since that amount represents an income item that would have been taxed to the recipient when received, why should the damage payment received in lieu thereof escape taxation?

Frequently, the damages received for a personal injury, whether received pursuant to a settlement or to a jury's award, are obtained as an undifferentiated lump sum. The portion that represents back pay and the portion that represents the estimated loss of future income are not separately identified. If those amounts were to be treated differently for tax purposes than are damages for nonpecuniary losses, it would be necessary to determine how much of the award was attributable to lost income. Such treatment would impose a significant administrative burden on the taxpayer and on the Service. While it would not be an insurmountable burden, it would be substantial. Perhaps, the wish to avoid having to make that determination is a factor in the decision to exclude such items from income.

In some cases, however, the amount of damages received for lost income (past and future) is separately identified. Why should those amounts not be taxed? If those amounts were taxed when separately identified but not when the damage is paid as an undifferentiated lump sum, the recipients of personal injury damages would be taxed differently depending upon the happenstance of whether the lost income item is separately identified. The extension of the exclusion to such cases may stem from an unwillingness to tax differently two sets of victims who received the same amount of damages but with different labels.

It is noteworthy that when Congress amended IRC § 104(a) in 1996 to restrict the exclusion to damages for physical injuries, the House Report stated as one of its reasons for the amendment that the damages in nonphysical cases are generally for lost profits or wages that would have been taxed. H. Rept. 104–586, p. 143 (104th Cong. 2d Sess. 1996). Why is it different when there is a physical injury? One difference is that the loss of wages or profits can be seen as merely a convenient indicator of the personal loss that the victim suffered. In other words, the victim receives compensation for the physical personal loss, and the income reduction is just one means of attaching a monetary figure to a loss that cannot be valued as a commodity can.

§ 2.1350. Sale of Parts of Taxpayer's Body. The exclusion from income provided by IRC § 104(a)(2) applies only to *damages* received on account of a personal physical injury or illness. It has no application to payments received by a taxpayer for the voluntary sale of a part of the taxpayer's body, and such payments will be included in the gross income of the taxpayer. (Note that a provision of the National Organ Transplant Act [42 U.S.C. § 274e] prohibits the sale of human organs for use in human transplantation, but the statute does not prohibit the sale of a person's blood).

When a taxpayer voluntarily sells a body part, he has chosen to dispose of that part in a commercial transaction. One difference between a sale and a receipt of damages is that in the latter case the taxpayer never even had an opportunity to decide whether to commercialize the body part.

In *Garber* [cited below], the taxpayer had a rare type of blood that she was able to sell on a regular basis for a substantial profit of thousands of dollars per year. The taxpayer failed to report to the Service her profit from the sale of her blood, and she was convicted by a jury verdict of the crime of having willfully attempted to evade and defeat the income tax. Holding that IRC § 104(a)(2) does not apply to the payment that the taxpayer received for her blood, a divided panel of the Fifth Circuit affirmed her conviction [*United States v. Garber*, 589 F.2d 843 (5th Cir. 1979)], but on a rehearing en banc, the Fifth Circuit reversed the conviction and remanded the case to the district court for further proceedings to determine whether the taxpayer acted willfully. *United States v. Garber*, 607 F.2d 92 (5th Cir. 1979). The majority of the Fifth Circuit determined that since the question of the taxability of the sale of blood is a novel issue and since a defendant in a criminal case should be given great latitude in presenting her case, the district court erred in rejecting the taxpayer's attempt to have a "tax expert" testify that the payments to the taxpayer for her blood are excluded from gross income (the "expert" did not rely on IRC § 104 for his conclusion). The majority also held that the district court erred in its instructions to the jury by indicating that the payments clearly were income to the taxpayer who simply refused to pay the tax thereon. The majority did not resolve the question of whether the payments to the taxpayer were gross income to her; they dealt instead with the question of whether there was sufficient doubt about the taxability to preclude a criminal prosecution for a willful act. The majority did suggest as a possible ground for excluding such payments that since the taxpayer could not prove that she had any basis in her blood, perhaps it should be assumed that her basis equalled the amount paid to her: but, the majority expressly refrained from resolving that question. The suggestion appears frivolous; there is authority for assuming that the properties exchanged in an arms-length exchange are of equal *value*, but there is no justification in reason or in precedent for assuming that the *basis* of property transferred is equal to the value of property received in exchange. In his concurring opinion in *Garber*, Judge Hill stated that the payments received by the taxpayer were gross income to her; and the four dissenting judges in *Garber* reached the same conclusion.

In *Green v. Commissioner*, 74 T.C. 1229 (1980), the Tax Court held that payment received from the sale of blood is included in gross income. The taxpayer in *Green* did not dispute the taxability of such payments; the issue she raised concerned the deductibility of certain expenses related to the sale of her blood. Nevertheless, the Tax Court passed on the issue of taxability [74 T.C. at p. 1233]. In *Lary v. United States*, 787 F.2d 1538 (11th Cir. 1986), the court denied a charitable deduction for a contribution of blood on the ground that the taxpayer's sale of his blood at fair market value would have caused the taxpayer to recognize ordinary income equal to the amount he would receive from such a sale. See § **9.5100.**

§ **2.1360. Installment Payments of Damages.** When IRC § 104(a)(2) applies to damages, it applies to periodic payments as well as to a lump sum payment. If a damage award is payable over a period of years, a portion of each installment payment represents interest to the recipient for the delay in receiving the money. In most installment sales, for example, when the installment payments do not provide for an adequate rate of interest, a portion of the installment payments is recharacterized as interest to reflect the unstated interest on the deferred payments. IRC § 483. The installment payments of damages are exempted from any recharacterization, and the entire amount of the installment payments is excluded from gross income.

It is difficult to discern a reasonable policy justification for the exclusion of the interest element in periodic payments of damages. The administrative difficulty of setting an interest rate has not proved to be much of an obstacle in the other areas in which interest is imputed when the stated interest on deferred payments is inadequate. See e.g., § **2.1540** et seq. Perhaps, this is an excessive response to the concern for the plight of a victim of physical injury.

§ **2.1400. Alimony, Separate Maintenance, and Child Support.** The terms "alimony and separate maintenance" have a special meaning for tax purposes. An item that constitutes "alimony" for state law purposes will not necessarily constitute "alimony" for federal tax purposes, and vice versa. E.g., *Human v. Commissioner*, 75 T.C.M. 1990 (1998). As used herein, any reference to "alimony" will refer to alimony and separate maintenance as defined for federal income tax purposes. If a payment from a payor spouse to a spouse or former spouse qualifies as alimony for tax purposes, the payment will constitute ordinary income to the recipient and will be deductible by the payor. IRC §§ 71(a), 215. The deduction allowable for such payments is taken from the payor's gross income in determining his adjusted gross income—that is, it is a nonitemized deduction [see § 3.2000]. IRC § 62(a)(10). For convenience, we sometimes refer herein to the wife (W) as the recipient of such payments and to the husband (H) as the payor, but the same rules apply when the roles are reversed. The Tax Reform Act of 1984 made extensive changes in the treatment of alimony through the amendment of IRC § 71. For example, the requirements that previously existed that alimony payments be "periodic" and be made in discharge of a legal obligation arising out of a marital or family obligation were eliminated. The Tax Reform Act of 1986 (the 1986 TRA) made additional changes to IRC § 71. The following discussion outlines the requirements under the current version of IRC § 71. You should note that all the regulations to IRC § 71 (including the temporary regulation), were promulgated prior to the adoption of the 1986 TRA, and so do not reflect the changes made by that Act.

§ 2.1410. Alimony or Separate Maintenance Payment. The general rule under IRC § 71(b)(1) is that payments are "alimony or separate maintenance payments" if they are *in cash* and received by or on behalf of a spouse under a "divorce or separation instrument" which does not designate the payments as not includable under IRC § 71 and nondeductible under IRC § 215. IRC § 71(b)(1)(A), (B). Thus, if the parties do not wish cash payments to be treated as alimony, they can elect "non-alimony" treatment by stating in the divorce or separation instrument that IRC §§ 71 and 215 (the alimony provisions) do not apply. The term "divorce or separation instrument" is defined at § 2.1417. If H and W are legally separated under a decree of divorce or of separate maintenance, with one exception, they must not share the same household at the time the payments are made if the payments are to qualify as alimony. See § 2.1414. A payment will not qualify as alimony if the payor is obligated to make any such payment after the death of the payee spouse or to provide a substitute for such payments after the death of the payee spouse. § 2.1415. Note that IRC §§ 71 and 215 do not apply to payments made between married taxpayers in a taxable year in which they elect to file a joint return. IRC § 71(e).

§ 2.1411. Payments of Property in Kind. If H makes payments to W by giving her property in kind (i.e., property other than cash), such a payment will not qualify as alimony. Temp. Reg. § 1.71–1T(b), A–5.

§ 2.1412. Cash Paid to a Third Party Pursuant to a Divorce or Separation Instrument. If the divorce or separation instrument provides for *H* to make a payment of cash to a third party which payment will inure to the benefit of *W*, that payment can qualify as alimony. However, any payments made to maintain property that is owned by *H* and used by *W* are not payments on behalf of *W* even if made pursuant to the terms of the divorce or separation instrument, and so such payments are not income to *W* under IRC § 71. Premiums paid by *H* pursuant to the terms of the divorce or separation agreement for term or whole life insurance on *H*'s life will qualify as payments on behalf of *W* only if *W* is the owner of the policy. Temp. Reg. § 1.71–1T(b), A–6.

§ 2.1413. Cash Paid to a Third Party at *W*'s Request or Ratification. Cash payments made by *H* to a third party, even though not made pursuant to a divorce or separation instrument, can qualify as alimony if *W* makes a timely written request, consent, or ratification which expressly states that IRC § 71 is to apply to that payment so that *W* will be taxed thereon. Temp. Reg. § 1.71–1T(b), A–7. To be effective, *W*'s request, consent or ratification must be received by the payor spouse prior to the date of filing the payor spouse's first tax return for the taxable year in which the payment was made. *Ibid.* The regulation does not state that such a payment must be one that is made in substitution for an obligation to make a payment of a like amount that is required to be made to *W* pursuant to a divorce or separation instrument. Perhaps the regulation will be construed as requiring that condition, but there is no explicit authority for imposing it.

§ 2.1414. Not Members of the Same Household. Generally, if spouses are legally separated under a decree of divorce or of separate maintenance and payment is made at a time when *H* and *W* are members of the same household, the payment cannot qualify as alimony. IRC § 71(b)(1)(C). If, however, one spouse is preparing to leave the household when the payment is made and does in fact leave within one month after the date of payment, the spouses will not be treated as members of the same household. Temp. Reg. § 1.71–1T(b), A–9. Note that if the spouses are not separated under a decree of divorce or separate maintenance, a payment made pursuant to a written separation agreement or decree ordering support or maintenance for *W during* a divorce or separation proceeding can qualify as alimony even though the spouses are members of the same household. *Ibid.*; *Venham v. Commissioner*, RIA TC Memo ¶ 2000–165.

§ 2.1415. No Liability to Make Payments After Death of Payee Spouse.

H's liability to make payments to *W* must terminate upon *W*'s death. IRC § 71(b)(1)(D). The termination of *H*'s obligation at *W*'s death may be a consequence either of a provision in the "divorce or separation instrument" or of the operation of local law. Prior to the 1986 amendment, there had to be a provision in the divorce or separation instrument terminating *H*'s liability on *W*'s death, but the 1986 TRA amendments changed that requirement so that it is sufficient if the liability is terminated either by local law or by the express terms of the divorce or separation instrument.

If the payor spouse's liability to make a payment will terminate if the payee spouse dies before it becomes payable, that will comply with the termination at death requirement. If the payor spouse fails to make a timely payment on the date that his liability becomes payable (i.e., all events have occurred to make the liability currently payable), the fact that the defaulted liability will not be terminated by the subsequent death of the payee spouse before actual payment is made does not violate the termination at death requirement. See § 2.1415–3. An obligation to make a payment, subject to termination on certain conditions such as death, can arise before the date on which the payment is to be made. In the view of the authors, the critical date for the termination at death requirement is the date on which the obligation first becomes *payable*; the death of the donee spouse before that date must terminate the obligation.

§ 2.1415–1. Lump Sum Payment Required by Divorce or Separation Instrument.

Since the 1984 Act eliminated the requirement that a payment be "periodic" to qualify as alimony, there is nothing to prevent a lump sum payment required by a divorce or separation agreement from qualifying as alimony if the terms of IRC § 71 are satisfied. However, the requirement (noted above) that the payor spouse's liability to make the payment must terminate on the payee spouse's death can be an obstacle. If neither local law nor the divorce or separation instrument provide that the liability to make the payment terminates if the payee spouse dies before the donor spouse is required to make the payment, the donor spouse's payment will not qualify as alimony because it will not comply with IRC § 71(b)(1)(D). It does not matter whether the payee spouse actually does die before the liability was payable; the crucial factor is whether the death of the payee spouse before that date would have terminated the liability if it had occurred.

The decision of the Tax Court in *Webb v. Commissioner*, 60 TCM 1024 (1990) is worthy of note. In that case, *H* agreed in a written separation agreement with *W* to pay *W* a lump sum of $200,000, to be paid on the execution of the agreement. The parties executed the agreement, and *H* paid the $200,000 to *W* at the time that the agreement was executed. The agreement created an obligation for *H* to pay *W* $200,000, and there was no provision in the agreement terminating that liability if *W* should die before payment was made. Consequently, if *W* had died after execution of the agreement but before the payment was made, her estate could have enforced the liability and required *H* to make the payment. The Tax Court held in *Webb* that the payment of the $200,000 did not qualify as alimony for tax purposes. It did not matter that payment was made simultaneous with the execution of the written separation agreement or that *W* actually was alive when the payment was made. The court deemed it determinative that the liability would be enforceable if payment had not been made before *W*'s death, regardless of when the payment was actually made.

In the authors' view, the Tax Court's decision in *Webb* is incorrect. The terms of the agreement made the liability payable on the execution of the agreement, and *W* had to be alive at that time or she could not have executed the agreement. The fact that the liability would be enforceable after *W*'s death if the payment were not timely made and if *W* died before the tardy payment took place appears to be irrelevant. The correct issue is whether *H*'s liability could be terminated by *W*'s death before it became payable, and it could not because the liability arose when *W* executed the agreement, and she had to be alive to do that. It should not matter that if H defaulted by failing to pay the sum at the time of execution when it was due, the defaulted liability could be enforced by W's estate if she died before payment was made. However, *Webb* was cited with approval by the Service in a 1995 Technical Advice Memorandum (TAM 9542001). As discussed in § **2.1415–3**, however, the conclusions expressed in the 1995 Technical Advice Memorandum cannot be reconciled with the result in *Webb*.

§ **2.1415–2. Payment of Spouse's Legal Fees Pursuant to Divorce or Separation Instrument.** If a divorce or separation instrument requires H to pay the attorney fees that W incurred in the divorce or separation, can H's payment of those fees qualify as alimony? Unless the divorce or separation instrument, or local law, provides that H's obligation to make that payment terminates on W's death, the Service concluded that the payments do not qualify as alimony because of the failure to comply with IRC § 71(b)(1)(D). TAM 9542001. The Service's view has been upheld in court. See *Berry v. Commissioner*, RIA T.C. Memo ¶ 2000–373; *Tobkin v. Commissioner*, T.C. Summ. 2004–42. If the parties wish to have the payments qualify as alimony, they could include a provision in the instrument that, after W's death, H has no obligation to make any payments to W or to her attorney; and, even then, if W does not die, the payments would be subject to the front-loading recapture rules of § 71(f). Note that H's liability to pay attorney fees would not become payable before W's attorneys submitted their bill, and W's death before the bill was submitted would not terminate H's obligation.

§ **2.1415–3. Late Payment of Defaulted Alimony.** Consider the following illustration. H is required by a divorce decree to pay W $10,000 a month for so long as W lives. After paying on time for a year, H fails to make the required payments for three consecutive months and thus falls into arrears. W dies, and her estate demands that H pay the sum due for the three months in which he is in arrears. A court enforces that demand, and H makes the payments to W's estate. This raises two questions. First, do the late payments themselves qualify as alimony? Second, while H's liability to make payments for subsequent months ceases on *W*'s death, his obligation to make any payments that previously became due does not terminate on *W*'s death, and the question arises as to whether that fact disqualifies all of the payments that *H* made (including those paid during *W*'s life) from being treated as alimony. The answer is that the payments, including the late payments of the defaulted amount, can qualify as alimony for federal income tax purposes.

As noted in § **2.1415–1**, the Tax Court held in *Webb* that even though a payor spouse's liability to make a lump sum payment became due at the time of the execution of the relevant instrument, the fact that payment could be enforced after the payee spouse's death prevented the lump sum payment from being alimony. If the same approach were applied to the monthly payments described in the paragraph above, it would render IRC § 71 meaningless since virtually no obligation would qualify as alimony. Obviously, that cannot be. Accordingly, in TAM 9542001, the Service purported to distinguish the circumstance of the late payment of a defaulted item from that of the obligation to pay a lump sum or attorney fees. As to the situation presented in *Webb* (i.e., a lump sum payment was required to be made at the time of execution of the agreement), the Service's purported distinction is elusive at best; but the Service surely is correct that the right of a payee spouse's estate to enforce the payment of defaulted "alimony" does not prevent either prior "alimony" payments or the late payments themselves from qualifying as alimony for tax purposes.

In the authors' view, the Service's conclusion that the enforceability of defaulted alimony payments does not violate the termination at death requirement is correct. However, the Service failed in its effort to disassociate that conclusion from the result reached by the Tax Court in *Webb*. The Service should repudiate the *Webb* decision and acknowledge that it is incorrect. Until it does so, a question can remain as to whether the crucial date for the wife's death to terminate a liability is the date (as the authors maintain is correct) on which the liability becomes *payable* rather than the date on which payment is actually made. It is inconceivable that the Service would retract its conclusion that the failure of a governing instrument or local law to terminate a defaulted liability if the payee spouse dies before payment is made does not violate the termination at death requirement of IRC § 71(b)(1)(D).

§ 2.1416. No Substitute Payments. *H* must not be required to make any payment (in cash or property) after *W*'s death that constitutes a substitute for payments that *H* was required to make during *W*'s life. IRC § 71(b)(1)(D). Whether or not a payment made after *W*'s death constitutes a substitution for payments which terminate on *W*'s death depends upon all the facts and circumstances in the case, but provisions requiring initiation, increase, or acceleration of payments upon *W*'s death will indicate the use of substitute payments. Temp. Reg. § 1.71–1T(b), A–14. If *H* is obligated to make a substitute payment, then the payments for which the substitute is provided will not qualify as alimony, and, of course, any such substitute payment also will not qualify. Temp. Reg. § 1.71–1T(b), A–13.

> **§ 2.1416–1. Illustration.** Under the terms of a divorce decree, *H* is obligated to make an annual cash payment to *W* of $40,000 terminating on the earlier of the expiration of ten years or *W*'s death. The decree also provides that at *W*'s death, if there are any living minor children of *H* and *W*, *H* will be obligated to make annual payments of $15,000 to a trust for the benefit of the children until the youngest child reaches the age of majority. According to Treasury's regulations, these facts indicate that the $15,000 payments to be made to the trust after *W*'s death are a substitute for $15,000 of the $40,000 annual payment to be made to *W*. Thus, $15,000 of the $40,000 annual payments that are made to *W* will not qualify as alimony or separate maintenance payments. The remaining $25,000 of the $40,000 annual payments can qualify as alimony. Of course, the payments to the trust after *W*'s death will not qualify as alimony. Temp. Reg. § 1.71–1T(b), A–14, Ex. (1).

§ 2.1417. Divorce or Separation Instrument. The term "divorce or separation instrument" refers to divorce decrees, written separation agreements, and decrees for support. IRC § 71(b)(2).

§ 2.1420. Front–Loading of Payments—Definitions of 1st, 2nd and 3rd, "Post–Separation Years." You will recall that the payor spouse is given a nonitemized deduction for alimony payments under IRC §§ 215 and 62(a)(10). In the 1984 TRA, Congress restricted the extent to which alimony deductions could be concentrated in the early years of payment. Those restraints on the "front-loading" of alimony payments were substantially liberalized by amendments adopted as part of the 1986 TRA. Note that the changes made by the 1986 TRA are not reflected in the current regulations and temporary regulation. As amended, the sole restriction on such payments is a provision for recapturing certain alimony deductions granted to H for payments made in the first two years in which alimony is paid. Before considering that restriction, it is useful to define several terms that are employed in that provision. The term "1st post-separation year" refers to the first *calendar* year in which H makes a payment to W that qualifies as alimony under IRC § 71. IRC § 71(f)(6). The "2nd post-separation year" is the first calendar year following the 1st post-separation year; the "3rd post-separation year" is the first calendar year following the 2nd post-separation year. IRC § 71(f)(6).

§ 2.1430. Recapture Rules. If the amount of alimony paid to W in the 2nd post-separation year is more than $15,000 greater than the amount of alimony paid to W in the 3rd post-separation year, a certain amount of the deduction granted to H for such payments in the 2nd post-separation year will be "recaptured" by requiring H to include that amount in his gross income for his taxable year that begins in the 3rd post-separation year. IRC § 71(f)(1)(A). The amount so included in H's gross income is called an "excess payment," which term is defined in §§ **2.1433–2.1433–2.** If the amount of alimony paid to W in the 1st post-separation year is more than $15,000 greater than the *average* of the amount of alimony paid to W in the 2nd and 3rd post-separation years (after taking into account the excess alimony payment of the 2nd post-separation year that is recaptured), the "excess payment" for the 1st post-separation year also is recaptured in the taxable year of H that begins in the 3rd post-separation year. IRC § 71(f)(3). The sum of the excess payments for the 1st post-separation year and the 2nd post-separation year is referred to as the "excess alimony payments." IRC § 71(f)(2). The "excess alimony payments" (i.e., the sum of the excess payment for the 1st and 2nd post-separation years) is included in H's gross income in his taxable year that begins in the 3rd post-separation year.

The manner in which the "excess payment" for a post-separation year is determined is described at §§ **2.1433–2.1433–2.** Note that the amount of alimony payments made in years subsequent to the 3rd post-separation year, or indeed whether any alimony payments are made after the 3rd year, has no effect on the recapture rules. The recapture rules relate only to the first three post-separation years.

§ **2.1431.   Payee's Deduction of Recaptured Amount.** As stated in § **2.1430**, the sum of the "excess payments" for the 1st and 2nd post-separation years are included in H's gross income for his taxable year that begins in the 3rd post-separation year. The inclusion of that amount in H's gross income essentially negates that amount of the deduction that H was allowed in the first two post-separation years. Since H is effectively denied a deduction for that amount, there is no reason for that amount to be treated as gross income to W. Yet, since the deductions that are recaptured by H represent alimony payments that previously were made to W, those payments were included in W's gross income in the first two post-separation years. In order to wash-out that amount of gross income from W's tax position, W is granted a deduction equal to the amount that H recaptured by including it in his gross income. IRC § 71(f)(1)(B). This deduction is allowable to W in her taxable year that begins in the 3rd post-separation year. This deduction is taken from gross income in determining W's adjusted gross income—i.e., it is a nonitemized deduction. IRC § 71(f)(1)(B).

§ **2.1432.   Taxable Year of Payor and Payee.** The taxable year of an individual typically is a calendar year. So, an individual's taxable year in which excess payments of the first two post-separation years are either to be included or deducted from gross income typically will be the 3rd post-separation year itself.

§ **2.1433.   "Excess Alimony Payments."** The term "excess alimony payments" refers to the sum of a payor's excess payments for the 1st and 2nd post-separation years. IRC § 71(f)(2). To determine that amount, it is necessary first to determine the "excess payments for the 2nd post-separation year," and then to determine the "excess payments for the 1st post-separation year."

§ 2.1433–1. Excess Payments for the Second Post–Separation Year.

Because of the manner in which the statutory formula operates, it is necessary to determine the excess payments for the second post-separation year before computing the excess payments for the first year. The "excess payment for the second post-separation year" is the excess of the amount of alimony *paid* by H in the second post-separation year over the sum of $15,000 and the amount of alimony paid by H in the third post-separation year. IRC § 71(f)(4).

§ 2.1433–2. Excess Payments for the First Post–Separation Year.

The excess payments for the first post-separation year is the excess of the amount of alimony paid by H in the first post-separation year over the sum of $15,000 and the average amount of alimony paid by H in the second and third post-separation years. In determining the average amount of alimony paid in the second and third post-separation years, the amount of alimony paid in the second post-separation year is reduced by an amount equal to the excess payments for the second post-separation year as determined in the manner described in § 2.1433–1. IRC § 71(f)(3).

§ 2.1434. Illustration 1.

H and W, who report their income on a calendar year basis, were divorced in Year One. The divorce decree requires H to make the following cash payments to W, all of which were made in a timely fashion: Year One, $50,500; Year Two, $42,000; Year Three, $10,000. Apart from the recapture rules, all of the requirements of IRC § 71 are satisfied. Under IRC § 215, in years One, Two and Three, H will deduct $50,500, $42,000, and $10,000 respectively. In each of those same years, W will include a like amount in her gross income. Since the first alimony payment was made in Year One, that year is the 1st post-separation year, and Years Two and Three are the 2nd and 3rd post-separation years respectively. In addition to the amounts of income and deductions described above, in Year Three H will be required to include $35,000 in his gross income, and W will be allowed to deduct $35,000, computed as follows:

Excess Payments in Second Post–Separation Year

Payment in Year 2 $42,000

Minus payment in Year 3 plus $15,000	(25,000)
Amount recaptured in Year 3 from Year 2 payment	$17,000

Average Unrecaptured Payments Made in Years Two and Three

Payment in Year 3	$10,000
Payment in Year 2 ($42,000) minus amount of Year 2 payment recaptured in Year 3 ($17,000)	25,000
Total for Years 2 and 3	$35,000
Average unrecaptured amount paid in Years 2 and 3 (1/2 × $35,000)	$17,500

Excess Payments in First Post–Separation Year

Payment in Year 1	$50,500
Minus the sum of $15,000 and the average unrecaptured payments made in Years 2 and 3 ($17,500)	(32,500)
Amount recaptured in Year 3 from Year 1 payment	$18,000
Excess alimony payments for Years 1 and 2 ($18,000 + $17,000)	$35,000

In summary, in Year Three, *H* will deduct the $10,000 alimony payment that he made to *W* in that year, and *W* will include $10,000 in her gross income. In addition, in that same year, *H* will include $35,000 in his gross income as the recapture of alimony deductions that he took in Years One and Two; and *W* will deduct $35,000 from her gross income in determining her AGI for Year Three. Note that it is irrelevant to the determination of *H*'s recapture income (and of *W*'s deduction) whether *H* made any alimony payments to *W* in years subsequent to Year Three.

§ 2.1435.   Illustration 2. The facts are the same as those set forth in **§ 2.1434** except that the amount of cash payments that *H* was required by the divorce decree to make, which payments were timely paid by *H*, were: Year One, $30,000; Year Two, $40,000; Year Three, $13,000. The amounts paid in those years will be included in *W*'s gross income and deductible by *H*. In addition, *H* will include $12,000 in his gross income for Year Three, and *W* will deduct $12,000 from her gross income for that year, computed as follows:

Excess Payments in Second Post–Separation Year

Payment in Year 2	$40,000
Minus payment in Year 3 plus $15,000	(28,000)
Amounted recaptured in Year 3 from Year 2 payment	$12,000

Average Unrecaptured Payments Made in Years Two and Three

Payment in Year 3	$13,000
Payment in Year 2 ($40,000) minus amount of Year 2 payment recaptured in Year 3 ($12,000)	28,000
Total for Years 2 and 3	$41,000
Average unrecaptured amount paid in Years 2 and 3 (1/2 × $41,000)	$20,500

Excess Payments in First Post–Separation Year

Payment in Year 1	$30,000
Minus the sum of $15,000 and the average unrecaptured payments made in Years 2 and 3 ($20,500)	(35,500)
Amount recaptured in Year 3 from Year 1 payment	$0
Excess alimony payments for Years 1 and 2 ($0 + $12,000)	$12,000

§ 2.1436. Illustration 3. The facts are the same as those stated in **§ 2.1434** except that the amount of cash payments that *H* was required by the decree to make, and which were timely paid, were: Year One, $30,000; Year Two, $40,000; Year Three, $3,000. The amount of deduction recaptured in Year Three (as gross income of *H* and as a deduction for *W*) is $26,500, computed as follows:

Excess Payments in Second Post–Separation Year

Payment in Year 2	$40,000
Minus payment in Year 3 plus $15,000	(18,000)
Amount recaptured in Year 3 from Year 2 payment	$22,000

Average Unrecaptured Payments Made in Years Two and Three

Payment in Year 3	$3,000
Payment in Year 2 ($40,000) minus amount of Year 2 payment recaptured in Year 3 ($22,000)	18,000
Total for Years 2 and 3	$21,000
Average unrecaptured amount paid in Years 2 and 3 (1/2 × $21,000)	$10,500

Excess Payments in First Post–Separation Year

Payment in Year 1	$30,000
Minus the sum of $15,000 and the average unrecaptured payments made in Years 2 and 3 ($10,500)	(25,500)
Amount recaptured in Year 3 from Year 1 payment	$4,500
Excess alimony payments for Years 1 and 2 ($4,500 + $22,000)	$26,500

§ 2.1440. Exceptions to the Recapture Rules. You will recall that the recapture rules apply where the amount of alimony *paid* in either the first or second post-separation year, or both, is significantly greater than the amount *paid* in the third post-separation year. There are certain circumstances in which smaller payments in the third post-separation year will not trigger a recapture because of statutory exceptions. For example, the recapture rules do not apply where the alimony payments terminate because of the death of either spouse or because of the payee spouse's remarriage. IRC § 71(f)(5)(A). The recapture rules do not apply to payments received under a support decree. IRC § 71(f)(5)(B). Another exception applies where payments may fluctuate because of certain external events. Payments made by *H* to *W* under an obligation to pay a "fixed portion or portions of the income from a business or property or from compensation for employment or self-employment," which obligation continues for a period of three years or more, are not subject to the recapture rules. IRC § 71(f)(5)(C). Thus, a payor spouse whose payments fluctuate due to *certain* circumstances that are beyond his control will not be required to recapture income. However, the temporary regulation states that fluctuations caused by an external event that is beyond the payor's control will trigger recapture if the event is not one of those listed above. Temp. Reg. § 1.71–1T(d), A–25.

§ 2.1450. Payments Made After Remarriage. If the source of a spouse's obligation to pay alimony is a divorce decree, the local law of *some* states terminates that obligation upon the remarriage of the payee spouse. Nevertheless, a written separation agreement may require a payor spouse to continue making payments after the payee's remarriage. If the local statutes override the parties' separation agreement so that the payor has no legal obligation to make payments to the payee after the latter's remarriage, and if there is no subsequent written agreement requiring the payor to make payments [see **§ 2.1451/2**], then any such payments made after remarriage will not qualify as alimony. The tax treatment of payments that do not qualify as alimony is discussed in **§ 2.1451.** However, if the payor has a continuing legal obligation under a divorce or separation instrument to make payments to the payee after remarriage, the payments will be alimony and so will be income to the payee and deductible by the payor, assuming all the requirements of IRC § 71 have been met. See *Spector v. Commissioner*, 71 TCM 3224 (1996); *Mass v. Commissioner*, 81 T.C. 112 (1983). Thus, in *Blakey v. Commissioner*, 78 T.C. 963 (1982), the Tax Court treated payments made after *W*'s remarriage as income to her and as deductible by *H* where the payments were required by a separation agreement that continued to be viable after W's remarriage even though the agreement was approved in the parties' divorce decree. The agreement in *Blakey* was not incorporated into the divorce decree, but the Tax Court said that it would have reached the same result if the agreement had been incorporated. Under local law (Virginia) the contractual obligation to make payments to W after her remarriage was not superseded by the divorce decree and survived the termination of the Court's jurisdiction. See also TAM 8642008 providing the same treatment on similar facts, except that the settlement agreement was incorporated (but not merged), into the divorce decree. The characterization of the payments by state law does not affect the tax law's characterization; even if state law does not label the post-remarriage payments as "alimony," they will be treated as alimony for tax purposes if they are required to be made. *Spector v. Commissioner*, 71 TCM 3224 (1996); TAM 8642008.

When payments are made pursuant to a separation agreement that is incorporated and merged into a divorce decree, and when the local law provides that a decree cannot require that alimony payments continue after the payee spouse's remarriage, payments made after a marriage do not qualify as alimony. *Sherwood v. Commissioner*, 38 T.C.M. 660 (1979). In such cases, the payor would have no legal obligation to make the payments which therefore would either be made voluntarily or under a mistaken belief of liability. In *Mass v. Commissioner*, 81 T.C. 112 (1983), a separation agreement was incorporated into the divorce decree, but it was not merged into the decree under state law. Thus, H's contractual obligation to pay continued after W's remarriage. The court held that the payments were alimony and so were includable in W's gross income under IRC § 71 and deductible from H's gross income under IRC § 215. See also, TAM 8642008.

§ 2.1451. Treatment of Payments That Do Not Qualify as Alimony. In Rev. Rul. 81–8, the Commissioner determined that payments made pursuant to a divorce decree, after the remarriage of the payee spouse, cannot qualify as alimony if, under local law, there is no legal obligation to make payments after that spouse's remarriage. However, the Commissioner further determined that the payments to such a remarried spouse constitute gross income under IRC § 61, unless there is evidence that the payments are a gift (i.e., that they were made out of detached and disinterested generosity). Thus, under the Commissioner's ruling, the payor receives no deduction in such circumstances and, typically, the payee will recognize gross income. The ruling was amplified and superseded by Rev. Rul. 82–155, which treated such payments as income to *W* if paid by *H*'s mistake but not income to *W* if *H* knew that he had no obligation to make the payment and intended to make a gift thereby. When *H* makes a payment for which he knows he is not obligated, it is likely that the payment will be a gift unless there is evidence that *H* had some compensatory purpose.

Rev. Rul. 82–155 (discussed above) was promulgated at a time when payment had to be in discharge of a legal obligation arising out of a marital or family relationship to qualify as alimony. Although that requirement was eliminated by the 1984 TRA, the ruling is still valid under current law. To qualify as alimony, a payment must be received under a divorce or separation instrument (IRC § 71(b)(1)(A)); if the payor has no legal obligation to make the payment, it will not satisfy that requirement.

§ 2.1452, Modification of Agreement.

In *Hollander v. Commissioner*, 248 F.2d 523 (9th Cir. 1957), prior to their divorce, *H* and *W* executed an agreement settling their property interests and providing for annual payments to be made by *H* to *W* until *W* either died or remarried. They were divorced some three months later. Two years after the agreement had been executed, *W* informed *H* that she wished to remarry. *H* and *W* then executed an agreement which modified their first agreement by requiring *H* to make monthly payments to *W* after her remarriage. The Ninth Circuit held that the second agreement was incident to the prior divorce of *H* and *W*, and so the court held that the payments made by *H* to *W* after her remarriage constituted alimony.

If spouses who have been divorced for several years and have previously settled all legal obligations to each other voluntarily enter into a written agreement that requires *H* to make annual payments to *W*, can such payments qualify as alimony? The answer turns on whether the subsequent written agreement that *H* and *W* made several years after their divorce can qualify as a divorce or separation instrument as that term is defined in IRC § 71(b)(2). See *Hollander v. Commissioner*, *supra*; and Temp. Reg. § 1.71–1T(b), A–7, discussed at **§ 2.1413**, both of which may provide support for the construction that a subsequent written agreement can constitute a divorce and separation instrument. Also, cf., Temp. Reg. § 1.71–1T(b), A–8.

§ 2.1460.   Property Settlements. Prior to the Tax Reform Act of 1984, the distinction between alimony payments and payments relating to a property settlement had important tax consequences. Property settlement payments were not covered under IRC §§ 71 and 215. The 1984 Amendment's elimination of the requirements (previously applicable) that payments be periodic and that they be attributable to obligations arising out of the marital relationship has obviated the need to make the distinction between alimony and payments relating to a property settlement. A single cash payment to W can qualify as alimony under current law, subject to recapture rules if the payment is greater than $15,000, and subject to satisfying the termination at death requirement discussed at **§§ 2.1415** to **2.1415–3**. In general, however, Congress chose to deny alimony treatment to payments that were likely to be property settlement when it is administratively simple to identify them. To that end, some of the restrictions imposed by IRC § 71 on qualifying for alimony are intended to deny alimony treatment for payments that are likely to be made pursuant to a property settlement. For example, any transfer of property in kind is excluded from alimony treatment. The apparent purpose of disqualifying cash payments from alimony treatment when such payments are to continue after W's death or when substitute payments are to be made upon W's death is that such payments are more likely to represent property settlements than support for W.

§ 2.1461.   Transfers of Property in Kind. As noted in **§ 2.1411**, a transfer of property in kind cannot qualify as alimony. The question arises as to whether a transfer of property in kind, made in connection with a marital split-up, might be treated as a taxable sale or exchange in which the transferor received property interests for the release of marital rights. Under IRC § 1041, a transfer to a spouse (or a former spouse if the transfer is made within one year after the marriage ceases, or if the transfer is related to the cessation of the marriage) will not cause the recognition of gain or loss to either the transferor or the transferee. In such cases, the transferee's basis in the transferred property is equal to the adjusted basis that the transferor had at the time that the transfer took place. Thus, the transferee is treated in the same manner as a donee of a gift except that the transferee's basis is not limited by the fair market value of the transferred property (as could apply to a gift where basis is determined by IRC § 1015(a)). IRC §§ 1015(e), 1041(b)(2). Note that a transfer to a nonresident alien will not qualify under IRC 1041 for non-recognition of gain or loss. IRC 1041(d).

Transfers of property in trust for the benefit of a spouse (or former spouse) may also be covered by IRC § 1041. However, a transfer in trust of an installment obligation can cause the transferor to recognize income. IRC § 453B(g). Similarly, a transfer in trust can cause the transferor to recognize income if the sum of liabilities assumed or accepted by the trust exceeds the total adjusted basis of the transferred properties. IRC § 1041(e).

§ 2.1462. Related to the Cessation of Marriage. A transfer to a former spouse is related to the cessation of the marriage if it is made pursuant to a divorce or separation instrument as defined in IRC § 71(b)(2) or to an amendment or modification of such an instrument, and if the transfer occurs within six years after the end of the marriage. [Temp. Reg. § 1.1041–1T(b)].

For convenience, we will sometimes refer to the transferor spouse of property as H and to the transferee spouse (whether a spouse or former spouse) as W. A transfer by H to a third party will be treated as having been made to W if the transfer is made on behalf of W *and* if either: (1) the transfer is required by a divorce or separation instrument, (2) the transfer is pursuant to the written request of W, or (3) H receives from W a written consent or ratification of the transfer to the third party (which consent or ratification must state that the parties intend the transfer to qualify under § 1041 as a transfer to W and must be received by H prior to H's filing of the first tax return for the year in which the transfer was made). Temp. Reg. § 1.1041–1T(c).

§ 2.1462–1. Illustration 1. *W* sold to her husband, *H*, 100 shares of stock of the *X* Corporation and Blackacre (unimproved land). The fair market value of the 100 shares of *X* stock was $10,000, and *H* paid that amount to *W* in cash. *W* had a basis of $16,000 in the 100 shares of stock. Although *W* realized a loss of $6,000 on that sale, none of her loss is recognized because of IRC § 1041.

Two years later, *H* sold the 100 shares of *X* stock to *B*, an unrelated third party, for $12,000. *H* recognized a loss of $4,000 on that sale, and he is permitted to deduct that loss in determining his taxable income. *H*'s basis in the 100 shares of *X* stock was $16,000—the same basis that *W* had at the time of the sale to *H*. In determining his loss on the sale to *B*, *H*'s basis is not limited to the fair market value that the stocks had at the time that *W* transferred them to *H*. *H*'s holding period for the stock includes the time that *W* held the stock prior to selling it to *H*. IRC § 1223(2). Note that the tax consequence to *H* of the sale to *B* would not be changed if two years earlier *W* had made a gift to *H* of the 100 shares of *X* stock instead of having sold those shares to *H*. Even if *H* had acquired the stocks as a gift from *W*, IRC § 1041 will override IRC § 1015, and so *H*'s basis in the stocks for loss purposes will not be limited to the stocks' value at the time that he acquired them. IRC § 1015(e).

Consider the tax consequences on a different set of facts. The fair market value of Blackacre at the date of the sale to *H* was $30,000, and *H* paid *W* that amount in cash. *W*'s basis in Blackacre was $18,000. So, *W* realized a gain of $12,000 on the sale, but she did not recognize any gain because of IRC § 1041. *H*'s basis in Blackacre is $18,000, the same basis that *W* had therein. *H*'s holding period includes the time that *W* held Blackacre. IRC § 1223(2).

§ 2.1462–2. Illustration 2. *H* and *W* each owned 100 shares of the outstanding stock of the *Y* Corporation. *Y* had 200 shares of stock outstanding, and so *H* and *W* each owned 50% of *Y*'s stock.

H and *W* divorced. The divorce decree ordered the *Y* Corporation to redeem the 100 shares of *Y* stock that *W* held. The fair market value of those 100 shares of *Y* stock was $400,000, and *W* had a basis of $100,000 in those shares. Pursuant to the divorce decree, *Y* paid *W* $400,000 in redemption of her shares of *Y* stock. The Commissioner contended that *W* recognized a gain of $300,000 on that redemption. *W* contended that her transfer of her 100 shares of *Y* stock to *Y* was made on behalf of *H* pursuant to a divorce decree and so should be treated as a transfer to *H* himself. *W* therefore contended that the redemption of her *Y* stock was merely a circuitous sale to *H*, and so IRC § 1041 precludes her recognition of any income from that "sale." [Note, that if *W*'s analysis is correct, then the amount paid by *Y* to *W* should be treated as a constructive distribution to *H* followed by a transfer from *H* to *W*; if so, *H* would have dividend income from the constructive distribution that was made to him.] A majority of the Tax Court rejected *W*'s contention in *Blatt v. Commissioner*, 102 T.C. 77 (1994) (reviewed by the court) and held that she did recognize a gain from the redemption of her stock. The Tax Court distinguished and disapproved of a contrary decision by the Ninth Circuit in *Arnes v. United States*, 981 F.2d 456 (9th Cir. 1992).

The *Arnes* case has an interesting follow up. After the wife prevailed in the 1992 Ninth Circuit case, the Service sought to tax the husband on the basis that the corporate distribution to the wife constituted a constructive dividend to the husband. In a decision reviewed by the court, a majority of the Tax Court held that there was no constructive dividend to the husband because he did not have a primary obligation to purchase *W*'s stock. *Arnes v. Commissioner*, 102 T.C. 522 (1994). Consequently, neither Mr. nor Mrs. Arnes will recognize income from the redemption!

In an attempt to resolve the inconsistent standards used by the courts and avoid situations where the IRS was whipsawed in that it could not tax either party, Treasury finalized Treas. Reg. § 1.1041–2. The regulations follow the primary and unconditional obligation standard. If H has a primary and unconditional obligation to purchase W's stock then the transaction is treated as a constructive distribution to H followed by a 1041 exchange (thus, W would not recognize any gain on the transaction). However, if H does not have such an obligation, W would be taxed under the normal redemption rules. However, the regulations provide H and W the ability to elect either treatment as long as they both agree and the elected treatment is expressed in the appropriate agreement. Treas. Reg. § 1.1041–2(c)(1) and (2).

§ 2.1463. Divorce Trusts. Prior to the Tax Reform Act of 1984 there were two alternative statutory provisions that applied to trusts which provided support for a former spouse, IRC §§ 71 and 682. Trusts which were covered by IRC § 71 are hereinafter referred to as "alimony trusts" and the other trusts are referred to as IRC § 682 trusts. Since payments from an alimony trust met all of the requirements for alimony treatment under IRC § 71, the income from an alimony trust was excludable from the gross income of the settlor (H) and the amount distributed to W was includable in her gross income. The income from an IRC § 682 trust also is excludable from H's income but the amount distributed to W from an IRC § 682 trust will be includable in W's gross income only to the extent of the trust's income. Under the amended version of IRC § 71, Congress eliminated alimony trusts and provides that such trusts are covered exclusively by IRC § 682. Under IRC § 682, the recipient of payments made out of a divorce trust is treated as a beneficiary of that trust. IRC § 682(b). Thus, payments in excess of the trust's income will not be included in the recipient's gross income. No amount is included in the settlor's gross income. IRC § 682(a).

§ 2.1470. Child Support. Any payment fixed in a divorce or separation instrument as payable for the support of children of H (the payor) will not be included in the gross income of W or deductible by H. IRC §§ 71(c)(1), 215(b).

§ 2.1471. Contingency Relating to a Child. Payments which are to be reduced upon the happening of a specific contingency relating to a child, or at a time clearly associated with the happening of a contingency relating to a child, will be treated as payments fixed for child support to the extent of such reduction. IRC § 71(c)(2)(A), (B). Reductions which are to occur when a child reaches a certain age, marries, or graduates from high school are examples of specific contingencies relating to a child. There are only two situations in which reductions will be presumed to be clearly associated with the happening of a contingency relating to a child of H. The first is where payments are to be reduced not more than six months before or after a child of *H* is to reach the age of 18, 21, or the local age of majority. The second is where payments are to be reduced on two or more occasions which occur not more than one year before or after a different child of *H* reaches a certain age between 18 and 24, inclusive. The certain age must be the same for each child but need not be a whole number of years. The presumption can be rebutted by a showing that the time for reduction was determined independently from any contingency relating to a child. Temp. Reg. § 1.71–1T(c).

§ 2.1472. Illustration. On May 1, 1986, *H* and *W* were divorced. Their two children, *X* (born February 10, 1976) and *Y* (born April 20, 1979), were 10 and 7, respectively. The divorce decree requires *H* to pay *W* $3,000 a month until July 1, 1996, at which time payments are to be reduced to $2,000 a month. On July 1, 2001, the payments are to be further reduced to $1,000 a month. On the date of the first reduction, *X* will be 20 years 4 months and 21 days old. On the date of the second reduction, *Y* will be 22 years 2 months and 11 days old. Each reduction is to occur not more than one year before or after a different child of *H* reaches any of the ages 21 years 2 months and 11 days through 21 years 4 months and 21 days. For example, the first reduction is within one year of the time *X* will reach the age of 21 years 3 months and the second reduction is within one year of the time *Y* will reach the age of 21 years 3 months. Thus, the reductions will be presumed to be clearly associated with the happening of a contingency relating to a child. Unless the presumption is rebutted, $2,000 of the $3,000 in monthly payments will be treated as fixed for child support and so will not be deductible by *H* or includable in *W*'s gross income.

§ 2.1480. Income Splitting. *H* can claim a deduction from his gross income equal to the amount that is included in *W*'s gross income. IRC § 215. This is a nonitemized deduction which is taken from gross income in determining adjusted gross income. IRC § 62(a)(10). In effect, this permits *H* and *W* to split *H*'s income between them in a manner roughly similar to the splitting of income between spouses who file a joint return, except that *H* and *W* have more flexibility for tax planning. If only partial payment of a required amount is made and if a provision has been made for child support, the amount paid is applied first to the nondeductible support of a minor child. IRC § 71(a)(3).

§ 2.1490. Marital Status. A question may arise as to whether a man and woman who claim to have been married and later divorced will qualify as such for tax purposes. This question often turns on the validity of a divorce from a prior marriage. For example, *H* and *W–1* obtained a divorce decree in Year One; *H* married *W–2* in Year Two, and *H* and *W–2* obtained a divorce decree in Year Three pursuant to which *H* was obligated to pay *W–2* $200 a month for the rest of her life. For the $200 monthly payments to *W–2* to qualify as alimony, *W–2* must have been a lawful wife of *H* prior to their purported divorce, and *W–2* could not have been *H*'s lawful wife unless the divorce decree obtained by *W–1* was valid. The question of the validity of a prior divorce can arise in a variety of other tax contexts (e.g., the determination of whether either party to the putative divorce can file a joint return with a "second" spouse after a second marriage and whether gifts or bequests to a "second" spouse will qualify for the gift tax or estate tax marital deduction).

§ 2.1491. Rule of Validation. When spouses obtain a divorce decree, the Service will not challenge the validity of the decree so long as it has never been declared invalid by a court of competent jurisdiction; but if a state court, having jurisdiction of the parties or of the subject matter of the action, declares the prior divorce decree to be invalid, the Service generally will follow the later court decree and treat the divorce as invalid. Rev. Rul. 67–442. See also Rev. Rul. 76–255. In so ruling, the Commissioner expressly rejected two decisions of the Second Circuit: *Borax v. Commissioner*, 349 F.2d 666 (2d Cir. 1965); and *Wondsel v. Commissioner*, 350 F.2d 339 (2d Cir. 1965). In *Borax* and *Wondsel*, the Second Circuit had held that the validity of a divorce for federal tax purposes was to be determined under a "rule of validation" which treats putative divorces as valid in all but a few cases. Under the "rule of validation," a divorce will be deemed invalid if declared so by a court of the jurisdiction that granted the divorce, but a declaration of invalidity by any other court would be disregarded. The purpose of this "rule of validation" was to promote certainty and uniformity which the court deemed to be important goals of the tax system.

§ 2.1492. Status of the Rule of Validation. As noted above, the Commissioner rejected the *Borax* and *Wondsel* "rule of validation." Rev. Rul. 67–442. The rule has fared badly in litigation since the Second Circuit adopted it in 1965.

The Tax Court, the Ninth Circuit and the Seventh Circuit have rejected the rule of validation and essentially accepted the Commissioner's position. See *Lee v. Commissioner*, 64 T.C. 552 (1975), aff'd 550 F.2d 1201 (9th Cir. 1977); and *Estate of Steffke v. Commissioner*, 64 T.C. 530 (1975), aff'd 538 F.2d 730 (7th Cir. 1976). Even the Second Circuit had criticized the rule and apparently has retreated from its earlier decisions. In *Estate of Goldwater v. Commissioner*, 64 T.C. 540 (1975), the Tax Court held that a divorce which was subsequently declared invalid by a state court of the state in which the spouse in question was domiciled (but not of the jurisdiction that granted the divorce) rendered the divorce invalid for federal estate tax purposes. Because an appeal in *Goldwater* would lie in the Second Circuit, the Tax Court deemed itself obligated to apply the law of the Second Circuit under its *Golsen* rule (see *Golsen v. Commissioner*, 54 T.C. 742 (1970), aff'd 445 F.2d 985 (10th Cir. 1971)). The Tax Court suggested that the "rule of validation" of the Second Circuit might apply only to income tax issues and not to estate tax questions. In affirming the Tax Court, the Second Circuit was somewhat critical of its earlier decisions in *Borax* and *Wondsel*, and the court did not rest its affirmance exclusively on the Tax Court's ground that the rule of validation applied only for income tax purposes. *Estate of Goldwater v. Commissioner*, 539 F.2d 878 (2d Cir.), cert. denied, 429 U.S. 1023 (1976). In so doing, the Second Circuit distinguished an earlier 1976 decision of that court which appeared to have adhered to the rule of validation—i.e., *Estate of Spalding v. Commissioner*, 537 F.2d 666 (2d Cir. 1976). In *Spalding*, on a decedent's death, the issue arose as to whether she was validly married to her "husband" in light of a New York court's judgment that the decedent's husband's divorce from his first wife was invalid. The decedent lived and died a resident of California. The Tax Court held that the decedent was not validly married to her putative "husband," but the Second Circuit reversed the Tax Court. In *Goldwater*, the Second Circuit explained its reversal in *Spalding* as resting on the fact that the New York court's decree could not bind the decedent's estate since she had never been a resident of New York. Thus, while the Second Circuit has not yet adopted the Commissioner's position, there is reason to question the extent to which that court will adhere to a strict rule of validation in the future. However, in a 1987 Tax Court decision that lay within the appeal jurisdiction of the Second Circuit, the Tax

Court held that the "rule of validation" was the established rule of the Second Circuit, and the Tax Court followed that rule pursuant to its *Golsen* principle. *Estate of Felt v. Commissioner*, 54 T.C.M. 528 (1987), appeal to 2d Cir. dismissed.

§ 2.1493.   Sham Divorces. The Commissioner ruled in Rev. Rul. 76–255, that where a married couple obtained a divorce from a foreign jurisdiction, and where the motivation for obtaining the divorce was tax reduction and where the parties intended to remarry promptly and did so, the divorce will be disregarded for tax purposes even if it is a valid divorce under state law. The Fourth Circuit, in a 2–1 decision, adopted the Commissioner's view in *Boyter v. Commissioner*, 668 F.2d 1382 (4th Cir. 1981), holding that whether a divorce should be considered a sham was a factual issue to be determined by the lower court.

§ 2.1500.   Compensation for Services.

§ 2.1510.   Cash Compensation. Cash compensation for services rendered is income to the recipient. A bonus (including a holiday bonus), vacation pay, severance pay, and similar compensation payments are included in an employee's gross income. See Treas. Reg. § 1.61–2(a)(1). Compensation for services paid in some form other than cash ordinarily will be treated as income in the amount of the fair market value of the property or service received. Treas. Reg. § 1.61–2(d)(1).

§ 2.1511.   Tips. Tips and similar "gratuities" given for services are included in the recipient's gross income. Treas. Reg. § 1.61–2(a)(1). Indeed, tips are income even if the taxpayer's receipt of such additional compensation violates state law. *Killoran v. Commissioner*, 709 F.2d 31 (9th Cir. 1983). Utilizing a formula grounded on an estimated amount of sales per hour worked and an estimated ratio of tips to sales (based on a discount of the percentage of tips on charged sales), the Service may determine that a food service employee underreported tip income, and the Service may impose a negligence penalty on the employee. See *McQuatters v. Commissioner*, 32 TCM 1122 (1973). The type of formula utilized in that case has been applied in subsequent cases and is referred to as the "McQuatters Formula." For a determination of the deductibility of expenses incurred in connection with tip income and with splitting of tips, and for a rejection of the Service's attempt to impose an accuracy-related penalty, see *Brown v. Commissioner*, 72 T.C.M. 59 (1996).

To obtain greater compliance with the tax law by those receiving tips, in 1982 Congress amended IRC § 6053 to impose reporting requirements on certain employers of persons who customarily receive tips for serving food and beverages to customers. In general, the requirement applies only to employers who operate a large food and beverage establishment. See IRC § 6053(c)(4). If required to report, the employer must declare its gross receipts (including charged amounts) from the sale of food and beverage, exclusive of carry out sales and sales for which a substantial service charge is added, and it must allocate a portion of such gross receipts among the tipped employees to reflect the employer's estimate of the amount of their tips. The aggregate amount of tips so allocated among the employees must equal a specified percentage of the employer's gross receipts (as described above), usually eight percent but never less than two percent. IRC § 6053(c)(3)(A), (C). This reporting requirement was adopted by Congress in response to an estimate by the Service that only 16 percent of tips received by employees was being reported by them.

§ 2.1520. Services in Exchange for Services. Where each of two persons perform services for the other, and the performance of each person is intended as consideration for the performance of the other's service, the value of the service received is income to each recipient. Treas. Reg. § 1.61–2(d)(1). Where services are received in connection with a trade or business and the payment therefor (including the fair market value of any services performed) is greater than or equal to $600, the individual receiving such services is subject to the information reporting requirements for the payment for such services under IRC §§ 6041(a) and 6041A(a). Rev. Rul. 85–101.

§ 2.1521. Illustration. *X*, an attorney, performed legal services for *Y*, a doctor; and *Y* performed medical services for *X*. *X* and *Y* agreed not to bill each other since the value of services performed by each was about equal. *X* will realize income in an amount equal to the value of the medical services he received from *Y*; and *Y* will realize income equal to the value of the legal services he received from *X*.

§ 2.1530. Property in Kind. Where payment for services is made in property (other than cash), the fair market value of the property is included in the recipient's gross income, and the recipient's basis in the property so received is equal to its fair market value. In effect, the recipient of the property is treated as if he had received for his services an amount of cash equal to the fair market value of the property and had then purchased the property from his employer for that cash amount (for special rules concerning the furnishing of meals and lodging to an employee, see § **2.1740** et seq.).

§ **2.1531.   Illustration 1.** *X* is an employee of World Wide Widgets, Inc. World Wide gave *X* a holiday bonus of 100 shares of IBM stock having a market value of $500 per share. *X* will realize gross income of $50,000. *X*'s basis in the 100 shares will be $50,000. Note that World Wide is treated as having received payment of $50,000 for the IBM stock, and so World Wide can recognize a gain or loss on the transaction depending upon its basis in the IBM stock. In addition, World Wide may be allowed a business expense deduction of $50,000 for paying a bonus of that amount to its employee.

§ **2.1532.   Illustration 2.** In Year One, World Wide gave *X* as a bonus 100 shares of World Wide's common stock having a value of $20 per share. Prior to that year, *X* owned no stock in World Wide. *X* recognized gross income of $2,000. Attempts to avoid taxable compensation by placing restrictions or conditions on property transferred for services (especially restrictions as to transferability and conditions creating a substantial risk of forfeiture) are covered by IRC § 83.

§ **2.1540.   Interest–Free and Below Market Interest Rate Loans.** Prior to the Tax Reform Act of 1984, it was held by the Tax Court and seven Circuit Courts of Appeals that the recipient of a loan with a below-market interest rate did not receive income for the value of receiving such a loan even when there was a compensatory purpose for not requiring the borrower to pay adequate interest. The rationale for excluding the value of receiving a loan for which little or no interest was charged was that in such cases the borrower constructively received income of an amount equal to the present value of the use of the borrowed funds and constructively paid interest to the lender of a like amount. Since, prior to the adoption of IRC § 163(h) as part of the Tax Reform Act of 1986, interest payments typically were deductible under IRC § 163, the borrower's income and deduction were a wash, and the borrower had no net income from the

transaction. However, there was a timing problem which prevented that construction of the transaction from being a wash. If the
loan was for a term of years, the borrower received income in the
year that the loan was made of an amount equal to the value of
his right to use those funds for the entire term of the loan. Thus,
in the year in which the loan was made, the borrower would
recognize income of an amount equal to the entire value of the
right to use the loaned funds over the term of the loan, and would
be treated as making a payment of a like amount of interest to
the lender in the same year. But, a portion (typically a large
portion) of the constructive payment to the lender would constitute a prepayment of interest which cannot be deducted at the
time of payment. IRC § 461(g). Deductions for the prepayment of
interest typically are allowed only in the subsequent years to
which those deemed payments relate, but the borrower's income
would be reported in the year that the loan was made. Thus,
while the borrower would have an equal amount of income and
deduction, the income would be recognized immediately and the
deduction might be deferred for some years. A number of courts
felt that the borrower's income and deduction should be matched
in the same year, and they accomplished that match by excluding
from the determination of the borrower's taxable income the
borrower's constructive income and his constructive interest deduction. The following discussion indicates the reason for the
Congressional decision to change the treatment of loans bearing
below-market interest and explains the current treatment of such
loans under IRC § 7872.

§ 2.1541. **The Time Value of Money.** The value associated
with the right to receive money depends upon both the
amount of money to be paid and the time at which payment is
to be made. That is, one dollar received by X today is worth
more than one dollar to be received by X one year from now.
Just how much more a current dollar is worth than the value
of a dollar to be received one year from now depends upon
what the market requires a lender to pay for the use of a
dollar. Thus, if the current market interest rate is 10 percent
simple interest, X would need to receive $1.10 one year from
now to put her in the same position she would be in if she
were to receive the one dollar today. Similarly, an obligation to
make a payment at a future date is a lesser liability than is an
obligation to make that payment currently. If X is obligated to
pay Y $1,000 two years from today and if the obligation is a

deductible item, a grant to X of a current deduction of $1,000 would not account for the value to X of having the use of that $1,000 for two years prior to the time that payment must be made.

§ 2.1541–1. Increased Significance of Deferral. Years ago, the time value of money was of less importance than today because interest rates were relatively low (three to four percent). In the interest of simplicity, the tax law typically ignored the benefits accruing to a taxpayer because of time value. However, once market interest rates rose to double digits, the time value of money took on much greater significance and caused the Service to focus on this problem. Congress responded by enacting a number of provisions that require income reporting to reflect more accurately the economic reality of the value of the use of money. One of these provisions is IRC § 7872 which requires taxpayers to recognize the value associated with the use of money on the receipt of a loan bearing an inadequate interest rate. Another example of this concern is the treatment of original issue discount that is described at § 5.5000.

§ 2.1542. Loans to Which IRC § 7872 Applies. IRC § 7872 covers only the following types of "below-market loans": gift loans, compensation-related loans (i.e., a loan between an employer and an employee or between an independent contractor and a person for whom he provides services), corporate-shareholder loans, tax avoidance loans, loans to a qualified continuing care facility, and any other below-market loan in which the interest arrangement has a significant effect on the federal tax liability of the lender or the borrower. IRC § 7872(c). A "below-market loan" is either: a demand loan bearing interest at a rate that is less than the "applicable Federal rate," or a term loan in which the amount loaned exceeds the present value of all payments to be made under the loan. IRC § 7872(e)(1). The meaning of "present value" is explained at § 2.1545–1 to § 2.1545–1D. For purposes of IRC § 7872, the word "loan" is broadly defined. Prop. Reg. § 1.7872–2. For example, many refundable deposits are treated as loans. Prop. Reg. § 1.7872–2(b). See § 2.1110. A prepayment for services or property, an advance to an employee to defray anticipated expenses, and an advance or draw on a partner's share of partnership income may be excluded from the statutory reference to "loans." Prop. Reg. § 1.7872–2(b)(3).

§ 2.1542–1. Constructive Payment To Borrower. In general, IRC § 7872 treats the lender of a below-market loan as making a constructive payment to the borrower of an amount equal to the foregone interest (see **§ 2.1544–2**), and this constructive payment will be treated as: a gift (in the case of a gratuitous transaction), a dividend (in the case of a loan from a corporation to its shareholder), paid compensation (in the case of a loan to a person providing services), or as some other payment characterization in accordance with the substance of the transaction. The constructive payment will be included in the borrower's gross income unless it is a gift or falls within some other exclusion from income. If an actual payment of the same character would have been deductible or amortizable by the lender (e.g., a payment for services rendered in connection with the lender's business), the amount of the constructive payment similarly will be deductible or amortizable by the lender. For most tax purposes, the parties will be treated as if the constructive payment had actually been made. For example, if a constructive payment from the lender to the borrower is treated as a gift, the lender may have gift tax consequences.

§ 2.1542–2. Constructive Interest Payment to Lender. The same amount that the borrower is deemed to have received from the lender is deemed to have been repaid simultaneously by the borrower to the lender. Note that in certain circumstances concerning a gift loan between individuals, the amount of repayment to the lender may be less than the payment to the borrower. See **§ 2.1544–4**. This constructive repayment is treated as an actual payment of interest by the borrower to the lender. The constructive interest payment is included in the lender's gross income. The constructive interest payment may be deductible or amortizable by the borrower if an actual payment would qualify as an interest deduction. Note that as a consequence of amendments made by the 1986 TRA, many types of interest payments are nondeductible. See **§§ 5.1000–5.1700**. If the constructive interest payment on a term loan can be deducted, the aggregate amount of the deduction will be allocated among the years of the loan's term as if the interest were "original issue discount"—i.e., the constructive interest will be compounded rather than simple interest, and so the amount of interest allocated to each successive year of the term will be greater than the interest allocated to the prior year. See **§ 2.1545** and **§ 5.4200** for a description of the manner in which original issue discount is allocated.

§ 2.1543. Definitions. For the purposes of IRC § 7872, a "gift loan" is a loan bearing below-market interest where the foregone interest qualifies as a gift. IRC § 7872(f)(3). A "gift loan" may be either a demand loan or a term loan. A "demand loan" is a loan which is payable in full at any time on the demand of the lender. IRC § 7872(f)(5). A "term loan" is any loan which is not a demand loan. IRC § 7872(f)(6). The market interest rate is set at the "applicable Federal rate" which is described at **§ 2.1545–1D** and **§ 5.5130.** A different applicable Federal rate is used for demand loans than is used for term loans. IRC § 7872(f)(2). The Federal short-term rate is used for demand loans, and the Federal rate for term loans depends upon the length of the term of the loan.

§ 2.1544. Gift Loans and Demand Loans. If a gift or demand loan is a below-market loan, the foregone interest will be treated as having been transferred from the lender to the borrower and retransferred from the borrower to the lender as an interest payment on the last day of the calendar year to which such foregone interest is attributable. IRC § 7872(a). Note that both the transfer to the borrower and the retransfer to the lender are treated as having been made on the last day of that calendar year. IRC § 7872(a)(2). In appropriate circumstances, the recipient of a constructive transfer or retransfer will recognize income thereby and the deemed payor of a transfer or retransfer will qualify for a deduction, but there are many circumstances where a transfer or retransfer will not be deductible.

§ 2.1544–1. Below–Market Loans. In the case of a demand loan, a "below-market loan" is a loan for which the interest payable is at a rate less than the applicable Federal rate. IRC § 7872(e)(1)(A). The applicable Federal rate for demand loans is the Federal short-term rate (compounded semiannually) in effect under IRC § 1274(d) for the period for which the amount of the foregone interest is being determined. IRC § 7872(f)(2)(B). For a term loan, a "below-market loan" is one where the amount loaned is greater than the present value of all payments due under the loan. IRC § 7872(e)(1)(B). For the meaning of "present value," see §§ **2.1545–1** to **2.1545–1D.**

§ **2.1544–2. Foregone Interest.** Foregone interest is defined as the difference between the amount of interest which would be payable in a given period under the applicable Federal rate and any interest actually payable on the loan during the same period. IRC § 7872(e)(2).

§ **2.1544–3.** *De Minimis* **Exception for Gift Loans Between Individuals.** IRC § 7872 will not apply to a gift loan between two individuals on any day on which the aggregate amount of loans outstanding between the two individuals is not greater than $10,000. IRC § 7872(c)(2)(A). However, this *de minimis* exception does not apply to a loan that is made for the purpose of purchasing or carrying an income-producing asset. IRC § 7872(c)(2)(B).

§ **2.1544–4. Amount Treated as Retransferred Limited to Net Investment Income.** In the case of a gift loan between individuals, the amount treated as retransferred by the borrower to the lender for any year shall not exceed the borrower's net investment income for that year, unless one of the principal purposes for the interest arrangement is tax avoidance. IRC § 7872(d)(1)(A) and (B). Simply stated, the net investment income is the excess of investment income over investment expenses. See IRC §§ 163(d)(4) and 7872(d)(1)(E). This limitation will not apply on any day on which the aggregate amount of outstanding loans between the borrower and the lender exceeds $100,000. IRC § 7872(d)(1)(D). If the net investment income for a borrower does not exceed $1,000, the net investment income will be treated as zero for that year. IRC § 7872(d)(1)(E)(ii).

§ **2.1545.   Treatment of Term Loans That Are Not Gift Loans.** In the case of a below-market term loan that is not a gift loan, the lender will be treated as having transferred, and the borrower will be treated as having received, cash in an amount equal to the excess of the amount loaned over the present value of all payments required to be made under the terms of the loan. IRC § 7872(b)(1). This constructive cash payment from the lender to the borrower is deemed to take place on the date that the loan is made (or on a later date that IRC § 7872 first becomes applicable to the loan). IRC § 7872(b)(1). In addition to this constructive payment of such excess amount from the lender to the borrower, the excess amount also will be treated as an original issue discount (OID). This constructive OID is in addition to any other original issue discount (OID) arising under the terms of the loan. IRC § 7872(b)(2). The OID constitutes an interest payment from the borrower to the lender and so is income to the lender and, in certain (but not all) cases, may be deductible by the borrower. The manner in which the interest payments arising from OID are allocated among the years comprising the term of the loan is described at § 5.4200. In general, OID is allocated to the term of the loan as if interest accrued daily at a fixed rate compounded semiannually. Thus, the amount of interest that is allocated to the later years of the loan's term is greater than the amount allocated to the earlier years. You will recall that a term loan is a below-market loan if the amount loaned exceeds the present value of all payments due under the loan. IRC § 7872(e)(1)(B).

§ 2.1545–1. Present Value. The current value of the right to receive a dollar amount at a future date is referred to as the "present value" of that right. The present value of a right to receive a dollar in the future is the amount that when invested at a specified rate of interest would yield by the date on which the dollar payment will be received the amount of dollars to be received at that future date. For example, in § 2.1541, the authors note that if $1 is invested for one year at 10% simple interest, the investor will have $1.10 at the end of that year. So, the present value of the right to receive $1.10 at the end of one year is $1 if the interest rate is 10% simple interest.

§ 2.1545–1A. Discount Rate. A key factor in determining present value is the rate of interest that is used to arrive at the dollar figure that will produce the amount receivable at the time at which payment is due. The figure payable at the future date must be discounted to arrive at the present value of the right to receive that amount, and the discount is determined by the rate of interest that is utilized. This assumed interest rate is referred to as the "discount rate." The choice of the discount rate depends upon market conditions. The greater the risk of loss or that the lender will not collect the required payment, the higher the discount rate will be. That reflects the fact that the greater the risk to which an investor is subject, the higher will be the rate of return that the investor will demand as a condition of making that investment.

§ 2.1545–1B. Simple or Compounded Interest. In addition to choosing a specified interest rate as the discount rate, it is also necessary to agree as to whether that interest rate will be a simple rate or a compounded rate. If a compounded interest rate is adopted, the frequency of compounding must be settled—i.e., daily, monthly, semiannually, annually or some other period.

§ 2.1545–1C. Computation of Present Value. Once the discount rate is determined, the computation of present value is merely an application of mathematical principles. It is not necessary, however, to understand those principles or to be skilled in mathematics to make that computation. Numerous tables are available which make the computation easy to make in most cases. For example, the following table provides the current value of the right to receive $1 at a specified future year where the discount rate is one of a number of alternative interest rates that are compounded annually.

Year	6%	7%	8%
1	.943	.935	.926
2	.890	.873	.857
3	.840	.816	.794
4	.792	.763	.735
5	.747	.713	.681
6	.705	.666	.630

Thus, referring to the table above, the current value of the right to receive one dollar six years from today, where the discount rate is eight percent compounded annually, is 63 cents. In other words, if 63 cents were invested for six years at an interest rate of eight percent compounded annually, it would produce an aggregate interest of 37 cents which, when added to the 63 cent investment, would provide the investor with one dollar at the end of that six-year period. If the amount to be received at the end of a six year period is greater than one dollar, the present value of that right (at a discount rate of eight percent compounded annually) is the product of multiplying .63 times the amount to be received in six years. For example, the present value of the right to receive $10,000 in six years, discounted at eight percent compounded annually, is $6,300 (i.e., .63 × $10,000). Similarly, the present value of the right to receive $10,000 in six years, discounted at six percent compounded annually, is $7,050 (i.e., .705 × $10,000).

§ 2.1545–1D. Choosing the Discount Rate. The discount rate that is chosen to determine the present value of a right to payment at a future date should reflect the rate of return that the market provides for investments involving similar risks. However, for tax purposes, it would be administratively infeasible for the Service to determine the extent of risk in a taxpayer's right to a future payment and to determine the current market rate of return for investments with comparable risks. Instead of requiring ad hoc determinations, for purposes of applying IRC § 7872 to term loans, Congress pegged the discount rate to the "applicable Federal rate" compounded semiannually. IRC § 7872(f)(2)(A). The "applicable Federal rate" is the average market yield (during a one-month period) of marketable securities issued by the United States government. IRC §§ 7872(f)(2)(A), 1274(d)(1). There are separate rates for short-term, mid-term, and long-term United States securities, and the applicable rate will depend upon the length of the term of the loan—i.e., if payment is due within three years, the Federal short-term rate will be employed; if the term of the loan is greater than three years but no more than nine years, the Federal mid-term rate will be employed. IRC § 1274(d)(1). The applicable Federal rates are determined and published monthly by the Treasury Department; and so it is easy for a taxpayer to determine the discount rate that is applicable at the time that a term loan is made to which IRC § 7872 applies.

§ 2.1545–2. *De Minimis* Exception for Compensation– Related Loans and Corporation–Shareholder Loans.

IRC § 7872 will not apply to a compensation-related loan or a corporation-shareholder loan on any day on which the aggregate amount of outstanding loans between the borrower and the lender does not exceed $10,000 and the interest arrangement does not have as one of its principal purposes the avoidance of a federal tax. IRC § 7872(c)(3). However, if the loans are *term* loans, if the aggregate amount of such loans between a borrower and a lender that are outstanding exceeds $10,000 on any day, and if IRC § 7872 applied to that day, a subsequent reduction of such loans to an amount of $10,000 or less will not excuse the parties from IRC § 7872 for those subsequent days, and that provision will continue to apply to the loan. IRC § 7872(f)(10).

§ 2.1546. Exception for Certain Loans to Qualified Continuing Care Facilities. IRC § 7872 will not apply to certain below-market loans to a "qualified continuing care facility" (as defined in IRC § 7872(g)(4)) pursuant to a contract that provides life-time care for the lender or the lender's spouse and that meets the conditions described in IRC § 7872(g)(3). This exception applies to such below-market loans only to the extent that the aggregate amount of loans between the lender and the facility does not exceed $90,000. This exception applies to a calendar year only if either the lender or the lender's spouse is 65 years of age or older by the close of the year. See IRC § 7872(g).

§ 2.1547. Exclusion of Certain Loans. Temporary regulation § 1.7872–5T lists several types of loans which will not be subject to IRC § 7872—for example, loans made by a life insurance company to an insured under a loan right in the policy typically are excluded from IRC § 7872. These loans are excluded because typically they have no significant effect on the tax liability of the borrower or the lender. However, if one of the principal purposes for the transaction is the avoidance of tax, the loan will be recharacterized as a tax avoidance loan under IRC § 7872(c)(1)(D). Temp. Reg. § 1.7872–5T(a)(2).

§ 2.1550. Uncompensated Loan of Property in Kind. If an employer permits an employee to use an automobile that the employer owns for the personal use of the employee and if the employer fails to charge a fair rental for the automobile, the difference between the rental that the employee paid for the automobile (if any) and the fair rental value of the car will constitute gross income to the employee. See *Keeter v. Commissioner*, 36 T.C.M. 1018 (1977). Similarly, an employee's use of other non-cash properties of his employer without charge or for an inadequate rental will cause the employee to recognize income.

The bargain element in an employer's rental to an employee can reasonably be viewed as a constructive receipt of rent by the employer and an immediate repayment to the employee as part of the employee's wages. Since the employee uses the rented property for personal purposes, no deduction is available to the employee for the constructive rental payment. While the constructive rental payment will constitute income to the employer, the income will be washed out by the deduction allowable for the constructive repayment to the employee as part of the latter's wages.

§ 2.1560.   Bargain Purchases. If an employee (or independent contractor) purchases property from his employer (or principal) for less than the value of the property, the difference constitutes disguised compensation and is taxable. IRC § 83. But see IRC § 132(c) and §§ **2.1620–2.1628.**

> **§ 2.1561.   Illustration 1. Disguised Compensation** *X* is an employee of Win All, Inc. *X* purchases Blackacre from Win All for $20,000, when the value of Blackacre is $35,000. The $15,000 "bargain" in *X*'s purchase is disguised compensation and is included in *X*'s gross income. *X*'s basis in Blackacre is $35,000. Win All is treated as having received $35,000 for Blackacre and will compute its gain or loss accordingly. Win All also is treated as having paid $15,000 compensation to *X*, and that amount likely will qualify as a business expense deduction.

> **§ 2.1562.   Illustration 2. Fringe Benefit Exception.** *Y* is an employee of Hudmaker's Department store. *Y* is employed as a salesperson in the store's toy department. The store permits all of its employees to purchase goods from the store at a ten percent discount. *Y* purchases a $200 washing machine for $180. The store's "gross profit percentage" (as defined in IRC § 132(c)(2)) for the sale of all its goods to its customers in the normal course of business is forty percent. As a consequence of IRC § 132(c) (a fringe benefit exception), *Y* will not realize any gross income because of making this

bargain purchase. See §§ **2.1622–2.1622–2.** *Y*'s basis in the washing machine is $180.

§ 2.1563. Illustration 3. Arms' Length Sale. *A* owns Blackacre which has a value of $40,000. Because of financial problems, *A* needs to sell Blackacre quickly. *B*, an unrelated party, knows of *A*'s financial distress. By shrewd bargaining, *B* purchases Blackacre from *A* for $35,000. Although *B* bought at a bargain price, the transaction was at arm's length and *B* will not realize income by making the bargain purchase. When the relationship between the purchaser and the seller does not suggest disguised compensation, no income will be realized. *B*'s basis in Blackacre is $35,000.

§ 2.1570. Stock Options. In the absence of a special statutory provision, when an employee of a corporation is granted an option to purchase the employer's capital stock at a favorable price, and the market value of the option can readily be determined, the employee will recognize gross income in an amount equal to the value of the option over the amount (if any) that the employee paid for it. Treas. Reg. § 1.421–6(c)(1). However, the Code does provide special tax treatment for so-called "incentive stock options." See **§ 2.1573.**

§ 2.1571. Problems of Valuation. In many circumstances, an option will not have a "readily ascertainable fair market value" at the time that it is granted to an employee. In such cases, the employee will not be taxed when he acquires the option; the transaction is kept open for tax purposes. See Treas. Reg. § 1.461–6(c)(1),(d); IRC § 83(e)(3). If the employee subsequently exercises the option, he will usually recognize gross income at that time in an amount equal to the difference between the market value of the stock when purchased by the employee and the amount paid for the stock by the employee. Treas. Reg. §§ 1.421–6(d); 1.83–7(a). The price at which the stock can be purchased under the option is referred to as the "strike price."

If an option is actively traded on an established market, it will be deemed to have a readily ascertainable fair market value. Treas. Reg. §§ 1.421–6(c)(2); 1.83–7(b)(1). If an option is not actively traded on an established market, it will not have a readily ascertainable fair market value unless *all* of the requirements set forth in Treas. Reg. § 1.421–6(c)(3) are satisfied. See also, Treas. Reg. § 1.83–7(b)(2).

§ 2.1572. **Restrictions on Acquired Property.** If property (including stock) that is acquired by an employee from his employer (whether or not acquired pursuant to an option) is subject to significant restrictions that affect the property's value, the time when the employee will be taxed and the extent to which the restriction will be taken into account in valuing the property are determined under special rules set out in IRC § 83. In general, the value of the property less the consideration paid by the employee will be taken into account on the first date that the property is not subject to a substantial risk of forfeiture of the employee's interest (or on the first date that the employee's interest can be transferred by him so that the transferee is not subject to a substantial risk of forfeiture). IRC § 83(a). Until such property becomes substantially vested, the transferor (rather than the transferee) continues to be treated as the owner of the property, and any income that the transferee receives during that period (or right of the transferee to use the property during that period) is treated as compensation paid to the transferee. Treas. Reg. § 1.83–1(a)(1).

Section 83 applies to the receipt of "property" in connection with the performance of services. IRC § 83(a). "Property" is defined in Treas. Reg. § 1.83–3(e) as including real and personal property other then cash "or an unfunded and unsecured promise to pay money or property in the future." Section 83 applies to such transfers regardless of whether made to the person who performed the services;but, for convenience, we will refer to the transferees as employees.

When property so acquired by an employee becomes taxable to the employee, the value of the property is determined by excluding all so-called "lapse restrictions" as if they were not present. IRC § 83(a). A "nonlapse restriction" is a permanent limitation on the transferability of property which will require the holder of the property to sell or offer to sell the property at a price determined by a formula and which will continue to apply to and be enforced against the holder or any subsequent holder (other than the employer). A "lapse restriction" is a restriction other than a nonlapse restriction and includes, but is not limited to, a restriction that carries a substantial risk of forfeiture. Treas. Reg. § 1.83–3(h), (i).

For purposes of IRC § 83, it is a factual question whether a risk of forfeiture is substantial, but the regulations do provide some guidance. For example, a risk of forfeiture is substantial when rights in transferred property are conditioned upon the future performance (or refraining from performance) of substantial services by any person. IRC § 83(c)(1); Treas. Reg. § 1.83–3(c). If an employee is required to return the property to the employer on the occurrence of a condition, that *may* create a substantial risk of forfeiture. For example, if the employee must return the property to the employer if the earnings of the employer do not increase, that will constitute a substantial risk of forfeiture; but if the employee must return the property only if the employee is discharged for cause or for committing a crime, that will not be considered a substantial risk of forfeiture. Treas. Reg. § 1.83–3(c)(2). If the employee is required to return the property if he accepts employment with a competitor of the employer (i.e., a covenant not to compete), that will not usually constitute a substantial risk of forfeiture, but particular facts may cause it to be so treated. Facts to be considered in such cases include: the age and health of the employee, the availability of other employment opportunities, the degree of the employee's skill, and the practice of the employer in enforcing such conditions. *Ibid.* If, on the required return of property pursuant to a restriction, the employer is required to pay the employee an amount equal to the fair market value of the property, the restriction will not constitute a substantial risk of forfeiture. Treas. Reg. § 1.83–3(c)(1).

If IRC § 83(a) otherwise prevents an employee from being taxed on the receipt of property, the employee has an election under IRC § 83(b) to have the fair market value of such property (less any consideration paid by the employee to acquire it) included in his income at the time of his receipt. The value of the property for this purpose is determined by treating all lapse restrictions as nonexistent. IRC § 83(b)(1)(A). If the election is made, the employee is treated as the owner of the property, and no additional amount is included in the employee's income when and if his interest in the property becomes substantially vested. On the other hand, if the property subsequently is forfeited, no deduction is allowable because of that forfeiture. IRC § 83(b)(1).

If property becomes taxable to an employee under either IRC § 83(a) or (b), and if the payment by the employer meets the requirements of IRC §§ 162 or 212, the employer will be allowed a deduction for the amount included in the employee's income. IRC § 83(h); Treas. Reg. § 1.83–6(a). No deduction is allowed under § 83(h) to the extent that the transfer constitutes a capital expenditure, a deferred expense or an amount properly included in the value of inventory, but in the first two circumstances, the transfer *may* permit an amortization of the amount transferred if that is appropriate. Treas. Reg. § 1.83–6(a)(4).

Section 83(b) is a kind of tax gamble. If a taxpayer makes that election, he must incur a tax liability at an earlier date than would otherwise be required. The taxpayer will benefit from the election if the value of the property to be included in taxpayer's income is significantly higher when the restriction terminates or is removed than the value that the property had at the time that the election was made.

Surprisingly, the Tax Court and the Ninth Circuit held that IRC § 83 applies even if the employee pays consideration for the property equal to the property's fair market value. *Alves v. Commissioner*, 79 T.C. 864 (1982), aff'd 734 F.2d 478 (9th Cir. 1984). In *Alves* the taxpayer acquired stock from a corporation in connection with the taxpayer's performance of services. Some of the acquired shares of stock were subject to restrictions which created a substantial risk of forfeiture and some shares were not. The taxpayer paid an amount for the stock that equalled the stocks' fair market value without any reduction in value because of the restrictions on some of taxpayer's shares. The majority of the Tax Court and the Ninth Circuit held that the taxpayer was subject to IRC § 83 when the stock was sold or when the restrictions were removed [under IRC § 83 the value of the stock at the time when the sale or restriction removal took place is compared to the consideration paid by the employee to determine the amount of income recognized by the employee]. Because of the application of IRC § 83, taxpayer recognized ordinary income at those times. The taxpayer could have prevented that consequence by making a timely election under IRC § 83(b) to have the excess of the fair market value of the acquired stock at the date that taxpayer acquired those shares over the amount that taxpayer paid for such stock included in his gross income in the year that taxpayer acquired the stock. Even though the amount of such excess would have been zero so that the election would not have caused taxpayer to recognize any income, the election would have made IRC § 83(a) inapplicable when the stock was sold or the restrictions were removed. Note that Treas. Reg. § 1.83–2(a) expressly authorizes a taxpayer to make an election under IRC § 83(b) even though the taxpayer paid full value for the acquired stock so that the taxpayer's acquisition was not a bargain purchase. Consequently, when an employee purchases property (which is subject to a restriction that constitutes a substantial risk of forfeiture) from his employer at a price that constitutes fair value for the property without regard to the restriction, the employee should make a protective election under IRC § 83(b).

§ 2.1572–1. Illustration 1. On March 5, Year One, *X* Corporation transferred 100 shares of its stock to *A*, an employee, as a bonus for *A*'s services. The transfer was made subject to a condition that if *A* failed to remain in the employ of *X* for three years (other than a termination caused by *A*'s health or death), the 100 shares of *X* stock had to be returned to *X*. *A* was allowed to transfer the stock, but the condition that *A* remain in *X*'s employ for three years will apply to all subsequent transferees. At the time of the transfer, the fair market value of a share of *X*'s stock was $200, and so the value of the 100 shares that *A* received (without taking into account the restriction to which those shares were subject) was $20,000. Since *A* could not keep the stock unless he continued to provide services for *X* in the latter's employment for three years, and since he could not terminate that condition by transferring the stock to a third party, that condition is a lapse restriction and also constitutes a substantial risk of forfeiture. *A* did not make an IRC § 83(b) election. *A* did not recognize income at the time that he received the stock in Year One because the substantial risk of forfeiture prevents the realization of that income.

Although for property law purposes *A* is the owner of the 100 shares of *X* stock, for federal income tax purposes *A* is not treated as the owner of those shares. Consequently, any "dividends" paid to *A* by *X* while *A* is not considered the owner of those shares of stock will not be treated as such, but instead will be treated as compensation paid to *A* for his services. Treas. Reg. § 1.83–1(a)(1). Presumably, the amount so included in *A*'s gross income as compensation will be deductible by *X* as a business expense.

§ 2.1572–2. Illustration 2. The same facts as those stated in **Illustration 1.** *A* continued in the employ of *X* for five years. The restriction on the 100 shares of *X* stock terminated on March 4, Year Four. At the date on which the restriction terminated, the fair market value of the stock is included in *A*'s income, and *A* thereafter is treated as the owner of those shares of stock for tax purposes. The fair market value of a share of *X* stock on March 4, Year Four was $300, and so the value of the 100 shares that *A* holds was $30,000. *A* must include $30,000 in his gross income. In the corporation's taxable year in which A recognized the $30,000 of gross income, the corporation will be allowed a deduction of $30,000 by IRC § 83(h). Treas. Reg. § 1.83–6(a).

§ 2.1572–3. Illustration 3. The same facts as those stated in **Illustration 1.** *A* died on June 23, Year Two. *A*'s death terminated the restriction and caused the then fair market value of the 100 shares of stock to be included in income. The income will be taxed to the estate of *A* as income in respect of a decedent. Treas. Reg. § 1.83–1(d). Income in respect of a decedent (IRD) is discussed at Chapter 21. In the corporation's taxable year in which the estate had income, the corporation will be allowed a deduction of a like amount.

2.1572–4. Illustration 4. The same facts as those stated in **Illustration 1** except that *A* made a timely election under IRC § 83(b) to recognize income when he received the 100 shares of *X* stock. *A* must include $20,000 in his gross income for Year One. *A* will be treated as the owner of the *X* stock for tax purposes, and so any dividends received by *A* will be treated as such for tax purposes. Neither *A* (nor his estate) will incur additional income taxes when the restriction terminates. However, if *A* leaves his employment within the prescribed three-year period and thereby forfeits the *X* stock, *A* will not be allowed a deduction for that forfeiture loss. In the corporation's taxable year in which A had gross income (Year One), the corporation will be allowed a deduction of a like amount.

§ 2.1573. Incentive Stock Options. The receipt and exercise of certain stock options ("incentive stock options") are granted special tax treatment by IRC § 422. An incentive stock option can be an option to purchase the stock of the taxpayer's corporate employer or of a parent or subsidiary of a corporate employer.

§ 2.1573–1. Holding and Employment Requirements.
If an option qualifies as an incentive stock option, and if no sale or other disposition of the stock takes place within one year after the taxpayer acquired the stock or within two years after the taxpayer acquired the option, the taxpayer will recognize no income either on the receipt, or on the exercise, of the option, and the employer will not be allowed a deduction for the bargain element in its sale of its stock to the taxpayer. IRC §§ 421(a), 422(a)(1). In addition, the taxpayer must have been in the continuous employ of the corporation granting the option (or of a parent or subsidiary of that corporation) for the period beginning with the grant of the option and ending three months prior to the exercise of the option (unless the taxpayer is disabled in which event the period ends one year prior to the exercise). There are some exceptions to these holding and continuous employment rules. In addition to excluding from gross income the bargain element in a taxpayer's exercise of an investment stock option, the taxpayer's gain on the subsequent sale of the stock will be a long-term capital gain.

§ 2.1573–2. Other Requirements.
In addition to holding and employment requirements, there are a number of other requirements that must be satisfied for an option to qualify as an incentive stock option. For example:

(a) the plan for issuing options was approved by the shareholders of the issuing corporation within a two-year period beginning twelve months before the plan was adopted;

(b) the option must be granted within ten years after a plan for issuing options was adopted by the issuing corporation or was approved by its shareholders, whichever is later;

(c) by its terms, the option must be exercisable within ten years;

(d) the option price must be at least equal to the fair market value of the stock at the time that the option is granted;

(e) the option is not transferable by the taxpayer except at death; and

(f) if the taxpayer owns stock possessing more than ten percent of the voting power of the outstanding stock of the employer (or of the employer's parent or subsidiary), the option price must be equal to at least 110 percent of the fair market value of the stock at the time of granting the option, and the option by its terms must be exercisable within five years.

§ 2.1580. Deferred Compensation.

§ 2.1581. Nonqualified Plans.
A cash method taxpayer does not report income until he has actually or constructively received cash or its equivalent. See **§§ 1.6210–1.6212** for discussion of the "constructive receipt" and "economic benefit" doctrines. Income is constructively received by a taxpayer in the year that it is credited to his account, or set apart for him, or otherwise made available so that he has the unrestricted right to draw upon it. Treas. Reg. § 1.451–2(a). When a taxpayer's right to draw funds is subject to substantial restrictions or a possibility of forfeiture, the taxpayer will not be deemed to have constructively received the income until his control is unrestricted and free from significant contingencies. *Ibid.* A mere unsecured promise to pay a taxpayer for services will not invoke the constructive receipt doctrine or constitute the equivalent of cash. Rev. Rul. 69–650; Rev. Rul. 60–31. See Treas. Reg. § 1.83–3(e). But if the promise is secured or if it is evidenced by a negotiable note, it likely will be treated as equivalent to cash and be included in the taxpayer's income. The treatment of the receipt of an unsecured nonnegotiable note is unresolved, but there is some authority for treating it as equivalent to cash if its fair market value is ascertainable. See **§ 2.1581–1.**

The principle under which a commitment to an employee becomes taxable if the value to the employee is ascertainable is called the "economic benefit" doctrine. See **§ 1.6212.** To a considerable extent, the economic benefit doctrine (a judicially created principle) has been replaced by IRC § 83, which provides rules for the taxation of an employee or independent contractor who receives property or an interest in property in connection with the performance of services. See § **2.1572.**

A taxpayer's right to a payment that is secured by an escrow deposit is covered by the economic benefit doctrine and is treated as a receipt of cash by the taxpayer; if the taxpayer is an employee or independent contractor, the transferred amount may be taxable under IRC § 83. Treas. Reg. § 1.83–3(e). However, if the obligor, while contractually bound to deposit a specified amount in escrow, fails to make the deposit, there is no economic benefit or constructive receipt to the taxpayer until funds are actually deposited in escrow. *Vaughn v. Commissioner*, 87 T.C. 164 (1986). If funds are deposited in the escrow account, but the account can be reached by creditors of the transferor (the employer), the escrow may qualify for the "rabbi trust" doctrine described in § **2.1581–5** and therefore may not cause the employee to be taxed.

The circumstances and conditions in which the Commissioner will issue an advance ruling on the tax treatment of a proposed unfunded deferred compensation arrangement are set forth in Rev. Proc. 92–65, amplifying Rev. Proc. 71–19.

§ **2.1581–1. Illustration 1.** *X*, a cash method taxpayer, executed an employment contract with World Wide Widgets, Inc. under which World Wide agreed to pay *X* a salary of $80,000 per year; and to pay *X* or his estate—commencing with the termination of *X*'s employment or his retirement—$20,000 per year for a period of years equal to the number of years *X* worked for World Wide prior to his retirement or the termination of his employment. Thus, in effect, *X* receives an annual salary of $100,000 ($80,000 to be paid currently and $20,000 to be deferred). In fact, the salary is less than $100,000 since the deferred $20,000 payment should be discounted to determine its present value (i.e., the loss of present use of the funds has an economic value). *X* must rely on World Wide's *unsecured* promise to make the deferred payments, and *X* must accept the risk that World Wide may not have the financial means of making those payments when they are due. World Wide's promise, which is not represented by notes, does not constitute the equivalent of cash; therefore, *X* will not include any of the deferred $20,000 payments in his gross income until they are actually paid to him. Rev. Rul. 60–31; Treas. Reg. § 1.83–3(e). The delivery of a negotiable promissory note or check typically will be treated as a cash equivalent. In *Warren Jones v. Commissioner*, 524 F.2d 788 (9th Cir. 1975), rev'g 60 T.C. 663 (1973), the Ninth Circuit treated the receipt of a nonnegotiable promissory note as an amount realized by a cash method taxpayer (i.e., as a cash equivalent), but that issue is unsettled. The promissory note is an unfunded and unsecured promise to pay money in the future and so is not "property" for purposes of IRC § 83, which therefore does not apply. Treas. Reg. § 1.63–3(e).

§ 2.1581–2. Illustration 2. The same facts apply as Illustration 1, but World Wide secures its obligation to make the deferred payments to *X* or his estate by transferring an appropriate amount each year to an escrow fund held by a local bank. According to *X*'s employment contract, the bank, as escrow agent, is to make the deferred payments when due. Since *X* receives an ascertainable economic benefit each year when World Wide deposits a sum with the escrow agent, that benefit constitutes a cash equivalent and *X* must include the amount actually deposited in his gross income. This is an application of the economic benefit doctrine. Also, § 83 will apply to require *X* to recognize income. Treas. Reg. § 1.83–3(e). The distinction between this and the prior illustration rests on the secured or unsecured nature of the deferred compensation. To the extent that the payments are secured, the economic benefit to the employee is reasonably ascertainable and is sufficiently similar to a cash payment that those amounts are taxable. Unless interest on the sums deposited is payable to *X* either currently or at some future date, the amount of gross income recognized by *X* when World Wide deposits a sum in the escrow fund should be reduced to reflect the present value of that sum to *X*.

§ 2.1581–3. Illustration 3. In Year One, Win All, Inc. paid the Friendly Insurance Company a $5,000 premium on an annuity policy for Win All's president, *X*. The policy provides a benefit payable to *X* or his estate upon his attaining his 65th birthday or upon his death. In Year One, *X* was 52 years old. The policy is to be held and owned by Win All until *X* reaches age 65 or dies, but Win All cannot cancel or assign the policy or change the beneficiary. *X* has received an economic benefit of $5,000 in Year One which he must report as gross income. *United States v. Drescher*, 179 F.2d 863 (2d Cir. 1950). See § 83.

§ 2.1581–4. Illustration 4. *X* maintains a savings account in the Friendly National Bank. On December 30, Year One, the Bank credited *X*'s account with $100 interest. Even though *X* did not withdraw any funds from the Bank in Year One, *X* constructively received the $100 interest in that year since he had an unrestricted right to withdraw the interest at any time after it was credited to his account. Accordingly, *X* recognized $100 interest income in Year One. See Treas. Reg. § 1.451–2(a).

§ 2.1581–5. Rabbi Trust. *X* establishes a plan to provide monthly payments to its employee, *A*, to commence when *A* retires or to be payable to *A*'s estate if *A* dies before retirement. *A*'s interest in the deferred payments are vested. As previously noted, if *X* does not fund or otherwise provide security for the deferred payments, *A* will not be taxed until he receives payment. However, *X* funds the plan by transferring cash to an irrevocable trust (or an escrow account) which secures that the payments will be made. *A* cannot assign, transfer, or pledge his interest in the trust or escrow account. The trust assets (or escrow account) cannot be withdrawn by *X* (the employer) or distributed to it. The trust instrument (or escrow agreement) provides that the trust's assets (or escrow funds) are subject to the claims of general and judgment creditors of *X*, and that provision will permit *X*'s creditors to reach the trust's assets (or escrow funds) under local law. In a number of letter rulings, the Commissioner has held that since creditors of *X* can obtain the trust's assets (or escrow funds) to satisfy the employer's debts, IRC § 83 will not cause *A* to recognize income [§ 83 taxes an employee for the receipt of a beneficial interest in assets "which are transferred or set aside from the claims of creditors of the transferor," Treas. Reg. § 1.83–3(e)], and there will be no constructive receipt or economic benefit to *A*, who will not be taxed on the deferred amounts until paid. E.g., PLR 8113107, PLR 8509023. The Commissioner has even approved such arrangements when creditors of the employer can reach the trust's assets only if the employer becomes insolvent or bankrupt. E.g., PLR 9822030, PLR 8703061, and PLR 8844020.

Since the first ruling on the taxation of a trust of this kind involved a trust for a rabbi, such trusts have become known as "rabbi trusts." They constitute one type of a nonqualified deferred compensation plan. An explanation for the Commissioner's approval of rabbi trusts is that the employer retains a significant reversionary interest in such trusts by his power to incur debts and thereby create creditors (and even insolvency) who can satisfy the employer's debts by taking the trust's assets. This power over the trust so intrudes upon the employee's security as to prevent the trust from providing an economic benefit of ascertainable value to the employee. Another explanation (and one adopted by the Commissioner in some of his rulings) is that the access of the employer's creditors to the trust's assets causes the employer to be treated as the owner of those assets under IRC § 671 (the so-called grantor trust provision).

In Rev. Proc. 92–64, the Commissioner set forth a model trust document that can be used to establish a rabbi trust.

§ 2.1582. **Qualified Retirement Plans.** To encourage the establishment of retirement plans for employees, Congress has granted favorable tax treatment for deferred compensation plans that comply with a number of statutory requirements. Thus, qualified pension and profit-sharing programs have been widely adopted by employers. See IRC §§ 401–404. In general, contributions made by an employer to a qualified pension or profit-sharing plan are deductible by the employer but are not included in the gross income of the employees who are beneficiaries of the plan, even though their interests are vested, until actually distributed to them from the fund. In addition, income earned by the fund is not taxed when earned. In effect, the tax on the employer's contributions and the income earned by the fund is deferred until payment is made to the beneficiary.

§ 2.1582–1. **Self–Employed.** Self-employed persons can adopt a qualified deferred compensation plan for themselves and their employees under the so-called Keogh or HR–10 provisions. See IRC § 401(c). The annual amount that can be contributed to a Keogh plan is much more limited than the amounts that can be contributed to ordinary employee plans. A self-employed individual may also qualify to use an Individual Retirement Arrangement, which defers a limited amount of income in certain circumstances.

§ 2.1582–2. Individual Retirement Arrangements. There are four kinds of Individual Retirement Arrangements (IRAs)—individual retirement accounts, individual retirement annuities, individual retirement bonds, and Roth IRAs. Certain contributions to the first three types may be deductible, but contributions to a Roth IRA are not deductible. The amount that can be contributed annually to an IRA is severely limited. The income earned by an IRA (other than a Roth IRA) generally is not taxed until distributed, and the income earned by a Roth IRA may never be taxed. There are limitations on the amount of AGI that a TP can have to qualify to make contributions to a Roth IRA, and an excise tax is imposed on excessive contributions.

§ 2.1583. Employee Life Insurance. If an employer purchases insurance on the life of an employee and if the proceeds are payable to a beneficiary selected by the employee, the premium paid or the value of the insurance coverage will be included in the employee's gross income. Treas. Reg. § 1.61–2(d)(2)(ii)(a).

§ 2.1583–1. Illustration. Win All, Inc. provides $20,000 individual term insurance coverage for its president, *X*, who names his wife as beneficiary. The annual premium for the policy is $200. Win All's payment of a $200 premium causes *X* to recognize $200 gross income.

§ 2.1583–2. Group–Term Exception. If an employer purchases group-term life insurance for its employees, the premium paid for a particular employee's coverage will be excluded from the employee's gross income to the extent that the premium does not exceed the cost (as determined under the Regulations) of $50,000 insurance. IRC § 79(a), (c). The premium paid in excess of the cost of $50,000 coverage is included in the employee's gross income. IRC § 79. For the meaning of "group term life insurance," see Treas. Reg. § 1.79–1(a); and Rev. Rul. 75–528. If a group term life insurance plan discriminates in favor of "key employees," either in terms of eligibility to participate or in terms of the type or amount of benefits, the exclusion from gross income will not apply to any key employee. IRC § 79(d). This exception does not apply to a "church plan" that is maintained for church employees. IRC § 79(d)(7). The meaning of "key employee" is defined in § 416(i). IRC § 79(d)(6).

§ 2.1600.   Fringe Benefits. An important means of compensating an employee is to provide the employee with a fringe benefit that is excluded from the employee's gross income. Fringe benefits include such items as free parking space, use of a company automobile, and reduced fares for air travel. Benefits provided to an employee are included in the employee's gross income unless they are expressly excluded by statute. IRC § 61(a)(1). For many years, some fringe benefits were excluded from gross income by the Code (e.g., group term life insurance coverage and furnishing of meals and lodging) and some were excluded by administrative practice of the Service. While the Tax Reform Act of 1984 extended the list of statutory nontaxable fringe benefits [e.g., IRC §§ 132, 117(d)], the 1984 Act eliminated the availability of administrative exclusions from gross income. After 1984, an employee's benefit is included in the employee's gross income unless a *statutory* exclusion is available.

§ 2.1610.   Medical Insurance Payments. An employer's contribution to an accident or health plan or to purchase medical insurance to compensate employees for personal injuries or illness of the employees, their spouses, and dependents, is excluded from the gross income of the employees. IRC § 106. The tax consequences of receiving medical insurance benefits or health plan benefits are discussed at **§ 2.4300** et seq.

§ 2.1620.   Certain Fringe Benefits. IRC § 132 allows an employee to exclude from his gross income any fringe benefit which qualifies as a "no-additional-cost service," a "qualified employee discount," "a working condition fringe," a "*de minimis* fringe," a "qualified transportation fringe," a "qualified moving expense reimbursement," or a "qualified retirement planning service." These are terms of art that are defined in IRC § 132. Also, an employee's use of an "on-premises athletic facility" that is provided by his employer will not cause the employee to recognize gross income. IRC § 132(j)(4). The requirements for qualifying an athletic facility for that exclusion are discussed in PLR 9029026.

Note that any fringe benefit which is not covered by a specific Code provision becomes taxable. IRC § 61(a)(1). If a benefit is taxable, the taxpayer will include in his gross income the difference between the fair market value of the benefit and the amount paid (if any) for such benefit.

§ 2.1621. No–Additional–Cost Service. Services which are provided to, or on behalf of, an employee by his employer may qualify as no-additional-cost services if two requirements are met. First, the services provided must be of the type offered by the employer to customers in the ordinary course of the line of business in which the employee performs substantial services. IRC § 132(b)(1). Thus, if a corporate employer offers a free ride on the company's commercially operated passenger train to an employee who works as a waitress in a restaurant that her corporate employer owns and operates as a separate business, the benefit will not qualify as a no-additional-cost service because the employee is not working in the passenger train line of her employer's business. However, if free train service were offered by the employer to an accountant who deals with all areas of the corporation's business, the "same line of business" test would be satisfied. Treas. Reg. § 1.132–4(a)(1)(iv)(A). The "same line of business" requirement is discussed at **§ 2.1623.** Second, the employer must not incur a substantial additional cost (including foregone revenue) by providing such a benefit. IRC § 132(b)(2). This determination is made without regard to any payment made by the employee for the service. In certain circumstances, where several employers execute a written agreement to provide services to employees of both parties, the services furnished by one employer to an employee of the other employer can be covered by the "no-additional-cost" exception, provided that neither employer incurs any substantial additional cost (including foregone revenue) in providing such services. IRC § 132(i). The exclusion from gross income of a no-additional-cost service is subject to the anti-discrimination rules [described at **§ 2.1622–2**] which prevent highly compensated employees from obtaining this exclusion if the employer's plan discriminates in favor of them.

§ 2.1622. Qualified Employee Discount. Employers often offer property or services to an employee at a price lower than that charged to the employer's customers; the difference in such prices is referred to as an "employee discount." IRC

§ 132(c)(3). Some or all of the value of an employee discount will be excluded from the gross income of the employee if the discount is offered on qualified property or service. IRC § 132(c). To the extent that a discount is excluded from the employee's gross income, it is referred to as a "qualified employee discount." Property or services are qualified if they are offered for sale to customers in the ordinary course of the line of business in which the employee performs substantial services; however, qualified property does not include personal property that is held for investment and does not include any real property. IRC § 132(c)(4). Thus, where a corporation owns and operates a department store chain and also owns and operates an automobile dealership as a separate business, a discount on the price of an automobile offered by the corporate employer to a sales clerk in its department store chain will not be a qualified employee discount. The "same line of business" requirement is discussed at **§ 2.1623.**

§ 2.1622–1. Limitation. There are separate limitations that apply to discounts on qualified property and those that apply to discounts on qualified services. An employee discount on *qualified property* is excluded from a taxpayer's gross income only to the extent that the discount does not exceed the "gross profit percentage" of the price charged to customers. IRC § 132(c)(1)(A). The "gross profit percentage" is defined as the amount by which the difference between the aggregate sales price of all property sold to customers in the line of business in which the employee is engaged and the aggregate cost of such property is a percentage of the aggregate sales price of such property. IRC § 132(c)(2)(A). The gross profit percentage is determined by reference to the employer's sales experience over a representative period. IRC § 132(c)(2)(B). An employee discount on *qualified services* is excluded to the extent that the discount does not exceed 20 percent of the price charged to the employer's customers for such services. IRC § 132(c)(1)(B).

§ 2.1622–2. No Discrimination. No-additional-cost services and qualified employee discounts will be excluded from the gross income of highly compensated employees only if they are offered to other employees on substantially the same terms. IRC § 132(j)(1). That is, fringe benefit plans which discriminate in favor of highly compensated employees will disqualify those employees for treatment under IRC § 132(a)(1) and (2). The employees who constitute the "highly compensated" classification are described in IRC § 414(q). IRC § 132(j)(6).

§ 2.1622–3. Certain Individuals Treated as Employees. Some individuals who are not actual current employees may receive free or discounted property or services from an employer and still qualify for exclusionary treatment under the no-additional-cost service and qualified employee discount provisions. For example, under these provisions, retired and disabled employees, spouses and dependent children of employees or of certain former or deceased employees are all treated as employees. IRC § 132(h). For purposes of this provision, "dependent child" of an employee or deceased employee is specially defined by IRC § 132(h)(2)(B).

§ 2.1623. Same Line of Business Requirement. The exclusion from an employee's income for either a "no-additional cost service" or a "qualified employee discount" fringe benefit is limited to property or services that are provided by the employer in the ordinary course of the same line of business in which the employee performs substantial services. The classification of a group of activities as a single line of business is determined by reference to categories established in the Enterprise Standard Industrial Classification Manual that is prepared by the U.S. Office of Management and Budget. A range of connected activities may be classified as a single line of business. For example, a general retail merchandise store is a single line of business, and so the retail sale of clothes, appliances, stationary, toys etc. at a department store are all part of a single line of business. A few other examples of a single line of business are: hotel and other lodging places, auto repair services and garages, and food stores. Treas. Reg. § 1.132–4(a)(2).

In certain circumstances, two or more lines of businesses conducted by an employer will be aggregated and treated as a single line of business. Treas. Reg. § 1.132–4(a)(3). For example:

(1) If it is uncommon in the industry of the employer for the several lines of businesses of the employer to be operated without the others, they will be treated as one line of business;

(2) If it is common for a substantial number of employees (other than those who work at the headquarters or main office of the employer) to perform substantial services for more than one line of business of the employer so that it is difficult to determine which employees perform substantial services for which business, then the several businesses in which the employees perform substantial services are treated as a single line of business.

If an employee performs services in more than one line of businesses that the employer conducts, the employee can exclude no-additional cost services and qualified employee discounts in any line of business for which the employee provides substantial services. Treas. Reg. § 1.132–4(a)(1)(i), (iii). An employee who performs substantial services that benefit more than one line of an employer's business is treated as performing substantial services for each such line of business. If an employee of a minor line of an employer's business that is significantly interrelated with a major line of the employer's business performs substantial services that directly benefit both the minor and the major lines of business, the employee is treated as providing substantial services to both lines of business. Treas. Reg. § 1.132–4(a)(1)(iv)(A). The following examples are drawn from Treas. Reg. § 1.132–4(a)(1)(iv)(B).

§ 2.1623–1. Illustration 1. *A* works for an employer who sells retail merchandise. *A* works in a department that provides repairs for purchased products of the employer. *A* is treated as providing substantial services to the retail merchandising line of business.

§ 2.1623–2. Illustration 2. *X* operates a hospital and a laundry service. While the laundry service handles the hospital's laundry, it also has gross receipts for laundry services provided to customers other than the hospital. *B* and *C* work for the laundry service. Approximately 40% of the work performed by *B* is in connection with servicing the laundry of the hospital. Since *B* performs substantial services that directly benefit the hospital's line of business, *B* is treated as providing substantial services to that line of business. *C* spends an insubstantial amount of work time dealing with the laundry services provided to the hospital; almost all of *C*'s time is spent on work for other customers. Since *C* does not perform substantial services that directly benefit the hospital line of business, *C* does not qualify for a no-additional cost service or qualified employee discount from the hospital's line of business.

§ 2.1624.   Working Condition Fringe. Property or services offered to an employee will not be included in an employee's gross income to the extent that the employee would be allowed a deduction for such items under IRC §§ 162 or 167 (i.e., business expense deductions and depreciation deductions) had the employee paid for them himself. IRC § 132(d). But, the deduction must be allowable because the item would be an expense of conducting the trade or business of being an employee of the employer who provided the fringe. Treas. Reg. § 1.132–5(a)(2). Note that the anti-discrimination requirement of IRC § 132(j)(1) [see § **2.1622–2**] does not apply to working condition fringe benefits.

For the possible application of the working condition fringe to educational or training assistance provided by an employer, see § **2.4560.**

§ 2.1625.   *De Minimis* Fringe. Where the value of the property or services provided to the employee is so small that accounting for it would be unreasonable or administratively impracticable, the employee will not be required to include such items in his gross income. IRC § 132(e)(1). The value of the property or services is determined after taking into account the frequency with which these benefits are provided by the employer to his employees. Note that while the anti-discrimination requirements of IRC § 132(j)(1) [see § **2.1622–2**] do not apply to *de minimis* fringe benefits, the special treatment accorded to eating facilities [§ **2.1626**] is subject to a similar anti-discrimination restriction.

§ 2.1626.   Eating Facilities. The operation of an eating facility by an employer may be treated as a *de minimis* fringe if the facility is located on or near the business premises of the employer and if the revenue derived from the facility normally equals or exceeds the direct cost of such operation. IRC § 132(e)(2). The benefits of an eating facility will qualify as a *de minimis* fringe for highly compensated employees only if they are available on substantially the same terms to each member of a group of other employees which is defined under a reasonable, nondiscriminatory classification. IRC § 132(e)(2).

Meals that are provided an employee on the business premises of the employer and for the convenience of the employer are excluded from the employee's gross income by IRC § 119, which therefore can overlap with IRC § 132(e)(2). These two statutory provisions are coordinated by the last sentence of IRC § 132(e)(2). When an employee's meal is excluded from income by IRC § 119, the employee is deemed to have paid for the meal; the constructive payment is equal to the direct operating cost of the facility that is attributable to that meal. That constructive payment brings the meal within IRC § 132(e)(2). The reason for constructing a payment lies in IRC § 274(n) which limits the deduction for the cost of a meal to 50% of that cost. By treating the employee's meal as having been purchased by the employee, the employer can deduct 100% of the cost of providing that meal, since § 274(n) will not apply to the employer.

§ 2.1627. Qualified Transportation Fringe. A qualified transportation fringe consists of any of the following three items:

(A) Qualified parking;

(B) Transportation in a commuter highway vehicle if such transportation is between the employee's residence and place of employment; and

(C) Any transit pass. IRC § 132(f).

While these three fringes are excluded from the employee's gross income, there is a dollar limitation on the monthly value that can be excluded. There is a ceiling on the amount of qualified parking that can be excluded in a month, and there is a ceiling on the aggregate amount of transit passes and commuter transportation that can be excluded in a month. But, both of those ceilings are indexed to inflation; i.e., they increase when the cost of living rises. IRC § 132(f)(2), (6). For years beginning in 2005, the maximum amount of qualified parking for a month that can be excluded is $200; and the maximum aggregate amount of transit passes and commuter transportation for a month that can be excluded is $105. Rev. Proc. 2004–71.

The qualified transportation fringe need not be furnished in kind to be excluded from income. An employer's cash reimbursement of an employee's cost also is excluded from income. IRC § 132(f)(3). Also, a qualified transportation fringe is excludable even if the employee has a choice to either take that benefit or to receive additional compensation. IRC § 132(f)(4).

The definitions of the three items that comprise the qualified transportation fringe and of other terms are set forth in IRC § 132(f)(5). "Qualified parking" includes parking provided to an employee on or near the business premises of the employer. IRC § 132(f)(5)(C).

Note that there is no prohibition against providing a qualified transportation fringe that discriminates in favor of highly compensated employees.

§ 2.1628. Qualified Moving Expense Reimbursement. The term "qualified moving expense reimbursement" means an amount received (directly or indirectly) by an individual from an employer as a reimbursement for (or payment of) expenses that would be deductible under IRC § 217 as moving expenses if directly paid or incurred by the individual. Such amounts are excluded from the individual's gross income unless the individual had deducted the expense in a prior year. IRC § 132(g). Any reimbursements or payments of an employee's moving expenses that are not excluded from income by IRC § 132(g) are included in the employee's gross income under IRC § 82. For example, since meals are not deductible under IRC § 217, the receipt of a reimbursement or payment for meals will be included in income. IRC § § 82, 217(b)(1). The extent to which unreimbursed moving expenses are deductible under IRC § 217 is discussed at **§ 10.3400** et seq.

§ 2.1629. Qualified Retirement Planning Services. In 2001, Congress added IRC § 132(a)(7) and (m) to exclude "qualified retirement planning services." The term "qualified retirement planning services" means any retirement planning advice or information provided to an employee and his spouse. IRC § 132(m)(1). Note that while the anti-discrimination requirements of IRC § 132(j)(1) [see **§ 2.1622–2**] do not apply to qualified retirement planning benefits, the special treatment accorded to such services is subject to a similar anti-discrimination restriction. IRC § 132(m)(2).

§ 2.1700.   Reimbursed Expenses. In general, if an employer reimburses an employee for personal expenses of the latter (or directly pays such personal expenses), the reimbursement (or direct payment) will be included in the employee's gross income. But, when an employee incurs an expense in the conduct of his employer's business, which expense qualifies as an allowable tax deduction of the employee, the employer's reimbursement or direct payment of such expense items will not constitute income to the employee provided that the employee is required to account (and does so) to the employer for all such expenses. Treas. Reg. §§ 1.62–2, 1.162–17(b) and 1.274–5(e)(2); Rev. Ruls. 76–71, 76–65, 76–62 and 77–351. Some specific expense items are discussed in the following sections.

An employer may pay a per diem amount in lieu of reimbursing the employee's actual expenses and such amount will be considered substantiated if the per diem is equal to or below the appropriate Federal per diem rate. Rev. Proc. 2000–9.

§ 2.1710.   Rationale. It is worth noting that the reason that the Service will permit an employee to exclude from his gross income certain amounts of reimbursement that he receives from his employer for expenses that he incurred in the conduct of his employer's business solely for the employer's benefit is that such expenses are deductible under IRC § 62(a)(2)(A) in determining the employee's adjusted gross income [see Chapter Three]. Thus, regardless of whether the employee elects to itemize his deductions, such reimbursed expenses would be deductible and would wash out the income that the employee recognized on receiving the reimbursement. Note also that since reimbursed expenses of an employee qualify as nonitemized deductions, the deduction of those expenses is not subject to the limitations that otherwise would be imposed by IRC § 67 (a floor on miscellaneous itemized deductions) and IRC § 68 (an overall limitation on itemized deductions).

§ 2.1720.   Moving Expenses. If an employer reimburses an employee for the expenses of moving to a new place of work to commence his employment at a new location, the reimbursement will be excluded from the employee's gross income as a fringe benefit to the extent that the reimbursed expenses would be deductible by the employee as moving expenses under IRC § 217 if directly paid or incurred by the employee. IRC § 132(a)(6); and see **§ 2.1628.** The reimbursement of the cost of an employee's meals are included in the employee's gross income as are reimbursements of other expenses that would not be deductible under IRC § 217. IRC § 82.

§ 2.1730. Travel Expenses. If an employee is required to travel while on his employer's business, the employer's reimbursement of the employee's actual travel expenses (including meals and lodging) will not be included in the employee's gross income. The employee must retain records and proof of expenditures in accordance with the requirements of IRC § 274. Note that the provision in IRC § 274(n)(1) limiting the deduction of meals to 50 percent of the cost does not apply to an employee whose meal expenses (on travel status) are reimbursed by his employer, but the employer can deduct only 50 percent of the cost of the meal for which the employee was reimbursed. IRC § 274(e)(3), (n)(1), (2)(A).

§ 2.1731. Expenses of Interviewing for a Job. Although no deduction is allowable for the travel or other expenses incurred by a taxpayer to interview for a job in a trade or business in which the taxpayer was not previously engaged, if a prospective employer reimburses a taxpayer for, or directly pays, the travel expenses incurred to interview for a job at the invitation of the prospective employer, the reimbursement and payments are excluded from the taxpayer's gross income to the extent that they do not exceed the actual expenses. Rev. Rul. 63–77. The expenses to which this provision applies include the taxpayer's round trip transportation costs and the costs of meals and lodging in the city at which the interview takes place. See § **10.1475.**

§ 2.1732. Expenses Incurred on Behalf of Another in a Non–Employment Context. The reimbursement of expenses incurred by a taxpayer on behalf of a person or entity in a non-employment context is excluded from the taxpayer's gross income. Rev. Rul. 80–99. For example, when the expenses of a taxpayer (who was a state employee) to attend and speak at a political fund-raising event were reimbursed by the political organization, the reimbursement was not included in the taxpayer's gross income. *Ibid.* See § **10.1475.**

However, Treas. Reg. § 1.61–21(a)(3) states that a "fringe benefit provided in connection with the performance of services shall be considered to have been provided as compensation for such services." At one time, in audits, the Service raised the question as to whether the person or entity's reimbursement of the taxpayer's expenses constitutes a fringe benefit that is taxable to the taxpayer to the extent not excluded by IRC § 132. While this question was raised, the Service has not yet replaced or revoked Rev. Rul. 80–99, and the authors know of no instances in which the Service has actually adopted that approach and sought to collect taxes in reliance on it.

§ 2.1740. Meals and Lodging. In the absence of a statutory exception, the fair market value of meals and lodging furnished to an employee as consideration for his services will be included in the employee's gross income. Reg. § 1.61–2(d)(3). The principal statutory exclusion of meals and lodging is provided by IRC § 119, the terms of which are described below. As noted in **§ 2.1626**, a statutory exclusion is granted for an employer's operation of an eating facility for his employees if the benefits to the employees qualify as a *de minimis* fringe under IRC § 132(e)(2).

§ 2.1741. Excluded Meals and Lodging. Under IRC § 119, the value of meals and lodging furnished by an employer to an employee, his spouse and dependents are excluded from the employee's gross income if they were: (1) furnished for the convenience of the employer, and (2) furnished on the business premises of the employer. As to lodging, there is the additional requirement that the employee was required to accept the lodging as a condition of his employment so that the employee will be better able to perform his services (e.g., the requirement that a maintenance man for an apartment house live in one of the apartments is appropriate for his job since the employee must be available to tenants at any time of day or night). An employer's furnishing of necessary utilities to an employee as part of the furnishing of lodging to the employee can be excluded from the employee's gross income by IRC § 119 as being within the exclusion for lodging. Rev. Rul. 90–64; *Turner v. Commissioner*, 68 T.C. 48, 50 (1977).

§ 2.1742. Meaning of Convenience of Employer. Meals or lodging is "for the convenience of the employer" if there is a substantial noncompensatory purpose even if there is also a compensatory purpose. If an employer provides meals on its business premises for its employees, and if the meals for more than half of the employees to whom meals are provided are provided for the convenience of the employer, then the meals provided to *all* of the employees are treated as provided for the convenience of the employer. IRC § 119(b)(4). In other words, if more than half of the employees who are provided meals can exclude them under IRC § 119, then all of the employees who are furnished those meals can exclude the value that they received thereby.

§ 2.1742–1. Illustration. The Friendly National Bank allows its employees only 30 minutes for lunch. So that the employees can have lunch at that time, the bank operates a cafeteria and provides a free lunch for its employees. Most of the employees who eat lunch at the cafeteria are restricted to a 30–minute lunch period. Even though the employees are not required to eat in the cafeteria, the bank does provide lunch on its premises for a substantial noncompensatory reason. Since the meals provided to more than half of the bank's employees who partake of it are furnished for a noncompensatory purpose, the president and other officers of the bank (whose lunch periods are not restricted) may also take their meals at the bank without incurring tax liability even though there is no noncompensatory purpose for the bank to furnish meals to that small minority. IRC § 119(b)(4).

§ 2.1743. Meaning of Business Premises. The term "business premises" refers to the place of employment of the employee. Thus, the business premises of a domestic servant's employer is the home in which the servant works. Treas. Reg. § 1.119–1(c)(1).

"Business premises" has been construed to mean "either (1) living quarters that constitute an integral part of the business property or (2) premises on which the company carries on some of its business activities." *Lindeman v. Commissioner*, 60 T.C. 609 (1973), Acq. See also, *Vanicek v. Commissioner*, 85 T.C. 731 (1985), Acq; PLR 9801023. The question of whether the furnishing of lodging that is physically separated from the business premises can qualify for the IRC § 119 exclusion will depend upon whether the premises at which the employee resides is utilized in the conduct of the employer's business. This is a factual question the resolution of which depends upon a consideration of the employee's duties and of the nature of the employer's business. *Ibid*; PLR 8938014; and TAM 9404005. In *Lindeman v. Commissioner*, *supra*, a house leased by the employer across the street from its business site for the use by an employee as the residence for himself and his family was held to be part of the employer's business premises. The employee had an office in his home and conducted some business there. In *Commissioner v. Anderson*, 371 F.2d 59 (6th Cir. 1966), a home provided to an employee several blocks from the business site was held not to be part of the business premises. Cf., *Benninghoff v. Commissioner*, 71 T.C. 216 (1978), aff'd per curiam, 614 F.2d 398 (5th Cir. 1980). In PLR 8938014, the Commissioner held that lodging furnished to a hospital employee across the street from the hospital was not part of the business premises. However, the physical proximity of the lodging to the business site is not the important datum; it is the extent to which business of the employer is conducted at that site that is most important.

§ 2.1744. Furnished in Kind. In order to be excluded from the employee's gross income, the meals and lodging must be actually furnished (furnished *in kind*) and not merely reimbursed or purchased. If the employer *reimburses* the employee for expenses in purchasing food or lodging rather than supplying them, the reimbursement may be taxed as gross income to the employee. *Commissioner v. Kowalski*, 434 U.S. 77 (1977).

§ 2.1744–1. Furnishing of Groceries. An unresolved question is whether an employer's furnishing of groceries to his employee will constitute the furnishing of meals in kind. In *Tougher v. Commissioner*, 51 T.C. 737 (1969), aff'd 441 F.2d 1148 (9th Cir. 1971), the Tax Court held that groceries do not qualify as meals in kind. However, in a later case, by a 2–1 divided court, the Third Circuit rejected the *Tougher* position and excluded groceries furnished to a taxpayer from his gross income under IRC § 119. *Jacob v. United States*, 493 F.2d 1294 (3d Cir. 1974). PLR 9126063.

§ 2.1744–2. Reimbursement for Employee's Meals Taken When Working Late. When an employee works late at his employer's office and is reimbursed for his dinner at a downtown restaurant, the Service ruled in 1920 that the reimbursement will be excluded from gross income. OD 514, 2 Cum. Bull. 90 (1920). The question is whether, and to what extent, that exclusion from gross

income is applicable today. Since it is a cash reimbursement for the cost of food that was not obtained on the
business premises of the employer, it is clear that IRC
§ 119 is inapplicable. As a consequence of the 1984 amendments, a fringe benefit is not excluded from an employee's
gross income unless a statutory exclusion is applicable. IRC
§ 61(a)(1). So, supper money will be included in an employee's gross income unless it fits within a statutory provision.
If reimbursed supper money is to be excluded from an
employee's gross income, it most likely will have to qualify
as a *"de minimis* fringe" benefit under IRC § 132(a)(4).
See PLR 9148001. The Joint Committee Staff's *General
Explanation of the Revenue Provisions of the Deficit Reduction Act of 1984* states at p. 858 that a *"de minimis* fringe"
includes "occasional supper money or taxi fare because of
overtime work." See also Reg. § 1.132–6(d)(2). Typically,
an employee will have to show that his reimbursements for
meals are infrequent; but if it is administratively difficult
to determine frequency for each individual employee, the
determination can be made by reference to the frequency
that reimbursement is provided to all the employees. PLR
9148001; and Treas. Reg. § 1.132–6(b)(2). The Joint Committee Staff's *Explanation* also states at (p. 856) that
reimbursed supper money will not qualify for exclusion as a
"working condition fringe" under IRC § 132(a)(3).

§ 2.1745. Payment by Employee. Where an employee is
furnished meals or lodging and a fixed amount is deducted
from the employee's salary as payment for the meals or
lodging, the amount so deducted is excluded from the employee's gross income, and the fair market value of the furnished
meals or lodging are either excluded from or included in gross
income depending upon whether IRC § 119 applies. Treas.
Reg. § 1.119–1(a)(3). But see IRC § 119(b)(3); *Cox v. Chaco*,
650 F.2d 174 (9th Cir. 1981).

   § 2.1745–1. Illustration. *X* manages a motel for Sleep-
well, Inc. *X* is required to live in a room at the motel. *X*
receives a salary of $800 per month, and Sleepwell with-
holds $100 of that monthly salary as payment for the room.
X will include only $700 per month in gross income, and
the value of the room will be excluded from *X*'s gross
income under IRC § 119. If IRC § 119 did not exclude the
value of the room, the $100 withheld from *X* would be

excluded from his gross income, but the rental value of the room would be included.

§ 2.1746.   Qualified Campus Lodging. The value of lodging provided by an educational institution to an employee, his spouse, and any of his dependents may be excluded under IRC § 119(a) if the conditions of that provision are satisfied. If IRC § 119(a) does not apply, all or part of the cost of lodging provided to such persons at or near the campus of the educational institution nevertheless may be excluded from the employee's gross income under IRC § 119(d), which excludes from gross income the value of "qualified campus lodging" furnished to an employee. A certain portion of the value of such lodging will be included in the employee's gross income to the extent that the amount of such portion exceeds the rent paid by the employee. IRC § 119(d)(2).

§ 2.1800.   Annuities. An annuity is a contractual right to receive payments for a fixed term or for the life or lives of some person or persons. The contract under which these rights are obtained may be an annuity, endowment, or life insurance contract.

§ 2.1810.   Percentage of Annuity in Gross Income. When a taxpayer purchases a commercial annuity, each payment made to the taxpayer (or to a surviving beneficiary of a joint annuity or a survivor's annuity) consists partly of a return of the taxpayer's capital and partly of income earned on his investment in the annuity. A percentage of each annuity payment (the "exclusion ratio") is excluded from the taxpayer's gross income, and the balance of the payment is included in gross income. IRC § 72(b)(1). Once the aggregate amount of annuity payments that have been excluded from the taxpayer's gross income equals the amount of the taxpayer's investment in the annuity contract, all additional annuity payments will be included in the taxpayer's gross income. IRC § 72(b)(2).

§ 2.1811.   Exclusion Ratio. The exclusion ratio is a fraction: the numerator is the taxpayer's *investment in the annuity contract*, and the denominator is the taxpayer's total *expected return from the annuity over the period for which payments will be made* (usually the period is for someone's life or for a fixed term). The regulations employ two different sets of life expectancy tables for determining a taxpayer's expected return—one set of tables applies for the portion of an annuity that is attributable to a pre-July 1, 1986 investment, and the second set of tables applies to the portion of an annuity that is attributable to a post-June 30, 1986 investment. If an annuity payment is received after June 30, 1986, the recipient can make an irrevocable election to have his expected return determined under the post-June 30, 1986 tables regardless of when the investment was made. Treas. Reg. § 1.72–9. If investments in the annuity were made both before and after July 1, 1986, the taxpayer can elect to have separate computations made for the portions of annuity payments that are attributable to the two separate periods of investment.

For certain annuity plans for employees (referred to an "qualified employer retirement plans"), IRC § 72(d) provides a simplified method for determining the amount of annuity payments that are a recovery of the employee's investment. The method is explained in Notice 98–2, 1998–2 I.R.B. 22, which also provides examples.

§ 2.1811–1. Illustration. X purchased an annuity in 1967 which will pay her $10,000 per year, beginning with her 61st birthday in 1987, until she dies. The annuity is to be paid in monthly installments. X paid $140,000 for the annuity. X's expected return from the annuity is $210,-000—i.e., $10,000 × 21 (the number of years of X's life expectancy under tables provided in the Regulations that can apply to X). Using the cost ($140,000) as the numerator and the expected return ($210,000) as the denominator, the exclusion ratio is 140,000/210,000; so 2/3 of each monthly payment is excluded from her gross income and 1/3 is included. Thus, X must include in her gross income $3,333 of each year's payments; that is the amount that represents income on her investment. She will exclude $6,667 of each year's payments. This exclusion will apply to monthly payments made during the 21–year period beginning with the date on which the first monthly payment is made to X. As shown in § 2.1820, the entirety of annuity payments made to X after her 82nd birthday will be included in her gross income. Note that because X paid for the annuity contract prior to 1986 (and so all of the investment was made prior to July 1, 1986), the author used Table I of Reg. § 1.72–9 to determine X's life expectancy and that table distinguishes between males and females. Because X will receive annuity payments after June 30, 1986, X can elect to determine her life expectancy under Table V of Reg. § 1.72–9, which table provides a sex-neutral table for determining life expectancy. It is unlikely that X would wish to elect to use Table V since that would provide a larger figure for her life expectancy (23.3 years) and so would increase her expected return to $233,000 and accordingly would reduce her exclusion ratio to 140,000/233,000 or 61.4 percent.

§ 2.1820. Termination of Exclusion Ratio. The exclusion ratio will be used to exclude a percentage of annuity payments from gross income until the taxpayer has recovered his investment. Thereafter, annuity payments will be included in the taxpayer's gross income. However, if the first annuity payment under the annuity contract is made to the taxpayer on or before December 31, 1986, the exclusion ratio will apply to all payments made under the contract including payments made after the taxpayer's investment has been recovered. Thus in the illustration above, after X attains her 82nd birthday, she will have received $210,000 in total payments of which $140,000 will have been excluded from her gross income because it represents a return of her $140,000 cash investment. X will have recaptured her entire cost investment by that time. Since X's first annuity payment was received after December 31, 1986, all payments received by X after she has recovered her $140,000 investment will be included in her gross income.

§ 2.1830. Deduction Allowable for Unrecovered Investment. If the payments under an annuity contract cease by reason of the annuitant's death and if at the time of such cessation there is an "unrecovered investment" in the annuity contract, the annuitant is granted an itemized deduction for the amount of the "unrecovered investment." IRC § 72(b)(3). This deduction is taken on the annuitant's income tax return for his last taxable year. IRC § 72(b)(3)(A). The deduction is not subject to the 2% of adjusted gross income floor that applies to certain itemized deductions referred to as "miscellaneous itemized deductions" [IRC § 67(b)(10)], but the general limitation on itemized deductions that is imposed by IRC § 68 does apply. The "unrecovered investment" in an annuity contract is the difference between the amount of investment in the annuity contract as of the annuity starting date and the aggregate amount of distributions made under the contract that were excluded from the recipient's gross income. IRC § 72(b)(4). The "annuity starting date" is the date on which the first payment under the contract is received by an annuitant. § 72(c)(4). This provision for a deduction applies only if the annuity starting date was after July 1, 1986.

§ 2.1840. Employee Annuity. Prior to the enactment of the 1986 TRA, when part of the purchase price of an annuity contract was paid by the taxpayer's employer and the amount was not then included in the employee's gross income, a special rule applied in determining the employee's income from annuity distributions. If the total amount payable to the employee under the annuity contract in the first three years (commencing with the date of the first annuity payment) was equal to or greater than the consideration contributed by the *employee* for the contract, then each annuity payment to the employee was excluded from gross income *until* the total amount excluded equals the total consideration paid by the employee. The full amount of all subsequent annuity payments was included in the employee's gross income. This special provision for certain employee annuities was repealed by the 1986 TRA. The repeal applies to employee annuities for which the first annuity payment (the "annuity starting date") is made after July 1, 1986. Under the 1986 TRA, distributions from employee annuities are treated the same as those from a commercial annuity that was purchased by the annuitant, except for the simplified calculation that IRC § 72(d) provides for certain employee annuities.

§ 2.1850. Private Annuity. A private annuity is a contractual obligation of a person or organization not regularly in the business of selling annuity contracts. Typically, a private annuity will be purchased from a member of the annuitant's family or from a charitable organization. Some charitable organizations are so involved in providing annuities that they are treated the same as a commercial annuity company. Since the value of a private annuity contract may be speculative and it may be "purchased" by the exchange of appreciated property, the tax rules are more complex than those for commercial annuities. For the current position of the Service, see Rev. Rul. 69–74, and Rev. Rul. 71–492.

§ 2.1860. Annuity Contract Not Held by a Natural Person. The income reporting provision supplied by IRC § 72 for annuity contracts apply only if the contract is owned by, or held on behalf of, a natural person. IRC § 72(u). If an annuity contract is held by a fictional entity (such as a corporation) and is not held on behalf of a natural person, the holder of the contract will be required to report income on the contract annually. Such income is reported on a method similar to the accrual method. IRC § 72(u).

§ 2.1900. Life Insurance.

§ 2.1910. Lump–Sum Proceeds. Normally, life insurance proceeds payable in a lump sum by reason of the death of the insured are not included in the gross income of the beneficiary. IRC § 101(a)(1). But see **§ 2.1950** and IRC § 101(f).

§ 2.1920. Life Insurance Proceeds Payable in Installments. If life insurance proceeds are payable to a beneficiary in installments over a period of a life or a term of years, part of each payment represents the principal amount payable by reason of the insured's death which is excludable under IRC § 101; part of the payment represents interest earned by that portion of the principal amount of the insurance proceeds that has been left on deposit with the insurance company. In essence, in such cases, the principal amount of the death benefit that is payable under the policy is left with the insurer to fund the insurer's payment of an annuity to the beneficiary. The tax rules for inclusion of such installment payments in gross income are similar to the rules that govern annuities. Thus, where life insurance proceeds are to be paid in installments over the lifetime of the beneficiary, a percentage of each installment that represents the principal sum of the insurance proceeds will be excluded form the gross income of the beneficiary.

Prior to the adoption of the 1986 TRA, the exclusion of a percentage of each installment payment continued to apply to installments received after the period of the beneficiary's life expectancy if the beneficiary outlived that period. While changing the treatment of annuity payments received under IRC § 72, the 1986 TRA did not expressly change the treatment of life insurance proceeds received in installments under IRC § 101. It is possible that the regulations to the 1986 TRA will restrict the exclusion of a percentage of installment payments to an aggregate amount that does not exceed the principal sum that was left with the insurer to provide installment payments; such a limitation would comport with the restriction on the exclusion of annuity payments that is imposed by IRC § 72(b)(2). The language of the amendments made by the 1986 TRA do not expressly impose that restriction, but it is possible that such a restriction can be inferred from the amendment. See Conference Report to the 1986 TRA, H.Rept. 99–841, 99th Cong., 2d Sess. (1986), p. II–338.

If the beneficiary had an option to have received a lump sum settlement on the insured's death, that lump sum will be deemed to be the principal sum that was left with the insurer; if no option for a lump sum settlement was available, the principal sum that was left with the insurer is deemed to be the present value of the payments to be made to the beneficiary as determined by using the interest rate applied by the insurer and by using mortality tables, promulgated by Treasury, that do not distinguish persons by sex. Conference Report to the 1986 TRA, H.Rept. 99–841, 99th Cong., 2d Sess. (1986), pp. II–338–II–339; Treas. Reg. § 1.101–7. The mortality figures that are employed are those in Treas. Reg. § 1.72–7(c)(11) and set forth in tables in Treas. Reg. § 1.72–9. Treas. Reg. § 1.101–7.

> **§ 2.1921. Illustration.** *F* purchased a $100,000 life insurance policy on his life and named his son, *S*, as beneficiary. Upon *F*'s death, if *S* received the $100,000 proceeds in a lump sum, nothing would be included in *S*'s gross income. Suppose *S* elected to leave the $100,000 with the company and to receive an annuity of $8,000 a year for the rest of his life. Under the applicable mortality tables, *S* had a life expectancy of 15 years. During the first 15 years that the $8,000 annual payments are made, *S* will exclude 1/15 × $100,000 = $6,666 of each annual payment, and the $1,334 balance of each annual payment will be included in *S*'s gross income. Treas. Reg. § 1.101–4. It is possible that if new regulations are promulgated under IRC § 101, they will provide that if *S* lives longer than 15 years, no part of the annual payments made after the expiration of that 15–year period will be excluded from *S*'s gross income. No such regulations have been proposed as yet. Even if such regulations are adopted, their validity may have to be tested in court.

§ 2.1930. Cessation of Installment Payments before the Entire Amount of the Death Benefit is Distributed. If the proceeds of a life insurance policy are left with the insurer to make installment payments for the life of a beneficiary (or for the lives of several beneficiaries) and if all payments from the insurer are to cease upon the death of the beneficiary, the death of the beneficiary prior to the expiration of his life expectancy will leave undistributed some portion of the principal amount of the death benefit that was left with the insurer. Will the beneficiary or the beneficiary's estate be allowed a deduction for the unrecovered amount? In the comparable circumstance where an annuitant for life dies prematurely, the 1986 TRA amended IRC § 72 to grant a deduction to the annuitant for his unrecovered cost. IRC § 72(b)(3); **§ 2.1830.** However, no amendment was made to the provisions dealing with installment payments of life insurance proceeds that were left on deposit with the insurer. It appears, therefore, that the pre–1986 law denying a deduction to the beneficiary in such cases will continue to apply. Perhaps Treasury will promulgate new regulations to IRC § 101 that will clarify this question.

§ 2.1940.   Insurance Proceeds Earning Interest. If life insurance proceeds are held by the insurance company under an agreement to pay interest when the insurance proceeds are withdrawn by the beneficiary, the proceeds are excluded from the gross income of the beneficiary; but, the interest payments are included. IRC § 101(c).

§ 2.1950.   Transfer for Value. If the original owner of a life insurance policy assigns the policy to another for valuable consideration prior to the death of the insured, part of the insurance proceeds may be taxable.

> **§ 2.1951.   Permissible Assignees.** None of the insurance proceeds will be included in the gross income of the beneficiary of the policy if the assignee of the policy was the insured, a partner of the insured, a partnership in which the insured was a partner, or a corporation in which the insured was an officer or shareholder. IRC § 101(a)(2)(B). Note that a co-shareholder is *not* within this exception.

> **§ 2.1952.   Tax–Free Transfers.** If the assignment of an insurance policy was a tax-free transfer (e.g., a gift or a corporate merger), the insurance proceeds are not taxable unless they would have been taxable if there had been no such assignment and the policy had continued to be held by the assignor. IRC § 101(a)(2)(A).

> **§ 2.1953.   Amount Taxable.** If the assignment of the policy was made for valuable consideration and if the above exceptions are inapplicable, the beneficiary may exclude from gross income an amount of the proceeds equal to the consideration paid for the policy by the assignee plus the net premiums paid

by the assignee (i.e., the beneficiary excludes an amount equal to his basis in the policy). The balance of the insurance proceeds will be included in the beneficiary's gross income.

§ 2.1954. Illustration 1. *H* purchases a $100,000 face amount life insurance policy from the Reliable Insurance Co. insuring his life. *H* paid an annual premium of $5,000. *H* died after paying premiums for three years, and the $100,000 proceeds were paid to *H*'s wife whom *H* had named as the beneficiary. Since *H* was the original owner of the policy and since he never assigned the policy to anyone, the $100,000 insurance proceeds are excluded from *W*'s gross income.

§ 2.1955. Illustration 2. Two years after *H* purchased the policy in the above illustration, *H* assigned the policy to *Y* who paid *H* $10,000 consideration for the policy. *Y* was *H*'s partner in a partnership which owned and operated a hardware business. Upon acquiring the policy, *Y* changed the beneficiary and designated himself as beneficiary. *Y* paid one $5,000 premium before *H* died. After *H*'s death, the insurer paid the $100,000 proceed to *Y* as the beneficiary of the policy. Since, at the time that *Y* purchased the policy from *H*, *Y* was *H*'s partner, the "transferee for value" rule is inapplicable. IRC § 101(a)(2)(B). The $100,000 insurance proceeds that *Y* received are excluded from his gross income.

§ 2.1956. Illustration 3. The same facts apply as in the second illustration, except that *Y* was not a partner in a partnership with *H*; instead *Y* and *H* were shareholders in Y-H, Inc., a corporation which owned and operated a hardware business. Since *Y* is a purchaser for value and since co-shareholders are not exempted from the "transferee for value" rule, *Y* can exclude from his gross income only the $10,000 consideration he paid for the policy plus the $5,000 premium he paid. The remaining $85,000 of the proceeds is included in *Y*'s gross income.

§ 2.2000. MISCELLANEOUS INCLUSIONS IN GROSS INCOME.

§ 2.2100. Income of Child. Income earned by a child is included in the child's gross income; it is *not* included in the parent's gross income even if the child's income is paid to the parent and is subject to the control of the parent. IRC § 73.

§ 2.2200. Prizes and Awards. In general, the fair market value of a prize or an award is gross income to the recipient. Quiz show and most contest prizes are taxable. However, there are several exceptions to this general rule. IRC § 74.

§ 2.2210. Exception: Awards Transferred to Charities. A prize or award is excluded from gross income if: (a) the prize or award was given in recognition of religious, charitable, scientific, educational, artistic, literary or civic achievement; (b) the recipient did not take any action to enter the contest or proceeding; (c) the recipient is not required to render future services as a condition to receiving the prize or award; and (d) the recipient assigns the prize or award to a governmental unit or tax exempt charitable or like organization. IRC § 74(b).

§ 2.2211. Effect of Transfer. If the assignment is properly made, the prize or award is not included in the winner's gross income and no charitable deduction is allowed to the winner or to the payor. The taxpayer's assignment of the prize or award must be made before the taxpayer uses the awarded item; for a cash award, the transfer must occur before the winner spends, deposits, or otherwise invests the funds. Otherwise, the award is taxable.

§ 2.2220. Exception: Employee Achievement Awards. The 1986 Tax Reform Act provides an exclusion for employees who receive "achievement awards" that satisfy certain requirements. The fair market value of an achievement award is *fully* excludable from gross income by the employee only if the cost of the award is fully deductible by the employer. IRC § 74(c). If part of the employer's cost is not deductible, then only part of the award is excluded from the employee's gross income. In such a case, the employee must include in his gross income the greater of: (1) the amount of the employer's cost that is nondeductible (but this amount cannot exceed the value of the award), or (2) the amount by which the value of the award exceeds the deduction allowable to the employer.

The employer's cost for providing an "employee achievement award" typically will be a deductible business expense under IRC § 162, but the amount of deduction allowable to the employer is restricted by IRC § 274(j). Since the employee's exclusion of the award depends upon the amount of deductions allowable to the employer, this restriction on deductibility also affects the amount of the employee's exclusion. The operation of the IRC § 274(j) limitation on the employer's deduction is described in **§§ 2.2225– 2.2225–2.** In appropriate circumstances, an employer's award to an employee will be excluded from the employee's gross income as a *de minimis* fringe benefit under IRC § 132(e). See **§ 2.2226.**

§ 2.2221. Employee Achievement Award Defined. An "employee achievement award" is an item of tangible personal property that an employer transfers to an employee for "length of service achievement" or "safety achievement." The property must be awarded as part of a meaningful presentation, under conditions and circumstances that do not create a significant likelihood of the payment of disguised compensation. IRC § 274(j)(3)(A). An example of facts that suggest disguised compensation is an employee award made at the time of annual salary adjustments as an apparent substitute for a previous program of awarding cash bonuses. Note that the award must consist of tangible personalty. An award of cash or a gift certificate will not qualify.

§ 2.2222. Length of Service Awards. An employee cannot exclude an award given for length of service if it is received during the employee's first five years of employment, or if the employee had previously received an award that year or during the past four years while working for that employer. IRC § 274(j)(4)(B). For this purpose, previously made employee awards that were excludable by the employee as a *de minimis* fringe benefit under IRC § 132(e) are disregarded.

§ 2.2223. Safety Achievement Awards. All employees are eligible for this award except managers, administrators, clerical workers, and other professional employees. If, however, the employer has made safety awards to more than ten percent of the eligible employees in one year, there is no exclusion for the award.

§ 2.2224. Qualified Plan Award. A qualified plan award is an employee achievement award provided under an established or written plan of the employer that does not discriminate in favor of highly compensated employees. An employee achievement award will not qualify as a qualified plan award if the *average* cost of all such awards that were made by the employer in that year exceeds $400. IRC § 274(j)(3)(B).

§ 2.2225. Dollar Limitations on the Employer's Deduction. The dollar amount of an employer's cost for an achievement award that can be deducted by the employer depends upon whether the award is a "qualified plan award." As noted in **§ 2.2220**, the amount excludable by the employee depends upon the amount of the employer's cost that is deductible.

§ 2.2225–1. Other Than Qualified Plan Awards. If an employee achievement award is not a qualified plan award, the maximum amount of cost that the employer can deduct for making such an award to an employee is $400. IRC § 274(j)(2)(A). If in a taxable year an employer made to one employee more than one employee achievement award that were not qualified plan awards, the maximum deduction allowable for the aggregate cost of making such awards to that employee cannot exceed $400. IRC § 274(j)(2)(A).

§ 2.2225–2. Qualified Plan Awards. If an employer makes one or more "qualified plan awards" [see **§ 2.2224**] to an employee in a taxable year, the maximum amount of deduction allowable for the aggregate cost of all employee achievement awards made such employee (including employee achievement awards that are not "qualified plan awards") is $1,600. IRC § 274(j)(2)(B).

§ 2.2226. *De Minimis* Fringe Benefit. In appropriate circumstances, an award to an employee will be excluded from the employee's gross income as a *de minimis* fringe benefit under IRC § 132(e). Typically, this exception will apply only to an award of an item having a small value that is given to an employee who has not received a number of such awards. However, the Report of the Senate Finance Committee to the 1986 TRA stated that the *de minimis* fringe benefit exception ordinarily will apply to a traditional retirement gift presented to an employee on retirement after completing a lengthy service. If otherwise applicable, the *de minimis* fringe benefit exception can apply to such awards even if the employee achievement award exclusion of IRC § 74(c) does not apply. See Conference Report to the TRA 1986, H.Rept. 99–841, 99th Cong., 2d Sess. (1986), p. II–19; Senate Finance Committee's Report on TRA 1986, S.Rept. 99–313, 99th Cong., 2d Sess. (1986), pp. 53–54.

§ 2.2230. Exceptions: Scholarship. Where the prize or award consists of a "qualified scholarship" under IRC § 117, the amount received is excluded from the recipient's gross income to the extent that the amount is used by degree candidates at an educational organization for "qualified tuition and related expenses" in accordance with the conditions of the grant or scholarship. IRC §§ 74(a), 117. This exception is subject to the tax rules specifically governing scholarships and fellowships discussed in § 2.4500.

§ 2.2240. **Fair Market Value.** If a prize or award is included in the recipient's gross income, the amount included is determined by reference to the fair market value of the property. Treas. Reg. § 1.74–1(a)(2). The fair market value of property is defined, for tax purposes, as "the price at which the property would change hands between a willing buyer and a willing seller, neither being under any compulsion to buy or to sell and both having reasonable knowledge of relevant facts." Treas. Reg. § 1.170A–1(c)(2). One difficulty with this definition is that there is more than one market at which an item can be sold (e.g., retail market, wholesale market, private sale market) and a choice must be made as to the proper market to use. The fair market value of an item is the cost of replacing it rather than the amount that could be realized on the liquidation of the item. So, it is necessary to determine the price that a member of the public would pay to purchase the item. Thus, if an item is generally obtainable by the public in the retail market, the fair market value of such an item is the price at which the item or a comparable item would be sold at retail. In *Anselmo v. Commissioner*, 757 F.2d 1208 (11th Cir. 1985), aff'g 80 T.C. 872 (1983), the court affirmed the Tax Court's determination that the "public" for low quality unmounted gems is jewelry manufacturers and jewelry stores that create jewelry items, rather than the individual consumer. The fair market value therefore was determined by the wholesale rather than the retail market. In most cases, the retail market will control.

§ 2.2300. **Income Received by Error.** When property or funds are received under a mistake of fact or law, the property or funds are included in the gross income of the recipient notwithstanding that the recipient may be required to return the item to the payor when the error is discovered. The item is included in income under the so-called "claim of right" doctrine: the recipient acquired the property without a consensual recognition (express or implied) of an obligation to repay and without restriction as to his disposition of the property at least until the error is discovered. If there are substantial restrictions on disposition or use or if there is an unconditional obligation to return the item, then the item will not be included in income. See § **2.1110.**

> § **2.2310. Illustration.** In Year One, Win All, Inc. erroneously computed the bonus to be paid X, an employee. Accordingly, Win All over-paid X by $2,500. The error was discovered in Year Three, and X returned the $2,500. The $2,500 is included in the gross income of X for Year One, and X is entitled to a $2,500 deduction for Year Three when he repaid that amount of the bonus. *United States v. Lewis*, 340 U.S. 590 (1951). See IRC § 1341 on repayment rules. §§ **13.4000–13.4350.**

§ **2.2400. Illegally Obtained Income.** Income obtained by embezzlement or other illegal means is included in the wrongdoer's gross income even though he is obligated to return it when discovered. *James v. United States*, 366 U.S. 213 (1961); *United States v. Sullivan*, 274 U.S. 259 (1927); Treas. Reg. § 1.61–14(a); see § **13.4000.** In 1982, the Service estimated that the compliance rate for reporting illegal income is only five percent. S.Rept. 97–494, 97th Cong., 2d Sess. (July 12, 1982), page 251.

In *Kreimer v. Commissioner*, 47 T.C.M. 260 (1983) (appeal to 11th Cir. dismissed in 1984), the taxpayer obtained a loan by fraud. The court held that the taxation of such a loan depends upon whether the taxpayer intended to repay the fraudulently obtained loan. If the taxpayer did intend to repay the loan, the taxpayer is treated as a borrower and will not be taxed on the borrowed funds. If there was no intention to repay the loan, the taxpayer is treated as having received income and is therefore taxed on the loan. It appears to the authors that the "borrowed" funds should be included in the taxpayer's gross income regardless of his intention to repay; the lender's participation in the consensual recognition of the obligation to repay was obtained by fraud and so should be disregarded.

> § **2.2410. Control As a Practical Matter.** The issue of when illegally obtained income is to be taxed was addressed in *United States v. Dixon*, 698 F.2d 445 (11th Cir. 1983). In *Dixon*, the taxpayer transferred funds from a client's account into his own account in 1975. The court held that the illegally obtained funds became income to the taxpayer in the year in which the taxpayer obtained "practical control" (control as a practical matter) over the funds. Thus, the criminal conviction for willful tax evasion for 1976 was upheld, even though the taxpayer received the funds in 1975, because "practical control" was not established until 1976.

§ 2.2500. Interest. Interest income is usually included in the recipient's gross income.

§ 2.2510. Exclusion of Certain Interest. Interest received from obligations of a state, territory, or a possession of the United States, or any political subdivision thereof will usually be excluded from gross income. IRC § 103. For example, interest received on a state or municipal bond (other than an arbitrage bond and certain private activity bonds) will be excluded from gross income.

All or a portion of interest or gain received from the redemption of certain qualified United States Savings bonds that are used to pay tuition and fees for the taxpayer, the taxpayer's spouse and dependents to attend an eligible education institution are excluded from the taxpayer's income by IRC § 135. This exclusion is phased out if the taxpayer's adjusted gross income (AGI), as modified by IRC § 135(c)(4), exceeds specified amounts (for 2005, $61,200 or $91,850 if a joint return is filed) indexed for cost-of-living increases. IRC § 135(b)(2); Rev. Proc. 2004–71.

§ 2.2520. Imputed Interest. Where property is sold under a deferred payment plan or where a loan of cash is made, there may be no provision for interest payments or the stated interest payable on the deferred payments or loan may be less than the then current market rate of interest. In certain cases where this occurs, the Code imputes interest payments of a sufficient amount to raise the interest rate to a reasonable figure. The circumstances in which interest payments are imputed and the manner in which such imputed interest is allocated over the years that the loan or deferred payments are to be made are discussed at **§ 5.4000** et seq. In certain cases, a debt instrument which was issued at a discount will be subject to the imputed interest income rules covering "original issue discount." See IRC §§ 1272, 1273. See **§ 5.5000** et seq.

§ 2.2600. Dividend Income. Income which can be characterized as a dividend *for tax purposes* is usually includable in gross income. While dividends constitute ordinary income, most dividends received by a *noncorporate* taxpayer will be taxed at capital gains rates (typically at a 15% rate). IRC § 1(h)(11).

§ 2.2610. Definition of Dividend. "Dividend" is a term of art in tax law. It does not include some types of distributions which are characterized as dividends for non-tax purposes; conversely, it does include some types of income that are not characterized as dividends for non-tax purposes. The term "dividend" is defined in IRC § 316 as a distribution by a corporation to its shareholders out of the "earnings and profits" of the corporation. The term "earnings and profits" is a federal tax concept that is used to measure the amount of corporate distributions that are to be treated as dividends. The definition of earnings and profits is designed to provide a measurement of a corporation's net earnings over the period of its existence that more closely represents economic reality than does the "taxable income" concept.

§ 2.2611.   **Illustration 1.** *X* is a shareholder of Win All, Inc., but *X* is not employed by the corporation. *X* pays Win All $10,000 as consideration for *X*'s purchase of Blackacre which has a value of $25,000. Win All has earnings and profits in excess of $50,000. *X* has received a dividend of $15,000—the excess value of Blackacre over the amount *X* paid for it.

§ 2.2612.   **Illustration 2.** The same facts as those stated in § 2.2611 except that Win All's earnings and profits were only $5,000. While *X* received $15,000 of value from Win All, only $5,000 of that amount is a dividend. The dividend cannot exceed the corporation's earnings and profits. The remaining $10,000 of the value received by *X* is treated as a return of his basis in his Win All stock and will be treated as a gain to the extent that it exceeds that basis.

§ 2.2613.   **Illustration 3.** *Y* purchased a $100,000 life insurance policy from Friendly Life Insurance Co., Inc., a mutual insurance company. The policy insures *Y*'s life. In Year One, *Y* paid Friendly a premium of $6,000. In Year Two, Friendly paid *Y* a "dividend" of $500 on the policy. While the company refers to the $500 payment as a dividend, it is actually a refund to *Y* of part of the premiums she previously paid—the amount of the refund being determined by the company's experience both in earnings and in claims. Consequently, the $500 payment made to *Y* in Year Two will be excluded from *Y*'s gross income as a return of her capital.

§ 2.2620.   Deduction for Receipt of Dividend By A Corporate Shareholder. A *corporate* shareholder may claim a deduction equal to a percentage of the dividend received from a domestic corporation subject to the limitations imposed by IRC § 246. IRC § 243. In some cases, a corporate shareholder is entitled to a deduction equal to 100 percent of the dividend received, thus

washing it out entirely. IRC § 243. No deduction or exclusion is provided for a dividend received by a noncorporate shareholder, but those dividends typically are taxed at capital gains rates. See § 2.2600.

§ 2.2700. Unemployment Compensation. A taxpayer's gross income includes his receipt of unemployment compensation payments. IRC § 85.

§ 2.2800. Payment in Kind for Services or Property. If payment for property or services are made with property in kind, then there is a taxable gain or loss on the difference between the fair market value of the property and the payor's basis in that property. *International Freighting Corp. v. Commissioner*, 135 F.2d 310 (2d Cir. 1943).

§ 2.3000. TAX BENEFIT RULE.

§ 2.3100. General Rule of Inclusion. If a taxpayer deducted an item on his federal tax return and enjoyed a tax benefit thereby and in a subsequent year recovers all or part of that item, he will recognize gross income in the year the deducted item is recovered. *Dobson v. Commissioner*, 320 U.S. 489 (1943). The rule has both an inclusionary and an exclusionary component, i.e., the recovery is included in the taxpayer's gross income to the extent that the taxpayer obtained a tax benefit from the prior year's deduction, and the recovery is excluded to the extent that the prior year's deduction did not provide a tax benefit. See *Hillsboro National Bank v. Commissioner*, 460 U.S. 370 (1983), pp. 380–381, fn. 12. The *Hillsboro National Bank* case is a landmark decision for the tax benefit rule. The Supreme Court's decision in *Hillsboro* involved two consolidated cases, one of which was the *Bliss Dairy* case. See §§ 2.3130 and 2.3140. Since the principal holding in the Supreme Court's decision in *Hillsboro* dealt with the *Bliss Dairy* case, the Supreme Court's decision often is referred to by courts and commentators as the "*Bliss*" or "*Bliss Dairy*" case. In this text, the Supreme Court's decision is referred to as "*Hillsboro*."

For an item received in one year to be excluded from income under the tax benefit rule because it constitutes a recovery of an item that had been deducted in a prior year without obtaining a tax benefit, there must be a nexus between the prior year's deduction without tax benefit and the item that was received in the subsequent year. See *Allstate Ins. Co. v. United States*, 936 F.2d 1271 (CAFC 1991), excluding from gross income amounts obtained by an insurance company from the enforcement of subrogation rights the company acquired when it satisfied claims (and took deductions for those payments) in a prior year. The exclusion from income was allowed to the extent that the deductions that the company took in the prior year did not produce a tax benefit for the company.

§ 2.3110.   Illustration 1. *X* loaned *Y* $10,000 in a business transaction. In 1979, *Y*'s $10,000 debt to *X* became worthless, and *X* deducted $10,000 from her 1979 tax return as a bad debt deduction under IRC § 166. *X* enjoyed a tax benefit from the deduction. In 1981, *Y* paid *X* $3,000 as a partial payment on his $10,000 debt. Even though the $3,000 paid to *X* in 1981 was a partial return of a loan *X* had previously made and, therefore, was a return of *X*'s capital, the $3,000 is, nevertheless, included in *X*'s gross income since *X* had enjoyed a tax benefit by taking a deduction for the debt in 1979. Moreover, the $3,000 will be included in *X*'s gross income for 1981 even if *X* is in a higher (or a lower) marginal tax bracket in 1981 than she was in 1979 when she took the deduction.

§ 2.3120.   Illustration 2. In Year One, *X* donated Blackacre (unimproved land) to the city of Flint, Michigan on condition that a library building be constructed on the land within ten years. *X*'s basis in Blackacre was $16,000. *X* deducted the value of Blackacre ($18,000) from his Year One tax return, and let us assume that deduction was properly allowed [the question of deductibility turns on whether the possibility that the building would not be constructed is so remote as to be negligible (Treas. Reg. § 1.170A–1(e))]. *X* obtained a tax benefit from the entire $18,000 deduction. In Year Seven, Blackacre is returned to *X* because the city decided not to build a library. The value of Blackacre in Year Seven was $22,000. *X* must include $18,000 of Blackacre's value in his gross income (it appears that the additional $4,000 in value of Blackacre is not included in *X*'s gross income since he never had a tax benefit for that portion of Blackacre). While there is no explicit authority as to the manner in which *X*'s basis in the recovered Blackacre is to be determined, it would seem that *X*'s basis in the recovered Blackacre would be $16,000—that is, *X*'s basis at the time of transfer will be reinstated.

If the value of Blackacre in Year Seven (when it was returned to *X*) had fallen to $14,000, it is unsettled whether *X* would be required to include only $14,000, or the full $18,000 deducted in

Year One, in his gross income. It may be that *Hillsboro* [see § **2.3100** and §§ **2.3130–2.3140**] requires recognition of income in the amount for which a prior tax benefit was received regardless of the fair market value of the property at the time it was returned, but the authors doubt that *Hillsboro* will be applied in that manner. *Hillsboro* held that a subsequent event which is fundamentally inconsistent with a prior deduction requires recognition of income. The question here involves the extent of the inconsistency. In fn. 37 of the *Hillsboro* decision, the Supreme Court noted that the taxpayer in that case did not raise the question of whether the amount of income to be recognized by the taxpayer because of the tax benefit rule should be less than the amount of deduction taken by the taxpayer in a prior year; and so, the Court expressly refrained from addressing that issue. For a pre-*Hillsboro* decision that limits *X*'s income to the $14,000 value that Blackacre had when the city returned it to *X*, see *Rosen v. Commissioner*, 611 F.2d 942 (1st Cir. 1980). In a post-*Hillsboro* decision, the Tax Court followed *Rosen* and limited the taxpayer's income on the return of property previously donated to a charity to the fair market value of the property when returned, but only *up to* the amount of charitable deduction previously taken. *885 Investment Co. v. Commissioner*, 95 T.C. 156, 166 (1990). Under the Tax Court's decision, only $14,000 is included in *X*'s income. Regardless of whether *X* is required to include $14,000 or $18,000 in his gross income, it is unclear what basis *X* will have in Blackacre—is *X*'s original $16,000 basis reinstated or is *X*'s basis equal to the amount included in his gross income? Cf., Treas. Reg. § 1.83–6(c).

If only $14,000 is included in *X*'s gross income (in accordance with the decisions of the Tax Court and of the First Circuit), it might seem appropriate to reinstate *X*'s original basis of $16,000 reduced by the $4,000 of deduction that *X* obtained that was not recaptured when the property was returned. So, in that case, *X* would have a basis of $12,000 in Blackacre. On the other hand, the amount of deduction allowable for many charitable gifts does not depend upon the basis of the donated property; rather, the measure of the deduction is the fair market value of the donated property. The $4,000 of unrecovered deduction relates to a decline in value while the property was in the hands of the charity. That amount can be viewed as a kind of charitable contribution itself. In certain circumstances described in IRC § 170(e), the amount of charitable deduction is limited to the taxpayer's basis in the donated property; and if such property is recovered, perhaps the taxpayer's basis in the recovered property should be reduced by any unrecaptured deduction. But, when the charitable deduction was not a type that is limited by the taxpayer's basis, it seems to the authors that the taxpayer should reinstate his original basis for the recovered property; in that case, there should be no reduction of basis because of an unrecaptured deduction.

§ 2.3130. Actual Recovery vs. Fundamental Inconsistency.
The question arose as to whether there has to be an actual physical recovery of a deducted item before the tax benefit rule can be applied. In *Tennessee-Carolina Transportation, Inc. v. Commissioner*, 582 F.2d 378 (6th Cir. 1978), a 2–1 decision affirming a divided Tax Court decision, the majority stated that "there need not be an actual physical 'recovery' of some tangible asset or sum in order to apply the tax benefit rule. The tax benefit rule should be applied flexibly in order to counteract the inflexibility of the annual accounting concept which is necessary for administration of the tax laws. The rule should apply whenever there is an actual recovery of a previously deducted amount or when there is some other event inconsistent with that prior deduction.... [An] inconsistency is enough to invoke the tax benefit rule." The Supreme Court subsequently adopted (in the *Hillsboro* case) a modified version of the view taken by the Sixth Circuit in the *Tennessee-Carolina* case.

In *Hillsboro National Bank v. Commissioner*, 460 U.S. 370 (1983), reversing a Ninth Circuit decision in *Bliss Dairy v. United States*, 645 F.2d 19 (9th Cir. 1981), the Supreme Court held that the tax benefit rule does not depend upon there being an actual recovery of the deducted item. While the Supreme Court held that an inconsistent subsequent event could trigger a tax benefit rule application, the Court held that only a certain type of inconsistent event did so. The test (under *Hillsboro*) is whether the subsequent event is "*fundamentally inconsistent* with the premise on which the deduction was initially based."(Emphasis added.) A subsequent event is fundamentally inconsistent with a deduction if it would have prevented the deduction from being allowable if it had occurred in the same year that the deductible event took place.

In *Hillsboro*, the Supreme Court said, "the tax benefit rule must be applied on a case-by-case basis. A Court must consider the facts and circumstances of each case in light of the purpose and function of the provision granting the deductions." *Hillsboro, supra*, at 385–386.

One difficulty in applying the *Hillsboro* standard is that it requires an examination of the Congressional purpose for granting the deduction to determine whether the subsequent event is "fundamentally inconsistent" with that purpose or with the factual assumptions on which the allowance of that deduction was based. For examples of that difficulty, see *Byrd, Transferee v. Commissioner*, 87 T.C. 830 (1986), aff'd without opinion, 829 F.2d 1119 (4th Cir. 1987); *Rojas v. Commissioner*, 90 T.C. 1090 (1988) (reviewed by the court), aff'd 901 F.2d 810 (9th Cir. 1990). See §§ **2.3141–2.3143.**

The Court's approach in *Hillsboro* is that if a later event would have prevented the taking of a tax deduction if it had occurred in the same year as did the deductible item, then the tax benefit rule will apply to the later event. However, if the later event occurs in a context in which nonrecognition provision prevents the recognition of income, a determination must be made as to which has priority—the nonrecognition provision or the tax benefit rule. *Hillsboro National Bank v. Commissioner, supra*, 460 U.S. at p. 386, fn. 20.

The decision in *Hillsboro* gave the tax benefit rule priority over a nonrecognition provision that then applied to a corporation's liquidating distributions. But the court's opinion states that some nonrecognition provisions will prevail over the tax benefit rule, and a determination must be made in each such case as to which is to prevail. *Ibid.* The Court gave no guidance as to the standards to be employed in making that determination.

§ **2.3140. Inconsistent Use of Expensed Goods.** In some circumstances, the amount paid for the purchase of goods to be used in a business can be deducted in the year in which the purchase price is paid or accrued rather than to be capitalized. In such cases, the item is sometimes referred to as an "expensed" item, and the deduction is sometimes referred to as an "expense." The assumption underlying the expensing of an item is that the item will be utilized in the taxpayer's business in a certain way. If subsequent events make clear that an expensed item will not be used in the assumed manner that underlay the granting of an expense deduction, will the tax benefit rule operate to require the taxpayer to include in income that amount of deduction previously allowed as an expense? In other words, does the change in use of an expensed asset constitute an event that is fundamentally inconsistent with the expense deduction that the taxpayer previously was allowed?

As previously noted, one of the two consolidated cases in the Supreme Court's *Hillsboro* decision was the *Bliss Dairy* case. *Bliss Dairy* involved a corporation that was in the dairy business and owned cattle for that purpose. The corporation purchased cattle feed and expensed the cost of that feed. An underlying assumption of permitting the corporation to expense the cost of the feed was that the feed would be consumed by the corporation's cattle over a period of time. Before all of the feed was eaten by the cattle, the corporation was liquidated and its assets, including the unused cattle feed, were distributed to the corporation's shareholders. Relying on the tax benefit rule, the Commissioner contended that the previously expensed cost of the unused cattle feed is included in the liquidating corporation's gross income since the liquidation erased the possibility that the remaining feed would be used by the corporation. The Supreme Court sustained the Commissioner's position and held that the liquidating distribution of the feed was fundamentally inconsistent with the corporation's previous deduction of the cost of that feed as an expense. As construed by the Supreme Court in *Hillsboro*, the tax benefit rule can be viewed as a device to recapture a deduction that was based on an assumption that certain events would occur if it subsequently becomes clear that neither the assumed events nor any comparable events will occur.

The *Hillsboro* decision did not include in the corporation's income the cost of the feed that was eaten by the cattle prior to the liquidation. If the cattle in *Bliss Dairy* had not been held for dairy purposes but rather had been held for sale, would the cost of the feed that was consumed by the unsold cattle also be subject to the tax benefit rule? Consider the discussion below of two Tax Court cases (and the Circuit Courts of Appeals decisions affirming those cases) that dealt with that issue.

§ 2.3141. Expensed Cost of Having Purchased Unsold Inventory. *Byrd, Transferee v. Commissioner*, § 2.3130, involved a corporation engaged in the plant nursery business. The corporation grew plants for sale. The corporation deducted (i.e., expensed) the cost of purchasing young plants which the corporation would grow to maturity and then sell. In the taxable year in question, the corporation was liquidated and distributed its unsold plants as liquidating distributions. The Commissioner contended that the expensing of the young plants was based on the assumption that the plants would be grown to maturity and then sold. The liquidating distribution of the unsold plants was fundamentally inconsistent with the allowance of an expense deduction for the purchase of the plants, and so the liquidating corporation must include in income the amount of its unwarranted deduction for the purchase of those plants. Relying on the *Hillsboro* doctrine, the Tax Court sustained the Commissioner, and the Fourth Circuit affirmed.

§ 2.3142. Expensed Costs of Maintaining and Cultivating Unsold Inventory. In *Byrd*, the Commissioner did not raise the question of whether the tax benefit rule should also have caused the recapture of the costs that the corporation incurred and deducted for materials and supplies used to nurture the unsold plants. The Tax Court did not address that issue in *Byrd*. In a subsequent decision in *Rojas*, discussed below, the dissenting eight judges of the Tax Court expressed their view that the tax benefit rule would apply to the expenses for nurturing the unsold plants that the corporation in *Byrd* had deducted prior to its liquidation. *Rojas v. Commissioner*, § **2.3130**. However, the majority of the Tax Court and the Ninth Circuit held that the tax benefit rule does not extend to those expenses. *Ibid.*

Rojas v. Commissioner, § **2.3130**, involved a corporation that was in the business of farming row crops. The corporation was liquidated and made liquidating distributions of harvested and unharvested crops. The Commissioner contended that, pursuant to the tax benefit rule, the previously deducted expenses that the corporation incurred for materials and services to cultivate those unsold crops (and for the seeds that grew into the crops) must be included in the corporation's income in the year of liquidation. The Commissioner relied on the *Hillsboro* doctrine. A majority of the Tax Court repudiated the Commissioner and held that the tax benefit rule did not apply. The court distinguished its earlier decision in *Byrd* on the ground that the expenses involved in *Byrd* were the expenses of purchasing the unsold plants, and so the purchased plants themselves were held by the corporation at the time of its liquidation. In *Rojas*, the materials and services for which the deductions were taken were consumed or used up by the time that the corporation liquidated. *Rojas* did not involve deductions for the cost of purchasing the unsold crops; it involved deductions for the cost of nurturing and growing those crops. [Note, however, that one of the previously deducted items was the cost of purchasing seeds, and the majority's failure to apply the tax benefit rule to that item might be inconsistent with *Byrd*'s application of the rule to the purchase of young plants.] Eight Tax Court judges dissented in *Rojas*. The dissenting judges would have applied the tax benefit rule.

In affirming the Tax Court's majority, the Ninth Circuit stressed that the position adopted by the Commissioner would require a recapture of a portion of general and administrative overhead and maintenance costs whenever an unfortunate event "frustrated the sale of any products which would otherwise have been completed and sold." The Ninth Circuit held that *Hillsboro* adopted a "limited rule," and the court refused to construe it as expansively as the Commissioner sought to do. *Rojas v. Commissioner*, 901 F.2d 810, 813, fn. 3 (9th Cir. 1990).

§ 2.3143. Expense Research Costs. TP, who was engaged in the business of manufacture and sale of consumer products, engaged in extensive research and experiments to develop patented and unpatented technology to be used in its business. In a subsequent year, TP discontinued a product line and sold some of the patented and unpatented technology that it had developed from its research and experiments. TP had deducted the costs of the research and experimental work under IRC § 174, which permits such costs to be expensed. In Rev. Rul. 85–186, the Service ruled that the sale of the technology was not fundamentally inconsistent with the purpose for allowing the costs of development to be expensed, and so the tax benefit rule does not apply.

The ruling does not discuss how the proceeds that TP received for the sale of the technology should be taxed. Since TP had no basis in the property, all of the proceeds (less expenses of sale) will be income to TP. How should that income be characterized—ordinary, capital gain, or section 1231 gain? The reasoning of the Service in Rev. Rul. 85–186 suggests that the *Arrowsmith* doctrine (**§ 12.4420**) should not apply. Also, the recapture rules of IRC § 1245 do not apply because no depreciation or amortization deductions were allowable, and IRC § 174 is not listed in IRC § 1245(a)(2)(C) as providing a deduction that is treated as an amortization deduction.

§ 2.3150.   Expenses Incurred in the Year in Which the Inconsistent Event Occurred. In *Rojas*, the expenses which the Commissioner sought to recapture through the tax benefit rule were incurred in the same taxable year that the liquidation took place. The taxpayers contended that the tax benefit rule does not apply unless the inconsistent event occurs in a subsequent taxable year. Of course, an alternative approach would be to deny the deduction to the corporation since inconsistent events occurred in the same year. The Tax Court held that regardless of whether the deduction is denied or is recaptured by the tax benefit rule, the principle to be applied is the tax benefit principle. *Rojas v. Commissioner*, *supra*, 90 T.C. at p. 1099. As already noted, the Tax Court and the Ninth Circuit held in *Rojas* that the tax benefit principle did not apply to the expenses incurred in that case, and so the courts allowed the corporation to deduct those expenses.

§ 2.3160.   Liquidation of a Corporation. *Hillsboro*, *Byrd*, and *Rojas* all involved liquidating distributions of a corporation. At the time that the facts of those cases arose, the general rule, subject to certain exceptions such as the tax benefit rule, was that a liquidating corporation did not recognize income because of distributing appreciated assets to its shareholders. The Tax Reform Act of 1986 changed that general rule and amended IRC § 336 to require a corporation (subject to a few exceptions) to recognize a gain equal to the amount of appreciation of any asset that it distributed in liquidation. As a consequence of that amendment, the application of the tax benefit rule to most liquidating distributions likely is moot. Regardless of the application of that rule, the liquidating corporation will recognize a gain in an amount equal to the difference between the fair market value of a distributed asset and the corporation's adjusted basis in that asset. As to liquidating distributions, the tax benefit rule will be significant only in the unlikely event that the tax benefit rule will be construed as requiring the recapture of previously deducted costs that exceed the fair market value of the distributed asset. See **§ 2.3120.**

§ 2.3200.   Exclusion Where No Tax Benefit. If a taxpayer deducted an item from his tax return but did not obtain a tax benefit

for the entire amount of the deduction, the recapture of all or part of
the item in a subsequent year will be excluded from the taxpayer's
gross income to the extent that he did not enjoy a tax benefit from
the prior year's deduction. IRC § 111. A tax benefit is obtained from
a deduction if it was useful in reducing the taxpayer's income tax for
the year he claimed the deduction or for some other year to which
the deduction was carried as a net operating loss or capital loss. If a
deduction caused a net operating loss carryover (or a capital loss
carryover) which, although unused, has not yet expired, it will be
treated as having provided the taxpayer with a tax benefit, and so the
recovery of that amount will not be excluded from the taxpayer's
gross income. IRC § 111(c). The provision in § 111 for an exclusion
from gross income can apply to virtually any recaptured item that
was previously deducted except for deductions allowed for depreciation, depletion, amortization, and amortizable bond premiums.

§ **2.3210.** **Illustration.** In Year One, X paid a property tax of
$8,000 to the Commonwealth of Virginia. In Year One, X had a
salary of $14,000 and had no other income. In his Year One tax
return, he claimed deductions of: $1,000 for state income tax,
$4,400 for interest payments on a home mortgage, $4,000 for
personal exemptions. In addition, X claimed an $8,000 deduction
for the payment of a property tax. Consequently, X's Year One
return showed a net loss of $3,400. This was not a "net operating
loss" which could be carried over to offset income in other years.
X elected to deduct his itemized deductions in that year since his
itemized deductions were greater in amount than his standard
deduction. In Year Four, X received a refund of $4,500 from the
Commonwealth of Virginia as a return of part of X's payment of
the Year One property tax which had been redetermined. Although X had deducted the entire $8,000 payment from his Year
One return, only $4,600 of it gave him a tax benefit (i.e., if X had
deducted only $4,600 of the real property tax, his tax bill for Year
One would have been $0, so X got no tax benefit from the
additional $3,400 of the property tax deduction). Therefore, under
IRC § 111, X will exclude $3,400 of the $4,500 refund he received
in Year Four from his gross income, and only $1,100 of the refund
is included in X's gross income.

§ **2.3220.** **Standard Deduction.** In lieu of deducting itemized
deductions (i.e., deductions other than exemption deductions and
other than those deductions listed in IRC § 62(a)) an individual
taxpayer can deduct a specified dollar amount referred to as the
"standard deduction." See § **3.3000.** Thus, an individual has a

minimum amount of deductions available regardless of the actual amount of his itemized deductions. Consequently, only the amount of an individual's itemized deductions that exceed his standard deduction can provide him with a tax benefit. See Rev. Rul. 93–75, and Rev. Rul. 92–91.

§ 2.3221. **Illustration.** In Year One, *Y*, who was unmarried and had no dependents, properly deducted $5,000 for a state income tax payment. *Y* paid that amount of tax under protest because he claimed that his correct state tax liability was only $450. The $5,000 payment qualified as an itemized deduction. *Y* had no additional itemized deductions for that year. *Y*'s only other deduction for that year was a personal exemption deduction of $2,000. See §§ **4.1000–4.1210.** The personal exemption deduction is not an itemized deduction. *Y*'s only gross income for that year was a salary of $23,000. *Y* had no nonitemized deductions. *Y*'s standard deduction in that year was $3,000. Since his itemized deductions ($5,000) were greater than his standard deduction allowance ($3,000), *Y* elected to deduct his itemized deductions in lieu of taking a standard deduction. For Year One, *Y* reported taxable income of $16,000 (i.e., $23,000 gross income minus $7,000 itemized deductions and personal exemption). [Note that *Y*'s adjusted gross income was too small to invoke the IRC § 68 limitation on itemized deductions. For the treatment of the recovery of an item the deduction of which had been reduced in a prior year because of IRC § 68, see Rev. Rul. 93–75.]

In Year Three, *Y*'s state income tax liability for Year One was redetermined to be only $800 instead of the $5,000 that *Y* paid in Year One. Accordingly, in Year Three, the state refunded $4,200 of *Y*'s Year One tax to him. Of that $4,200 refund, *Y* will exclude $2,200 from his gross income, and so only $2,000 will be included in his gross income. If *Y* had paid a state income tax of only $800 (the correct amount) in Year One, he would have used his $3,000 standard deduction in that year instead of deducting his itemized deductions. So, of the $5,000 state income tax deductions that he took in Year One, only $2,000 of that item reduced his tax liability since the remaining $3,000 was available to him as a standard deduction in any event. Accordingly, only the $2,000 of *Y*'s refund that constituted a recovery of a deduction from which *Y* derived a tax benefit is included in *Y*'s gross income.

Since Y elected to itemize his deduction for Year One under IRC § 63(e), will Y be permitted to reverse that election and qualify for the standard deduction? IRC § 63(e)(3) authorizes a taxpayer to change that election after the year in question in accordance with regulations. Treas. Reg. § 1.63–1 permits a taxpayer to change an election from utilizing itemized deductions to the standard deduction and vice versa simply by recomputing the taxable income for the year for which the original election was made. The regulation does not expressly state that such a change of election can be made even after the statute of limitations for the earlier year has expired; but Treas. Reg. 1.63–1(b) states that a change of election does not effect the limitations period for claiming a credit or refund—thereby separating the period for claiming a refund from the period for changing the election. In the view of the authors, it would be unduly harsh to require a taxpayer to abide by an election that was made for an amount of itemized deductions that effectively was reduced by the operation of the tax benefit rule. The failure to use the standard deduction is not comparable to the taxpayer's failing to claim a deduction that was available when the return was filed. Rev. Rul. 93–75 and Rev. Rul. 92–91 provide support for the view that, in applying IRC § 111, the standard deduction can be used to compute the amount of tax benefit that the taxpayer derived in the prior year.

§ **2.3300. Gratuitous Recovery.** The Commissioner has maintained that a taxpayer will recognize income on the recovery of a previously deducted item (for which a tax benefit was enjoyed) even though the recovery is obtained by a gift or other gratuitous transfer. In Rev. Rul. 76–316, the Commissioner ruled that an accrual method debtor was obliged to recognize gross income on the amount of interest it had previously accrued and deducted when the creditor gratuitously forgave the debt. The Tax Court and the Fifth Circuit, however, held that a taxpayer's gratuitous recovery of an item will not cause gross income to the taxpayer even though the taxpayer had previously deducted the item and obtained a tax benefit from that deduction. *Putoma Corp. v. Commissioner*, 66 T.C. 652 (1976), aff'd 601 F.2d 734 (5th Cir. 1979).

In *Hillsboro* [§ **2.3130**], the Supreme Court indicated its approval of the analysis used by the courts in *Putoma*. The Court noted that Congress has excluded gifts from the recapture rules of IRC §§ 1245 and 1250, and the Court extrapolated from these exceptions a possibility that similar exceptions apply to the tax benefit rule.

In *Putoma*, a 50 percent shareholder of a corporation had sold property to the corporation and had received in payment an interest-bearing note of the corporation. The corporation reported its income on the accrual method of accounting and thus deducted the interest owing on its note at each due date even when it failed to make payment. Note that IRC § 267 did not bar the taking of such deductions since the shareholder did not own more than 50 percent of the corporation's stock. After a few years, the shareholder forgave the corporation its obligation to pay the interest then in default. A majority of the Tax Court held in *Putoma* that the cancellation of the corporation's debt did not cause the corporation to recognize income under either the tax benefit rule or the discharge of debt rule because the cancellation was made gratuitously (i.e., as a contribution to the corporation's capital which is exempt from tax by IRC § 118). The Commissioner appealed only on the tax benefit rule issue, and a divided panel of the Fifth Circuit affirmed.

Congress responded to the *Putoma* decisions by amending IRC § 108 to require a corporation to recognize income in certain circumstances where a debt of the corporation is canceled as a contribution to capital [see **§ 2.1271**]. However, this statutory amendment deals only with contributions to capital. It seems unlikely that the spirit of the amendment will be extended to affect other types of gratuitous cancellations of debts such as gifts [see **§ 2.1280**]. Note, however, that when a debt canceled by a creditor would have been income to the creditor if it had been paid and when the debtor previously obtained a tax benefit from the debt by means of a tax deduction, a proper application of the transactional approach to a cancellation of indebtedness would not permit the transaction to go untaxed since the remaking of the transaction by novation would not put the parties in the same place they would have stood initially if the original agreement had conformed to the final result. In other words, the deduction enjoyed by the debtor prevents a reworking of the arrangement unless the deduction is taken into account. Perhaps the better way to treat this type of transaction is to tax the creditor on anticipatory assignment of income principles, but Congress chose a different route when it dealt with contributions to capital in IRC § 108(e)(6). See **§ 20.2300.**

§ 2.3400. Recovery of Erroneously Deducted Item. When a deduction for an expenditure was erroneously claimed and allowed and the taxpayer later recovers the expenditure after the statute of limitations for amending the return has expired, the Tax Court holds that the tax benefit rule does not apply. *Canelo v. Commissioner*, 53 T.C. 217 (1969), aff'd on another ground, 447 F.2d 484 (9th Cir. 1971). *Hughes and Luce L.L.P. v. Commissioner*, 68 TCM 1169 (1994), aff'd on another ground, 70 F.3d 16 (5th Cir. 1995); *Davoli v. Commissioner*, 68 TCM 104 (1994). The courts of appeals that have considered this issue have uniformly rejected the Tax Court's position and have held that the tax benefit rule applies without regard to whether the deduction in question was properly or erroneously taken. E.g., *Hughes and Luce, L.L.P. v. Commissioner*, 70 F.3d 16 (5th Cir. 1995); *Unvert v. Commissioner*, 656 F.2d 483 (9th Cir. 1981).

While the Tax Court continues to adhere to its position that the tax benefit rule does not apply directly when the deduction was erroneously taken, the court applies another doctrine that, in many cases, reaches the same result by invoking the tax benefit rule through a more indirect route. The Tax Court has adopted a "rule of consistency" (or sometimes called a rule of "quasi estoppel") that prevents a taxpayer from successfully asserting that a claimed deduction was erroneous. E.g., *Hughes and Luce, L.L.P. v. Commissioner*, 68 TCM 1169 (1994); and *Davoli v. Commissioner*, *supra*. If the taxpayer is estopped from claiming that the prior treatment was incorrect, then the tax benefit rule will apply to the subsequent event. Since the application of the rule of consistency has the same result to the taxpayer as a direct application of the tax benefit rule, courts of appeals have affirmed Tax Court decisions applying the duty of consistency rule; but they have done so on the ground that the tax benefit rule should be applied directly. *Hughes and Luce L.L.P. v. Commissioner*, 70 F.3d 16 (5th Cir. 1995); and *Unvert v. Commissioner*, 656 F.2d 483 (9th Cir. 1981).

The duty of consistency or quasi estoppel rule that the Tax Court applies is not as broad as a direct application of the tax benefit rule and so may not apply in some situations in which the tax benefit rule would. The duty of consistency arises (according to the Tax Court) when: (1) the taxpayer made a representation or reported an item in one year, (2) the Commissioner acquiesced in or relied on that representation or report, and (3) the taxpayer attempts to change that representation or treatment of the prior item in a later year after the statute of limitations for amending the earlier return has expired. *Hughes and Luce L.L.P. v. Commissioner*, *supra*. If all of the relevant facts were reported by the taxpayer in his return, and reported correctly, but the taxpayer came to the wrong conclusion as to the correct tax treatment of the item, the duty of consistency rule likely will not be applied by the Tax Court; whereas, a direct application of the tax benefit rule would cause the recognition of income to the taxpayer. For example, in *885 Investment Co. v. Commissioner*, 95 T.C. 156 (1990), the taxpayer erroneously claimed a deduction for a contribution to a charity subject to a reversionary interest, the possibility of occurrence of which was more than negligible. On the return of the property to the taxpayer after the statute of limitations had run, the court applied the tax benefit rule because an appeal would lie to the Ninth Circuit which had previously rejected the erroneous deduction exception to the tax benefit rule. The court followed the Ninth Circuit's view under the court's *Golsen* rule (see *Golsen v. Commissioner*, § **2.1492**). A reasonable inference from the court's opinion is that the court would not have applied the rule of consistency to that case if the court had not been constrained by the Ninth Circuit's position to follow the tax benefit rule. The question of the validity of the Tax Court's view that the tax benefit rule does not apply to erroneously taken deductions therefore is important, notwithstanding the court's adoption of the rule of consistency.

Whether the rule of consistency is needed or not, there is good justification for finding it valid. The purpose of having a statute of limitations for amending or challenging tax returns is to prevent the changing and litigation of the items reported on the return once the time period has run. Once that period has run, the parties should not be allowed to challenge the accuracy of items on the return even for purposes of determining the tax treatment of events occurring subsequently. If that is not so, the accuracy of the tax return could be litigated in a subsequent year even though that would run counter to the purpose of the statute of limitations.

§ 2.4000. ITEMS EXCLUDED FROM GROSS INCOME.

A number of provisions excluding items from gross income already have been referred to (e.g., the exclusion for life insurance proceeds [IRC § 101]; the Tax Benefit Recovery Exclusion [IRC § 111]). Some additional statutory exclusions are listed below.

§ 2.4100. Inherited Property.

Property received by bequest, inheritance or devise will be excluded from gross income and the recipient is not subject to tax. IRC § 102. In addition, property received as part of a bona fide settlement of a dispute over a decedent's will is excluded from gross income as if it were property received by inheritance. *Lyeth v. Hoey*, 305 U.S. 188 (1938).

In *Estate of Brandon v. Commissioner*, 828 F.2d 493 (8th Cir. 1987), reversing 86 T.C. 327 (1986), the Eighth Circuit held that for purposes of determining whether a transfer from a decedent's estate to the decedent's surviving spouse (pursuant to the spouse's claim under a state statute that was subsequently held to be invalid on constitutional grounds) qualified for the estate tax marital deduction, it was not sufficient for the Tax Court to find that the transfer was made pursuant to a bona fide settlement of a colorable claim; it was necessary for the court to determine whether the surviving spouse's claim for the property was valid. See the Tax Court's decision on remand in *Brandon v. Commissioner*, 91 T.C. 829 (1988). Regardless of whether the Eighth Circuit's decision is correct, the court rested its conclusions on the special requirements that must be satisfied to qualify a transfer for a marital deduction under the estate and gift tax laws; it appears that the Eighth Circuit's holding does not apply to income tax issues.

IRC § 102(c) includes in an employee's income a bequest that the employee received from an employer. There is reason to doubt whether the policy considerations that induced Congress to require that gifts to employees be included in income is applicable in the case of bequests. A putative donative transfer from an employer to an employee can serve business motives as well as, or even to the exclusion of, disinterested generosity. A "gift" to an employee can provide motivation for the employee to continue to expend great effort in his work. Such "gifts" can also provide incentive to other employees to work harder in anticipation of receiving like gifts. Even when an employee receives a gift on retirement, the knowledge of that gift may influence the work habits of other employees. Because of the difficulty of demonstrating the intent of the donor of such gifts, Congress adopted a flat rule that denies gift treatment to all such transfers. IRC § 102(c). This statute also denies income exclusion to bequests to employees. But, an employer is much less likely to have business motives for making a testamentary disposition than is the case for transfers made when the employer is still conducting the business.

In this connection, consider a bequest to a person who had worked as a domestic for the decedent for many years. It is possible to think of such a bequest as merely being additional consideration for services performed, but the likelihood that personal elements controlled the decision to make that bequest are quite strong. Nevertheless, the current version of IRC § 102(c) will tax the beneficiary of that bequest. However, if the employee was a relative of the decedent and was a natural object of the decedent's bounty, a bequest to the employee will not be included in the employee's income. See Prop. Reg. § 1.102–1(f)(2).

§ 2.4110. Income Earned from Inherited Property. While the inherited property itself will not be taxed, income attributable to an inherited asset will be included in gross income. IRC § 102(b). Thus, the income from a testamentary trust normally will be included in the recipient's gross income.

§ 2.4120. Decedent's Unrecognized Income. Income earned by a decedent during his life but not recognized until after his death will be treated as gross income to the ultimate recipient of the income. For example, when X was entitled to a commission from his employer at the time of his death, but the amount of the commission had not been computed at X's death and was not payable until a date one month after X's death, the commission will be included in the gross income of the person to whom it is paid. IRC § 691. Such income is called "income in respect of a decedent." Income in respect of a decedent (IRD) is discussed at **§ 21.0000**, et. seq.

§ 2.4130. Basis of Property Acquired from a Decedent. Under IRC § 1014(a), subject to a few exceptions, the basis of property that was included in a decedent's gross estate for tax purposes is equal to the fair market value of the property at the date of the decedent's death or, if the decedent's executor elects the alternate estate tax valuation method under IRC § 2032, the basis will equal the fair market value at the date that the property was valued for estate tax purposes under IRC § 2032. If the executor made an election for certain real properties to be valued for estate tax purposes pursuant to the special valuation provided by IRC § 2032A, the basis of such properties will be the same valuation figure as is used for estate tax purposes. IRC § 1014(a)(3). If decedent's executor elects under IRC § 2031(c) to reduce the value of land subject to a "qualified conservation easement," the basis of the excluded portion of the land will be the same basis that the decedent had in that portion. IRC § 1014(a)(4). However, in TAM 199933001, the Service held that a beneficiary was not estopped from claiming a higher basis in inherited property than the value agreed upon by the estate and the Service.

The basis rules of IRC § 1014 apply to property acquired by the taxpayer from a decedent in whose gross estate the property was included even if the taxpayer had acquired the property from the decedent as a gift made by the decedent during his life. (In such cases, the donee's original basis in the donated property would equal that of the donor, but the donee's basis would be changed under IRC § 1014 as of the date of the decedent's death.) If a donee sold, exchanged or otherwise disposed of the donated property prior to the donor's death, the death of the donor will not cause any adjustment to be made to the donee's basis, and the determination of the donee's gain or loss on such disposition is not altered. IRC § 1014(a).

IRC § 1014 basis rules apply to property in the hands of a person who either acquired that property from a decedent or "to whom the property passed from a decedent." IRC § 1014(a). The definition of property acquired from or passed from a decedent is set forth at IRC § 1014(b).

Under IRC § 1014(b)(1), property acquired by bequest, devise, or inheritance, or by the decedent's estate from the decedent, is treated as having passed from the decedent for purposes of IRC § 1014(a). So, foreign real property acquired by a U.S. citizen by inheritance from a nonresident alien gets a basis equal to the fair market value of the property at the decedent's death even though the property is not included in the gross estate of the decedent. Rev. Rul. 84–139.

§ 2.4131. Property Acquired by Decedent As a Gift Within One Year of Death.

If appreciated property (i.e., property whose value exceeds its basis) was acquired by a decedent by gift within a year prior to the decedent's death and if such property (or the proceeds from the sale of such property by the decedent's estate) pass to the person who originally gave the property to the decedent or to the spouse of such person, the basis of the property will equal the basis that the decedent had therein immediately prior to his death. IRC § 1014(e). The purpose of this provision is to prevent the step-up in basis of appreciated property by giving it to a dying person who bequeaths it back to the donor.

§ 2.4132. Income in Respect of a Decedent.

The basis rules for property which was included in a decedent's gross estate do *not* apply to a right to receive "income in respect of a decedent." IRC § 1014(c). For the meaning of "income in respect of a decedent," see §§ **2.4120** and **21.0000**, et seq. To the extent that an item constitutes the right to receive income in respect of a decedent, the transferee will have no basis therein.

§ 2.4133. Illustration. In Year One, *D* purchased an interest-bearing United States bond for $70. No interest is payable on the bond until it is surrendered by the holder. *D* did not elect to include the appreciation of the bond's value as interest income over the term of the bond, and so the interest income from the bond is deferred until the bond is surrendered. *D* died in Year Five, and his executor did not elect the alternate valuation date. At that time, the bond could be surrendered for $100, and the bond had a value of $100, which is the amount included in D's gross estate for estate tax purposes. Thirty dollars of that amount is the right to receive income in respect of a decedent so that *D*'s estate (and the transferee of the estate) will have a zero basis therein. The estate's basis in the bond (and the basis of the beneficiary to whom the bond is distributed from the estate) is $70—the fair market value (at the time of D's death) of that portion of the bond that does not constitute the right to receive income in respect of a decedent.

§ 2.4134. Penalty for Valuation Overstatement. The penalty imposed on a taxpayer for underpaying his tax as a consequence of overstating the value or adjusted basis of property (this is part of the "accuracy-related penalty") applies to a taxpayer whose basis in property that is determined under IRC § 1014 is overstated because the value of the property at the applicable valuation date was overstated. Rev. Rul. 85–75; see IRC § 6662(e). Under IRC § 6662(e), a valuation overstatement occurs if the value or adjusted basis reported is 200 percent or more of the amount determined to be the correct value or adjusted basis, and if the resulting underpayment of tax is at least $5,000 ($10,000 for most corporations). The penalty will not apply if the taxpayer had a reasonable basis for the reported valuation and the claim was made in good faith. IRC § 6664(c)(1). When the beneficiary of an estate adopted a basis equal to the value reported for the property on the decedent's estate tax return, the beneficiary's reliance on the estate tax return was not deemed a reasonable justification for the beneficiary's overstatement of value. Rev. Rul. 85–75.

§ 2.4135. Generation–Skipping Transfers. In addition to estate and gift taxes, the Code imposes a tax (called a "generation-skipping tax") on certain transfers that pass to a person who is more than one generation removed from the transferor. IRC § 2601 et seq. When that tax is imposed, the basis of the property that triggers the tax will be adjusted according to the terms of IRC § 2654(a). The basis adjustment for certain types of generation-skipping transfers is the same as that applied by § 1014(a) for inherited property; and the basis adjustment for other types of generation-skipping transfers is similar to the adjustments made for gift taxes on donated property [see § 2.4230]. *Ibid*.

§ 2.4140. Holding Period. When a taxpayer recognizes a gain or loss on the sale or exchange of an asset, the period of time in which the taxpayer is deemed to have held the asset prior to disposing of it may be significant. A taxpayer's "holding period" determines whether the gain or loss from the sale or exchange of a capital asset is a long-term or a short-term capital gain. In addition, a taxpayer's holding period will determine whether gain or loss from certain involuntary conversions or from the sale or exchange of certain property used in a trade or business will be characterized under IRC § 1231, and will determine the rate of tax on such gains. The tax consequences of having long-term or short-term capital gain or of having gain or loss under IRC § 1231 are discussed later in this work. See Chapters 18 and 19.

§ 2.4141. Holding Period of Inherited Property. Where the basis of property acquired from (or passing from) a decedent is determined under IRC § 1014, the transferee will be treated as having held the property for more than one year, which is a sufficient period of time to qualify gain or loss from the sale of such property as long-term capital gains or loss or as IRC § 1231 gain or loss. IRC § 1223(10). So, even if the transferee disposes of the property within one year of obtaining it, the transferee's gain or loss will either be long-term or IRC § 1231 gain or loss.

§ 2.4200. Taxation of Gifts. Property received as a gift (other than a gift from an employer to an employee) will be excluded from the donee's taxable income. IRC § 102. With one exception, a donor will not recognize gross income on making a gift for which no consideration is received and to which IRC § 102 applies. The donor's immunization from recognizing income is a common law rule; it is not provided by any statute. The one exception is that a donor will recognize a gain on his donation of appreciated property to a political organization. IRC § 84; see § **16.5000.** For an extensive examination of the tax treatment of gifts, see Douglas A. Kahn and Jeffrey H. Kahn, *"Gifts, Gafts and Gefts"–The Income Tax Definition And Treatment of Private and Charitable "Gifts" And A Principled Policy Justification for the Exclusion of Gifts from Income,* 78 Notre Dame L. Rev. 441 (2003).

§ 2.4210.   Examples.

§ **2.4211.   Illustration 1.** *X* made a gift to *Y* of stocks having a fair market value of $100,000. *Y* is not an employee of *X*. *Y* does not include the $100,000 in her gross income. *X* had a basis of $26,000 in the donated stocks. *X* does not recognize a gain on making the gift.

§ **2.4212.   Illustration 2.** *X* transferred stocks having a value of $100,000 to T in trust. *X* had a basis of $58,000 in the stocks. The income from the trust is payable to *Y* for life, and upon *Y*'s death the corpus is to be distributed to *Z*. Neither *Y* nor *Z* is an employee of *X*. Neither the trusts, *Y* nor *Z* will recognize any income because of *X*'s transfer of the stocks. IRC § 102. The income distributed from the trust to *Y* is not excluded from *Y*'s gross income by IRC § 102.

Unless the income is excluded by some other statutory provision (e.g., if part of the income was attributable to interest from municipal bonds and thus excluded under IRC § 103), the income will be included in *Y*'s gross income. IRC § 102(b). *X* did not recognize any income from making the transfer to the trustee. Upon *Y*'s death, the trust assets are distributed to *Z*, and *Z* does not recognize any income (except that if any trust income earned in the trust's last year is distributed to *Z* rather than to *Y*'s estate, that income will be taxed to *Z*).

§ **2.4220.   Definition of a Gift.** A gift for income tax purposes is a transfer without adequate consideration which is made out of the donor's "detached and disinterested generosity." If the donor is motivated to make the transfer "out of affection, respect, admiration, charity, or like impulses," the transfer is a gift, but if the donor makes the transfer as a consequence of "the constraining force of any moral or legal duty" or from "the incentive of anticipated benefit," the transfer will not qualify as a gift for income tax purposes. *Commissioner v. Duberstein*, 363 U.S. 278 (1960). For example, tips or gratuities given for services rendered will be included in the recipient's gross income. *Cracchiola v. Commissioner*, 643 F.2d 1383 (9th Cir. 1981).

Routinized and periodic cash "gifts" from members of a congregation to their pastor were deemed to be additional compensation to the pastor and so were included in his gross income. *Godwin v. United States*, 67 F.3d 149 (8th Cir. 1995). The Court decided the case on *Duberstein* principles and explicitly declined to decide whether IRC § 102(c) [See § **2.4224**] applies. The court questioned whether the members of the congregation (as contrasted to the church entity itself) were the pastor's employer, and it refrained from resolving that issue. *Ibid*, f.n. 5.

Olk v. United States, 536 F.2d 876 (9th Cir. 1976), raised the question of whether "tokes" (i.e., chips used in gambling houses) that were given by patrons of a gambling casino to a dealer, who was an employee of the casino, are includable in the dealer's gross income. In *Olk*, the Ninth Circuit accepted the district court's determination that "tokes were given to dealers as a result of impulsive generosity or superstition on the part of the players," that this was the dominant motive for such transfers, and that those determinations were findings of fact requiring the clearly erroneous standard of review. *Olk v. United States*, 536 F.2d at p. 878. However, the Ninth Circuit determined that the tokes were a form of wages received because of their regularity and because of the dealers' anticipation of such payments as a form of compensation. The Court's analysis suggests that the donor's intent is not the exclusive test for determining whether a transfer qualifies as a gift. Tokes to crap dealers have been treated as income in subsequent Tax Court cases. *Tomburello v. Commissioner*, 86 T.C. 540, 1986 WL 22105 (1986); *Catalono v. Commissioner*, 81 T.C. 8, 1983 WL 14910 (1983), aff'd without opinion sub. nom. *Kroll v. Commissioner*, 735 F.2d 1370 (9th Cir. 1984).

§ **2.4221. Mixed Motivations.** Where the motives of the donor are mixed, the gift being made partly out of generous affection and partly out of the anticipation of economic benefit, the tax consequences turn on the dominant purpose of the donor. *Commissioner v. Duberstein, supra*. In one case where the dominant motive of a number of donors could not be determined, the Tax Court apportioned the property transferred—treating most of it as income and part of it as an excludable gift. *Kralstein v. Commissioner*, 38 T.C. 810, 1962 WL 1156 (1962), Acq.

§ 2.4222. Term of Art. For tax purposes, "gift" is a term of art whose definition does not necessarily turn upon the common law concept of gift. Moreover, the term "gift" has a different meaning in the income tax laws than it has in the gift tax laws. *Farid-Es–Sultaneh v. Commissioner*, 160 F.2d 812 (2d Cir. 1947); and *United States v. Davis*, 370 U.S. 65 (1962).

§ 2.4223. Factual Issue. In general, the question of whether a transfer qualifies as a gift (and thus is excluded from gross income under IRC § 102) is treated as a factual issue. So, the determination of a trial court on this issue will be dispositive unless clearly erroneous. See *Commissioner v. Duberstein*, *supra*. However, in the Ninth Circuit's decision in *Olk v. United States*, 536 F.2d 876 (9th Cir. 1976), the court did not apply the clearly erroneous standard of review. The Ninth Circuit made a distinction between a finding of a transferor's dominant purpose for making a transfer and the conclusion that that purpose qualified the transfer as a gift. The former was said to be a factual issue and the latter, a conclusion of law which does not require the clearly erroneous standard of review. This aspect of the *Olk* case is questionable. The Second Circuit has held "Mixed questions of law and fact, entailing the application of a legal standard to a given factual pattern, are reviewed under the clearly erroneous standard." *Bausch & Lomb, Inc. v. Comm'r*, 933 F.2d 1084, 1088 (2nd Cir. 1991). See also *Merrill Lynch & Co. v. Comm'r*, 386 F.3d 464, 469 (2nd Cir. 2004).

§ 2.4224. Employee Gifts. A transfer made by or for an employer to or for the benefit of an employee will not qualify as a gift for income tax purposes. IRC § 102(c). In some circumstances, it may pose an issue as to whether a transferor is an employer of the transferee. See, e.g., *Goodwin v. United States*, **§ 2.4220**, where the court finessed the question of whether individual members of a congregation are the employers of their pastor.

For the treatment of bequests to an employee, see the last two paragraphs of **§ 2.4100.**

A Proposed Regulation states that an extraordinary transfer to a person who, although an employee, is a natural object of the transferor's bounty, will be a gift if the transferee can show that the transfer was not made because of the transferee's employment. Prop. Reg. § 1.102–1(f)(2). The Proposed Regulation further states that transfers between related parties will not be income to the transferee under IRC § 102(c) if attributable to their familial relationship and not to the employment. *Ibid.*

§ 2.4225.   Illustration 1. *H* transfers Blackacre to his son, *S. H* received no consideration for the transfer. Presumably, *H* made the transfer out of love and affection (i.e., detached and disinterested generosity), and consequently the value of the gift will be excluded from the gross income of *S*. The presumption may, of course, be rebutted if evidence of a contrary intent is available. Even if *S* worked for his father as an employee, despite the literal terms of IRC § 102(c), it is likely that Blackacre will be excluded from *S*'s gross income. Prop. Reg. § 1.102–1(f)(2).

§ 2.4226.   Illustration 2. *X* dies while employed by Win All, Inc. Win All pays $12,000 to *X*'s widow, *W*, as a measure of the esteem and affection in which *X* was held by the corporation. Win All had no legal obligation to make the payment. The payment will not be a gift to *W* regardless of whether the corporation made the payment out of detached and disinterested generosity. IRC § 102(c). Since *W* was never an employee of Win All, should IRC § 102(c) apply? It appears that it should since the reason for the transfer is the former employment of *X*. Of course, *X* is not a current employee of Win All. In the authors' view, IRC § 102(c) should apply to former employees as well as to current ones.

§ 2.4230.   Basis of Gifts. For purposes of determining a donee's gain on the donee's subsequent disposition of donated property, the donee's original basis in the donated property is equal to the basis that the donor had at the time of the transfer. IRC § 1015. For purposes of determining the donee's *loss* on a subsequent disposition of the donated property, the donee's original basis is the lesser of: (a) the donor's basis at the time of transfer or (b) the fair market value of the donated property on the date of transfer. IRC § 1015(a).

If a gift tax was paid on the transfer of an item (other than a gift to a spouse), the donee's basis in that item will be increased by the portion of such gift tax that is attributable to the appreciated element of the property (the excess of the value of the property over the donor's basis). IRC § 1015(d)(6). The basis can not be increased to a figure that is greater than the fair market value of the property at the time of the gift. The portion of the gift tax that is attributable to the appreciated element of the donated property is determined by multiplying the gift tax by a fraction—the numerator of which is equal to the appreciated element of the gift and the denominator of which is equal to the amount of the gift. Treas. Reg. § 1.1015–5(c)(5), Ex. (1). For this purpose, the amount of a gift is equal to the fair market value of the donated item less any annual exclusion and gift tax deductions (i.e., marital and charitable deductions) attributable thereto. Treas. Reg. § 1.1015–5(c)(2).

Note that, for *gift tax* purposes, a donor is granted an exclusion for a specified amount of gifts the donor made during a calendar year to an individual. Each individual donee who received gifts from the donor in that year will qualify for the exclusion, but only gifts that do not constitute future interests can qualify. Currently, the amount of the exclusion is $11,000 per donee per year [the amount of exclusion effectively is increased if a gift is treated as having been made equally by a husband and wife]. For purposes of applying the basis adjustment rules, when more than one gift is made to the same donee in a calendar year, the exclusion is applied to the gifts in the order of time that they were made. Treas. Reg. § 1.1015–5(c)(2).

If a donor made more than one taxable gift in a calendar year, the gift tax on the aggregate amount of taxable gifts made that year is allocated among the several taxable gifts according to the amount of each gift to determine the tax on each donated item. See, Treas. Reg. § 1.1015–5(c)(3)(5), Ex. (1). A "taxable gift" is defined in IRC § 2503.

A donor has the primary responsibility to pay any gift taxes, but donees are secondarily liable for such taxes if the donor fails to pay. The adjustment to basis that is provided for gift taxes paid on a gift applies regardless of whether the gift tax was paid by the donor or the donee. See Treas. Reg. § 1.1015–5(b)(2).

§ 2.4231. Illustration 1. *X* gave *Y* 100 shares of Win All, Inc. stock having a fair market value of $10,000. *X* had a basis of $8,000 in the stock, and no gift tax was paid on the gift. If *Y* subsequently sold the stock for $12,000, *Y* will realize a $4,000 gain on the sale. If Y sold the stock for $7,000, she will realize a $1,000 loss on the sale.

§ 2.4232.   Illustration 2. X gave Y 100 shares of Win All, Inc. stock having a fair market value of $8,000. X had a basis of $10,000 in the stock. No gift tax was paid on the gift. If Y subsequently sold the stock for $12,000, she will realize a $2,000 gain on the sale. If Y sold the stock for $7,000, Y's basis for purposes of computing loss will be $8,000 (the lower of X's basis or the fair market value of the gift at the date of transfer), and she will realize a $1,000 loss on the sale. Finally, if Y sold the stock for $9,000, Y will not realize a gain because her basis for computing gain was $10,000, and Y will not realize a loss because her basis for computing loss was $8,000. Consequently, Y will not realize either a gain or a loss.

§ 2.4233.   Illustration 3. X gave Y Blackacre which had a fair market value of $38,000. X had a basis of $20,000 in Blackacre, and X paid a gift tax of $3,000 on the transfer. No gift tax deductions or credits were allowable for the gift, but $11,000 of the gift is excluded by virtue of the annual exclusion. Y's basis in Blackacre is the same as X's basis ($20,000) plus two-thirds (the fraction of the value of the gift representing the appreciated element) of the $3,000 gift tax paid. Y's basis in Blackacre, therefore, is $22,000.

Note that the appreciated element of the gift is determined without regard to the $11,000 annual gift tax exclusion, but the exclusion is taken into account in determining the amount of the gift, which therefore is $27,000. Treas. Reg. § 1.1015–5(c)(5), Ex. (1). So, the applicable fraction is:

$$\frac{\$18,000 \text{ (appreciation)}}{\$27,000 \text{ (taxable gift)}} \quad \times \quad \$3,000 \text{ (gift tax)} = \$2,000 \text{ (added to basis)}$$

§ 2.4234.   Illustration 4. In Year One, M made a gift to F of Blackacre having a fair market value of $101,000, and M had a basis of $71,000 in Blackacre. In that same year, M made a gift to G of a painting having a fair market value of $71,000. M made no other gifts that year. M is allowed two $11,000 exclusions for gift tax purposes—one for the gift of Blackacre and one for the gift of the painting. M was not allowed any deductions for those gifts, and she was not entitled to any gift tax credits. The gift taxes for the two gifts totalled $55,500. M

reported making a $101,000 gift to F; and, after deducting the $11,000 exclusion, she reported a taxable gift of $90,000. M also reported a $71,000 gift to G; and, after deducting the $11,000 exclusion, she reported a taxable gift of $60,000. So, the total of M's taxable gifts for Year One was $150,000. The total gift tax on the two gifts was $55,500.

To determine F's basis in Blackacre, it is first necessary to determine the amount of the $55,500 gift tax that is attributable to the gift of that item. The transfer of Blackacre constituted a taxable gift of $90,000 (after deducting the $11,000 annual exclusion). The total amount of taxable gifts made by M in that year was $150,000. So, the gift of Blackacre constitutes 90,000/150,000 or 60% of the taxable gifts made by M that year. Treas. Reg. § 1.1015–5(c)(3). Therefore, 60% of the $55,500 gift tax incurred by M is attributable to Blackacre— i.e., $33,300 of gift tax is attributable to Blackacre.

But, not all of the $33,300 gift tax that is attributable to the gift of Blackacre can be added to F's basis in that property. Only the portion of the gift tax that is attributable to the appreciated element of Blackacre (in the hands of M) can be added to basis. The appreciated element of Blackacre at the time of the gift was $30,000—the value of Blackacre was $101,000 and M had a basis of $71,000 therein. But, the gift tax that M incurred is attributable to a gift of only $90,000 (the extra $11,000 of value was excluded from gift taxation by the annual exclusion). So, the fraction of the $33,300 gift tax that is attributable to the appreciated element of Blackacre is the percentage of the amount of taxable gift that was made because of the transfer of Blackacre that is represented by the amount of Blackacre's appreciation. Thus, the addition to Blackacre's basis is determined as follows:

$$\frac{\$30,000 \text{ (appreciation)}}{\$90,000 \text{ (taxable gift)}} \quad x \quad \$33,300 \text{ (gift tax for Blackacre)} =$$

$$\$11,100 \text{ (gift tax attributable to appreciation)}$$

F's basis in Blackacre equals the $71,000 basis that M had therein plus the $11,100 addition for the gift tax paid on account of the appreciated element of Blackacre. So, F obtains a basis of $82,100 in Blackacre. See Treas. Reg. § 1.1015–5(c)(5), Ex.(1).

§ 2.4240. Bargain Purchases. Where X (an individual) purchases property from Y and the consideration paid by X for the property is less than the property's value, the difference will constitute gross income to X in circumstances where the bargain price appears to be a disguised compensation to X (e.g., where Y is X's employer or where Y is a corporation of which X is a shareholder). In some cases (for example, where the two parties have a close familial relationship), the difference will constitute a gift from Y to X. If there is no relationship between X and Y that indicates that the bargain element was compensation or a gift to X, the bargain element has no tax consequence.

When the bargain element in a sale constitutes a gift to the purchaser, the donor-vendor will realize and recognize a gain only to the extent that the amount realized on the bargain sale exceeds the donor-vendor's basis in the property. Treas. Reg. § 1.1001–1(e)(1). In no circumstance, however, can a donor-vendor realize a loss on making a bargain sale. Even if the amount realized by a donor-vendor is less than his basis, and even if the fair market value of the transferred property also is less than the basis of the donor-vendor, no loss can be realized on a gift bargain sale transaction. Treas. Reg. § 1.1001–1(e).

§ 2.4241. Illustration 1. Intending to make a gift, H sells Blackacre to his son, S, for $20,000. Blackacre has a value of $50,000, and H had a basis of $65,000 therein. H will not realize a loss on the bargain sale. Treas. Reg. § 1.1001–1(e). S received a gift of $30,000 (less an $11,000 annual exclusion for gift tax purposes), which is the difference between the value of Blackacre ($50,000) and the purchase price paid by S ($20,000). No gift tax was paid on the gift. For the purpose of determining gain, S has a basis in Blackacre equal to the greater of the purchase price paid by S ($20,000) or the donor's basis ($65,000). Treas. Reg. § 1.1015–4. Thus, S will have a basis of $65,000 in Blackacre. For purposes of determining loss, S will have a basis of $50,000 in Blackacre since the value of the donated property ($50,000) was less than the donor's basis. If a gift tax had been paid on the transaction, S's basis for gain or loss would be unchanged since there was no appreciated element to the transferred property. See **§ 2.4230.**

§ 2.4242. Illustration 2. If S had paid $70,000 for Blackacre in Illustration 1 and if Blackacre had a value of $90,000 at the time of the "sale," H would recognize a $5,000 gain on the sale; S would receive a gift of $20,000 (less an $11,000 annual exclusion) and would have a basis of $70,000 in Blackacre for purposes of both gain and loss. If a gift tax had been paid on the transaction, S's basis would be increased by the amount of that tax since all of the tax would be attributable to an appreciated element of the property.

§ 2.4243. Basis in Bargain Purchase Situation. When the purchaser-donee of a bargain purchase arrangement (part-gift and part-sale) pays less than the donor-vendor's basis, the purchaser-donee will assume the basis of the donor. Note, however, that the purchaser-donee's basis for purposes of determining *loss* cannot exceed the fair market value of the property at the date of transfer. When the purchaser-donee of a bargain purchase pays more than the donor-vendor's basis, then the purchaser-donee's basis equals the consideration he paid. Note also that the purchaser-donee's basis will be increased (but not above fair market value) by any gift tax paid on the appreciated element of the gift.

§ 2.4244. Illustration. In Year One, M had a basis of $30,000 in Greenacre which had a value of $60,000. In that year, intending to make a gift, M sold Greenacre to his daughter, D, for $25,000. M did not realize a loss on that bargain sale. Treas. Reg. § 1.1001–1(e). M reported having made a gift of $35,000 to D, and M paid a gift tax of $7,000 on that gift. Because of gifts made to D earlier that year, no annual exclusion was allowable for the bargain element of the sale-gift of Greenacre. D's basis in Greenacre is equal to $30,000 (the donor's adjusted basis since that is greater than the $25,000 paid by D) plus the gift tax paid on the appreciated element of the donated property. At this writing, no regulation has yet been promulgated explaining how to determine the amount of gift tax paid on the appreciated element of property transferred pursuant to a part-gift, part-sale transaction. In the author's opinion, the gift tax adjustment likely will be determined in the following manner:

The $25,000 paid to M did not cause M to recognize a gain because M offset $25,000 of his adjusted basis in Greenacre against the amount so paid. M's remaining $5,000 of basis in Greenacre should be allocated to the part-gift portion of the transaction. Since M had a basis of $5,000 in the $35,000 portion of Greenacre which constituted a gift to D, the appreciated element of the donated property is $30,000. Thus, 30,-000/35,000 or 6/7 of the $7,000 gift tax is attributable to the appreciated element. D's basis in Greenacre is $30,000 plus $6,000 of the gift tax payment which provides D with a total basis of $36,000.

§ 2.4250.   Bargain Purchase in Commercial Setting. In a commercial setting, the employer will recognize gain or loss on the difference between the fair market value of the property (not the bargain price paid by the employee) and the employer's basis in the property. See *International Freighting Corp. v. Comm'r*, 135 F.2d 310 (2nd Cir. 1943).

§ 2.4260.   Political Contributions. In general, contributions made to a political organization as dues or fees or proceeds from a fund-raising event will not constitute gross income to the political organization to the extent that such amounts are segregated for a proper political purpose such as the attempt to influence the selection or election of an individual to a federal, state, or local office. IRC § 527. If a politician uses contributed funds for personal use, the funds will be income to him unless he can prove that the donor intended the contribution to be an unrestricted gift within the meaning of *Commissioner v. Duberstein*, [**§ 2.4220**]. Rev. Proc. 68–19; *United States v. Pisani*, 773 F.2d 397 (2d Cir. 1985). The presumption is that political contributions are not intended to be unrestricted gifts, and the taxpayer has the burden of proving otherwise. Rev. Proc. 68–19.

§ 2.4300.   Accident and Health Benefits.

§ 2.4310.   Medical Insurance. When a taxpayer purchases a medical or accident insurance policy with his own funds, any benefits (including reimbursements) received by him under the policy because of an accident or illness will generally be excluded from the taxpayer's gross income. IRC § 104(a)(3). The fact that the taxpayer had previously deducted the payment of premiums for the policy will not prevent exclusion from gross income. However, medical benefits will be included in the taxpayer's gross income if they are received as a reimbursement for medical expenses that had *previously been deducted* by the taxpayer. IRC § 104(a); Treas. Reg. § 1.213–1(g).

A practice arose of engaging in so-called "insurance speculation," in which multiple medical insurance policies are purchased by a taxpayer who hopes to become ill enough to require hospitalization so that he can reap a profit from collecting payments on all of his policies. Some hospitalization insurance plans provide for payments to the insured without regard to other coverage the insured may have, and so it is possible to earn a profit from an illness. If a taxpayer who engages in insurance speculation is legitimately hospitalized for an illness, current law does not cause any of the insurance proceeds collected by the taxpayer to be included in his income—i.e., there is no limitation in IRC § 104(a)(3) that restricts the exclusion from income to the amount of expenses actually incurred by the taxpayer. However, in such cases, a question can arise as to whether the taxpayer's illness was bona fide. It is possible for an insurance speculator to conspire with a doctor to receive a diagnosis of illness and an order for hospitalization; if that occurs, none of the insurance payments received by the taxpayer will be excluded from income.

In *Dodge v. Commissioner*, 96 T.C. 172, 1991 WL 15439 (1991), the taxpayer had collected from a number of medical insurance policies that had been purchased as part of an insurance speculation program. The Tax Court held that taxpayer can exclude the insurance proceeds only if the claims made on the policies were legitimate and only if the claims related to actual injuries or sickness of the taxpayer. The court further held that the taxpayer has the burden of proof on those issues, and that taxpayer's burden is not satisfied by the fact that the insurance companies honored the taxpayer's claims. The court held that the circumstantial evidence in that case raised serious questions concerning the legitimacy of taxpayer's "alleged injuries and sickness." The court found that the testimony given by taxpayer and by his doctor lacked credibility, and the court was not convinced that the insurance proceeds "related to actual, legitimate personal injuries or sickness." The court held that the insurance proceeds are included in taxpayer's gross income.

§ 2.4320. Disability Insurance. When a taxpayer purchases a disability insurance policy with his own funds, any disability benefits received by him under the policy are excluded from his gross income. IRC § 104(a)(3). Disability benefits received by a taxpayer are included in gross income if the premiums were paid by the employer. Rev. Rul. 73–155.

§ 2.4330. Workman's Compensation Benefits. Generally, any amount received by a taxpayer under a workman's compensation act as compensation for personal injuries or sickness will be excluded from gross income. IRC § 104(a)(1). However, to the extent that such compensation constitutes a reimbursement of medical expenses that were *previously deducted* by the taxpayer, the payments will be included in gross income.

§ 2.4340. Employee Health and Accident Plans. When an employer provides a health or accident plan for an employee, or when an employer pays the premiums on an accident or medical insurance policy covering an employee and the employee's family, the tax consequences from receiving benefits under that plan or policy depend upon the nature of the benefits.

§ 2.4341. Benefits Attributable to Employer. If an employee receives health or accident benefits directly from an employer or from a third party who was compensated by the employer to provide those benefits (and the compensation was not included in the employee's gross income), the exclusion (or inclusion) of the benefits in the employee's income is determined by the provisions of IRC § 105. See IRC §§ 104(a)(3), 105. Such benefits will be included in the employee's income unless certain statutory requirements are satisfied. IRC § 105(a). One of the requirements that must be met is that the benefit must either be paid pursuant to an insurance policy or the benefit must be payable under a plan that was previously adopted by the employer. IRC § 105(e). The plan can be informal; it need not be written nor need the employee have the right to enforce the benefits provided by the plan. However, if the employee has no enforceable right to the benefits, then (at the time of the employee's illness or injury) the employee must have been included within the plan and the employee must have had actual or constructive knowledge of the plan (i.e., information about the plan was reasonably available to the employee). Treas. Reg. § 1.105–5(a).

The requirement that the benefit be made pursuant either to insurance or to a plan is a *sine qua non* for excluding such a benefit from the employee's income; it is not sufficient. The additional requirements that must be met depend upon the nature of the benefit received. These additional requirements are described below at **§§ 2.4342** and **2.4343.** Note that a self-employed person will not be treated as an "employee" for purposes of IRC § 105, and so no health or accident benefits received by a self-employed person (e.g., a partner who is employed by his partnership) can be excluded from income under that section. IRC § 105(g). However, the benefits may be excluded by IRC § 104(a)(3), which is a more expansive provision than § 105.

§ 2.4342. Reimbursement or Payment of Medical Expenses. Amounts paid under an employee health or accident plan, or under an employer-paid insurance policy, will be excluded from the employee's gross income to the extent that such payments are made in satisfaction of, or to reimburse the employee for, undeducted medical care costs that were incurred by the employee for medical care of the employee, the employee's spouse or dependents. IRC § 105(b). For purposes of IRC § 105(b), the term "medical care costs" is defined in IRC § 213(d) and is not subject to the limitation on the deduction of medicines and drugs in IRC § 213(b). Therefore, reimbursements for the cost of nonprescription medicine and drugs are excluded from gross income, but dietary supplements (e.g., vitamins) are not. Rev. Rul. 2003–102. If such payments reimburse an employee for medical expenses that the employee had deducted on his income tax return for a prior year, the reimbursement will be included in the employee's gross income to the extent that the prior deductions were allowed to the employee. IRC § 105(b). For purposes of this provision, a "dependent" is defined a little more broadly than it is in IRC § 152. IRC § 105(b).

If the reimbursement or payment of medical expenses of a type described above are made from a plan of which the employer is a self-insurer, then such payments to or for the benefit of a so-called "highly compensated individual" are subject to certain anti-discrimination requirements. IRC § 105(h). A self-insured plan includes any plan for which reimbursement is not provided by an accident or health insurance policy. IRC § 105(h)(6). See Treas. Reg. § 1.105–11(b). A "highly compensated individual" is an individual who either: (1) is one of the five highest paid officers of the employer, (2) after applying certain stock attribution rules, owns more than 10% of the stock of a corporate employer, or (3) is among the highest paid 25% of all employees (other than shareholders included within (2) who are not covered by the plan). IRC § 105(h)(5).

A reimbursement or payment from a self-insured plan to a highly compensated individual will not be fully excluded from the employee's income unless the self-insured plan does not discriminate in favor of highly compensated individuals. If the self-insured plan does so discriminate, then the payments or reimbursements made to a highly compensated individual can be excluded only to the extent that they do not exceed the benefits that are payable under the plan for employees who are not highly compensated. In other words, to the extent that a highly compensated individual receives benefits in excess of what would be payable to a less compensated employee, the excess cannot be excluded. The manner in which the excess amount is determined is described in IRC § 105(h)(7) and in Treas. Reg. § 1.105–11(e). Note that a reimbursement for routine medical diagnostic procedures for the employee (not for his dependent) is not subject to the anti-discrimination requirements. Treas. Reg. § 1.105–11(g). Note also that if a plan is discriminatory, that will have no effect on the exclusion of benefits provided to or for the benefit of employees who are not highly compensated individuals. Finally, note that if medical reimbursements are paid under an insurance policy the premiums for which were paid by the employer, the anti-discrimination requirements are inapplicable since the payments or reimbursements are not made under a self-insured plan.

§ 2.4343. Payments Unrelated to Medical Expenses and to Absence from Work. Gross income does not include amounts received under an employee accident or health plan (or an employer paid insurance policy) to the extent that such amounts constitute compensation for permanent loss (or the loss of use) of a member or function of the body, or the permanent disfigurement of the employee, his spouse, or his dependent. IRC § 105(c). To qualify for this exclusion the compensation must be computed by reference to the injury sustained and without regard to the period of the employee's absence from work. The meaning of IRC § 105(c) is explored in *Watts v. United States*, 703 F.2d 346 (9th Cir. 1983). In *Watts*, the taxpayer was prevented from continuing work due to severe hypertension. In denying the taxpayer an exclusion, the court held that the taxpayer had to show a permanent loss (or loss of the use) of a member or function of the body or a permanent disfigurement for IRC § 105(c) to be applicable.

[For a similar view, note Rev. Rul. 63–181, where a lump sum disability payment to a taxpayer suffering from terminal cancer that totally and permanently disabled him was excluded from gross income under IRC § 105(c). The Commissioner ruled that the disability was so acute as to constitute a permanent loss (or loss of the use) of a member or function of the taxpayer's body.] The payment involved must not be determined by reference to the period of the employee's absence from work for IRC § 105(c) to apply. Note that the exclusion of payments described in this paragraph is *not* subject to any anti-discrimination requirements. The anti-discrimination requirements of IRC § 105(h) do not apply to IRC § 105(c).

§ 2.4344. **Premiums Paid for Medical Insurance.** Premiums paid by an employer for accident or health insurance to compensate employees for personal injuries or sickness are excluded from the gross income of the employees. IRC § 106. Similarly, amounts paid by an employer to fund an accident or health plan for employees is excluded from the employees' gross income. If the employees are to be taxed at all, it will be when they receive benefits from the plan; and, as shown above, even then the benefits may be excluded from an employee's gross income. There are no anti-discrimination requirements as a condition to the exclusion of insurance premiums. Treas. Reg. § 1.105–11(b)(2).

§ 2.4400. **Improvements Made by a Tenant on Lessor's Realty.**

§ 2.4410. **Construction of the Improvement: Rent Substitute.** Where land is leased to a tenant who constructs an improvement on the land, the lessor does not recognize gross income thereby unless the improvement is intended as a *rent substitute*. Factors which would indicate that the tenant's improvement was intended as a rent substitute are: (a) a leasehold term which is significantly shorter than the useful life of the improvement, or (b) a leasehold term subject to the power of the lessor to terminate the lease at his option. In most circumstances, the tenant's construction of an improvement will *not* constitute income to the lessor at the time of construction. See *M. E. Blatt Co. v. United States*, 305 U.S. 267 (1938).

§ 2.4420. **Termination of the Lease.** In *Helvering v. Bruun*, 309 U.S. 461 (1940), the Supreme Court held that upon termination of a lease, the lessor recognizes gross income in an amount equal to the fair market value of improvements previously constructed on the demised land by the tenant. Two years later, Congress adopted the antecedent of IRC § 109 which specifically excludes the value of such improvements from the lessor's gross income upon termination of the lease, *unless* the improvements represent a liquidation in kind of lease rentals. IRC § 109 is a nonrecognition provision (not a complete exclusion) because the gain realized by the lessor on termination of the lease is deferred. IRC § 1019 prohibits any adjustments to the lessor's basis as a consequence of income which is realized on termination of a lease but is not recognized because of IRC § 109. Thus, while the lessor does not recognize income on receiving the leasehold improvements, he does not acquire any basis for the improvements, and consequently his depreciation deductions for using the improvements in a trade or business will be lower than they would be if the improvements had been included in gross income. Similarly, if he sells the improvements, his gain will be increased or his loss decreased.

> § 2.4421. **Illustration.** In Year One, L leased land in which he had a basis of $40,000 to T for 50 years at an annual rental of $4,000. T erected a building on the land at a cost of $100,000. Upon the expiration or termination of the lease, all improvements on the land will become the property of L. Twenty years later, L terminated the lease because of T's failure to pay rent, and L thereby acquired the property including the building constructed by T. The lease could not be terminated under its terms for any reason other than nonpayment of rent. At the time of termination, the fair market value of the building was $60,000. L did not recognize any gain on the termination of the lease. IRC § 109. L's basis in the land is $40,000, and L's basis in the building is $0.

§ 2.4500. **Qualified Scholarships.** Prior to 1954, scholarships were treated as a type of gift and usually were excluded from gross income. Since 1954, they have not been treated as gifts and have been dealt with in several Code provisions (e.g. IRC §§ 117 and 127). The most important of these provisions is IRC § 117.

IRC § 117 excludes from gross income any amount received as a "qualified scholarship" by an individual who is a candidate for a degree at an "educational organization" as defined in IRC § 170(b)(1)(A)(ii). A "qualified scholarship" is an amount received by an individual as a scholarship or fellowship grant to the extent that the aggregate amounts of scholarship and fellowship grants received by that individual do not exceed the amount of that individual's "qualified tuition and related expenses," which term is explained at § 2.4510. There is no requirement that the funds received by a taxpayer be traced to the payment of tuition and related expenses or that the scholarship grant require the taxpayer to use the funds for that purpose. It is sufficient that the scholarship or grant does not prohibit such use or earmark the grant for a different use. Conference Report on the Tax Reform Act of 1986, H.Rept. 99–841, 99th Cong., 2d Sess. (1986), p. II–16. To the extent that the amount of scholarship or fellowship grant received by an individual exceeds his qualified tuition and related expenses, the excess is included in his gross income. Note that there are several credits and deductions allowed for qualified educational expenses.

§ 2.4510. Qualified Tuition and Related Expenses. Qualified tuition and related expenses are limited to: (a) tuition and fees required for the enrollment or attendance of a student at an educational organization, and (b) fees, books, supplies, and equipment required for a course of instruction at the educational organization. IRC § 117(b)(2). No exclusion is permitted for scholarship or grant money provided for room and board, allowances, or for expenses for travel, research, or clerical help. A recipient's recordkeeping requirements that must be satisfied to exclude a scholarship from the recipient's gross income are set forth in Prop. Reg. § 1.117–6(e). However, there is no requirement that the actual dollars of the grant be traced to a qualified expenditure. The taxpayer merely needs to show that money was spent on qualified tuition and related expenses. *Id*. The grant need not specify that it is for tuition, but if it specifies that it is for room and board or other nonexcludable items, then the taxpayer must include the amount in income. Prop. Reg. § 1.117–6(c)(1).

§ 2.4520. Degree Candidates. The exclusion under IRC § 117 applies only to degree candidates. A candidate for a degree includes students attending a primary or secondary school and students who are pursuing a degree at a college or a university. A candidate for a degree also includes a student, full or part-time, who receives a scholarship for study at an educational institution that: (a) provides an educational program that is acceptable for full credit towards a bachelor's or higher degree, or offers a program of training to prepare students for gainful employment in a recognized occupation; (b) is authorized under Federal or State law to provide such a program; and (c) is accredited by a nationally recognized accreditation agency. General Explanation of the Tax Reform Act of 1986, Prepared by the Staff of the Joint Committee on Taxation, 99th Cong., pp. 42–43 (1987); Prop. Reg. § 1.117–6(c)(4)(iii).

§ 2.4530.   Payments for Teaching, Research or Other Services. Recipients of scholarships or fellowship grants are not permitted to exclude from their gross income that portion of a scholarship or grant representing payment for teaching, research or other services provided by the student. IRC § 117(c). A student must include in gross income amounts received that represent payment for the student's services required as a condition of receiving the scholarship or grant. Also, a qualified tuition reduction (see § 2.4540) will be included in the student's gross income to the extent that the reduction constitutes a payment for the student's services. IRC § 117(c).

§ 2.4531.   Athletic and Other Extracurricular Activity Scholarships. If a scholarship is granted by an educational institution because of a student's participation in a varsity sport or in some other extracurricular activity (such as a musical, dramatic or journalistic activity), a question might be raised as to whether the scholarship is granted for services rendered or to be rendered to the grantor institution. To date, the Service has not even attempted to include such scholarships in a student's gross income. In several Tax Court cases involving the tax characterization of athletic scholarships, but not directly involving the taxability of such scholarships, the Commissioner agreed that an athletic scholarship can be excluded from the recipient's gross income under IRC § 117. See e.g., *Jolitz v. Commissioner*, 73 T.C. 732, 1980 WL 4541 (1980).

In Rev. Rul. 77–263, the Commissioner passed upon the exclusion from gross income of a one-year athletic scholarship that was awarded to an incoming freshman in anticipation of the student's participation in a varsity sport. The student was not required to participate in the sport; the scholarship could not be canceled in that year just because the student failed to participate in the sport; and the student was not required to undertake some other activity in lieu of participating in that sport. The Commissioner ruled that such an athletic scholarship is excluded from the student's gross income by IRC § 117. A negative inference of the Commissioner's emphasis on the facts that the scholarship could not be canceled during that year because of the student's nonperformance in the sport and that no alternative service is required is that an athletic scholarship will be taxable to a student if the educational institution can cancel the scholarship in the event that the student fails to participate in the sport (or, even worse, if the institution can cancel the scholarship if the student's effort or performance in the sport is deemed to be sub-par).

The Service has not expressly addressed the question of whether such a scholarship will qualify for exclusion from gross income if the institution has no obligation to renew it for each of the student's subsequent years at the institution and if the institution has not, in fact, renewed such scholarships when a student voluntarily chose not to continue to participate in the sport or if the student's performance was deemed to be inadequate. While some athletic scholarships might fail such a test if it were adopted, for political reasons it does not seem likely that the Service will seek to tax athletic scholarships at this time or in the foreseeable future.

Of course, like all other scholarships, athletic scholarships will be taxable to the extent that they exceed qualified tuition and related expenses.

§ 2.4540. Qualified Tuition Reduction. The amount of an individual's "qualified tuition reduction" is excluded from his gross income. IRC § 117(d). A "qualified tuition reduction" is the amount of reduction in tuition provided to an employee of an educational organization described in IRC § 170(b)(1)(A)(ii) for education below the graduate level at the employer's or other qualified educational institution. The exclusion of tuition reduction not only applies to tuition reductions for the education of employees but also applies to such reductions for the education of any person who is treated as an employee under IRC § 132(h) (such as an employee's spouse or dependent child).

In PLR 9431017, the Service addressed the question of whether IRC § 117(d) would apply if a university extended its tuition deduction polity to include a "domestic partner" of that employee. The Service ruled that IRC § 117(d) will apply only if the state in which the employee resides recognizes the relationship of the employee and the domestic partner as a valid marital relationship. In that latter circumstance, the domestic partner will qualify as a spouse under IRC § 132(h). Otherwise, IRC § 117(d) will not apply and any tuition reduction afforded the domestic partner will constitute gross income to the employee.

A qualified tuition reduction that is provided with respect to a highly compensated employee will not be excluded from income unless such reductions are available to employees on a basis that does not discriminate in favor of highly compensated employees. IRC § 117(d)(3). The term "highly compensated employee" is defined in IRC § 414(q).

As noted in § 2.4530, a qualified tuition reduction will be included in the student's gross income to the extent that the reduction represents payment for the student's services.

§ 2.4541. **Teaching and Research Assistants.** The rule limiting the "qualified tuition reduction" exclusion to education below the graduate level does not apply to a graduate student at a qualified educational institution who is engaged in teaching or research activities for that institution. IRC § 117(d)(4). Thus, qualified tuition reduction can be provided for graduate studies for such teaching and research assistants. However, to be excluded from a student's gross income, the reduction must comply with the requirement of IRC § 117(c) that it does not represent a payment for the student's teaching or research services.

The principal standard for determining whether a tuition reduction was granted as compensation for a student's services is whether the services are primarily for the grantor's benefit rather than in furtherance of the student's education. If the services performed by the student are primarily for the benefit of the grantor, an amount of tuition deduction that is equal to the value of those services will be included in the student's gross income. Prop. Reg. § 1.117–6(d)(2), (3). If the grantor also made a cash payment to the student for the student's services, that payment will be taken into account in determining the amount of tuition reduction that constitutes compensation to the student for such services. *Ibid.* Since, in some cases, only a portion of a tuition reduction will constitute compensation to a student for services, it is possible for a tuition reduction to be divided into two portions: a compensatory portion that is included in the student's gross income, and a noncompensatory portion that is excluded from the student's gross income if it qualifies under IRC § 117(d).

In determining the value of a student's services, the amount paid by the grantor for the same or similar services provided by comparable students who do not receive a tuition reduction or by non-student employees will be given considerable weight. Also, the amount paid by other educational organizations for similar services will be taken into account. Prop. Reg. § 1.117–6(d)(3).

§ 2.4550. Considered Earned Income. The amount of scholarships, and tuition reductions that are includable in a taxpayer's gross income are considered earned income for the purpose of the standard deduction rule applicable to a taxpayer who may be claimed as a dependent by another person. Conference Report on the Tax Reform Act of 1986, H.Rept. 99–841, 99th Cong., 2d Sess. (1986), p. II–17; Prop. Reg. § 1.117–6(h). For the limitations on a dependent's use of his standard deduction, see **§§ 3.3120–3.3123.** Consequently, where such amounts plus other earned income exceed the figure established by IRC § 63(c)(5)(A), a taxpayer will be permitted to use his basic standard deduction to the extent of his income from such amounts plus his other earned income.

§ 2.4560. Educational Assistance Program. IRC § 127 excludes from an employee's income certain educational assistance provided by the employer. The maximum amount of educational assistance that an employee can exclude in a calendar year is $5,250. The exclusion for educational assistance initially was scheduled to expire at the end of 1983, but Congress continually extended the termination date. Currently, the provision is scheduled to expire at the end of 2010.

To qualify for the exclusion, the educational assistance must be provided pursuant to a written plan of the employer. The plan must specify the classification of employees who qualify for benefits, and that classification must not discriminate in favor of highly compensated employees [the meaning of "highly compensated employee" is set forth at IRC § 414(q)]. IRC § 127(b). The plan can benefit certain self-employed persons, subject to the anti-discrimination provision noted above. IRC § 127(c)(2). Not more than 5% of the amount of such benefits can be paid or incurred during a year for individuals who are significant shareholders or owners of the employer (i.e., an individual who owns more than 5% of the stock or the capital and profits interest in the employer is a significant shareholder or owner of the employer). IRC § 127(b)(3). If the plan is to qualify, eligible employees cannot be given the choice of receiving other remuneration in lieu of the educational assistance, and reasonable notification as to eligibility and terms of the program must be provided to all eligible employees. IRC § 127(b)(4), (6).

The benefits that can be excluded from income under this provision are: (1) the payment by the employer of the employee's educational expenses, including (but not limited to) tuition, fees, books, supplies, and equipment, and (2) the provision by the employer of courses of instruction for the employee (including books, supplies and equipment). The statute does not permit the exclusion of certain expenses; for example, the statute does not exclude from income the payment or provision of: meals, lodging and transportation, and the payment or provision of tools or supplies which can be retained by the employee after the instruction is completed. Also, the statute does not exclude payments or provisions made with respect to education involving sports, games or hobbies. IRC § 127(c)(1).

To the extent that educational assistance does not qualify for exclusion under IRC § 127, it will be included in the employee's gross income unless it can qualify for exclusion as a fringe benefit under IRC § 132. One fringe benefit category that can apply to educational assistance in certain circumstances is the "working condition fringe." IRC § 132(j)(8). See § **2.1624**, *supra*.

§ 2.4570.   Tax Policy Justification for Scholarship Exclusion. Congress has not made clear its rationale for excluding certain scholarships from gross income. Since educational expenses generally are not deductible (except for certain educational expenses that qualify as business expenses, see §§ **10.4100– 10.4270**), there is even greater reason to question why certain scholarships are excluded. A variety of justifications have been suggested by commentators, and we will consider a few of those.

Many educational institutions (especially state schools) do not charge an amount for tuition that equals the value of the education that is purchased thereby. The tuition cost effectively is subsidized to the extent that it is less than market value. There has never even been a suggestion that a student should include in income the amount of subsidy he receives. It would be very difficult to measure the amount of that subsidy, but administrative difficulty is only one of the reasons that the bargain element in tuition is not taxed. For example, state universities typically charge nonresident students a higher tuition than they charge their resident students, and so the latter could be said to be subsidized at least to the extent of that difference in cost. Yet, resident students are not taxed on that subsidy. One reason for this may be a federal policy to encourage education. Another reason may be that a state's provision of goods or services in kind typically has not been taxed to the recipient. For example, the receipt of free secondary education and of police and fire protection services are not taxed. A state's subsidization of university education can be placed in the same category.

Given that the subsidy element in tuition charges is not taxable, the suggestion has been made that tuition reductions through scholarships also should be excluded. This is put on grounds of equity—that is, if the recipients of one type of educational subsidy are not taxed, the recipients of similar types of subsidies should be treated the same. While equity considerations are relevant, one should be cautious about the amount of weight to be accorded them. Often, the wish to provide comparable tax treatment for similar, but nevertheless different, items is not a sufficient reason by itself to warrant extending a favorable tax treatment. Assuming that a tuition reduction by a state school should be treated as a nontaxable grant of services by a state, there must still be a reason to extend that treatment to scholarships granted by private schools and by third parties.

One of several justifications offered by Professor Dodge is that tuition reductions (and a scholarship granted by an educational institution can be viewed as a tuition reduction to the extent that the amount of the scholarship does not exceed the student's tuition) is a type of price discrimination, and as such is not taxable. See, Dodge, *Scholarships Under the Income Tax*, 46 The Tax Lawyer 697 (1993). Professor Dodge points out that when a taxpayer purchases an airline ticket at a discount because of a special offering, he is not taxed on the difference between the special price that he obtained and the higher price paid by passengers who did not qualify for that bargain. He suggests that the price differential in tuition (even when that is accomplished through scholarships provided by the educational institution) should also be treated as a nontaxable bargain purchase. But, there are important differences between an airline's price discrimination and a school's tuition reduction through the grant of scholarships. The former is provided by a carrier to increase its revenue by selling seats that otherwise would remain empty. That has not been the reason for providing scholarships. Typically, they are not designed to sell places in the school's student body that would go unclaimed if sold at the usual price. The price set for the airline passenger is set for revenue maximization purposes, and so the usual rule of treating an arms' length exchange as one of equal values should and does apply. The reason for providing a scholarship (and so a lower tuition cost) is not because business judgment dictates that price as the best that can be obtained; rather, the scholarship is provided as a means to accomplish some educational or political goal of the institution. Consequently, since the price of the student's education has been set to accomplish a goal of the institution rather than at the education's market value, the presumption of equality that adheres to an arms' length bargain is inapplicable.

For example, if the 1,000,000th customer to purchase a ticket on an airline was given a special bargain price as part of a goodwill campaign, the bargain element should be taxable income. A scholarship granted to a student is more like the latter circumstance than a commercial price discrimination.

It is tempting to treat a scholarship as similar or analogous to a gift, but the reasons for excluding gifts from a donee's gross income do not apply to scholarships, regardless of whether the grantor of the scholarship is the educational institution itself or some other entity. It is unlikely that the educational institution at which the student is attending has the requisite "detached and disinterested generosity" for granting the student a scholarship. When the scholarship is provided by a third party, the funds from which the scholarship is paid usually will have been obtained by a contribution for which a tax deduction was allowed, and so the justification for excluding a gift from income is not applicable to scholarship grants.

The best (and perhaps the only viable) justification for excluding certain scholarships from income may be the previously mentioned policy not to tax services received in kind from a state. While that policy apparently does not apply when the educational institution in question is not a state school, the same reasoning might be applicable there as well. A private college or university typically is a non-profit organization that serves a governmental function. The provision of services in kind (i.e., education) by such an entity is analogous to the provision of services directly by a governmental body. While there may be flaws in that analogy, when it is combined with the equitable consideration of giving the same tax treatment for subsidies to students that are granted by private, non-profit educational entities as is applied to subsidies that are granted by state institutions, and with the federal goal of encouraging education, the combined considerations may be sufficient to justify the exclusion. The same or similar considerations apply when the scholarship is granted by a third party, especially if the third party is a tax-exempt, non-profit organization.

§ 2.4600. General Welfare Fund Distributions. Amounts received as distribution from a general welfare fund (typically a distribution made by a federal or state agency pursuant to a statute to provide help for needy persons in the interest of the general welfare) do not constitute gross income to the recipient. See Rev. Rul. 73–87, and Rev. Rul. 63–136. But, welfare funds obtained by fraud are included in the recipient's gross income, Rev. Rul. 78–53.

§ 2.4610. Illustration 1. *J* received welfare payments from the State of *Y* to support himself and his three children. The payments are excluded from *J*'s gross income. Rev. Rul. 57–102. The exclusion will apply even if *J* were required to perform some work under a state welfare work relief program as a condition to receiving the payments. Rev. Rul. 71–425.

§ 2.4620. Illustration 2. *K* purchased a house that is included as an historic building in the National Register of Historic Places. *K* plans to use the building as an office at which *K* will conduct his professional work. *K* applied for and received a grant from the state to restore the house. The grant was made pursuant to section 101 of the National Historic Preservation Act of 1966. In Rev. Rul. 80–330, the Commissioner held that the grant received by *K* is included in *K*'s gross income. The Commissioner stated that the purpose of the grant was to preserve historically significant buildings as contrasted to a grant based on need which is made under a social benefit program to promote the general welfare.

§ 2.4630. Social Security Benefits. Prior to 1984, the entire amount of payments received as Federal social security benefits were excluded from gross income. From 1984 to 1993, inclusive, a portion of social security benefits, which could not exceed 50% of the benefits received, was included in income if the taxpayer's modified income exceeded a specified figure. As a consequence of an amendment adopted as part of the Omnibus Budget Reconciliation Act of 1993, the amount of an individual's social security benefits that is included in gross income is now determined under a two-tier structure. The maximum amount of social security benefits that can be included in gross income is 85% of the benefits received in a taxable year, but the percentage can be smaller than that figure and can even be zero.

§ 2.4631. **Definition of "Social Security Benefit."** For this purpose, a "social security benefit" refers to a monthly benefit received under Title II of the Social Security Act (which includes old age and survivors benefits) and to certain railroad retirement benefits.

§ 2.4632. **Benefits From Another Country.** If a taxpayer receives benefits under a social security program of a foreign country, all of those benefits are included in the taxpayer's gross income. Rev. Rul. 66–34. No portion of such benefits is excluded from gross income. The typical circumstance in which this occurs is when a citizen or former citizen of a foreign country becomes a resident of the United States and retires in this country.

§ 2.4640. **Unemployment Benefits.** A taxpayer's unemployment benefits are included in his gross income. IRC § 85; § 2.2700.

§ 2.4700. **Rental Value of Parsonage.** The rental value of a home provided to a minister or a rental allowance actually used by the minister to rent a home, is excluded from the minister's gross income. IRC § 107.

§ 2.5000. **RECEIPT OF WINDFALLS AND PENALTIES.** In *Eisner v. Macomber*, 252 U.S. 180 (1920), The Supreme Court quoted from an earlier case that "income may be defined as the gain derived from capital, from labor, or from both combined." Since the receipt of a windfall or a penalty is not derived from capital or from labor, prior to 1955 several courts held that such receipts were outside the scope of the income tax. That view was repudiated and laid to rest by the Supreme Court in *Commissioner v. Glenshaw Glass Co.*, 348 U.S. 426 (1955) where punitive damages were held to be included in gross income. In *Glenshaw*, the Court stated that the definition of income employed in *Eisner v. Macomber* was useful to the analysis of that case but "was not meant to provide a touchstone to all future gross income questions."

CHAPTER THREE

ADJUSTED GROSS INCOME AND THE STANDARD DEDUCTION

§ 3.0000. ROLE OF AGI AND STANDARD DEDUCTION IN DETERMINING TAXABLE INCOME. Taxable income is defined in § 63 as either (1) gross income minus allowable deductions other than the standard deduction or (2) as "adjusted gross income" minus the standard deduction and the deduction for personal and dependent exemptions. The manner in which taxable income is computed is described at § **1.6310.**

§ 3.1000. CONCEPT OF ADJUSTED GROSS INCOME. Adjusted gross income (AGI) is the gross income of an individual less certain specified deductions, primarily those listed in IRC § 62(a). There are only a few deductions that are not listed in IRC § 62(a) that are allowed in determining AGI. E.g., IRC §§ 71(f)(1)(B), 164(f), and 165(h)(4)(A). The deductions taken into account in determining AGI are called "nonitemized deductions" or more commonly "above the line deductions." All other deductions, except for the personal and dependent exemption deductions, are called "itemized deductions." Itemized deductions are sometimes referred to as "below the line deductions."

The AGI concept applies only to individuals and estates and trusts. AGI is applied to estates and trusts only for very special and limited purposes. IRC § 67(e). Hereafter in this book, the term is used exclusively as it applies to individuals.

The legislative history to the predecessor of § 62 states that the purpose of the adjusted gross income concept is to create a standard of measurement of income that will provide figures that are as nearly equivalent as is practicable when the standard is applied to different types of taxpayers who derive their income from different sources. S. Rep. No. 78–885, at 24–25 (1944). The Ways and Means Committee, discussing the adoption of the concept, said that "adjusted gross income means gross income less business deductions." Although that purpose is frequently cited by the Service in ruling on whether specific items are to be taken into account in determining AGI, it has very little predictive value. Many items are included in or excluded from the determination of AGI for political or financial reasons, and their treatment does not conform to the goal of having a standardized measurement of economic income. For example, subject to a few minor exceptions, the unreimbursed business expenses of an employee (other than moving expenses) cannot be deducted in determining the employee's AGI; even though, when the same expenses are incurred by a self-employed individual, they are deducted in determining AGI. The determination of whether an individual is an employee for tax purposes rests on the common law of agency. *Alford v. United States*, 116 F.3d 334 (8th Cir. 1997).

§ 3.1100. Function of AGI. An individual's adjusted gross income (AGI) serves a number of functions. One function is that AGI determines the deductions that are available to a taxpayer who utilizes the standard deduction. **§ 3.2000.** Another is that AGI serves as an element of the formulas that apply to determine the amount of certain expenditures or payments that are deductible. For example, the maximum amount of charitable contributions that an individual may deduct in a taxable year is a percentage of the individual's contribution base which is determined by reference to his AGI; an individual's deductions for medical care in a taxable year are limited to the excess of his medical care expenses over seven and one-half percent of the individual's AGI; and certain itemized deductions (including the unreimbursed business expenses of an employee) are characterized as "miscellaneous itemized deductions" and are deductible only to the extent that the aggregate of such deductions exceeds 2% of the taxpayer's AGI. IRC §§ 170(b)(1), 213(a), 67. See *McKay v. Commissioner*, 102 T.C. 465, 493, 1994 WL 97734 (1994) (holding that the unreimbursed business expenses of an employee are subject to the 2% of AGI floor). If the alternative minimum tax (See Chapter 15) applies to a TP, no deduction is allowable for the TP's miscellaneous itemized deductions. IRC § 56(b)(1)(A)(i).

§ 3.1110. Miscellaneous Itemized Deductions. "Itemized deductions" are deductions (other than the personal and dependent exemption deductions) that are not taken into account in determining AGI. **§ 3.1000** In this book, the deductions that are taken into account in determining AGI are called nonitemized deductions. Those itemized deductions that are not listed in IRC § 67(b) constitute a subcategory of itemized deductions that are called "miscellaneous itemized deductions." Miscellaneous itemized deductions are deductible only to the extent that the aggregate of those deductions in a taxable year exceeds 2% of the TP's AGI. If the alternative minimum tax applies to a TP, no deduction is allowable for the TP's miscellaneous itemized deductions. IRC § 56(b)(1)(A)(i).

§ 3.1120. Overall Limitation on Itemized Deductions. In addition to the floor imposed on "miscellaneous itemized deductions," if an individual's AGI for a taxable year exceeds an "applicable amount"—i.e., for the year 2005, the applicable amount is $145,950 ($72,975 for a married taxpayer who files a separate return) adjusted upward each year for any increase in the cost-of-living—then that individual's itemized deductions for that year are reduced by the *lesser* of: (1) 3% of the excess of the individual's AGI over the applicable amount, or (2) 80% of such itemized deductions that are otherwise allowable. IRC § 68; Rev. Proc. 2004–71 (Sec. 3.11). The IRC § 68 limitation on the amount of an individual's allowable itemized deduction is referred to as the "overall limitation on itemized deduction." IRC § 68 does not apply to the following four deductions: medical expenses, investment interest (as defined in IRC § 163(d)), personal casualty and theft losses, and wagering losses. IRC. § 68(c).

The overall limitation of IRC § 68 is scheduled to be phased out beginning in the year 2006. The limitation will not apply to the year 2010. However, the limitation of IRC § 68 is scheduled to spring back in full force in the year 2011. IRC § 68(f), (g), and section 901, Pub. Law 107–16 (the sunset provision).

§ 3.1200. IRC § 62 Deductions. AGI equals gross income minus the deductions listed in IRC § 62(a) plus a few other deductions. See **§ 3.1000.** The deductions taken into account in determining AGI, most of which are listed in IRC § 62(a), are referred to in this book as "nonitemized deductions." Other than the exemption deductions, deductible items that are not deductible in determining AGI are referred to as "itemized deductions." A number of the deductions listed in IRC § 62(a) (all of which are nonitemized deductions) are business expense deductions, but most of the unreimbursed business expenses of an employee (other than moving expenses) are excluded and so must be itemized. The business expenses of an employee qualify as nonitemized deductions to the extent that they are reimbursed by the taxpayer's employer; thus, the income from the reimbursement and the deduction for the business expense will be a wash. A few designated employee expenses incurred in one of several specified businesses are nonitemized deductions. IRC § 62(a)(2)(B)–(E). Also, the deduction allowed by IRC § 217 for unreimbursed moving expenses (the expense of moving to a new locality because of a change in the taxpayer's place of work) is a nonitemized deduction regardless of whether the taxpayer is an employee or self-employed. IRC § 62(a)(15). A few nonbusiness expense deductions qualify as nonitemized deductions. For example, deductible losses from the sale or exchange of property, and the deduction allowed under IRC § 215 for alimony payments are nonitemized deductions. Deductions are discussed at length later in this work. Note that IRC § 62(a) does not make an expenditure deductible; rather, IRC § 62(a) lists those items which are deductible under other Code provisions that are to be deducted from gross income in determining an individual's AGI.

An expense that falls within a specific statutory category for deduction may also constitute a business expense. For example, state taxes on realty are deductible under IRC § 164 as a state and local real property tax. But, if the realty is used in the taxpayer's business, the state tax will also constitute an expense of conducting that business and so is deductible under IRC § 162. While a deduction for taxes under IRC § 164 is an itemized deduction, a business expense deduction is a nonitemized deduction unless the business is that of being an employee. In cases where two Code provisions overlap, the courts and the Service have permitted taxpayers to use the more favorable provision. *McNutt-Boyce Co. v. Commissioner*, 38 T.C. 462, 1962 WL 1124 (1962), aff'd per curiam, 324 F.2d 956 (5th Cir. 1963), Acq.; Rev. Rul. 92–29. See also, Temp. Reg. § 1.62–1T(d). Therefore, the payment or accrual of a state tax on realty that is used in a taxpayer's self-employed business is treated as a nonitemized deduction. Temp. Reg. § 1.62–1T(d). Other business-related items are treated similarly if they are directly connected with the conduct of a business (other than an employee's business).

The Service's position is that for an expense to qualify as a nonitemized business expense deduction, it must be directly, and not merely remotely, connected with the conduct of a trade or business (other than an employee's business). Temp. Reg. § 1.62–1T(d). The tax must be imposed on the business itself as contrasted to a tax on an individual who owns and conducts the business. To illustrate how the Service distinguishes a "direct" connection with a business from a "remote" one, the temporary regulation asserts that while state property taxes imposed on realty used in a self-employed business are nonitemized deductions, state income taxes imposed on an individual's self-employed business income are itemized deductions. *Ibid.* The Service's position that the state income tax on an individual's business income is an itemized deduction was sustained by the Tax Court and the Fourth Circuit in *Tanner v. Commissioner*, 45 T.C. 145, 1965 WL 1300 (1965), aff'd per curiam, 363 F.2d 36 (4th Cir. 1966).

§ 3.2000. STANDARD DEDUCTION.

In lieu of taking itemized deductions, an individual taxpayer can deduct a specified dollar amount which is referred to as the "standard deduction." Thus, where an individual taxpayer elects to utilize the standard deduction, the taxpayer will deduct his nonitemized deductions from his gross income in order to arrive at his AGI, and the taxpayer will then deduct his standard deduction from his AGI. In addition, an individual taxpayer who utilizes the standard deduction can deduct the amount (if any) of deductions permitted for the exemptions available to the taxpayer. See Chapter Four. The nonitemized deductions and the exemption deductions are available to an individual regardless of whether he utilizes the standard deduction, but itemized deductions can be taken only if the taxpayer does not use the standard deduction. If a taxpayer does not utilize the standard deduction or is not permitted to use a standard deduction, the taxpayer is said to have "itemized" his deductions—i.e., the taxpayer will deduct his itemized deductions in lieu of the standard deduction.

§ 3.2100. Qualification for the Standard Deduction.

The standard deduction is available only to individuals. There is no standard deduction for corporate taxpayers or for trusts or estates. Not all individuals are permitted to utilize a standard deduction.

§ 3.2110. Individuals Who Are Barred from Using the Standard Deduction.

Certain individuals are not eligible to use the standard deduction. IRC § 63(c)(6). For example, a nonresident alien is not granted a standard deduction. If a married couple files separate returns and if one spouse elects to "itemize" deductions [see § 3.2000], the other spouse is barred from using a standard deduction. IRC § 63(c)(6)(A).

§ 3.2120. Dependent's Use of Standard Deduction.

If an individual taxpayer qualifies as a dependent exemption deduction for another person, the basic standard deduction [See § 3.2210] allowable to that taxpayer *cannot exceed* the taxpayer's earned income plus a specified amount (for 2005, the amount is $250) or a specified dollar amount (for 2005, the amount is $800), whichever is greater. IRC § 63(c)(5); Rev. Proc. 2004–71 (Sec. 3.10). Thus, in 2005, a dependent's basic standard deduction is available to reduce $250 of income plus the amount of income earned by that dependent from employment and from the active conduct of a trade or business. Alternatively, the dependent can deduct $800.

These figures are increased annually to reflect changes in the cost of living. IRC § 63(c)(4).

§ **3.2121.　Illustration 1.** B is an unmarried dependent child of P who is entitled to a dependent exemption deduction for B. In 2005, B had interest income (which is unearned income) of $400. B had no other income that year. B is not allowed a personal exemption deduction. IRC § 151(d)(2). B is allowed a basic standard deduction of $800, and so B has $0 of taxable income in that year. IRC § 63(c)(5); Rev. Proc 2004–71.

§ **3.2122.　Illustration 2.** The same facts as those stated in § **3.2121** except that B also had $500 of earned income in 2005. B's basic standard deduction is limited to $800, and so B's taxable income for 2005 is $100. As noted in §§ **20.4221– 20.4222, 20.4310**, even if B is under the age of 14, B will be taxed on that $100 at rates applicable to B himself without regard to the marginal tax bracket of B's parents.

§ **3.2123.　Illustration 3.** The same facts as those stated in § **3.2121** except that B' also had earned income of $750 for 2005. B is allowed a basic standard deduction of $1,000 ($B$'s earned income plus $250) or $800, whichever is greater. So, B's taxable income for 1998 is $150.

§ **3.2124.　Illustration 4.** The same facts as those stated in § **3.2121** except that B also had earned income of $7,000 for 2005. While B's basic standard deduction is limited to the greater of his earned income plus $250 or $800, it cannot exceed the amount that is allowable for taxpayers of his filing status. B is an unmarried taxpayer, and the 2005 basic standard deduction for such a taxpayer is $5,000. So, in 2005, B had gross income of $7,400 and a standard deduction of $5,000. B's taxable income for that year is $2,400.

§ **3.2200.　Amount of the Standard Deduction.** The standard deduction is divided into two separate parts: a "basic standard deduction," and an "additional standard deduction" for the aged and blind.

§ **3.2210.　Basic Standard Deduction.** The amount of the basic standard deduction depends upon the tax return filing status of the taxpayer who is utilizing it. IRC § 63(c)(2). For taxable years beginning in 2005, the basic standard deduction amounts are [Rev. Proc. 2004–71]:

$10,000—joint return or surviving spouse
 $7,300—head of household
 $5,000—unmarried taxpayer (other than surviving spouse or head of household)
 $5,000—married taxpayer filing separate return

The amounts listed above are indexed annually (i.e., they are increased to reflect cost-of-living increases if any). IRC § 63(c)(4).

§ 3.2220. Additional Standard Deduction. Prior to the 1986 Act, an additional exemption deduction was granted for being aged or blind. This exemption was repealed by the 1986 TRA. In lieu of exemption deductions, Congress provides a taxpayer an additional standard deduction allowance of a specified dollar amount for each of the following circumstances: the taxpayer is 65 years of age or older, the taxpayer is blind, the taxpayer's spouse is 65 years of age or older and qualifies as an exemption of the taxpayer under IRC § 151(b), the taxpayer's spouse is blind and qualifies as an exemption of the taxpayer under IRC § 151(b). IRC §§ 63(c)(3), and 63(f). The personal exemption deductions are described in Chapter Four. The dollar amount for the additional standard deduction is indexed annually for inflation; for 2005, the dollar amount is $1,000. Rev. Proc. 2004–71. If a taxpayer has no spouse (and does not qualify as a "surviving spouse" as defined by IRC § 2(a)), the additional standard deduction for being elderly or blind is a larger figure; for the year 2005, the amount of the deduction is $1,250, instead of the $1,000 amount that otherwise would be applicable. IRC § 63(f)(3); Rev. Proc. 2004–71.

§ 3.2300. Illustration. In 2005, Mary Ryan, a 30–year-old unmarried taxpayer with no dependents and with good eyesight had the following income and deductible expenditures:

Income	*Deductible Expenditures*
$32,000—salary	$2,000 —nonitemized deductions
$2,000—dividends	$1,800 —itemized deductions
$800—interest	
$34,800—total	

Mary's gross income is $34,800. Her AGI is $32,800—i.e., the difference between her gross income ($34,800) and her nonitemized deductions ($2,000). None of Mary's deductions is a miscellaneous itemized deduction. Mary's taxable income is determined as follows:

$32,800 —AGI
($2,700)—personal exemption deduction
($7,300)—standard deduction
$22,800 —taxable income

Mary will deduct a $7,300 basic standard deduction because that figure is greater than her itemized deductions which total only $1,800. Mary is not entitled to an additional standard deduction since she is neither aged nor blind.

§ 3.2400.   Illustration. H was divorced from Y in Year One, and he married Z in Year Two. In October of Year Six, H and Z separated physically, but they were not divorced or legally separated in that year. Neither H nor Z has any children. Z filed a separate income tax return for Year Six, and she elected to deduct her itemized deductions instead of taking a standard deduction. Because Z deducted her itemized deductions, H is not permitted to utilize a standard deduction on his separate tax return for Year Six. IRC § 63(c)(6)(A). The standard for determining whether a couple will be treated as married is determined at the close of a taxable year in accordance with IRC § 7703. IRC § 63(g).

§ 3.2500.   Illustration. R is the unmarried 15–year-old daughter of M. R has good eyesight. M provides over one-half of R's support, and M is entitled to a dependent exemption deduction for R. § 4.1220. In 2005, R had $4,000 of dividend and interest income from stocks and bonds that R had received as gifts from her grandparents two years earlier, and R earned $100 from her part-time employment as a babysitter. The only deductible expense that R had in 2005 was $300 in state income taxes. The deduction permitted for an individual's state income taxes is an itemized deduction (i.e., it is not included in the IRC § 62(a) list), but it is not a miscellaneous itemized deduction. R's taxable income is determined as follows:

$4,100 —gross income
($ 0)—IRC § 62(a) deductions
$4,100 —AGI

$4,100
($ 800)—standard deduction
($ 0)—personal exemption
$3,300 —taxable income

R is not allowed a personal exemption for 2005 because she qualifies as a dependent exemption deduction for *M*. IRC § 151(d)(2). Also, because *R* qualifies as a dependent exemption deduction for *M*, the amount of *R*'s standard deduction is limited to $800. Since that amount is greater than *R*'s itemized deductions (which totaled only $300), *R* will utilize an $800 standard deduction in lieu of taking her itemized deduction.

*

CHAPTER FOUR

PERSONAL AND DEPENDENT EXEMPTION DEDUCTIONS

§ 4.0000. EXEMPTIONS AND DEDUCTIONS IN GENERAL. Once the basic concepts relating to the determination of income are mastered, the student must develop a solid working knowledge of deductions. An exemption is merely one type of deduction that is available. There are *two classes* of exemptions—*personal* exemption deductions and *dependent* exemption deductions. Remember *deductions* are items which may be subtracted from gross income (or from adjusted gross income) as part of the calculation of taxable income; they are to be distinguished from *exclusions* which, as previously noted, relate to items which are not included in gross income in the first instance. The personal and dependent exemption deductions are described in this chapter. Most of the other tax deductions are described in subsequent chapters.

§ 4.1000. DEDUCTIBLE FROM ADJUSTED GROSS INCOME (AGI). The amount of deduction allowable for an exemption is deducted from the AGI of an individual regardless of whether he utilizes a "standard deduction." The "standard deduction" is described at **§§ 3.2000–3.2500.** The exemptions do not constitute *itemized* deductions and so do not affect the availability of the standard deduction. The exemptions are not deducted in determining AGI and so do not affect the size of a TP's AGI. An exemption constitutes a statutorily prescribed amount of allowable deduction. As noted at **§ 4.2000** et seq., the amount of an individual's deductions for exemptions is phased out if the individual's AGI exceeds a specified dollar amount.

§ 4.1100. Corporations. In determining a corporation's regular tax liability, a corporation has no exemptions. If a corporation's tax liability is determined under the Alternative Minimum Tax system (IRC § 55), the corporation will have a $40,000 exemption, but that exemption is phased out if the corporation's Alternative Minimum Taxable Income exceeds $150,000. IRC § 55(d)(2), (3). Note that certain small corporations are not subject to the Alternative Minimum Tax. IRC § 55(e).

§ 4.1200. Types of Exemptions and the Exemption Amount.

There are two general types of exemptions available to an individual taxpayer: (a) *personal* (taxpayer and spouse); and (b) *dependents*. An individual is allowed a deduction of a specific dollar amount (an "exemption amount") for each exemption to which he is entitled. The exemption amount is increased annually to reflect increases in the cost-of-living; that is, the exemption amount is tied to the cost-of-living index. IRC § 151(d). For the year 2005, the exemption amount is $3,200. Rev. Proc. 2004–71 (Sec. 3.17).

§ 4.1210. Personal Exemption.

An individual is entitled to one exemption for himself unless he is a dependent of another person who is entitled to take a deduction for him as a dependent. An individual who qualifies as a dependent exemption deduction for another person is not allowed a personal exemption deduction for himself or an exemption for his dependents. IRC § 151(d)(2).

On a joint return, the exemptions of both spouses are deductible. A married taxpayer who files a separate return can take an exemption for a spouse only if the spouse had no gross income and is not a dependent of another person. IRC § 151(b). The determination of whether a taxpayer's spouse had gross income or was the dependent of another person is made in relation to the calendar year in which the taxable year of the taxpayer begins. IRC § 151(b). The meaning of "dependent" is explained at §§ 4.1220–4.1243.

§ 4.1211. Marital Status of Taxpayer.

Marital status is determined on the last day of the taxable year. A taxpayer who is divorced or legally separated at that time is not treated as married for tax purposes. However, if a taxpayer's spouse dies during a taxable year, an exemption can still be claimed for that year if the marital status requirements were satisfied at the time of death. IRC § 7703(a)(1). In certain circumstances described in IRC § 7703(b), a married individual who lives apart from his or her spouse for the last six months of a taxable year and who maintains a household that is the principal abode of a child of the individual for more than one-half of the taxable year is treated as an unmarried individual. A "child" of an individual is a person related to the individual as described in IRC § 152(f)(1). See § 4.1231.

§ 4.1211–1. Legal Separation.

For a court decree to effect a legal separation, it "must expressly and affirmatively provide that the parties live apart in the future and, thereby, alter the original and normal marital relationship." *Boettiger v. Commissioner*, 31 T.C. 477, 1958 WL 937 (1958); *Capodanno v. Commissioner*, 69 T.C. 638, 647, 1978 WL 3352 (1978), aff'd, 602 F.2d 64 (3d Cir. 1979). Whether a decree of separate maintenance will qualify as a decree of legal separation depends upon the local state law; in most circumstances, a decree of separate maintenance will not qualify. Compare *Capodanno v. Commissioner*, *supra* with *Legett v. Commissioner*, 329 F.2d 509 (2d Cir. 1964).

§ **4.1211–2. Validity of Divorce.** The standards for determining whether the validity of a divorce can be challenged in a tax proceeding and the tax consequences of obtaining a tax avoidance divorce (i.e., a divorce obtained for tax reasons when the parties plan to remarry promptly) are discussed at §§ **2.1490–2.1493.**

§ **4.1220. Dependent Exemption Deduction.** The exemption deduction that is granted to a taxpayer for having dependents is sometimes referred to as the "dependent exemption deduction." An individual taxpayer is entitled to one exemption for each person who meets the definition of a "dependent" of that person. IRC § 151(c). A "dependent" is defined as a person who is not excluded by one of the specific statutory exclusions described at § **4.1240** and who fits within one of two categories: (1) qualified children, and (2) qualified relatives. IRC § 152(a). The meaning of those two terms is set forth below. The several statutory exclusions from dependent classification are described in § **4.1240.** Before examining those exclusions, we will define three relevant terms: "child," "qualified child," and "qualified relative." Unless one of the exclusions applies, a TP will have an exemption for each of the TP's qualified children and qualified relatives.

§ **4.1230. Definition of "Child," "Qualified Child," and "Qualified Relative."**

§ **4.1231. Child.** A child of an individual is a son, daughter, stepson or stepdaughter of that individual. IRC § 152(f)(1)(A)(i). An individual who has been legally adopted by a person or who has been lawfully placed with a person for a lawful adoption is treated as a child of that person. IRC § 152(f)(1)(B). An "eligible foster child" (defined in IRC

§ 152(f)(1)(C)) of an individual is treated as a child of the individual. IRC § 152(f)(1)(A)(ii).

This definition of a "child" is utilized in some other provisions of the Code. See e.g., IRC § 7703(b)(1).

§ 4.1232. Qualifying Child. A "qualifying child" with respect to a TP is defined in IRC § 152(c) and includes persons whose relationship to the TP is not that of a "child" as the latter term is defined in **§ 4.1231.** Since it refers to more than the children of the TP, perhaps Congress might have chosen a more appropriate term. Nevertheless, the term "qualifying child" is the one that is used.

The definition of a "qualifying child" is a uniform definition that is adopted in other provisions of the Code. It is not limited to the dependent exemption provision. The same term and definition, with some modifications, are used in the provisions for: the child tax credit (IRC § 24), the earned income credit (IRC § 32), the dependent care credit (IRC § 21(b)(1)(A)), and head of household filing status (IRC § 2(b)(1)(A)).

There are four categories of tests that an individual must satisfy to be a qualifying child. The individual must satisfy all four tests. Those four categories are: relationship, age, residency, and support.

(1) *Relationship Test.* To be a qualified child of a TP, an individual must be either: a child of the TP (as defined in **§ 4.1231**), a descendant of such a child, a brother, sister, stepbrother, or stepsister of the TP, or a descendant of any such relative. IRC § 152(c)(2).

(2) *Age Test.* To be a qualified child of a TP, the individual must not have attained the age of 19 before the end of the calendar year in which the taxable year of the TP begins. Alternatively, an individual will satisfy the age test if the individual is a full-time student at an educational organization (or is pursuing a full time course of institutional on-farm training) *and* if the individual has not attained the age of 24 before the end of the calendar year in which the taxable year of the TP begins. If an individual is permanently and totally disabled at any time during the calendar year described above, the individual will satisfy the age

test, regardless of the age of the individual. IRC § 152(c)(3)(B).

(3) *Residence Test.* To be a qualified child of a TP, the individual must have the same principal place of abode as the TP for more than one-half of the TP's taxable year. IRC § 152(c)(1)(B).

(4) *Support Test.* To be a qualified child of a TP, an individual must not have provided over half of the individual's own support for the calendar year in which the taxable year of the TP begins. IRC § 152(c)(1)(D) In determining the percentage of support provided by an individual, a scholarship of the individual to study at an educational organization is not taken into account *if* the individual is a child of the TP and a student. IRC § 152(f)(5). Note that there is no requirement that the TP have provided over half of the individual's support; it is sufficient that the individual did not provide over half of the individual's own support.

When an individual could qualify as a qualifying child of more than one TP, the Code provides a tie-breaking system to determine which TP will prevail. IRC § 152(c)(4). An individual can be a qualifying child of only one person.

§ 4.1233. Qualifying Relative. In addition to a qualifying child, a qualifying relative can provide a TP with a dependent exemption deduction. IRC § 152(a)(2). There are four categories of tests that must be satisfied for an individual to be a qualifying relative of a TP. IRC § 152(d)(1). The individual must satisfy all four tests. These four categories are: a relationship test, a gross income test, a support test, and a non-qualifying child test. Id.

(1) *Relationship Test.* To be a qualified relative of a TP, the individual must, with respect to the TP, be: (a) a child or descendant of a child (as defined in **§ 4.1231**), (b) a brother, sister, stepbrother, or stepsister, (c) a son or daughter of a brother or sister, (d) the father or mother of the TP or an ancestor of either, (e) a brother or sister of the father or mother of the TP, (f) a stepfather or stepmother, (g) a son-in-law, daughter-in-law, father-in-law, mother-in-law, brother-in-law, or sister-in-law, (h) an individual (other than the TP's spouse) who for the taxable

year has the same principal place of abode as the TP and is a member of the TP's household whose relationship with the TP does not violate local law. IRC § 152(d)(2)(H), (f)(3).

(2) *Gross Income Test.* The individual's gross income for the calendar year in which the taxable year of the TP begins must be less than the exemption amount. IRC § 152(d)(1)(B). For the year 2005, the exemption amount is $3,200. See § **4.1200.** While a TP's exemption amount is reduced if the TP's AGI exceeds a threshold amount (See § **4.2000**), the statute does not refer to any specific person's exemption amount, and therefore refers to the exemption amount for that taxable year without any reduction because of a person's AGI. The exemption amount changes yearly to reflect changes in the cost-of-living.

(3) *Support Test.* The TP must provide more than half of the individual's support in the calendar year in which the TP's taxable year begins. IRC § 152(d)(1)(C). In determining the percentage of support provided to an individual by a TP, a scholarship of the individual to study at an educational organization is not taken into account *if* the individual is a child of the TP and a student. IRC § 152(f)(5). If no one person contributed over half the support for an individual, but two or more persons together contributed more than half of that support, under certain conditions, the members of that group are permitted to designate one person from the group who will be deemed to have provided over one-half of the individual's support. IRC § 152(d)(3). Such an agreement is called a "multiple support agreement."

(4) *Non-Qualifying Child Test.* The individual must not be a qualifying child of the TP or of any other person in the taxable year. IRC § 152(d)(1)(D). The term "qualifying child" is defined in § **4.1232.**

§ **4.1240. Exclusions from Dependent Classification.** There are three conditions that must be met for a qualifying child or a qualifying relative to be a dependent of a TP. If any of those three conditions is not satisfied, the individual will not be a dependent.

§ 4.1241. Joint Return Exclusion. An individual who files a joint return with his or her spouse cannot qualify as a dependent of any person. IRC § 152(b)(2).

§ 4.1242. Citizenship. With one exception, an individual cannot qualify as a dependent unless the individual is either a citizen, national or resident of the United States, or a resident of a country that is contiguous to the United States. IRC § 152(a)(3). The one exception to that requirement is that an adopted child of a United States citizen or national can qualify as a dependent if the child has the same principal place of abode as the adoptive parent and is a member of the parent's household. Id.

§ 4.1243. Ineligible Taxpayer. If a TP qualifies as a dependent of someone for a taxable year, the TP is deemed not to have any dependents in that taxable year. IRC § 152(b)(1). See also, IRC § 151(d)(2). So, an individual who otherwise would have been a dependent of that TP will not be a dependent.

§ 4.1250. Divorced or Separated Parents. When a married couple with a young child or children divorce or separate, a question can arise as to which parent is entitled to claim a dependent exemption deduction for the children. If no special statutory provision applies, such a child typically will be a "qualified child" or a "qualified relative" of the parent who has custody of the child for more than one-half of the calendar year. But, what if the parents wish to have the dependent exemption deduction taken by the noncustodial parent (i.e., the parent who does not have custody of the child for more than one-half of the calendar year)? The Code permits the parents to elect to have the noncustodial parent qualify for the exemption deduction if the conditions specified in IRC § 152(e)(2) are satisfied. This provision applies only if the child receives over half of his support during the calendar year from his parents and the parents are either: (1) divorced or legally separated under a decree of divorce or separate maintenance, or separated under a written separation agreement, or live apart at all times during the last six months of the calendar year, and (2) the child is in the custody of one or both parents for more than one-half of the calendar year. IRC § 151(e)(1).

If a child can qualify a parent for a dependent exemption deduction only if the child is a qualifying relative (**§ 4.1233**), and if the obstacle to that qualification is that the support test of IRC § 152(d)(1)(C) cannot be satisfied, the parents might be able to execute a "multiple support agreement" to qualify one of the parents for that deduction. See IRC § 152(d)(3). And see § **4.1233 (3).** If a multiple support agreement applies to a child, regardless of whether the parents are a party to that agreement, then IRC § 152(e) will not apply to that child. IRC § 152(e)(4). In other words, the multiple support agreement has priority.

§ **4.1260.   Old Age and Blindness Exemption.** Prior to 1987, an additional exemption was granted to a taxpayer for old age and for blindness and for the old age and blindness of the taxpayer's spouse. The 1986 TRA repealed that provision and substituted an additional standard deduction amount as described at § **3.2220.**

§ **4.2000.   PHASE–OUT OF EXEMPTION AMOUNT.** As noted in § **4.1200**, the amount of deduction for each exemption (personal and dependent) to which a taxpayer is entitled is increased annually to reflect inflation. For the year 2005, the exemption amount is $3,200. Rev. Proc. 2004–71 (Sec. 3.17). The amount of a taxpayer's exemption deduction for a taxable year is reduced if the taxpayer's adjusted gross income (AGI) for that year exceeds a specified figure, which figure is referred to as the "threshold amount." The threshold amount is indexed to reflect inflation. IRC § 151(d)(4). The amount of the reduction to each exemption deduction to which the taxpayer would otherwise be entitled is equal to a percentage (called the "applicable percentage") of the exemption amount that otherwise would apply. The applicable percentage is two percentage points for each $2,500 (or fraction thereof) by which the taxpayer's AGI for that year exceeds his threshold amount. [If the taxpayer is a married person filing a separate return, the $2,500 figure is reduced to $1,250.] The exemption amount cannot be reduced below zero. IRC § 151(d)(3).

§ **4.2100.   Threshold Amount.** The threshold amounts for the year 2005 are as follows:

$218,950—joint return or surviving spouse

$182,450—head of household

$145,950—unmarried taxpayer

$109,475—married taxpayer filing a separate return

§ **4.2200.   Illustration 1.** In 2005, individual *G* had AGI of $168,950. *G* was unmarried and did not qualify as a surviving spouse or as a head of household. *G* had two children, and he was entitled to two dependent exemptions for those children. So, *G* had three exemption deductions—two dependent exemption deductions and one personal exemption deduction. Before applying the phase-out provision, each exemption deduction was $3,200 (in other words, in 2005 the "exemption amount" was $3,200). The exemption amount for each exemption deduction is reduced by two percentage points for each $2,500 (or fraction thereof) by which *G*'s AGI of $168,950 exceeds his threshold amount of $145,950 (a difference of $23,000). Dividing $2,500 into the $23,000 difference provides a figure of 9.2. Since a fraction of a $2,500 excess is treated as a whole $2,500 excess, there are ten $2,500 steps in the excess over *G*'s threshold amount. The exemption amount is reduced by two percentage points for each $2,500 step. Since there are ten steps, the exemption amount is reduced by 20%. The reduction of the exemption amount is $640 (20% × $3,200 = $640). So, the exemption amount becomes $2,560 ($3,200 reduced by $640). Since *G* had three exemption deductions, the aggregate amount of deduction allowed to *G* for his exemptions is $7,680 (3 × $2,560).

§ 4.2300. Illustration 2. The same facts as those stated in Illustration 1, except that *G*'s AGI for 2005 was $270,950. The excess of *G*'s AGI over his threshold amount was then $125,000, and there are 50 steps of $2,500 increments in that figure. *G*'s exemption amount is reduced by two percentage points for each of those 50 steps. Therefore, the exemption amount is reduced by 100% of that amount, and *G* will have no deduction for his three exemptions.

§ 4.2400. Illustration 3. The same facts as those stated in Illustration 1, except that *G*'s AGI for 2005 was $295,950. The excess of *G*'s AGI over the threshold amount was then $150,000, and there are 60 steps of $2,500 increments in that figure. Ordinarily, *G*'s exemption amount is reduced by two percentage points for each of those 60 steps; however, that would result in a 120% reduction. Since the applicable percentage is not to exceed 100%, the result is the same as in Illustration 2. The exemption is reduced by 100%, leaving *G* with no deductions for his three exemptions.

§ 4.3000. STANDARD DEDUCTION. In lieu of deducting itemized deductions (i.e., deductions other than those listed in IRC § 62(a) and other than exemption deductions), an individual can deduct a specified dollar amount, which is referred to as a "standard deduction." The standard deduction is described at **§§ 3.2000–3.2500.** The standard deduction is available to most individuals, but certain persons are barred from using that deduction or are limited as to the amount of standard deduction that is available to them [see §§ **3.2110–3.2120**]. The standard deduction is available only to a taxpayer who is an individual—i.e., it is available only to a natural person. The standard deduction is divided into two elements—a basic standard deduction and an additional standard deduction for the aged and blind. § **3.2200.**

§ **4.4000. BUSINESS AND NONBUSINESS DEDUCTIONS IN GENERAL.** Chapters Five through Thirteen deal with deductions other than exemptions and the standard deduction. Some deductions are related to the taxpayer's business activities, some are not, and some have both business and personal attributes. While many textbooks group business and nonbusiness deductions separately, there is sufficient overlap to warrant treating them together. Consequently, while the first group of deductions listed in the following chapters are nonbusiness deductions, no effort has been made to group the deductions discussed in this work into airtight compartments, and the reader will find the discussion of business and nonbusiness deductions interspersed.

§ **4.5000. BURDEN OF PROOF.** The reader should note that (with a few exceptions) no deduction for gross income will be permitted unless it is authorized by a statutory provision. Consequently in the typical case, the taxpayer must establish that his claim for a deduction is authorized by the Code. The Government is not required to demonstrate that there is no provision in the Code which authorizes the deduction.

CHAPTER FIVE

INTEREST EXPENSE

§ 5.0000. DEDUCTION FOR INTEREST EXPENSES. Prior to the adoption of the 1986 TRA, subject to a few exceptions, most interest paid or accrued in a taxable year was deductible. IRC § 163. Interest was deductible even though incurred in connection with the acquisition of property for personal, nonbusiness uses (e.g., interest on deferred payments for the purchase of household goods or for the purchase of a family car, interest on a home mortgage loan); but, subject to several exceptions, the principal one being for so-called "qualified residence interest" (**§ 5.1320**), that is no longer so. Even under prior law, there were (and still are) provisions that deny deductions for interest connected with certain types of transactions; for example, interest incurred or continued to purchase or carry tax-exempt bonds is not deductible [IRC § 265(a)(2)], and interest payable on debts relating to certain life insurance coverage or to certain endowment or annuity contracts is nondeductible under IRC § 264(a)(2) and (a)(4).

An interest payment (otherwise qualifying for a deduction) is deductible only if the taxpayer has an unconditional and legally enforceable obligation to repay the underlying debt. *Linder v. Commissioner*, 68 T.C. 792, 1977 WL 3613 (1977). However, interest paid by a taxpayer on a nonrecourse debt secured by property that the taxpayer owns can qualify for an interest deduction so long as the debt is considered to be bona fide. **§ 5.2100.** Except for short-term consumer loans, the amount of interest for a taxable year that can be deducted cannot exceed the economic accrual of the interest obligation for that period. Rev. Rul. 83–84; Rev. Proc. 83–40.

When the only Code section under which an interest expense of an individual can be deducted is IRC § 163, it constitutes an itemized deduction. However, if an interest expense is directly connected with the conduct of a trade or business (other than the business of being an employee), it can be deducted under IRC § 162 as a business expense and so qualifies as a nonitemized deduction. See *Standing v. Commissioner*, 28 T.C. 789, 1957 WL 1159 (1957), aff'd, 259 F.2d 450 (4th Cir. 1958). The Service's nonacquiescence in *Standing* (1958–1 Cum. Bull. 7) was withdrawn in 1992–2 Cum. Bull. 1, which also substituted an acquiescence on other issues in that case, but made no reference to the treatment of interest. Since the Service concedes that similar statutory overlaps concerning the deductibility of state real estate taxes and of legal and accounting expenses incurred in contesting income taxes that are imposed on a self-employed business permit such taxes and expenses to qualify as nonitemized deductions, the prospects for obtaining a like result for interest expenses connected with a self-employed business are favorable. See § **3.1200.** For the nondeductibility of interest on a tax deficiency that is attributable to an income tax on the income of an unincorporated business, see § **5.1300.** As we will see, five courts of appeals have denied a deduction for such tax deficiency interest.

While an interest expense typically is an itemized deduction, it is excluded by IRC § 67(b)(1) from the category of "miscellaneous itemized deductions." Consequently, interest expense deductions are not subject to the 2% of AGI floor that applies to many other itemized deductions. See § **3.1110.** Also, the interest expense deduction is allowed in determining the TP's alternative minimum tax. IRC § 56(b)(1)(A)(i).

You will recall (§ **3.1120**) that the aggregate itemized deductions of a taxpayer for a taxable year are subject to an overall limitation imposed by IRC § 68, which reduces the amount deductible according to a specified formula. Three itemized deductions are excluded from that overall limitation, and one of those exclusions is the deduction for *investment interest.* IRC § 68(c)(2). Investment interest is described at §§ **5.1200–5.1220.** Since interest that is directly connected with a self-employed trade or business (other than tax deficiency interest) is deductible as a nonitemized business expense, the only itemized interest deductions that are subject to the overall limitation of IRC § 68 are the qualified residence interest deduction (§§ **5.1320–5.1332**), interest on certain deferral of estate tax liability, interest on certain educational loans, and possibly certain interest deductions that are taken into account under IRC § 469 in determining the income or loss from a passive activity (§ **5.1210**). While the limitation imposed by IRC § 68 will be phased out beginning in the year 2006, the limitation is scheduled to return in full force beginning with the year 2011. IRC § 68(f), (g), Section 901 of P.L. 107–16 (Sunset of Provisions of the Economic Growth and Tax Relief Reconciliation Act of 2001).

§ 5.1000. INTEREST INCURRED BY NONCORPORATE TAX-PAYER.

The 1986 TRA expanded the circumstances in which interest incurred by a noncorporate taxpayer is not deductible.

§ 5.1100. Material Participation in Trade or Business.

When interest (other than tax deficiency interest) is incurred in connection with the taxpayer's conduct of a trade or business (other than the trade or business of providing services as an employee) in which the taxpayer materially participates, the interest is deductible. IRC

§ 163(d)(5), and IRC § 163(h)(2)(A). "Material participation" in an activity by a taxpayer requires that the taxpayer is engaged in that activity in a regular, continuous and substantial basis. IRC §§ 163(d)(5)(C) and § 469(h)(1).

§ 5.1200. Trades and Businesses in Which Taxpayer Does Not Materially Participate and Investments. When interest of a noncorporate taxpayer is incurred in connection with an investment of the taxpayer or with a trade or business in which the taxpayer does not materially participate, the deductibility of such interest is subject to several limitations. See **§ 5.1220.** Such interest is referred to as "investment interest." IRC § 163(d)(3). Interest incurred in connection with a "passive activity," as defined in IRC § 469(c), is not treated as investment interest. IRC § 165(d)(3)(B)(ii).

> **§ 5.1210. Passive Activities.** Interest incurred by a noncorporate taxpayer in connection with an investment is subject to the limitations described in **§ 5.1220.** In lieu of the investment interest limitations, some interest of that type will be subject to the limitations imposed by IRC § 469 on losses incurred by a taxpayer in passive activities. IRC § 163(d)(3)(B). See **§ 7.9000** et seq. When interest is connected with a passive activity, as that term is defined in IRC § 469(c), it will be aggregated with other deductions connected with such activities and subjected to the limitations described in **§ 7.9000** et seq. Note that not all passive investments constitute a "passive activity" for purposes of IRC § 469; for example, portfolio investments (including stocks and bonds) are excluded from the passive activity category [IRC § 469(e)], and the interest incurred in connection with portfolio investments is treated as investment interest and is subject to the investment interest limitations. IRC § 163(d)(5)(A)(i). Note also that the passive activity loss limitations of IRC § 469 apply to personal service corporations and certain closely held corporations as well as to noncorporate taxpayers. **§ 7.9160.**

§ 5.1220. Deduction of Investment Interest. "Investment interest" for a taxable year can be deducted only to the extent of the TP's "net investment income" for that year. IRC § 163(d)(1). Net investment income is the excess of the taxpayer's investment income over investment expenses (other than interest expenses). IRC § 163(d)(4). The excess of investment interest over net investment income that is not deductible in a current year is carried over and treated as investment interest incurred in the next taxable year. IRC § 163(d)(2). If any of the carryover is not deductible in the next year because of the net investment income limitation, the unused carryover can be carried forward to subsequent years.

For purposes of the investment interest limitation, property held as an investment includes portfolio property (as described in IRC § 469(e)(1)) and property held by a taxpayer in connection with a trade or business that is not a passive activity and in which the taxpayer does not materially participate. IRC § 163(d)(5). Income and expenses from a passive activity that is covered by IRC § 469 are not treated as investment income and expenses for purposes of IRC § 163. IRC § 163(d)(4)(D). Investment interest does not include any "qualified residence interest," which is described at §§ 5.1320–5.1332. IRC § 163(d)(3)(B)(i).

Prior to 1993, investment income included the net gain recognized on the disposition of investment property. As a consequence of a 1993 amendment, the net gain from the disposition of investment property is treated as investment income only to the extent that it is not a long-term capital gain. IRC § 163(d)(4)(B)(ii). However, a taxpayer is provided with an election to treat all or part of the net gain from the disposition of investment property as investment income, and the amount of gain for which that election is made will be excluded from net capital gain and so will not qualify for the capital gains tax preferential rate. IRC §§ 1(h)(2), 164(d)(4)(B).

In 2003, Congress provided that "qualified dividend income" is taxable at capital gains rates (typically at a 15% rate). Qualified dividend income is defined in IRC § 1(h)(11). Qualified dividend income is excluded from investment income by IRC § 163(d)(4)(B). However, the TP can elect to treat qualified dividend income as investment income under IRC § 163(d), in which case that dividend income will not qualify for the capital gains rates. IRC §§ 1(h)(11)(D)(i), 163(d)(4)(B).

As noted above, while the amount of a taxpayer's investment interest that exceeds his net investment income for a taxable year is not deductible in that year, it can be carried over to the next year. But, what if the excess investment interest that is not deductible in a taxable year is greater than the taxpayer's taxable income for that year? Should the taxpayer be permitted to carry over that amount of the excess investment interest that exceeds his taxable income? If there were no limitation in IRC § 163 on the deductibility of investment interest, the amount of taxpayer's investment interest that exceeds his taxable income could not be deducted or carried over to another year; the excess interest expense would not create a net operating loss that could be carried over to subsequent years pursuant to IRC § 172. IRC § 172(d)(4). The carryover provision in IRC § 163(d)(2) was intended to provide relief for a taxpayer who was denied a deduction for investment interest because of the net investment interest limitation. If the carryover provision applies to investment interest in excess of taxable income, it will do far more than merely provide such relief; it will permit the carryover and ultimate deduction of an expense item that could never have been deducted by the taxpayer if the net investment interest limitation had not been adopted. For this reason, initially, the Commissioner determined that the carryover provision of IRC § 163(d) does not apply to investment interest in excess of the taxpayer's taxable income for the year in which the interest expense was incurred. Rev. Rul. 86–70, revoked by Rev. Rul. 95–16. While the Tax Court initially held for the Commissioner on this issue, the Fourth Circuit Court of Appeals reversed and held that the carryover of investment interest is not limited by the taxpayer's taxable income. *Beyer v. Commissioner*, 916 F.2d 153 (4th Cir. 1990), rev'g 92 T.C. 1304, 1989 WL 66555 (1989). In a subsequent case, a majority of the Tax Court overruled its earlier decision and adopted the Fourth Circuit's view that the carryover of investment interest is not limited by the taxpayer's taxable income. *Lenz v. Commissioner*, 101 T.C. 260, 1993 WL 393870 (1993) (reviewed by the court). After losing three more Court of Appeals cases, the Service threw in the towel and conceded that the carryover disallowed investment interest is *not* limited by taxpayer's taxable income for the year in which the interest was paid or accrued. Rev. Rul. 95–16.

§ 5.1300. Personal Interest. The 1986 TRA eliminated a deduction for interest of a noncorporate taxpayer that is incurred in connection with most consumer purchases. Thus, interest on a personal loan taken out to finance the purchase of a family car or of household goods is no longer deductible. IRC § 163(h)(1). Similarly, interest on income tax deficiencies or payment extensions are not deductible. But see **§ 5.1311.** A major exception to this denial of an interest deduction for consumer loans is that a deduction is allowed for "qualified residence interest," which is defined in **§ 5.1320.** IRC § 163(h)(2)(D). Several additional exceptions are noted in **§ 5.1310.** Note that interest incurred in connection with a trade or business in which the taxpayer materially participates as a non-employee (i.e., the TP is self-employed) is deductible; but if the taxpayer's business is that of an employee, no deduction will be allowed (i.e., such interest of an employee is treated as personal interest). IRC § 163(h)(2)(A); *McKay v. Commissioner*, 102 T.C. 465, 1994 WL 97734 (1994), appeal vacated, 84 F.3d 433 (5th Cir. 1996). There is no justification for denying a deduction for an employee's business interest, but Congress has done so.

§ 5.1310. Exceptions. The denial of a deduction for personal interest does not apply to investment interest, which is subject to the limitations described in **§ 5.1220**, nor to interest that is covered by IRC § 469 as incident to a passive activity. IRC § 163(h)(2)(C). Nor does the denial apply to the deduction allowable under IRC § 221 for interest on education loans. IRC § 163(h)(2)(F). Also, interest on certain estate tax obligations, the payment of which has been deferred, is deductible, but no deduction is allowable for the especially low interest rate provided for an extension of time under IRC § 6166 for payment of estate tax in certain circumstances. IRC § 163(h)(2)(E), (k). An important exception to the denial of a deduction for personal interest is that a deduction is allowed for "qualified residence interest," as described in **§ 5.1320** et seq. IRC § 163(h)(2)(D).

§ 5.1311. Interest on Tax Deficiency or Deferral Attributable to Self–Employed Income. Prior to the Code's disallowance of a deduction for personal interest, which was added to the Code by the Tax Reform Act of 1986, the interest that an individual incurred on an income tax deficiency or an extension of time for payment of the tax was deductible. Typically, the deduction that was allowed an individual for such interest was an itemized deduction. However, if the income tax deficiency could be traced to the taxpayer's self-employed business, the Tax Court and several Courts of Appeals treated the interest deduction as a nonitemized deduction on the ground that it was a business deduction under IRC § 62(a)(1). E.g., *Commissioner v. Standing*, 259 F.2d 450 (4th Cir. 1958), aff'ing 28 T.C. 789, 1957 WL 1159 (1957). Such interest was also held to be a business deduction for purposes of computing the taxpayer's net operating loss carryover. *Commissioner v. Polk*, 276 F.2d 601 (10th Cir. 1960), aff'ing 31 T.C. 412, 1958 WL 1213 (1958).

After the 1986 Act eliminated a deduction for personal interest, and thereby disallowed a deduction for interest on income tax deficiencies, the question arose as to whether the interest on an income tax deficiency that is traced to the conduct of a self-employed trade or business continues to be deductible as a business expense. The *Standing* and *Polk* line of cases, while dealing with a different issue, did characterize such interest as a business expense, and therefore would seem to support allowing a deduction for post–1986 interest of that nature. However, in a Temporary Regulation promulgated in 1987, Treasury treated all such interest as nondeductible personal interest. The Temporary Regulation (Temp. Reg. § 1.163–9T(b)(2)(i)(A)) states that personal interest includes interest "paid on underpayments of individual Federal, State or local income taxes and on indebtedness used to pay such taxes . . . , regardless of the source of the income generating the tax liability." The Temporary Regulation accords with a similar statement in the Blue Book for the Tax Reform act of 1986. Staff of the Joint Committee on Taxation, 99th Cong., 2d Sess., *General Explanation of the Tax Reform Act of 1986*, p. 266 (1987). If valid, the Temporary Regulation establishes that neither interest on such an income tax deficiency nor interest on a loan taken to obtain the funds to pay an income tax on self-employed business income can be deducted.

In *Redlark v. Commissioner*, 106 T.C. 31, 1996 WL 10243 (1996) (reviewed by the court), rev'd 141 F.3d 936 (9th Cir. 1998), a majority of the Tax Court held that Temp. Reg. § 1.163–9T(b)(2)(i)(A) is invalid, and that interest on an income tax deficiency that can be traced to self-employed business income is deductible. In reversing the Tax Court, the Ninth Circuit deemed the language of the statute to be so broad and generalized that there was an implicit legislative delegation to the Commissioner to set the standards for what constitutes personal interest. The court therefore held that the Temporary Regulation is a permissible application and construction of the statute and must be sustained. Accordingly, the Ninth Circuit held that interest payable on an individual's income tax deficiency is not deductible regardless of the source of the deficiency. *Ibid.* Four other circuit courts of appeals came to the same conclusion that the Ninth Circuit reached, and held that such interest is not deductible. *Kikalos v. Commissioner*, 190 F.3d 791 (7th Cir. 1999);, *Allen v. United*

States, 173 F.3d 533 (4th Cir. 1999); *McDonnell v. United States*, 180 F.3d 721 (6th Cir. 1999); *Miller v. United States*, 65 F.3d 687 (8th Cir. 1995).

It is noteworthy that Temp. Reg. § 1.163–9T(b)(2)(iii)(A) provides that interest paid with respect to sales, excises, and similar taxes incurred in connection with a trade or business or an investment is not personal interest. Accordingly, such interest is deductible; but the interest incurred in connection with an investment is subject to the limitations on the deduction of investment interest described in § **5.1220.**

§ 5.1320. Deduction for Qualified Residence Interest. Qualified residence interest is deductible as an itemized deduction, but it is not a miscellaneous itemized deduction. IRC §§ 67(b)(1), 163(h)(2)(D). It is, however, subject to the overall limitation on itemized deduction imposed by IRC § 68. See **§ 5.0000.** "Qualified residence interest" refers to interest on a debt that constitutes either an "acquisition indebtedness" or a "home equity indebtedness" with respect to a "qualified residence" of the taxpayer. IRC § 163(h)(3)(A). A "qualified residence" is the principal residence of the taxpayer (within the meaning of IRC § 121), and one other residence which the taxpayer selects and which the taxpayer uses as a residence for a specified part of the year. IRC § 163(h)(5)(A). As to the second residence, if the taxpayer rents it for part of the year, for the property to be a qualified residence, the taxpayer must use the property for personal purposes for longer than the greater of: (1) 14 days, or (2) ten percent of the number of days that it is rented. IRC §§ 163(h)(5)(A)(i)(II), 280A(d)(1). If the taxpayer does not rent the selected property at all during the year, it will be a qualified residence regardless of the amount of personal use to which the property is put. IRC § 163(h)(5)(A)(iii).

§ 5.1330. Qualified Residence Interest. As noted above, qualified residence interest is interest on one or two types of indebtedness which is incurred with respect to a qualified residence—"acquisition indebtedness" and "home equity indebtedness."

§ 5.1331. Acquisition Indebtedness. Acquisition indebtedness is a debt which was incurred in acquiring, constructing, or substantially improving a qualified residence of the taxpayer and which is secured by such residence. The term also includes a debt, secured by the residence, which was incurred as the result of the refinancing of an acquisition indebtedness but only to the extent of the amount of the acquisition debt that was refinanced. IRC § 163(h)(3)(B). The aggregate amount of a taxpayer's acquisition indebtedness for a given period cannot exceed $1,000,000 ($500,000 for a married taxpayer who files a separate return); but this limitation does not apply to any indebtedness (hereinafter referred to as "pre-October 14, 1987 indebtedness"), whether or not an acquisition indebtedness, that was incurred on or before October 13, 1987, and that was secured by a qualified residence on October 13, 1987, and at all times thereafter until the interest is paid or accrued. IRC § 163(h)(3)(B)(ii), (D). Interest paid or accrued on such pre-October 14, 1987 indebtedness, or (subject to time limitations) on a debt incurred to refinance such pre-October 14, 1987 indebtedness, is deductible. IRC § 163(h)(3)(D). The $1,000,000 (or $500,000) limitation on the amount of post-October 13, 1987 indebtedness that can constitute acquisition indebtedness is reduced (but not below zero) by the amount of such pre-October 14, 1987 indebtedness of the taxpayer. IRC § 163(h)(3)(D)(ii). While not subject to the dollar ceiling of $1,000,000 (or $500,000), a taxpayer's pre-October 14, 1987 indebtedness is treated as an acquisition indebtedness [IRC § 163(h)(3)(D)(i)(I)] and so can affect the amount of the dollar ceiling on home equity indebtedness and on post-October 13, 1987 acquisition indebtedness. See **§ 5.1332.**

§ 5.1332. Home Equity Indebtedness. Home equity indebtedness means a post-October 13, 1987 indebtedness (other than an acquisition indebtedness) that is secured by a qualified residence to the extent that the aggregate amount of such indebtedness does not exceed the difference between the fair market value of such qualified residence and the amount of the taxpayer's acquisition indebtedness with respect to such residence. The aggregate amount that is treated as a taxpayer's home equity indebtedness for any period cannot exceed $100,000 ($50,000 for a married taxpayer who files a separate return). IRC § 163(h)(3)(C).

§ 5.1400. Illustrations.

§ 5.1410. Illustration 1: Net Investment Income Limitation. In Year One, B, a cash method individual, had interest income of $3,500 from corporate bonds that *B* owned. *B* had an outstanding debt of $30,000 which *B* had incurred in order to obtain part of the funds that he used to purchase the corporate bonds. The interest that *B* incurred and paid on that debt in Year One was $4,000. *B* had no other investment income or expenses in that year. *B*'s taxable income for Year One was $40,000. *B* is permitted to deduct $3,500 of his interest expense (the amount equal to his net investment income) as an itemized deduction. The $500 of interest that cannot be deducted in Year One is carried forward and treated as an investment interest payment of $500 in Year Two. The $500 carryforward will be added to the investment interest that *B* paid in Year Two, and *B* can deduct the aggregate amount of Year Two investment interest only to the extent of *B*'s net investment income for Year Two.

§ 5.1420. Illustration 2: Interest on Consumer Loan. In Year One, *C*, a cash method individual, purchased an automobile for his personal use. *C* obtained a bank loan of $10,000 to purchase the automobile, and the loan was secured by the purchased vehicle. In Year One, *C* incurred and paid interest of $1,000 on the automobile loan. No part of the $1,000 interest payment is deductible. This is nondeductible personal interest.

§ 5.1430. Illustration 3. Interest on Loan for Employee's Business. The same facts as those stated in **§ 5.1420**, except that the automobile that *C* purchased was exclusively used by *C* to travel on his route as a traveling salesman for his employer, a clothing manufacturer. Since the car is used in *C*'s trade or business of being an employee, the interest on the car loan is treated as personal interest that is nondeductible. IRC § 163(h)(2)(A).

§ 5.1440. Illustration 4. Home Equity Indebtedness. The same facts as those stated in **§ 5.1420**, except that the loan for the automobile is secured by a mortgage on *C*'s personal residence, which has a fair market value of $110,000 and is subject to an acquisition indebtedness of $45,000. The $10,000 automobile loan is a home equity indebtedness, and so the interest payments on that debt constitute "qualified residence interest" and, therefore, are deductible.

§ 5.1500. Loan to Cash Method Taxpayer to Obtain Funds to Pay Interest on Another Loan from the Same Creditor. No deduction is allowed a cash method taxpayer for interest paid on a loan (Loan #1) to the extent that the payment of the interest is derived from the proceeds of another loan (Loan #2) from the same lender. This is an application of the substance vs. form rule, and it applies when the court finds that the purpose of Loan #2 was to provide the funds to pay the interest on Loan #1. To deny the deduction, the court must determine that the interest payment on Loan #1 was derived from the proceeds of Loan #2, and that that was the purpose of undertaking Loan #2. In such a case, the form of the transaction is ignored. It is treated as a deferral of the interest due on Loan #1, and no deduction is allowable to a cash method taxpayer for the accrual of unpaid interest. In effect, no payment has been made to the creditor; instead, the amount of the debt to the creditor has been increased. *Davison v. Commissioner*, 107 T.C. 35, 1996 WL 479682 (1996), aff'd per curiam, 141 F.3d 403 (2d Cir. 1998). See also, *Battelstein v. IRS*, 631 F.2d 1182 (5th Cir. 1980) (en banc); *Wilkerson v. Commissioner*, 655 F.2d 980 (9th Cir. 1981); Ann. 83–130, 1983–32 IRB 30.

Of course, a debtor can borrow from a third party to obtain the funds to pay the interest on a debt. The problem of deductibility arises when the debtor borrows from the same lender that made the original loan.

§ 5.1510. Illustration. *G*, a cash method individual, borrowed $100,000 from *L*. Simple interest of 8% is payable on the debt each year. At the end of the year, *G* borrows $8,000 from *L*, and gives *L* a note bearing 8% simple interest. Immediately afterwards, *G* pays $8,000 to *L* as the interest due on the $100,000 debt.

On those facts, it is likely that a court would find that the interest paid on the $100,000 debt was derived from the second loan made by *L*, and that the purpose of making that loan was to provide *G* with the funds to pay the interest. In that case, *L* will not be treated as having paid the interest, and no deduction will be allowed. It will be treated as if the interest accrued but was not paid.

§ 5.2000. DEFINITION OF INTEREST. Interest is the amount paid or accrued for the use of another's money. An interest deduction is allowed only for interest paid or accrued for the taxpayer's use of money; no deduction is allowed for an interest payment made by a taxpayer for money borrowed by someone else. See *Secunda v. Commissioner*, 36 T.C.M. 763 (1977).

§ 5.2100.   Illustration 1: Nonrecourse Debt. A nonrecourse debt is one for which the debtor has no personal obligation to repay and which, upon default, the debtor can collect only by foreclosing on the property securing the debt. Individual X owns Blackacre (improved rental realty) which is subject to a mortgage of $50,000. X has no personal liability on the mortgage. If X makes an interest payment to the mortgagee of $4,000, his payment will be treated as interest for tax purposes if the underlying debt is bona fide. See Treas. Reg. § 1.163–1(b). A nonrecourse loan will be considered bona fide if it is reasonable to assume that the debt will be paid. For example, the debt will be bona fide if the underlying security bears a reasonable relationship to the amount of the purported indebtedness. Rev. Rul. 84–5; *Estate of Franklin v. Commissioner*, 544 F.2d 1045 (9th Cir. 1976), aff'g 64 T.C. 752, 1975 WL 3035 (1975). Assuming that X's debt is bona fide, the deductibility of the interest payment will depend upon the application of the passive activity loss limitation. See IRC § 469(c)(2).

§ 5.2200.   Illustration 2: Interest on Another's Debt. X purchased Whiteacre from Y. X paid Y $10,000 and assumed an outstanding mortgage of $30,000. In addition, X assumed the obligation to pay $1,000 defaulted interest on the mortgage obligation which Y had failed to pay. On X's subsequent payment of the $1,000 of defaulted interest, X cannot treat that payment as interest because the payment is not made for money borrowed by X, but rather is made as part of the purchase price X paid to Y for the property.

§ 5.2300.   Illustration 3: Interest on Tax Deficiency. Individual X owes an income tax deficiency of $10,000 to the federal government. The income to which the income tax deficiency is attributable was not earned in a self-employed business. The interest payable on this tax deficiency is treated as personal interest, which is not deductible. IRC § 163(h). Even if the income to which the tax deficiency is attributable was earned in a self-employed business, five courts of appeals have held that the interest payment is not deductible. See **§ 5.1311.**

§ 5.2400.   Illustration 4: Finder's Fee. Individual A desires to borrow $1,000,000 for a business in which A materially participates as a self-employed person. B locates a lender who is willing to lend A the $1,000,000. A pays B $10,000 as a "finder's fee." The payment to B is not interest; it is made for B's services in locating an available source for a loan and is not a cost of the use of the money. However, since the loan is related to A's business, A can amortize the $10,000 finder's fee payment over the term of the loan and deduct an aliquot (i.e., proportional) part of the fee each year as a business expense under IRC § 162.

§ 5.2500. Penalty for Prepayment of Debt. Under the terms of some loans, a borrower is charged a fee (sometimes called a "prepayment penalty") if the borrower wishes to pay all or part of the principal before that payment becomes due (i.e., a prepayment of the principal). The "penalty" payable for such a prepayment is treated as interest for tax purposes. Rev. Rul. 57–198; PLR 199951037; PLR 199951038.

§ 5.2600. Guarantor's Payment of Interest. If, after a debtor's default, a taxpayer who guaranteed the repayment of the debt fulfills his obligation by paying the creditors the amount due, including the unpaid interest, the taxpayer will *not* be allowed an interest deduction for the interest payment. A guarantor is only secondarily liable for the debt, and the borrowed funds typically are used by the primary debtor rather than by the guarantor. The guarantor's interest payment is treated as a payment for another's use of money and so is not deductible as interest. *Rushing v. Commissioner*, 58 T.C. 996, 1972 WL 2529 (1972), Acq. Whether the payment is deductible on some other ground will depend upon the circumstances under which the taxpayer guaranteed the debt.

§ 5.2700. Credit Card Annual Fee. The annual fee paid for the use of a credit card is not interest. Rev. Rul. 2004–52.

§ 5.3000. ASCERTAINING PORTION OF CARRYING CHARGES FOR CERTAIN INSTALLMENT PURCHASES THAT CONSTITUTE INTEREST. If personal property or educational services are purchased under an installment contract which states carrying charges separately, but for which the interest charge cannot be ascertained, then payments equal to six percent of the average unpaid balance of the contract during the taxable year are treated as interest. IRC § 163(b)(1). The amount treated as interest, however, cannot exceed the aggregate carrying charges attributable to that year. IRC § 163(b)(2). Whether such interest is deductible depends upon whether the purchased personal property or educational services is connected with the taxpayer's business or investment. Personal interest is not deductible.

§ 5.4000. INADEQUATE INTEREST. In certain cases where the stated interest payable on deferred purchase payments or on a loan of cash is less than market rates, the Code imputes interest payments of a sufficient amount to raise the interest rate to a reasonable figure. The deductibility of such imputed interest is determined by the rules described in §§ **5.0000–5.1510.**

§ 5.4100. Deferred Purchase Payments. If a contract of sale allows deferred payments for a period of greater than one year, payments made more than six months after the sale may be treated under IRC § 483 as including *unstated interest,* which may be deductible as interest by the buyer-debtor and is included as ordinary income to the creditor-vendor. The total unstated interest is equal to the excess of the total payments to be made over the present value of those payments. The present value is computed by using a discount rate that is equal to the applicable Federal rate as determined by reference to IRC § 1274(d). IRC § 483(b). See **§ 5.5130.** In many cases, the discount rate will be limited to a maximum rate of nine percent compounded semiannually. IRC § 1274A. In certain cases where land is sold on a deferred payment arrangement between family members, the maximum discount rate is six percent compounded semiannually. **§ 5.4110.**

The total unstated interest is apportioned among the payments that are due to be made more than six months after the sale in a similar manner to that employed in determining original issue discount (OID); that is, the interest allocated to a payment reflects the interest accrued to that date on a compounded basis. See §§ **5.5000** and **5.5200.**

In many cases when a debt instrument is given as partial or full consideration for property in kind, the OID rules of IRC §§ 1272–1274 are applicable to the debt instrument. **§ 5.5300.** In those cases, IRC §§ 1272–1274 take priority and IRC § 483 does not apply. IRC § 483(d)(1). As noted in **§ 5.5300,** when a debt instrument is received as partial or full payment for property in kind, in some circumstances the provisions of IRC § 483 will apply; in others, the OID rules of IRC §§ 1272–1274 will apply, and, in some cases, neither will apply.

§ 5.4110. Exceptions. As to the purchaser of personalty or of educational services to which IRC § 163(b) applies [see **§ 5.3000**], IRC § 163(b) takes priority over IRC § 483. IRC § 483(d)(3). As noted in **§ 5.4100,** in most cases, IRC § 483 will not apply to a debt instrument to which the OID rules of IRC § 1272 apply. IRC § 483(d)(1). IRC § 483 does not apply in certain other circumstances described in IRC § 483(d), including a sale or exchange in which the sale price does not exceed $3,000. Neither IRC § 483 nor the OID rules of IRC §§ 1272–1274 apply to the *obligor* on a debt instrument given as consideration for the purchase of personal use property. IRC § 1275(b)(1).

If an individual sells land under a deferred payment contract to a member of his family (as defined in IRC § 267(c)(4)), the imputed interest rate cannot exceed six percent compounded semiannually. IRC § 483(e)(1). This maximum rate limitation does not apply if one of the parties to the transaction is a nonresident alien. IRC § 483(e)(4). For any one calendar year, the aggregate amount of sales price between two related individuals that can qualify for this maximum rate limitation is $500,000. IRC § 483(e)(3).

§ 5.4200. Loans Bearing Inadequate Interest. When a loan, which is made without a discount, either bears no interest or bears below-market-rate interest, the OID rules do not apply, but it is clear that an item of value has been passed by the lender to the borrower. The reason that inadequate interest is charged to the borrower may be compensatory or it may be donative. In any event, in many (but not all) such circumstances, Congress has chosen to recharacterize the transaction by constructing a transfer to the borrower of all or a part of the amount by which the stated interest (if any) is inadequate (as compared with market rate interest) and by constructing an interest payment from the borrower to the lender. IRC § 7872. The market rate interest is determined by reference to the "applicable Federal rate," which is described at **§ 5.5130.** IRC § 7872(f). The constructive transfers and interest payments that are deemed to have been made under IRC § 7872 can cause income tax consequences and (in certain cases) gift tax consequences. See **§ 2.1540** for a discussion of IRC § 7872 and of the timing problems that can arise under that provision.

§ 5.5000. ORIGINAL ISSUE DISCOUNT. A debt instrument is sometimes issued at a discount price; that is, the issue price is less than the amount of principal that is payable by the debtor over the term of the debt. The amount of such discount is called "original issue discount" or "OID." IRC § 1273(a)(1). There is a *de minimis* exception: if the original issue discount is less than the product of multiplying 1/4 of 1 percent times the number of complete years to maturity, then the debt will be treated as not having any original issue discount. IRC § 1273(a)(3). The OID represents additional interest that effectively is payable by the debtor over the period of the loan. The period of the loan is divided into "accrual periods," each of which typically is a six-month period. IRC § 1272(a)(5). The tax law allocates a portion of the OID to each day of each accrual period and treats the amount so allocated as interest received by the creditor and paid by the debtor. With a few exceptions, this imputation of interest payments is made regardless of the method of accounting employed by the creditor and by the debtor. The interest so allocated is included in the creditor's gross income and, in proper circumstances, is deductible by the debtor. IRC §§ 163(e), 1272(a). The deductibility of such interest depends upon the debtor's use of the loan proceeds. Certain debt instruments are excluded from OID treatment: tax-exempt obligations, United States savings bonds, short-term debts, (i.e., debts with a term period of one year or less [but note that the discount on a short-term debt may have to be accrued and recognized by the holder under IRC § 1281]), and certain nonbusiness loans between natural persons if the aggregate amount of loans between those persons does not exceed $10,000. IRC § 1272(a)(2). Note that interest (including OID) of a cash-method debtor on a short-term debt is deductible only when paid. IRC § 163(e)(2)(C). Also, if the obligor of a debt instrument having OID is on the cash method and if the debt is incurred in connection with personal use property, the obligor cannot deduct interest until paid [IRC § 1275(b)(2)]; this provision will apply primarily to qualified residence interest in view of the current law's disallowance of a deduction for personal interest. See §§ **5.1330–5.1332.** For an excellent treatment of the function of present value and the operation of the OID rules, see Posin, *The Time Value of Money in Corporate Takeovers*, 21 Conn.L.Rev. 49, 53–62 (1988).

§ 5.5100. Definitions of Terms. OID is defined as the difference between the "stated redemption price at maturity" of a debt instrument and the issue price. IRC § 1273(a)(1).

A debt instrument refers to a bond, debenture, note, certificate, or other evidence of indebtedness. IRC § 1275(a)(1). The term "debt instrument" does not include certain annuity contracts. IRC § 1275(a)(1)(B).

§ 5.5110. Stated Redemption Price at Maturity. The "stated redemption price at maturity" is the *total* amount payable on a debt instrument over the term of the debt. It includes interest payments other than payments that are based on a fixed rate and are payable unconditionally during the term of the loan at fixed periodic intervals of no greater than one year. IRC § 1273(a)(2).

§ 5.5120. Issue Price. A debt instrument's "issue price" depends upon whether the debt instrument was publicly offered and upon whether it was issued in exchange for cash, property, or services. For purposes of the OID rules, any reference to "property" is deemed to refer to property, services, and the right to use property; but it does not refer to cash. IRC § 1273(b)(5).

If a publicly-offered debt instrument is issued for cash, the issue price is the price at which the debt instrument was first offered to the public at a price at which a substantial amount of such debt instruments were sold. IRC § 1273(b)(1). If a debt instrument which is not publicly offered is issued for cash, the issue price of each such debt instrument is the price paid by the first buyer of that debt instrument. IRC § 1273(b)(2).

If a debt instrument is issued for "property," and if the debt instrument either is part of an issue that is traded on an established securities market or is issued in exchange for stocks or securities that are so traded or (in certain cases) is issued in exchange for other "property" of a kind that is regularly traded on an established market, then the issue price of such debt instrument is equal to the fair market value of the "property" for which the debt instrument was issued. IRC § 1273(b)(3). In all other cases when a debt instrument is issued for "property," if the stated interest payable under the debt instrument provides an interest rate that is equal to or greater than the "applicable Federal rate," compounded semiannually, the issue price will equal the stated redemption price at maturity, and so, there will be no OID. IRC §§ 1273(b)(4), 1274. However, in such cases when the debt instrument does not provide an adequate interest rate, the Commissioner will impute the issue price under IRC § 1274. With one minor exception, this imputed issue price is the sum of the present values of *all* payments due under the debt instrument. IRC § 1274(b)(1). The present value of a payment is determined as of the date of the sale or exchange by applying a discount rate equal to the "applicable Federal rate" (defined in **§ 5.5130**) compounded semiannually. IRC § 1274(b)(2).

As previously noted, the significance of the "issue price" is that OID is equal to the difference between the "stated redemption price at maturity" and the "issue price." Thus, the smaller the issue price, the greater that the OID can be. For a discussion of OID, see Posin, *The Time Value of Money in Corporate Takeovers*, 21 Conn.L.Rev. 49, 53–62 (1988).

§ 5.5130. Applicable Federal Rate. The "applicable Federal rate," which is used as the discount rate, is determined and published monthly by the Treasury Department on the basis of the average market yields of market obligations of the United States. IRC § 1274(d). There are separate Federal rates for short-term, mid-term and long-term debt instruments. IRC § 1274(d).

The applicable Federal rate is sometimes used to impute the issue price of a debt. As noted in § 5.5120, the Commissioner will impute the issue price of a debt by discounting the payments to be made only if: (1) the debt is given as partial or full payment for "property," and (2) there is not adequate stated interest. Even then, there are a number of exceptions set forth in IRC §§ 1274(c)(3), and 1273(b)(3), which will bar the application of this discount method.

When the issue price is imputed under IRC § 1274, the discount rate is the applicable Federal rate (compounded semiannually) at the date of sale or exchange of the property for which the debt instrument is issued. IRC § 1274(b)(2). In the case of sales and leaseback transactions, the discount rate for imputing the issue price of a debt instrument is 110 percent of the applicable Federal rate. IRC § 1274(e). In certain sales or exchanges, the discount rate cannot exceed nine percent compounded semiannually. IRC § 1274A.

§ 5.5140. *De Minimis* Exception. If the amount of OID for a debt instrument is so small that it does not warrant making periodic allocations of interest accruals, it would be an administrative nuisance to require that treatment. The Code responds to that concern for administrative convenience by establishing a *de minimis* rule under which a relatively small amount of OID is disregarded. Specifically, the Code provides that if the amount of OID for a debt instrument is less than the product of multiplying the number of complete years to the instrument's maturity times one-fourth of one percent of the stated redemption price at maturity, then the amount of OID will be treated as zero. IRC § 1273(a)(3). The figure, as so computed, that constitutes the ceiling on the *de minimis* rule is referred to as the *"de minimis* amount." Treas. Reg. § 1.1273–1(d)(2).

§ 5.5150. Illustrations.

§ 5.5151. *De Minimis* Rule. A debt instrument that provides for a payment of $100 after 10 years is issued for $98. Before applying the *de minimis* rule, the OID is $2—the difference between the stated redemption price at maturity ($100) and the issue price ($98). One-fourth of one percent of the $100 stated redemption price at maturity is 25 cents. Multiplying 25 cents times the number of complete years to maturity (10) provides a $2.50 ceiling for the *de minimis* rule—i.e., $2.50 is the *de minimis* amount. IRC § 1273(a)(3). Since the OID for the instrument is less than $2.50, it is treated as zero. If the debt instrument had been issued for $97.50 or less, the OID would not have been less than the *de minimis* amount, and so the OID would not be treated as zero.

§ **5.5152. Issue Price When Debt or Property is Traded on an Established Securities Market.** *R* Corporation exchanged its bond (a debt instrument) for 50 shares of the stock of the *X* Corporation. The fair market value of the 50 shares of *X*'s stock is $10,000. If either the *X* stock is traded on an established securities market or the *R* bond is part of an issue a portion of which is traded on an established securities market, the issue price of the *R* bond will be $10,000, since that is the fair market value of the property for which the bond was issued. IRC § 1273(b)(3).

§ **5.5153. Imputed Issue Price.** In Year One, *C* transferred a truck with a fair market value of $8,500 to *H* in exchange for a debt instrument issued by *H* that was not traded on an established securities market. The principal amount of the debt instrument is $10,000 to be paid in a lump sum in 5 years. The debt instrument provides for 5% interest to be paid semiannually. The applicable Federal rate for mid-term securities at that time was 10%. The issue price of the debt instrument is the sum of the present values of the interest payments and the present value of the $10,000 amount payable at maturity. The present value of each payment is determined by discounting that payment at 10% compounded semiannually, determined as of the date on which the exchange took place.

In determining the stated redemption price at maturity of *H*'s debt instrument, the 5% interest payments are excluded since they are based on a fixed rate and are payable unconditionally during the term of the loan at fixed periodic intervals of no greater than one year. So, the stated redemption price at maturity is $10,000. In contrast, the issue price of *H*'s debt instrument includes the present values of the interest payments. Consequently, the OID equals the difference between

$10,000 (the stated redemption price at maturity) and the sum of the present value of the $10,000 required payment plus the present values of the interest payments that are required to be made over the 5–year term of the debt instrument.

§ 5.5200. Accrual and Allocation of OID. Once the amount of OID is determined, that amount is allocated among the accrual periods for the term of the debt instrument. The OID is allocated on a daily basis for each such accrual period (typically a six-month period). In general, the daily amount of OID is determined by treating the debt instrument as earning interest at a fixed rate, compounded semiannually, so that the amount of annual interest increases over the term of the debt instrument. The portion of OID that is allocated to a taxable year is included in the creditor's gross income for that year and is treated as paid or accrued by the debtor in that year. The deductibility of interest allocated to a debtor is determined by the rules described at **§§ 5.0000–5.1500.** In effect, the creditor and debtor are placed on the accrual method for purposes of reporting OID regardless of whether they otherwise report their income on that method. But see, IRC §§ 163(e)(2)(C), 1275(b)(2) discussed at **§ 5.5000.**

§ 5.5210. Yield to Maturity. The fixed rate which is used to determine the daily OID allocations is the "yield to maturity" of the debt instrument (i.e., the rate that if applied to the issue price and compounded semiannually would provide by the maturity date an amount equal to the OID). IRC § 1272(a)(3).

§ 5.5220. Computation of OID. The daily allocation of OID typically is determined separately for each six-month period (the accrual period) in the term of the debt. If the debt instrument does not provide for an acceleration of the payment of principal, the method of computing the daily allocation of OID for each six-month period in the term of the debt is to multiply the fixed rate (the yield to maturity) times the "adjusted issue price" (the issue price plus previously accrued OID) as determined at the beginning of the six-month period and then allocate the resulting figure (less interest paid in that six-month period) on a daily basis within that six-month period. IRC § 1272(a)(3)–(5). For illustrations of these computations, see **§ 2.1213–5(D)**, Exs. (1)–(3). If the debt instrument permits prepayments of principal or certain other accelerations of principal payments, IRC § 1272(a)(6) adopts a more complex formula for determining the daily portion of OID.

§ 5.5230. Adjustment to Creditor's Basis. A creditor's basis in a debt instrument is increased by the amount of OID that is included in his gross income. IRC § 1272(d)(2).

§ 5.5240. Illustration. For an illustration of some of the principles set forth in **§§ 5.5000–5.5230**, see the examples in **§ 2.1513–5(D)** which demonstrate how OID operates in conjunction with cancellation of indebtedness.

§ 5.5300. Sale or Exchange of Property. As indicated in **§ 5.5120**, the IRC § 1272 OID principles are not restricted to debt instruments that are acquired for cash. Sections 1272 and 1274 OID rules can also apply to debt instruments acquired in connection with the sale or exchange of property or services. The IRC § 1272 and § 1274 OID rules, therefore, overlap with the treatment of deferred payment sales in IRC § 483. While the treatment of IRC § 1272 and § 1274 OID rules is similar to the treatment under IRC § 483 of deferred payment sales, there are differences—for example, the amount of unstated interest is computed differently for purposes of IRC §§ 1272 and 1274 than it is for purposes of IRC § 483 deferred payment sales, and (more importantly) a cash method taxpayer will include interest under IRC § 483 in income when received as contrasted to the treatment of OID by IRC § 1272 which requires that the interest be taken into income as it accrues. The Code excludes certain sales or exchanges of property from the imputed issue price rules of IRC § 1274; for example, exclusions are provided for: debt instruments received for the sale of a principal residence; certain sales of land between family members; the sale by an individual, estate or testamentary trust of a farm for less than $1,000,000; certain sales of patents; and the sale of property for which the aggregate consideration does not exceed $250,000. IRC § 1274(c)(3). The imputed issue price rules do not apply if none of the payments on the debt instrument are due to be made more than six months after the sale or exchange of the property for which the instrument was given. IRC § 1274(c)(1). In many sales in which one of the exceptions to IRC § 1274 applies, the deferred payment rules of IRC § 483 will apply; however, there are a few types of transactions that are exempt from both IRC § 1274 and IRC § 483. For example, when a taxpayer gives his personal note as consideration for the purchase of personal use property, neither IRC § 483 nor IRC § 1274 will apply to the taxpayer (the *obligor*). IRC § 1275(b).

§ 5.5400. Subsequent Holder of Debt Instrument. The OID rules not only apply to the original holder of the debt instrument, but also apply to any subsequent holder. So, if a taxpayer purchases a debt instrument from the holder of that instrument and if there was OID when that instrument was issued, the OID will continue to be allocated to the purchaser on a daily basis as described at §§ **5.5200–5.5230.** However, if the amount paid by the purchaser for the debt instrument is greater than the sum of the issue price of the instrument and the aggregate OID previously included in the gross income of any holder, the daily OID allocation that is treated as income to that purchaser will be reduced by an allocated portion of that excess (the purchaser's "acquisition premium"). IRC § 1272(a)(7). A holder will not recognize any OID as income if he purchased the debt instrument at a premium (i.e., if he paid more for the debt instrument than its stated redemption price at maturity). IRC § 1272(c)(1). The sale of a debt instrument (for a premium or otherwise) has no effect on the amount of *deduction* that continues to be allowable to the issuer; only the holder's income can be affected. A change in the issuer's deduction allowance would place a great administrative burden on the issuer. For an illustration of the treatment of an acquisition premium, see § **2.1213–5(D)**, Ex. (2).

§ **5.5500. Characterization of Gain from the Retirement, Sale or Exchange of Debt Instrument.** Amounts received on retirement of a debt instrument are treated as having been received in exchange therefor. IRC § 1271(a)(1). In the absence of an explicit provision to the contrary, the gain recognized on a sale or exchange of a debt instrument usually will constitute a capital gain since the instrument usually will be a capital asset. Exceptions to capital gains treatment are set forth in IRC § 1271.

In general, IRC § 1271(a)(2) characterizes the gain from the sale or exchange of debt instruments as ordinary income to the extent that the gain represents previously unreported OID. This provision does not apply to a debt instrument if there was no intention by the issuer to call the debt instrument before maturity. IRC § 1271(a)(2)(A). An intention to call an instrument before maturity means that there was an understanding between the issuer and the original purchaser that the issuer will redeem the instrument before maturity. Treas. Reg. §§ 1.1271–1(a)(1), 1.1232–3(b)(4)(i). This provision does not apply if the holder of the debt instrument purchased it at a premium, nor does it apply to tax-exempt obligations. IRC § 1271(a)(2)(B). However, the gain recognized on the sale or exchange of short-term government obligations will cause ordinary income to the extent that the gain represents the ratable share of acquisition discount. IRC § 1271(a)(3).

Acquisition discount is the excess of the stated redemption price at maturity over the taxpayer's basis in the debt instrument. IRC § 1271(a)(3)(C). The ratable share of that discount is determined by comparing the number of days the taxpayer held the debt instrument to the number of days in the period from the taxpayer's acquisition of the instrument to its maturity. IRC § 1271(a)(3)(D).

§ 5.6000. MARKET DISCOUNT. IRC § 1276 requires that any gain on the disposition of a "market discount bond" that was acquired in the marketplace (i.e., it was not acquired from the issuer) shall be treated as ordinary income to the extent that the gain is attributable to accrued "market discount." A "market discount bond" is a bond having a market discount except: obligations payable in no more than one year; United States savings bonds; tax-exempt obligations such as debts of a local government; installment obligations; and a few other exceptions. IRC § 1278(a)(1). The term "bond" refers to any bond, debenture, note, certificate of indebtedness, or other evidence of debt. IRC § 1278(a)(3).

"Market discount" is equal to an excess of the stated redemption price at maturity over the taxpayer's basis when the obligation was acquired. IRC § 1278(a)(2). If the purchased bond had original issue discount, a "revised issue price" (i.e., issue price plus OID recognized prior to the purchase in question) will be used in determining market discount in lieu of using the stated redemption price at maturity. IRC § 1278(a)(2)(B), (4).

Unless the taxpayer elects otherwise, the "accrued market discount" will be determined by first allocating the market discount ratably to each day over the period that begins with the taxpayer's acquisition of the bond and ends on the date that the bond matures, and second, multiplying that daily accrued discount times the number of days that the taxpayer held the bond. IRC § 1276(b)(1). In lieu of a ratable daily allocation of market discount, the taxpayer can elect under IRC § 1276(b)(2) to determine accrued market discount by applying a constant interest rate, compounded semiannually, to the taxpayer's basis in the bond. If the bond's principal can be paid in more than one payment, accrued market discount is determined in a manner set forth in regulations. IRC § 1276(b)(3).

The holder of a market discount bond can elect under IRC § 1278(b) to accrue and recognize a portion of the market discount each year that he holds the bond, and if that election is made, the provisions of IRC § 1276 will not cause ordinary income on the sale of the bond. IRC § 1278(b)(1)(A). Also, if that election is made, taxpayer's basis in the bond will be increased by the amounts included in his gross income. IRC § 1278(b)(4). If made, the election will apply to all market discount bonds that were acquired by the taxpayer in the taxable year in which the election was made, and the election will apply to subsequent taxable years until revoked by the taxpayer with the consent of the Secretary (or his delegate). IRC § 1278(b)(2), (3).

§ 5.6100. Partial Principal Payments. If a distribution of a portion of the principal of a market discount bond is made to the holder of the bond, the distributee will recognize ordinary income to the extent that the amount of the distribution does not exceed the accrued market discount on the bond. IRC § 1276(a)(3). In such an event, the amount of the bond's accrued market discount will be reduced by the amount of the distribution that is treated as ordinary income to the holder of the bond. IRC § 1276(a)(3)(B). This latter provision prevents the holder of the bond from being taxed twice on the same amount of discount.

§ 5.6200. Stripped Bonds or Coupons. If the holder of a bond separates some of the interest coupons from the bond and then disposes of either the bond or the stripped coupons, the transferor must recognize interest income as provided in IRC § 1286. For this provision to apply, it is not necessary that the bond actually contain coupons, which are rarely found on bonds currently. For purposes of that statute, the right to receive interest on a bond is treated as a "coupon." IRC § 1286(e)(5). So the statute can apply to a circumstance where the interest element of a bond has been separated from the right to repayment of the principal.

§ 5.7000. DENIAL OF DEDUCTION. In addition to the denial of deductions described at **§§ 5.1200–5.1500**, deductions are disallowed from certain kinds of interest payments, such as:

(a) interest on a debt incurred to purchase a single premium life insurance policy [IRC § 264(a)(2)];

(b) interest on debts incurred in connection with a plan to systematically borrow part or all of the annual increments in a life insurance policy's cash value (or of the increments in cash value of an annuity or endowment contract) [IRC § 264(a)(3) (there are some exceptions to this rule)];

(c) interest on debts incurred in connection with the purchase or *holding* of an obligation when the income from the obligation is wholly exempt from federal income tax (e.g., interest on a loan used to purchase municipal bonds which provide tax-free income) [IRC § 265(a)(2)].

§ 5.7100. Construction Period Interest.
Interest paid or accrued by a taxpayer on an indebtedness incurred or continued for the purposes of constructing or producing tangible property (or for the purchase of certain property to be held for sale to customers) must be capitalized and added to the basis of such property (or added to the inventory costs of produced or purchased inventory). IRC § 263A. As to produced or constructed property, this provision applies only to interest paid or incurred during the production period which is allocable to produced property that either: (a) is real property, (b) is property with a class life (as determined by IRC § 168) of at least 20 years, (c) has an estimated production period exceeding two years, or (d) has an estimated production period exceeding one year and a cost exceeding $1,000,000. IRC § 263A(f). This capitalization requirement does not apply to the production of property for the taxpayer's personal use; for example, the interest connected with the construction of a personal residence for the taxpayer is not capitalized. IRC § 263A(c)(1).

§ 5.8000. PREPAID INTEREST.
A prepayment of interest (that is otherwise deductible) made by an accrual-method taxpayer must be amortized over the period of the loan. A cash-method taxpayer also must capitalize a prepaid interest payment and amortize that amount. IRC § 461(g). Thus, a cash-method taxpayer effectively is put on the accrual method for purposes of deducting prepaid interest payments. Prepaid interest must be allocated ratably over the period of the loan. *Zidanic v. Commissioner*, 79 T.C. 651, 1982 WL 11171 (1982).

§ 5.8100. "Points"—Current Deduction.
IRC § 461(g)(2) permits a current deduction in certain cases for "points" paid by a cash method taxpayer *in connection with* a loan incurred for the purchase or improvement of the taxpayer's principal residence and secured thereby. "Points" are dollar obligations that are imposed by the lender on the borrower (typically at the closing of the loan) in lieu of charging a higher annual interest rate. Each "point" is equal to 1% of the total amount loaned. The payment of points is currently deductible if incurred in connection with a loan for the purchase or improvement of the taxpayer's principal residence (and secured by such residence) if the use of points and the amount charged are in accord with the established practice in that community. To be deductible, the points must be charged for the loan; if payment is for appraisal fees, title fees, inspection fees, attorney fees, or property

taxes, it will not be deductible regardless of how the parties attempt to characterize the payment. Rev. Proc. 94–27. This provision for a current deduction constitutes an exception to the general rule that prepaid interest must be amortized.

§ 5.8200.   Safe Harbor for the Current Deduction of Points. In Rev. Proc. 94–27, the Service provided a safe harbor for a cash method taxpayer to obtain a current deduction for the payment of points for a loan undertaken in connection with the acquisition of the taxpayer's principal residence. This safe harbor provision does not apply to points incurred in connection with the *improvement* of a principal residence. To come within this safe harbor provision, all of the following conditions must be satisfied:

(1) The Uniform Settlement Statement that is prescribed by the Real Estate Settlement Procedures Act of 1974 must clearly designate the amount of points that are incurred in connection with the indebtedness.

(2) The amount of points must be stated as a percentage of the indebtedness.

(3) The amount of points must conform to an established business practice for charging points for loans for the acquisition of personal residences in the area in which the residence is located, and the amount of points must not exceed the amount generally charged in that area.

(4) The points must be paid in connection with the acquisition of the taxpayer's principal residence and must be secured by it.

(5) The points must be paid directly by the taxpayer. If a taxpayer who purchases a principal residence uses the cash method of accounting, points paid by the seller of the residence (including points charged to the seller) will be treated as paid directly by the taxpayer provided that the taxpayer excludes the seller-paid points from his purchase price for the residence in computing his basis in the residence.

The 1994 Revenue Procedure specifies a number of circumstances in which the safe harbor will not apply. For example, it does not apply to points paid for a refinancing loan, a home equity loan, or a line of credit even when such loans are secured by the personal residence. It does not apply to a loan obtained in order to make improvements to taxpayer's residence. It also does not apply to points paid for a loan to acquire property that is not the taxpayer's principal residence, such as a second home, vacation property, and investment or trade or business property.

§ 5.8300. "Points" Paid on Refinancing a Home Mortgage.

In Rev. Rul. 87–22, the Commissioner announced that points paid on the refinancing of a home mortgage (at least to the extent that the amount of the "new" refinanced mortgage does not exceed the balance of the "old" mortgage at the time of refinancing) is not protected by IRC § 461(g)(2) since the loan is not incurred for the purchase or improvement of the taxpayer's home. Since the Commissioner determined that the exception provided by IRC § 461(g)(2) does not apply to refinanced loans, he held that the points paid for refinancing home mortgages must be amortized over the period of the loan. Rev. Proc. 87–15. A majority of the Tax Court sustained the Commissioner's position in *Huntsman v. Commissioner*, 91 T.C. 917, 1988 WL 122291 (1988) (divided decision), but because of the special facts of that case (described below), the Eighth Circuit Court of Appeals reversed, 905 F.2d 1182 (8th Cir. 1990).

Huntsman involved the refinancing of a short-term "bridge loan" (i.e., an acquisition loan to purchase taxpayer's principal residence that was taken for a short period during which the borrower seeks to obtain permanent financing) which was secured by a first mortgage on taxpayer's principal residence plus a second mortgage taken one year later to make home improvements. The first mortgage acquisition loan was repayable in full in three years (i.e., it was a so-called balloon loan). A little more than two and one-half years later, taxpayer obtained permanent financing (a 30–year variable rate mortgage) and used the proceeds to pay off the bridge loan and the home improvement loan. The taxpayer paid the lender three points (amounting to $4,440) for making the permanent financing loan. The question in *Huntsman* was whether taxpayer's payment of points for the permanent refinancing could be deducted in the year of payment or whether it must be amortized over the 30–year period of that loan. The Tax Court held that the points must be amortized. In reversing the Tax Court, the Eighth Circuit stressed that the refinancing of the bridge and home improvement loans were made *in connection with* the purchase or improvement of the taxpayer's principal residence since the taxpayer's obvious expectation at the time he obtained a three-year bridge loan was to replace it with permanent financing. The court's opinion suggests that the fact that the refinanced loan was a short-term bridge loan was critical to its decision; it is doubtful that the Eighth Circuit would allow a current deduction for points paid for the refinancing of a long-term acquisition loan. Nevertheless, in an AOD (CC–1991–02) promulgated on February 11, 1991, the Service stated that while it would not seek Supreme Court review of the Eighth Circuit's decision in *Huntsman* because there is no conflict among the circuit courts, the Service will not follow that decision in jurisdictions outside of the Eighth Circuit.

§ 5.8400.   Unamortized Loan Costs Deductible on Taxpayer's Death. In Rev. Rul. 86–67, the Commissioner stated that unamortized loan costs (which include unamortized interest prepayments) that exist at a taxpayer's death can be deducted in the decedent's final return. The taxpayer's death ends the period during which he can benefit from the loan.

§ 5.9000.   SHAM TRANSACTIONS. The interest deduction has played a prominent role in a number of tax reduction schemes. Many such plans consist of mere paper transactions in which bookkeeping entries are made but very little of substance occurs. In most of these cases, courts will disallow the claimed interest deduction. E.g., *Knetsch v. United States*, 364 U.S. 361 (1960). Several cases have suggested that even where a loan transaction was not a sham, if the taxpayer's sole motive in taking the loan was tax-oriented, the deduction might be denied. E.g., *Goldstein v. Commissioner*, 364 F.2d 734 (2d Cir. 1966). The *Goldstein* approach is an application of the "economic substance" doctrine. See **§ 5.9100** below. While the subsequent Congressional adoption of restrictions on deductibility of interest paid on loans incurred in connection with an investment [see IRC § 163(d)] would seem to cast doubt on the continuing vitality of the *Goldstein* approach, the case has been cited with approval. See *Sheldon v. Commissioner*, 94 T.C. 738, 1990 WL 69233 (1990) (reviewed by the court). The *Sheldon* decision is discussed below.

§ 5.9100.   Economic Substance Doctrine. In a number of cases, courts have held that a transaction which lacks economic substance will be disregarded for tax purposes. *E.g., Sheldon v. Commissioner*, 94 T.C. 738, 1990 WL 69233 (1990) (reviewed by the court); *ACM Partnership v. Commissioner*, 73 T.C.M. 2189 (1997); *Yosha v. Commissioner*, 861 F.2d 494 (7th Cir. 1988). To have economic substance, a transaction must be imbued with independent, nontax consideration. See *Frank Lyon Co. v. United States*, 435 U.S. 561, 572 (1978). Accordingly, interest on loans or other financial transactions will be deductible only if there is an independent purpose, other than tax benefits, for the transaction. *Sheldon v. Commissioner*, *supra*. The doctrine of economic substance is separate and distinct from the sham transaction doctrine.

In a 9–7 decision in *Sheldon*, a majority of the Tax Court applied the economic substance doctrine to deny interest deductions where the potential profit from a transaction was relatively small in comparison to the tax benefits that were expected. The seven dissenting Tax Court judges also adopted the economic substance doctrine and also cited the *Goldstein* case (see § **5.9000**) with approval. However, the dissenters determined that the application of the economic substance doctrine should not turn on the sufficiency of the expected profits of the transaction. The dissenters would have the sole test be whether there was a tax-independent purpose to the transaction. Even if the doctrine does turn on sufficiency of profits (and the dissenters thought that it did not), the dissenters believe that the expected profits should then be compared to the amount of *investment* rather than to the amount of anticipated tax benefits. The nontax benefits should at least be commensurate with the costs expended in the transaction. See *ACM Partnership v. Commissioner, supra.*

*

CHAPTER SIX

STATE AND LOCAL TAXES

§ 6.0000. DEDUCTION FOR PAYMENT OF TAXES. Except for the generation-skipping tax that is imposed by IRC § 2601 on certain income distributions and for the environmental tax imposed by IRC § 59A, payments of federal taxes (e.g., federal income, estate or gift taxes, or federal excise taxes) are not deductible. IRC § 164(a). Some state and local taxes and foreign taxes are deductible. One-half of the self-employment social security tax paid by a *self-employed* taxpayer is deductible as a nonitemized deduction. (IRC § 164(f)).

§ 6.1000. DEDUCTIBLE TAXES. State and local income taxes and real and personal property taxes are deductible as are foreign income and real property taxes. IRC § 164(a). However, as noted in the paragraph below, a taxpayer can elect to deduct state and local sales taxes instead of deducting state and local income taxes. In addition, state, local, and foreign taxes incurred in connection with a trade or business or a profit-seeking venture are deductible even if such taxes are not listed in IRC § 164(a)(1)–(5); however, no deduction is permitted for any tax that is paid or accrued in connection with the acquisition or disposition of property. IRC § 164(a). If a tax is paid or accrued in connection with the acquisition of property, the tax is added to the taxpayer's basis in the property; if a tax is paid in connection with the sale or other disposition of property, the tax is deducted from the amount realized by the taxpayer on making that disposition. IRC § 164(a). This requirement that the state taxes connected with the acquisition or disposition of an asset be capitalized applies only to taxes incurred in connection with the conduct of a trade or business or profit-seeking activity; and presumably applies only if the deduction is claimed under IRC §§ 162 or 212 rather than under IRC § 164. If an asset is acquired for personal use, and if the taxpayer elects to deduct state and local sales taxes (as described in the paragraph below), those taxes are deductible rather than capitalized. It would appear that even if a state or local sales tax were incurred in connection with a trade or business or profit-seeking activity, the tax would be deductible (rather than capitalized) if the taxpayer elected to deduct the tax under IRC § 164(b)(5) by electing not to take a deduction for state and local income taxes.

For many years, state and local sales taxes were deductible, but that provision for a deduction was deleted by the 1986 TRA. For the years after that deletion and prior to 2004, state and local sales taxes were not deductible, but could be capitalized in certain circumstances. In the American Jobs Creation Act of 2004, Congress amended IRC § 164 to permit a taxpayer to elect either to take a deduction for state and local income taxes or instead to deduct state or local sales taxes. IRC § 164(b)(5). The motivation for granting that option is to permit a deduction for the payment of state taxes to citizens of states that do not have an income tax and derive their revenue primarily from sales taxes. If a taxpayer elects to deduct state and local sales taxes, the taxpayer has an option of either deducting the actual taxes paid, or the taxpayer can use the tax stated in tables the IRS provides, which tables are based on the average amount of sales taxes paid by persons in that state whose filing status, adjusted gross income, and number of dependents is similar to the taxpayers. IRC § 164(b)(5)(H). If the taxpayer elects to use the tables, the taxpayer can add a deduction for the actual state and local sales tax the taxpayer paid on the purchase of an automobile, boat or other item designated by the IRS. IRC § 164(b)(5)(H)(i). That provision permits a taxpayer to use the tables for his aggregate small purchases, and still get a deduction for the tax actually paid for large ticket items such as an automobile. This provision for an election to deduct state and local sales taxes will sunset in 2006; so, as currently written, the provision applies only for the years 2004 and 2005.

Taxes assessed against realty for local benefits of a kind tending to increase the value of the assessed property generally are not deductible. IRC § 164(c)(1); Treas. Reg. § 1.164–4. To the extent that such taxes are for the purpose of maintenance or repair or for the purpose of meeting interest charges, they can be deducted. Treas. Reg. § 1.164–4; GCM 37927. The taxpayer may be able to capitalize the nondeductible portion of such taxes, and, if the property whose value is increased is used in a trade or business and is depreciable, the taxpayer can depreciate that portion of the tax. Rev. Rul. 73–188.

If there is no election to deduct state and local sales taxes, estimated state income tax payments are deductible in the year made if the taxpayer is on the cash method and made the payment in good faith. If the taxpayer had no reasonable basis at the time of payment to believe that any additional tax liability will be incurred, the estimated tax payment is not deductible. Rev. Rul. 82–208. The federal environmental tax on corporate taxpayers and the generation-skipping tax (GST) imposed on certain income distributions are deductible. IRC § 164(a)(4),

(5). For the allocation of real estate taxes for the year in which the realty is sold, see § **6.3000.**

As noted in §§ **3.1200** and **6.4000**, a state tax that is deductible only under IRC § 164 will usually be an itemized deduction; but it will not be a miscellaneous itemized deduction. IRC § 67(b)(2). However, a state tax on property used in a trade or business will also qualify as a business expense deduction under IRC § 162, and so will be a nonitemized deduction if the TP is self-employed. The state *income* tax on an individual's business income will be an itemized deduction, regardless of whether the taxpayer is self-employed or an employee. See § **3.1200.**

§ **6.1100.   Definition of "Tax."** The question sometimes arises as to whether a payment required to be made to a state (or to a foreign government) should be treated as a "tax" for federal income tax purposes. A "tax" has been defined (for Federal income tax purposes) as an enforced contribution, exacted pursuant to legislative authority in the exercise of the taking power, and imposed and collected for the purpose of raising revenue to be used for public or governmental purposes and not as a payment for some special privilege granted or service rendered. See Rev. Rul. 61–152.

The Commissioner contends that there is a federal standard for determining whether an expenditure qualifies as a tax under IRC § 164 regardless of whether state law characterizes the payment as a tax. However, the Commissioner's attempts to deny a deduction for payments which are *required* to be made by New Jersey and California employees to a state disability fund was unsuccessful. *McGowan v. Commissioner*, 67 T.C. 599 (1976); *Trujillo v. Commissioner*, 68 T.C. 670 (1977). The Tax Court treated the payments as a state tax for which a deduction is allowed by IRC § 164. The Commissioner has conceded this issue and now allows a deduction for such payments. Rev. Ruls. 81–191 through 81–194. But, contributions of employers or employees to *voluntary* plans to provide disability benefits are not taxes within the meaning of § 164.

A New York law attempted to make tenants personally liable for real estate taxes imposed on the demised property so that the tenants could qualify a portion of their rent for an income tax deduction. In Rev. Rul. 79–180, the Commissioner determined that, in fact, the realty taxes were not imposed on tenants, whose only liability was to pay their rent; therefore no deduction is allowed to the tenants.

§ 6.2000.   TAXES NOT DEDUCTIBLE. Death and gift taxes (other than generation-skipping state and federal taxes imposed on certain income distributions [IRC § 164(a)(4), (b)(4)]) are not deductible whether imposed by the federal or state government. IRC § 275. The payment or accrual of state and local sales taxes that are not connected with the conduct of a trade or business or a profit-seeking activity is not deductible unless the taxpayer elects to deduct them in lieu of deducting state and local income taxes. State and local taxes on gasoline and other motor fuels are not deductible (unless such fuels are used by the taxpayer in his business or investment activities, in which event they may qualify as business or profit-oriented expenses).

Taxes assessed against realty for local benefits of a kind tending to increase the value of the assessed property generally are *not* deductible. IRC § 164(c); Treas. Reg. § 1.164–4. To the extent that such taxes are nondeductible, they can be capitalized [see Treas. Reg. 1.164–4(a)]; and, if the property is used in a trade or business or profit-oriented activity and is depreciable, the capitalized tax may be depreciated over the period that the improvements which caused the tax to be assessed are of use to the taxpayer's business or profit activity. Rev. Rul. 73–188. To the extent that such taxes are for the purpose of maintenance, repair, or to meet interest charges, and so are not for value added to taxpayer's property, they can be deducted under IRC § 164. Treas. Reg. § 1.164–4(b); GCM 37927. The burden is on the taxpayer to show the amount of the tax that is allocable to such purposes.

§ 6.2100.   Capitalization of Taxes Allocable to the Production of Commercial Realty. The direct cost of producing or constructing tangible property are capitalized and added to the basis of the produced property. IRC § 263A. Prior to the adoption of the 1986 TRA, which added § 263A to the Code, some of the indirect costs incurred in producing property were currently deductible and some were required to be capitalized. The 1986 TRA amended the Code to require that most of the indirect costs of producing property must be capitalized. The indirect costs that are required to be capitalized include taxes which are allocable to the produced property. IRC § 263A(a)(2)(B). So, real property taxes incurred with respect to realty on which a commercial building is being constructed will not be deductible but instead will be added to the taxpayer's basis in the building and deducted as part of the depreciation allowance for that building. Only taxes incurred or paid during the construction period (the period beginning with the date on which construction begins and ending with the date that the constructed property is ready to be placed in service) will have to be capitalized. If the building that the taxpayer constructs is for the personal use (as contrasted to an investment or business use) of the taxpayer (e.g., the construction of a personal residence), the capitalization requirements do not apply; in such cases, real estate taxes are currently deductible. IRC § 263A(c)(1).

§ 6.2200. Tax Imposed on Another. A person cannot deduct a payment of a tax which was imposed on someone else. So, if a taxpayer purchases realty which is encumbered by a lien for unpaid real property taxes which had accrued prior to the taxpayer's purchase of the realty, the taxpayer's subsequent payment of the overdue taxes constitutes part of the cost of the property to the taxpayer and is not deductible by him. *Reinhardt v. Commissioner*, 75 T.C. 47 (1980). To the extent that a real estate tax for the year of sale is allocated to the buyer under IRC § 164(d) [see **§ 6.3000**], it is treated as a tax imposed on the buyer and is deductible by him.

§ 6.3000. APPORTIONMENT OF REAL ESTATE TAX. Upon the sale of real property, the real property tax for the real property tax year of sale will be allocated between the buyer and seller according to the number of days of the taxable year during which each held the property. IRC § 164(d).

§ 6.3100. Illustration: Method of Apportionment. *D* sold Blackacre to *B* on February 28, Year One, which was not a leap year. On July 15 of that year, the State of *X* assessed a real property tax of $1,000 on Blackacre for that calendar year. *B* paid the tax on January 10, Year Two. *D* is entitled to an income tax deduction for Year One equal to 58/ 365 x $1,000 since *D* is deemed to have held Blackacre until one day prior to the day of sale. *B*, a cash-basis taxpayer, is entitled to a deduction of 307/365 x $1,000 in Year Two.

§ 6.4000. ITEMIZED DEDUCTIONS. For a tax payment (or accrual) to qualify as a nonitemized deduction, the expense must be directly, and not merely remotely, connected with a trade or business; and the taxpayer's business must not be that of being an employee. Property taxes imposed on realty that is used in a trade or business (other than the trade or business of being an employee) constitute nonitemized deductions, but state taxes imposed on an individual's *income* are an itemized deduction even when the individual's income is derived from the conduct of a self-employed trade or business. See **§ 3.1200.** Thus, most state and local taxes that are deductible will be itemized deductions. Even when treated as an itemized deduction, most such taxes are *not* subject to the 2% of AGI floor on the deduction of miscellaneous itemized deductions because taxes that are deductible under IRC § 164 are excluded from that limitation by IRC § 67(b)(2). However, if an individual's taxes are treated as itemized deductions, they are included with other itemized deductions of the taxpayer and subjected to the overall limitation on itemized deductions that is imposed by IRC § 68 when an individual's AGI exceeds a specified amount. See § **3.1120.**

Employee business expenses that are not reimbursed by the employer are miscellaneous itemized deductions and are subject to the 2% of AGI floor. See § **3.1100.** If an employee incurs state taxes in connection with his business of being an employee, those taxes qualify for deduction under both IRC §§ 164 and 162. If taken under § 164, the deduction is not a miscellaneous itemized deduction, and so is not subject to the 2% of AGI floor that applies to individual taxpayers. But, if the deduction is taken as a business expense under IRC § 162, it will be a miscellaneous itemized deduction. The question is which of those two provisions takes priority, or is the taxpayer allowed to choose? When both IRC §§ 162 and 164 have applied to the tax expense of a self-employed taxpayer, the courts and the IRS have allowed the taxpayer to use § 162 so that the item would be a nonitemized deduction. That benefitted the taxpayers in those cases. In the instant situation, the taxpayer would be benefitted if the deduction is characterized by IRC § 164 so that it is not subject to the 2% of AGI floor. The authors believe that since the deduction is allowable by IRC § 164, the exception in IRC § 67(b)(2) is applicable, and the tax is not subject to the 2% of AGI floor.

§ **6.5000.   LIMITATIONS ON DEDUCTION.** As noted in § **6.4000,** a tax deductible under IRC § 164 is excluded from the list of miscellaneous itemized deductions, and so is not subject to the 2% of AGI floor; but such taxes are subject to the overall limitation on an individual's itemized deductions imposed by IRC § 68. With only three exceptions, taxes deductible under IRC § 164 cannot be deducted in determining an individual's alternative minimum tax. IRC § 56(b)(1)(A)(ii). One of the exceptions is that a tax which can be deducted as a nonitemized deduction will be allowed in determining the alternative minimum tax. The other two exceptions are that the deduction for the generation-skipping tax imposed on income distributions and the deduction for the environmental tax imposed by IRC § 59A are allowed in determining the alternative minimum tax. IRC §§ 56(b)(1)(A), 164(a)(4), (5). All other deductible state and local and foreign taxes, including state and local sales taxes when the election is made to deduct those taxes, are disallowed in determining the alternative minimum tax.

The disallowance of a deduction for most taxes in determining the alternative minimum tax applies only to individual taxpayers; corporations are not denied a deduction for taxes. Similarly, the limitations on the deduction of miscellaneous itemized deductions and the overall limitation on itemized deductions (imposed by IRC §§ 67 and 68) do not apply to corporate taxpayers.

The alternative minimum tax is discussed in Chapter 15. An individual TP must compute both his regular income tax liability and his alternative minimum tax liability, and then the individual TP must pay whichever of those two is greater. The scope of the alternative minimum tax is expanding, and a significant percentage of individual taxpayers pay the alternative minimum tax rather than the regular tax. This expansion of the scope of the alternative minimum tax greatly increases the significance of the denial of a deduction for most taxes in determining an individual's alternative minimum tax liability.

*

CHAPTER SEVEN

LOSSES

§ 7.0000. DEDUCTION OF LOSSES. A corporation or other business entity typically is allowed a deduction for its losses since such losses are *presumed* to be incurred in connection with business activities. IRC § 165(a). An *individual* is allowed a deduction for a loss incurred by him only if the loss was incurred in connection with: (a) the individual's trade or business, (b) a transaction entered into for profit, or (c) a casualty or a theft of the individual's property. IRC § 165(c). No deduction is allowed a taxpayer for a loss to the extent that the taxpayer is compensated by insurance or otherwise. IRC § 165(a).

§ 7.1000. DENIAL OF DEDUCTION ON PUBLIC POLICY GROUNDS. The Commissioner maintains that no deduction will be allowed for a loss incurred as a consequence of a theft or as an incident of a trade or business or of a transaction for profit if the loss was incurred in connection with an illegal activity of the taxpayer. The Commissioner contends that a deduction must be denied in such cases to prevent a frustration of public policy. Rev. Rul. 77–126. Despite the fact that claimed deductions for *business expenses* cannot be denied on public policy grounds (Treas. Reg. § 1.162–1(a)), the Tax Court has sustained the Commissioner's position that the public policy exception does apply to *losses* for which a deduction is sought under IRC § 165 and accordingly has denied claims for theft loss deductions and for casualty loss deductions. See **§ 10.5400** and **§ 10.5500.** It is not sufficient for nondeductibility that an expenditure merely bears a relationship to an illegal act; "the test for nondeductibility always is the severity and immediacy of the frustration" of a sharply defined national or state policy that would result if a deduction were allowed. GCM 37985 (1977). See *Commissioner v. Tellier,* 383 U.S. 687. 694 (1966). In this connection, it is noteworthy that the Tax Court has held that a loss incurred in conducting an illegal business (i.e., the confiscation by the government of a truck, horse trailer, and marijuana owned by a marijuana dealer) could be deducted only under IRC § 165 as a loss if it were deductible at all, and, because of public policy considerations, the court disallowed the deduction. *Holt v. Commissioner,* 69 T.C. 75 (1977), aff'd per curiam, 611 F.2d 1160 (5th Cir. 1980). See also *Santilli v. Commissioner,* 69 T.C.M. 2974 (1995). The courts in *Holt* rejected the taxpayer's attempt to claim the loss as a business expense deduction under IRC § 162 (which is not subject to the public policy exception [see §§ **10.5000– 10.5500**]) because the loss provision is the more specific statutory direction.

The decisions of the Tax Court and the Court of Appeals for the Second Circuit in *Stephens v. Commissioner*, 93 T.C. 108 (1989), rev'd 905 F.2d 667 (2d Cir. 1990) are worth noting. *Stephens* involved a taxpayer who had been convicted of fraud and conspiracy in violation of federal statutes and who had been sentenced to prison plus several relatively small fines on each of five counts. One of the prison terms was suspended and taxpayer placed on probation on condition that taxpayer make restitution to his victim. The court chose that device to pressure the taxpayer to draw on funds in a Bermuda bank account that only the taxpayer could reach. The amount of restitution was $1 million, of which about $530,000 had been obtained by fraud, and the rest was interest. The taxpayer had paid income tax on the $530,000 of fraudulently obtained funds. Taxpayer sought to deduct the restitution payments of the $530,000 fraudulently obtained funds under IRC § 165(c)(2) as a loss incurred in a transaction entered into for a profit. IRC § 162(f) prohibits the allowance of a business expense deduction under IRC § 162(a) for the payment of a fine or similar penalty to a government for a violation of a law. While the Tax Court noted that IRC § 162(f) does not apply to a deduction claimed under IRC § 165, the court held that the Congressional policy that underlies the adoption of IRC § 162(f) should be applied to deny a deduction under IRC § 165 for a fine or similar penalty of a type that would preclude an IRC § 162 deduction. In other words, the Tax Court adopted a public policy limitation on the deductibility of losses under IRC § 165, and the court incorporated the terms of IRC § 162(f) into that public policy limitation. The Tax Court held that the taxpayer in *Stephens* is not allowed a deduction for the restitution payments he made because, the payments having been ordered in lieu of a prison term, they constituted a fine or similar penalty. Of course, the payments were made to a private person, and IRC § 162(f) applies only to payments to a "government." The Tax Court held that IRC § 162(f) does not require that the payment be made directly to a government; it is sufficient that the origin of the taxpayer's liability to make the payment is his criminal violation and that the payment satisfies a criminal penalty otherwise imposed on the taxpayer. See also *Waldman v. Commissioner*, 88 T.C. 1384 (1987), aff'd in a one-sentence order, 850 F.2d 611 (9th Cir. 1988); and *Bailey v. Commissioner*, 756 F.2d 44 (6th Cir. 1985).

In reversing the Tax Court's decision in *Stephens*, the Second Circuit held that the restitution payments are deductible by the taxpayer under IRC § 165(c)(2). *Stephens v. Commissioner*, 905 F.2d 667 (2d Cir. 1990). The Second Circuit concurred with the Tax Court's view that the policy underlying IRC § 162(f) should be imposed as a limitation on IRC § 165 as well. However, the Court of Appeals determined that the restitution payments made to the victim were compensatory in nature, not punitive. The Second Circuit distinguished *Waldman* on the basis that restitution was the only penalty imposed in that case, and distinguished *Bailey* on the basis that the payment in that case originally was imposed as a fine and subsequently was applied to claims for restitution, and was deemed by the Sixth Circuit to have retained its status as a penalty. The Second Circuit did not say that it would follow *Waldman* or *Bailey* in like circumstances.

The Second Circuit also held that IRC § 162(f) applies only to payments to a government and that the policy incorporated into IRC § 165 is similarly limited. The Second Circuit held that the policy of IRC § 162(f) that is incorporated into IRC § 165 as a public policy limitation does not apply to the taxpayer's restitution payment to his victim since the victim is a private person, not a government. Finally, the Second Circuit held that no national or state policy would be frustrated by allowing the deduction that the taxpayer claimed, and so the general terms of the public policy limitation on IRC § 165 deductions are inapplicable. For a contrary view, treating as a fine or penalty a restitution payment made to a non-governmental party pursuant to a criminal preceding, see *Kraft v. United States*, 991 F.2d 292 (6th Cir. 1993); and *Waldman v. Commissioner, supra*.

Perhaps the most important aspect of the *Stephens* decisions is that both the Tax Court and the Second Circuit Court of Appeals accepted the view that there are public policy limitations on deductions claimed under IRC § 165, albeit they disagreed as to how one of those public policy limitations was to be construed. The Commissioner contends that public policy limitation on deductions applies to every Code section except IRC §§ 61, 162, 212, and 471. GCM 36962 (1976). Consequently, the Commissioner contends that it applies to limit deductions claimed under IRC § 165, and the courts have adopted that view.

Casualty loss deductions also have been denied on public policy grounds. For example, no deduction will be allowed for fire damage that is attributable to a deliberate act of arson by the taxpayer even when the spread of the fire was not intended or anticipated by the taxpayer. In *Blackman v. Commissioner*, 88 T.C. 677 (1987), aff'd without published opinion, 867 F.2d 605 (1st Cir. 1988), the taxpayer deliberately set fire to his wife's clothes (apparently as an act of spite), and the fire spread and caused substantial damage to the house and to its contents. In denying the taxpayer a casualty loss deduction, the Tax Court relied on the public policy limitation as one of two alternative grounds for its decision. See also, § **7.2300.**

§ **7.2000. CASUALTY AND THEFT LOSSES.** A deduction is allowed for a loss of property arising from a fire, storm, shipwreck, or other casualty or from theft even though the property is used for purely personal purposes and is not used in connection with a business or profit-seeking activity. IRC § 165(c)(3). When the damaged or stolen property was neither business nor investment property, the loss is sometimes referred to as a personal casualty or theft loss. The deductibility of personal casualty and theft losses is subject to restrictions described at §§ **7.2500–7.2551.** A deduction is allowed under the casualty or theft loss provision only for damage or loss suffered by the taxpayer on property owned by him; no deduction is allowed under that provision for a taxpayer's liability for damages caused by the taxpayer to the property of another. See, e.g., *Miller v. Commissioner*, 34 T.C.M. 528 (1975).

A personal casualty or theft loss deduction will be allowed only to the extent of the loss in value of the damaged or stolen property; and, as we shall see, the amount allowed may be even less than that. No deduction is allowed for out-of-pocket costs incurred in connection with a personal casualty or theft loss. For example, no deduction is allowed for the additional living expenses incurred as a consequence of the unavailability of a damaged residence. Some expenses of this type, such as repairs of damaged property, can be used as a measurement of the amount of decline in value that the damaged property suffered. See § **7.2410.**

It is worth noting that IRC § 123 excludes from gross income the amounts received by a taxpayer, pursuant to an insurance contract, to reimburse the taxpayer for the extra living costs incurred for the taxpayer and his household while his residence is unavailable for occupancy because of a casualty (or because of the threat of a casualty). The amount of such insurance reimbursements that is excluded is limited to the excess of the actual living expenses incurred during the unavailability of the residence over the amount of living expenses that would have been normal for the taxpayer and his household to incur if the residence were occupied. Note that the Code excludes the reimbursement of such expenses from income even though, if not reimbursed and therefore borne by the taxpayer, the expenses would not be deductible. As previously noted, a reimbursement of a nondeductible expense is not always given parallel tax treatment to the treatment that would have been accorded to the expense if unreimbursed—such reimbursements sometimes are excluded from gross income even though the expenditure is nondeductible. See, e.g., § **10.1475** discussing the treatment of reimbursements received by a taxpayer to interview for a job.

Subject to specific exceptions such as the denial of a deduction for the payment of a fine, if a taxpayer incurs a loss of property which is used in a business or profit-seeking venture, he is entitled to a deduction for the amount of that loss whether or not it was caused by a casualty or theft. See Rev. Rul. 90–61; Rev. Rul. 87–59. Similarly, a taxpayer may be permitted to deduct as a business expense [IRC § 162] the amount he paid to another for damages that taxpayer caused if his liability was incurred in the course of his trade or business. See, *Milller v. Commissioner, supra*.

Casualty and theft losses incurred by an individual with respect to property that was used in a business or profit-seeking venture are deductible under IRC § 165(c)(1) or IRC § 165(c)(2) rather than IRC § 165(c)(3). Unless expressly mentioned otherwise, any reference hereafter to a casualty or theft loss refers to a loss incurred with respect to property that an individual had used exclusively for personal purposes.

§ 7.2100. Illustration: No Deduction for Loss Incurred on Condemnation of Residence.

X's personal residence was condemned by the city which paid *X* $20,000 as compensation. *X* had a basis of $25,000 in the property, so he realized a $5,000 loss. The loss does not constitute a casualty or theft loss, and, since the residence was not property held in a trade or business or in a profit-seeking venture, *X* is *not* entitled to a deduction.

§ 7.2110. Rationale.

The exhaustion of personally used property through ordinary use or deterioration constitutes personal consumption. While personal consumption does reduce a taxpayer's wealth, it does not affect his "ability to pay" for the purpose of determining his tax under a progressive rate structure. A taxpayer cannot reduce his share of the nation's tax burden merely by consuming his wealth. However, when a taxpayer's wealth is reduced as a consequence of some sudden outside force, such as a storm or fire, his "ability to pay" taxes is affected in a way that is different from the decline in wealth caused by normal deterioration. Even though the item damaged or lost by a casualty or theft was purchased by the taxpayer for his consumption, the loss that the taxpayer suffered does not reflect his consumption of the item, but rather reflects a loss caused by external forces. Consequently, subject to substantial dollar limitations, Congress has granted a deduction for losses caused by a casualty or by theft to reflect the decline in the taxpayer's "ability to pay." Indeed, a deduction is allowed even if the taxpayer's negligence was a factor in causing the casualty or in allowing the theft to occur since his carelessness does not constitute a personal consumption of the item. Treas. Reg. § 1.165–7(a)(3)(i). For the effect of a taxpayer's negligence on the deductibility of a loss, see § **7.2300.** Of course, if a taxpayer deliberately set fire to an item or wantonly sat by and permitted a fire to destroy it, that would constitute a personal consumption of the item, and no deduction will be allowed for such a loss. Such a loss would not be "unexpected," which is one of the requirements for qualifying as a casualty. See § **7.2200.** In *Blackman v. Commissioner*, 88 T.C. 677 (1987), aff'd without published opinion, 867 F.2d 605 (1st Cir. 1988), the courts denied the taxpayer's claim for a casualty loss for fire damage when the taxpayer started the fire and either intentionally or out of gross negligence allowed it to spread.

§ **7.2200. Definition of Casualty.** In IRC § 165(c)(3), Congress provides a casualty loss deduction for losses arising from fire, storm, shipwreck or "other casualty." The Commissioner and the courts have made their determination of whether a loss was caused by an "other casualty" on the basis of whether the nature of the event that caused the loss is analogous to one of the three types of casualties that are named in the statute (i.e., fire, storm, and shipwreck). The Commissioner maintains that an event is an "other casualty" only if it is of a "sudden, unexpected and unusual nature." Rev. Rul. 72–592. The Commissioner defines those terms as follows: "To be sudden" the event must be swift and precipitous, and not gradual or progressive. To be "unexpected," the event must be one that is ordinarily unanticipated, that occurs without the intent of the one who suffers the loss. To be "unusual," the event must be one that is extraordinary and nonrecurring, one that does not commonly occur during the activity in which the taxpayer was engaged when the destruction or damage occurred, and one that does not commonly occur in the ordinary course of day-to-day living of the taxpayer. The "unexpected" and "unusual" standards are sufficiently similar that, in the authors' view, they could be combined into a single standard of foreseeability; that is, the event causing the loss must not be one that could or should have been anticipated. The manner in which the foreseeability of an event should be weighed in determining the deductibility of losses is discussed at §§ **7.2211–7.2213.**

§ 7.2210. Requirement That a Loss Be Sudden. A loss incurred as a consequence of a gradual deterioration of an asset is attributable to the consumption or use of that asset, and so such losses are not treated as casualties. For example, damage caused by rust or by moths is not deductible. While the courts have divided on the issue, the Commissioner maintains that termite damage is not a casualty because the damage is the result of a gradual deterioration caused by a steadily operating cause. Rev. Rul. 63–232.

In *Short v. Commissioner*, 55 T.C.M. 54 (1988), the taxpayers' residence was damaged due to a severe drought. The drought occurred in mid–1980, and taxpayers first noticed the damage to their home in 1981. The damage progressed and became more of a problem in 1982. Taxpayer claimed a casualty loss deduction for the year 1982. The Tax Court denied the claim for a deduction because the loss was not sudden; it resulted from progressive deterioration. The court acknowledged that a drought can constitute a casualty under appropriate circumstances, but not when there is a substantial time lag between the drought and the damage. The court suggested that the taxpayers might have had a stronger case if they had claimed a loss deduction in 1981 when they first noticed some damage since that would have been a shorter time after the drought occurred. For the treatment of the loss of plants, shrubs and trees because of a drought, see **§ 7.2214.**

The death of trees caused by an insect-carrying disease was held not to be a casualty in *Maher v. Commissioner*, 680 F.2d 91 (11th Cir. 1982). Yet in Rev. Rul. 79–174, the Commissioner allowed a deduction when ornamental trees died five to ten days after a massive beetle attack occurred in an area where such attacks are unusual.

§ 7.2211. The Application of the Foreseeability Standard. As previously noted, the Commissioner's requirements that the event causing a loss be one that is unexpected and unusual actually constitutes a single standard of foreseeability. Let us consider how rigidly this requirement of nonforeseeability is applied. If, for personal use, a taxpayer purchases an asset that he knows is likely to be destroyed in a few years by a regularly recurring event, the destruction of the item can be regarded as part of the cost of the taxpayer's consumption for the period of time that he used it. The extent to which foreseeability will prevent the deduction of a loss is unclear. A deduction will not be denied merely because a taxpayer knew that damage or loss had a statistical probability. For example, the likelihood that a taxpayer who regularly drives an automobile in a large metropolitan area will someday suffer collision damage may be high, but that probability will not preclude the taxpayer from deducting such a loss when it is incurred. Treas. Reg. § 1.165–7(a)(3). The Tax Court has held that foreseeability of damage is merely one factor to be weighed in determining whether a deduction will be allowed. E.g., *Heyn v. Commissioner*, 46 T.C. 302 (1966), Acq., allowing a casualty loss deduction for a landslide caused by an excavation.

§ 7.2212. Weighing Foreseeability. It is difficult to determine what weight should be accorded to the foreseeability of an event that causes a loss. Foreseeability does not appear to have influenced the Congressional decision to allow a deduction for losses caused by the three categories of events that are expressly named in IRC § 165(c)(3). There are areas of the United States where severe storms are common occurrences, and yet Congress expressly provided for the deductibility of storm damage. As noted in **§ 7.2211**, the regulations permit a deduction for damage to an automobile resulting from a collision regardless of the statistical probability that such damage will occur. Automobile collisions are deemed to be sufficiently analogous to shipwrecks (which are expressly named in the statute) to be deductible. Perhaps, the standard *should be* that foreseeability will preclude casualty characterization whenever the likelihood of the taxpayer's suffering such a loss, viewed at the time that the property was first put to use by the taxpayer, was so high that the taxpayer took (or should have taken) that probable loss into account as a cost of the intended personal use of the property. See Rev. Rul. 90–61.

§ 7.2213. Examples of the Commissioner's Application of the Foreseeability Requirement. In PLR 8247060, the Commissioner denied a deduction for the damage incurred when the engine to taxpayer's automobile froze during an extremely cold period. There was some indication that the amount of anti-freeze in the car was insufficient. The Commissioner held that the damage did not result from a casualty because below freezing temperatures are not so unusual in the middle Atlantic states where the taxpayer resided as to make the occurrence of those temperatures an unanticipated event. In PLR 8227010, the Commissioner denied a deduction for the damage to taxpayer's uninsured automobile which was incurred in an automobile race. Taxpayer had been racing cars as a competitive amateur sport for some years prior to the loss in question. The Commissioner reasoned that collisions are not unusual in automobile races, and so taxpayer's loss was not so unexpected as to permit casualty characterization.

§ 7.2214. The Treatment of Droughts. The criteria for distinguishing a deductible casualty loss from a nondeductible loss is based on whether the event that caused the loss is one that is associated with the normal exhaustion of the item that was damaged or destroyed. The treatment accorded to losses incurred when ornamental trees or shrubs are killed by a drought is instructive in determining what constitutes a casualty. If a taxpayer, who lives in an area where droughts are unusual, purchases shrubbery and trees to landscape his home, he may be aware that a drought could destroy them, but he likely does not expect that a drought will occur. If a drought does occur and destroys his shrubbery and trees, the taxpayer will wish to claim a casualty loss deduction. The Commissioner asserts that damage caused to property through "progressive deterioration" is not a casualty loss. The Commissioner contends that the destruction of ornamental trees and shrubs because of a drought will not usually qualify as a casualty because the drought typically kills gradually over a long period of time. Rev. Rul. 66–303; Rev. Rul. 76–521. See also Rev. Rul. 90–61. In Rev. Rul. 77–490, the Commissioner modified his position somewhat by acknowledging that a drought loss can constitute a casualty in certain circumstances which he did not identify.

In *Ruecker v. Commissioner*, 41 T.C.M. 1587 (1981), the Tax Court allowed a casualty loss deduction for a loss of ornamental plants and shrubs because of a severe drought that took place in California. The death of the plants and shrubs took place over a three to four-month period, and the court held that it was swift and unusual and so was not a consequence of gradual deterioration. See also, *Short v. Commissioner* at **§ 7.2210.**

In Rev. Rul. 90–61, an abnormal drought caused the death of tree seedlings that had been planted for use in taxpayer's lumber business. The Commissioner allowed the taxpayer a deduction under IRC § 165(a) for the loss of the seedlings even though the Commissioner determined that the loss did not constitute a casualty because it lacked suddenness. Since the loss occurred in connection with taxpayer's trade or business, it was deductible as a business loss [under IRC § 165(c)(1)]. The Commissioner stated that since the deaths caused by the abnormal drought were "unexpected, unusual and identifiable," the loss qualified as a business loss deduction.

§ 7.2215. Damage to or Destruction of Property Contrasted with Losing Property. As noted at § 7.2110, the fact that the damage to a taxpayer's property was attributable to the negligence of the taxpayer will not bar a deduction. But, the courts have drawn a line between events, on the one hand, when carelessness caused the loss of property and, on the other hand, when carelessness resulted in property of the taxpayer being damaged or destroyed because of the introduction of a sudden destructive force. For example, a deduction was denied when a taxpayer placed a diamond ring in tissue paper and her husband then mistakenly disposed of the tissue paper with the ring inside down a toilet. *Keenan v. Bowers*, 91 F.Supp. 771 (E.D.S.C. 1950). On the other hand, when a taxpayer placed her diamond ring in a waterglass next to the sink and her husband then poured the contents of the glass down the drain and activated the garbage disposal which damaged the ring so severely as to render it worthless, the Tax Court allowed a casualty loss deduction. *Carpenter v. Commissioner*, 25 T.C.M. 1186 (1966). If property is lost as a consequence of the exertion of a sudden force, a deduction may be allowed. For example, in *White v. Commissioner*, 48 T.C. 430 (1967), Acq., a taxpayer was allowed a casualty loss deduction for a diamond that was lost when her husband accidentally slammed a car door on the taxpayer's hand, breaking the prongs of the setting for the diamond and dislodging the stone, which was never found despite a diligent search.

§ 7.2216. Timing of Deduction. A casualty loss deduction usually is taken in the taxable year that the casualty loss was incurred or in a later year when a prospect for reimbursement

has ceased to exist. See § **7.2510** and § **7.2550.** One exception
to that general rule occurs when the President declares an
area a disaster area under the Disaster Relief and Emergency
Assistance Act. In that event, under IRC § 165(i), a taxpayer
may be permitted to elect to deduct the loss in the taxable year
prior to the year in which the disaster occurred.

§ **7.2217.   Itemized or Nonitemized Deduction.** The deduction allowable for a casualty or theft loss of property that
was used by the taxpayer for nonbusiness, personal purposes
will be an itemized deduction, except that it will be a nonitemized deduction to the extent that the taxpayer has a "personal
casualty gain" (see § **7.2531**) in that taxable year. § **7.2532.**
When a casualty or theft loss of personally used property is an
itemized deduction, it will not be a "miscellaneous itemized
deduction" and so is not subject to the 2% of AGI floor, and it
will not be subject to the overall limitation on itemized deductions that is imposed by IRC § 68. IRC §§ 67(b)(3), 68(c)(3).

§ **7.2220.   Caveat.** There are commentators who contend that
casualty and theft losses of personally used property are personal
consumptions and so no deduction should be allowed for them.
Regardless of the merits of that view, Congress has allowed a
deduction, but it sometimes is difficult to determine whether an
event is covered by the statutory provision. The best guide for
making that determination is to ascertain the likely Congressional
purpose for allowing a deduction and to examine the event in the
light of that likely purpose. It should be noted that in recent years
the detractors of the deduction have influenced Congress to limit
severely the amount that can be deducted for losses incurred in
connection with personally used property. §§ **7.2530–7.2540.**

§ **7.2230.   Judicial Construction.** The courts have adopted a
mechanistic approach in their construction of the term "casualty." They have looked to the three events specifically mentioned
in the statute (fire, storm, and shipwreck) and have found the
common characteristics of those events to be that they are sudden
and unanticipated. The courts then require that an event which is
not one of the three enumerated in the statute be sudden and
unanticipated in order to qualify for the deduction. Since such
events typically will not constitute personal consumption, that
distinction generally works well. However, it should not be applied so mechanically that the courts lose sight of the reason that
sudden and unanticipated events are deductible. Otherwise, a

court may resolve such questions as whether termite damage constitutes a casualty on the basis of the time elapsed before the damage was discovered. The proper question to be asked is whether termite damage constitutes an anticipatible deterioration (similar to rust) or whether it constitutes an external force which a person would not expect to occur, even though such person recognizes the possibility that that event might occur.

§ 7.2300. Taxpayer's Negligence. A casualty loss deduction will not be allowed if the casualty was caused by the "willful act or willful negligence" of the taxpayer or someone acting on his behalf. Treas. Reg. § 1.165–7(a)(3)(i). "Willful negligence" means "reckless disregard of the safety or the rights of others" or a "willful determination not to perform a known duty." Black's Law Dictionary 1186 (4th ed. 1968). It refers to a more aggravated form of negligence than gross negligence. However, in *Blackman v. Commissioner*, 88 T.C. 677 (1987), aff'd without published opinion, 867 F.2d 605 (1st Cir. 1988), the Tax Court stated that a taxpayer's gross negligence would bar a casualty loss deduction. Other than cases of willful or perhaps gross negligence, a taxpayer's negligence will not bar him from deducting the casualty loss that he suffered thereby. A taxpayer's deliberate destruction of his own property will not qualify as a deductible casualty loss. See § **7.1000.**

§ 7.2400. Computation of Amount of Deductible Loss.

§ 7.2410. Alternate Methods. Once there has been a casualty loss, it is necessary to determine the amount of the loss in order to determine the amount of deduction that is allowable. The allowable deduction is dependent upon, but not necessarily equal to, the amount of the casualty loss. For purposes of this deduction, the amount of casualty loss is the lesser of: (a) the difference between the fair market value of the damaged property immediately before and immediately after the casualty, or (b) the adjusted basis of the damaged property. Treas. Reg. § 1.165–7(b)(1). In many instances the cost of repairs will be accepted as evidence of the decline in value caused by the casualty. Treas. Reg. § 1.165–7(a)(2)(ii), and see *Turecamo v. Commissioner*, 64 T.C. 720 (1975), aff'd, 554 F.2d 564 (2d Cir. 1977). The cost of removing debris that was a product of a casualty is included in the determination of the cost of repairing the damage. Rev. Rul. 71–161. For the meaning of "fair market value," see § **2.2240.**

§ 7.2411. Replacement Cost. When an item is completely destroyed, the taxpayer can establish the fair market value immediately before the event by establishing the replacement cost of the destroyed item and then reducing that replacement cost by a depreciation allowance for the time that the item was held by the taxpayer. *Pfalzgraf v. Commissioner*, 67 T.C. 784 (1977), Acq. This replacement cost minus depreciation method is used principally for evaluating the loss to household goods. It is worth emphasizing that the amount of loss incurred is not necessarily the amount which may be deducted. See § **7.2500** and following.

§ **7.2412. No Replacement Is Available.** In *Zardo v. Commissioner*, 43 T.C.M. 626 (1982), the Tax Court adopted a modified version of the replacement cost method in valuing the amount of loss suffered because of the destruction of mature trees on land on which a residence is situated. Essentially, as the measurement of the amount of loss, the court used replacement cost (which included the cost of removing the trunks of the old trees) for purchasing the tallest trees available, although the only available trees were shorter than the trees that were lost. In addition, the court included in its measurement of the loss a small amount for the decline in the fair market value of the property that would result from replacing the destroyed trees with shorter ones; it appears that the court may have simply plucked a figure out of the air to represent the estimated decline in fair market value.

§ **7.2420. Business Property.** If the damaged property is used in a trade or business, the amount of the casualty loss will be determined in the same manner as is used to determine the amount of casualty loss suffered by nonbusiness property as set forth in § **7.2410**; except that if such business property is totally destroyed, the amount of loss is the adjusted basis of the destroyed property irrespective of whether the adjusted basis was greater or lesser than the value of the damaged property prior to the casualty. Treas. Reg. § 1.165–7(b)(1)(ii).

§ **7.2421. Illustration 1: Partial Loss.** *X*'s automobile was damaged in a collision. *X*'s negligence caused the accident, but *X* was not grossly negligent. The value of *X*'s automobile immediately before the accident was $2,200, and the value immediately after the accident was $1,500. *X* had a basis of $2,500 in the car. *X* has no insurance coverage and no prospect of being reimbursed for his loss. Whether *X*'s car is used by him solely for personal purposes or in his trade or business, the amount of his casualty loss is $700 ($2,200 value before the accident minus $1,500 value after the accident), since the difference in value before and after the accident was a lesser amount than X's adjusted basis. The amount of this loss which is deductible is determined according to the limitations described in § **7.2600.**

§ **7.2422. Illustration 2: Complete Destruction When Basis Exceeds Value.** Assume the same facts as in § **7.2421** except that X's car was completely destroyed by the collision and had no salvage value. If X used the car for personal purposes, the amount of his loss would be $2,200 ($2,200 value before the accident minus the $0 value afterwards), but if X used his car for business purposes, the amount of his loss would be $2,500 (the adjusted basis of the car).

§ **7.2423. Illustration 3: Complete Destruction When Value Exceeds Basis.** The same facts apply as those stated in § **7.2422** except that X's adjusted basis in the car was only $2,000. Whether the car was used for business or personal purposes, the amount of X's loss is $2,000 since the adjusted basis of the car is less than the decline in value.

§ **7.2424. Application to Business Property.** On its terms, the casualty loss deduction provided by IRC § 165(c)(3) does not apply to business property. The statute refers to "losses of property not connected with a trade or business." However, business property losses clearly are deductible. For an individual, such losses are deductible under IRC § 165(c)(1) as a loss incurred in a trade or business; for a corporate taxpayer, such losses are deductible under IRC § 165(a). Since a casualty or theft constitutes an event of sufficient significance to warrant recognition of the loss incurred, the treatment of casualty losses on business property is discussed in the same regulations that deal with casualty losses on non-business property, and there is every reason to consider them together. However, the consolidated consideration of business and nonbusiness properties should not obscure the fact that a deduction is allowed for those two types of properties under quite different statutory provisions. It is for this reason, for example, that the limitations on the deduction of casualty losses that are imposed by IRC § 165(h) do not apply to losses suffered with respect to business property.

§ 7.2500. Limitations on Deduction. The amount of casualty and theft losses that can be deducted is subject to three limitations—two of which apply only to losses incurred with regard to personally used property and one of which (the prospect of reimbursement limitation) applies to losses incurred with regard to all properties regardless of how they are used. The three limitations are: (1) the prospect of reimbursement [§§ **7.2510–7.2515**], (2) the $100 floor [§§ **7.2520–7.2521**], and (3) the ten percent of AGI floor [§§ **7.2530–7.2534**].

§ 7.2510. Prospect of Reimbursement. A loss is deductible in the taxable year in which it was "sustained." Treas. Reg. § 1.165–1(d)(1). A casualty or theft loss is not sustained and, therefore, cannot be deducted in a taxable year to the extent that, at the end of the year, there is a reasonable prospect of the taxpayer's being reimbursed by the wrongdoer or by an insurer. Treas. Reg. § 1.165–1(d)(2). For an example, of the application of the reasonable prospect of reimbursement principle to prevent the deduction of a theft loss, see *Jeppsen v. Commissioner*, 128 F.3d 1410 (10th Cir. 1997). If, at the end of a taxable year, there is a reasonable prospect of reimbursement for only a portion of a casualty or theft loss, the remaining portion for which no reimbursement is anticipated is deemed to have been sustained in that taxable year. Any amount of casualty or theft loss that was treated as not being sustained in a taxable year because of a prospect of reimbursement will be treated as having been sustained in the first subsequent taxable year at the end of which it can be determined with reasonable certainly that reimbursement will not be obtained. Treas. Reg. § 1.165–1(d)(2)(ii). The prospect of reimbursement limitation is based on the provision in IRC § 165(a) that limits the deduction under that section to a loss that is "not compensated for by insurance or otherwise." This limitation applies to all types of losses regardless of whether they are incurred in connection with a trade or business or with personally used property.

§ 7.2511. Refusal to Seek Reimbursement from Insurer. Prior to 1986, a majority of the Tax Court and the Sixth and Eleventh Circuit Courts of Appeals held that when a taxpayer chooses not to obtain reimbursement from an insurer for a casualty or theft loss which was covered by insurance, the loss is nevertheless sustained and deductible by the taxpayer. *Hills v. Commissioner*, 691 F.2d 997 (11th Cir. 1982) (divided decision), aff'g 76 T.C. 484 (1981) (reviewed by court);

Miller v. Commissioner, 733 F.2d 399 (6th Cir. 1984) (en banc divided decision). The amendments made by the Tax Reform Act of 1986 repudiated that position. An individual taxpayer's loss on personally used property that is covered by insurance cannot be included in the taxpayer's casualty or theft losses unless the taxpayer files a timely insurance claim. IRC § 165(h)(4)(E). In this connection, note *Campbell v. Commissioner*, 54 T.C.M. 632 (1987), where the Tax Court denied a claim for a deduction for a business loss to the extent that the taxpayer's loss was covered by insurance even though the taxpayer did not claim reimbursement from the insurer.

Note, however, that the statute (IRC 165(h)(4)(E)) applies only to a failure to enforce an insurance claim. If a taxpayer fails to pursue a claim against a tortfeasor, that may not prevent a deduction, especially in light of the uncertainties of success in litigation and in collection. The deductibility may rest on a weighing of the risks of litigation against the amount of the claim.

§ 7.2512.   Effect of Suing for Recovery. The question of whether a reasonable prospect of recovery exists is a question of fact to be determined from all the existing facts and circumstances. Treas. Reg. § 1.165–1(d)(2)(i). If a taxpayer files suit to recover a loss (whether the suit is filed before or shortly after claiming a deduction for that loss), the filing of the suit raises a presumption that the taxpayer believed that he had a reasonable prospect of recovering the loss which, therefore, would not be deductible. *Dawn v. Commissioner*, 675 F.2d 1077 (9th Cir. 1982); *Gale v. Commissioner*, 41 T.C. 269 (1963); *Lapin v. Commissioner*, 60 T.C.M. 59 (1990), aff'd 956 F.2d 1167 (9th Cir. 1992); but see the dictum in *Parmelee Transportation Co. v. United States*, 351 F.2d 619 (Ct. Cl. 1965). To obtain a deduction for the loss prior to a settlement of the suit, the taxpayer has the burden of showing that no reasonable prospect of recovery exists despite the taxpayer's prosecution of the suit. See *Marx v. Commissioner*, 62 T.C.M. 1370 (1991), allowing a casualty loss deduction for damage to taxpayer's home that was caused by a contractor's negligence even though taxpayer had obtained a judgment against the contractor and was continuing to attempt to collect on that judgment. The court determined that taxpayer's prospects for collecting on the judgment were slim at best.

§ 7.2513. Insurance as an Indirect Reimbursement.
When a taxpayer collects insurance proceeds (such as fire
insurance or life insurance) on the occurrence of an event, a
question may arise as to whether the insurance reimburses the
taxpayer for a loss suffered by him and so prevents the
taxpayer from taking a deduction for that loss. In *Johnson v.
Commissioner*, 66 T.C. 897 (1976), aff'd per curiam by a
divided court, 574 F.2d 189 (4th Cir. 1978), the taxpayer
collected life insurance proceeds on the death of his partner
pursuant to a policy the taxpayer had acquired to insure his
partner's life. The taxpayer then liquidated the partnership
business and received an amount which was less than his
basis. The Tax Court held that the loss realized on that
liquidation was reimbursed by the life insurance proceeds,
which the court determined was purchased to protect against a
decline in value of the business caused by the partner's death.
The court disallowed the deduction claimed by the taxpayer
for the loss incurred on the liquidation. See § **2.1323.** As
noted in § **2.1323**, there are reasons to doubt that the *Johnson* decision will be followed; and, to date, it has not been.

§ 7.2514. Subsequent Recovery. The fact that a taxpayer
who took a loss deduction recovers all or part of that loss in a
subsequent year does not prove that there was a reasonable
prospect of recovery in the year in which the loss was incurred. If there was no reasonable prospect in the year of loss,
a subsequent recovery by the taxpayer of a previously deducted item will usually be treated as income to him in that year
under the tax benefit rule. Treas. Reg. § 1.165–1(d)(2)(iii). See
§ **2.3000** et seq. See also, Rev. Rul, 71–161 allowing a casualty
loss deduction for an item for which an unexpected reimbursement was received in a subsequent year; *Montgomery v. Commissioner*, 65 T.C. 511 (1975) where the court held that a
taxpayer's collection of insurance proceeds on a claim for
hurricane damage to a building was gross income to the
taxpayer who had taken a casualty loss deduction in an earlier
year.

As an administrative matter, requiring that a recovery be
included in income in the year of recovery is preferable to
requiring that the prior year be kept open so that an amended
return could be filed deleting the casualty or theft deduction.
The position adopted by the tax law of including the recovery

in income conforms with the annual accounting concept and is easier to administer.

§ **7.2515. Inventory.** A theft loss to the inventory of a taxpayer's business has been held to be deductible without regard to the likelihood that the taxpayer will be reimbursed for the loss. *National Home Products, Inc. v. Commissioner*, 71 T.C. 501 (1979). This is because the deduction is allowed under IRC § 471 (as a downward adjustment of closing inventory) rather than under IRC § 165 (as a theft loss). Treas. Reg. § 1.165–7(a)(4). The Tax Court determined in *National Home* that there are good policy reasons not to apply the "prospect of reimbursement" limitation to inventory adjustments even if caused by a theft. Of course if a deduction is so allowed, a subsequent reimbursement (such as the receipt of insurance funds) will be included in the taxpayer's gross income. *National Home Products, Inc. v. Commissioner, supra.*

§ **7.2520. $100 Floor.** A second limitation on deductibility, the $100 floor, applies only to casualty and theft losses that an individual incurred with regard to personally used property. If damaged or stolen property was not used in the taxpayer's trade or business or in an income-producing activity, the amount of loss incurred in connection with one casualty or theft can be deducted only to the extent that the amount exceeds $100. IRC § 165(h)(1). The $100 floor applies to the total amount of loss incurred in a casualty or theft; it does not apply to each item that was damaged or stolen in a single casualty or theft.

§ **7.2521. Illustration.** In Year One, *F*'s house was burgled, and the thief stole $25,000 in cash from *F*'s safe. Later that year, *F*'s automobile was totally destroyed in an accidental collision. In that same collision, a rare vase that *F* was transporting in the automobile also was destroyed. At the time of the accident, *F* had a basis of $15,000 in the automobile and a basis of $6,000 in the vase. Immediately before the collision occurred, the fair market value of the automobile was $10,000, and the value of the vase was $18,000. Neither the automobile nor the vase were insured, and both items were worthless after the collision. *F* had no prospect of receiving reimbursement for any of these losses. *F*'s adjusted gross income for Year One was $100,000. None of the items that were stolen or destroyed were used in *F*'s trade or business or in a profit-seeking venture. In determining the amount of deduction allowable to F for the loss of his car and vase, we will ignore the "10% of AGI" floor for a net casualty loss [see § **7.2530**] because the large amount of theft loss that F suffered in that year is itself sufficient to satisfy that floor. The amount of loss sustained by F because of the collision is $16,000 (i.e., $10,000 from the destruction of the automobile, and $6,000 from the destruction of the vase). The $100 floor is applied against the entire $16,000 loss since both items were destroyed in the same casualty; the floor is not applied separately to each of the two items destroyed in that casualty. Consequently, without regard to the 10% of AGI floor for a net casualty loss, F is entitled to deduct $15,900 because of the damage caused by the collision. Note that an additional $100 floor will apply to the $25,000 theft loss that F suffered when his house was burgled.

§ **7.2530. The Ten Percent of AGI Floor for a Net Casualty Loss.** The third and final limitation on an individual's deduction of casualty and theft losses applies only to personally used property. This third limitation is comprised of two distinct parts, each of which is discussed separately below.

§ **7.2531. Definitions.** Before examining this third limitation, it is useful to define several terms. A "personal casualty gain" is the gain recognized by a taxpayer from the involuntary conversion of personally used property which occurred as a consequence of a fire, storm, shipwreck, or other casualty, or from theft. A personal casualty gain can arise from a reimbursement from an insurer or from the person causing the loss. A "personal casualty loss" is the amount of loss to personally used property that the taxpayer sustained by reason of fire, storm, shipwreck, or other casualty, or from theft. In determining a taxpayer's "personal casualty loss," the $100 floor [described in § **7.2520**] for each separate casualty and theft is deducted. IRC § 165(h)(3)(B). The excess of a taxpayer's aggregate personal casualty losses for a taxable year over the taxpayer's aggregate personal casualty gains for such year are referred to as the taxpayer's "net casualty loss" for that year. Note that personal casualty gains and losses include theft gains and losses.

§ **7.2532. Personal Casualty Gain Limitation.** A taxpayer's aggregate personal casualty losses for a taxable year (which amount, you will recall, reflects a reduction for the

$100 floor) are deductible to the extent of the taxpayer's aggregate personal casualty gains for that year. IRC § 165(h)(2). The characterization of such gains and losses is discussed at **§ 7.2534.** If there is a net casualty loss (see **§ 7.2531**) in a taxable year, the amount of personal casualty losses (after reduction for the $100 floor) that does not exceed the taxpayer's personal casualty gains for that year are treated as nonitemized deductions. IRC § 165(h)(4)(A). If there is *not* a net casualty loss in a taxable year, all personal casualty gains and losses will be treated as gains and losses from the sale of capital assets; and so the losses will be nonitemized deductions. IRC §§ 165(h)(2)(B), 62(a)(3).

§ 7.2533. The 10% of AGI Floor. As stated above, if the taxpayer's aggregate personal casualty losses for a taxable year exceed the taxpayer's aggregate personal casualty gains for that year, the excess is referred to as the "net casualty loss" for that year. See **§ 7.2531.** A taxpayer's net casualty loss for a taxable year can be deducted only to the extent that that amount exceeds 10% of the taxpayer's AGI for that year. IRC § 165(h)(2)(A)(ii). To the extent that a net casualty loss is deductible, it will be an itemized deduction. See **§ 7.2217.**

§ 7.2534. Characterization of Personal Casualty Gains and Losses. If a taxpayer's aggregate personal casualty gains for a taxable year exceed the taxpayer's aggregate personal casualty losses for that year, all such gains and losses will be treated as capital gains and capital losses respectively. IRC § 165(h)(2)(B). If a taxpayer's aggregate personal casualty gains do not exceed the taxpayer's personal casualty losses for a taxable year, the losses will be ordinary and the gains also will be ordinary since they are excluded by IRC § 1231(a)(4)(C) from that section and since there will have been no sale or exchange as required by IRC § 1222. Capital gains and losses are discussed in Chapter Eighteen, and section 1231 gains and losses are discussed in Chapter Nineteen.

§ 7.2535. Illustration 1. In Year One, *J* had adjusted gross income (AGI) of $150,000. In that year, she had $40,000 of personal casualty gains and $32,000 of personal casualty losses after taking off the $100 floor. *J* is allowed to deduct the entire $32,000 of her personal casualty loss. Since she can deduct her personal casualty losses to the extent of her personal casualty gains, and since those gains exceed her losses, the 10% of AGI floor is inapplicable. All of her personal casualty gains and losses are treated as capital gains and losses. The $32,000 of deductible personal casualty losses are a nonitemized deduction. IRC §§ 165(h)(2)(B), 62(a)(3).

§ 7.2536. Illustration 2. The same facts as those stated in **Illustration 1** except that, after taking off the $100 floor, *J*'s personal casualty losses for that year were $62,000. In that case, *J* is allowed a $47,000 deduction for the losses she suffered. She can deduct $40,000 because she had that amount of personal casualty gains, and she can deduct the $7,000 excess of her net casualty loss ($22,000) over the 10% of AGI floor ($15,000). The remaining $15,000 of her personal casualty loss is not deductible. Since her personal casualty losses exceed her personal casualty gains, both will be treated as ordinary. However, $40,000 of *J*'s deduction (the amount that equals *J*'s personal casualty gain) is a nonitemized deduction, and the remaining $7,000 of *J*'s deduction is an itemized deduction.

§ 7.2537. Illustration 3. The same facts as those stated in **Illustration 1** except that, after applying the $100 floor, *J*'s personal casualty losses for that year were $52,000. In that case, *J* will be allowed to deduct only $40,000 of her losses— i.e., the amount that is equal to her personal casualty gains. Since her net casualty loss ($12,000) is less than the 10% of AGI floor ($15,000), no amount of her net casualty loss is deductible. Both her deductible casualty losses and her casualty gains are treated as ordinary. *J*'s deduction will be a nonitemized deduction.

§ 7.2540. Separate Application. With one exception, the floors of $100 per casualty and theft and of 10% of AGI for a net casualty loss apply separately to each taxpayer. Thus, if John and Ralph were joint owners of a recreational motorboat that was destroyed by fire, and if they had no other losses or personal casualty gains in that year, John can deduct only the amount of his loss in excess of the sum of $100 plus 10% of John's AGI for that taxable year, and Ralph's deduction is subject to the floor of $100 plus 10% of Ralph's AGI. The one exception to this separate treatment is that a husband and wife *who file a joint return* will be treated as a single individual, and so the deduction for the properties of a husband and wife (whether co-owned or separately owned) that were damaged or stolen in the same event will be subjected to a single $100 floor. IRC § 165(h)(4)(B). Of course, the spouses' loss in excess of their $100 floor will be aggregated with the spouses' other personal casualty losses for that year, and the aggregate amount will be deductible only to the extent of their aggregate personal casualty gains plus the excess of their net casualty loss over 10% of their combined AGI.

§ 7.2550. Reimbursement Prospects. As noted in § 7.2510, a property loss incurred by a taxpayer from a casualty or theft is deemed not to have been sustained in the year of the casualty or theft to the extent that the taxpayer has a reasonable prospect of reimbursement. In such event, the loss will be treated as having been sustained in a subsequent year when it is determined with reasonable certainty that all or some part of the hoped-for reimbursement will not be received. Treas. Reg. § 1.165–1(d)(2). It appears that the floor of 10% of AGI for the deduction of a net casualty loss that was incurred by an individual in a year in which a reasonable prospect of reimbursement existed and that is deemed to have been sustained in a later year in which the prospect of reimbursement is negated will be measured by the individual's AGI in the later year.

§ 7.2551. Illustration: Effect of Reimbursement Prospect on the AGI Floor. In Year One, X had AGI of $20,000; thus 10% of X's AGI for that year is $2,000. In that year, Y became intoxicated while a guest in X's home, and Y negligently set fire to and thereby totally destroyed a painting that X had recently purchased for $5,600. X's basis in the painting was $5,600 and that was its value immediately prior to its destruction. The painting was not insured. X claimed reimbursement from Y. Because of Y's poor financial condition, X agreed in Year One to a settlement with Y under which Y would pay $4,000 for the damage he caused. This payment was to be made in installments to commence in Year Two. In his tax return for Year One, X reported a loss of $1,600 since there was no reasonable prospect of recovering that amount of his $5,600 loss. X had no other losses or personal casualty gains in that year. The deductibility of the $1,600 loss sustained in Year One is subject to a $100 floor. Treas. Reg. § 1.165–7(b)(4)(ii). The remaining $1,500 of the sustained loss is not deductible because it is less than $2,000 (10% of X's AGI). So, X is not entitled to a casualty loss deduction in Year One.

Y never made any of the payments to X that were required by the settlement agreement. In Year Three, X determined that he could not collect anything from Y, and X abandoned his claim for the $4,000 that Y had agreed to pay. X had AGI of $45,000 in Year Three; 10% of that figure is $4,500. In his tax return for Year Three, X reported that he sustained a $4,000 loss as a consequence of its having become clear in that year that X would not receive any reimbursement for the destruction of his painting. Treas. Reg. § 1.165–1(d)(2). X sustained no other losses and had no personal casualty gains in Year Three. The $4,000 loss that X sustained in Year Three is not subject to the $100 floor since the $100 limitation for the destruction of the painting had been applied in Year One (i.e., the deduction of the casualty loss is subject to a single $100 limitation even though the loss is deemed to have been sustained in two separate years.) Treas. Reg. § 1.165–7(b)(4)(ii). The remaining question is how should the 10% of AGI floor be applied? While the result is extremely harsh, it appears likely that the deduction of X's loss will be subject to two AGI floors—$2,000 for the loss sustained in Year One and $4,500 for the loss sustained in Year Three. If so, none of the loss sustained by X can be deducted.

§ 7.2560. Itemized and Nonitemized Deductions. To the extent that a taxpayer's aggregate "personal casualty loss" for a taxable year does not exceed the taxpayer's aggregate "personal casualty gain" for such year, the personal casualty losses qualify as nonitemized deductions. **§ 7.2532.** Thus, a "personal casualty loss" will reduce a "personal casualty gain" regardless of whether the taxpayer utilizes the standard deduction.

For the significance of classifying a deduction as nonitemized, see Chapter Three. Personal casualty losses and gains are defined at **§ 7.2531.** A taxpayer's "net casualty loss" (i.e., the excess of personal casualty losses over personal casualty gains) is an itemized deduction; but the 2% of AGI floor that applies to certain itemized deductions does not apply to personal casualty losses. IRC § 67(b)(3). Also, the special limitation imposed by IRC § 68 on the amount of itemized deductions that can be taken does not apply to personal casualty losses. IRC § 68(c)(3). See **§ 3.1120.**

§ 7.2600.   Table of Deductible Casualty and Theft Losses. The following table shows the amount of loss that an individual taxpayer may deduct as a consequence of a casualty where: there is no reasonable prospect of reimbursement, the taxpayer sustained no other losses and had no personal casualty gains in that year, and the taxpayer had AGI of $20,000 in that year. In this table, references to "casualty" losses includes both casualty and theft losses.

TABLE 1—PROPERTY HELD FOR PERSONAL USE

a Basis	b FMV	c Salvage	d Casualty Loss
8,000	6,000	2,000	1,900
8,000	12,000	2,000	5,900
8,000	6,000	–0–	3,900
8,000	12,000	–0–	5,900

TABLE II—PROPERTY HELD FOR BUSINESS USE

a Basis	b FMV	c Salvage	d Casualty Loss
8,000	6,000	2,000	4,000
8,000	12,000	2,000	8,000
8,000	6,000	–0–	8,000
8,000	12,000	–0–	8,000

a.   Taxpayer's adjusted basis in the damaged property.

b.   Fair market value of the damaged property immediately before the casualty.

c.   Fair market value of the damaged property immediately after the casualty occurred.

d.   Amount deductible under IRC § 165 because of the casualty.

§ 7.2700.   Adjustment to Basis. When a taxpayer claims a deduction for a casualty loss, the taxpayer's basis in the property will be reduced by the amount of the deduction. IRC § 1016(a)(1) requires that basis be adjusted for a loss "properly chargeable to capital account." A reasonable construction of that provision would not reduce a taxpayer's basis for a casualty loss to the extent that the loss is nondeductible because of a floor or other limitation. See e.g., Rev. Rul. 71–161. To the extent that a deduction was allowable but the taxpayer failed to take the deduction on the taxpayer's tax return, it is a harder question whether the taxpayer's basis should be reduced. There is little authority on this issue, but there is a mild suggestion in Treas. Reg. § 1.165–1(c)(1) that basis is reduced only for casualty losses that are actually "claimed" as deductions by the taxpayer.

However, in Rev. Rul. 71–161, the Commissioner said that in the case of property damaged or destroyed by a casualty, basis "must be reduced by the amount of *allowable* loss deduction under section 165 of the Code." (Emphasis added.) Rev. Rul 71–161 further states that basis must also be reduced by the amount of insurance or other compensation "received or *recoverable* (i.e., there exists a claim for reimbursement with respect to which there is a reasonable prospect of recovery)." (Emphasis added.) Both of those statements in the ruling are open to question in that they call for a reduction of basis that can exceed the amount of deduction that was allowed. Under that ruling, the taxpayer's basis will be increased by the amount expended by the taxpayer in repairing the damaged property.

§ 7.2700A. Costs of Repairing Business Property.

If a deduction is allowed (or allowable) for damage suffered by business property because of a casualty, will the cost of repairing that property also be deductible as a business expense? The Service maintains that to the extent that the repairs are merely replacing the damaged property, they must be capitalized. Rev. Rul. 71–161; GCM 34438 (1971). In the view of the authors, the Service's position is questionable. The deductibility of the repair should not be affected by the allowance of a deduction for the damage suffered by the property. The Service's position to the contrary is based on the principle that an event should not provide duplicate deductions. To the extent that a deduction is allowed for a casualty loss, the Service's ruling considers an allowance of a deduction for the cost of replacing the damaged parts of the property as a duplication of the deduction already allowed. Of course, if the replacement is one that would be required to be capitalized in any event (even when there had been no preceding casualty), then it should be capitalized in this circumstance as well. But if the "replacement" or other repair otherwise qualifies as a deductible "repair" of business property (see § 10.1440 *et seq*.), then the cost should be deductible. As discussed in § 7.2700A–1, the allowance of a deduction for the costs of repairs does not constitute a duplication of deduction for the damage suffered. In this regard, a District Court has stated that the Service's assertion in Rev. Rul 71–161 that, in such circumstances, the repair should be capitalized is a "dubious proposition." *Waldrip v. United States*, 48 AFTR2d 81–6031, n.5 (N.D. Ga. 1981).

IRC § 263(a)(2) denies a deduction for an amount expended in restoring or in making good the exhaustion thereof for which an allowance is or has been made in the form of a deduction for depreciation, amortization, or depletion. Treas. Reg. § 1.263(a)–1(a)(2). In the authors' view, this provision is not applicable in determining the deductibility of a repair of an item for which a casualty loss deduction was allowed. On its terms, the statute is limited to restoration of the exhaustion of an asset's life for which depreciation or other amortization deductions were taken. Such a restoration would lengthen the life of the property beyond that which it had after the exhaustion took place. The provision has no application to the restoration of a loss incurred because of a casualty. Moreover, the description of a repair in Treas. Reg. § 1.162–4 supports the construction of IRC § 263(a)(2) that the latter applies only to expenditures that lengthen the life of the property. That regulation recognizes that a repair in the nature of a *replacement* must be capitalized, but only if the item "appreciably prolongs the life of the property." If the expense appreciably prolongs the life of the repaired property beyond the life it would have had if the repair had not become necessary, it would not be a "repair" for tax purposes. So, if the expense constitutes a true repair, as defined for tax purposes, IRC § 263(a)(2) will not apply.

If the Service's position for capitalization of expenses incurred to repair a deductible loss caused by a casualty were adopted, a question can arise as to the proper treatment of the costs of repairs that exceed the amount of deduction that was allowable for the casualty loss. This problem did not arise in Rev. Rul. 71–161, because the cost of repairs (and debris removal) in that case exactly matched the amount of deduction allowed for the casualty (a hurricane). They matched exactly because the taxpayer in that ruling elected to use the cost of repairs (and debris removal) as the measure of the amount of loss caused by the hurricane. See Treas. Reg. § 1.165–7(b)(1). Since it was business property and the taxpayer had a sufficient basis, the entire amount of the loss was deductible. The problem of the cost of repairs being greater than the amount of the deduction allowed for damage to business property will arise only when the loss in value due to the casualty is greater than the taxpayer's basis in the property. If that does occur, it seems that, even under the Service's position, the amount of repair cost in excess of the casualty loss deduction should be deductible.

§ 7.2700A–1. Double Deduction. As noted above, the Service has ruled that the cost of repairing damaged business property for which a casualty deduction is allowable cannot be deducted as a business expense because the allowance of one deduction for the loss suffered and a second deduction for the cost of repairs would contravene the prohibition in Treas. Reg. § 1.161–1 that "double deductions are not permitted" In the authors' view, that regulatory prohibition is not applicable. A reasonable construction of the regulation is that a single item of loss or expense cannot be deducted twice. In the question in point, there are two separate items involved albeit both are the result of a single casualty (i.e., the first item is a decline in value of the damaged property and the second item is the expenditure of cash to repair that property). There is no tax windfall in allowing both deductions since the casualty deduction causes a reduction of the taxpayer's basis in the damaged property, and the repair constitutes a cash outlay. While, as is the case with all repairs, the cash outlay will increase the value of the damaged property by curing the damage, it will not increase the taxpayer's basis unless the policy that the Commissioner adopted in Rev. Rul. 71–161 is validated.

§ 7.2700B. Costs of Repairing Personally Used Property. On the other hand, when personally used property is damaged by a casualty for which a deduction is allowed in part, what should be the tax consequence of the cost of making repairs to that property? The cost of repairs is not deductible since it is neither a business nor a profit oriented expense. If the author is correct in asserting (contrary to the Service's ruling) that the cost of repairing business property should not be capitalized, will that preclude capitalizing the cost of repairing personally used property? As a policy matter, it would seem desirable to retain the basis of the damaged property to the extent that an amount is expended on repairs. In other words, the optimum treatment would seem to be to reduce the basis of the damaged property by the difference between the amount of deduction that was *allowed* and the amount expended in repairing the property. However desirable that result may be, there is no statutory or other authority for that treatment. It is likely, therefore, that the repair will have no effect on the taxpayer's basis unless the position adopted in Rev. Rul. 71–161 is adopted.

§ 7.2710. Cost of Removal of Business Property. When business property (other than a building) ceases to be used in the business, the adjusted basis of the property, plus the cost of removing it from its location, are deductible as a business loss. Rev. Rul. 2000–7. The loss deduction is allowed regardless of whether the retired property was depreciable. Treas. Reg. §§ 1.165–2(c), 1.167(a)–8, and Rev. Rul. 2000–7.

§ 7.2720. Cost of Removal of Business Property Pursuant to a Replacement. If an item used in a business is removed to make way for a replacement, the general rule is that the cost of removal is attributed to the discarded item and is allowed as a business loss deduction. Rev. Rul. 2000–7. The deduction is allowable regardless of whether the item was depreciable. One exception to this general rule is that the cost of demolishing a building must be added to the basis of the land, but that is a special statutory provision. IRC § 280B. See **§ 7.9000A.**

If a component of a depreciable asset is removed and replaced, the deduction of the cost of removal depends upon whether the cost of the component is a deductible repair or a capitalized improvement. Rev. Rul. 2000–7. See **§ 10.1440.**

§ 7.2800. Theft Losses. A theft loss is deemed to have been sustained in the year that the taxpayer *discovers* the loss. IRC § 165(e). The amount of a theft loss is determined in the same manner as the amount of a casualty loss, but the value of the property immediately after the theft is treated as zero. Treas. Reg. § 1.165–8(c). The amount deductible is subject to the same restrictions as are imposed on casualty losses (i.e., the $100 floor, the 10% of AGI floor on a net casualty loss, and the prospect of reimbursement rules apply also to theft losses of personally used property).

§ 7.2810. Illustration: Inconsistent Treatment. *X*, an employee of *Y*, embezzled $10,000 from *Y* in Year One. For the purpose of hiding her embezzlement, *X* altered *Y*'s books to reflect a cost of *Y*'s inventory that was $10,000 greater than the actual amount paid to purchase that inventory. Ignorant of the falsification of his books, *Y* claimed and was allowed a cost of goods sold for Year One that was based on the falsified books and that resulted in *Y*'s reporting taxable income for Year One that was understated by $10,000. In Year Six (after the statute of limitations had run on *Y*'s tax return for Year One), *Y* discovered *X*'s embezzlement and became aware of the fact that the cost of his inventory for Year One was $10,000 less than the amount he had reported to the Service. There was no prospect that *Y* could obtain reimbursement of the $10,000 that *X* stole. On his tax return for Year Six, the year in which *Y* first discovered the embezzlement, *Y* claimed a theft loss deduction of $10,000. Since the loss was claimed under IRC § 165(c)(1) as a business loss, none of the floors that apply to IRC § 165(c)(3) is applicable. In a similar situation, the Commissioner contended that no theft loss deduction should be allowed to *Y* because *Y* had already obtained the benefit of reduced taxable income in Year One, and to permit a deduction in Year Six would allow a double reduction of taxable income. A majority of the Tax Court, however, allowed a taxpayer a theft loss deduction in such a circumstance. *B.C. Cook & Sons, Inc. v. Commissioner*, 59 T.C. 516 (1972).

In *Cook*, the Tax Court concluded that the Commissioner's only remedy, if any, was to assess a deficiency for Year One if either the statute of limitations for that year was open or if the defense of the statute of limitations was barred by the mitigation provisions of IRC §§ 1311–1315. The Tax Court's decision in *Cook* was repudiated by a district court in *Stahl Specialty Co. v. United States*, 551 F.Supp. 1237 (W.D.Mo. 1982) which disallowed the claim for a theft loss deduction. Indeed, Judge Dawson, who wrote the majority opinion in the 1972 *Cook* decision, stated in his concurring opinion in a subsequent (1975) related *Cook* case that he had changed his mind and now believed that he had erred in the first *Cook* case when he allowed the taxpayer a theft loss. *B.C. Cook & Sons, Inc. v. Commissioner*, 65 T.C. 422, 432 (1975), Nonacq., aff'd, 584 F.2d 53 (5th Cir. 1978), in which the courts held that the mitigation statutes do not apply to this circumstance and so the Commissioner was barred by the statute of limitations from assessing a deficiency for Year One. The Comissioner nonacquiesced in the Tax Court's decision.

§ **7.2820. Definition of Theft.** For tax purposes, "theft" covers any criminal appropriation of another's property to the benefit of the taker, including theft by swindling, false pretenses and any other guile. Whether a theft occurs depends upon the law of the jurisdiction where it was sustained, but the exact nature and nomenclature of the crime (e.g., larceny, embezzlement, or obtaining money under false pretenses) is of little importance so long as it amounts to theft. Rev. Rul. 77–18.

§ **7.2821. Illustration: Importance of State Law Definition of Theft.** *X*'s loss from the purchase on the open market of stocks of Equity Funding Corporation (Equity), which purchase was made in reliance on false statements issued by Equity, did not qualify as a theft loss because, under the applicable state law, Equity's fraud did not constitute a "theft" since Equity did not acquire any of *X*'s assets through its fraudulent statements. However, *X*'s loss on other Equity stocks, which he had purchased directly from Equity pursuant to a stock option plan for Equity's employees, did qualify as a theft loss deduction subject to the requirement that there be no reasonable prospect of reimbursement. *De Fusco v. Commissioner*, 38 T.C.M. 920 (1979).

§ 7.3000. PROOF THAT CASUALTY OR THEFT OCCURRED.

While proof that an item of the taxpayer has mysteriously disappeared is not sufficient to establish that a casualty or theft loss occurred, it is not necessary for the taxpayer to identify the specific event that caused the loss. To qualify for a casualty or theft loss deduction, a taxpayer need only present evidence sufficient to support a reasonable inference that the loss was due to a casualty or theft. In *Kielts v. Commissioner*, 42 T.C.M. 238 (1981), the testimony of an expert witness that it was improbable that a diamond stone would fall out of its setting unless a substantial force were applied to the ring was sufficient evidence to establish that a casualty loss had occurred even though the taxpayer could not identify the precise event that dislodged the missing diamond from the setting. The court allowed the taxpayer a deduction for the loss of her diamond stone. However, a taxpayer was not allowed a deduction for household goods that disappeared during the process of moving because the taxpayer was unable to prove the cause of the disappearance. *Owens v. Commissioner*, 45 T.C.M. 156 (1982). In *Jacobson v. Commissioner*, 73 T.C. 610 (1979), Acq., a taxpayer was granted a theft loss deduction even though she could not prove who committed the theft or precisely when it occurred. The taxpayer did prove that a number of valuable items in her house were gone and that there was some evidence that the house had been entered during her extended absence. The court suggested that while several items might disappear from a house without explanation, it was highly unlikely that a large number of valuable personal items would be mislaid or otherwise disappear without the involvement of some outside agency. The Tax Court deemed it sufficient for granting the deduction that a reasonable inference from the taxpayer's evidence is that a theft, rather than a mere mysterious disappearance, had occurred. Had the facts pointed to no more than a mysterious disappearance, no deduction would have been allowed.

§ 7.4000. NET OPERATING LOSS.

When a taxpayer's deductions exceed his gross income, his deductions for casualty and theft losses may be included in computing his *net operating loss* which may be carried back or forward and deducted from gross income recognized in other taxable years. IRC § 172(d)(4)(C); see §§ **13.6000–13.6300.**

§ **7.5000. WAGERING LOSSES.** Gambling losses sustained in a taxable year are deductible only to the extent that the taxpayer had gambling winnings in that same year. IRC § 165(d), and Treas. Reg. § 1.165–10. Thus, if a taxpayer lost $5,000 at a race track but won $1,000 in a poker game in the same year, he may deduct $1,000 of his loss. Similarly, if in that year the taxpayer had instead won $8,000 in a poker game, he would have to pay taxes only on his net winnings of $3,000. If a taxpayer had $10,000 gambling winnings in Year One, and had $6,000 gambling losses in Tear Two, the taxpayer would include all $10,000 of his winnings in his gross income for Year One, and the taxpayer would not be allowed any deduction for his $6,000 gambling loss in Year Two.

§ **7.6000. RESIDENCE AND OTHER NON–INCOME PRODUC-ING PROPERTY.** No deduction is allowed for a loss recognized on the sale of a taxpayer's personal residence or on the sale of any other personal (non-income) property. Treas. Reg. § 1.165–9(a). The fact that no provision of the Code grants a deduction for such losses is sufficient to deny a deduction; in addition, IRC § 262 has been cited as authority for denying a deduction.

§ **7.7000. CONVERSION TO BUSINESS PROPERTY.** If a taxpayer converts to a business or income-producing use his personal residence or other property which had formerly been used by him for personal purposes, a loss recognized on the taxpayer's subsequent sale of the converted property will be deductible. The actual rental of a residence may constitute such a conversion, but the mere unsuccessful offering for rent will not likely qualify as a conversion for *this* purpose. See § **10.1370.** In determining the amount of *loss* so recognized by a taxpayer, the taxpayer's basis at the time of conversion is the lower of: (a) his adjusted basis at that date; or (b) the fair market value of the property at that date. Treas. Reg. § 1.165–9(b). The taxpayer's basis at the time of conversion (as so computed) is then further adjusted for depreciation or other appropriate items incurred after the date of conversion. Cf., Treas. Reg. § 1.165–7(a)(5) for a similar rule when converted property is damaged in a casualty.

The above method for determining the taxpayer's basis at the time of sale is only for purposes of measuring the taxpayer's recognized *loss* (if any) on a sale. The normal rules for determining basis are used in measuring the taxpayer's gain (if any) on a sale.

§ 7.8000.   AT RISK LIMITATION. The extent to which deductions (otherwise allowable) that arise in connection with the conduct of a single trade or business or investment activity are disallowed or deferred because they exceed the amount of the taxpayer's investment in that activity is set forth in IRC § 465 (the "at risk" limitation provision). IRC § 465 applies only to "losses" as defined in IRC § 465(d), which adopts a different meaning for the term "loss" than that which is used in IRC § 165. For purposes of the "at risk" limitation, a loss from an activity is the excess of the taxpayer's deductions (otherwise allowable) that are attributable to that activity over the taxpayer's income from that activity. The treatment of such losses (including the restriction on their deductibility, the carryover provision, and the recapture of previously deducted losses) is discussed at §§ **10.7000–10.7420.** Prior to the adoption of the 1986 TRA, the "at risk" limitation provision did not apply to real estate investments. The 1986 TRA extended the "at risk" limitation to real estate investments, but the application to realty is more limited than it is to other types of activities. See §§ **10.7230– 10.7234.**

§ 7.9000.   LIMITATIONS ON THE DEDUCTIBILITY OF LOSS- ES AND CREDITS GENERATED BY A PASSIVE ACTIVITY. In the 1986 TRA, Congress adopted a number of provisions to eliminate (or at least to minimize) tax shelter investments. One of the most important of those anti-shelter provisions is the adoption of IRC § 469 which limits the amount of loss deductions and credits that can be utilized when arising out of a "passive activity." For convenience, we will sometimes refer to these limitations on passive activity losses and credits as a "PAL" (i.e., a passive activity limitation). While aimed at tax shelters, the PAL provision also reaches other investments. In general, subject to some exceptions, the losses arising out of a passive activity can be deducted only from the income produced by that activity or by other passive activities. Similarly, certain tax credits (other than the foreign tax credit) arising out of a passive activity can be utilized only to reduce income taxes incurred as a consequence of income produced by passive activities.

If an item of a passive activity is one that reduces a taxpayer's basis in a property interest, the taxpayer's basis will be so reduced even if no deduction is allowable for the item because of the IRC § 469 PAL rules. See Temp. Reg. § 1.469–1T(d)(1). In other words, IRC § 469 can deny or defer a deduction or credit, but it will not prevent the reduction of basis that the loss or deduction otherwise requires.

Keep in mind that the purpose of the PAL is to match deductions and credits from passive activities with the income from such activities. The aim of the provision is to prevent an acceleration of deductions and credits so that they are obtained in a year prior to the year in which the income from that activity is recognized. The concern is with the *timing* of deductions and credits rather than with the question of whether the taxpayer will ever incur the expenditure or loss for which the deduction or credit is allowed. The PAL was adopted to deal with a gap in the tax law that arose because of the time value of money—i.e., if a taxpayer's deduction in one year is offset by an equal amount of income in a later year, which income arose because of the deduction that was previously allowed, the taxpayer will benefit (even if both the income and the deduction are subject to the same marginal tax rate) because of the time value of money. So, the aim of the PAL is different from the aim of the at risk rules, which are designed to insure that a taxpayer will bear the loss or expenditure for which a deduction is allowed.

Except for closely held corporations, the passive activity loss of a taxpayer for a taxable year is the amount by which the "passive activity deductions" exceed the "passive activity gross income" for that year. Temp. Reg. § 1.469–2T(b)(1). Those terms are discussed at **§ 7.9142** and **§ 7.9143.**

§ 7.9100. Division of Investment and Business Activities Into Three Categories. The "PAL" provision divides a taxpayer's investment and business activities into three separate categories.

§ 7.9110. Passive Activity Category. The passive activity category, which is defined in **§ 7.9200**, constitutes one of those divisions.

§ 7.9120. Portfolio Activity. A second category can be characterized as a "portfolio" activity. While the Code does not employ the term "portfolio," it is convenient to designate those activities with a term that reasonably describes them, and the term "portfolio" is used in the committee reports. A portfolio activity includes investments that produce: interest, dividends, annuities, or royalties (other than royalties derived in the ordinary course of a trade or business). IRC § 469(e)(1). In addition, gain or loss attributable to the disposition of portfolio property or of any property held for investment is treated as gain or loss from a portfolio activity; for this purpose, an interest in a passive activity is not an investment. IRC § 469(e)(1)(A). For convenience, we will refer to income arising out of a portfolio activity as "portfolio income."

§ 7.9130. Third Category and Material Participation. Any activity that is not a passive activity or a portfolio activity [see § 7.9120] is in the third category. Thus, the third category includes investment activities that are not portfolio investments, and it includes a trade or business activity. For this purpose, a trade or business activity is a profit-oriented activity or an activity connected with a trade or business. IRC § 469(c)(6). However, an activity cannot qualify for the trade or business category unless the taxpayer "materially participates" in the conduct of that activity—i.e., the taxpayer is involved in the operations of the activity on a basis that is: "regular, continuous, and substantial." IRC §§ 469(c)(1), 469(h)(1). In determining whether a taxpayer materially participates in an activity, the participation of the taxpayer's spouse is taken into account. IRC § 469(h)(5). The seven tests for determining whether a person materially participates in an activity are set forth in Temp. Reg. § 1.469–5T. According to that temporary regulation, an individual materially participates in an activity for a taxable year if (and only if) any one of the following seven tests is satisfied:

(1) the individual participates in the activity for more than 500 hours during the taxable year;

(2) the individual's participation in the activity constitutes substantially all of the participation in the activity that takes place that taxable year;

(3) the individual participates in the activity for more than 100 hours that taxable year, and the individual's participation for that year is not less than that of any other individual;

(4) the activity is a "significant participation activity" (as that term is defined in Temp. Reg. § 1.469–5T(c)) of the individual for that taxable year, and the individual's aggregate participation in all significant participation activities for that year exceeds 500 hours.

(5) the individual materially participated in the activity for any five taxable years (that need not be consecutive) during the ten taxable years that immediately precede the taxable year;

(6) the activity is a personal service activity, and the individual materially participated in the activity for any three taxable years (that need not be consecutive) preceding the taxable year; or

(7) based on all the facts and circumstances the individual participates in the activity on a regular, continuous, and substantial basis during the taxable year.

§ 7.9140. Significance of Division Into Categories. The purpose of the PAL provisions is to isolate the income, deductions and most of the credits arising from certain passive activities so that the deductions and credits from such activities can be used only to reduce the income or tax liability from the same or other passive activities. The first step to accomplish that purpose is to define "passive activity" and then to divide all activities into passive and non-passive categories and to permit the deductions and credits from passive activities to be taken only against the income or income tax incurred from passive activities. That discourages the making of investments in activities for the purpose of creating tax deductions and credits that otherwise could be utilized to lower the taxpayer's tax liability from income-producing activities. But Congress determined that the division of activities into only two categories (passive and non-passive) would not be adequate to accomplish its goal. Certain types of passive activities typically produce income rather than a net loss—for example, an investment in stocks and bonds will usually produce dividend and interest income. If the investment in such income-producing properties were treated as a passive activity, the losses produced by tax shelter investments could then be utilized to reduce or eliminate the income tax that otherwise would be incurred on the income-producing passive investments. If that were permitted, there would still be an incentive to invest in tax shelters. To prevent that, Congress carved a third category (generally referred to as a "portfolio activity") out of the passive activity category, and the income, deductions, and credits generated by portfolio activities are treated the same as those generated by other non-passive activities. Thus, the losses and credits generated by the narrowed category of passive activities cannot be offset against the income generated by portfolio activities. In addition, certain types of income that otherwise would be classified as passive activity income instead are recharacterized by the regulations as non-passive. See Temp. Reg. § 1.469–2T(f).

§ 7.9141. Recharacterization of Passive Income. Temporary regulations list six types of passive activities the gross income from which can be recharacterized as non-passive. Temp. Reg. § 1.469–2T(f)(2)–(7). This provision can apply only to a taxpayer's gross income for a year to the extent that it is attributable to all or a portion of the taxpayer's "net passive income" from one or more of the six types of passive activities that are listed in the temporary regulations. While it is *gross income* that is recharacterized, the amount of gross income that is so treated is measured by all or a portion of the taxpayer's net passive income from an activity for that year. If an activity, which is one of the six types listed in the temporary regulations, produces a "net passive loss" for a year, that activity will not cause any gross income to be recharacterized, but its net passive loss may cause a *reduction* of the amount of gross income that is attributable to the taxpayer's net passive income from an activity that is recharacterized. See Temp. Reg. § 1.469–2T(f)(2). A taxpayer's "net passive income" from an activity for a taxable year is the amount by which the taxpayer's passive activity gross income (as specially determined) exceeds the taxpayer's passive activity deductions from the activity for that year. Conversely, the taxpayer's "net passive loss" from an activity for a taxable year is the amount by which the taxpayer's passive activity deductions from the activity exceed the taxpayer's passive activity gross income (as specially determined) from the activity for that year. Temp. Reg. § 1.459–2T(f)(9)(i), (ii). The meanings of the terms "passive activity deductions" and "passive activity gross income" are explained at §§ **7.9142** and **7.9143.**

Five of the six passive activities that are listed in the temporary regulations are:

(1) a trade or business activity in which the taxpayer is a "significant" participant but not a "material" participant [the terms "significant" and "material" participation in a trade or business activity are defined in Temp. Reg. § 1.469–5T; an individual significantly participates in a trade or business activity if the individual participates in the activity for more than 100 hours during the year and if the individual does not materially participate in the activity.];

(2) the rental of nondepreciable property [this provision for the recharacterization of net passive income applies if less than 30 percent of the unadjusted basis of the properties leased to taxpayer's customers is depreciable under IRC § 167];

(3) a passive equity-financed lending activity;

(4) the rental of certain properties incidental to development activity.

(5) the rental of property to a trade or business in which taxpayer materially participates.

§ 7.9142. Passive Activity Deductions—Exclusion of Certain Deductions. "Passive activity deductions" are defined in Temp. Reg. § 1.469–2T(d). In determining the amount of passive activity deductions of an activity, certain deductions are disregarded. The types of deductions to be disregarded are set forth at Temp. Reg. § 1.469–2T(d)(2)–(6). A few examples of excluded deductions are: charitable contributions; casualty and theft losses; state, local or foreign tax payments or accruals; a miscellaneous itemized deduction as determined by IRC § 67(b); a carryover or carryback of a net operating loss; and an expense that is allocable to portfolio income.

§ 7.9143. Passive Activity Gross Income. This term is defined at Temp. Reg. § 1.469–2T(c). In general, income from a passive activity, including the gain recognized on the disposition of an interest in a passive activity and gain recognized on the disposition of property used in a passive activity, will be included in the taxpayer's passive activity gross income. However, the temporary regulation cited above excludes certain items of income from passive activities from the taxpayer's passive activity gross income. Some of the exclusions are listed in Temp. Reg. § 1.469–2T(c)(7).

§ 7.9150. Carryover of Disallowed Losses and Credits. The losses and credits from a passive activity that are disallowed to a taxpayer by PAL can be carried forward to the immediately succeeding taxable year and treated as if they were incurred in that year. IRC § 469(b); Treas. Reg. § 1.469–1(f)(4). Such carryover losses and credits are subject to PAL restrictions in the year to which they are carried.

§ 7.9151. Disposition of Passive Activity. The typical attribute of a tax shelter activity was that the deductions and credits from that investment were concentrated in the early term of the activity. This often resulted in the taxpayer's recognition of substantial income from that activity in its later years. Consequently, most tax shelters operated as a deferral of tax obligations. A tax deferral is of benefit to an investor principally because of the time value of money. The passive activity limitation (PAL) restricts the benefit to be derived from such deferrals by deferring the tax benefit from net losses and credits that are attributable to passive activity investments until such activities produce taxable income. Thus, such losses and credits are held in abeyance to be matched with the income from those activities that effectively was deferred by preferential tax treatment.

When a taxpayer disposes of his entire interest in a passive activity in a taxable transaction (i.e., a transaction in which all realized gain or loss is recognized), any deferred gain from that activity will then be recognized. Consequently, any remaining carryover losses that are attributable to *that* activity can be deducted in the year of such taxable disposition unless the sale or other disposition is made to certain persons who are related to the taxpayer. IRC § 469(g). A disposition does not permit the allowance of carryover credits. If the sale of taxpayer's interest in a passive activity is made on an installment basis, then the taxpayer's carryover losses from that activity are deductible on an installment basis. IRC § 469(g)(3). If the carryover loss is greater than the gain that taxpayer recognized on the disposition of his interest in the passive activity, it demonstrates that, to the extent of such difference, the activity resulted in a real economic loss. Therefore, there is no reason to continue any further the deferral of the carryover losses from that activity. So, in such cases, the entire amount of a taxpayer's carryover losses from a passive activity are allowed to be deducted in the year of such taxable disposition. IRC § 469(g). Of course, this provision requires that where losses of several passive activities are deferred, it is necessary to allocate the carryovers among the several activities that produced them so that the carryovers attributable to any single activity can be identified. When carryover losses are deducted in a year of disposition of that activity, the deduction is applied in the following order:

(1) income or gain from that passive activity (including gain from the disposition of the property),

(2) income or gain from other passive activities,

(3) any other income or gain.

In certain circumstances noted below, a disposition of an interest in property that was used in a passive activity at the time of disposition is given special treatment.

§ 7.9151A. The Twelve–Month Rule. As noted above, it is advantageous for a taxpayer to have passive income since that permits the taxpayer to utilize passive losses and credits that otherwise would be deferred. A taxpayer who has held a non-passive activity for some years might seek to convert that activity to a passive one shortly before selling it so that the gain recognized on the sale would constitute passive income since the characterization of the gain from a disposition of property usually is made according to the use of the property at the time of disposition. To restrain that manipulation, the regulations provide that when a taxpayer disposes of an interest in property that had been used in more than one activity in the twelve-month period that ends on the date of the disposition, the amount realized from the disposition and the adjusted basis of the property must be allocated among the several activities according to the number of days of use in each activity during such twelve-month period. The gain or loss that is so determined to be from a non-passive activity will be treated as non-passive income or loss. Temp. Reg. § 1.469–2T(c)(2)(ii). However, in lieu of that allocation, the taxpayer may elect to allocate the disposed-of interest entirely to the activity in which the property was predominantly used during that twelve-month period *if* the value of the disposed-of interest does not exceed the lesser of (1) $10,000, or (2) 10% of the sum of the fair market values of such interest and of all other properties used in that activity during the twelve-month period. *Ibid.*

§ 7.9151B. Substantially Appreciated Property. In addition to the twelve-month rule, the regulations impose an even more extensive restriction on gain recognized from the sale of substantially appreciated property (SAP). Substantially appreciated property (SAP) is defined as property which has a fair market value that is greater than 120% of the adjusted basis of such property. Treas. Reg. § 1.469–2(c)(2)(iii)(C). All of the gain recognized from the disposition of substantially appreciated property is treated as non-passive income unless the property was used in a passive activity either (1) for the entire 24–month period ending on the date of disposition, or (2) for a time equal to 20% of the period during which the taxpayer held such property. Treas. Reg. § 1.469–2(c)(2)(iii)(A).

§ 7.9152.   Transfers at Death or by Gift. When the taxpayer dies before disposing of his interest in a passive activity, the unused carryover losses from that activity can be deducted in the year of the taxpayer's death, but only to the extent that such unused losses exceed the step-up in basis (if any) that the transferee of such interest obtained because of the taxpayer's death (i.e., the excess, if any, of the transferee's basis over the basis that the taxpayer had at the time of his death is a "step-up" in basis). IRC § 469(g)(2). The amount of such carryover loss that is equal to the transferee's step-up in basis can never be deducted. Any unused carryover of tax credits that were disallowed by IRC § 469 will be lost on the taxpayer's death.

If a taxpayer makes a gift of an interest in a passive activity, the unused carryover loss from that activity (and probably the losses incurred by the taxpayer from that activity in the year of disposition) can never be deducted, but that unused loss is added to the donee's basis in the transferred interest. IRC § 469(j)(6). If the basis acquired by the donee is greater than the fair market value of the property at the date that the gift was made, IRC § 1015(a) limits the donee's basis to such fair market value for the purpose of determining a *loss* recognized by the donee on a subsequent disposition. It appears that an addition to the donee's basis that is attributable to the donor's unused passive losses is subject to that limitation for the purpose of determining any loss recognized by the donee on a subsequent disposition. The addition to the donee's basis merely reinstates some of the donor's basis that was reduced by a passive activity loss that was not deductible. If the donor had retained that basis (i.e., if it had not been reduced by the passive activity loss), the donee's loss basis in the transferred asset would have been limited to the property's fair market value at the time of the gift, and there is no reason not to apply that same limitation to the addition to basis that the donee obtains by IRC § 469(j)(6).

§ 7.9153.   Former Passive Activity. An activity is a "former passive activity" in a taxable year if, with respect to the taxpayer, the activity is not a passive activity for the taxable year, but was a passive activity for any prior taxable year. IRC

§ 469(f)(3). The unused deductions from passive activity years can be taken against the income from the activity in the current taxable year, and the unused credits from passive activity years can be offset against the regular tax liability from the activity in the current taxable year (after utilization of carryover deductions from that activity). Any excess deductions and credits continue to be treated as arising from a passive activity. IRC § 469(f)(1). If the activity produces portfolio income in the current taxable year, it would seem that the carryover losses and credits from prior passive activity years should not be permitted to offset such portfolio income or the tax liability therefrom; but the literal language of IRC § 469(f)(1) makes no exception for portfolio income.

§ 7.9160. Persons Subject to Passive Activity Limitations. The passive activity provisions apply to individuals, estates, trusts, personal service corporations, and certain closely-held corporations. IRC § 469(a)(2). The passive activity limitations operate more generously for certain closely-held corporations than they do for other taxpayers. IRC § 469(e)(2).

§ 7.9200. Definition of "Passive Activity." A passive activity is an activity (other than a portfolio activity) which involves the conduct of a trade or business (which, for this purpose, includes a profit-orientated investment) in which the taxpayer does not materially participate. IRC § 469(c)(1). The meaning of "material participation" is explained in **§ 7.9130.** Except as provided otherwise by regulation, a taxpayer will not be deemed to materially participate in an activity in which he has only a limited partnership interest. IRC § 469(h)(2). The definition of a limited partnership interest is set forth in Temp. Reg. § 1.469–5T(e)(3). Temp. Reg. § 1.469–5T(e)(2) explains the circumstances in which a limited partner will be treated as having materially participated in an activity. Note that the regulation distinguishes between "material participation" and "significant participation." See **§ 7.9141.** A working interest in oil or gas property (other than a limited partner's interest) generally will *not* be treated as a passive activity regardless of whether the taxpayer materially participated in that activity. IRC § 469(c)(3), (4).

§ 7.9210. Rental Activity. Prior to the amendments made by the Omnibus Budget Reconciliation Act of 1993 (OBRA), a "rental activity" was treated as a passive activity even if the taxpayer materially participated in the conduct of that activity. IRC § 469(c)(2), (4); Temp. Reg. § 1.469–1T(e)(1)(ii). Even after the

1993 amendment, that continues to be true for all rental activities other than rental real estate activities. The definition of "rental activity" is explained below. As a consequence of the 1993 amendments, while the rental activities of many taxpayers will continue to be treated as passive activities, the rental real estate activities of many (but not all) of those who materially participate in a real property trade or business will not be treated as a passive activity. IRC § 469(c)(7). The requirements for the exclusion of a rental real estate activity from passive activity classification are explained at **§ 7.9212.** This provision has no affect on the question of whether a limited partner materially participates in the business of the limited partnership. IRC § 469(c)(7)(A).

§ 7.9211. Definition of "Rental Activity." Subject to specified exceptions listed below, a "rental activity" is one where payments are received principally for the use of tangible property. IRC § 469(j)(8). According to the regulations, an activity is a rental activity for the taxable year if (1) during the year, tangible property held in connection with the activity is used by customers or is held for use by customers, and (2) gross income or (in the case of property held for use by customers) anticipated gross income attributable to the conduct of the activity represents (or will represent) amounts paid or to be paid principally for the use of such tangible property. Temp. Reg. § 1.469–1T(e)(3)(i).

§ 7.9211–1. Exclusions From Rental Activity. The regulations contain a number of exceptions which preclude certain activities that involve the rental of tangible property from qualifying as "rental activities" for purposes of PAL. Temp. Reg. § 1.469–1T(e)(3)(ii). According to the regulations, an activity involving the use of tangible property is not a rental activity for a taxable year if for that taxable year any one of the following six conditions exists:

(1) The average period of customer use for such property is seven days or less;

(2) The average period of customer use for such property is 30 days or less, and "significant personal services" (i.e., services performed by individuals of a type described in Temp. Reg. § 1.469–1T(e)(3)(iv)) are provided by or on behalf of the owner of the property in connection with its rental;

(3) "Extraordinary personal services" (as defined by Temp. Reg. § 1.469–1T(e)(3)(v)) are provided by or on behalf of the owner in connection with the rental regardless of the average period of customer use;

(4) The rental of such property is incidental to a nonrental activity of the taxpayer as determined by Temp. Reg. § 1.469–1T(e)(3)(vi);

(5) The taxpayer customarily makes such property available during defined business hours for nonexclusive use by various customers (this exception is probably designed to exclude facilities such as a golf course or a health club whose customers will normally be invitees or licensees rather than tenants or lessees); or

(6) The taxpayer rents the tangible property for use by a partnership, S corporation or joint venture (which conducts an activity other than a rental activity) in which the taxpayer owns an interest [Temp. Reg. § 1.469–1T(e)(3)(vii)].

§ 7.9211–2. Exception for Certain Losses and Credits from Rental Real Estate Activity.

If the exclusion from passive activity characterization that is described at § 7.9212 is applicable to an individual, then IRC § 469 will not apply to that individual's share of losses and credits from a rental real estate activity. But, if that exclusion is not applicable to an individual, and if the individual's AGI is not too large, a certain amount of losses and credits from a rental real estate activity *may* be excluded from the IRC § 469 limitation.

If a *natural person* who has AGI that is less than $150,000 "actively" participates in one or more rental real estate activities, that person will be permitted to deduct a certain amount of the net loss from those activities against any of his income (i.e., the PAL of IRC § 469 does not apply to that amount of loss). IRC § 469(i). No regulations defining active participation have been promulgated as yet, but there are some guidelines. A taxpayer cannot qualify as an active participant in an activity unless the aggregate value of the interests in that activity held by the taxpayer and his spouse is ten percent or more of the value of all the interests in that activity. IRC § 469(i)(6)(A). In determining whether a taxpayer actively participates in a rental activity, the participation of the taxpayer's spouse is taken into account. IRC § 469(i)(6)(D). Except as provided otherwise in Temp. Reg. § 1.469–5T(e)(2), a person whose only interest in a rental activity is a limited partnership interest is not an "active" participant in that activity. IRC § 469(i)(6)(C). The maximum amount of loss from rental real estate activities that a taxpayer can deduct under the active participant exception is $25,000, and that figure is reduced by 50 percent of the excess of the taxpayer's modified AGI over $100,000. IRC § 469(i)(3)(A). A taxpayer's AGI is modified by excluding deductions for passive activity losses, interest on education loans, qualified tuition payments, and for IRA contributions; and by including the income, that is otherwise excluded by IRC § 135, from the redemption of U.S. Savings bonds used to pay higher education costs, the amounts received by an employee to help pay for adoption expenses; and by excluding social security income. IRC § 469(i)(3)(F).

§ 7.9211–2A. Low Income Housing and Rehabilitation Credits.

A passive activity may generate tax credits, and such credits are subject to the IRC § 469 limitations. IRC § 469(a). Special rules apply if the credits are generated by a rental real estate activity and are otherwise available to a natural person who "actively" participated in the activity. When tax credits are attributable to a rental real estate activity, the amount of such credits that exceeds the amount of income tax attributable to passive activities is allowable to the extent that such excess credit does not exceed the "deduction equivalent" of $25,000. IRC § 469(i)(1), (2). With two exceptions the $25,000 amount is phased out when the individual's modified AGI exceeds $100,000 (the same phase-out provision that is described in § 7.9211–2). IRC § 469(i)(3)(A). The two tax credits that receive special treatment insofar as the phase-out is concerned are: (1) the tax credit for new construction and rehabilitation of low income housing [IRC § 42] and (2) the tax credit for certain expenses of rehabilitating historical and certain other buildings [IRC § 47]. For credits allowed by IRC § 42, there is no reduction of the $25,000 amount. IRC § 469(i)(3)(D). For credits allowed by IRC § 47, the $25,000 amount is reduced by 50 percent of the excess of the taxpayer's modified AGI over $200,000. IRC § 469(i)(3)(B). One other important difference in those two credit allowances from the allowance of loss deductions from such a rental real estate activity is that the IRC §§ 42 and 47 credits are allowable to a natural person who owns an interest in such a rental real estate activity regardless of whether that person "actively" participated in the activity. IRC § 469(i)(6)(B). In addition, the portion of the passive activity loss from such activity that is attributable to a commercial revitalization deduction under IRC § 1400I also is allowable without regard to whether the taxpayer "actively" participated in the activity. Ibid.

§ 7.9212. Special Rules for a Taxpayer Who Materially Participates in a Real Property Trade or Business. As to individuals, the automatic classification of rental activities as passive activities does not apply to rental real estate activities if the following two requirements are satisfied:

(1) more than one-half of the personal services performed by the taxpayer in trades or businesses is performed in "real property trades or businesses" in which the taxpayer materially participates [the meaning of material participation in a trade or business is explained at **§ 7.9130**, and that definition is applicable to this provision; and so the participation of spouses in a real estate trade or business are combined to determine whether either spouse materially participated]; and

(2) the taxpayer performs more than 750 hours of services during the taxable year in real property trades or businesses in which the taxpayer materially participates.

While the participation of spouses can be combined in determining material participation of either spouse, they cannot be combined for the purposes of the other requirements. So, each person's own performance of service must satisfy the 750–hour requirement and the more-than-one-half of taxpayer's services requirement. IRC § 469(c)(7)(B).

The term "real property trade or business" means any real property development, redevelopment, construction, reconstruction, acquisition, conversion, rental, operation, management, leasing, or brokerage trade or business. IRC § 469(c)(7)(C).

Personal services that are performed as an employee do not qualify as services performed in a real property trade or business unless the employee has more than a 5% ownership interest in the employer. IRC § 469(c)(7)(D)(ii).

As to corporate taxpayers, if the taxpayer is a closely held C corporation, it will qualify for the exclusion from passive activity characterization if more than 50% of the corporation's gross receipts are derived from a real estate trade or business in which the corporation materially participates. IRC § 469(c)(7)(D)(i). The meaning of material participation for a closely held C corporation is defined in IRC § 469(h)(4).

If the requirements of this provision are satisfied, then any rental real estate activity of the taxpayer is not treated as a passive activity. This provision is applied by treating each rental real estate activity of the taxpayer as a separate activity unless the taxpayer elects to treat all such interests as one activity. IRC § 469(c)(7)(A).

§ 7.9220. Earned Income. A taxpayer's earned income (that is, income earned by the taxpayer from his services) is not treated as passive activity income. IRC § 469(e)(3).

§ 7.9300. Interests in Passive Activities Acquired Prior to Adoption of the 1986 TRA.

The limitations on the deduction of passive activity losses and credits apply to such losses and credits that arise in taxable years beginning after 1986, regardless of when the taxpayer acquired an interest in that activity. For interests purchased prior to the adoption of the 1986 TRA, the imposition of limitations that did not exist at the time of purchase is harsh. To mitigate that harshness, Congress phased-in the disallowance of losses or credits arising from an interest acquired prior to the enactment of the 1986 TRA. IRC § 469(m). Only a percentage of such losses or credits (that otherwise would be disallowed by IRC § 469) are disallowed in the years 1987–1990 (i.e., 35% in 1987, 60% in 1988, 80% in 1989, and 90% in 1990). The phase-in is now complete, and IRC § 469 will operate the same for interests acquired prior to the date of adoption of the 1986 TRA as it operates on interests acquired after that date.

§ 7.9400. Regulatory Exclusion From Passive Activity Category.

Those taxpayers that have passive activity investments that generate losses (especially those taxpayers that acquired interests in such activities prior to the adoption of the 1986 TRA) will seek passive activity investments that generate taxable income so that they can utilize their loss deductions from their passive activity investments. To that end, taxpayers may structure a new investment in a manner that would cause the income therefrom to constitute passive activity income. To prevent an abusive use of such arrangements, Congress has given Treasury broad authority to exclude certain types of income from the passive activity category when it is necessary to do so to prevent a frustration of the Congressional purpose in adopting the passive activity limitations. IRC § 469(*l*). Treasury exercised that authority by promulgating Temp. Reg. § 1.469–2T(f), which is discussed at §§ **7.9141–7.9143.**

§ 7.9500. Interaction with At Risk Rules. The At Risk rules [IRC § 465] are applied first, and any deduction that would be permitted after applying the At Risk rules will then be subject to the passive activity limitation imposed by IRC § 469. Temp. Reg. § 1.469–2T(d)(6).

§ 7.9600. Operation of the PAL. The following examples illustrate the operation of the PAL.

§ 7.9610. Illustration 1. *X*, a natural person, has interests in two passive activities—PA–1 and PA–2. In Year One, *X* has salary income of $170,000, and *X* has a net loss of $30,000 from PA–1 and a net loss of $20,000 from PA–2. A deduction of those losses is not barred by the at risk rules. *X* also has dividend income of $8,000 from publicly held stocks that *X* owns. *X* is not permitted to deduct any amount for the losses incurred by his interest in PA–1 and PA–2. Those losses are carried forward and treated as having been incurred in *X*'s next taxable year.

§ 7.9620. Illustration 2. The facts are the same as those stated in § **7.9610.** In Year Two, *X* had salary income of $180,000, and he had dividend income of $9,500. *X* had a loss of $8,000 from PA–2. A deduction of that loss is not barred by the at risk rules. In Year Two, *X* sold his interest in PA–1 for a recognized gain of $18,000. *X* had no other income or loss from PA–1 in that year. *X* can deduct from his gain on the sale of PA–1 $18,000 of his $30,000 carryover loss from PA–1. This washes out that gain. *X* can deduct the $12,000 balance of PA–1 carryover loss from his salary and dividend income. The $8,000 loss that *X* incurred with respect to PA–2 is not deductible in that year. For Year Three, *X* has a carryover loss from his PA–2 investment of $28,000 (i.e., $20,000 from Year One and an additional $8,000 from Year Two).

§ 7.9000A. DEMOLITION OF STRUCTURE. When a taxpayer razes a building that he owns and uses in a trade or business or in a profit-seeking venture, he incurs expenses in demolishing the building (or other structure) and may have an unrecovered basis in the demolished structure (i.e., a basis that has not been recovered through depreciation or other deductions). Since the building (or other structure) was used in the taxpayer's business or profit venture, should he be permitted a deduction for the expenses of razing the structure and for his remaining adjusted basis in the structure? At one time, a deduction would be allowed unless the taxpayer had purchased the property with the intention of razing it (for example, so that a more efficient building might be constructed on the lot in its place). In such cases, the cost of razing the building and all or much of the unrecovered basis was not deductible and instead was added to the taxpayer's basis in the underlying land. The current rule, which is set forth at IRC § 280B, prohibits a deduction for the cost of demolishing a structure and denies a deduction for any unrecovered basis regardless of what purpose the taxpayer had when he acquired the property. Any amount of the expenses of demolishing the structure and of the unrecovered basis of the structure that would have been deductible if it were not for IRC § 280B, will instead be added to the taxpayer's basis in the land. One aspect of this provision is that it eliminates what had been a difficult factual issue to resolve— namely, what intention a taxpayer had when he acquired improved realty and subsequently demolished the structure.

CHAPTER EIGHT

MEDICAL EXPENSES

§ 8.0000. MEDICAL EXPENSES. Expenses *paid* for the medical care of a taxpayer, his spouse, and dependents are deductible subject to certain limitations described below. IRC § 213(a). The term "dependent" in this provision adopts the definition of that term in IRC § 152 (the provision for a dependent exemption deduction) except that several of the requirements imposed by IRC § 152 are deleted. IRC § 213(a). Consequently, an individual can be a TP's dependent for purposes of the medical expense deduction even though that individual does not qualify for a dependent exemption deduction for the TP.

Note that the reimbursement that a taxpayer receives from an insurer pursuant to medical care insurance typically is excluded from the taxpayer's gross income except to the extent that the taxpayer had previously deducted the expenses. See **§§ 2.4300–2.4342.**

In certain cases, a child of divorced or legally separated parents is treated as the dependent of both parents for purposes of determining whether a parent's payment of the child's medical expenses qualifies for the medical expense deduction. IRC § 213(d)(5). If a tax credit is taken under IRC § 21 for a medical expense that was incurred for the care of a dependent, that expense cannot also be deducted. IRC § 213(e). In other words, those expenses that qualify both for a tax credit and for a medical expense deduction can be taken as one or the other, but not as both.

A medical expense is deductible only in the taxable year in which it was *paid*, regardless of when the expense was incurred and regardless of whether the taxpayer is on the cash or the accrual method of accounting. Treas. Reg. § 1.213–1(a)(1).

§ 8.1000. DEFINITION OF MEDICAL CARE. For purposes of IRC § 213, "medical care" refers to amounts paid for the "diagnosis, cure, mitigation, treatment, or prevention of a disease, or for the purpose of affecting any structure or function of the body." An expenditure that is merely beneficial to the general health of an individual (as contrasted to an expense designed to alleviate or cure a specific illness) is not an expenditure for medical care.

As discussed below, transportation costs incurred primarily for and essential to the medical purposes described above constitute medical care expenses. § **8.1200–8.1220.** Subject to requirements described below, premiums paid on certain medical insurance coverage qualify for a deduction. § **8.1400.**

Not every expenditure that constitutes a medical care expense is deductible. For example, the costs of medicines and drugs are medical care expenses. Rev. Rul. 2003–102. The regulations state that "medicines and drugs" refer to items that are legally procured and generally accepted as falling within the category of medicines and drugs, regardless of whether they can be obtained only with a prescription. Treas. Reg. § 1.213–1(e)(2). The term does not include toothpaste, hand lotions and similar items. But, the statute does not allow a deduction for all medicines and drugs. The cost of insulin is deductible. The only other costs for medicines and drugs that are deductible are those for "prescribed drugs." IRC § 213(b). A "prescribed drug" is a drug or "biological" which can be obtained only with a physician's prescription. IRC § 213(d)(3). A "biological" is described in Blackstone's *Pocket Medical Dictionary* as a biological product such as a serum or vaccine.

While the cost of nonprescription drugs is not deductible, it is significant that they nevertheless are classified as medical care expenses. In addition to § 213, other Code provisions apply to medical care expenses. For example, IRC § 105(b) excludes from an employee's gross income reimbursements of medical care expenses that the employee received from a health insurance plan funded by the employee's employer. See § **2.4342.** In Rev. Rul. 2003–102, the Commissioner ruled that an employer's reimbursements of an employee's cost of purchasing nonprescription drugs was a reimbursement of medical care costs that is excluded from the employee's gross income under § 105(b) even though those expenses would not have been deductible under § 213 if they had not been reimbursed. The ruling further held that expenses for vitamins and other dietary supplements are for the benefit of the taxpayer's general health and therefore are not medical care expenses; and so the employer's reimbursement of those expenses is included in the employee's gross income.

Amounts paid for the care (including personal care services), treatment, mitigation, and rehabilitation of a "chronically ill individual" (and, subject to a ceiling, the premiums for insurance to cover such costs) constitute medical care expenses. IRC §§ 213(d)(1)(C),(D), (10), 7702B(c). A "chronically ill individual" is defined in IRC § 7702B(c)(2) as including an individual who has been certified by a licensed health care practitioner as being unable to perform (without substantial assistance) at least two activities of daily living for a 90–day period due to a loss of functional capacity. It would seem that this provision, which was added to the Code in 1996, will provide a deduction for the cost of personal care services for individuals who are unable to care for themselves because of Alzheimer's or dementia.

§ 8.1100. Personal Expenditure. The line between a medical expense and a personal expense which relates in part to a physical or mental condition is sometimes difficult to draw. For example, in Rev. Rul. 75–319, the Commissioner ruled that the expenses incurred by a husband and wife for marriage counseling services performed by a clergyman associated with a counseling center were personal, nondeductible expenses. The ruling stressed that the expense was not incurred for the prevention or alleviation of a physical or mental defect or illness, but rather to help improve the taxpayer's marriage. However, in that same year, the Commissioner ruled that the fees paid by a husband and wife for psychiatric treatment for their "sexual inadequacy and incompatibility" were deductible medical expenses. Rev. Rul. 75–187.

§ 8.1110. Cosmetic Surgery. In Rev. Rul. 76–332, the Commissioner ruled that an expense incurred for cosmetic plastic surgery (a face lift) for the purpose of improving the taxpayer's personal appearance was deductible. The face lift operation had not been recommended by a physician, and the taxpayer was not suffering from a mental disorder. The Commissioner determined in Rev. Rul. 76–332 that since the face lift operation affected a structure of the human body, it constituted medical care according to Treas. Reg. § 1.213–1(e)(1)(ii). The Commissioner cited with approval his earlier ruling on the deductibility of a vasectomy, abortion, and similar operations. See **§ 8.1700.** In Rev. Rul. 82–111, the Commissioner sustained the deductibility of expenses incurred for a cosmetic hair transplant and for hair removal by electrolysis, but denied a deduction for the cost of tattooing and for the cost of having a taxpayer's ear pierced. Both Rev. Rul. 76–332 and Rev. Rul. 82–111 were vitiated by an amendment adopted as part of the Omnibus Budget Reconciliation Act of 1990. As amended, IRC § 213(d)(9) expressly precludes a medical expense deduction for cosmetic surgery (or similar procedures) unless the surgery or other procedure is necessary to ameliorate a deformity attributable to "a congenital abnormality, a personal injury re-

sulting from an accident or trauma, or disfiguring disease."
"Cosmetic surgery" is defined in IRC § 213(d)(9)(B) as a "procedure which is directed at improving the patient's appearance and
does not meaningfully promote the proper function of the body or
prevent or treat illness or disease."

§ **8.1120. Religious Cure.** The question has arisen as to
whether expenses incurred in seeking a cure of a disease or illness
from a religious source constitutes a medical expense. A treatment need not be administered or proscribed by a licensed medical doctor to qualify as a medical deduction. See § **8.1140**, For
example, a taxpayer's transportation costs of attending meetings
of an Alcoholics Anonymous Club are deductible. Rev. Rul. 63–
273. The amount paid for services rendered by an authorized
Christian Science Practitioner qualifies as a medical expense. Rev.
Rul. 55–261. The expense of taking a child suffering with a
malignant tumor to the Shrine of Our Lady of Lourdes in
Lourdes, France was held to be primarily for the purposes of
spiritual help rather than to alleviate a physical defect and so was
nondeductible. *Ring v. Commissioner*, 23 T.C. 950 (1955). Similarly, the expenses of a trip by the taxpayer's wife to Samoa (her
original homeland) for the purpose of being treated for a stroke
by native "doctors" were held to be nondeductible. *Tautolo v.
Commissioner*, 34 TCM 1198 (1975). The wife's case had been
diagnosed as hopeless by her doctors in California where she
lived. The Samoan "doctors" had no medical school training, and
their treatment consisted of prayers to the spirits, herbs and
massages. They gave the same treatment to all persons regardless
of the nature of the illness. The Tax Court determined that the
taxpayer probably did not have a "reasonable expectation" that
the Samoan trip would cure his wife, and that the trip was a "last
resort." The relevance of those two determinations is unclear, but
perhaps they influenced the court's view as to the bona fides of
the purported medical purpose of the trip as contrasted to making
a final trip to the wife's homeland. Although the court did not
speak on that subject, it may have been the actual rationale for
the result the court reached.

§ **8.1130. Divided Purpose.** Frequently, in medical expense
cases, the purpose of incurring the expense is clear. If, however,
the taxpayer claims a medical reason for incurring an expense
that would normally be a personal item, the taxpayer may obtain
a medical expense deduction, but he must bear a heavy burden of
proof to show that it was undertaken for a medical reason. The

Tax Court has held that in such cases, the taxpayer's burden is to prove that he would not have incurred the expense but for the medical care need. In *Huff v. Commissioner*, 69 T.C.M. 2551 (1995), the Court said,

> Certain treatments are inherently medical in nature (i.e., surgery), and taxpayers have little difficulty convincing the Commissioner or courts that such procedures fit within the section 213 definition. Other treatments ... are more commonly recognized as nonmedical procedures intended for an individual's general well-being. In those instances where a normally nonmedical procedure is claimed as a basis for a medical deduction, the burden is on such taxpayers to show that the procedure comes within the requirements of the statute.

Thus, in *Jacobs v. Commissioner*, 62 T.C. 813 (1974), the Tax Court denied a man a medical deduction for the cost of divorcing his wife even though his marriage impaired his mental health and his psychiatrist recommended the divorce as vital to his treatment. See also *Rabb v. Commissioner*, 31 T.C.M. 476 (1972), where the court denied a deduction for the amounts spent on shopping excursions recommended by the taxpayer's psychiatrist. While the cost of the construction of a swimming pool to meet the medical needs of the taxpayer or his dependent generally is deductible subject to the limitations discussed in **§ 8.3000**, no deduction will be allowed unless the principal reason for constructing the pool was medical care. Compare *Evanoff v. Commissioner*, 44 T.C.M. 1394 (1982) (no deduction) with *Ferris v. Commissioner*, 582 F.2d 1112 (7th Cir. 1978) (discussed in **§ 8.3300**) (deduction for part of the cost).

A doctor's instruction to undertake an expenditure of this type is a significant factor in meeting the burden of proving that it was done for a medical reason. See **§ 8.1140.** Indeed, in some cases of this nature, a doctor's recommendation may be necessary, albeit not sufficient, to qualify the expenditure for a deduction. A doctor's opinion is sometimes necessary to prove that a disease exists or that a typically personal expenditure constitutes a treatment for a disease. Info 2001–0155 (June 29, 2001). A doctor's opinion is not always required and sometimes is merely one among several factors to be weighed. In Info 2001–0155, the Service said,

Among the objective factors that indicate that an otherwise personal expense is for medical care are the taxpayer's motive or purpose, recommendation by a physician, linkage between the treatment and the illness, treatment effectiveness, and proximity in time to the onset or recurrence of a disease.

In Rev. Rul. 87–106, the Commissioner stated that while capital expenditures incurred for medical reasons are currently deductible as medical expenses (See § **8.3000**), the amount of such expenditures that are incurred for non-medical reasons (such as architectural and aesthetic compatibility with the taxpayer's residence) is not deductible. See also *Ferris v. Commissioner, supra*; and § **8.3300.** The Commissioner will not provide an advance ruling on the question of whether a proposed capital expenditure for an item that is ordinarily used for personal purposes is primarily intended for a medical purpose. Rev. Proc. 2004–3, Sec. 3.01(18). But see, § **8.3000**

§ 8.1140. Doctor's Instruction. An expense need not have been incurred on the advice of a medical doctor to qualify as a deductible medical expense. The nature of the services rendered controls the determination of whether it is medical care; the determination does not rest on the experience, title, and qualification of the person rendering the service. *Brown v. Commissioner*, 62 T.C. 551 (1974), aff'd per curiam, 523 F.2d 365 (8th Cir. 1975); *Tautolo v. Commissioner*, 34 T.C.M. 1198 (1975). However, when the purposes for making an expenditure may be divided between medical and personal reasons, a doctor's instruction (while not conclusive) will be a significant factor. See § **8.1130.** In Info 2001–0155 (June 29, 2001), the Service stated that a doctor's opinion is sometimes necessary to show that a disease is present or that a typically personal expenditure constitutes a treatment for a disease. For example, in Rev. Rul. 2002–19, the Service suggests that one of the conditions for deducting the cost of a weight loss program is that a physician have diagnosed that the taxpayer is suffering from obesity or from some other disease that requires weight loss for treatment. See § **8.1620.** The Internal Revenue Code itself explicitly requires that to qualify an individual's long-term care expenses for a deduction under IRC § 213(d)(1)(C), the individual must be certified by a licensed health care practitioner to satisfy certain conditions specified in IRC § 7702B(c)(2). See § **8.1000.** Note Rev. Rul. 76–80, where the Commissioner held that a taxpayer could not deduct the cost of purchasing a special type of vacuum cleaner that would alleviate the taxpayer's allergy to household dust by removing dust from the air. Although use of an air cleaner had been recommended to the taxpayer by his physician, the physician had not suggested using this type of vacuum cleaner as an air cleaner. Relying in part on the fact that no medical recommendation had been made to the taxpayer to purchase the machine, the Commissioner ruled that there was "no evidence, such as a medical prescription, that the vacuum cleaner was purchased primarily for medical care."

§ 8.1150. Illegal Expenditures. The regulations deny a deduction for medical care expenditures that are illegal. Treas. Reg. § 1.213–1(e)(1)(ii). In Rev. Rul. 97–9, the Service ruled that even though a taxpayer's purchase of marijuana pursuant to physician's prescription was legal under the local state law, it nevertheless was nondeductible because it violated the federal Control Substance Act (21 U.S.C. §§ 801–971) which lists marijuana as a controlled substance (21 U.S.C. § 812(c)). However, in an earlier ruling, the Service allowed a deduction for the purchase of laetrile where the sale and use of the item was legal in the state in which the purchase took place. Rev. Rul 78–325. The 1978 ruling does not discuss the question of whether the purchase violated federal law or the policy of the Food and Drug Administration against the use of laetrile.

§ 8.1200. Transportation. Medical expenses include the cost of transportation incurred primarily for and essential to medical care. IRC § 213(d)(1)(B). "Transportation costs," the cost of transporting a person from one location to another, must be distinguished from the broader term "travel expenses." While travel expenses include transportation costs, they also include living expenses (meals and lodging) incurred at the new location. The extent to which travel expenses are deductible is discussed at **§ 8.1500.**

The Commissioner ruled in Rev. Rul. 78–266 that child care expenses incurred to permit a patient to visit a physician for medical treatment are personal, nondeductible expenses. The Commissioner did not treat the child care expenses as part of the cost of visiting the doctor. See *Ochs v. Commissioner*, 195 F.2d 692 (2d Cir. 1952). See also, *Estate of Levine v. Commissioner*, 43 T.C.M. 259 (1982), aff'd 729 F.2d 1441 (2d Cir. 1983).

§ 8.1210. Limitations on Deduction of Transportation Expenses. The statute permits a deduction only for expenses "paid" during the taxable year. When a taxpayer uses his own vehicle for transportation for medical care purposes, the Commissioner contends (and the courts have held) that the taxpayer cannot claim a medical expense deduction for depreciation of the vehicle so used because the Commissioner asserts that a depreciation allowance is not an amount paid. See Rev. Proc. 64–15, citing *Gordon v. Commissioner*, 37 T.C. 986 (1962). In *Commissioner v. Idaho Power Co.*, 418 U.S. 1 (1974), the Supreme Court treated a depreciation allowance on equipment being used by the taxpayer in the construction of a capital asset to be used in the taxpayer's business as an amount paid for the construction of the capital asset and, therefore, a nondeductible capital expenditure. It might appear that a depreciation allowance on a vehicle being used for medical care purposes similarly should be treated as an amount paid for medical care and thus be deductible. However, in a split decision, the Tenth Circuit denied a claim for a medical expense deduction for the depreciation of a vehicle which was so used. *Weary v. United States*, 510 F.2d 435 (10th Cir. 1975). The Tenth Circuit did not deem *Idaho Power* to be controlling. Accord, *Henderson v. Commissioner, 80 T.C.M. 517 (2000)*; *Pfersching v. Commissioner*, 46 T.C.M. 424 (1983); and *Elwood v. Commissioner*, 72 T.C. 264 (1979). Of course, the transportation costs actually paid by the taxpayer in using his own vehicle (e.g., gas, parking fees and tolls) for a medical purpose are deductible.

§ 8.1220. Standard Mileage Allowance. If a taxpayer uses his own car as a means of transportation for medical purposes, in lieu of itemizing his actual transportation expense, the taxpayer may elect the optional standard mileage rate which, at present, is fifteen cents per mile. The optimal mileage allowance can be taken in lieu of deducting operating expenses (including gas and oil). However, parking fees and tolls are not reflected in the mileage allowance, and so can be deducted separately. Rev. Proc. 2004–64 (Secs. 7.02–7.04). The mileage allowance also does not reflect any amount for depreciation of the vehicle since depreciation is not allowed as a medical care deduction. See **§ 8.1210.**

§ 8.1300. Payment with Borrowed Funds. While a medical expense must actually be paid to be deductible, the timing of the deductibility of the payment of a medical expense does not turn upon whether the taxpayer used his own funds or whether he used borrowed funds. If a taxpayer used borrowed funds, the expense is allowed as a deduction in the taxable year that the payment was made rather than in the year that the taxpayer repaid the loan. *Granan v. Commissioner*, 55 T.C. 753 (1971).

§ **8.1310. Credit Cards.** If a taxpayer uses a bank's credit card to pay a medical expense, he creates a creditor-debtor relationship between the payee and the bank, and he retains no control over that relationship. The use of the credit card is equivalent to the payment of the medical expense with borrowed funds, and so the deduction is allowable in the year in which the credit card charge is made rather than in the year in which the taxpayer repays the bank. Rev. Rul. 78–39.

§ **8.1400. Insurance Premiums.** Premiums for medical insurance are included in a taxpayer's allowable medical expenses. If an insurance policy provides for coverage other than medical care insurance (e.g., a lump sum payment for loss of life or limb), only the amount of the premium which is attributable to the medical care insurance is deductible. Even that amount cannot be deducted unless the insurance company provides an explicit statement of the amount of the premium that is paid for medical care and unless the amount charged by the insurance company for medical care is not an unreasonably large portion of the entire premium. IRC § 213(d)(6). As noted in § **8.1000**, premiums paid for insurance to cover the cost of medical care for a "chronically ill individual" (such as the cost of care for a person suffering from Alzheimer's or dementia) qualify as deductible medical care expenses, subject to a dollar ceiling. IRC § 213(d)(1)(D), (10).

§ **8.1410. Disability Insurance.** Premiums paid to provide specified amounts of payments to the insured in the event that the insured becomes disabled are not deductible as medical care expenses. Treas. Reg. § 1.213–1(e)(4). If the purpose of the insurance is to protect the existence of a business from the harm that the business would suffer because of the loss of the individual's services, the premiums *might* then be deductible under IRC § 162 as business expenses; but that is far from certain. Note that the payments that an individual receives from an insurer pursuant to a disability insurance policy are excluded from the individual's gross income by IRC § 104(a)(3). See § **2.4320**.

§ **8.1420. Premiums Paid by Self–Insured Individual.** The premiums paid by a self-employed person for medical insurance to cover himself, his spouse and dependents are deductible as business expenses under IRC § 162(*l*). The insurance must be provided pursuant to a plan for the trade or business in which the taxpayer is self-employed. The dollar amount that is deductible cannot exceed the individual's "earned income" from the trade or business with respect to which the plan providing the medical care coverage is provided. IRC § 162(l)(2)(A). The deduction is not available for the premium for any month in which the taxpayer is eligible to participate in a subsidized health plan maintained by an employer of the taxpayer or his spouse. IRC § 162(l)(2)(B). Any amount of premium deductible for a self-employed taxpayer under IRC § 162(l) cannot be taken as a medical care expense under IRC § 213. IRC § 162(l)(3).

§ 8.1500. Travel Expenses. "Travel expenses" refer to all of the expenses incurred in making a trip including: the transportation costs, the costs of meals and lodging, and other expenses incurred at the new location. As noted in **§ 8.1200**, transportation costs incurred primarily for and essential to medical care are deductible. However, subject to the several exceptions described in **§ 8.1510** and **§ 8.1520**, other travel expenses (including the cost of meals and lodging) are not deductible. Treas. Reg. § 1.213–1(e)(1)(iv). See *Commissioner v. Bilder*, 369 U.S. 499 (1962).

§ 8.1510. Institutional Care. The cost of in-patient hospital care, including the cost of meals and lodging that are provided to an in-patient, are treated as deductible medical expenses. Treas. Reg. § 1.213–1(e)(1)(v). Similarly, expenses (including meals and lodging) incurred while residing in an institution that is not a hospital are deductible medical care expenses if the principal reason for residing at that institution is to receive medical care. Treas. Reg. § 1.213–1(e)(1)(v). It appears unlikely that the costs of meals received in connection with such medical care will have to be separately stated and subjected to the 50% of cost limitation of IRC § 274(n).

Whether medical care is the principal reason for a person's residing at an institution is a question of fact the determination of which rests on an examination of the condition of the person in question and of the services received by that person at the institution. For example, the cost of institutional care for a mentally ill person who is unsafe when left alone is deductible. Treas. Reg. § 1.213–1(e)(1)(v)(a).

A frequently litigated issue is whether the cost of a child's attending a private boarding school is deductible when the child suffers with physical or emotional disorders. In general, when a child with emotional problems is boarded at a school because that school provides a strictly ordered environment, but provides no special services for the child's disorder, no deduction will be allowed for the expense of boarding the child even if the child's doctor recommends that the child be sent to such a school. However, when a boarding school caters to a specific illness or infirmity of a child, all the expenses (including meals, lodging, and educational costs) of the child's boarding and matriculation at that school are deductible. For example, in PLR 8401024, the Commissioner allowed a medical expense deduction for the costs of having a child who suffered with dyslexia attend a school for handicapped students with special learning disabilities. The school provided the services of a number of professional specialists who deal with various aspects of the handicaps of those with learning disabilities. Since the determination of deductibility rests on factual issues, there has been considerable litigation concerning various types of boarding school experiences, and the Commissioner has had mixed success in litigating this issue.

§ 8.1511. Primary Purpose Not Medical. When the primary purpose of a person's residing at an institution is not to receive medical care, then only the cost of actual medical care received by such person is deductible. In such cases, none of the costs of meals and lodging are deductible. Treas. Reg. § 1.213–1(e)(1)(v)(b).

§ 8.1520. Limited Deduction for Lodging Expenses. In general, unless an individual resides in an institution (**§ 8.1510**), lodging expenses incurred while away from home for medical care purposes are not deductible. There is a limited exception to that general rule. Amounts paid for lodging while away from home primarily for and essential to medical care are deductible if: (1) the medical care is provided by a physician in a licensed hospital or in a medical care facility that is related to, or the equivalent of, a licensed hospital; (2) the lodging is not lavish or extravagant; and (3) there is no significant element of personal pleasure, recreation, or vacation in the travel away from home. IRC § 213(d)(2). The amount deductible for lodging under this provision cannot exceed $50 per night for each individual. IRC § 213(d)(2). For a deduction to be allowed under IRC § 213(d)(2), the *primary* purpose of the taxpayer must be to receive treatment from a physician; if a physician's treatment is merely an incidental purpose and the primary purpose is to alleviate a health problem by staying in a locality with a favorable climate, no deduction for lodging will be allowed. *Polyak v. Commissioner*, 94 T.C. 337 (1990).

§ 8.1530.   Illustration: Travel Expenses. *X* suffers from an asthmatic condition and a heart condition. *X*'s doctor recommended that *X* reside in Arizona for the months of August and September each year since those months are the worst periods for *X*'s asthmatic attacks and the climate in Arizona will mitigate *X*'s attacks. *X* followed his doctor's advice and went to Arizona for those two months. While residing in Arizona, *X* did not visit a doctor or receive any treatment. *X* spent the following sums:

(a) *X* paid the doctor a fee of $200.

(b) On August 1–3, *X* drove from New York to Phoenix in his automobile, and *X* expended $80 for gas and oil while traveling on the road.

(c) In addition, *X* spent $150 for food and lodging while traveling on the road.

(d) While living in Arizona, *X* spent $2,000 on lodging and $1,200 on food.

(e) *X* returned to New York in October, and his return expenses were $85 for gas and oil and $175 for food and lodging.

Subject to the limitation as to the amount of medical expenses that can be deducted, *X*'s $200 payment to his doctor is a deductible medical expense. Since *X* went to Arizona to mitigate a specific medical condition rather than merely to benefit his general health, *X*'s $165 costs for gas and oil in driving to Arizona and back are also deductible medical expenses. (In lieu of that amount, *X* could deduct a standard mileage allowance. (See **§ 8.1220.**)) *X* is not allowed any depreciation deduction for the use of his car. The $2,000 spent for lodging and the $1,200 spent for food while in Arizona are not deductible, because food and lodging while living away from home for medical purposes are not treated as medical expenses unless one of the exceptions described at **§ 8.1510** and **§ 8.1520** is applicable. Neither of those exceptions applies to the instant facts.

It is probable that the $325 that *X* expended on food and lodging in transit to and from Phoenix qualify as deductible medical care expenses. While the Service contends that food and lodging expenses incurred in transit to a place being visited for medical care purposes are not deductible, the Tax Court and the Sixth Circuit have allowed a deduction for such expenses. *Montgomery v. Commissioner*, 51 T.C. 410 (1968), aff'd 428 F.2d 243 (6th Cir. 1970). Accord, *Pfersching v. Commissioner*, 46 T.C.M. 424 (1983). If the expense of meals on travel status is determined to be deductible, only 50% of the cost of such meals can qualify for a deduction. IRC § 274(n).

§ 8.1600. Specific Illness. In general, an expense incurred to improve the general health of a taxpayer will not be deductible. Instead, the expense must either relate to a specific illness or it must be incurred for the purpose of affecting a structure or function of the body. Treas. Reg. § 1.213–1(e)(1)(ii). Notwithstanding that general rule, it is likely that fees paid to a doctor for any medical services, including an annual check-up, will be deductible even though the services are not attributable to a specific illness. See *Murray v. Commissioner*, 43 T.C.M. 1377 (1982).

In GCM 37115 (1977), the Commissioner stated that for an expense to qualify for a medical care deduction, it must either be for the purpose of affecting a structure or function of the body, or: "(1) the taxpayer must show the present existence or the imminent probability of a mental or physical disease, defect, or illness;" and "(2) the expense must be for goods or services directly or proximately related to the diagnosis, cure, mitigation, treatment or prevention of the disease."

§ 8.1610. Illustration: Luxury Vacation. *Y* was feeling run-down and visited his doctor. *Y*'s doctor advised him to take a cruise on the Mediterranean as a rest cure and *Y* did so. The cost of the cruise is not a deductible medical expense since it was not incurred in connection with a specific illness, but rather was for the general good health of the taxpayer. Regs. §§ 1.213–1(e)(1)(ii) and (iv).

§ 8.1620. Weight Reduction and Stop–Smoking Programs. In Rev. Ruls. 79–151 and 79–162, the Commissioner ruled that the cost of participation, pursuant to a doctor's recommendation, for general health improvement purposes in either a weight reduction or stop-smoking program is not deductible. However, the Commissioner subsequently revered his position on those issues.

In Rev. Rul. 2002–19, the Commissioner officially accepted that obesity itself is a disease. Consequently, the ruling concluded that the cost of a weight loss program by a person who has been diagnosed as obese by a physician is a medical care expense. Even if the person is not obese, if he suffers from a disease (such as hypertension) for which a physician has directed him to lose weight, the cost of participating in a weight loss program is a medical care expense. The ruling distinguished Rev. Rul 79–151 because the taxpayer in that latter ruling did not suffer from a specific disease, and participated in the weight loss program merely to improve his general health and appearance. However, the 2002 ruling held that the taxpayers could not deduct the cost of reduced-calorie diet food because those foods substitute for the foods the taxpayers would normally have had and because they satisfy the taxpayers' nutritional needs. See § **8.4000.** In an earlier pronouncement, in Info 2001–0155 (June 29,2001), the Service indicated that to the extent that a special diet for weight loss exceeds the cost of the taxpayer's regular diet, the additional cost is a medical care expense. The latter position accords with the Tax Court's view. See § **8.4000.** Even if the Service adopts that view, the taxpayer's burden to show that there is an additional cost and the amount thereof will be very difficult to meet. If a deduction is allowed for the additional cost of meals, only 50% of that additional cost will be deductible. IRC § 274(n).

The medical standard that is used to determine whether a person is obese is referred to as the "Body Mass Index" or "BMI." The BMI is the product of the person's weight in pounds times a specified figure divided by the person's height in inches.

As to smoking, Rev. Rul. 99–28 revoked Rev. Rul. 79–162. In Rev. Rul. 99–28, the Service acknowledged that scientific studies had determined that nicotine is addictive and is harmful to the health of the smoker. The Service determined that the cost of treatment for an addiction to a harmful substance is a medical care expense. The Service held that one of the taxpayers who was the subject of that ruling could deduct as medical care expenses the cost of participating in a smoking-cessation program even though the taxpayer had no specific disease and even though a doctor had not instructed the taxpayer to cease smoking. Another taxpayer, who was also the subject of that ruling, was allowed to deduct as medical care expenses the cost of prescription drugs to alleviate the effects of nicotine withdrawal. However, the cost of nicotine gum and nicotine patches were held not to be deductible because they contain a drug (other than insulin) and do not require a prescription from a physician. The cost of a nonprescribed drug is disallowed as a deduction by IRC § 213(b). See § **8.1000.**

§ **8.1700. Abortion.** The Commissioner has ruled that the cost of a legal abortion or vasectomy is a medical expense. Rev. Rul. 73–201. See also Rev. Rul. 73–603, allowing a deduction for the cost of a legal operation to render a woman incapable of bearing children. Such expenses are incurred for the purpose of affecting a structure or function of the body and so were held to be deductible.

§ **8.1800. Itemized Deduction.** The medical expense deduction is an itemized deduction, but is not a miscellaneous itemized deduction and so is not subject to the 2% of AGI floor. IRC § 67(b)(5). See §§ **3.1000–3.1110.** The medical expense deduction is not subject to the overall limitation on itemized deduction that applies when an individual's AGI exceeds a specified figure. IRC § 68(c)(1). See § **3.1120.** As stated in § **8.2100,** medical expenses for a taxable year are deductible only to the extent that they exceed 7.5% of taxpayer's AGI, and so there is no reason to apply any additional limitations or floors. However, for purposes of applying the Alternative Minimum Tax, which tax applies if it is greater than the taxpayer's regular tax, the floor for the deduction of medical expenses is 10% of the taxpayer's AGI instead of the 7.5% of AGI that is the floor for the purposes of the regular tax. See § **15.2511.**

§ **8.1900. Business Expense.** An expense for services or goods which mitigate a taxpayer's illness or physical defect may also be appropriate and helpful to the taxpayer's conduct of his trade or business. Cf., § **8.1410.** The question may arise as to whether such an expense is deductible as a medical expense under IRC § 213 or as a business expense under IRC § 162. A business expense is not subject to the limitations on deductibility (such as the 7.5% of AGI floor [see §§ **8.2000–8.2100**]) that apply to medical expenses. The Commissioner has ruled that for such an expense to qualify as a business expense deduction (rather than as a medical expense) all three of the following elements must be present: (1) the nature of the taxpayer's work clearly requires that he incur the expenses to satisfactorily perform such work; (2) the goods or services purchased by such expense are clearly not required or used, other than incidentally, in the conduct of the taxpayer's personal activities; and (3) the Code and regulations are otherwise silent as to the treatment of such an expense. Rev. Ruls. 75–316, 75–317. The provision in IRC § 162(*l*) for a business expense deduction for certain medical insurance premiums paid by a self-employed person is discussed at § **8.1420.**

§ **8.2000. LIMITATIONS ON MEDICAL EXPENSE DEDUC-TIONS.** Once the amount of medical care expenses is determined, it is necessary to determine the extent to which the expenses are deductible. For example, as noted in § **8.1000**, the medical expense of purchasing nonprescription drugs is not deductible. As a basic rule, it should be remembered that no deduction is permitted for expenses for which the taxpayer has been compensated by insurance or otherwise. The amount of uncompensated medical care expenses that can be deducted by a taxpayer in a taxable year is subject to a "floor" so that only the excess of such expenses over the "floor" can be deducted. IRC § 213(a). The "floor" is described below in § **8.2100.**

§ **8.2100. Amount Deductible.** Medical care expenses of a taxpayer are deductible only to the extent that the aggregate amount of such expenses for the taxpayer's taxable year exceeds 7.5% of the taxpayer's adjusted gross income (AGI) for that year. IRC § 213(a). Thus, no deduction is allowed for an amount of medical care expenses that is equal to 7.5% of the taxpayer's AGI for that year, and that amount is the "floor" for the medical care expense deduction. As stated in § **8.1800**, medical care expense deductions are itemized deductions, but are not miscellaneous itemized deductions, and are not subject to the overall limitation that IRC § 68 imposes on most itemized deductions. Note that for the purpose of determining a taxpayer's Alternative Minimum Tax (see Chapter 15), the floor for the deduction of medical expenses is 10% of the taxpayer's AGI. See § **15.2511.** The Alternative Minimum Tax applies to a TP in a year in which that tax is greater than the TP's regular tax liability.

§ **8.2200. Illustrations of Computation.** In each of the following illustrations assume that X has AGI of $15,000 for Year One. Thus, 7.5% of X's AGI for the year is $1,125. Assume also that the Alternative Minimum Tax is not applicable to the TP that year.

§ **8.2210. Illustration 1.** In Year One, X's only medical care expense is the $800 premium he paid for medical insurance covering X, his wife, and their four dependent children. The premium payment qualifies as a medical care expense. The premium payment ($800) plus other medical care expenses ($0) is less than 7.5% of X's AGI ($1,125), so no deduction will be allowed.

§ **8.2220. Illustration 2.** The same facts as in § **8.2210** except that in Year One X also expended $240 on medicines for his wife and his dependent son, and X was not compensated for those expenses. Of the amount expended by X on medicines, $50 was spent on cough medicine, aspirin, salves for muscle aches and similar items all of which can be purchased at a pharmacy without a physician's prescription. The remaining $190 was spent on drugs prescribed by X's doctor and which can be obtained only with a physician's prescription. Only the $190 spent on drugs for which a prescription was required qualify as a medical care expense. Since X's total medical care expense of $990 ($800 for insurance premiums plus $190 for prescribed drugs) is less than 7.5% of X's AGI ($1,125), no deduction is allowed.

§ 8.2230.   Illustration 3. The same facts as in **§ 8.2220** except that in Year One X also paid a dentist $285 for dental work performed on X's dependent daughter. This payment qualifies as a medical care expense. X's medical expenses for Year One total $1,275 ($800 for insurance premiums plus $190 for prescribed drugs plus $285 dental expenses). This figure exceeds 7.5% of X's AGI ($1,125) by $150, and so X is allowed an itemized deduction of $150 for medical care expenses. This deduction is not subject to the 2% of AGI floor on miscellaneous itemized deductions, and it is excluded from the itemized deductions that are subject to the overall limitation imposed by IRC § 68.

§ 8.2300.   Reimbursed Expenses. The medical expenses of many taxpayers are paid wholly or partly by insurance that is purchased by the taxpayer himself or by his employer on his behalf. In general, when a taxpayer's medical costs are paid by such insurance or directly paid by the taxpayer's employer, the taxpayer will not recognize gross income unless the TP had previously taken a deduction for those expenses. See **§§ 2.4330** and **2.4341–2.4344.** Note that there is no floor or dollar limitation as to the amount that can be so excluded from a taxpayer's gross income.

§ 8.3000.   CAPITAL ACQUISITIONS FOR MEDICAL CARE. Although capital expenditures typically are not currently deductible for Federal income tax purposes (they may be amortized in appropriate cases), capital acquisitions or improvements made primarily for medical care purposes are currently deductible medical expenses (subject to the limitations discussed in **§§ 8.2100–8.2230**) if the purchased asset does not constitute a permanent improvement or betterment of property. Thus, the costs of purchasing eye glasses, a seeing eye dog, artificial teeth and limbs, a wheelchair, and crutches are currently deductible medical care expenses. Treas. Reg. § 1.213–1(e)(1)(iii). Such expenses are deducted (subject to the usual floor and limitations) in the year paid and are not amortized over the useful life of the asset. When a capital acquisition that was made primarily for medical care purposes constitutes an improvement or a betterment of the taxpayer's property, only the difference between the cost of the asset and the increase in value of the improved property as a consequence of the acquisition is a medical care expense. Rev. Rul. 83–33.

Since 1982 [Rev. Proc. 82–65], the Commissioner has stated that he will not provide advance rulings on the factual question of whether a capital expenditure for an item that ordinarily would be used for personal, living, or family purposes (such as a swimming pool) was primarily motivated by medical care objectives. Rev. Proc. 2004–3 (Sec. 3.01(18)). Despite that asserted refusal to rule, in 1983 the Commissioner ruled that a taxpayer was entitled to a medical care expense deduction for the amount by which the taxpayer's cost of adding a swimming pool to his property exceeded the increase in value of the taxpayer's property resulting from that addition. Rev. Rul. 83–33. The taxpayer's purpose in adding the pool was to comply with his physician's instruction that taxpayer swim several times a day as a treatment for osteoarthritis. Also, in Rev. Rul. 87–106, the Commissioner listed thirteen specific expenditures which will qualify as a medical expense if made for the primary purpose of accommodating a personal residence to the handicapped condition of the taxpayer, his spouse, or one of his dependents. The ruling expressly states that the list is not intended to preclude a deduction for other such expenditures. The listed expenditures are considered by the Commissioner to be ones that generally do not increase the value of the residence, and so the entire amount of the listed expenditures is a deductible medical expense.

If part of a capital expenditure that otherwise qualifies as a medical care expense is made for a non-medical purpose, that portion of the expenditure will not be deductible. For example, if in constructing a swimming pool for a medical purpose, the TP expends an additional amount to make the pool more attractive so that it will not detract from the architectural and aesthetic splendor of the home, the additional amount is not a deductible expense. See § **8.3300.**

§ 8.3100. Illustration 1: Improvement of Taxpayer's Property.

X has a heart condition, and her doctor advised her to construct a bathroom on the first floor of her two-story home so that *X* will not have to climb the stairs more than once a day. *X* has the bathroom constructed at a cost of $5,000 for the primary purpose of protecting her health. The value of X's home is increased by $3,000 as a consequence of making the improvement; $2,000 of X's cost constitutes a deductible medical care expense (subject to the floor described in § **8.2100**).

§ **8.3200. Illustration 2: Improvement of Rented Property.** The same facts as those stated in § **8.3100** except that X rents her two-story home from Y (an unrelated party), and X nevertheless builds the bathroom (with Y's permission) at a cost of $5,000. Since no property of X was improved by the expenditure, the entire $5,000 cost is a medical care expense. Rev. Rul. 70–395.

§ **8.3300. Excessive Costs.** If a taxpayer constructs or purchases a facility that is more lavish than is needed for medical purposes, the additional cost incurred above that needed to construct or purchase a functionally adequate facility may not qualify as a medical expense. In *Ferris v. Commissioner*, 582 F.2d 1112 (7th Cir. 1978), a taxpayer constructed a swimming pool that was needed for medical purposes. The taxpayer spent over $190,000 to construct the pool so that it was architecturally and aesthetically compatible with the taxpayer's luxury home. The Court held that the additional cost incurred to achieve that compatibility was not incurred primarily for medical purposes and so did not qualify for a medical expense deduction. See also Rev. Rul. 87–106.

§ **8.3400. Illustration 3: Accommodation to Handicap.** The taxpayer cannot walk and is confined to a wheelchair. To accommodate his home to his handicap, the taxpayer incurred expenses to: (1) construct entrance and exit ramps to the residence; (2) widen interior doorways; (3) lower kitchen cabinets and equipment; and (4) install handrails throughout the house. All of those expenses qualify as medical expenses. Rev. Rul. 87–106.

§ **8.4000. SPECIALLY PREPARED FOOD.** The Commissioner contends that the cost of obtaining food or beverage which is prepared specially for medical reasons is not deductible if the food or beverage is taken as a substitute for food or beverage normally consumed by the taxpayer and satisfies his nutritional requirements. Rev. Rul. 55–261; Rev. Rul. 2002–19. In those rulings, the Commissioner did not expressly discuss whether the taxpayer could deduct, as a medical expense, the additional cost of obtaining specially prepared foods over the cost that he otherwise would have incurred for his food. The Tax Court has consistently held that the excess cost is deductible if the taxpayer can prove that the special diet is needed for medical purposes and can prove the amount of extra cost incurred to have that diet. By way of analogy, the

Commissioner has allowed a medical expense deduction for the extra cost incurred on obtaining a braille text book for a blind child over the cost of a regular printed edition. Rev. Rul. 75–318. Perhaps the Commissioner has not authorized a deduction for the excess cost of food because of the administrative difficulty of determining what amount the taxpayer would have expended for his food if he did not need the special diet. But see Info 2001–0155 (June 29, 2001) in which the Service said that the excess of the cost of special meals required for medical reasons over the cost that the taxpayer would have incurred for regular meals is deductible as a medical expense. The burden of the taxpayer to prove the amount of the excess cost is so difficult to sustain that few taxpayers will be able to qualify for a deduction for any part of the cost of meals.

The taxpayers who have litigated this issue have had mixed results. While the Tax Court consistently holds that the excess cost of such meals is a deductible medical expense, the taxpayers often have foundered on failing to meet the burden of proving the amount of the excess cost, if any. Compare *Cohn v. Commissioner*, 38 T.C. 387 (1962), (Nonacq.) (allowing a deduction for the additional cost of having a restaurant prepare salt-free food so as to comply with a salt-free diet) with *Harris v. Commissioner*, 46 T.C. 672 (1966) (denying a deduction for the cost of specially prepared food for a diabetic); *Huff v. Commissioner*, 69 T,C.M. 2551 (1995) (denying a deduction for the cost of vitamins and food supplements): *Massa v. Comissioner*, 77 T.C.M. 1484 (1999), aff'd 208 F.3d 226 (10th Cir. 2000) (denying a deduction to a taxpayer with Crohn's disease for the cost of a special diet because, among other reasons, the taxpayer failed to prove any excess cost).

In *Randolph v. Commissioner*, 67 T.C. 481 (1976), the Tax Court allowed a medical expense deduction for the additional cost incurred by the taxpayer in obtaining chemically uncontaminated food where the taxpayer was allergic to a variety of chemicals found in pesticides and herbicides. The Court determined the amount deductible by comparing the taxpayer's cost for the organic (uncontaminated) food he obtained with statistics showing the average price of similar contaminated food in the Chicago area. Accord, *Von Kalb v. Commissioner*, 37 T.C.M. 1511 (1978), allowing a deduction for the additional cost of a high-protein diet required by the taxpayer for medical reasons. In *Van Kalb*, the taxpayer was allowed to deduct the additional amount she spent on groceries to meet her special dietary needs, but she was not allowed to deduct any portion of the amount she spent at restaurants for meals. The taxpayer's evidence of an additional cost for meals was provided by comparing the cost of her groceries to those of her friends.

To qualify for a deduction, a taxpayer must prove: (1) that he has a specific medical condition that requires a special diet, and (2) the actual amount of the additional cost incurred because of that dietary need. *Nehus v. Commissioner*, 68 T.C.M. 1503 (1994), aff'd 108 F.3d 338 (9th Cir. 1997). This is a difficult burden to meet, especially as to the requirement of showing the additional cost incurred.

If the additional cost of specially prepared food can qualify as a medical expense, only 50% of that additional cost is deductible. IRC § 274(n).

§ 8.5000. HEALTH SAVINGS ACCOUNTS. Many health coverage plans provided by employers for their employees have low deductible features so that the employee will bear only a small amount of any medical expense incurred. That circumstance gives the employee little incentive to make a cost benefit calculation when determining whether to undergo a medical procedure. This leads to expensive expenditures for unnecessary medical procedures.

In an effort to remedy that situation, in 1997, Congress adopted IRC § 220 to provide special tax treatment for "Medical Savings Accounts." In general, this provision permitted an employee who was a participant in a high deductible medical plan provided by his employer to deduct contributions to a fund which would be available to pay for medical expenses not covered by the employer's plan. The amount deductible is subject to a dollar limitation. To the extent that the funds in the Account are used to pay for qualified medical services, they are not taxable to the employee. The purpose of this provision and of its replacement provisions is to encourage employers to use high deductible insurance plans and to provide tax relief for employees to fill in the gap in their insurance coverage with their own funds. Since the employees will be using their own funds to pay for medical services, it is expected that they will be more prudent in their purchase of those services.

The name of Medical Savings Accounts was changed in the year 2000 to "Archer MSAs." IRC § 220. The Archer MSA's provision was replaced in the year 2003 by the "Health Savings Accounts" provision, which is set forth in IRC § 223. While there are differences between the Health Savings Accounts and the Archer MSAs, the general operation of the two is similar. The Archer MSAs provision continues to apply to those who previously set up those accounts. If an employee wishes to establish a new account, to qualify for a beneficial tax treatment, the new account must be established as a Health Savings Account under IRC § 223.

*

CHAPTER NINE

CHARITABLE CONTRIBUTIONS

§ 9.0000. CHARITABLE CONTRIBUTIONS IN GENERAL. Contributions or gifts of cash or other property to, or for the use of, qualified charitable organizations may be deductible from the donor's AGI as an itemized deduction. IRC § 170. The meaning of "gift" or "contribution" is discussed in **§ 9.1100.** As noted there, in this context, the two words are synonymous and are used interchangeably.

Only gifts of property are deductible; a contribution of services is not deductible. Treas. Reg. § 1.170A–1(g). See **§ 9.5200.** Unless specifically provided otherwise, the amount of a charitable gift or contribution is equal to the fair market value of the donated property at the time of the contribution. The special treatment accorded to gifts to a charity of appreciated property (i.e., property whose value exceeds its basis) is discussed at **§§ 9.2300–9.2434–2.** The meaning of "fair market value" is discussed at **§ 2.2240.** In *Anselmo v. Commissioner*, 757 F.2d 1208 (11th Cir. 1985), the court affirmed the Tax Court's determination that the value of a contributed item of property is the price of such item in the market in which items of that type are most commonly sold to the public. The court also concluded that in determining fair market value, the choice of the relevant market is a question of fact.

Note that the deductibility of contributions to an organization is determined by IRC § 170. The tax exempt status of an organization (i.e., whether it is taxable on its income) is determined by other sections of the Code—principally IRC § 501.

§ 9.1000. DEFINITION OF CHARITABLE CONTRIBUTION. As defined in IRC § 170(c), a charitable contribution means a contribution or gift which is paid to or for the use of:

> (a) a state, a United States' possession, any political subdivision of any of the foregoing, the United States, or the District of Columbia, provided that the contribution or gift is made exclusively for public purposes;
>
> (b) a corporation, trust, community chest, fund, or foundation
>
> > (i) created or organized in the United States or any possession of the United States, or under the law of the United States, or

of any state or possession of the United States or of the District of Columbia;

(ii) organized and operated exclusively for religious, charitable, scientific, literary, or educational purposes, or to foster national or international amateur sports competition (but if it is not a "qualified amateur sports organization" as defined in IRC § 501(j), only if no part of its activities involve the provision of athletic facilities or equipment), or for the prevention of cruelty to children or animals;

(iii) no part of the earnings of which inures to the benefit of any private individual or shareholder;

(iv) no substantial part of the activities of which is attempting to influence legislation, but certain charities will be permitted a greater amount of lobbying and lobbying-type expenses if the charity makes a valid election under IRC § 501(h); and

(v) which does not participate or intervene in any political campaign on behalf of, or in opposition to, any candidate for public office; and

(c) certain other organizations (e.g., veterans organizations, fraternal lodges, non-profit cemeteries) listed in IRC § 170(c)(3), (4), and (5).

§ 9.1100.   Contribution or Gift. A "contribution" or "gift" to a charity is a payment of cash or property without adequate consideration and made for the purpose of conferring a benefit on the charity. *Mason v. United States*, 513 F.2d 25 (7th Cir. 1975). For purposes of the deduction, the words "contribution" and "gift" are synonymous, and are used interchangeably. *DeJong v. Comissioner*, 309 F.2d 373, 376 (9th Cir. 1962). Since the meanings of the two words are the same, we will focus on the meaning of the word "gift."

In determining whether an uncompensated transfer to an individual is excluded by IRC § 102 from the transferee's gross income as a gift, the definition of a "gift" was established by the Supreme Court's decision in *Commissioner v. Duberstein*, 363 U.S. 278 (1960). Under the *Duberstein* rule, the principal characteristic of a private gift is that it was made by the transferor out of "detached and disinterested generosity." See **§ 2.4220.** The courts are divided as to whether the same standard is to be applied in determining whether a transfer to a charity constitutes a gift for charitable deduction purposes. Some courts have applied the *Duberstein* standard, and others have rejected it. Compare, *DeJong v. Commissioner*, 309 F.2d 373 (9th Cir.

1962); *Fausner v. Commissioner*, 55 T.C. 620 (1971) (adopting the *Duberstein* standard) with *Crosby Valve & Gage Co. v. Comissioner*, 380 F.2d 146 (1st Cir. 1967) *Singer Co. v. United States*, 449 F.2d 413 (Ct. Cls. 1971) (rejecting that standard). While the Supreme Court has not expressly passed on this issue, its opinions in *United States v. American Bar Endowment*, 477 U.S. 105 (1986); and, *Hernandez v. Commissioner*, 490 U.S. 680 (1989) suggest that the Court does not favor the use of the *Duberstein* standard for this purpose. Indeed, the Ninth Circuit, which adopted the *Duberstein* standard in the *DeJong* case, subsequently held that that standard is not applicable when the transferor to the charity is a corporation. *United States v. Transamerica Corp.*, 392 F.2d 522, 524 (9th Cir. 1968).

If the *Duberstein* standard is inapplicable, what then is the standard for determining a charitable gift? The standard is whether the transferor received a substantial *quid pro quo* flowing from the transfer. In *Hernandez v. Commissioner*, supra, the Supreme Court said that gifts are "payments made with no expectation of a financial return commensurate with the amount of the gift." The cumulative benefits, both direct and indirect, that the transferor received are taken into account, but only benefits that have financial significance are considered. In other words, psychic benefits, such as enjoying the pleasure derived from making the gift, are ignored. Also, the benefits that the transferor shared with other members of the general public are ignored. For example, a gift to a theater company that allows it to perform for the general public is not treated as a benefit to the transferor merely because he can enjoy their performances along with other members of the public.

Indirect benefits are taken into account. An example of an indirect benefit is found in *Singer Company v. United States*, supra. In that case, the Singer company sold sewing machines at a significant discount to a number of charities. The question was whether the company could take a charitable deduction for the amount of the discount. When property is transferred to a charity for less than adequate consideration, the transaction is referred to as a "dual payment," and that type of transaction is discussed in **§ 9.1200.** The court allowed the company a deduction for the discount it gave on the sale of sewing machines to certain charities (churches, the Red Cross, and hospitals), but denied a deduction for the discounts given to schools. The court held that Singer obtained an indirect benefit from its bargain sales to the schools in that many of the pupils who used the sewing machines would become attached to them and would constitute a pool of potential future customers.

The determination of whether a transferor has received a substantial benefit is made by examining "the external features of the transaction" rather than by conducting "imprecise inquiries into the motivations" of the transferor. *Hernandez v. Commissioner*, 490 U.S. 680 (1989). The receipt of religious benefits in exchange for a transfer poses special issues. Those issues are discussed in § **9.1210.**

§ **9.1200. Dual Payments.** A deduction may be allowed for a transfer to a charity even though the transferor receives consideration for the transfer if the value of the property transferred to the charity is greater than the value of the consideration received. A transfer of that nature is called a "dual payment." See *United States v. American Bar Endowment*, 477 U.S. 105, 119 (1986). The transfer is partly a sale or purchase and partly a contribution to the charity. The dual payment transaction is similar to the part-gift part-sale transaction that applies to a bargain sale to an individual for a donative purpose as described in §§ **2.4240–2.4244.** Of course, the amount of the charitable deduction for a dual payment is the amount by which the value transferred to the charity exceeds the value of the consideration received. If the taxpayer transferred appreciated property to the charity, the statutory limitations on the amount of deduction permitted for contributions of appreciated property will apply. See §§ **9.2300, 9.2400–9.2434.**

For a transfer to a charity for consideration to qualify as a dual payment for which a charitable deduction is allowable, a two-pronged test must be satisfied. First, the transfer to the charity will be deductible only to the extent that it exceeds the market value of the benefits received in return. Second, the transferor must have intended to transfer that excess to the charity as a gift—that is, the transferor deliberately transferred excess value to the charity for the purpose of making a gift. This two-pronged test was first stated in Rev. Rul. 67–246, and it was expressly adopted by the Supreme Court in *United States v. American Bar Endowment*, supra. If a taxpayer fails either of those two prongs, no deduction will be allowable. The taxpayer has the burden of proving that the transfer satisfies both prongs. While the second prong raises a subjective issue, resting on the transferor's intent, the Supreme Court has emphasized that the determination of that issue should be made exclusively on the basis of identifiable external facts. *Hernandez v. Commissioner,* supra at p. 691.

The application of both of those prongs can be difficult when the benefits received are ones that are not purchased in a commercial market. This problem is especially difficult to resolve when the benefits received are religious services. The receipt of intangible religious benefits is discussed in § **9.1210.**

A donor's receipt of a benefit from the charity will be ignored if the benefit is insubstantial. The standard for determining substantiality is discussed at § **9.1300.**

§ **9.1210. Intangible Religious Benefits.** In *Hernandez v. Commissioner,* supra, the Supreme Court rejected the contention that the receipt of intangible religious benefits is to be ignored in determining whether a payment to a religious organization is deductible. The Court refused to adopt a blanket exception for intangible religious benefits. The *Hernandez* case involved religious benefits provided by the Church of Scientology for a stated fee.

The Church of Scientology treats the human spirit by providing "auditing" and "training" sessions to its members, which constitute one-on-one counselling and the education of a member by a person known as an "auditor." The auditing process is part of the religious teaching and practice of the organization. It is intended to identify the spiritual difficulty of the member and to help the member deal with that difficulty. The organization set fixed fees for these auditing sessions, the amount of which varied with the length and sophistication of the sessions. These fixed fees were referred to by the organization as a "price" or "fixed contribution." The prices were set forth in schedules promulgated by the organization.

In a 1978 ruling, the Commissioner determined that the fees paid by Church of Scientology members for auditing were not deductible as charitable contributions. Rev. Rul. 78–189. For purposes of considering the merits of that ruling, it can be assumed that the Church of Scientology qualifies as a religious organization. The 1978 ruling was inconsistent with the long-standing practice of the Service to allow a charitable deduction for fixed payments where the quid pro quo for the payment was exclusively a religious benefit. For example, the Service ruled in 1970 that "pew rents, building fund assessments and periodic dues paid to a church" are deductible contributions. Rev. Rul. 70–47. The 1970 ruling superseded and was merely a restatement of the published position taken by the IRS more than 50 years earlier in A.R.M. 2, 1 Cum. Bull. 150 (1919). While no other rulings were promulgated, there is every reason to believe that the Service allowed deductions for set fees to attend Jewish services at High Holy Days, and tithes paid by Mormons and for similar fees.

The question of deductibility of auditing fees came to a head when the issue reached the Supreme Court in *Hernandez v. Commissioner*, 490 U.S. 680 (1989). In a 5–2 decision, the Court held that the fees were not deductible. The Court rejected the taxpayer's contention that the receipt of an intangible religious benefit does not constitute consideration that precludes a charitable deduction for a payment to the charity. As pointed out by the dissents in *Hernandez*, a problem with treating religious benefits, especially intangible religious benefits, as consideration in dual payment cases is that those benefits are not bought and sold on a commercial market, and there is no reasonable means to determine their dollar value.

In commercial transactions, if a fee is expressly set for a service, and if the parties are at arms' length, the tax law treats the value of the service as equal to the amount of the fee. But, it is doubtful that that approach is appropriate for determining the value of a religious service for which a set fee is paid. Even though the religious organization established a specified fee for the service, the transaction is not at arms' length because the taxpayer may have donative motives for agreeing to pay the amount of that fee—i.e., the TP may be willing to pay the stated amount because part or all of it represents a gift to the organization. It is difficult to determine how much of the fee is a gift and how much of the fee (if any) is paid in order to receive the service. The difficulty of characterizing payments ostensibly made for religious services is similar to the problem of characterizing a "contribution" that a taxpayer makes to a college when the "contribution" entitles the TP to purchase tickets to athletic events. As we shall see, Congress expressly allows the TP to deduct 80% of that contribution. IRC § 170(*l*). See **§ 9.1240.**

A similar issue arises when a charity auctions items or services that were donated to the charity for that purpose. The bidders in such auctions typically are people who have reasons to make a contribution to the charity. The successful bid often is significantly higher than the value of the item or service purchased. This should be treated as a dual payment (see **§ 9.1200**) in which the excess over the value of the item constitutes a charitable gift. The value of the item or service should not be deemed to be equal to the amount of the successful bid. In other words, the price agreed upon by the buyer and seller is not determinative of the value of the item or service. While in most cases, the commercial value of the purchased item or service can be determined because it is sold on the commercial market, but some will not be. For example, if the bidder purchased the opportunity to have dinner with a prominent author, how would the value of that opportunity be determined? The point is that the amount paid by the bidder is not a reliable indicator of the actual value.

In *Hernandez*, the taxpayer raised on appeal for the first time the contention that the Service's position on auditing fees was discriminatory in that the Service allowed deductions for fees charged by other religious groups. The Court held that the record before it was inadequate for the Court to resolve the issue of whether there was an administrative inconsistency and whether that should bar the government from denying a deduction in that case. The two dissenters in *Hernandez* emphasized the administrative inconsistency of the Service's positions.

A taxpayer is not entitled to receive a benefit contrary to the tax law merely because that treatment was erroneously accorded to another by the Service at some time in the past. *Mid-Continent Supply Co. v. Commissioner*, 571 F.2d 1371 (5th Cir. 1978). However, if the Service has consistently allowed a benefit to one class of taxpayers, there is support for the view that the benefit cannot then be denied to a similarly situated taxpayer unless the current denial of the benefit is the consequence of a change of position by the Service. *Powell v. United States*, 945 F.2d 374 (11th Cir. 1991). Cf., *Church of Scientology Flag Service Org. v. City of Clearwater*, 2 F.3d 1514 (11th Cir. 1993). But see, *Sklar v. Commissioner*, 282 F.3d 610 (9th Cir. 2002).

The question of administrative inconsistency in the Service's treatment of the Church of Scientology was subsequently raised by the taxpayers in *Powell v. United States*, 945 F.2d 374 (11th Cir. 1991). The taxpayers' claim that the Service wrongly disallowed their deduction for payment to the Church of Scientology had been dismissed by the district court. The Court of Appeals held that the claim of administrative inconsistency made a valid cause of action if factually established, and so the court vacated the district court's order and remanded the case to the district court. The Service then backed away from its victory in *Hernandez*; and, in a nonpublic agreement with the Church of Scientology, the Service agreed to allow members of that church to deduct fees paid for auditing and training sessions. In that same year, the Service issued Rev. Rul. 93–73 in which it declared obsolete its earlier Revenue Ruling 78–189 which had stated that no charitable contribution deduction will be allowed for payments to the Church of Scientology for auditing and similar services. The 1993 ruling does not include any discussion as to what position the Service now takes on this issue; it merely revokes the 1978 ruling as obsolete. The meaning of obsoleting a ruling is described by the Service in its Cumulative Bulletins. In 2003–1 Cum. Bull. iii, the Service states as follows:

> *Obsoleted* describes a previously published ruling that is not considered determinative with respect to future transactions. The term is most commonly used in a ruling that lists previously published rulings that are obsoleted because of changes in law or regulations.

The Service has not said why its 1978 ruling is now obsolete. After all, the Supreme Court sustained the ruling in the *Hernandez* case. But, in *Hernandez*, the Court declined to pass on the question of whether the 1978 ruling was inconsistent with the administrative position that the Service has taken with respect to other religious organizations; and the Eleventh Circuit subsequently held that the Service is not permitted to treat one religion differently from others. *Powell v. United States, supra.* It is possible that the Service came to recognize the inconsistency in its positions and has chosen not to apply the *Hernandez* principle to any religious organizations. It is possible therefore that the Service will no longer maintain that the receipt of a religious benefit is consideration that prevents a payment from being a charitable contribution.

The Service's agreement with the Church of Scientology raises questions as to the treatment of fees paid to attend a parochial school providing both religious and secular education or for solely religious education such as a fee to attend Sunday school. That issue is discussed next.

§ 9.1220. Tuition or Fees for Religious and Secular Education. The question has arisen whether a "contribution" to a religious organization that operates a school in which the TP's child attends, and for which no or inadequate tuition is charged, can qualify for a charitable deduction, and, if so, in what amount? In *DeJong v. Comissioner*, 309 F.2d 373 (9th Cir. 1962), which preceded *Hernandez* by some 27 years, the taxpayers claimed a charitable deduction for contributions to a religious organization that owned and operated a grammar and high school at which two of the taxpayer's children attended. The school charged no tuition, and raised most of its funds by soliciting contributions from parents of enrolled students. The taxpayers contributed $1,075 to the school, and the Service allowed all but $400 of it as a charitable deduction. The Service treated $400 as the value of the two children's education, and denied a deduction for that amount. The Tax Court and the Ninth Circuit upheld the Service's denial of that deduction. The courts and the Service treated the claimed "contribution" as a dual payment, only part of which is deductible.

The most recent decision involving this situation is *Sklar v. Commissioner*, 282 F.3d 610 (9th Cir. 2002). The taxpayers in *Sklar* were Orthodox Jews who sent their children to a Jewish parochial school. The students devoted 55% of their time in school to religious education. The taxpayers claimed a deduction for 55% of the tuition they paid to the school on the ground that it was paid for religious education. The Ninth Circuit affirmed the Tax Court's decision denying any deduction to the taxpayers.

While the court discussed several issues, its holding rested on the ground that the taxpayers did not meet their burden of proving that the benefit of the secular part of the students' education had a market value that was less than the amount of their tuition. The court held that the value of the secular education was to be determined by reference to tuition paid to private schools rather than to the zero cost of a public school education. In other words, the court held that the taxpayers failed to satisfy their burden to show that the contribution met the first prong of the two-pronged test for deducting part of a dual payment. See § **9.1200.**

While the court's opinion in *Sklar* suggests that it would not allow a deduction for the cost of religious education, the court did not pass on that issue. Even if it were decided to allow a deduction for the cost of religious education, a question would arise whether there are not secular aspects of that education. For example, history and languages can be part of a religious education. How can those subjects be distinguished from secular education just because they are taught in the context of religious training? For more discussion of these issues, see Douglas Kahn and Jeffrey Kahn, *"Gifts, Gafts and Gefts"—The Income Tax Definition and Treatment of Private and Charitable "Gifts" and a Principled Justification for the Exclusion of Gifts from Income,* 78 Notre Dame L.Rev. 441, 495–524.

The taxpayers in *Sklar* also raised the issue of administrative inconsistency. They contended that the Service's agreement to allow the members of the Church of Scientology to deduct the fees paid for religious education (auditing and training) made it unconstitutional for the Service to deny a deduction for the cost of religious training provided by other religions. The holding in *Sklar* avoided that issue by finding that the taxpayers had failed to establish the value of the secular education that their children received. However, the language of the majority opinion in that case, and of the concurring opinion of Judge Silverman, indicates that the court would reject the taxpayers' contention if the court were subsequently to reach that issue. Instead of expanding the Service's concession to other religions, the court indicated that it would hold unconstitutional the Service's allowance of a deduction to members of the Church of Scientology as violating the Establishment clause.

§ 9.1230. Tickets as Compensation. If a taxpayer who makes a contribution to a charity receives tickets to a performance as a consequence of making the contribution, part of the "contribution" will be treated as a payment for the tickets. It does not matter whether the taxpayer uses the tickets to attend the performance; it is sufficient if he retains the tickets, rather than refusing them or promptly returning them. Rev. Rul. 67–246. In that same ruling, the Commissioner urged charities to indicate in their solicitations and on any ticket, receipt or other evidence of payment that they give to donors, the amount of payment to the charity that constitutes a payment for the ticket or other benefit and the amount that is a gift. As to the circumstances in which a charitable donee is *required* to provide such information to a donor, see § **9.9300.**

§ 9.1240. Contributions to Colleges that Entitle the Taxpayer to Purchase Tickets to Athletic Events. If a taxpayer makes a payment to a college or university and, as a result, receives the right to purchase preferred or difficult-to-obtain tickets to athletic events in a stadium of that school, and if the payments otherwise would have qualified as charitable contributions, 80% of the amount paid by the taxpayer will qualify as a charitable contribution. IRC § 170(*l*). If any portion of the taxpayer's payment is for the purchase of tickets (as contrasted to obtaining a right to purchase tickets), that portion must be separated and treated as a straight purchase. Only 80% of the remaining portion of the payment is deductible. IRC § 170(*l*).

§ 9.1300. Substantial Benefit to Donor. If the benefits received or expected to be received by a donor from a gift to a charitable organization are substantial, no deduction will be allowed unless the taxpayer can prove that the value of the benefit received is less than the value of the donated property and that the taxpayer made the gift with the knowledge of that difference. *Stubbs v. United States*, 428 F.2d 885 (9th Cir. 1970); *Dowell v. United States*, 553 F.2d 1233 (10th Cir. 1977). See **§ 9.1200** for the treatment and qualification of "dual payments." A "substantial" benefit is one that is greater than those benefits that accrue to the general public. *Ottawa Silica Co. v. United States*, 699 F.2d 1124 (Fed. Cir. 1983). In *Ottawa Silica*, a deduction was denied for a gift of land to a city to be used for the construction and placement of a high school. The construction of a high school on that land would increase the value of other land that the taxpayer owned in that area, and the court deemed that a sufficient benefit to preclude a deduction. The benefit to the taxpayer in that case might be classified as "indirect" in that it was not something transferred to the taxpayer by the donee. It is clear that the benefit to a transferor need not be direct to warrant denying a charitable deduction. The Federal Circuit's view on that question is that the benefit need only flow from the donee's use of property even though no direct compensation is paid to the donor. See also *Singer Co. v. United States*, 449 F.2d 413 (Ct. Cl. 1971). If the monetary value of the substantial benefit received by the taxpayer is less than the value of the property transferred to the charity, the difference in value will be deductible as a charitable contribution if the external features of the transaction demonstrate that the taxpayer knew of that difference and nevertheless effected the transaction for the purpose of conferring a benefit on the charity.

The Commissioner has recognized that in many cases the value of a benefit given to a donor is very small in comparison with the amount of the donor's contribution. For administrative reasons, there is good cause to ignore such benefits when they are inconsequential. Accordingly, the Commissioner has determined that if the fair market value of the benefits that a donor receives for making a contribution to a charity is insubstantial, then those benefits will be ignored, and the entire amount of the contribution will qualify for a charitable deduction. Rev. Proc. 90–12. In that 1990 Revenue Procedure, the Commissioner set forth several safe harbors in which a benefit from a charity will be deemed to be insubstantial. For example, if a donor's payment to a charity occurs pursuant to a fund-raising campaign in which the charity informs its donors of the amount of their contributions that are deductible and if the fair market value of all the benefits received by a donor because of the contribution is no more than either 2% of the payment made by the donor or $83, whichever is less, the benefit received by that donor will be treated as insubstantial. Rev. Proc. 90–12 as modified by Rev. Proc. 2004–71 (Sec. 3.24). The dollar figures in the 1990 revenue procedure have been changed from time to time to reflect increases in the cost-of-living.

§ 9.1400.   Gift Subject to Contingency. If a gift to a charity is subject to a contingency that will deprive the charity of the donated property if it occurs, the question arises whether any charitable deduction will be allowed for that gift. A deduction will be allowed for such a gift only if the likelihood that the contingency will occur is "so remote as to be negligible." Treas. Reg. § 1.170A–1(e). The language "so remote as to be negligible" has been construed to mean "a chance which persons generally would disregard as so highly improbable that it might be ignored with reasonable safety in undertaking a serious business transaction." *885 Investment Co. v. Commissioner*, 95 T.C. 156, 161 (1990), quoting from, *United States v. Dean*, 224 F.2d 26, 29 (1st Cir. 1955).

§ 9.1500.   Reward Money. The Commissioner ruled that a contribution by the parents of a murder victim of reward money to the police department for information leading to the conviction of the murderer is a contribution to a political subdivision for exclusively public purposes and is deductible pursuant to IRC § 170. Rev. Rul. 81–307.

§ 9.1600.   Indirect Payment for Lobbying. As a consequence of the amendments made by the 1993 Act, no deduction is allowed to a business for expenses incurred to lobby for legislation or rules of a benefit to the taxpayer's business. Congress feared that taxpayers might circumvent that restriction by utilizing a tax-exempt entity as a conduit to pay for the lobbying activities. To prevent a taxpayer from obtaining a deduction for contributions to a tax-exempt organization which pays for lobbying of a business interest to the taxpayer, Congress adopted IRC § 170(f)(9).

§ 9.1700.   Nondeductibility of Depreciation Allowances. No charitable deduction is allowed for a taxable year unless actual payment to the charity was made in that year (subject to an exception for *corporate* donors that report on the accrual method). Taxpayers are not allowed a charitable deduction for depreciation allowances for property used for charitable purposes because depreciation does not constitute a "payment." *Orr v. United States*, 343 F.2d 553 (5th Cir. 1965). As noted in connection with the medical expense deduction in § **8.1210**, one might question whether the Supreme Court's decision in the *Idaho Power* case will cause depreciation allowances to be treated as a payment, but it is virtually certain that *Idaho Power* will not be so extended. See IRC § 170(f)(3) denying a deduction for a taxpayer's contribution to a charity of the right to use property.

§ **9.1710. Travel Expenses.** Subject to limitations described below, travel expenses (including the cost of meals and lodging while away from home) that are incurred and paid by a taxpayer for a charitable purpose, and for which personal pleasure, recreation, or vacation was not a significant element, are deductible. No deduction is allowed for depreciation of a car that is used by the taxpayer for a charitable purpose. The taxpayer may deduct the actual expenses incurred in operating the car or the taxpayer may elect to use the optional standard mileage rate which currently is fourteen cents per mile. IRC § 170(i); Rev. Proc. 2004–64 (Sec. 7.01). The mileage allowance does not reflect depreciation since depreciation deductions are not permitted for the charitable use of an asset. If a taxpayer elects to use the mileage allowance, the taxpayer can deduct his actual costs for parking fees and tolls in addition to the allowance. Rev. Proc. 2004–64 (Sec. 7.04). A deduction is not allowed for a travel expense unless there is no significant element of personal pleasure, recreation, or vacation involved. IRC § 170(j). If the TP's allowable travel expenses include meals that the taxpayer purchased while on travel status, only 50% of the cost of such meals is deductible. IRC § 274(n)(1).

§ **9.1800. Borrowed Funds and Credit Card Payments.** A contribution is deemed made when the payment is made to the charity regardless of whether the donor used his own funds or borrowed funds. If a contribution is made to a charity through the use of a bank credit card, the contribution is deemed to have been made at the time that the charge was made rather than when the donor repaid the sum to the bank. Rev. Rul. 78–38; see § **8.1300** and § **8.1310** for a discussion of the use of borrowed funds or a credit card to pay a medical expense.

§ **9.2000. LIMITATIONS ON AMOUNT OF DEDUCTION.**

§ **9.2100. Percentage Limitation on an Individual's Charitable Deduction.** The limitation on the maximum amount of deduction that will be allowed an individual for charitable contributions turns upon the nature of the charitable donee and the nature of the gift. The limitation is expressed in the statute as a percentage of the taxpayer's "contribution base."

§ 9.2110. Definition of Contribution Base. The term "contribution base" refers to a taxpayer's adjusted gross income (AGI) computed without taking into account any net operating loss that the taxpayer may incur in a subsequent year that will be *carried back* to the taxable year and deducted from the taxpayer's gross income for that year. IRC § 170(b)(1)(F). In other words, a taxpayer's contribution base equals his AGI computed without regard to any net operating loss *carryback* authorized by IRC § 172.

§ 9.2120. Maximum Limitation. Gifts or contributions (other than gifts of appreciated capital gain property) of an amount up to 50 percent of the taxpayer's contribution base are deductible provided that the gifts or contributions are made *to* (but not "for the use of") a qualified charitable organization that is one of the types listed in IRC § 170(b)(1)(A). Examples of such organizations are: churches, educational organizations, hospitals, medical care institutions, and organizations that are substantially supported by the public or the government and that perform a charitable or educational function. The donee organizations to which the 50% of contribution base limitation applies are defined in IRC § 170(b)(1)(A) and are hereafter referred to as "A" charities. A qualified charitable organization that does not constitute an "A" charity is referred to as a "B" charity. "B" charities are comprised principally of posts or organizations for war veterans and of certain, but not all, private foundations.

A gift in trust, the income or an annuity from which is payable to an "A" charity, does not qualify as a gift *to* the "A" charity, but rather is a gift for the use of the "A" charity; therefore the gift of the income or annuity interest does not qualify for the 50% limitation. However, a gift of a remainder interest in a trust to an "A" charity will qualify for the 50% deduction if the conditions of **§ 9.4200** are satisfied. Treas. Reg. § 1.170A–8. There are special requirements that must be met before a gift of a partial interest can qualify for a charitable deduction. Those requirements are discussed at **§§ 9.4000–9.4540.**

§ 9.2130. Limitation on Other Charitable Gifts. Any charitable contribution or gift (other than a gift of appreciated capital gain property) which does not qualify for the 50% of contribution base limitation (i.e., a gift to a "B" charity or a gift for the use of an "A" or "B" charity) is subject to a maximum limitation of whichever is less—either: (a) 30% of the taxpayer's contribution base, or (b) the difference between 50% of the taxpayer's contribution base and the amount of deduction allowed to the taxpayer for the tax year for contributions to "A" charities determined without regard to IRC § 170(b)(1)(C) limits (discussed at **§§ 9.2430–9.2432–1**) on the amount of deduction allowable for gifts to "A" charities of certain appreciated capital gain property. IRC § 170(b)(1)(B). As noted above, gifts *for the use of* a charity (whether an "A" or "B" charity) are also subject to the 30% limitation. Stating the limitation on gifts to "B" charities differently, the taxpayer can deduct an amount up to 30% of his contribution base provided that his total amount of charitable deductions for the taxable year (including gifts to both "A" and "B" charities) cannot exceed 50% of the taxpayer's contribution base. When a gift of appreciated property is made to an "A" charity, the determination of the limitation on gifts made to a "B" charity involves additional considerations discussed in the Illustrations in **§ 9.2432–2** and **§ 9.2434–2.**

§ 9.2131. Illustration 1: Fifty Percent Limitation. *X*, an individual, has $60,000 AGI and contribution base in Year One. *X* gave $30,000 cash to Zion Lutheran Church, an "A" charity, and $2,000 cash to a private foundation which constitutes a "B" charity. *X* can deduct the $30,000 he gave the church since that complies with the 50% limitation on gifts to "A" charities, but *X* cannot deduct any part of the $2,000 contributed to the private foundation since his total deductions for the year cannot exceed 50% of his contribution base. However, the $2,000 contribution to the "B" charity may be carried over to *X*'s next five taxable years and deducted in the earliest year allowable under the limitations provided in IRC § 170(b)(1)(B). See **§ 9.2200.** In most cases, a taxpayer's contribution base will equal his AGI since it is only when he is entitled to a net operating loss carryback deduction in that year that any modification of AGI must be made in computing the contribution base.

§ 9.2132.   Illustration 2: Thirty Percent Limitation. In Year One, *X*, an individual, had $60,000 AGI and contribution base. *X* gave $5,000 cash to a church, and he gave $20,000 cash to a private foundation which constitutes a "B" charity. *X* can deduct the $5,000 given to the church, but *X* can deduct only $18,000 of the amount given to the foundation in that year (i.e., 30% of the taxpayer's contribution base ($60,000) = $18,000). *X* may carry over the remaining $2,000. See **§ 9.2200.**

§ 9.2133.   Maximum Limitation on Deductions for a Corporation's Charitable Gifts. The amount of charitable deductions for a taxable year that a corporate taxpayer can deduct is limited to 10% of the corporation's taxable income for that year computed with certain modifications described in IRC § 170(b)(2). For corporate donors, no distinction is made for gifts to "A" or "B" charities.

§ 9.2140.   Religious Purpose of an Organization. There are tax advantages for an organization to qualify as a church or a religious organization, including that it will then qualify for the 50% of contribution base limitation. There has been litigation over the question of whether an organization qualifies as religious.

In *Church of the Chosen People v. United States*, 548 F.Supp. 1247 (D.Minn. 1982), the court applied the three-part test set forth in the non-tax case of *Africa v. Commonwealth of Pennsylvania*, 662 F.2d 1025 (3d Cir. 1981), and, holding that the taxpayer did not qualify as a religious organization, denied tax-exempt status to the taxpayer. The test in *Africa* for determining whether an organization's goals are religious focuses on the following questions: (a) whether the beliefs address fundamental and ultimate questions concerning the human condition, (b) whether the beliefs are comprehensive in nature and constitute an entire system of belief instead of merely an isolated teaching, and (c) whether the beliefs are manifested in external forms. "The Gay Imperative," the plaintiff's only major doctrine in *Church of the Chosen People*, failed the *Africa* standard because it was neither comprehensive in nature nor manifested in external forms in ways analogous to other religions. Although not mentioned in its opinion, perhaps the district court was influenced by the fact that the "church" was also known by the name "Demigod Socko Pantheon."

§ 9.2150. Qualification as a Church. Not every religious organization qualifies as a "church." *Chapman v. Commissioner*, 48 T.C. 358, 363 (1967). In a speech by a former Commissioner, he listed fourteen criteria that the Service utilizes in determining whether a religious organization is a church; and the Tax Court listed those criteria in *First Church of In Theo v. Commissioner*, 56 T.C.M. 1045 (1989). While the Tax Court did not adopt those criteria, it found them helpful and gave them some weight. The court held that the taxpayer was not a church and was a private foundation. The Commissioner's fourteen criteria were listed and utilized by the Tax Court and the Eight Circuit in *Spiritual Outreach Society v. Commissioner*, 58 T.C.M. 1284 (1990), aff'd 927 F.2d 335 (8th Cir. 1991).

Contributions to a religious organization that fails to qualify as a church nevertheless may qualify for a charitable deduction. IRC § 170(c)(2)(B). The contributions to certain charitable organizations described in IRC § 170(b)(1)(A), and churches are included in that list, are given favored tax status; for example, the amount of an individual's contributions to those organization that are deductible is greater than the amount allowable for contributions to other qualified charities. See §§ **9.2120–9.2130.**

An individual's contributions to a religious organization that is not a church can qualify for the same preferential tax treatment that is accorded to gifts made to churches if the organization either: (1) receives a substantial part of its support in the form of contributions from the general public, or (2) qualifies as a private foundation of the type that is described in IRC § 170(b)(1)(E). IRC § 170(b)(1)(A)(vi), (vii). If not, the amount of an individual's contributions to that organization that can be deducted will be more restricted than are contributions to a church. Qualification as a church can exempt an organization from certain federal taxes and reporting requirements that apply to other tax-exempt entities.

§ 9.2200. Carryover of Unused Deduction. Under IRC § 170(d), when an individual makes a charitable contribution to "A" charities in excess of the maximum limitation of 50% of the taxpayer's contribution base, the excess may be carried over to the taxpayer's next five taxable years and deducted in the earliest year allowable under the 50% limitation applicable to that year. An individual also is allowed a five-year carryover for gifts made to "B" charities in excess of the amount allowed as a deduction for that year. IRC

§ 170(b)(1)(B). Similarly, an individual is granted a five-year carry-over for gifts made *for the use of* an "A" or "B" charity in excess of the amount allowed as a deduction. The carryover of gifts to or for the use of a "B" charity or for the use of an "A" charity are treated as gifts to a "B" charity in each of the five subsequent years to which the contribution is carried.

§ 9.2210.   Illustration 1: Computation of Amount of Carryover. X is an individual. In each of X's taxable years One through Four, X had AGI and a contribution base of $40,000. In Year One, X gave $22,000 cash to one "A" charity, $10,000 cash to a second "A" charity, and $4,000 cash to a "B" charity. X can deduct only $20,000 of the $32,000 he gave to "A" charities. None of the $4,000 that he gave to a "B" charity is deductible in Year One. X may carry forward for five years the difference between his gifts to "A" charities ($32,000) and 50% of his contribution base ($20,000) (i.e., X can carry forward $12,000). X also receives a carryover for his $4,000 gift to the "B" charity.

§ 9.2220.   Illustration 2: Limitation on Use of Carryover. The same facts apply as in **§ 9.2210.** In Year Two, X gives $15,000 to an "A" charity. In that year, X will use $5,000 of his carryover of contributions to "A" charities, and so his charitable deductions will total $20,000 (i.e., X will use his carryover contribution to the extent of the difference between 50% of his contribution base in Year Two ($20,000) and the amount actually contributed to "A" charities in that year ($15,000)). Thus, X has $7,000 of his carryover charitable gifts to "A" charities remaining after Year Two. X also has a $4,000 carryover remaining from the contributions that he made to a "B" charity in Year One since he cannot use any of that carryover in Year Two.

§ 9.2230.   Illustration 3: Effect of Carryover Deduction on Gifts to "B" Charities. The same facts apply as in **§ 9.2220.** In Year Three, X gave $14,000 to an "A" charity and $5,000 to a "B" charity. X must use $6,000 of his "A" charity carryover in Year Three (50% of X's contribution base ($20,000) minus the $14,000 contributed to an "A" charity). Thus, X deducts $20,000 in Year Three and carries forward $1,000 of unused "A" charity carryover from his Year One deduction. He also carries forward $4,000 in unused carryover from his Year One contribution to a "B" charity and $5,000 from his unused contribution to a "B" charity in Year Three.

§ 9.2240. Illustration 4: Use of Carryover Deduction. The same facts apply as in **§ 9.2230.** In Year Four, *X* gave $4,000 to an "A" charity. *X* will use his $1,000 remaining carryover from contributions that he made to "A" charities in Year One, and he will also use all $9,000 of his carryovers from contributions that he made to "B" charities in Years One and Three. Thus, *X* will deduct a charitable contribution of $14,000 in Year Four. *X* has no further carryover deductions after Year Four.

§ 9.2300. Gifts of Appreciated Property That Is Not Capital Gain Property. When a donor gives property to a charitable organization and the donor would have recognized ordinary income or short-term capital gain had he sold the donated property for its fair market value, the amount of the charitable contribution will be reduced by the amount of gain which the donor *would have* recognized as ordinary income or as short-term capital gain had he sold the property for its value. IRC § 170(e)(1)(A). Different limitations are imposed when a taxpayer makes a gift to a charity of appreciated property (property whose value is greater than its basis) the gain from the sale of which would have been taxed to him as either long-term capital gain or as gain under IRC § 1231 (such property is called "capital gain property"). See **§ 9.2400** and following. As explained at **§§ 9.2410** and **9.2420**, a contribution of appreciated tangible personal property to or for the use of a charity and a transfer of appreciated property of any kind (other than certain publicly traded stock) to or for the use of certain private foundations are subject to special limitations that apply regardless of whether the donated property is capital gain property.

In certain limited circumstances, IRC § 170(e)(3) allows a corporation a deduction for a portion of the appreciated element of a *corporation's* inventory (or certain other ordinary income property) which the corporation contributes to certain qualified charities. A similar deduction is allowed for the corporate contribution of certain scientific equipment or apparatus that was constructed by the corporation, provided that the original use of the property is by the charitable donee which must be an institution of higher learning that uses the property for research, experimentation or research training and provided that other statutory requirements are satisfied. IRC § 170(e)(4).

§ 9.2310. Illustration 1: Property with Zero Basis. *X* wrote a novel. Before publication, *X* assigned the copyright to the book to a qualified charity. *X* had no basis in the copyright, and the value of the copyright was $25,000. If *X* had sold the copyright for its value ($25,000), *X* would have recognized a $25,000 gain, none of which would have been long-term capital gain or IRC § 1231 gain. See IRC §§ 1221(3) and 1231(b)(1)(C). Consequently, the amount given by *X* to the charity is deemed to be the value of the copyright ($25,000) *reduced* by the amount of ordinary income that *X* would have recognized if he had sold the copyright for its value ($25,000). Thus, in this case, *X* is treated as having made a charitable gift of zero dollars.

§ 9.2320.   Illustration 2: Property with Dollar Basis. *X* is an art dealer who purchases and sells paintings. In Year One, *X* bought a painting for $25,000. By Year Three, the painting had a value of $40,000. If *X* had sold it for its value, *X* would have recognized a gain of $15,000, none of which would have been long-term capital gain or IRC § 1231 gain since *X* held the painting for sale to his customers. *X* donated the painting to an art museum that was a publicly supported organization. The amount of *X*'s contribution is the value of the painting ($40,000) *reduced* by the ordinary income that *X* would have recognized if he had sold the painting ($15,000). For charitable deduction purposes, *X* made a gift of $25,000 to the charity.

§ 9.2330.   Illustration 3: Appreciation is Partially Capital Gain and Partially Ordinary Income. *X* owned depreciable equipment which he gave to a qualified public charity that used the equipment in conducting its charitable function. The value of the equipment at the time of the gift was $30,000 and *X* had an adjusted basis of $15,000 therein. If *X* had sold the equipment for its value instead of making a gift of it, he would have recognized ordinary income of $5,000 (depreciation recapture under IRC § 1245) and *X*'s remaining gain of $10,000 would have constituted a gain under IRC § 1231. *X* is deemed to have made a gift of $25,000—that is, $30,000 minus $5,000 (the amount of *X*'s potential gain that would not have been treated as long-term capital gain or as an IRC § 1231 gain)—subject to the limitations on gifts of capital gain property described in **§ 9.2430.**

§ 9.2340.   Illustration 4: Installment Obligation. *Y* made a gift of an installment obligation [see **§ 20.5000** for a definition of "installment obligation"] to a qualified charity. Since *Y* is required to recognize as gross income, at the time of donation, the difference between the value of the obligation and *Y*'s basis therein [IRC § 453B], the gift is not treated as a gift of appreciated property and the special limitations on such gifts are not applicable. See Rev. Rul. 74–336.

§ 9.2400. Gift of Capital Gain Property. When a taxpayer makes a gift or contribution to a qualified charity of appreciated property, the sale of which at fair market value would have caused the taxpayer to recognize long-term capital gain (or gain under IRC § 1231), the charitable deduction will be subject to the restrictions described in §§ **9.2410–9.2434–2.** For convenience, appreciated property, the sale of which at fair market value would produce a long-term capital gain (or IRC § 1231 gain) is sometimes referred to as "capital gain property." For the treatment of a gift or contribution of appreciated property, the sale of which at fair market value would have caused the taxpayer to recognize ordinary income or a short term capital gain, see §§ **9.2300–9.2340**

§ 9.2410. Tangible Personal Property. When a taxpayer gives appreciated *tangible personal property* to or for the use of a qualified charity (whether the donee is an "A" charity or a "B" charity), the amount of the charitable contribution is limited to the donor's adjusted basis in the donated property. IRC § 170(e)(1)(B)(i). This limitation is not applicable if the donee's use of the donated property is related to its charitable function or purpose, but if the donee is a private foundation that is treated as a "B" charity, an identical limitation *may* be required by IRC § 170(e)(1)(B)(ii) which is described at § **9.2420.**

§ 9.2411. Illustration 1: Limitation of Amount of Gift. Since Year One, *X* (an individual) owned a painting by Titian in which he had a basis of $30,000. In Year Twelve, *X* gave the painting to the Zion Lutheran Church, an "A" charity. The value of the painting at the time of the gift was $50,000. If *X* had sold the painting for its value, he would have recognized a $20,000 long-term capital gain. Unless it can be demonstrated that the church's use of the painting is related to its charitable function, *X* will be deemed to have made a charitable contribution of only $30,000 (i.e., the amount of *X*'s gift is limited to his adjusted basis in the donated painting).

§ 9.2412. Illustration 2: Donee's Use of Property in Conduct of Charitable Function. The same facts apply as in § **9.2411** except that *X* gave the painting to the Corcoran Art Museum, a publicly supported organization that qualifies as an "A" charity. Since the museum's use of the painting is clearly related to its educational purposes, X is deemed to have made a contribution of $50,000 (the fair market value of the painting). However, the amount deductible by X will be subject to the limitations established in IRC § 170(b)(1)(C) discussed in § **9.2430**.

§ **9.2420. Gifts to Certain Private Foundations.** The amount of charitable contribution that is made by making a gift of appreciated property to or for the use of certain private foundations described in IRC § 170(e)(1)(B)(ii) is equal to the donor's adjusted basis in the donated property. IRC § 170(e)(1)(B)(ii). Note that there are some special exceptions to this rule; for example, contributions of "qualified appreciated stock" are not subject to the limitation described above. IRC § 170(e)(5). In general, the "qualified appreciated stock" exception permits a deduction for the full value of a gift to a private foundation of stocks that are listed on a securities market. Stock of a corporation will not constitute "qualified appreciated stock" if the aggregate amount of stock of such corporation that has been contributed by the taxpayer (and by certain persons related to the taxpayer) to private foundations described in IRC § 170(e)(1)(B)(ii) exceeds ten percent (in value) of such corporation's outstanding stock. Of course, if IRC § 170(e)(5) applies, the special percentage limitations [see §§ **9.2430–9.2433**] on gifts of appreciated property will also apply.

§ **9.2430. Other Gifts of Capital Gain Property.** When a taxpayer makes a gift to an "A" charity of "capital gain property" (i.e., property the sale of which at fair market value would cause the taxpayer to recognize a long-term capital gain or an IRC § 1231 gain), IRC § 170(b)(1)(C) establishes a separate percentage of contribution base limitation. This limitation on gifts of "capital gain property" applies only if the special limitation of IRC § 170(e)(1)(B) [described at §§ **9.2410–9.2420**] is not applicable. For example, if the amount of a gift to a charity of tangible personal property is limited by IRC § 170(e)(1)(B)(i) to the donor's basis in the donated property, then the special percentage of contribution base limitations imposed by IRC § 170(b)(1)(C) is inapplicable. It should be noted that most gifts of appreciated property to "A" charities will fall within IRC § 170(b)(1)(C), rather than within the narrower category listed in IRC § 170(e)(1)(B).

§ 9.2431. Thirty Percent Limitation. When a taxpayer makes a contribution of "capital gain property" [see § **9.2400**] to an "A" charity, the maximum amount of such contributions that may be included in the taxpayer's charitable deductions for that year is an amount equal to 30% of the taxpayer's contribution base. As noted above, this 30% limitation does not apply to a gift if the amount of that gift is limited by IRC § 170(e)(1)(B) to the donor's basis in the donated property. IRC § 170(b)(1)(C)(i).

§ 9.2432. Carryover of Excess Contributions. The amount of a taxpayer's contributions of capital gain property to "A" charities that is in excess of the 30% limitation may be carried forward by the taxpayer to the next five taxable years, and the carryforward deduction in each of those years is subjected to the 30% of contribution base limitation.

§ 9.2432–1. Illustration 1: Operation of Thirty Percent Limitation and Carryover. In Year One, *X* (an individual) had AGI and a contribution base of $80,000. In Year One, *X* gave Blackacre, land valued at $50,000, to the Zion Baptist Church, an "A" charity. *X* had a basis of $46,000 in Blackacre. Because Blackacre was "capital gain property," *X* can use only $24,000 of his gift (30% of his contribution base of $80,000) as a charitable contribution. This is so even though the appreciated value of Blackacre over *X*'s basis was relatively small in comparison with Blackacre's total value; it is sufficient that there is any appreciation in value. But see the election described at § **9.2434.** *X* carries forward $26,000 (the difference between Blackacre's value ($50,000) and $24,000 (30% of *X*'s contribution base)) for the next five years.

In Year Two, *X* had a contribution base of $70,000, and he gave $5,000 cash to the Salvation Army, an "A" charity. In Year Two, *X* will deduct $5,000 for the cash gift to the Salvation Army, and he will deduct $21,000 as a carryover from his Year One gift (i.e., *X* has a carryover of $26,000 which is subject to the 30% limitation so that 30% of $70,000 = $21,000 and, therefore, only that amount of the carryover can be deducted in Year Two).

In Year Three, *X* had a contribution base of $62,000, and *X* gave $30,000 cash to the Red Cross, an "A" charity. While

X had an unused carryover of $5,000 from Year One ($21,000 of the $26,000 carryover was used in Year Two), he can deduct only $1,000 of it in Year Three because the amount of *X*'s actual contributions was only $1,000 less than 50% of *X*'s contribution base. Thus, *X* deducts the $30,000 contribution to the Red Cross, and he deducts $1,000 of his carryover.

In Year Four, *X* made no gifts and had a contribution base of $40,000. *X* can deduct the $4,000 unused balance of his carryover from Year One in Year Four.

In computing the limitation on deductions for gifts made to "B" charities, the 30% limitation on gifts of capital gain property made to "A" charities is ignored.

§ 9.2432–2. Illustration 2: Effect that Gift of Capital Gain Property to an "A" Charity Has on Deductibility of a Cash Gift to a "B" Charity. The same facts apply as in **§ 9.2432–1** except that in Year One, *X* also gave $3,000 cash to a "B" charity. *X* is not allowed any deduction in Year One for his $3,000 gift to the "B" charity because the amount he gave to the "A" charity (the church), computed without regard to the 30% limitation, exceeded 50% of his contribution base. IRC § 170(b)(1)(B)(ii). However, *X* is permitted to carry forward the $3,000 contribution that he made to the "B" charity.

§ 9.2433. Gifts of Capital Gain Property to "B" Charities. A contribution base limitation also applies to charitable gifts of "capital gain property" to a "B" charity; the deduction for such gifts is subject to both a 20% limitation on gifts of "capital gain property" to "B" charities and a 30% limitation on gifts of "capital gain property" to both "A" and "B" charities. IRC § 170(b)(1)(D)(i). Stated another way, the donor of "capital gain property" to "B" charities may deduct the lesser of: (a) 20% of the taxpayer's contribution base, or (b) the difference between 30% of the taxpayer's contribution base and the amount of deduction allowed for that tax year for contributions of "capital gain property" to "A" charities. It is unclear whether the application of the 30% limitation requires that gifts of capital gain property to an "A" charity are to be taken into account if the taxpayer elects to exclude such gifts from the 30% limitation as described in **§ 9.2434.** It is likely that such gifts will not be taken into account.

The significance of imposing a 30% limitation on gifts to "B" charities lies in situations where the donor made gifts of capital gain property to "A" charities in the same year so that the amount allowed for the gift to the "B" charity is less under the 30% limitation than the amount allowed under the 20% limitation. The amount of a taxpayer's contribution of "capital gain property" to a "B" charity in excess of the percentage limitation imposed by IRC § 170(b)(1)(D) may be carried forward to the next five taxable years where such carryforward deduction will be subject to the same percentage limitations. IRC § 170(b)(1)(D)(ii).

Most "B" charities will be private foundations; the principal exception is veterans' posts or organizations which typically will be "B" charities. Since a gift of many types of capital gain property to a "B" charity (other than a veterans' post or organization) will be limited by IRC § 170(e)(1)(B) to the donor's adjusted basis in the donated property, it is surprising that Congress further restricted such gifts by imposing the 20% and 30% limitations.

§ 9.2434. Election to Reduce Amount of Gift. If, for a taxable year, a taxpayer does not wish to have his contributions to "A" charities of capital gain properties subjected to the 30% limitation provision, the taxpayer can elect to be exempted from the 30% limitation provision for that year. To so elect, the taxpayer must elect to have all his contributions of capital gain properties in that taxable year covered by the limitations imposed by IRC § 170(e)(1)(B). Thus, if a taxpayer makes that election, in lieu of the 30% of contribution base limitation, the amount of the taxpayer's gifts of capital gain properties will be restricted to the taxpayer's basis in those properties. IRC § 170(b)(1)(C)(iii). If a taxpayer makes this election, the computation of any carryforward charitable deductions for that taxable year which are traceable to a contribution of capital gain property in a prior tax year will be made as if the taxpayer had also made this election in the prior tax year. The principal use of this election is likely to be in situations where the amount of appreciation of donated capital gain property is relatively small.

§ 9.2434–1. Illustration 1: Acceleration of Timing of Deduction. X (an individual) had a contribution base of

$60,000 in Year One. In Year One, X donated Blackacre (land) to Temple Beth El, an "A" charity. X had a basis of $29,500 in Blackacre which had a value of $30,000. If X made no election, X would deduct $18,000 as a charitable gift in Year One and carry over $12,000 for a five-year period. Instead, X can elect to treat the gift under IRC § 170(e)(1)(B) so that the amount of the gift is limited to X's basis in Blackacre. Thus, under the election, X would deduct a charitable contribution of $29,500 in Year One, and X would have no carryover deductions.

§ 9.2434–2. Illustration 2: Effect on Gifts to "B" Charities. Y (an individual) had a contribution base of $60,000 in Year One. In Year One, Y donated Blackacre (land) to the American Red Cross, an "A" charity. Y had a basis of $14,000 in Blackacre which had a fair market value of $16,000. In Year One, Y also gave Whiteacre (land) to a publicly supported veterans' organization, which is a "B" charity. Note that the special limitation imposed by IRC § 170(e)(1)(B)(ii) does not apply to a "B" charity unless it is a private foundation. Y had a basis of $7,000 in Whiteacre, which had a value of $10,000. If Y made no election, she could deduct $18,000 as a charitable deduction for that year, and she would have a carryover of $8,000 from her contribution of Whiteacre to the veterans' organization (which carryover is subject to the 20% and 30% limitations described in IRC § 170(b)(1)(D)). If, instead, Y elects to treat the gifts that she made that year under IRC § 170(e)(1)(B), she can deduct $14,000 for the gift to the "A" charity and $7,000 for the gift to the "B" charity for a total deduction of $21,000 for that year. In that case, Y will have no carryover of unused contributions. Note that the 20% and 30% limitations of IRC § 170(b)(1)(D) apply to Y's gift of Whiteacre to the veterans' fund even though Y's election required that the amount of that gift be limited to Y's basis in Whiteacre. In this case, however, neither the 20% nor the 30% limitation restricted the amount of Y's deduction. In allowing a deduction of $7,000 for the gift of Whiteacre to the veterans' organization, the author assumes that the 30% limitation that is imposed by IRC § 170(b)(1)(D) will be applied without taking into account Y's gifts of capital gain property to an "A" charity since the taxpayer's election to reduce the amount of all of her gifts of capital gain property exempted the gift to "A" charities from the 30% limitation that is imposed by IRC § 170(b)(1)(C). If the author's construction of IRC § 170(b)(1)(D) is correct, the 30% limitation will never apply to gifts of capital gain property to "B" charities if an election is made under IRC § 170(b)(1)(C)(iii) since in such cases the 20% limitation will always be smaller than the 30% limitation.

§ 9.3000. BARGAIN SALES. As noted in **§ 9.1200**, when a taxpayer sells property to a qualified charity for less than the property's value and when the taxpayer intended to confer a benefit on the charity, the transaction is a dual payment—that is a part-sale and part-gift transaction. For purposes of determining the taxpayer's gain, if any, on the receipt of a payment from the charity, the taxpayer must allocate to the part of the property sold only that portion of his adjusted basis in the property which bears the same ratio to his adjusted basis as the amount realized bears to the fair market value of the transferred property. IRC § 1011(b). The remaining basis is allocated to the contributed portion of the property. Any limitation under IRC § 170(e)(1) on the amount of charitable contribution that is attributable to a gift of appreciated property is determined by reference to the amount of the taxpayer's basis that is allocated to the contributed portion of the property. See *Estate of Bullard v. Commissioner*, 87 T.C. 261 (1986) (reviewed by the court).

§ 9.3100. Illustration: Allocation of Basis.

X (an individual) owned Blackacre with a value of $40,000, and X had an adjusted basis of $10,000 in Blackacre. If X were to sell Blackacre for its fair market value, X would recognize a long-term capital gain of $30,000. For the purposes of conferring a $10,000 benefit on University Y, X sold Blackacre to University Y for $30,000. X made a charitable gift of $10,000 to Y. X received $30,000 consideration for that part of Blackacre that he sold to Y. As shown below, X must allocate $7,500 of his $10,000 adjusted basis in Blackacre to the portion of Blackacre that he sold.

$$\frac{\$30,000 \text{ amount realized}}{\$40,000 \text{ value of Blackacre}} \quad \times \quad \$10,000 \text{ adj. basis} = \$7,500$$

Thus, X recognized a gain of $22,500 ($30,000 amount realized minus $7,500 allocated basis), and X is entitled to a charitable contribution of $10,000. All of the limitations noted in **§§ 9.2430–9.2434–2** apply to the portion donated (i.e., the $10,000 donation constituted appreciated property since X had a basis of only $2,500 therein). In this case, none of the limitations of IRC § 170(e)(1) is applicable, and so only the percentage of contribution base limitation is applicable.

§ 9.4000.   GIFTS OF PARTIAL INTEREST IN PROPERTY. When a taxpayer gives a charity less than his entire interest in an item of property, the Code imposes special conditions on deductibility. Moreover, if the charitable gift is a partial interest in *appreciated property*, the donor's basis in that property must be apportioned between the contributed portion and the non-contributed portion of that property for the purpose of applying the rules concerning charitable gifts of appreciated property, described in **§ 9.2300**, **§ 9.2400**, and following. See also IRC § 170(e)(2) and Treas. Reg. § 1.170A–4(c)(1).

§ 9.4100.   Gifts of an Income Interest in a Trust. Under IRC § 170(f)(2)(B), subject to the exception described in **§ 9.4300**, no deduction is allowed for a gift of property to a trust in which the charity has an income interest unless:

(a) the charity's interest in the trust is either a guaranteed annuity interest or a fixed percentage of the value of the trust property valued and distributed annually (this latter interest is a form of unitrust); *and*

(b) the income earned by the trust is included in the taxpayer's gross income under IRC § 671 (the grantor trust provision).

As previously noted, a deductible gift of an income (or annuity or unitrust) interest in a trust does not qualify for the 50% limitation provision but, instead, is treated (for that purpose) as if it were made to a "B" charity irrespective of whether the beneficiary is an "A" o r a "B" charity. If a donor receives an income tax deduction for a gift in trust of an annuity interest to a charity and if, in a subsequent year prior to the termination of the charity's interest, the donor ceases to be taxed under IRC § 671 on the income earned by the trust (e.g., when the donor dies before possession passes to the remainderman), then on such subsequent date the donor shall be treated as having received an amount of income equal to the amount of deduction previously allowed the donor for the charitable gift *reduced by* the discounted value of all income earned by the trust and taxed to the donor prior to his ceasing to be taxed on the trust's income. IRC § 170(f)(2)(B) and Treas. Reg. § 1.170A–6(c)(4).

§ 9.4200.   Gifts of Remainder Interests in a Trust. Under IRC § 170(f)(2)(A), no deduction is allowed for a gift to a trust in which a charity has a remainder interest unless the trust is a charitable remainder annuity trust, a charitable remainder unitrust [as defined in IRC § 664(d)], or a pooled income fund [described in IRC § 642(c)(5)]. If a deductible gift of a remainder interest is made to an "A" charity, the gift will qualify for the 50% limitation. Treas. Reg. § 1.170A–8. If the donor has retained the power to change the recipient of the remainder interest from an "A" charity to a "B" charity, the 30% limitation on gifts to "B" charities will apply. Rev. Rul. 79–368.

§ 9.4210.   Charitable Remainder Annuity Trust. A charitable remainder annuity trust is a trust from which a sum certain (which must be no less than 5% of the initial value of all the property transferred to the trust) is payable at least annually to beneficiaries, at least one of whom is not a qualified charity, for a term of no more than 20 years or for the life or lives of such individual beneficiaries and, upon termination of the payments, the trust assets must be transferred to, or for the use of, a qualified charity. No payment (other than the fixed annuity payments) may be made to noncharitable beneficiaries. IRC § 664(d)(1).

§ 9.4220.   Charitable Remainder Unitrust. A charitable remainder unitrust is a trust from which a fixed percentage (which must not be less than 5%) of the net value of the trust's assets (valued annually) is payable at least annually to beneficiaries, at least one of whom is not a qualified charity, for a term of no more than 20 years or for the life or lives of individual beneficiaries and, upon termination of those payments, the trust assets must be transferred to, or for the use of, a qualified charity. The trust instrument may provide, in lieu of the percentage payment described above, for a distribution of the trust income to the income beneficiaries in any year in which the trust income is less than the percentage payment and for the distribution of annual trust income in excess of the percentage payment to the extent that the aggregate payments in prior trust years were less than the aggregate amount of percentage payments required for those years, but no other amounts may be distributed to the income beneficiaries. IRC §§ 664(d)(2) and 664(d)(3).

§ 9.4230.   Pooled Income Fund. Generally, a pooled income fund is a fund maintained by a public charity to which a person transfers property. The charity places the property in an investment pool and pays the donor (or his beneficiary) an aliquot share of the income for life. The charity maintains the investment pool and possesses the remainder interest therein. IRC § 642(c)(5).

§ 9.4300. Exceptions for Gifts of Complete Interests. If a taxpayer makes a gift to a trust all the beneficiaries of which are qualified charities, then the limitations i n §§ **9.4100–9.4200** are not applicable, and the entire amount donated by the taxpayer constitutes a charitable gift. IRC § 170(f)(2)(D).

§ 9.4400. Contributions Not Made in Trust of Partial Interest in Property. Where a taxpayer contributes less than his entire interest in property (other than a transfer made in trust) to a qualified charity, the taxpayer is not allowed a charitable deduction for the gift unless the gift would have qualified for a deduction under IRC § 170(f)(2), described in §§ **9.4100–9.4300**, if the gift had been made in trust. IRC § 170(f)(3)(A).

§ 9.4410. Exceptions. The restriction on gifts of a partial interest in property does not apply to the gift of a legal (i.e. non-trust) remainder interest in a personal residence or farm nor does it apply to the gift of an undivided portion of the taxpayer's entire interest in an item or property. IRC § 170(f)(3)(B)(i) and (ii). To qualify as a gift of an undivided portion of an interest in property, the charity must be given the right, as a tenant in common with the donor, to possession, dominion and control of the property for a portion of each year appropriate to its interest in such property. Treas. Reg. § 1.170A–7(b)(1). See *Winokur v. Commissioner*, 90 T.C. 733 (1988), Acq.

In a 1987 ruling, the Commissioner held that the restriction on gifts of partial interests does not apply to a gift of a portion of a legal remainder interest in a personal residence or farm. Rev. Rul. 87–37, revoking Rev. Rul. 76–544. Also, a deduction is allowed to a taxpayer for granting to an "A" charity, with respect to realty, either: (a) the entire interest of the donor other than a qualified mineral interest, (b) a restriction in perpetuity on the use which may be made of the realty (i.e., a permanent easement), or (c) a remainder interest in the realty, if the grant is made exclusively for "conservation purposes" (as defined in the statute). IRC § 170(f)(3)(B)(iii), (h). Such a contribution is referred to as a "qualified conservation contribution."

§ 9.4420. Illustration: Uncompensated Lease of Property. *X* (an individual) owns improved Blackacre having a rental value of $3,000 per year. In Year One, X contributes the use of Blackacre to his local church for a period of one year. Since X has given only a portion of his interest in Blackacre to the church, and the church's right to use the property (akin to an income interest) would not have qualified for a deduction under IRC § 170(f)(2)(B) if the gift had been made in trust since the church did not receive an annuity or unitrust interest, IRC § 170(f)(3) prohibits X from deducting the rental value of the property.

§ 9.4500. Contribution of a Future Interest in Tangible Personalty. The contribution to a charity of a future interest in tangible personalty will not be treated as complete until all intervening interests in the property either expire or are possessed by persons other than the donor or persons standing in a relationship to the donor described in IRC § 267(b) or IRC § 707(b). IRC § 170(a)(3). When the specified intervening interests expire or terminate, the gift will then be complete; and the determination of the qualification of the gift for a charitable deduction will be made on the basis of the facts that exist at that time. A gift of an undivided interest in property (such as a painting) to a charity that grants the donee charity the right to the property for a portion of each year does not constitute a gift of a future interest. *Winokur v. Commissioner*, 90 T.C. 733 (1988).

§ 9.4510. Illustration 1: Retention of Possession by Donor. Mary owned a valuable painting by Monet. In Year One, Mary gave a remainder interest in the painting to the Phillips Art Museum, a publicly supported organization that qualifies as an "A" charity. Mary retained the right to possess the painting for ten years, after which time possession passes to the museum. Mary is not deemed to have made a gift in Year One. In Year Eleven, when Mary's possessory interest expires, Mary is treated as having made a gift of the painting to the museum.

§ 9.4520. Illustration 2: Donation of Possessory Interest to a Related Party. The same facts apply as in **§ 9.4510** except that in Year One Mary gave her son, Randolph, the possession of the painting for ten years, and then the possession of the painting passes to the museum. Since Randolph is within the group of relatives of Mary described in IRC § 267, Mary is not deemed to have made a gift of the painting until Randolph's possessory interest expires.

§ 9.4530. Illustration 3: Donation of Possessory Interest to a Nonrelated Party. The same facts apply as in **§ 9.4510**

except that in Year One, Mary gave her son, Randolph, possession of the painting for five years, then the right to possession passes to Mary's close friend, Alice, for five years, and then possession passes to the museum. Mary is not deemed to have made a gift in Year One. In Year Six, when possession passes to Alice, who is not within the list of Mary's relatives stated in IRC § 267(b), Mary is deemed to have made a gift of the remainder interest to the museum. However, IRC § 170(f)(3) will deny Mary a charitable deduction for making the gift, since the charity's remainder interest (viewed as of Year Six) was not a charitable remainder annuity trust or unitrust, nor was it a pooled income fund. See Rev. Rul. 73–610. In this case, Mary will never be allowed a charitable deduction.

§ 9.4540.   Illustration 4: Restrictions on Donee's Use of Property. Robert made a gift to a museum of a rare book collection. Under the terms of the gift, the museum is required to store the books in a locked room, Robert retained the right for life to full access to the collection, and Robert retained for life the right to deny access to the collection to any person seeking to use the books. Robert's gift likely will be treated as a gift of a future interest in tangible personalty in which Robert retained an intervening interest, and so Robert is not entitled to a charitable deduction. See Rev. Rul. 77–225. Also see Treas. Reg. § 1.170A–7(b)(1)(i).

§ 9.5000.   CONTRIBUTION OF SERVICES. A charitable deduction is allowed only for contributions of property; the value of a contribution of personal services is not deductible. Treas. Reg. § 1.170A–1(g). In *Grant v. Commissioner*, 84 T.C. 809 (1985), aff'd without opinion, 800 F.2d 260 (4th Cir. 1986), a negligence penalty (currently imposed by IRC § 6662 as part of the accuracy-related penalty) was imposed on an attorney who claimed a deduction for the fair market value of services contributed to a charity. The court held that the regulation disallowing such a deduction [Treas. Reg. § 1.170A–1(g)] was valid. The Service has narrowly construed the meaning of property.

§ 9.5100.   Donation of Blood to a Charity. A donor's contribution of blood is generally treated as a contribution of a service and therefore is not deductible. In *Lary v. United States*, 787 F.2d 1538 (11th Cir. 1986), the court held that a donation of blood was not deductible regardless of whether it was characterized as the performance of a service or the contribution of property. Even if the blood donation is treated as a contribution of property, the taxpayer has the burden of proving the amount of his basis in his blood; only the amount of taxpayer's basis in his donated blood is deductible. If taxpayer had sold the donated blood for its fair market value, any amount received in excess of basis would be ordinary income, and, therefore, the excess of the value of taxpayer's donated blood over taxpayer's basis is nondeductible under IRC § 170(e)(1)(A). It is highly unlikely that a taxpayer can prove that he has any basis in his blood.

§ **9.5200. Expenses Incurred in Providing Services.** While a taxpayer's contribution of services itself to a charity are not deductible, the unreimbursed, out-of-pocket expenses incurred by the taxpayer in connection with providing those services are deductible. For example, subject to limitations described in § **9.1710**, a taxpayer's expenditures for uniforms, transportation, and travel away from home which are necessary to the rendition of gratuitous services by the taxpayer for a qualified charity are deductible. Treas. Reg. § 1.170A–1(g). However, a taxpayer is not permitted to deduct expenses that the taxpayer paid on behalf of another person in connection with the latter's performance of services for a charity. § **9.5210.** The Commissioner has ruled that child care expenses incurred to free the taxpayer to perform services for a charity are personal, nondeductible expenses. Rev. Rul. 73–597.

§ **9.5210. Payment of Expenses of Other Persons Performing Services for a Charity.** As noted in § **9.5200**, the unreimbursed expenses incurred and paid by a person in connection with that person's performance of services for a charity are deductible. But, what if a person who does not perform services for a charity pays the expenses incurred by another person in connection with the latter's performance of services for the charity? In *Davis v. United States*, 495 U.S. 472 (1990), the Supreme Court held that no deduction will be permitted for paying the expenses of another when the payor is not himself providing services to the charity. As part of its holding in *Davis*, the Court held that the payment of another's expenses does not constitute a contribution "for the use of" the charity as that phrase is used in IRC § 170 because that phrase refers to contributions made in trust for a charity.

§ **9.6000. ASSIGNMENT OF INCOME.** A taxpayer may assign to a charity income from services performed by the taxpayer or income earned by property owned by the taxpayer. The usual anticipatory assignment of income rules [discussed in Chapter 20] apply equally to gifts to a charity. If a gift is treated as an anticipatory assignment of income, the income will be included in the taxpayer's gross income. Taxpayer will be allowed a charitable deduction, but the amount of that deduction will be subject to the percentage limitations imposed on charitable deductions.

§ 9.7000. PUBLIC POLICY EXCLUSIONS FROM EXEMPT STATUS. The Supreme Court has held that an organization having an exempt purpose specified in IRC § 501(c)(3) may, nevertheless, be denied exempt status because the organization practices racial discrimination. In *Green v. Connally*, 330 F.Supp. 1150 (D.D.C. 1971), aff'd per curiam sub nom., *Coit v. Green*, 404 U.S. 997 (1971), the court construed the word "charitable" in IRC § 501(c)(3) as incorporating a public policy limitation defined by federal public policy against racial discrimination in education. The Supreme Court subsequently affirmed decisions in two cases where tax-exempt status was denied to private educational institutions whose discriminatory policies were based on asserted religious beliefs. *Bob Jones University v. United States*, 639 F.2d 147 (4th Cir. 1980), aff'd, 461 U.S. 574 (1983); *Goldsboro Christian Schools, Inc. v. United States*, 644 F.2d 879 (4th Cir. 1981), aff'd sub nom., *Bob Jones University v. United States*, 461 U.S. 574 (1983). The Supreme Court based its denial of tax-exempt status on statutory construction and public-policy grounds, stating that "to warrant exemption under IRC § 501(c)(3), an institution must fall within a category specified in that section and must demonstrably serve and be in harmony with the public interest." *Bob Jones University v. United States*, 461 U.S. at p. 592. The question remains open as to whether this denial can be extended to groups which discriminate on bases other than race (e.g., gender or religion).

§ 9.8000. ITEMIZED DEDUCTION. The charitable deduction is not listed in IRC § 62(a), and so it is treated as an itemized deduction. The 2% of AGI floor does not apply to charitable deductions. IRC § 67(b)(4). Charitable contributions are subject to the limitation on the deduction of itemized deductions that is imposed by IRC § 68 when an individual's AGI exceeds a specified amount. See **§ 3.1120.**

§ 9.9000. OVERVALUATION. There is evidence that taxpayers sometimes overvalue the property donated to a charity and thereby overstate the amount deductible. Congress has imposed reporting and verification requirements to minimize that abuse.

§ 9.9100. Substantiation Requirements. For a charitable contribution of $250 or more, no deduction will be allowed unless the taxpayer obtains from the donee a contemporaneous written acknowledgement of the gift. IRC § 170(f)(8). The written acknowledgement must include:

(1) a statement of the amount of cash contributed and a description of any non-cash property that was contributed (but there is no requirement that the acknowledgement state the value of the donated non-cash property); and

(2) a statement as to whether the donee provided any goods and services in consideration, in whole or in part, of the donation, and a description of the goods or services provided to the donor and a good faith estimate of the value of those goods or services [however, if the only consideration provided to the donor was an "intangible religious benefit" that generally is not sold commercially, it need not be valued and the donee charity need only include a statement of the nature of the religious benefit].

The requirement of a contemporaneous written acknowledgement is waived if the donee organization files a return that conforms with requirements established by the Service in regulations. IRC § 170(f)(8)(D).

The Service is authorized to promulgate regulations that will describe circumstances in which the substantiation requirement need not be satisfied.

§ 9.9200. Information Required. If a TP makes a contribution to a charity for which a deduction of more than $500 is claimed, no deduction will be allowed unless the information and substantiation requirements described below are satisfied. IRC § 170(f)(11)(A). The deduction will not be denied if the failure to comply is due to reasonable cause and not to willful neglect. Id.

(1) The TP must include with the return for the taxable year in which the contribution was made a description of the contributed property and such other information as the Service may require.

(2) If the value of donated property exceeds $5,000, the TP is required to obtain a qualified appraisal and is required to include on his return information about the property and about the qualified appraisal. This requirement does not apply if the contributed property is cash, publicly traded securities, or a vehicle for which information is required by the provision described at **§ 9.9400.** IRC § 170(f)(11)(A)(i).

(3) If the value of the donated property is $500,000 or more, the taxpayer is required to attach the qualified appraisal to his return. This requirement does not apply if the contributed property is cash, publicly traded securities, or a vehicle for which information is required by the provision described at **§ 9.9400.** IRC § 170(f)(11)(A)(i).

In applying the dollar thresholds for the above reporting and appraisal requirements, all similar donated properties, whether donated to one or more donees, are aggregated. IRC § 170(f)(11)(F).

If a taxpayer contributes property to a charity, the claimed value of which (plus the value of similar items donated by the donor to one or more donees) exceeds $5,000, and if the charitable donee sells, exchanges or otherwise disposes of that property within two years after its receipt, the donee is required to file a return with the Internal Revenue Service disclosing specified items of information. The information to be disclosed on that return includes an identification of the donor and a statement of the amount received by the donee on its disposition of the donated property. IRC § 6050L. The donee is required to send a copy of that return to the donor.

§ 9.9300. Disclosure of Information. In addition to the substantiation and information requirements, the Code imposes a disclosure requirement on the donee organization when the amount transferred to the donee exceeds $75 and the donor received partial consideration for the transfer. IRC § 6115. The more than $75 figure applies to the amount transferred to the donee without reduction for the amount of any partial consideration that the donor received from the donee. This disclosure requirement does not apply to a contribution to a religious organization in return for which the transferor receives an intangible religious benefit that generally is not sold commercially outside of a donative context.

Specifically, the donee is required to provide the donor with a written statement that:

(1) explains that the contribution is deductible only to the extent of the excess of the value of the contribution over the value of any goods and services furnished to the donor in return; and

(2) provides the donor with a good faith estimate of the value of the goods and services that the donor received. IRC § 6115.

If the donee fails to comply with those disclosure requirements, a penalty may be imposed on the donee. IRC § 6714.

When the item or benefit received by a donor is of insubstantial value, the charitable donee may inform the donor that the donor's contribution is fully deductible. The Service has provided guidelines for the determination of whether an item or benefit is of insubstantial value.

§ 9.9400. Donation of a Vehicle. The Service has evidence that the donation of automobiles to charities has been a major source of overvaluations. To deter that practice, in the American Jobs Creation Act of 2004, Congress added § 170(f)(12) to the Code, which applies to the donation of certain vehicles (including automobiles, boats and aircrafts). If the claimed value of the vehicle exceeds $500, a number of substantiation, reporting and certification requirements are imposed on the donor and the donee. If the donee sells the vehicle (which had a claimed value greater than $500) without making any material improvement, the donor cannot take a deduction for the donation that is greater than the gross proceeds that the donee received. IRC § 170(f)(12)(A)(ii). The statute does not state whether there is a time limit for the period between the donation and the sale for this provision to be applicable, but it seems unreasonable to apply this provision to sales made after the vehicle has been used by the charity for some time.

§ 9.9500. Penalty For Overvaluation. If a taxpayer has an underpayment of income tax for a taxable year which is attributable to a significant overstatement of the value of property contributed in kind to a charity (i.e., the taxpayer overvalued the contributed property and thereby obtained a greater charitable deduction than was proper), a penalty may be imposed on the taxpayer under IRC § 6662. This penalty is part of the accuracy-related penalty that is described at **§ 1.6331.** The amount of the penalty and the criteria for imposing it are described in **§ 1.6331.**

§ 9.9A000. ADVANCE NOTICE REQUIREMENT. IRC § 508 requires *most* organizations seeking tax-exempt status under IRC § 501(c)(3) to notify the Secretary that they are applying for such status. What significance does that requirement have for the resolution of whether a contribution to an organization described in IRC § 170(c)(2) qualifies for a deduction? While the statute does not expressly require notification by IRC § 170(c)(2) organizations, most IRC § 170(c)(2) organizations also are IRC § 501(c)(3) organizations. If an IRC § 501(c)(3) organization fails to give timely notice to the Service that it is not a private foundation, it will be presumed to be a private foundation. IRC § 508(b). The classification of an organization as a private foundation may affect the amount of deduction allowable for contributions to that organization. See, e.g., IRC § 170(b)(1)(B), (D), (e)(1)(B)(ii). Organizations that are not required to notify the Secretary are listed in IRC § 508(c) and Treas. Reg. § 1.508–1(a)(3). For example, churches are excluded from this requirement. IRC § 508(c)(1)(A).

§ 9.9B000.   DECLARATORY JUDGMENT. The Code permits an organization to obtain a declaratory judgment as to whether it is a qualified charitable organization under IRC §§ 501(c)(3) or 170(c)(2) and as to certain similar questions. IRC § 7428. The organization can seek the declaratory judgment only after the Service has either rejected the organization's claim or has failed to make a determination of the claim. The petition for declaratory judgment can be brought in either the Tax Court, the United States Court of Federal Claims, or the United States District Court for the District of Columbia at the option of the organization. No judgment will be issued until the organization has exhausted its administrative remedies as defined in IRC § 7428(b)(2). A court's declaratory judgment under this provision is reviewable in the same manner as a final judgment or decree of that court. To mitigate the drying up of contributions to an organization whose administrative ruling of charitable status was revoked by the Service, IRC § 7428(c) permits an *individual* to deduct up to $1,000 of contributions made by him and his spouse to an organization whose administrative ruling of qualification as an IRC § 170(c)(2) organization was revoked by the Service if the organization has filed a timely petition for a declaratory judgment of that issue. Such contributions made after the notice of the Service's revocation of its determination of charitable status was published and prior to a court's final determination that the organization does not qualify for IRC § 170(c)(2) status will be deductible. This provision for a deduction of up to $1,000 will not apply to an individual who is wholly or partly responsible for the circumstances that constituted the basis of the revocation. IRC § 7428(c)(3).

§ 9.9B100.   Scope of Review. In *Houston Lawyer Referral Service, Inc. v. Commissioner*, 69 T.C. 570 (1978), the Tax Court examined the scope of the declaratory judgment proceeding that is authorized by IRC § 7428. Essentially, the proceeding is a review of the administrative determination of the Service rather than a de novo determination of the charitable status of the petitioner. Typically, the court's determination will be made on the administrative record, and only in rare circumstances will the court allow additional evidence to be introduced.

CHAPTER TEN

BUSINESS AND NONBUSINESS EXPENSES

§ 10.0000. BUSINESS AND NONBUSINESS EXPENSES. The federal income tax is imposed on taxable income (i.e., gross income reduced by allowable deductions). The most common and important deductions are the expenses of conducting a trade or business or other profit-seeking venture. Business-related expenses are usually deductible under the general rule of IRC § 162, but some business-related expenses are deductible under more specific provisions of the Code (e.g., business bad debts under IRC § 166). A deduction may be authorized by more than one section of the Code, but no more than one deduction is allowed for a single item. See **§ 7.2710.** No deduction is allowed for an expense for which the taxpayer has the right or an expectation of being reimbursed. Rev. Rul. 80–348. See *Campbell v. Commissioner*, 54 T.C.M. 632 (1987), where the Tax Court denied a business expense deduction for a business loss to the extent that the loss was covered by insurance even though the taxpayer did not claim reimbursement from the insurer.

§ 10.1000. ORDINARY EXPENSES: GENERAL. IRC § 162 grants a deduction for the *ordinary and necessary* expenses of conducting a trade or business. An expense is deductible under IRC § 162 if:

(a) the taxpayer is engaged in a "trade or business" (e.g., a "gentleman farmer" who operates a farm as a hobby rather than as a business is not engaged in the trade or business of farming);

(b) the expense was paid or incurred in connection with the conduct of the trade or business; and

(c) the expense was "ordinary and necessary" [a term of art explained at **§§ 10.1500–10.1521**].

§ 10.1100. Trade or Business. The term "trade or business" is not defined in either the Code or the Regulations and has no precise single definition. An individual may be engaged in more than one trade or business at the same time. The term "trade or business" is used in a number of Code sections, but it has a more restricted meaning in IRC § 162 than it does in most other sections in which it is employed. For example, in *Snow v. Commissioner*, 416 U.S. 500 (1974), the Supreme Court held that the term "trade or business" as used in IRC § 174 (providing a current deduction for research and experimental expenses) has a broader scope than that term has when used in IRC § 162.

In general, for purposes of IRC § 162, a "trade or business" is an activity entered into for the purpose of making a profit and with the expectation that the activity ultimately will produce a profit. It is sufficient if the taxpayer contemplates eventually turning a profit; he need not expect a profit at the outset—i.e., it is permissible to anticipate start-up losses. *Nickerson v. Commissioner*, 700 F.2d 402 (7th Cir. 1983). The test is whether the taxpayer's expectation of a profit is bona fide; it need not be a reasonable expectation. *Churchman v. Commissioner*, 68 T.C. 696 (1977); *Dreicer v. Commissioner*, 78 T.C. 642 (1982). A consistent history of losses over a number of years does not establish conclusively that a venture was not entered into for profit, but it is evidence of that possibility.

While a profit motive is essential to qualify for a business expense deduction, it is not sufficient. The "taxpayer must be involved in the activity with continuity and regularity and . . . the taxpayer's primary purpose for engaging in the activity must be for income or profit. A sporadic activity, a hobby or an amusement diversion does not qualify." *Commissioner v. Groetzinger*, 480 U.S. 23 (1987). If the activity is not a trade or business, the expense may qualify as a deduction under IRC § 212 if the activity is profit-motivated. See **§ 10.1200.**

In addition to a profit motive, a transaction must have economic substance on an objective basis to be recognized by the tax law. No recognition will be given to a transaction that is a sham arrangement for the purpose of creating beneficial tax consequences. *Johnson, Jr. v. Commissioner*, 966 F.2d 598 (10th Cir. 1992).

An exception to the profit motive requirement is that under IRC § 7701(a)(26), the performance of the functions of a public office constitutes a trade or business regardless of whether the taxpayer is compensated for his services. *Frank v. United States*, 577 F.2d 93 (9th Cir. 1978).

§ 10.1110. Facts and Circumstances Test. As a consequence of a statement made by Justice Frankfurter in his concurring opinion in a 1940 Supreme Court decision, a question arose as to whether an activity could qualify as a trade or business only if it constituted the offering of goods or services. This issue arose primarily in the context of whether a professional gambler could be engaged in the trade or business of gambling. The issue was laid to rest by the Supreme Court's repudiation in *Commissioner v. Groetzinger*, 480 U.S. 23 (1987) of the notion that there is a requirement that goods or services be offered. In *Groetzinger*, after the taxpayer lost his job in sales and market research, he turned to parimutuel wagering, primarily on greyhound racing. In the year 1978, he went to racing tracks six days a week for 48 weeks. Taxpayer gambled only on his own account; he made no bets for others, nor did he sell tips or function as a bookie. Taxpayer spent a substantial amount of time studying racing forms and similar materials. He devoted 60 to 80 hours per week on these gambling-related endeavors. In 1978, taxpayer had gross winnings of $70,000 on his gambling, but he lost $72,032 so he had a net loss for that year of $2,032. The Commissioner contended that taxpayer's gambling activity did not constitute a trade or business and so, under the state of the law as it existed at that time, a portion of taxpayer's gambling losses constituted a tax preference item that caused the taxpayer to incur an alternative minimum tax liability. The Supreme Court held that taxpayer was in the trade or business of gambling and so incurred no alternative minimum tax liability. The Court repudiated the suggestion that an activity must offer goods or services to constitute a trade or business. Rather than draw a bright line for classification as a trade or business, the Court determined that the facts and circumstances of each case must be examined. The activity must be profit-motivated, and the taxpayer must have a bona fide expectation of earning a profit (but a reasonable expectation is not required). Also, the taxpayer must be involved in the activity with regularity and continuity.

As to a gambling activity, note that gambling losses are deductible only to the extent of gambling winnings in the same taxable year. IRC § 165(d).

§ 10.1120. Stock Investment Activity and Rental Realty Activity.

§ 10.1121. Stock Investment Activity. Investing in stocks and securities does not constitute a trade or business even when the investment activity is extensive and involves many

dollars. *Higgins v. Commissioner*, 312 U.S. 212 (1941). However, investing in stocks and securities must be distinguished from "trading" in them, which is described in the next paragraph and is treated quite differently. Salaries, fees and other expenses incurred in connection with stock investments are not deductible under IRC § 162 as business expenses. While such expenses usually will be deductible under IRC § 212, they will be treated as miscellaneous itemized deductions under IRC § 67(b) and can be deducted only to the extent that such items exceed 2% of the taxpayer's AGI. Moreover, if the alternative minimum tax (AMT) applies to the taxpayer, no deduction is allowed for any of those expenses. IRC § 56(b)(1)(A)(i). If the AMT does not apply to the taxpayer, the deduction for those expenses is also subject to the overall limitation on itemized deductions that is imposed by IRC § 68 when an individual's AGI exceeds a specified amount. Note, however, that investment interest [defined in IRC § 163(d)(3)] that is deductible is not subject to the 2% of AGI floor or the § 68 limitation on itemized deductions. IRC §§ 67(b)(1), 68(c)(2); and is not disallowed by the alternative minimum tax system

If a person who buys and sells stocks and securities qualifies as a "trader," as contrasted to an investor, the trader's activity will constitute a trade or business. See *Commissioner v. Groetzinger*, in § **10.1110**; *Moller v. United States*, 721 F.2d 810 (Fed. Cir. 1983). A "trader" in stocks is one who buys and sells stocks frequently "in an endeavor to catch the swings in the daily market movements and profit thereby on a short term basis." *Moller v. United States*, *supra*; *Mayer v. United States*, 32 Fed. Cl. 149 (Fed. Cl 1994); *Purvis v. Commissioner*, 530 F.2d 1332, 1334 (9th Cir. 1976); *Chen v. Commissioner*, RIA TC Memo 2004–132 (2004).

§ **10.1122. Rental of Real Estate.** The question has arisen whether the rental of realty that the TP owns constitutes a trade or business. Before the adoption in 1942 of the antecedents to IRC §§ 212 and 167(a)(2), that question was of considerable significance since the expenses of operating the realty and depreciation deductions for a building would be allowable only if the rental activity constituted a trade or business. In the context of deductions, the question is much less significant now since not only will such expenses and depreciation be allowable by IRC §§ 212 and 167(a)(2), but they will be nonitemized deductions under IRC § 62(a)(4). However, the issue is still important because the determination of the character of a gain or loss on the sale of the realty will depend upon whether the realty was used in a trade or business rather than merely held as an investment. That issue is of particular importance if the TP recognizes a loss on the sale of the realty. A gain or loss recognized on the sale of rented realty will be a capital gain or loss if the rental activity was not a trade or business, but will be characterized by IRC § 1231 if the rental activity constituted a trade or business. IRC § 1231(b)(1). A § 1231 loss often qualifies as an ordinary loss, which typically is more useful to a TP than is a capital loss. IRC § 1231(a)(2). See § **19.2000** *et seq.* for a discussion of the operation of IRC § 1231.

The standard for determining whether rental realty was used in a trade or business has changed over the years. Initially, the Service and the Tax Court treated the mere rental of improved realty as a trade or business, but imposed greater requirements if the rental realty was not improved. The courts and the Service no longer use a different standard for improved and unimproved rental realty. In both cases, the test for determining whether the rental activity constitutes a trade or business turns on the degree of activity of the TP in the conduct of that activity. If the TP does not manage the property or incur costs and effort in advertising and renting it (for example, if the property is rented under a net lease in which the lessor does little more than collect the net rent), the property likely will be treated as an investment rather than as part of a trade or business. TAM 8350008. See, *Curphey v. Commissioner*, 73 T.C. 766 (1980).

IRC § 280A imposes special limitations on the amount that can be deducted for the rental of a dwelling unit if the TP uses all or part of the unit for personal purposes at any time during the taxable year. The operation of those limitations is discussed at § § **10.1180–10.1186.**

§ **10.1130. Time When Business Commences.** It is important to determine when a taxpayer commences the conduct of a trade or business since the expenses incurred prior to that date may not be deductible. A taxpayer is first deemed to be carrying on a business at the time that the facts show that there has been sufficient progress that the taxpayer will almost certainly engage in a profit-seeking activity. See *Aboussie v. United States*, 779 F.2d 424 (8th Cir. 1985). In *Aboussie*, the court denied a deduction for the premium paid by a limited partnership for mortgage insurance in connection with a housing project which the partnership was constructing. In the year in question, the construction had barely begun, and so the court determined that considerable uncertainty existed at that time as to whether and when the project would produce profits.

§ 10.1140.   Interruption of Business. If a taxpayer ceases to conduct a business for a period of time, the question can arise as to whether the taxpayer remains in the business for the period of time that he is inactive. If the hiatus is relatively brief and was intended to be temporary, the taxpayer will continue to be in the same business. *Furner v. Commissioner*, 393 F.2d 292 (7th Cir. 1968). If the taxpayer ceases to conduct a business for an indefinite period, the taxpayer will be deemed to no longer be in that business. *Damron v. Commissioner*, 46 T.C.M. (CCH) 903 (1983).

§ 10.1150.   Activity Not Engaged in for Profit. There have been many "hobby" cases concerning the deductibility of expenses incurred in activities such as farming, the owning and racing of horses, the writing of books, etc., and the results have been mixed but largely turn on factual findings as to the taxpayer's motive. The Tax Reform Act of 1969 (the 1969 TRA) added IRC § 183 to the Code which deals with the deductibility of expenses incurred in connection with an "activity not engaged in for profit." IRC § 183 does not affect the deductibility of expenses which are deductible without regard to whether they are incurred in connection with a profit-seeking activity (such as state income and property taxes), but it does *limit* the deductibility of other expenses of non profit-seeking activities. Since IRC § 183(c) defines an "activity not engaged in for profit" as one whose expenses are not allowable as deductions under IRC §§ 162, 212(1) or (2), on its face the language of IRC § 183 would not impose a significant limitation on deductibility (i.e., if such expenses do not qualify under IRC § 162 or IRC § 212, they would likely not be deductible in any event). Presumably, the congressional purpose for adopting IRC § 183 was to restrict the deduction of expenses connected with activities which lie in a marginal zone which might be characterized as either personal or income-related depending upon factual findings; therefore, courts may narrow their construction of the applicability of IRC § 162 or IRC § 212 as a consequence of the 1969 adoption of IRC § 183. See *Jasionowski v. Commissioner*, 66 T.C. 312 (1976) stating that IRC § 183 "has clearly placed a gloss on post–1969 judicial profit-motive inquiries."

§ 10.1160. Determining "Profit–Making Activity." In Treas. Reg. § 1.183–2(b), the Treasury lists nine factors to be taken into account in determining whether an activity is engaged in for profit. For an example of the court's use of those factors, see *Burger v. Commissioner*, 809 F.2d 355 (7th Cir. 1987). The Tax Reform Act of 1976 (the 1976 TRA) adopted a specific provision [IRC § 280A] dealing with the deductibility of expenses incurred in connection with the rental or other business use of realty that the taxpayer or certain related parties occupied as a personal residence for part of the taxable year. The provision is discussed at § 10.1180. See also §§ 10.1530–10.1534.

> **§ 10.1161. Presumption.** If a venture nets a profit in three or more of the five consecutive years ending with the taxable year in question, IRC § 183(d) establishes a rebuttable presumption that the venture is a profit-seeking venture. If the activity is the breeding, training, racing, or showing of horses, the period is two of seven years. A failure to qualify for the presumption does not create a negative inference that the activity was not profit-seeking. In *Churchman v. Commissioner*, 68 T.C. 696 (1977), the Court held that an artist was engaged in an activity for profit even though she failed to earn a profit in any of the six years in which she had engaged in artistic activities. The Court felt that the loss years were a less significant factor for an artist than for most trades because an artist often has to endure a long period of economic loss before achieving the public acclaim that leads to a profit. The Court was influenced by the extensive efforts made by the taxpayer to market her works so that her activity went beyond the creative stage and indicated a strong profit motive.

§ 10.1170. Taxable Income. Prior to the 1986 adoption of limitations on the amount of deduction allowable for itemized deductions, even when a venture did not qualify as a profit-seeking activity, only the net income from the venture was taxed. IRC § 183. In determining the net income from such an activity, expenses connected with the activity which are deductible without regard to whether the activity constituted a profit venture (e.g., state income and property taxes, and casualty losses) are deducted first, and other expenses of the activity are deductible only to the extent of the balance. IRC § 183(b). By definition, expenses which are deductible under IRC § 183 are not business expenses and, therefore, must be itemized; that is, they are not deducted in determining AGI. Rev. Rul. 75–14; Rev. Rul. 76–287. Also, those expenses are miscellaneous itemized deductions, the deductibility of which is subject to the 2% of AGI floor imposed by IRC § 67(a), and are not deductible at all in the alternative minimum tax system. Therefore, even when the income earned from a hobby exactly equals the expenses incurred in conducting the hobby, a TP may have a net income from the activity because the amount of deduction allowable for those expenses may be less than the amount of income from the activity. These expenses also are subject to the IRC § 68. overall limitation on the amount of itemized deductions that can be deducted. See § **3.1120**, *supra*.

§ **10.1171. Illustration 1: Hobby Expenses.** *X*, a successful chemist, is a talented and enthusiastic chess player who plays in four to six chess tournaments a year. In Year One, *X* won $350 in prizes from such tournaments. During the year, he incurred travel expenses of $650 in the course of his chess activities. Although *X* is not engaged in chess as a trade or business (it is a hobby), he may, nevertheless, treat $350 of his expenses, the amount of his winnings, as an itemized deduction (subject to the 2% of AGI floor), and he will receive no tax allowance for the $300 expenses he incurred in excess of his winnings. If *X*'s AGI exceeds a specified amount, his expenses that are otherwise deductible are subject to the limitation imposed by IRC § 68; and, if X's tax is determined under the alternative minimum tax system, none of X's expenses is deductible. IRC § 56(b)(1)(A)(i).

§ **10.1172. Illustration 2: Non Profit–Seeking Deductions.** The same facts apply as in § **10.1171** except that *X* won $365 and incurred $350 travel expenses. *X* paid $35 in state income taxes on his winnings. *X* had no other expenses in connection with this hobby. The $35 state tax expense is not a miscellaneous itemized deduction because of IRC § 67(b)(2), and, therefore, that expense is not subject to the 2% of AGI floor. Assuming that X's AGI is low enough that the IRC § 68 limitation is inapplicable *X* netted $330 (gross income minus state tax) from the venture without taking the travel expenses into account. Therefore, *X* may treat only $330 of his travel expenses as a miscellaneous itemized deduction.

§ 10.1180.   Rental of a Dwelling Unit. The 1976 TRA added IRC § 280A to the Code which (among other provisions) imposes restrictions on the deductibility of expenses incurred by a taxpayer in connection with the rental of a dwelling unit to another, or in connection with other business use of a dwelling unit, if the taxpayer is deemed to have used the dwelling unit for personal purposes at any time during the taxable year. For the limitations imposed on the deduction of expenses incurred in the business use of a dwelling, see §§ **10.1530–10.1536.**

A taxpayer is deemed to have used a dwelling unit for personal purposes for a day if for any part of such day the unit is used: (a) for personal purposes by the taxpayer or by another person who owns an interest in the unit or by certain members of the taxpayer's family (or the family of such other person); or (b) by any individual under a swap arrangement which enables the taxpayer to use some other dwelling unit; or (c) by any person (other than certain employees of the taxpayer) who rents the unit for less than a fair rental on such day. IRC § 280A(d)(2). As a consequence of a 1981 amendment to IRC § 280A, a taxpayer is permitted to rent a dwelling unit to a member of the taxpayer's family (or to anyone else) for use by the tenant as the tenant's principal residence provided that the tenant pays a fair rental to the taxpayer. IRC § 280A(d)(3)(A). In addition, a taxpayer can rent a dwelling unit to a person having an interest in the unit if the rental is fair and is made pursuant to a "shared equity financing agreement" as defined in IRC § 280A(d)(3)(C). IRC § 280A, which applies only to individuals and to so-called S corporations (a corporation that has validly elected to be taxed under specific provisions of the Code), has no effect whatsoever on the deductibility of expenses which are allowable without regard to whether the activity is profit-seeking (e.g., casualty losses and state income taxes)—such deductible expenses are sometimes referred to in this book as "non profit-seeking deductions."

§ 10.1181.   Allocation. When a taxpayer is deemed to have used a dwelling unit for personal purposes on any day during the taxable year, the amount of expenses incurred in connection with the dwelling unit (other than non profit-seeking deductions) must be allocated between the period of time in which the dwelling unit (or a portion thereof) was rented at a fair value and the period of time that the unit (or a portion thereof) was otherwise actually used. The amount deductible (other than non profit-seeking deductions) cannot exceed the amount of expenses so allocated to the fair rental use of the property. IRC § 280A(e); Prop. Reg. § 1.280A–3(c). The allocation of expenses described above is made according to the ratio between the number of days in the year that the dwelling was actually rented to the number of days that it was actually used for any purpose (including rental of the property); the days in which the unit was neither rented nor used for any other purpose are not taken into account in making this allocation. Prop. Reg. § 1.280A–3(c)(1), (d)(3) and (4), Ex. See also *Bolton v. Commissioner*, 77 T.C. 104 (1981), aff'd, 694 F.2d (9th Cir. 1982). For a discussion of the standards employed in determining whether the rental for a unit was for fair value, see Razavi v. Commissioner, 74 F.3d 125 (6th Cir. 1996).

§ 10.1182.   Limitation on Deductions. In addition to the allocation requirement described in **§ 10.1181**, IRC § 280A will impose additional limitations on deductibility (which are essentially identical to the limitations imposed under IRC § 183 described at **§ 10.1170**) if the taxpayer is deemed to have used the dwelling unit for personal purposes during that taxable year for the *greater* of (a) 14 days; or (b) 10% of the number of days during such taxable year in which the unit was rented at a fair rental. IRC § 280A(c)(5), (d)(1). For the purpose of determining whether (b) applies, any day on which a unit is deemed to have been used by the taxpayer for personal purposes will not constitute a day on which it was rented for fair value. In such cases, the deductions allocated to the fair rental use of the unit (other than non profit-seeking deductions) are deductible only to the extent that the gross income from rental use for that taxable year exceeds the amount of non profit-seeking deductions which are allocable to the period of fair rental use for that year. IRC § 280A(c)(5). The "gross income from rental use" (i.e., the "gross rental income") equals the gross receipts from rentals reduced by the expenses of obtaining tenants such as realtor's fees and advertising expenses. Prop. Reg. § 1.280A–3(d)(2). The reference to non-profit seeking deductions in this text is to deductions (such as mortgage interest on a principal residence and state property taxes) that are deductible regardless of whether connected to an income activity. The amount of deduction that is disallowed by this provision is carried over to the next taxable year of the taxpayer and treated as a deduction in that year, subject to the same limitations. IRC § 280A(c)(5).

The proposed regulations set forth an order for taking three classes of deductions. Prop. Reg. § 1.280A–3(d)(3). The order is described in the **Illustration** at § **10.1182–3.**

§ 10.1182–1. Allocation of Non Profit-Seeking Deductions.

One reason that the amount of non-profit oriented deductions that are allocated to the period of rental use is important is because the profit-seeking deductions allowable for that period cannot exceed the difference between the gross rental income and such non profit-seeking deductions. According to the Tenth and Ninth Circuits and the Tax Court, the amount of non profit-seeking deductions that are allocable to the period of rental use is the fraction of such deductions that reflects the fraction of the entire taxable year that is comprised of days of fair rental use. *McKinney v. Commissioner*, 732 F.2d 414 (10th Cir. 1983); *Bolton v. Commissioner*, *supra*, § **10.1181.** Thus, according to the courts, unlike the allocation of profit related expenses (which allocation, as described in § **10.1181**, is made by comparing the days in which the unit is rented with the days that it is actually used for any purpose), the allocation of non profit-seeking deductions is made by comparing rental days with the total number of days in the taxable year including days in which the unit is neither rented nor otherwise used.

In its proposed regulations, Treasury determined that non profit-seeking deductions are to be allocated to the period of rental use in the same manner that other expenses are allocated—i.e., Treasury would allocate such expenses according to the percentage of days of *use* of the unit that the number of fair rental days constitutes. Prop. Reg. § 1.280A–3(d)(3), (4), Ex. As noted above, in *Bolton* and in *McKinney*, the Tax Court and the Ninth and Tenth Circuits adopted a different formula for that allocation and the courts' formula is more favorable to taxpayers. The Tenth and Ninth Circuits expressly noted the proposed regulation and repudiated it as an invalid interpretation by Treasury. *McKinney v. Commissioner*, *supra*; *Bolton v. Commissioner*, *supra*.

§ 10.1182–2. Exception for Principal Residence. If a taxpayer rents his entire principal residence for an entire taxable year, there will be no limitations on his deductions because of IRC § 280A, but note that IRC § 183 may apply. If a taxpayer rented his principal residence for a 12–month period (or more) that straddled two calendar years, his use of the property as his residence for part of each of those two taxable years could cause IRC § 280A to apply to the deductions available for each year. IRC § 280A(d)(4) provides that the limitation on deductions described in § **10.1182** is not applicable if the taxpayer rents (or holds for rent) the property for a fair rent and for a consecutive period of at least 12 months (or a lesser period if the property is sold or exchanged at the end of the period). In such an event, the taxpayer will not be treated as using the property for personal purposes for those days in the taxable years in which the consecutive period lies that the taxpayer used the property as his principal residence. This exception does not, however, prevent the limitation on deductions caused by the allocation of expenses described at § **10.1181**; it only precludes the application of the limitation of deduction rules [IRC § 280A(c)(5)] that are described at § **10.1182.**

§ 10.1182–3. Illustration. *X* owns a vacation residence in Northern Michigan, and the property is not subject to a mortgage. In Year One, which is not a leap year, *X* and her family (i.e., her husband and children) occupied and used the residence for a total of 90 days; the residence was rented at a fair rental to unrelated parties for a total of 180 days, and the residence was unused and unoccupied for the remaining 95 days of that year. The rent that *X* received for the residence in that year was $2,600, and *X* expended $100 in advertising costs to rent the property. Therefore, the gross rental income that *X* received was $2,500. In that year, *X* incurred and paid a property tax of $1,000 because of her ownership of the residence. The portion of the property tax that is allocable to the rental of the residence qualifies as a nonitemized deduction [IRC § 62(a)(4)]; however, the portion of the property tax that is attributable to the non-rental period is treated as an itemized deduction. In addition, *X* incurred and paid $5,000 of expenses in connection with the residence, and only those expenses that are allocable to the rental period can be deducted (i.e., those expenses can be deducted only to the extent that they can be attributed to a profit-seeking activity). So, only the portion of those expenses that can be allocated to the rental of the residence is deductible, and even then the amount of deduction is limited by the provisions of § 280A. The amount of depreciation deduction allowable for the use of the residence during the rental period is $1,000, but the deductibility of the depreciation allowance also is subject to the limitations of § 280A.

The proposed regulations provide an order of priority for the deduction of the expenses connected to the rental use of the residence. Prop. Reg. § 1.280A–3(d)(3). First, the expenses attributable to that period that are deductible without regard to their connection to a profit-seeking activity (such as mortgage interest and state taxes) are taken into account. Second, the profit-seeking deductions (other than those that cause an adjustment to basis such as depreciation deductions) are taken into account. Lastly, the deductions attributable to the rental use that do cause an adjustment to basis (such as depreciation deductions) are taken into account.

The only expense of X that can be deducted without regard to whether it is connected to a profit-seeking activity is the state property tax. The proposed regulations clearly include property taxes in this category. It is noteworthy, however, that while the property tax is a deductible item regardless of whether it is connected with a rental activity, only that portion of the property tax that is attributable to the rental use of the property is a nonitemized deduction. The question then is how much of the $1,000 property tax is attributable to the rental period. If the allocation described in the proposed regulations is adopted, the allocation is made by comparing the portion of the rental period (180 days) to the portion of the year that the residence is used for any purpose (270 days). On that method of allocation, 180/270 x $1,000 = $667 is allocated to the rental period. However, according to the Tax Court, and to the Ninth and Tenth Circuit Courts of Appeals, the allocation should be made by comparing the number of days of the rental period (180 days) to the total number of days in that year (365 days). On that method of allocation, 180/365 x $1,000 = $493 is allocated to the rental period. We will use the method of allocation that was adopted by the Tax Court and by the two Circuit Courts, and so we will allocate $493 of the property tax to the rental income. That leaves $2,007 of gross rental income that can be offset by the other deductions.

The next item to be deducted is the portion of the $5,000 of expenses that are allocable to the leasing of the residence. In this case, there is no dispute over the correct method of allocation. The number of days of rental use (180) are to be compared to the number of days of total use (270). IRC § 280A(e). So, 180/270 x $5,000 = $3,333 is allocated to the rental use of the property. The $1,667 of those expenses that is disallowed as a deduction because of this allocation is not carried over; it is never deducted. But, even as to the $3,333 that is allocated to the rental period, the amount that can be deducted is limited by IRC § 280A(c)(5) to the amount of gross rental income ($2,500) less the non profit-seeking deductions that are attributable to the rental period ($493), and so only $2,007 of the $3,333 of allocated deduction can be deducted in Year One. The remaining $1,326 of disallowed deduction is carried over to Year Two and deductible then subject to the same limitations. IRC § 280A(c)(5).

Finally, since after taking the allowable deductions described above, there is no more gross rental income left, the $1,000 of depreciation deduction that is allocated to the rental period is not allowed because of the § 280A(c)(5) limitation. The $1,000 of depreciation is carried over to Year Two and can be deducted in that year subject to the same limitations.

§ 10.1183.   Rental for a Brief Period. If a dwelling unit which is deemed to have been used by the taxpayer as a residence in a taxable year is rented for fewer than 15 days of that year, no deductions (other than non profit-seeking deductions) will be allowed for expenses incurred in connection with the rental of that unit, but the rent received by the taxpayer will be excluded from his gross income. IRC § 280A(g).

§ 10.1184.   Coordination with IRC § 183. Although the consequences of IRC § 280A are similar to those imposed by

IRC § 183, the applicability of the two sections turns on quite different standards. While the application of IRC § 183 rests on the profitability of a venture, IRC § 280A turns more upon the number of days in which the taxpayer uses the dwelling unit for personal purposes. However, one of the limitations that IRC § 280A imposes does turn on profitability. IRC § 280A(c)(5). If IRC § 280A is applicable to the rental of a dwelling unit for a taxable year, then IRC § 183 does not apply. See IRC § 280A(f)(3).

§ 10.1185. Temporary Rental of Residence. In adopting the provisions of IRC § 280A that are applicable to a taxpayer's rental of a dwelling unit, Congress apparently was taking aim at the rental of a "vacation home" during all or part of the year that the taxpayer does not use it. However, the actual language of IRC § 280A is broader than that and will apply to a taxpayer who is away from his residence for a part of a taxable year and rents it to another for that period. Thus, if Professor X at Duke University teaches at the University of Virginia for the fall semester as a visiting professor, Professor X will be subject to IRC § 280A if he rents his home in Durham, North Carolina to another for that fall semester.

§ 10.1186. Nonitemized Deductions. Expenses incurred in connection with rental property that are deductible under IRC § 212 are nonitemized deductions. IRC § 62(a)(4). IRC § 280A operates as a limitation on the amount of otherwise allowable deductions that can be taken; it does not change the character of the deductions that are allowed. Consequently, such expenses (to the extent allowed) are not subject to the 2% of AGI floor that applies to miscellaneous itemized deductions.

§ 10.1200. Nonbusiness Expenses. Expenses incurred by an individual taxpayer in connection with a profit-seeking venture which is not a "trade or business" may be deducted. IRC § 212 authorizes a deduction for "ordinary and necessary" expenses paid or incurred: (a) for the production or collection of income; (b) for the management, conservation or maintenance of income-producing property; or (c) in connection with the determination, collection or refund of any tax. Such deductions are sometimes called "nonbusiness expense deductions," and they are to be distinguished from personal expense deductions such as medical expenses. Note, however, that many (but not all) items that are deductible under IRC § 212 will constitute miscellaneous itemized deductions under IRC § 67(b) and so will be subject to the 2% of AGI floor imposed by IRC § 67(a), and will not be deductible at all if the alternative minimum tax is applicable. Such expenses also are subject to the limitation on itemized deductions that is imposed by IRC § 68 when an individual's AGI exceeds a specified amount. See § **3.1000**, *supra*.

§ **10.1210. Compared with "Trade or Business" Expense.** For an expense to be deductible under IRC § 212(1) or IRC § 212(2), it must meet the same requirements that a trade or business expense must meet to qualify under IRC § 162 except that it will not be connected with a "trade or business." Thus, the expense must be "ordinary and necessary" and cannot constitute a capital outlay. For the meaning of "ordinary and necessary" see §§ **10.1500–10.1522.** A deduction for a payment claimed under IRC § 212 will be disallowed if the payment is of a type for which a deduction would be disallowed under IRC § 162(c), (f), or (g) if the deduction were claimed as a business expense (i.e., certain bribes, kickbacks, illegal payments, fines, and treble damages are not deductible). Treas. Reg. § 1.212–1(p).

§ **10.1220. Illustration 1: Expenses of Seeking Alimony.** *W* seeks a divorce and alimony from *H*, and she thereby incurs $2,000 in legal fees. Since alimony is includable in gross income, the expenses of seeking alimony are deductible as an expense for the production of income. Treas. Reg. § 1.262–1(b)(7); see *Hesse v. Commissioner*, 60 T.C. 685 (1973). This deduction will constitute a miscellaneous itemized deduction that is subject to the 2% of AGI floor and to the overall limitation on itemized deductions imposed by IRC § 68. See § **3.1120**, *supra*. However, the portion of *W*'s legal fees incurred in obtaining the divorce is not deductible; only the portion of the fees attributable to establishing her right to alimony and to the collection of the alimony is deductible. If the legal expenses for seeking alimony cannot be separately determined, no deduction is allowed. See Rev. Rul. 72–545; *Munn v. United States*, 455 F.2d 1028 (Ct. Cl. 1972). Note that W's establishment of her right to alimony creates a right to receive income over a period of years, the cost of establishing her right to that income is currently deductible, rather than capitalized. See § **10.1400** *et seq.* for a discussion of the requirement of capitalization.

§ **10.1230. Illustration 2: Expenses Incurred in Seeking Damages.** Since punitive damages are included in the recipient's gross income [see IRC § 104(a)(2)], the expenses incurred in seeking punitive damages, whether or not the TP's suit is successful, are deductible under IRC § 212(1), subject to the 2% of AGI floor and to the overall limitation on itemized deductions imposed by IRC § 68. See § **3.1120**, *supra*. If the TP's tax is determined under the alternative minimum tax system, no deduction is allowable for those expenses. IRC § 56(b)(1)(A). If the compensatory damages would be excludable from the plaintiff's gross income (and that will not always be the case), only the portion of a taxpayer's expenses that are attributable to seeking punitive damages is deductible. The allocation of the taxpayer's expenses may be made by using the proportion of punitive damages obtained by the taxpayer to the total amount of damages awarded to the taxpayer (or obtained by settlement). If a taxpayer loses his suit for damages or if the taxpayer obtains a lump sum settlement without apportionment between compensatory and punitive damages, the portion of the taxpayer's expenses that is attributable to seeking punitive damages is still deductible. Typically, the apportionment of expenses in such cases is made by using the proportion of punitive damages claimed in the taxpayer's complaint to the entire amount claimed in taxpayer's complaint. Rev. Rul. 85–98. Of course, if compensatory damages would be taxable to the plaintiff (as is true, for example, of compensatory damages for defamation), then all of the taxpayer's expenses in seeking damages (compensatory and punitive) are deductible.

§ **10.1231.   Costs Incurred in Discrimination Suits.** The question arose as to the proper treatment of legal fees received under a contingent fee arrangement in suits in which the damages sought were included in the plaintiff's taxable income. The Government contends that the entire amount of the plaintiff's award, including the amount paid to the attorney under the contingent fee arrangement, is taxable to the plaintiff. While the fee paid to the attorney is deductible, it constitutes a miscellaneous itemized deduction, and so is subject to the limitations imposed on those deductions. Much worse, the size of the fees typically was large enough to cause the TP to be taxed on the alternative minimum tax system, and no deduction at all is allowed for miscellaneous itemized deductions under that system. This is a harsh result, and there were even a few cases where a TP who won a sizeable award ended up having a large deficit after paying the attorney fees and the taxes on the entire award. Taxpayers litigated the issue of whether they were taxed on the portion of the award that was payable to the attorney under a contingent fee arrangement, but the Supreme Court held that the entire amount of the award is taxable to the plaintiff, and so resolved the issue for the government (albeit two issues raised in amicus briefs were left open by the Court). *Commissioner v. Banks*, ___ U.S. ___ (2005).While the *Banks* case was still pending in the Supreme Court, Congress addressed part of this problem by amending IRC § 62 to provide that attorney fees and court costs incurred in an action for damages under certain specified statutes involving some type of discrimination are nonitemized deductions. IRC § 62(a)(19). The nonitemized deductions are not subject to any of the limitations imposed on itemized deductions, and so the inclusion of the attorney's fee in income and the allowance of a nonitemized deduction for the fee is a wash. While the amendment covers all attorney fees, whether contingent fees or not, it reaches only fees and costs incurred in discrimination suits, and leaves the problem intact for plaintiffs in other suits. The problem of the treatment and classification of certain deductions is much larger than the discrimination suit problem on which Congress focused exclusively, and some reform is needed. For a discussion of those issues, see Jeffrey H. Kahn, *Beyond the Little Dutch Boy: An Argument for Structural Change in Tax Deduction Classification*, 80 Wash. L. Rev. 1 (2005).

§ 10.1240. Illustration 3: Expenses Incurred in Management of Income–Producing Property. *X* owns a portfolio of common stocks which is managed by a bank. The bank's fees are deductible by *X* (subject to the 2% of AGI floor and to the IRC § 68 overall limitation on itemized deductions) as expenses of managing, conserving or maintaining income-producing property. Similarly, trustee fees and commissions are usually deductible under IRC § 212(2), but also typically are classified as miscellaneous itemized deductions.

§ 10.1250. Expenses Incurred in Reducing Taxpayer's Obligation to Pay Deductible Expenses. When a taxpayer incurs an expense to reduce the extent to which he is obligated to make payments that are deductible in determining taxable income, the expense is incurred to obtain a result that would increase the taxpayer's taxable income. That is, a reduction of the taxpayer's deductions will increase the amount of his taxable income. The question arises as to whether such expenses can be deducted under IRC § 212(1) as expenses incurred for the "production of income." In *Hunter v. United States*, 219 F.2d 69 (2d Cir. 1955), the Second Circuit denied a deduction to a taxpayer for attorney fees incurred in defending against his wife's suit for alimony (the payment of alimony is deductible under IRC § 215). The court held that IRC § 212(1) applies to expenses incurred for the production of *gross* income. It is not sufficient to seek to increase taxable income.

§ 10.1260. Tax–Related Expenses. IRC § 212(3) grants a deduction for expenses incurred in connection with tax counseling or the preparation of a tax return or a claim for a tax refund or redetermination. See **§ 10.1360.** This is a miscellaneous itemized deduction that is subject both to the 2% of AGI floor and to the limitation imposed by IRC § 68. See **§ 3.1120.** However, the cost of having prepared that portion of a tax return that relates to the taxpayer's conduct of a self-employed trade or business is a nonitemized deduction and so is exempt from the limitations and ceiling imposed on certain itemized deductions. Rev. Rul. 92–29. Similarly, the expenses incurred in resolving asserted tax deficiencies relating to the taxpayer's trade or business are nonitemized deductions. Rev. Rul. 92–29.

It appears that the personal or perhaps even the capital nature of a transaction that caused the imposition of a tax will not affect the deductibility of expenses incurred in determining or reporting that tax. See *Sharples v. United States*, 533 F.2d 550 (Ct. Cl. 1976). There is a question whether expenses incurred in obtaining tax advice incident to a decision concerning the acquisition or disposition of an asset are deductible under IRC § 212. Compare *Honodel v. Commissioner*, 722 F.2d 1462 (9th Cir. 1984), aff'g 76 T.C. 351 (1981) (holding such expenses to be nondeductible because they are not "ordinary and necessary") with *Collins v. Commissioner*, 54 T.C. 1656, 1666 (1970), Acq. (allowing a deduction for the cost of tax advice incident to the acquisition of an asset).

§ 10.1300. Personal Expenses. No deduction is permitted for personal, living, or family expenses. IRC § 262.

§ 10.1310. Mixed Purposes. A taxpayer's motives for incurring an expense may be mixed (i.e., he may have both business and personal motives). Generally, the *primary* purpose of the taxpayer is decisive although the issue is not free of doubt. See *Shiosaki v. Commissioner*, 475 F.2d 770 (9th Cir. 1973).

§ 10.1320. Deductibility Determined from the Source of the Obligation or from the Immediate Objective of the Expense. A taxpayer may incur an expense for what appears on its face to be a personal or family purpose, but the taxpayer may contend that his actual purpose was connected with his business or investment activities. If the source of the taxpayer's obligation is personal (such as a marital relationship) no deduction will be allowed.

§ 10.1321. Illustration: Defense of Divorce Suit. *H* was sued for divorce by *W*, and he incurred legal expenses in defending the suit. *H* contended that his purpose in defending the suit was not to bar the divorce but rather to retain his controlling interest in the corporation which employed him. Consequently, *H* claimed his expenses to be deductible under IRC § 212(2) as having been incurred for the conservation of income-producing property. However, the Supreme Court held that the origin and character of a divorce action is personal and family-oriented and accordingly disallowed the claimed deduction. *United States v. Gilmore*, 372 U.S. 39 (1963). It is unsettled whether the portion of *H*'s expenses that is attributable to an effort to retain his ownership of stock is a capital expenditure to be added to *H*'s basis in those stocks. This issue was expressly left open by the Supreme Court's decision in *Gilmore*, but the tenor of that decision suggests that no addition to basis should be allowed. But see *Gilmore v. United States*, 245 F.Supp. 383 (N.D.Cal. 1965) (allowing *H* to increase his basis); *Serianni v. Commissioner*, 80 T.C. 1090 (1983) (allowing *W* to increase her basis in certain stocks by a portion of legal fees incurred in a divorce action to establish her equity interest in those stocks). See **§ 10.1350.**

§ 10.1330. Immediate Objective Controls Characterization. A taxpayer may have a personal immediate objective for incurring an expense, but his desire for that objective may be grounded on business considerations. For example, a taxpayer might contend that his ultimate purpose in defending an action against himself for assault and battery was to protect his job which he would lose if he were unsuccessful in defending the action. The proper test for deductibility is whether the origin of the action for assault and battery was personal, and, if so, no deduction should be allowed the taxpayer regardless of his motives for defending the suit. E.g., *Michaelis v. Commissioner*, 32 AFTR 2d 73–5859 (9th Cir. 1973), aff'g 30 T.C.M. 834 (1971).

Similarly, a taxpayer may incur an expenditure of a capital nature and claim a deduction on the ground that the ultimate purpose of the expenditure was to accomplish a current business objective. In general, taxpayers have been unsuccessful in making that contention, and the courts characterize such expenditures according to the immediate objectives of the taxpayer. In *Woodward v. Commissioner*, 397 U.S. 572 (1970) and *United States v. Hilton Hotels*, 397 U.S. 580 (1970), the Supreme Court held that the payments there in question (appraisal costs to determine the value of stock held by minority shareholders) were nondeductible capital expenditures and that the ultimate purpose of the taxpayer in acquiring the stock of the minority shareholders did not make the expenditures deductible. See *Michaelis v. Commissioner, supra*.

§ 10.1340. The Origin Test. The Supreme Court's adoption in *Gilmore* [**§ 10.1321**] of the "origin" test for determining whether an expense is personal or business-oriented is a reasonable test in certain circumstances. Thus, if *X* negligently operated his automobile and thereby injured *Y*, the deductibility of the damages *X* paid to *Y* will turn upon whether *X* was operating his car for personal purposes or in pursuit of his business. But not all expenses which have a personal origin should be nondeductible. For example, if a divorced wife sues her ex-husband for defaulted alimony, her legal fees are deductible even though the source or origin of her claim is her former marital relationship—that is, the alimony she will collect will be gross income to her and so she should be permitted to deduct the cost of obtaining it. See Treas. Reg. § 1.262–1(b)(7); *Wild v. Commissioner*, 42 T.C. 706 (1964), Acq.; *Hesse v. Commissioner*, 60 T.C. 685 (1973); Acq., aff'd without a written opinion, 511 F.2d 1393 (3d Cir. 1975). See also, *Nickell v. Commissioner*, 831 F.2d 1265 (6th Cir. 1987). Similarly, a plaintiff who obtains damages for libel of his personal reputation will be permitted to deduct his legal fees. See **§ 10.1230**. While the origin of such actions may be personal, the immediate objective of the suit is to obtain gross income for the taxpayer, and so the taxpayer's net income can be properly determined only by reducing the gross income so acquired by the amount expended in obtaining it. Allowing this deduction appears to conform with the congressional purpose for adopting IRC § 212(1).

§ 10.1341. Proper Use of the Origin Test. The proper operation of the origin test has not yet been resolved. The Tax Court has adopted a view of the operation of the origin test that is especially appealing. The Tax Court stated in *Boagni v. Commissioner*, 59 T.C. 708, 713 (1973), Acq.:

> Quite plainly, the "origin-of-the-claim" rule does not contemplate a mechanical search for the first in the chain of events which led to the litigation but, rather, requires an examination of all the facts. The inquiry is directed to the ascertainment of the "kind of transaction" out of which the litigation arose [(citation omitted)]. Consideration must be given to the issues involved, the nature and objective of the litigation, the defenses asserted, the purposes for which the claimed deductions were expended, the background of the litigation, and all facts pertinent to the controversy.

The above statement has been quoted with approval in several subsequent Tax Court decisions. E.g., *Mosby v. Commissioner*, 86 T.C. 190 (1986); *Lucas v. Commissioner*, 79 T.C. 1 (1982); *Duntley v. Commissioner*, 54 T.C.M (CCH) 1138 (1987); *Colvin v. Commissioner*, RIA TC Memo ¶ 2004–67 (2004).

The Tax Court's articulation of the origin test was criticized and rejected by the Ninth and Tenth Circuits. *Keller Street Development Co. v. Commissioner*, 688 F.2d 675 (9th Cir. 1982); *Dye v. United States*, 121 F.3d 1399 (10th Cir. 1997). The Ninth Circuit in *Keller Street* stated that the *Boagni* description of the origin test was actually a description of the "primary purpose of the litigation" test, which the Ninth Circuit noted had been rejected by the Supreme Court. In *Keller Street*, the Ninth Circuit held that the proper application of the origin test is a two-step process: first, the transaction from which the taxable event proximately resulted must be identified (e.g., the event that prompted the cause of action and was the basis of the suit), second, characterize the transaction that was identified in the first step. See *Dye v. United States*, *supra*; and *Glassman v. Commissioner*, 74 T.C.M. (CCH) 1106 (1997).

The author has the following suggestions as to how the rule should operate.

§ 10.1341–1. Business Deductions. It is proper to use the origin test to determine whether an expenditure or loss qualifies as a business expense or business loss. A business expense deduction (or business loss deduction) should not be allowed for an expenditure unless the transaction in question has business origins or is attributable to a previous change of purpose from a personal to a business activity (such as a permanent conversion of a personal residence to rental property). Even in respect to business expenses, the origin test is not always useful. For example, when *H* and *W* are seeking a divorce, and *W* telephones business clients of *H* and makes defamatory statements concerning *H*'s professional skills, the expenses that *H* incurs in obtaining an injunction prohibiting *W* from contacting *H*'s clients should be deductible notwithstanding the fact that the origin of the problem is the marriage of *H* and *W*. It is necessary to determine whether the expense is more closely related to *H*'s business than it is to his personal life since the expense relates to both parts of *H*'s life.

§ 10.1341–2. Nonbusiness Deductions. Despite the fact that the *Gilmore* case itself [**§ 10.1321**] involved a question of the availability of IRC § 212, the origin test is less helpful in distinguishing a personal expenditure from a nonbusiness expense deduction item under IRC § 212 and in distinguishing business and nonbusiness deduction items from a capital expenditure. The test for determining whether IRC § 212 applies should rest more on the character of the expenditure than on its origin. The character of an expenditure rests on a number of surrounding factors of which the origin is merely one. If the expenditure is directly related to the production of gross income, a deduction should be allowed regardless of the origin of the taxpayer's claim to that income item. The nexus between the expenditure and the collection of the income typically will be so immediate that there will be little or no uncertainty as to whether the expenditure is more closely attributable to the income production than to the activity from which the income claim was derived. Thus, a spouse's expenses to collect alimony are deductible. On the other hand, if an expenditure which has personal origins also relates to the conservation of income-producing property, it usually will be difficult to determine whether the expenditure should be treated as part of the cost of the personal activity or whether it is more closely attributable to the cost of retaining the income-producing property. The test for deductibility of such items could be made to turn on the primary

purpose of the taxpayer in making the expenditure as
determined subjectively for each taxpayer. The administrative difficulty of applying a subjective test is so great that
the Supreme Court rejected the primary purpose test and
instead adopted the origin test.

§ 10.1341–3. Summary. In summary, the origin test
may be useful in determining whether an expenditure
qualifies as a business expense or as an expense of maintaining or conserving income-producing property, but it is
not useful in determining whether an expenditure qualifies
as one for the production of income. An expenditure to
produce income bears such a proximate relationship to the
income that there is not the uncertainty of purpose that
exists for expenditures which satisfy personal goals.

§ 10.1341–4. Capital Expenditures. Courts have applied the origin test to determine whether an expenditure
is to be treated as capital or ordinary. E.g., *Anchor Cou-
pling Co. v. United States*, 427 F.2d 429 (7th Cir. 1970);
Entwicklungs und Finanzierungs A.G. v. Commissioner, 68
T.C. 749 (1977). The authors doubt that the distant origin
of an activity is the most appropriate determinant of
whether an expenditure is a capital item. Instead, the
inquiry might better focus on a number of considerations
such as the immediate objective of the expenditure (as
determined from objective facts rather than from the view
of the subjective goal of the taxpayer) and the character of
the transaction. The origin of a transaction is an important
input in determining the nature of the expenditure, but it
ought not be the exclusive criterion. The origin test can
work perfectly well to differentiate capital expenditures
provided that a related group of transactions can be separated so that the origin of each separate transaction is used
to characterize the events. This separation of related transactions is difficult to do, and the courts have often failed to
do so properly. Because of the difficulty of applying the
origin test alone, the author believes that several criteria,
such as the immediate objective and character of the expenditure, should be employed together with a consideration of
the origin of the activity. These several criteria should
merely be factors to help the court reach the ultimate issue
of whether an expenditure is more closely related to a

capital transaction or to an ordinary business or profit-seeking transaction.

§ 10.1341–5. Illustration 1: Expense Arising from Acquisition of a Capital Asset.

X was engaged in a manufacturing business. X sought to acquire a trademark from Y to use in X's business. The cost of acquiring the trademark is a capital expenditure. In bidding for the trademark, X made derogatory comments about Z, a competitor of X, who also was bidding to acquire the trademark. Z learned of the comments made by X, and Z sued X for defamation. X settled the suit by paying Z $100,000 damages. Was the origin of X's expenditure the capital acquisition of a trademark or was the origin the conduct of X's business? The origin test, in and of itself, provides little guidance. Perhaps a better way to frame the question is whether the acquisition of capital assets is an integral part of X's business so that expenses incurred while so engaged are business expenses unless they have a closer nexus to the immediate acquisition of the asset than they do to X's general business activity. In the authors' view, this type of expenditure should be allowed as a business expense.

§ 10.1341–6. Illustration 2: Expense Arising from Acquisition of a Capital Asset.

The same facts apply as in § 10.1341–5 except that X succeeded in purchasing the trademark from Y. Y subsequently filed suit against X for having made misrepresentations. X paid Y $10,000 damages to settle the suit. X was certain that he would prevail in the suit, but he settled in order to terminate the adverse publicity that the suit had generated. The origin test has been employed in similar cases to characterize X's payment as a capital expenditure. But, is the origin of X's payment his fear of adverse publicity or the representations that he made to induce Y to sell? The courts have resolved that question by focusing on the origin of Y's suit rather than on the origin of X's payment. In effect, the courts look to the immediate objective of the payment—to settle the suit brought by Y—and they will not look at X's subjective motives for settling the dispute. See Rev. Rul. 73–146, and TAM 200126008.

§ 10.1341–7. Illustration 3: Mixed Business and Personal Objectives.

Prior to completing his medical school

education, *W* executed an agreement with the Navy under
which he received a Naval reserve commission and a defer-
ment from active duty until completion of residency training in his specialty. Upon completing his residency, *W*
sought administrative and judicial relief from the order to
report to active duty, but the effort was unsuccessful. *W*
incurred $1,000 in legal fees in his attempt to avoid active
duty. While *W* could have earned more income from the
private practice of medicine than from serving on active
duty in the Navy, the desire to avoid Navy duty rests at
least as much on personal considerations as on financial
ones. The personal considerations are so integral to *W*'s
decision that they cannot readily be separated from *W*s
financial concerns (indeed it is likely that the personal
considerations are dominant). The analysis of the nature of
the transaction should be made from the objective facts and
should not be based on a subjective evaluation of *W*'s actual
thought process. No deduction should be allowed. On similar facts, the Tax Court utilized the origin test and held
that the origin of *W*'s expenditure was to obtain a deferral
from active duty, which is a personal matter, and so the
Court denied *W*'s claim for a deduction. *West v. Commissioner*, 71 T.C. 532 (1979).

**§ 10.1341–8. Illustration 4: Distinguishing Purposes
of Closely Held Corporation from Purposes of Its
Shareholder.** *W* sued *H* for divorce and *W* named as
additional defendants three corporations whose stock was
either owned by *H* or by a corporation owned by him. *W*
sought to restrain the business activities of the corporations and to gain control of them. The defendants successfully resisted *W*'s action, and they incurred legal fees and
expenses of approximately $1,300,000. On its motion, the
divorce court ordered that the legal fees and expenses be
incurred one-fourth by each defendant. The Commissioner
denied a deduction to the corporations for their payment of
their share of the fees and expenses. In *Dolese v. United
States*, 605 F.2d 1146 (10th Cir. 1979), the Tenth Circuit
allowed the corporations a deduction only for that part of
their fees and expenses that was attributable to freeing the
corporations from the restraint on conducting their business activities and for that part of their fees and expenses
that was incurred in resisting *W*'s effort to take over

control of the corporations since the takeover could be injurious to the well-being of the corporations. The balance of the fees and expenses paid by the corporations were not only nondeductible; they also were treated as a constructive dividend to H and taxable to him.

§ 10.1341–9. Illustration 5: Difficulty of Identifying Origin. H and W owned all of the stock of the X Corporation, and H served as its president. H loaned a car belonging to the corporation to his son, S, and S negligently injured B, an unrelated party, in an automobile accident. B sued H, W, S, and X for more than $4,000,000. As a consequence of B's filing suit, the bank froze X's credit line and demanded security for an outstanding note, and X suffered other financial threats. X settled the suit with B by having X's insurer pay B over $100,000, and X paid B over $50,000 from funds X borrowed from its bank. X's counsel advised X that if the suit went to trial, the company likely would be found liable for having negligently allowed S to use the car. In a divided decision of the Fourth Circuit in *Kopp's Co. v. United States*, 636 F.2d 59 (4th Cir. 1980), the majority of the court held that the settlement payments and legal fees paid by X are deductible business expenses. In dissenting, Judge Ervin stressed that the origin of the suit was H's loan of the company car to S, which was a personal (i.e., nonbusiness) transaction. Judge Ervin did not believe that the corporation was liable for damages and he felt that even if X were so liable and had business reasons to settle the suit, the personal origin of the suit prevents the corporation from qualifying for a deduction.

§ 10.1341–10. Illustration 6: Multiple Disputes. A, who was in the business of mining coal, mined and removed coal from two tracts of land owned by F. After several years, F brought suit against A. F claimed in his complaint that A had not paid F royalties that were due for coal taken from one of the tracts pursuant to a lease between the parties. F requested a judgment for the unpaid royalties. F also claimed that there was no lease between the parties for mining the second tract, and so A was a trespasser as to its mining operations on that tract. F sought compensatory and punitive damages for the trespass and taking of coal from the second tract. A raised several defenses in his answer, one of which was that the parties had made a valid oral lease which permitted *A* to mine the second tract. The parties arrived at an out-of-court settlement of their dispute. *A* sought to deduct the legal fees that he incurred in that litigation. In a somewhat similar case, the Tax Court held that the origin of *F*'s suit against *A* was partly a claim for royalties under a lease and partly a claim for trespass, and that *A*'s defense was partly to resist the claim for royalties and partly to defend his title to the oral leasehold of the second tract. The portion of the fee for resisting the royalty claim is deductible as a business expense, and the portion allocable to defending *A*'s title to the leasehold is a nondeductible capital expenditure. See §§ **10.1460–10.1461.** The court allocated the fee on a 50%–50% basis between those two disputes. *Frazee McCall Joint Venture v. Commissioner*, 60 T.C.M. 1466 (1990).

§ **10.1342. Misuse of the Origin Test.** Whatever may be the merits of the origin test, it has confused some courts and led them into making extraordinary decisions. For example, in *Brown v. United States*, 526 F.2d 135 (6th Cir. 1975), the taxpayer, her sister and her brother were shareholders of a corporation. The brother offered to purchase the stock of the taxpayer and her sister. The taxpayer became suspicious over the terms of the offer—particularly as mention was made of another corporation (wholly owned by the brother) which did business with the family corporation. The taxpayer and her sister consulted an attorney who, after an investigation, informed them that the brother's corporation had acquired the most valuable assets and operations of the family corporation in transactions which constituted a fraud upon the taxpayer and her sister as shareholders of the family corporation. The brother refused to divulge any information about his wholly owned corporation, and so the taxpayer and her sister brought a shareholder derivative suit. This suit was settled favorably for the taxpayer and her sister who thereby exchanged their stock holdings for debentures of the family corporation at a value 80% greater than the offer made for their stock by the brother. In addition, the settlement increased the taxpayer's annual income from the family corporation eightfold and guaranteed the taxpayer and her sister seats on the board of directors. The taxpayer sought to deduct her legal fees. The Sixth Circuit reversed a district court judgment allowing the deduction. The Sixth Circuit held that the origin of the taxpayer's suit was to determine the value of her stock so that she could properly respond to her brother's offer and so no deduction is allowable for the legal fees, which were capital expenditures. For another peculiar application of the origin test, see the divided decision of the Seventh Circuit in *Fischer v. United States*, 490 F.2d 218 (7th Cir. 1973).

§ 10.1350. Capital Expenditures in Defending a Divorce Action.

In several cases subsequent to the Supreme Court's decision in *Gilmore* [§ **10.1321**], expenses for seeking or defending a divorce action were treated as capital expenditures and were added to the taxpayer's basis in the property he wished to protect or obtain. *Gilmore v. United States*, 245 F.Supp. 383 (N.D.Cal. 1965). See also *George v. United States*, 434 F.2d 1336 (Ct. Cl. 1970). Those cases appear to be inconsistent with the Supreme Court's decision in *Gilmore*, but the issue is unsettled.

§ 10.1360. Tax Advice Incident to a Divorce.

The United States Court of Appeals for the Federal Circuit (as the successor to the Court of Claims) has consistently held that the expenses of obtaining tax advice incident to a divorce proceeding are deductible under IRC § 212(3) [*George v. United States*, § **10.1350**, *supra*; *Munn v. United States*, 455 F.2d 1028 (Ct. Cl. 1972)], and the Commissioner conceded this issue in Rev. Rul. 72–545, provided that a reasonable basis exists for determining the amount of taxpayer's legal fee that is allocable to tax advice. A contrary view was suggested by the opinions of three dissenting judges and two concurring judges in the Tax Court's decision in *Merians v. Commissioner*, 60 T.C. 187 (1973), Acq., where those five judges stated that a fee for tax advice in connection with estate planning is not deductible under IRC § 212(3), albeit the fee *might* be deductible in certain cases under IRC § 212(2) as a conservation of income-producing property. Those opinions imply that the deductibility of the cost of tax advice depends upon the underlying transaction to which the tax advice relates. The Commissioner conceded by stipulation in *Merians* that such fees are deductible under IRC § 212(3). The majority of the Tax Court accepted that stipulation and therefore did not discuss the wisdom of the Commissioner's concession. The comments of the five concurring and dissenting judges on this issue were largely dictum and were not adopted in the majority's opinion. Subsequent court decisions also have not adopted the dictum of the five concurring and dissenting judges. For example, in a subsequent decision, the Tax

Court allowed a deduction for the portion of the legal fees incurred in a divorce proceeding that is allocable to tax advice. *Goldaper v. Commissioner*, 36 T.C.M. 1381 (1977). In *Goldaper*, the Service did not contest the deductibility of such fees but contended that no part of the lawyer's services was allocable to tax advice. The Court allocated a portion of the fee to tax advice and allowed a deduction.

§ 10.1370. Conversion of Residence. When a taxpayer moves out of his personal residence and converts it to an income-seeking activity, he can thereafter deduct the costs of maintaining and repairing the property as well as a depreciation allowance. Treas. Regs. §§ 1.212–1(h) and 1.167(g)–1. In the taxable year in which the taxpayer moved out, the amount of such deductions may be subject to the limitations imposed by IRC § 280A. See § **10.1180.**

The question arises as to what action of a taxpayer is sufficient to constitute a conversion to an income-producing activity. Merely attempting to sell an unwanted prior residence will not usually qualify as a conversion to an income-producing activity. Actually renting the property usually will suffice. E.g., *Bolaris v. Commissioner*, 776 F.2d 1428 (9th Cir. 1985). However, a temporary renting of a former residence whole trying to sell the property likely will not be sufficient to constitute a conversion; the rental activity is merely an effort to reduce costs while endeavoring to sell the property. *Saunders v. Commissioner*, RIA Memo TC ¶ 2002–143 (2002). Regardless of whether actually rented, a bona fide offering of a former residence for rent (or offering it for rent or sale at the option of the tenant/purchaser) typically will be sufficient to constitute a conversion. See *Robinson v. Commissioner*, 2 T.C. 305 (1943). Note, however, that a mere offering to rent will not be a sufficient conversion to permit the taxpayer to deduct a loss recognized on the subsequent sale of the property even though it is a sufficient conversion for purposes of allowing the deduction of maintenance costs and depreciation. See § **7.7000.**

When the former residence is offered only for sale by the taxpayer (and not for rent), a deduction will not be permitted for maintenance costs in most cases; but in certain circumstances, a deduction will be allowed. See *Smith v. Commissioner*, 26 T.C.M. (CCH) 149 (1967), aff'd per curiam, 397 F.2d 804 (9th Cir. 1968); and *Lowry v. United States*, 384 F.Supp. 257 (D.N.H. 1974). In *Smith*, the Tax Court suggested that merely holding for sale is sufficient to effect a conversion, but later cases repudiated that view. In *Newcombe v. Commissioner*, 54 T.C. 1298 (1970), the Tax Court reconsidered this issue in a case where, immediately after moving out, the taxpayer had offered a former residence for sale at a price in excess of its then market value but not in excess of the taxpayer's basis in the property. The court disallowed the taxpayer's claim for a deduction for maintenance costs and depreciation; the case was reviewed by the entire court and there were no dissents. The majority opinion held that a number of factors must be examined to determine whether a formerly occupied residence has been converted into "property held for the production of income." If the residence is offered for sale only (and not for rent), it will be treated as converted if the taxpayer can show that he intended to hold the property until he could sell it for more than its basis and for more than its value at the date of "conversion" (post-conversion appreciation). If the property is offered for sale (even at a price in excess of its then value) immediately or shortly after the taxpayer moved out, that will ordinarily be strong evidence that he is not holding it for post-conversion appreciation. The larger asking price could merely be a bargaining ploy. The critical issue is the purpose or intention of the taxpayer.

In *Newcombe*, the majority found that the taxpayer did not in fact hold the property for post-conversion appreciation. While the court noted that its decision in *Smith v. Commissioner, supra* had reached a contrary result, it disapproved of that earlier decision and stated that the *Smith* case had "little precedential value."

Seven Tax Court judges in *Newcombe* concurred with the result reached by the majority opinion. The seven concurring judges stated, however, that property need only be held for post-conversion appreciation to qualify as property held for the production of income; they disagreed with the statement in the majority opinion that the property must also be held for sale at a price in excess of the taxpayer's basis.

"Whether an individual holds property for the production of income is a question of fact, and depends on the purpose or intention of the individual, as gleaned from all of the facts and circumstances of the particular case." *Grant v. Commissioner*, 84 T.C. 809, 825 (1985). In *Newcombe*, the court listed five factors to be considered in making that determination, and those five factors have been adopted in subsequent Tax Court cases. E.g., *Saunders v. Commissioner*, supra; The five factors are:

(1) the length of time the house was occupied by the TP as a residence

(2) whether the TP permanently abandoned personal use of the house

(3) the character of the property (recreational or otherwise)

(4) whether the house was offered for rent

(5) whether it was offered for sale.

Newcombe has been cited with approval in subsequent cases. E.g., *Quinn v. Commissioner*, 65 T.C. 523 (1975).

The question of whether a personal residence has been converted arises where the property was previously used by the taxpayer as a residence. If the taxpayer seeks to sell an inherited or purchased residence that was not so used by the taxpayer, there is no question of a conversion; and maintenance expenses and depreciation deductions will be allowed. E.g., *Mitchell v. Commissioner*, 47 T.C. 120 (1966).

§ 10.1380. Statutory Restrictions. IRC § 274 prohibits a deduction for certain entertainment and travel expenses which otherwise might be deductible as business expenses or as nonbusiness expenses under IRC § 212. Some expenses are disallowed only if the taxpayer fails to comply with a requirement of substantiation [IRC § 274(d)] but some are disallowed regardless of substantiation—for example, the cost of attending a convention or seminar that is held on a cruise ship is nondeductible under IRC § 274(h)(2) unless certain special requirements are satisfied. Typically, no deduction will be allowed for an expense for a facility (such as a yacht, hunting lodge, swimming pool, or tennis court) which is used in conjunction with an activity of a type that is generally associated with an entertainment, amusement or recreational activity. IRC § 274(a)(1). No deduction will be allowed for dues paid or incurred for membership in a club organized for business, pleasure, recreation or other social purpose. IRC § 274(a)(3).

§ 10.1390. 50 Percent Limitation on Deduction of Entertainment and Meal Expenses. Subject to limited exceptions listed in IRC § 274(n)(2), because of IRC § 274(n)(1), a taxpayer can deduct only 50% of his unreimbursed entertainment and meal expenses that are otherwise deductible. A more liberal deduction allowance is provided for meals purchased by employees in certain transportation industries. IRC § 274(n)(3).

§ 10.1391. Illustration. *D* conducts seminars for a fee. The price for each attendee includes food and beverages provided at the seminar. *F* who attends a seminar for business purposes is entitled to deduct the fee that he paid to *D*, other than any reduction of that deduction required by IRC § 274(n). The expenses that *D* incurred in presenting the seminar, including the expenses incurred in providing food and beverages, are deductible business expenses. The reduction imposed by IRC § 274(n)(1) does not apply to *D* because he is selling the food and beverages for full consideration in money or money's worth. IRC § 274(e)(8), (n)(2)(A). However, *F* will have to determine the amount of the fee he paid that is attributable to food and beverages, and *F* can deduct only 50% of that amount. It would be helpful to the attendees' determination of their deduction if *D* would provide a statement of the amount of the fee that is attributable to food and beverages, but such an allocation is not binding on the government, nor is it required. See PLR 9029015. If *F* were an employee who was reimbursed by his employer for the fee he paid to *D*, the entire amount would be deductible by *F* [and thus would wash out the income that *F* recognized because of the reimbursement], but the employer could not deduct 50% of the amount of the reimbursement that is attributable to the payment for food and beverages.

§ 10.1390A. Limitation on Deduction for Executive Compensation. There is a ceiling on the amount of deduction that is allowable for compensation paid or incurred to certain executive employees of a publicly held corporation. For this purpose, a "publicly held corporation" is a corporation issuing a class of common equity securities that is required to be registered under Section 12 of the Securities Exchange Act of 1934. IRC § 162(m)(2). The maximum amount of deduction allowable for compensation to a covered employee is $1,000,000. IRC § 162(m)(1). A covered employee is: the chief executive officer of a publicly held corporation (or a person acting in that capacity), or an employee whose compensation for that year must be reported under the Securities Exchange Act to the corporation's shareholders because the employee is one of the publicly held corporation's four highest compensated officers (other than the chief executive) for that year. IRC § 162(m)(3). The $1,000,000 ceiling applies to the deduction for all remuneration provided to a covered employee except that certain designated types of compensation are excluded and so are not subject to the $1,000,000 ceiling. For purposes of applying the $1,000,000 limitation, the following items are not treated as compensation of the covered employee [IRC § 162(m)(4)]:

(1) commissions payable solely because of income generated by the covered employee;

(2) remuneration received because of the attainment of one or more performance goals if certain outside director and share-holder approval requirements are satisfied;

(3) payments made to a tax qualified retirement plan;

(4) amounts that are excluded from the covered employee's gross income (such as excludable fringe benefits and employer-provided medical insurance coverage); and

(5) remuneration paid pursuant to certain binding contracts that were in effect on February 17, 1993.

The deduction for an employer's expenses in entertaining certain individuals (generally, officers, directors and owners) is limited to the amount that such persons include in their income. IRC § 274(e)(2).

§ 10.1400. Capital Expenditures. A capital expenditure cannot be deducted in the year in which it is paid or accrued. Instead, it must be capitalized. One of the goals of the income tax system is to match expenditures with the income that they produce. When an expenditure produces an income stream that will be received over a period of years, a current deduction of that expenditure would provide a distorted picture of the income actually earned each year. That is, the income reported in the year of the expenditure would be too low, and the income reported in the years in which the income stream is received would be too high. If, instead, the expenditure is capitalized and then amortized over the period in which the income stream is received, there would be a closer matching of income and expenses and a more accurate portrayal of the TP's yearly income.

However, matching of income and expenses is only one of the goals of the tax system. When that goal comes into conflict with others, a decision must be made as to which will take priority. It is for that reason that not all expenditures that produce a future income stream are capitalized. A principal reason for not capitalizing a particular expenditure is that it would impose a greater administrative burden then the benefit of matching would provide. It is essentially a cost-benefit analysis. As Judge Posner stated, "If one really takes serious-ly the concept of a capital expenditure as anything that yields income, actual or imputed, beyond the period (conventionally one year) in which the expenditure is made, the result will be to force the capitalization of virtually every business expense. It is a result courts naturally shy away from. The administrative costs of conceptual rigor are too great." *Encyclopaedia Brittanica, Inc. v. Commissioner*, 685 F.2d 212 (7th Cir. 1982). The determination of which expendi-tures are capitalized and which are currently deductible can be difficult to make and therefore has led to a significant amount of litigation, the holdings of which cannot always be reconciled.

The difference in consequence between an expense and a capital expenditure is the timing of the recovery of the taxpayer's cost. An expense is deducted in the year paid or accrued. A capital expendi-ture (if deductible at all) must be amortized over a period of time; if not amortizable, it is taken into account upon the disposition of the asset or the dissolution of the enterprise. See *FMR Corp. v. Commis-sioner*, 110 T.C. 402 (1998).

Generally, a current deduction is not allowed for an amount spent for the acquisition, creation, or improvement of an asset which will be used or enjoyed by the taxpayer over a period of more than 12 months. IRC §§ 161, 263. But see § **10.1410.** Typically, if the useful life of a business item is 12 months or less, the cost is deducted currently even when the item will be used in two taxable years. Rev. Ruls. 69–560 and 73–357.

In a 1971 decision, the Supreme Court appeared to have suggested that an expenditure was not a capital expenditure unless it created or enhanced a separate and distinct asset. *Commissioner v. Lincoln Savings & Loan Ass'n*, 403 U.S. 345 (1971). The Supreme Court subsequently repudiated that suggestion in *Indopco, Inc. v. Commis-sioner*, 503 U.S. 79 (1992). *Indopco* involved the question of the deductibility of expenses incurred in connection with a friendly corporate acquisition. The expenses in question were the fees paid to an investment banking company to determine the value of a corpo-rate target's stock and the fees paid to a law firm to conduct the acquisition and to obtain favorable tax treatment for the target's shareholders. The taxpayers contended that the fees were deductible business expenses rather than nondeductible capital expenditures. The Supreme Court held that the expenses were capital expenditures and therefore were not deductible.

The Supreme Court held that *Lincoln Savings* holds only that expenditures that serve to create or enhance a separate and distinct asset should be capitalized; it does not stand for the view that expenditures that do not create or enhance a separate asset cannot be capital expenditures. In other words, the creation or enhancement of a separate and distinct asset is a "sufficient but not a necessary condition to classification as a capital expenditure." The courts have not established standards for determining whether a separate and distinct asset has been created. *FMR Corp. and Subsidiaries v. Commissioner*, 110 T.C. 402 (1998).

In *PNC Bancorp. v. Commissioner*, 110 T.C. 349 (1998), rev'd, 212 F.3d 822 (3d Cir. 2000), the Tax Court held that a bank's loan origination fees must be capitalized and amortized because each loan that was consummated was a separate and distinct asset. The principal business of the banks was to accept deposits and to make loans. The "loan origination fees" for which the court denied a deduction included amounts paid to third parties for appraisals and reports on property offered as security for a proposed loan, credit reports on the borrower, salaries and fringe benefits paid to the bank's employees for evaluating the borrower's financial status, evaluating collateral and other security arrangements, negotiating the terms of a loan, processing loan documents, and closing the loan transaction. In the view of the Tax Court, the recurring nature of those expenses did not save them from capital expenditure characterization because the court deemed each loan to be a separate and distinct asset that was created by those expenses.

The Third Circuit reversed the Tax Court and authorized the bank to deduct currently the loan origination fees. *PNC Bancorp. v. Commissioner*, 212 F.3d 822 (3d Cir. 2000). The court held that while the fees were associated with a capital asset, they did not create that asset. Mere association of an expenditure with an asset is not a reason to require capitalization of the expenditure. In reaching its decision, the court appeared to have been influenced by the "recurring, routine, day-to-day" nature of the expenses in question. See *Encyclopedia Britannica, Inc. v. Commissioner*, supra, where the court stated, "The distinction between recurring and nonrecurring business expenses provides a very crude but perhaps serviceable demarcation between those capital expenditures that can feasibly be capitalized and those that can not be."

The Eighth Circuit's decision in *Wells Fargo & Co. v. Commissioner*, 224 F.3d 874 (8th Cir. 2000), may point the way to a proper application of the capitalization doctrine and may explain the result reached by the Third Circuit in the *PNC Bancorp* case. *Wells Fargo* dealt with the question of whether a portion of salaries paid to regular officers of the corporate TP should be capitalized because that portion of their salary is allocable to services the officers provided in exploring and negotiating a friendly consolidation with another corporation. The Tax Court had held that a portion of the officers' salaries had to be capitalized. The Eighth Circuit reversed the Tax Court and held that they were currently deductible. The court noted that the officers were regularly employed by the corporation and were not employed for the purpose of assisting with the proposed consolidation. There is a suggestion in the opinion that if the officers had been hired to work on the consolidation or if their compensation had been raised because of their work on the consolidation, their salaries (or the additional compensation they received) might then have had to be capitalized. The court stated, "payments made by an employer are deductible when they are made to employees, are compensatory in nature, and are directly related to the employment relationship (and only indirectly related to the capital transaction, which provides the long-term benefit." Referring to the "origin of the claim" doctrine, the court held that the origin of the expenditure was the regular employment of the officers; and their assignment to the consolidation issue was incidental to their work.)

If on every occasion in which an employee, whose normal work does not require capitalization of his salary, engages in a task that will produce a long-term benefit to the employer, a portion of the employee's salary would have to be allocated to that task and capitalized, that would impose a significant administrative burden on the employer and on the IRS. In that case, the benefit of better matching of income and expenses may not be sufficient to justify imposing that burden. On the other hand, if an employee spends all of his working time on a project that leads to the creation of an item, and if the period during which his time is spent on that project is significant, it would not be that difficult to determine how much of his salary is allocable to the item. Similarly, if an employee's salary is raised when he begins working on a project and is reduced when he completes the project, it is reasonable to conclude that the additional salary is payment for working on that special project, and therefore to allocate that amount of his salary to that project and to capitalize that amount if the project produces an identifiable income stream over a period of time.

In IRC § 263A, Congress has imposed the burden of allocation of costs for producing or purchasing certain specified properties. There is reason to question whether it would be appropriate to extend that allocation burden to properties not listed in that statute.

The Supreme Court noted in *Indopco* that the distinction between a current expense and a capital expenditure is one of degree and not of kind. The test is whether the expenditure will produce substantial benefits into the future. The Court conceded that not all future benefits (i.e., benefits that extend beyond the taxable year in which the expenditure occurred) are of sufficient significance to warrant capital expenditure treatment. The mere presence of an incidental future benefit will not be enough. It is necessary to weigh both the extent of the benefit and the length of time in the future that it will continue. This weighing process rests on a judgment that cannot be reduced to a quantifiable standard. See also, *FMR Corp. and Subsidiaries v. Commissioner*, 110 T.C. 402 (1998).

The Service has repeatedly suggested (e.g., Notice 96–7) that the *Indopco* decision does not change the tax rules relating to capitalization of expenses and merely eliminates the confusion that temporarily existed because of language in the *Lincoln Savings* decision. However, *Indopco* has placed a gloss on the capital expenditure issue that has tilted the decisions on that issue away from expense treatment. See e.g., *FMR Corp. and Subsidiaries v. Commissioner*, *supra*.

Subsequent to the *Indopco* decision, there have been numerous examples of a current deduction's being allowed for an expenditure that creates benefits that will be enjoyed in the future. For example, the expenses of so-called institutional advertising generally are deductible. Treas. Reg. § 1.162–20(a)(2) provides that the cost of institutional or goodwill advertising that keeps the taxpayer's name before the public generally is deductible. See *RJR Nabisco Inc. and Consolidated Subsidiaries v. Commissioner*, RIA Memo TC ¶ 98, 252 (1998). In Rev. Rul. 92–80, the Commissioner held that the *Indopco* decision did not affect the deductibility of advertising costs, which continue to be currently deductible. However, in the *RJR Nabisco* case, the Commissioner contended that while the expenses of executing an advertising campaign are currently deductible, the expenses of creating or developing an advertising campaign must be segregated and capitalized. The Tax Court held that no distinction was proper and that all advertising expenses are currently deductible so long as the benefits resulting from the advertising campaign "are among the traditional benefits associated with ordinary business advertising." Id.

In holding that *Indopco* did not change the rule that incidental repairs of business assets are deductible expenses "even though they may have some future benefit," the Commissioner stated in Rev. Rul. 94–12 as follows:

The *Indopco* decision clarifies that the creation or enhancement of a separate and distinct asset is not a prerequisite to capitalization. That clarification does not, however, change the fundamental legal principles for determining whether a particular expenditure can be deducted or must be capitalized. With respect to expenditures that produce benefits both in the current year and in future years, the determination of whether such expenditures must be capitalized requires a careful examination of all the facts.

In Rev. Rul. 94–77, the Commissioner allowed a deduction for severance pay made to employees in connection with a business downsizing even though that may produce future benefits through lower operating costs. In Rev. Rul. 96–62, the Commissioner confirmed that *Indopco* has no effect on the deductibility of the cost of training new employees, and that such expenses generally are deductible.

§ 10.1410.   Small Cost Exception.

If the cost of an item which will be used in a trade or business for more than 12 months is too small to warrant amortizing it over a period of years, it may be deducted currently. See Treas. Reg. § 1.162–12(a) permitting a current deduction for the cost of inexpensive ordinary farm tools such as shovels and rakes. In *Sharon v. Commissioner*, 66 T.C. 515 (1976), aff'd, 591 F.2d 1273 (9th Cir. 1978), the Tax Court held that a $25 fee paid for a license to practice law in New York could have been deducted currently because of the small size of the fee, but a fee in the hundreds of dollars paid by the taxpayer for a California license was sufficiently large to require amortization. See also *Kohen v. Commissioner*, 44 T.C.M. 1518 (1982), allowing a current deduction for a $90 bar application fee even though it was a capital expenditure.

§ 10.1420.   Allocation to Year of Use.

Capital expenditures are not "ordinary" expenses under IRC § 162, and so cannot be deducted under that section. Also, IRC § 263 expressly denies a deduction for such expenditures. If the benefits of the expenditure will not last indefinitely (or if a statute expressly provides for amortization), the portion of a capital expenditure which is allocable to the years of use may be deductible in those years under rules of amortization or depreciation discussed later in this work. See Chapters Eleven and Twelve.

§ 10.1421.   Illustration 1: Purchase of Tangible Property.

X paid $50,000 to purchase a machine which he expects to use in his business for ten years. The purchase price is a capital expenditure and is not currently deductible. Since the machine will be used over a ten-year period, part of the cost will be deductible in each of those years.

§ 10.1422.   Illustration 2: Purchase of Intangible Property. In Year One, Y paid $1,000 for a five-year term fire insurance policy to cover the building used in his business. The payment is a capital expenditure and is not currently deductible, but Y will be able to deduct $200 each year of the five-year term.

§ 10.1423.   Illustration 3: Purchase of Property with an Inexhaustible Life. Z purchased unimproved land for $50,000 to be used in his business. The payment is a capital expenditure, and none of it is deductible since land is not an exhaustible asset.

§ 10.1424.   Illustration 4: Use of Depreciable Property in Constructing an Asset. X, a public utility, used various items of equipment (such as cars, trucks, trailers, and radio equipment) in constructing new capital assets. X contended that it could depreciate the cost of such items over their useful lives and take a current deduction for the depreciation allowance in each year. The Commissioner contended that the depreciation allowance for such items could not be deducted currently, but instead must be added to the cost basis of the capital asset which was constructed with the equipment. The Supreme Court concurred with the Commissioner and treated the depreciation allowance as an amount paid for the construction of the new capital assets and therefore must be added to the basis of those newly constructed assets instead of being deducted currently. *Commissioner v. Idaho Power Co.*, 418 U.S. 1 (1974). The same treatment will be accorded to an accelerated cost recovery system (MACRS) allowance for the equipment under IRC § 168. See **§ 11.1200.**

> **§ 10.1424–1.   Wages.** The amount of wages paid to employees for their work in constructing or acquiring a capital asset, which is owned by the employer, is not a deductible expense but rather is a capital expenditure to be included in the employer's basis in the constructed or acquired property. See *Commissioner v. Idaho Power Co.* at **§ 10.1424.** For an example of the treatment of the payment of wages as a capital expenditure for the construction of improvements on realty, see *Chevy Chase Motor Co. v.*

Commissioner, 36 T.C.M. 942 (1977). For a discussion of whether a portion of wages paid to an employee who devotes part of his working time to the creation of income that will be received over some years, see § **10.1400.**

§ **10.1430. Prepaid Expenses and the Cost of Currently Consumable Assets.** A prepayment of expenses to be incurred in the future is essentially the same as purchasing an asset to be used in the future. The question of whether a prepaid expense is currently deductible or must be amortized over the period to which it relates hinges on whether the taxpayer has purchased a separate item and on the length of time of the prepayment. Similarly, the deductibility of the cost of acquiring an asset that will be used up over a period of 12 months or less rests on the same issue. However, when a cash method taxpayer seeks to deduct in the year of payment a prepaid expense (the benefit from which will be enjoyed in two taxable years), the resolution of the issue often depends on whether the Commissioner can require the allocation of the expense between the taxable years to which it relates on the basis of the Commissioner's authority under IRC § 446(b) to require that the taxpayer's method of accounting accurately reflects the taxpayer's income. This same issue can be raised in determining the propriety of expensing the cost of an asset that will be used for 12 months or less.

§ **10.1431. Determining the Propriety of Expensing Prepayments or the Cost of Consumable Assets.** As previously noted, the Supreme Court's *Indopco* decision stressed that the duration and extent of benefits obtained from an expenditure must be weighed to determine whether it must be capitalized. In *Zaninovich v. Commissioner*, 616 F.2d 429 (9th Cir. 1980), rev'g 69 T.C. 605 (1978), the Ninth Circuit adopted a mechanical rule that where a payment of a business expense relates to a period of 12 months or less, the payment is currently deductible in the taxable year in which the payment is made and need not be capitalized. In *Zaninovich*, the court allowed a deduction for the prepayment of rent for a 12–month period even though 11 of those months lay in the taxable year following the year in which the payment was made. The Tax Court, relying on IRC § 446(b), maintains that a prepaid expense (or the cost of acquiring an asset which will soon be exhausted) must be allocated among the months to which it relates if a significant portion of the expense (or of the use of the asset) is attributable to the taxable year subsequent to the year in which payment is made. It appears that the Tax Court will not require an expense (or cost of purchase) to be prorated if there is a good business reason for the taxpayer's having made the prepayment (or purchase) in the earlier year. *Van Raden v. Commissioner*, 71 T.C. 1083 (1979); *Pope v. Commissioner*, 43 T.C.M. 234 (1981). For the treatment of the prepayment of interest on a loan, which treatment is dictated by IRC § 461(g), see § **5.8000.**

§ 10.1440. Capital Expenditure Versus Repairs. One of the difficult factual issues in tax law is to distinguish a repair from a capital expenditure. A capital expenditure must be capitalized and so cannot be deducted in full in the year occurred. On the other hand, the cost of repairs on business property or property held for profit is a currently deductible expense. The regulations define a repair as "incidental repairs which neither materially add to the value of the property nor appreciably prolong its life, but keep it in an ordinary, efficient operating condition." Treas. Reg. § 1.162–4. Another factor is whether the expenditure made the item adaptable for a different use. See TAM 9315004. In contrast, a capital expenditure adds to the value of the property and frequently prolongs its life. The determination of whether a repair materially adds to the value of an asset is made by comparing the value of the asset after the repair is made with the value it had *before the repair became necessary. Plainfield-Union Water Co. v. Commissioner*, 39 T.C. 333, 338 (1962), Nonacq. In Rev. Rul. 94–38, the Service adopted the position on the definition of a repair that the Tax Court had formulated in the *Plainfield-Union Water* case—namely, that the proper test of whether value was added is to compare the status of the asset after the expenditure with the status it had before the condition arose that necessitated the expenditure. In that ruling, the Service said that its nonacquiescence in the *Plainfield-Union* case was on other grounds. See also *Jacks v. Commissioner*, 55 T.C.M. 968 (1988).

In general, the cost of replacing a major component of a property will have to be capitalized. TAM 9618004; Rev. Rul. 2000–7. Just how major the component must be is a difficult question. Under certain circumstances, for example, where the component was faulty when first installed, even the replacement of a major component might qualify as repair.

§ 10.1441. Caveat. It is far easier to state the distinction between repairs and capital expenditures than to apply it in practice.

§ 10.1442. Major Renovations. When expenditures are incurred in connection with a plan of capital improvement such as a major renovation of an apartment building, all such expenditures are capitalized even though some parts of it would have been deductible if incurred separately. *Ruttenberg v. Commissioner*, 52 T.C.M. 370 (1986). See *United States v. Wehrli*, 400 F.2d 686 (10th Cir. 1968).

§ 10.1443. The *Indopco* Decision Has No Effect on the Deductibility of Repairs. As discussed in **§ 10.1400**, the Supreme Court held in its *Indopco* decision that the creation or enhancement of a separate and distinct asset is not a prerequisite to treating an item as a capital expenditure. In Rev. Rul. 94–12, the Commissioner ruled that the *Indopco* decision has no effect on the determination of the deductibility of incidental repairs. The standards for deducting repairs were not altered by the Supreme Court's decision.

§ 10.1444. Repair of Damage Caused By A Casualty. In Rev. Rul. 71–161, the Commissioner said the repair of damage caused by a casualty for which a loss deduction had been allowed was in the nature of a replacement and so must be capitalized. See also, GCM 34438 (1971). It seems likely that the Commissioner's position is based on the principle that there should not be more than one tax deduction for the same event. See Treas. Reg. § 1.161–1. As discussed in **§ 7.2710**, the allowance of a deduction for the amount expended on repairing damage does not constitute a duplication of the deduction allowed because of the loss suffered from the casualty. One deduction is for the decline in value of property caused by a casualty, and the other is due to the amount of money expended in repairing the damage. There is dictum in a District Court decision stating that the Service's view that such repairs must be capitalized is a "dubious proposition." *Waldrip v. United States*, 48 AFTR2d 81–6031 (N.D. Ga. 1981).

§ 10.1445. Environmental Clean–Up Costs. *X* purchased uncontaminated land. *X* conducted a manufacturing business that discharged hazardous waste on to the land. X incurred expenses to clean-up the land and free it of contamination. X also incurred continuing expenses to keep the land free of subsequent contamination. The Service initially ruled that all of those expenses are currently deductible under IRC § 162, and are not capital expenditures under IRC § 263. Rev. Rul. 94–38. Subsequently, the Service revised its position. While agreeing that the expenditures do not fall within IRC § 263, the Service determined that the expenses were costs of the manufacturing of inventory, and so the costs are capitalized under IRC § 263A and added to inventory costs. Rev. Rul. 2004–18.

X also constructs groundwater treatment facilities (including wells, pipes, pumps, and other equipment) to extract, treat and monitor contaminated groundwater. X expects to operate these groundwater facilities for 8 years. The cost of constructing those facilities must be capitalized under IRC § 263 and cannot be deducted as a current expense. Rev. Rul. 94–38.

If the land that X purchased had been contaminated when he purchased it, would X be allowed a deduction for cleaning-up the land and freeing it from contamination or would those costs be capitalized as part of the cost of acquiring the land? If X knew of the contamination at the time that X purchased the land, then clearly the cost of cleaning-up should be capitalized. The purchase price paid for the land should have reflected the costs that the buyer would have to incur to put the land into useable condition, and so the costs incurred to accomplish that are part of the cost of acquiring the land in useable condition. But, what if X were unaware of the contamination at the time of purchase? In that case, the purchase price of the land probably did not reflect those costs since they were not antici-pated at the time. The question of deductibility in that case is unclear. The authors believe that, in those circumstances, a case can be made for treating the costs of cleaning-up as a repair, but the issue is far from settled.

§ 10.1446. Developing Or Purchasing Software. In Rev. Rul. 69–21, the Service ruled that the development of software is sufficiently akin to research and experimental expenditures (albeit it is not such an expenditure) that the expenses in-curred in developing software should be given similarly liberal cost recovery treatment. Accordingly, a taxpayer who develops software can treat its expenses as currently deductible provided that it has not previously treated such development costs differently (*i.e.*, by amortizing them). Alternatively, a taxpayer can choose to amortize such development costs over a period of 5 years (or less if taxpayer can show a shorter useful life). Amortization will be required if the taxpayer had previously elected to amortize such expenses. On the other hand, if the taxpayer purchases software, the cost must be capitalized and can be amortized over a 5–year period (or shorter if the software has a shorter useful life). *Ibid*, and Rev. Proc. 97–50. In some circumstances, such as where a taxpayer pays a consulting firm to develop software for the taxpayer, there will be a question whether the taxpayer developed the software (and hired an expert to do the work) or whether the taxpayer purchased the software. See TAM 8614004. The tax consequences can be quite different. The criteria for distinguishing developed software from purchased software are explained in Jeffrey Kahn's article, *Deducting Year 2000 Costs*, 79 Tax Notes 1621 (June 22, 1998). That article also discusses: (1) the tax treatment of the costs of fixing the software program problems faced by many taxpayers because of a failure in programs to anticipate the arrival of the Year 2000, and (2) the possibility that in certain (but not all) cases, the cost of purchasing software to cure the Year 2000 problem might be currently deductible as a repair.

§ 10.1450. Purchase or Sale of an Asset. When an expenditure is incurred in connection with the acquisition or sale of an asset, it is a capital expenditure that either is added to the basis of the asset or is subtracted from the amount realized on the sale. Whether an expense that is related to a sale or purchase is to be treated as a deduction, or instead is to be treated either as part of the acquisition cost of an asset or as an offset to the amount realized on the sale of an asset, is sometimes a difficult issue. See §§ **10.1341–4** to **10.1341–6.**

§ 10.1451. Start–Up Expenses of Beginning A Trade or Business. IRC § 162 allows a deduction for the ordinary and necessary expenses of carrying on a trade or business. In order to be deductible, the expenses must relate to a trade or business that was functioning at the time that the expense was incurred. *Hardy v. Commissioner*, 93 T.C. 684, 687 (1989). Unless expressly authorized by statute, start-up or pre-opening expenditures of a new trade or business are not deductible under IRC § 162. See § **10.1451–2** for a discussion of the special statutory provision dealing with those expenditures.

If an existing trade or business investigated whether to expand its business (for example, by opening a branch) and how to go about doing so, the pre-opening expenditures incurred in connection with that expansion are on a different footing than are the pre-opening expenditures of investigating whether to venture into a different trade or business from the one it is currently conducting. In the expansion situation, the expenditure is incurred in connection with a trade or business that is functioning at the time the expenditure is incurred, and so that obstacle is not present. Let us now consider how the pre-opening expenditures will be treated in each of those situations.

§ **10.1451–1. Expanding a Business.** The expenditures connected with a business can be divided into five stages: (a) expenses incurred in making an investigation to determine whether to enter a business and, if so, which business to acquire (these are referred to as investigatory expenses) ; (b) expenses incurred in attempting to purchase a specific business ; (c) expenses incurred in preparing to commence business operations ; (d) expenses incurred in the current conduct of the business; and (e) expenses incurred in terminating the business. Expenses incurred in the latter two stages (i.e., (d) and (e)) typically are deductible. Investigatory expenses (i.e., stage (a)) are deductible if they are ordinary and necessary and connected to the expansion of an already on-going business. *Wells Fargo & Co. v. Commissioner*, 224 F.3d 874 (8th Cir. 2000). The test for determining whether an expense is an investigatory expense is the "whether" and "which" test. So long as the TP is seeking to determine *whether* to enter a business or *which* business to acquire, the expenses are investigatory. *Wells Fargo & Co. v. Commissioner*, supra; Rev. Rul. 99–23. *Wells Fargo* allowed a deduction for investigatory expenses of one bank to explore whether to combine with another bank and, if so, which bank. Once a TP focuses on a specific business to acquire, the expenses to acquire that business are capitalized. Thus, the expenses in stage (b) are capitalized. In *Wells Fargo*, once the TP had focused on the specific bank it considered combining with, the expenses thereafter were capitalized. The expenses incurred in stage (c) also are capitalized.

In *FMR Corp. and Subsidiaries v. Commissioner*, 110 T.C. 402 (1998), the Tax Court denied a deduction (or any amortization) for the taxpayer's expenses of creating regulated investment companies, which taxpayer then advised and managed, even though that was a recurring activity in the conduct of taxpayer's business. The court held that *Indopco* had cut the ground out from cases that had held that expansion expenses of an existing business are deductible. Instead, the court held that, regardless of whether an expenditure is attributable to an expansion of a business, the proper test for its deductibility is whether either (1) a separate and distinct asset was created, or (2) future benefits of substantial duration and extent will be obtained. In other words, the expense must meet the "ordinary and necessary" requirement that applies to both IRC § 162 (business expenses) and IRC § 212 (nonbusiness expenses). Relying on the second standard, the Tax Court held that the expenses must be capitalized. The court did not allow amortization because the taxpayer could not prove an ascertainable useful life.

Investigatory expenses incurred in connection with a new trade or business (i.e., not incurred in expanding a trade or business already conducted by the TP) are capitalized. The statutory relief provided for such investigatory expenses is described in § **10.1451–2.**

§ **10.1451–2. Congressional Action.** In 1980, Congress added IRC § 195 to the Code, and in 1984 Congress significantly amended that provision, and amended it again in 2004. This provision authorizes a taxpayer to elect to take a current deduction for $5,000 of "start-up expenses," which amount is reduced by the extent to which the TP's start-up expenses for that year exceed $50,000. The remaining start-up expenses can be amortized over a 180–month period (i.e., 15 years). This deduction and amortization provision applies only if the TP elects it under IRC § 195(b). "Start-up expenditures" include an amount paid in connection with investigating the creation or acquisition of an active trade or business. The start-up expenses that can be deducted or amortized are only the investigatory expenses (i.e., the expenses incurred during the "whether" and "which" period. Rev. Rul. 99–23). The amortization of start-up expenditures commences with the month in which the active trade or business begins. IRC § 195(a) expressly bars a deduction for start-up expenditures except to the extent allowed by that section; therefore, such expenses must either be deducted or amortized under an IRC § 195(b) election or cannot be deducted at all. The election is available to a taxpayer only as to that amount of the expenditure which, if it had been paid or incurred in connection with the expansion of an existing trade or business in the same field, would be allowed as a current deduction in the year paid or incurred. IRC § 195(c)(1)(B). Thus, it would seem that § 195 applies only to the ordinary and necessary costs of investigating whether to enter into a new business and which business to acquire.

The Eight Circuit's holding permitting the current deductibility of an expenditure for the investigation of expanding an existing business is buttressed by the apparent Congressional assumption in adopting IRC § 195 that such expenses are usually deductible. See also H. Rept. 96–1278 on the Miscellaneous Revenue Act of 1980, at 11 (1980), 1980–2 Cum. Bull. 709, 712–713. However, once the investigation of the TP goes beyond the "whether and which" period, and focuses on the acquisition of a specific business, the expenses connected with acquiring that business or getting it started will be capitalized. However, the Tax Court's view is that IRC § 195 did not change the standard for the deductibility of expansion expenses,; and, given the *Indopco* standard, only expansion expenses that do not create a separate and distinct asset or provide future benefits of substantial duration and extent are deductible.

Deductions for interest, taxes, and research and experimental expenses are excluded from IRC § 195, and so are deductible, or not, without regard to that provision. IRC § 195(c)(1).

§ 10.1451–3. Date on Which Active Trade or Business Begins. The date on which an active trade or business begins plays an important role in the deductibility of expenses. One function of that date is that expenses incurred afterwards can be deducted currently under IRC § 162 as business expenses. Expenses incurred prior to that date will be capitalized, except for certain investigatory expenses for the expansion of an existing business. If a taxpayer elects to amortize his start-up expenses under IRC § 195(b), then the month in which the active trade or business begins will also serve as the date on which the amortization deductions commence.

Unfortunately, the date on which an active trade or business is deemed to begin is a question of fact which can be difficult to determine. Even the standard to be applied in determining that date is not settled. The Commissioner has adopted the standard employed by the Fourth Circuit in *Richmond Television Corporation v. United States*, 345 F.2d 901 (4th Cir.), vacated and remanded per curiam on other grounds, 382 U.S. 68 (1965), original holding on this issue reaff'd, 354 F.2d 410 (4th Cir. 1965). The *Richmond Television* case, which arose prior to the adoption of IRC § 195, dealt with the question of the deductibility of start-up expenditures as business expenses under IRC § 162. In the first *Richmond Television* case, the court stated that a taxpayer does not begin a trade or business "until such time as the business has begun to function as a going concern and performed those activities for which it was organized." The Commissioner has adopted this "going concern" standard in applying IRC § 195. E.g., TAM 9331001; PLR 9027002, PLR 9047032, and Rev. Rul. 81–150. A more liberal standard for determining the beginning of a business was suggested by the Senate Finance Committee's Report on the Miscellaneous Revenue Act of 1980 (which was the Act in which IRC § 195 was first adopted), but the Commissioner expressly rejected that suggestion in the letter rulings cited above. See S.Rept. No. 1036, 96th Cong., 2d Sess. 14 (1980). In any event, when a taxpayer purchases a going business, the taxpayer is deemed to begin the business at the date of acquisition. IRC § 195(c)(2)(B).

§ 10.1451–4. Nonbusiness Expenses. Prior to the 1984 adoption of IRC § 195, there was a question whether start-up expenditures of a noncorporate taxpayer to investigate a profit-seeking activity could be deducted under IRC § 212

as a nonbusiness expense. This issue may have been resolved by the addition of IRC § 195(a) to the Code in 1984.
That provision expressly denies a deduction for start-up
expenditures (as defined in that provision) other than those
permitted by § 195 itself, and that makes the deduction
and amortization election provided by IRC § 195(b) the
exclusive means of obtaining any deduction for such expenditures. *Hardy v. Commissioner*, 93 T.C. 684 (1989) (reviewed by the court). Because IRC § 195 applies only to the
start-up expenses of a trade or business, it will not preclude
deductions for start-up expenses of a profit-seeking activity
unless the exclusivity of that provision is extended to IRC
§ 212 expenses.

§ 10.1452. Abandoned Project. If, after investigating the
financial prospects of entering a business in which the taxpayer is not then engaged and after making preparations to
commence business activities, the taxpayer then abandons the
project before beginning operations, the question arises as to
whether the expenses incurred in the preliminary preparation
and investigation are deductible under IRC § 165 as a loss
incurred in a transaction entered into for a profit. The deductibility of such expenses may turn on how much the taxpayer
had done before abandoning the project. No deduction is
allowable for the loss under IRC § 165(c)(1) since the TP
never commenced a trade or business. A deduction will be
allowed for the loss under IRC § 165(c)(2) if the TP's actions
were sufficient to constitute a "transaction" entered into for
profit. If the taxpayer merely investigates whether to engage
in a business and does not focus on a particular business, he
may not have been sufficiently committed to the venture to
characterize it as a transaction for profit, and, consequently,
he may be denied a deduction for his expenses. See Rev. Rul.
57–418; *Frank v. Commissioner*, 20 T.C. 511 (1953). However,
if the taxpayer takes significant steps in preparation of entering the business so that it goes beyond a general search and
has focused on the acquisition of specific assets and if the
taxpayer then abandons the project, he will be allowed a
deduction. Rev. Ruls. 57–418, 71–191 as explained in Rev. Rul.
79–346. Note that IRC § 195 will not be of any help to the
taxpayer since the $5,000 deduction provided by that provision
is available for the taxable year in which the active trade or
business begins, and the amortization of investigatory ex-

penses there authorized commences with the month in which the active trade or business begins.

In *Larsen v. Commissioner*, 66 T.C. 478 (1976), Acq., the Tax Court allowed a geologist to deduct under IRC § 165 the cost incurred in unsuccessfully attempting to acquire oil and gas leases for certain properties. The Commissioner contended that these expenses were not deductible because at the same time that the taxpayer was unsuccessfully seeking the leases in question, the taxpayer was also successfully seeking oil and gas leases on other properties, and therefore the Commissioner contended that the costs in question should be treated as part of the capital expended in acquiring the leases on the other property. The Tax Court held that each lease was a separate transaction and allowed the taxpayer a current deduction.

§ 10.1453. Expenses of Producing Property—the Uniform Capitalization Rule. Subject to certain exceptions, a taxpayer's direct and indirect costs of producing real property or tangible personal property is required to be capitalized (if the produced property is not inventory) or included in inventory costs (if the produced property is inventory). IRC § 263A. For the purposes of this statutory provision, tangible property includes books, films, sound recordings, video tapes and similar properties. IRC § 263A(b). In certain circumstances, the cost of the taxpayer's purchasing inventory or inventory-type property to be resold by the taxpayer must either be capitalized or included in inventory costs. IRC § 263A(b)(2). For the treatment of expenses incurred by an author in producing a book (including the expenses incurred in research), see **§ 10.1490A.**

§ 10.1460. Defense of Title. Expenditures incurred by a taxpayer in acquiring title to property or in defending title to property are capital expenditures. See § **10.1341–10.**

§ 10.1461. Illustration: Dispute Over Title. *D* and *E* owned 1,000 shares of IBM common stock as joint tenants with rights of survivorship. *D* had purchased the IBM stock with his own funds. *E* was *D*'s housekeeper. *D* died and *E* claimed ownership of the stock as a surviving joint tenant. *D*'s heir, *X*, sued for the stock, claiming that *D* held the IBM stock jointly with *E* as a convenience, that *D* did not intend that the stock would become *E*'s property upon *D*'s death, and that *X*, as *D*'s heir, was entitled to the stock. *E*'s legal fees incurred in the successful defense of the suit are capital expenditures. See *Woodward v. Commissioner*, 397 U.S. 572 (1970), and *United States v. Hilton Hotels*, 397 U.S. 580 (1970). The fees were incurred by *E* to retain ownership of the stock as contrasted to maintenance or repairs to keep an item in operating condition. The expenses incurred by *X* in unsuccessfully prosecuting the suit are not deductible.

§ 10.1462. Protection of Goodwill. While the cost of purchasing goodwill (for example where goodwill is sold as part of a going business) is a nondeductible capital expenditure (which may be amortizable under IRC § 197), an expense incurred in protecting the taxpayer's existing goodwill is currently deductible. For example, in Rev. Rul. 76–203, a moving and storage company was allowed a deduction for compensation it voluntarily paid to customers whose uninsured goods were destroyed in a fire that consumed the taxpayer's warehouse.

§ 10.1470. Expense of Seeking or Obtaining Employment. Treas. Reg. § 1.212–1(f) provides that the expenses "of seeking employment or in placing oneself in a position to begin rendering personal services for compensation" are not deductible. Presumably this is because they constitute capital expenditures of entering a business in contrast to an expense of conducting an existing business activity. While the Service initially ruled that the fee paid to an employment agency for actually placing the taxpayer in a job is deductible [Rev. Rul. 60–223]; it revoked that ruling in Rev. Rul. 75–120 and adopted a different approach, which is described in **§ 10.1473.**

§ 10.1471. Taxpayer Already in the Business. At first, the Tax Court appeared reluctant to grant a deduction for a fee (or other expense) paid to an employment agency to locate a job opportunity (as contrasted to actually securing the taxpayer in a new job). *Louis v. Commissioner*, 25 T.C.M. 1047 (1966). In *Louis*, the Tax Court restricted Rev. Rul. 60–223 [§ **10.1470**] to allow a deduction only for fees paid to an employment agency "for having secured employment" for the taxpayer, and the court held that the ruling did not cover a fee to an employment agency which is payable for *seeking* a job for the taxpayer where no job was actually secured for him. The court did not expressly approve of Rev. Rul. 60–223; rather, the court held that even if that ruling was valid, it was of no help to the taxpayer. In subsequent holdings, even though a taxpayer did not obtain a job, the court allowed a deduction for such expenses when the taxpayer was already established in his trade and was seeking a position in the same trade. The fee is deductible in such case s as having been made incident to the taxpayer's conduct of his business of being an employee in that same trade. *Primuth v. Commissioner*, 54 T.C. 374 (1970); *Motto v. Commissioner*, 54 T.C. 558 (1970). It is now settled that the deductibility of an employment agency's fee does not depend upon whether the agency obtains an employment offer for the taxpayer. *Cremona v. Commissioner*, 58 T.C. 219 (1972), Acq.; *Black v. Commissioner*, 60 T.C. 108 (1973). The Commissioner's current position is explained at § **10.1473.**

§ **10.1472. The Expense of Obtaining or Retaining a Political Office.** A state court judge was permitted to deduct his expenses of defending a misconduct charge brought against him. The judge's defense of his right to his office is distinguishable from expenses of seeking reelection which constitute nondeductible expenses. Rev. Ruls. 74–394; 75–120. The fees and costs of a political campaign (including a campaign for a judicial office) are not deductible. *McDonald v. Commissioner*, 323 U.S. 57 (1944); *Nichols v. Commissioner*, 511 F.2d 618 (5th Cir. 1975). No deduction is allowable regardless of whether the taxpayer is seeking election to a new position or reelection to a position already held by the taxpayer. The reason for this disallowance is to prevent the tax law from tilting the availability of financial resources in favor of an incumbent. Similarly, the costs incurred in obtaining or securing a political appointment are not deductible even if the taxpayer has made a career of public service. *Estate of Rockefeller v. Commissioner*, 83 T.C. 368 (1984) (denying a deduction for costs incurred in connection with investigations and Congressional hearings on the confirmation of the taxpayer's nomination to be Vice–President of the United States).

§ **10.1473. The Commissioner's View.** In Rev. Rul. 75–120, the Commissioner revoked his earlier rulings on this subject, and he ruled that expenses incurred by an employee in seeking new employment in the employee's trade or business are deductible under IRC § 162 irrespective of whether the employee actually secures a new position. However, to be deductible, the employee must be seeking new employment in the same trade or business in which he is already established.

If the employee seeks employment in a new trade or business, his expenses of seeking that employment (including a fee to an employment agency) will *not* be deductible irrespective of whether the taxpayer actually obtains and accepts a new job. If a taxpayer is unemployed at the time he seeks employment, his trade or business will consist of the services he performed for his past employer if there is substantial continuity between his last employment and the seeking of a new job (i.e., the time lag cannot be too great). When deductible under Rev. Rul. 75–120, a taxpayer's *unreimbursed* costs are miscellaneous itemized deductions and so are subject to the 2% of AGI floor imposed by IRC § 67(a) and to the reduction of itemized deductions imposed by IRC § 68.

In Rev. Rul. 75–120, the Commissioner expressly notes that the expenses of a political campaign are not deductible. Thus, notwithstanding the rule that the expenses of seeking employment in the taxpayer's established line of business are deductible, the expenses of a campaign for election or reelection to a public office (including a judicial office) are not deductible. The reason for this is explained in § **10.1472.**

§ **10.1474. Administrative Feasibility.** The view adopted by the Commissioner in Rev. Rul. 75–120 is more consistent with the regulations than was Rev. Rul. 60–223, which was revoked. However, there can be substantial administrative burdens in determining what constitutes a *new* trade or business, and it remains to be seen how liberally the Commissioner or the courts will apply the requirement that an employee be seeking a job in the same trade or business. In Rev. Rul. 78–93, a taxpayer who had been engaged in the full-time practice of law and who also was a part-time lecturer at a law school incurred expenses for career counseling which led to the taxpayer's obtaining a position as a full-time assistant professor on the faculty of a law school. The Commissioner ruled that the taxpayer had been engaged in two trades or businesses and so the full-time law faculty position was not a new trade or business for the taxpayer. The Commissioner allowed a deduction for the taxpayer's expenses.

§ **10.1475. Reimbursed Expenses for Interviewing for a Job.** As noted above, a taxpayer's expenses in interviewing for a job in a new trade or business are not deductible. But if the prospective employer reimburses the taxpayer or pays those expenses directly, and if the employer had invited the employee to interview, the reimbursements and direct payments are excluded from the taxpayer's gross income. Rev. Rul. 63–77. The types of reimbursed expenses that can be excluded from gross income include the taxpayer's transportation costs and the cost of meals and lodging for the taxpayer's stay in the city where the interview takes place. In one sense, the taxpayer provides a service to the prospective employer by coming to that person's place of business to allow the prospective employer to interview the taxpayer.

Similarly, the Commissioner ruled that reimbursements of travel expenses made by a political organization to an appointed state government employee to permit the latter to attend and address a political fund raising event is excluded from the employee's gross income. Rev. Rul. 80–99. In that ruling, the Commissioner stated, "it is also a well-established position of the Internal Revenue Service that reimbursements for expenses incurred by a taxpayer on behalf of another in a nonemployment context are not includible in the taxpayer's income."

§ 10.1480. Deductibility of Capital Expenditures. Capital expenditures are not currently deductible. However, a capital expense often may be deducted by the taxpayer over the period of years during which it is estimated the taxpayer will use the asset or improvement for which the expenditure was incurred. This deduction will be permitted only if the asset or improvement is held in connection with a "trade or business" or a profit-seeking venture.

§ 10.1481. Depreciation and Amortization. In some cases, the taxpayer's deduction is taken as depreciation under IRC §§ 167 or 168 (discussed in Chapters Eleven and Twelve). The term "depreciation" includes deductions allowable under the accelerated cost recovery system (MACRS) provided by IRC § 168. In other cases, in lieu of depreciation, the deduction will be taken as amortization, possibly under IRC §§ 162 or 212, or as some other form of amortization that is expressly authorized by a statutory provision. Amortization is sometimes provided for items that otherwise could not be depreciated—for example, IRC § 197 allows the amortization of the capitalized costs of goodwill when purchased as part of the purchase of a going business.

§ 10.1482. Illustration 1: Allocation of Cost Between Depreciable and Nondepreciable Items. *X* paid $60,000 for the purchase of improved Blackacre. Of that price, $10,000 was paid for the land, and $50,000 was paid for a small apartment house situated on the land. *X* can take depreciation deductions for the $50,000 he paid for the building. However, since the useful life of the land will never terminate, *X* is not permitted any deduction for the cost of the land.

§ 10.1483. Illustration 2: Depreciation of Intangible Asset. On January 1, *X* paid $3,000 for a five-year fire insurance policy insuring the building used in his business. *X* can amortize the $3,000 payment over the five-year useful life of the insurance protection he bought. Consequently, *X* can deduct $600 in that year and in each of the four succeeding years as a depreciation deduction under IRC § 167.

§ 10.1490. Uniforms. An employee's cost of the acquisition and maintenance of his uniform is deductible if the uniform is required by his employer, is not readily adaptable to general use so that it could be used in place of regular clothing, and if it is not so used. Rev. Rul. 70–474. Where allowed, the cost of a uniform is currently deductible and need not be depreciated over the useful life of the garment. *Mortrud v. Commissioner*, 44 T.C. 208 (1965); *Loinaz v. Commissioner*, 34 T.C.M. 71, 77, n.2 (1975). A current deduction is allowed pursuant to the "small cost" exception to the treatment of capital expenditures. See **§ 10.1410.**

§ 10.1491. Itemized Deduction. If deductible at all, an employee's expense of purchasing a uniform is an itemized deduction (as contrasted to an IRC § 62 deduction) unless the taxpayer's employer reimburses him for the expense. If a taxpayer is reimbursed by his employer, the expense of purchasing the uniform (if deductible at all) is deductible under IRC § 62(a) from the taxpayer's gross income (i.e., it is a nonitemized deduction), thereby washing out the income that the taxpayer recognized on receiving the reimbursement. IRC § 62(a)(2)(A); Rev. Rul. 72–110. If not reimbursed, the cost constitutes a miscellaneous itemized deduction that is subject to the 2% of AGI floor imposed by IRC § 67 and to the reduction of itemized deductions required by IRC § 68.

§ 10.1492. Test for Determining "Adaptable to General Use." The question has arisen as to whether the determination that a type of clothing that an employee is required to purchase and wear is adaptable to general use by the employee outside of his work turns on the standards and tastes of the community (the so-called "objective" approach) or whether it turns on the individual standards and tastes of the employee (the "subjective" approach). The Tax Court adopted the subjective approach. In *Pevsner v. Commissioner*, 38 T.C.M. 1210 (1979), the court allowed the taxpayer to deduct the cost of Yves St. Laurent clothes that she bought to wear in her work as manager of a boutique selling only women's clothes designed by Yves St. Laurent. The taxpayer was expected to wear such clothes at work, but the court found that it would be inappropriate and out of keeping with the taxpayer's lifestyle for her to wear the clothes outside of her work (the taxpayer preferred a more conservative style of dress). See also *Yeomans v. Commissioner*, 30 T.C. 757 (1958), Nonacq. The Fifth Circuit reversed the Tax Court in *Pevsner*. Applying an objective standard, the court denied a deduction to the taxpayer for the cost of her clothes. *Pevsner v. Commissioner*, 628 F.2d 467 (5th Cir. 1980). If an objective approach is adopted, a question remains as to the identification of the community whose standards and tastes are to be adopted.

§ 10.1490A. Books, Films, Plays, Photographs, Sound Recordings, Fine Art Products, and Similar Properties. Prior to the adoption of the Technical and Miscellaneous Revenue Act of 1988, the uniform capitalization rule imposed by IRC § 263A (see § **10.1454**) required the expenses of an author in producing a book to be capitalized as part of the cost of producing the book. Similarly, the cost of producing a film, video tape, dramatic work or other artistic property had to be capitalized. In many cases, such capitalized costs could have been recovered by the artist or author over the recovery period of the asset if it were depreciable by its creator. Note that the special provision in IRC § 174 for the deduction of research and experimental expenditures does not apply to research performed in connection with literary or historical projects. Treas. Reg. § 1.174–2(a)(1).

However, as a consequence of the 1988 amendment adding subsection (h) to IRC § 263A, many of the expenses of authors, photographers and artists are exempt from the capitalization requirements of that section and so can be taken as current

deductions. The exemption from the uniform capitalization statute applies only to a "qualified creative expense," which is
defined in IRC § 263A(h)(2) as an expense:

> (1) that is paid or incurred by an individual in the trade or
> business (other than as an employee) of being a writer, photog-
> rapher, or artist [in certain circumstances, the term can also
> apply to the qualified expenses of a personal service corpora-
> tion substantially all of whose stock is owned by such an
> individual (IRC § 263A(h)(3)(D))]; and

> (2) that, in the absence of § 263A, would be allowable as a
> deduction.

The statutory exclusion does not apply to certain expenses; it does
not apply to expenses relating to printing, photographic plates,
motion picture films, video tapes and similar items.

The exclusion from IRC § 263A of certain creative expenses does
not necessarily make them currently deductible. It removes one
obstacle to taking them as current deductions, but they must also
pass muster as not being capital expenditures under IRC § 263.
See *Encyclopaedia Britannica v. Commissioner*, 685 F.2d 212 (7th
Cir. 1982). The likelihood, however, is that such expenses will not
be required to be capitalized, and the exclusion from IRC § 263A
is some evidence that Congress intended a more liberal treatment
of the expenses of those involved in artistic professions.

The exclusion applies to the qualified creative expenses of three
broad categories of professions: writers, photographers, and artists. Those three categories are defined as follows.

> *Writers*. A writer is an individual whose personal efforts create
> (or may reasonable be expected to create) a literary manu-
> script, a musical composition (including the accompanying
> words), or a dance score.

> *Photographer*. A photographer is an individual whose personal
> efforts create (or may reasonable be expected to create) a
> photograph or a photographic negative or transparency.

> *Artist*. An artist is an individual whose personal efforts create
> (or may reasonably be expected to create) a picture, painting,
> sculpture, statue, etching, drawing, cartoon, graphic design, or
> original print edition. IRC § 263A(h)(3).

§ 10.1500. Ordinary and Necessary. Only expenses that are
"ordinary and necessary" are deductible as business expenses under

IRC § 162 or as expenses incurred in connection with profit-seeking ventures under IRC § 212. The term "ordinary" and the term "necessary" have been construed as having separate independent significance.

§ 10.1510. **Necessary Defined.** Of the two terms, the requirement that the expense be "necessary" has proved to be less of an obstacle than the requirement that the expense be "ordinary." A "necessary" expense is merely one that is "appropriate and helpful" to the taxpayer's conduct of his trade or business or profit-seeking venture. *Welch v. Helvering*, 290 U.S. 111 (1933); *Commissioner v. Tellier*, 383 U.S. 687 (1966). Thus, the judicial construction of that requirement has been more modest than the term "necessary" might suggest.

§ 10.1511. **Failure to Seek Reimbursement.** If an employee pays for an item for which he is entitled to be reimbursed by his employer and if the employee fails to seek reimbursement, the employee cannot deduct his payment of the item because the expense was not "necessary." *Lucas v. Commissioner*, 79 T.C. 1 (1982); *Boser v. Commissioner*, 77 T.C. 1124 (1981), Acq., aff'd without published opinion (9th Cir. 1983); but see, *Heineman v. Commissioner*, 82 T.C. 538, 545 (1984) (allowing a deduction for costs incurred by an executive for which he did not seek reimbursement but for which no plan existed providing him with a right of reimbursement).

§ 10.1520. **Ordinary Defined.** The meaning of the term "ordinary" is less certain. Justice Cardozo defined the term "ordinary" as requiring that the expense not be unique in the experience of the group or community of which the taxpayer is a member. *Welch v. Helvering*, 290 U.S. 111 (1933); cf., *Brenner v. Commissioner*, 62 T.C. 878 (1974). In many subsequent cases, courts have applied Cardozo's definition. *United Draperies, Inc. v. Commissioner*, 340 F.2d 936 (7th Cir. 1964) (disallowing a deduction for lawful "kickbacks"). In other cases, the courts have indicated that the term "ordinary" merely distinguishes a capital expenditure, which sometimes may be amortized or depreciated, from a current expense which is to be deducted when paid or accrued. *Commissioner v. Tellier*, 383 U.S. 687 (1966); and *Commissioner v. Lincoln Savings and Loan Ass'n*, 403 U.S. 345 (1971). The latter view—a more sensible construction of the statute—has been gaining favor with the Service and with the courts. See Treas.

Reg. § 1.162–1(a); *FMR Corp. and Subsidiaries v. Commissioner*, 110 T.C. 402 (1998); and Rev. Rul. 74–323.

In *Brizell v. Commissioner*, 93 T.C. 151 (1989), and in *Raymond Bertolini Trucking Co. v. Commissioner*, 736 F.2d 1120 (6th Cir. 1984), the courts allowed a taxpayer to deduct "kickbacks" that were legal to make. In a subsequent Sixth Circuit case, a divided panel denied a deduction for kickbacks that were legal to make; the court held that the kickbacks were not "necessary" because the majority of the court thought that the taxpayer could have obtained its business without making the kickbacks. *Car-Ron Asphalt Paving Co. v. Commissioner*, 758 F.2d 1132 (6th Cir. 1985). See also *Diamond v. Commissioner*, 56 T.C. 530, 542–3 (1971), aff'd, 492 F.2d 286 (7th Cir. 1974) following and approving of the *United Draperies* approach. The *Car-Ron Asphalt* decision is unusual (and of doubtful validity) because courts typically do not second guess the business judgment of a taxpayer.

In *Trebilcock v. Commissioner*, 64 T.C. 852 (1975), aff'd by court order, 557 F.2d 1226 (6th Cir. 1977), the court denied a deduction for a salary paid to a minister to consult with the taxpayer and his employees concerning their spiritual, personal, and business problems. The minister had no expertise in business matters, and his advice came through prayer to God. The court held that even the portion of the minister's salary that was attributable to his business advice was nondeductible because the taxpayer failed to prove that such expenses were "ordinary" in the taxpayer's type of business.

§ 10.1521. Current View. In *Conley v. Commissioner*, 36 T.C.M. 1644 (1977), the taxpayer had controlled a corporation which owned and operated a public relations business. The business was unsuccessful and the corporation became insolvent. The taxpayer then obtained employment with several large public relations firms. To preserve his reputation in the public relations field, the taxpayer used his own funds to pay debts of the insolvent corporation, including the corporation's obligation for unpaid federal social security and withholding taxes and for state unemployment taxes due on account of its employees. The Tax Court held that the taxpayer's payments of the corporation's debts were made for the purpose of protecting his own reputation in the public relations field and therefore are deductible under IRC §§ 162, 165 or 212. See also, *Lohrke v. Commissioner*, 48 T.C. 679, 684–689 (1967). However, the court held that the taxpayer's payment of the corporation's liability for federal and state taxes was not deductible because to allow a deduction would "frustrate a well-defined public policy." The holding in the case is at odds with the Supreme Court's decision in *Welch v. Helvering* [§ **10.1510**] to disallow a deduction for a taxpayer's payment of his prior employer's debts, but the *Welch* decision justifiably has been subjected to criticism. The Tax Court's resort to public policy as a ground for denying the taxpayer a deduction for the payment of the corporation's tax liabilities is questionable [see § **10.5000**]. If the taxpayer's payments of the corporation's debts are otherwise deductible as having been made to protect his reputation, the corporation's benefit from the taxpayer's use of his funds should not affect the determination of taxpayer's right to a deduction.

§ **10.1522. Roles of the Term "Ordinary."** The Seventh Circuit stated that the term "ordinary" has two different uses: (1) "to prevent the deduction of certain expenses that are not normally incurred in the type of business in which the taxpayer is engaged ('ordinary' in this sense blends imperceptibly into 'necessary')," and (2) "to clarify the distinction between expenses that are immediately deductible and expenses that must first be capitalized." *Encyclopaedia Britannica v. Commissioner*, 685 F.2d 212 (7th Cir. 1982).

§ **10.1530. Office in Home.** Prior to the 1976 TRA, a taxpayer who maintained an office in his personal residence was sometimes permitted to deduct an aliquot share of his rent or to depreciate the portion of his house that was dedicated to office use, but the case law on this question (particularly for employees) was unsettled. Compare *Newi v. Commissioner*, 432 F.2d 998 (2d Cir. 1970); and *Green, Jr. v. Commissioner*, 59 T.C. 456 (1972) with *Bodzin v. Commissioner*, 509 F.2d 679 (4th Cir. 1975). The 1976 Act resolved much of this issue by adopting IRC § 280A which established severe restrictions on the deductibility of the cost of a home office. Under that provision, no deduction is allowed for the business use of all or part of a dwelling unit which was used by the taxpayer for personal purposes for more than 14 days of that taxable year unless one of the exceptions described below is applicable. For the limitations on the deductibility of expenses incurred in renting a dwelling to a tenant, see §§ **10.1180– 10.1185.**

§ 10.1531. Exceptions. A deduction for a home office will be allowed where a portion of the dwelling unit is *exclusively used* on a regular basis: (a) as the principal place of business for *any* trade or business of the taxpayer; or (b) as a place of business which is used by patients, clients, or customers in meeting or dealing with the taxpayer in the normal course of his trade or business. A deduction will also be allowed for the maintenance of a separate structure, which is not attached to the dwelling unit, in connection with the taxpayer's trade or business. IRC § 280A(c). If a home office is also used for personal, nonbusiness purposes, no deduction will be allowed. *Langer v. Commissioner*, 63 T.C.M. 1900 (1992), aff'd 989 F.2d 294 (8th Cir. 1993). A home office need not be used exclusively for only one business of the taxpayer for home office expenses to be deductible; but if the taxpayer uses the home office for more than one business, then no deduction for home office expenses will be allowed unless the use for *each* of those businesses qualifies under IRC § 280A(c). If any one of the businesses fails to qualify, no deduction will be allowed for any of the expenses. *Hamacher v. Commissioner*, 94 T.C. 348, 356–357 (1990).

If a deduction is allowable under IRC § 280A for the use of a home office, the amount of the deduction is limited by IRC § 280A(c)(5) to the difference between the gross income for that year from such use and the sum of the non profit-seeking deductions allocable to such use (see **§ 10.1180**) and the deductions of that trade or business that are not allocable to the home office use. Any deduction disallowed by this provision is carried over to the next year. IRC § 280A(c)(5).

§ 10.1532. Principal Place of Business. There can be only one principal place of business for each trade or business conducted by a taxpayer. When a taxpayer conducts a trade or business in more than one location (one of which is the taxpayer's home), there was some controversy as to the standard to be employed in determining which location was the *principal* place of that business. The Supreme Court initially resolved that dispute in *Commissioner v. Soliman*, 506 U.S. 168 (1993), but the Court's formula would have denied a deduction for home office use to thousands of small business owners. Dissatisfied with that consequence, Congress responded in the 1997 Act by amending IRC § 280A(c)(1) so as to effectively repudiate the result reached in *Soliman*.

Before examining the 1997 amendment, let us put it in context by considering the history of the litigation over this issue. The Tax Court took the view that the determination of the principal place of the taxpayer's business does not rest exclusively on a comparison of the number of hours spent at each location. Initially, the test that the Tax Court employed in determining whether the taxpayer's home office constitutes the taxpayer's principal place of business rested on whether the home office was the "focal point" of the taxpayer's conduct of that trade or business. *Baie v. Commissioner*, 74 T.C. 105 (1980). In general, the "focal point" of a taxpayer's business is the place where goods or services are provided to customers or where income is earned. Two Circuit Courts of Appeals (the Second and the Seventh) repudiated the "focal point" standard. *Weissman v. Commissioner*, 751 F.2d 512 (2d Cir. 1984); *Meiers v. Commissioner*, 782 F.2d 75 (7th Cir. 1986); *Cadwallader v. Commissioner*, 919 F.2d 1273 (7th Cir. 1990).

With six judges dissenting, the Tax Court abandoned its "focal point" test in *Soliman v. Commissioner*, 94 T.C. 20 (1990) (reviewed by the court), aff'd by a divided court, 935 F.2d 52 (4th Cir. 1991), reversed, 506 U.S. 168 (1993). In place of the "focal point" test, the Tax Court adopted a "facts and circumstances" test. The relative amount of time spent at the home office was only one factor to be taken into account. Other factors mentioned by the court are: the business exigencies for having a home office, whether the functions performed in the home office are essential to the conduct of the business, whether the office is suitable for those functions, and the appropriateness of the furnishings of the office.

The taxpayer in *Soliman* was an anesthesiologist who administered to patients at three hospitals. None of the hospitals provided him with an office. Taxpayer dedicated one room of his apartment exclusively for use as an office at which he performed numerous administrative functions (including maintaining medical records for his patients and billing and collections) and worked on his continuing medical education requirements. The office did not satisfy the "focal point" test that the Tax Court had used up to that time. Applying a more flexible "facts and circumstances" test, the Tax Court allowed deductions for the home office expenses. In a 2–1 decision, the Fourth Circuit affirmed. The court emphasized that: (1) the home office was essential to taxpayer's business, (2) he spent a substantial amount of time there, and (3) there was no other location available for the performance of the office functions of taxpayer's business.

In reversing the decisions of the Tax Court and the Fourth Circuit, the Supreme Court held that no deduction will be allowed for a home office unless that office is the most important, consequential and influential place at which the taxpayer conducts his business. *Commissioner v. Soliman*, 506 U.S. 168 (1993). There is no objective formula for making that determination; instead, it rests on an inquiry into the facts of each case. However, the Court did identify two considerations that it termed "primary" and to be given the greatest amount of weight in making this determination: namely, (1) the relative importance of the activities performed at each location, and (2) the amount of time spent at each place.

Under the *Soliman* standard, the analysis begins with an objective examination of the type of business which the taxpayer conducts. In order to determine which functions that are performed at different locations are the most important, the nature of the taxpayer's business must be understood. Most businesses will have a pattern in which certain functions are more significant than others.

The Court rejected the notion that the fact that the function conducted at the taxpayer's home office is an important element of the taxpayer's business is sufficient to authorize a deduction for his home office expenses. The determination of deductibility rests on a comparison of the relative importance of the functions conducted at the several locations at which the taxpayer works. If all of the function s conducted by the taxpayer are necessary to the business, only the location of the most important of those is the principal place of the taxpayer's business. The Court noted that some businesses have no principal place of business. If so, no deduction can be allowed for home office expenses. The home office does not become the principal place of business by default.

In the Taxpayer Relief Act of 1997, Congress added the last sentence to IRC § 280A(c)(1). This amendment creates a special exception to the *Soliman* standard for determining principal place of business and provides a home office deduction for many small business owners who otherwise would not qualify. The standard established by the Supreme Court in *Soliman* is applicable if the special exception created by the 1997 amendment does not apply.

The amendment provides that the principal place of business includes a place which is used by the taxpayer for the administrative or management activities of a trade or business of the taxpayer if there is no other fixed location of that trade or business where the taxpayer conducts substantial administrative or management activities for such trade or business. IRC § 280(c)(1)(last sentence). The legislative history to the amendment suggests that if the taxpayer does perform some administrative work at another fixed location, that will not prevent the application of the special exception *if* the administrative work done at the other location is insubstantial (i.e, minimal paperwork).

There is no requirement, in order for a home office to qualify as a principal place of business, that a taxpayer perform any management or administrative tasks there; but, if the taxpayer does so and does not perform substantial administrative tasks at any other fixed location of that business, that alone will be sufficient to qualify the home office as the principal place of that business, provided that the other requirements of IRC § 280A (such as the requirement of exclusive use) are satisfied. Had this provision been applicable at the time that the facts of *Soliman* took place, the taxpayer in *Soliman* would have qualified for a home office deduction. Many taxpayers (e.g., doctors, salespeople, and teachers) have no principal place of business, and conduct management and administrative functions of their businesses from an office in their home dedicated exclusively to that function. The *Soliman* decision would have prevented most of those people from obtaining a deduction for their home office, but the 1997 amendment will allow a deduction subject to the limitations otherwise imposed by IRC § 280A.

§ 10.1532–1. Illustration 1: Others Perform Administrative Tasks Too. *B* is a self-employed surgeon. She performs operations at the *X* hospital. While some administrative tasks are performed by *B*'s secretary in an office at the hospital, *B* has a room in her home that is used exclusively for *B*'s conducting administrative tasks, such as billing and maintaining medical records of her patients. One-fourth of the administrative work for *B*'s medical

practice is performed by the secretary at a room in the hospital, and the remaining 75% is performed by B in her home office. Although most of B's work (meeting patients and performing surgery) is performed outside her home, and although a significant portion (25%) of the administrative work is done by another person at the hospital, the home office will qualify as a principal place of B's medical practice. IRC § 280A(c)(1). The expenses of the home office will be deductible.

§ 10.1532–2. Illustration 2: Taxpayer Carries Out Minor Administrative Duties At Another Fixed Location. The same facts as those stated in **Illustration 1** except that B has no secretary and so she does the 25% of the administrative work at the room at the hospital as well as the 75% of the administrative work that she does in her home office. The home office will not qualify as the principal place of B's medical business, and so no deduction is allowable for home office expenses. The fact that B does more than a minimal amount of administrative work at a fixed location of her medical business (the room at the hospital) will prevent the special qualification of the last sentence of IRC § 280A(c)(1) from applying. In the absence of the operation of that special provision, the work that B performs at home likely will not satisfy the requirement that the home office be the most important, consequential, and influential place at which B conducts her business. When the special provision does not apply, the standard for determining whether a home office is the principal place of business is the standard established by the Supreme Court in *Soliman*. In other words, the 1997 amendment can be seen as creating a special exception to the *Soliman* standard, but otherwise *Soliman* is controlling.

§ 10.1533.   Place of Business Used by Patients, Clients, or Customers in Meeting or Dealing with the Taxpayer. In lieu of qualifying as the principal place of taxpayer's business, a home office can satisfy IRC 280A by being the place where patients, clients or customers meet or deal with the taxpayer in the normal course of taxpayer's trade or business. IRC § 280A(c)(1)(B). The use by such persons must be substantial and integral to the taxpayer's business. Prop. Reg. § 1.280A–2(c).

In *Green v. Commissioner*, 78 T.C. 428 (1982), rev'd 707 F.2d 404 (9th Cir. 1983), the taxpayer, an account executive for a real estate management firm, maintained a home office at which the taxpayer received numerous telephone calls on a regular basis from his clients. These telephone calls were a regular part of the conduct of the taxpayer's business. Only rarely did a client come to the taxpayer's home and meet with him in person. The taxpayer's employer provided the taxpayer with an office at which he spent approximately 20% of his eight-hour workday. Because the taxpayer was difficult to reach during the day, he received numerous phone calls from his clients in the evening, and he maintained a room in his house exclusively as his office. In a sharply divided decision, the Tax Court held that the phone conversations with clients was sufficient, on the facts of that case, to qualify as a "meeting or dealing" with clients. Seven judges dissented on the ground that "meeting or dealing" requires that the client be physically present at the home office. The Ninth Circuit reversed the majority's decision on the same ground as that asserted by the dissenting Tax Court judges.

§ **10.1534. Employee's Home Office.** If the taxpayer is an employee, no deduction will be allowed for a home office (even if one or more of the conditions described above are satisfied) unless the exclusive use of the home office is for the convenience of the taxpayer's employer. IRC § 280A(c)(1). In *Cadwallader v. Commissioner*, 919 F.2d 1273 (7th Cir. 1990), the court held that when an employee is provided by his employer with adequate facilities to perform his work, he cannot obtain a deduction for a home office because he chooses to perform work there. The home office is then for the convenience of the employee and not for the employer as required by the statute. In *Cadwallader*, the Seventh Circuit denied a deduction for home office expenses to a professor of psychology at a State university, even though the professor did most of his writing and research at that office, since the university provided the professor with an adequate office on campus. The court stated that if the university (the taxpayer's employer) had failed to provide him with adequate office facilities for his research and writing, and if the taxpayer had used the home office exclusively and regularly to do his research and writing, the taxpayer would then have been entitled to deduct his home office expenses. If that latter situation had existed (and it did not in that case), it would have indicated that the employer expected the professor to outfit an office for his use, and so the taxpayer's use of the home office would then have been for the convenience of the employer.

§ 10.1535.   Storage Use. In certain cases, a deduction may be allowed for the cost of maintaining space in a dwelling unit to store inventory of the taxpayer. IRC § 280A(c)(2).

§ 10.1536.   Limitation on Deductions. Of course, IRC § 280A does not prevent a taxpayer from deducting expenses attributable to the home office space which are deductible without regard to whether the space is employed in an income-seeking activity (e.g., real estate taxes). Such expenses are hereinafter referred to as "non profit-seeking deductions." If none of the exceptions to IRC § 280A is applicable, no deduction (other than non profit-seeking deductions) will be allowed for the use of a home office. If one or more of the exceptions is applicable, then IRC § 280A(c)(5) limits the amount of deduction allowed for the use of the office for the taxable year to the excess of the taxpayer's gross income for the taxable year from the use of the home office over the sum of: (1) the deductions for that year allocable to the use of the office which are allowable whether or not the office was so used and (2) the deductions for that year allocable to the trade or business in which the home office use occurs but which are not allocable to that use. Any expenses of the home office that are not deductible in a taxable year because of this limitation are carried over and treated as deductions allocable to such home use in the succeeding taxable year. IRC § 280A(c)(5).

§ 10.1600.   Unreasonably Large Expenses. If an expense is unreasonably large (i.e., an expense which is greater than the normal payment for such services or benefits), the unreasonable portion of the expense will not be allowed as a business deduction. For example, *ABC*, Inc. pays an annual salary of $100,000 to *X*, its sole shareholder, for his services as president. A reasonable salary, based on salaries paid to persons performing comparable services, would be $60,000. Therefore, $40,000 of the salary paid to *X* is not deductible since it was not an ordinary and necessary expense.

§ 10.1700.   Bribes, Illegal Kickbacks, and Other Illegal Payments.

§ 10.1710.   Payments to Government Officials. No deduction is allowed for a bribe or kickback to an official or employee of any government or governmental agency if the payment is unlawful. In addition, if a payment is made to an official or employee of a foreign government, and if the payment is unlawful under the Foreign Corrupt Practices Act of 1977, the payment is not deductible. IRC § 162(c)(1). The statute imposes a heavy burden of proof on the Service on the issue of whether the bribe, kickback or payment was illegal.

§ 10.1720. Other Bribes and Kickbacks. No deduction is allowed for other bribes, kickbacks and payments (i.e., those made to persons other than government officials or employees), if they are illegal under the law of the United States, or under any state law which is generally enforced, if such law subjects the payor to a criminal penalty or to the loss of license or privilege to engage in a trade or business. The Service bears a heavy burden of proof on the question of whether a bribe, kickback or payment is illegal. IRC § 162(c)(2). In addition, no deduction is permitted for a kickback, rebate, or bribe made by a person providing services or supplies under a medicare program if the payment is made in connection with the furnishing of such services or supplies. IRC § 162(c)(3).

§ 10.1730. Illegal Payments. As noted in **§ 10.1720**, IRC § 162(c)(2) denies a taxpayer a deduction for any payment that is illegal under a federal or state law which is generally enforced and which subjects the payor to a criminal penalty or the loss of a license or privilege to engage in a trade or business. A "state law which is generally enforced" refers to a statute of a state or the District of Columbia unless either the statute is never enforced or the only persons charged with violations thereof are either infamous or those whose violations are extraordinarily flagrant. Treas. Reg. § 1.162–18(b)(3). It would appear that IRC § 162(c)(2) overturns the holding in *Commissioner v. Sullivan*, 356 U.S. 27 (1958) [discussed at **§ 10.5100**].

§ 10.1731. No Penalty. When an employment agency specified gender in an advertisement, which made the ad illegal under the Civil Rights Act of 1964, the agency nevertheless was permitted to deduct the cost of the advertisement as a business expense. Since the Civil Rights Act did not impose a penalty for such violations, IRC § 162(c) is inapplicable; the public policy exception to deductibility of business expenses has been discarded. Rev. Rul. 74–323.

§ 10.1732. Applications of Illegal Payment Rule. For some interesting applications of the provisions of IRC § 162(c) denying a deduction for illegal expenses, see Rev. Rul. 82–149; *Max Sobel Wholesale Liquors v. Commissioner*, 69 T.C. 477 (1977), aff'd, 630 F.2d 670 (9th Cir. 1980). In *Sobel*, in violation of state law providing for minimum prices, the taxpayer (a wholesale liquor dealer) secretly transferred extra liquor to its customers. The Tax Court and the Ninth Circuit held that these transfers were a reduction of the purchase price for the liquor sold and so were not deductible expenses which would have been denied by IRC § 162(c). See also Rev. Rul. 82–149. This holding (permitting a reduction of purchase price) applies to rebates between a buyer and seller. The Tax Court and the Ninth Circuit have declined to extend that holding to rebates made by an agent to a buyer. See *Alex v. Commissioner*, 628 F.2d 1222 (9th Cir. 1980), aff'g 70 T.C. 322 (1978) (a divided decision). The question of whether public policy considerations can bar the taking of a deduction under IRC § 165 for a *loss* incurred in an illegal transaction is considered at § **10.5400** and at § **10.5500** and at § **7.1000.**

§ 10.1800. Miscellaneous.

§ 10.1810. Lobbying Expenses. Even prior to the adoption of the Omnibus Budget Reconciliation Act of 1993, most lobbying expenses could not be deducted. There were some important exceptions, however. The 1993 amendments deny deductions for virtually all lobbying expenses except for lobbying with a local council or similar governing body. IRC § 162(e).

§ 10.1820. Fines and Penalties. No deduction is allowed for the payment of a fine or similar penalty to a government because of a violation of the law. IRC § 162(f). For the tax treatment of the payment of expenses which are illegal to make, see § **10.1730** and § **10.5000.**

§ 10.1821. Illustration: Characterization of a Fine. The taxpayer, a public school teacher, engaged in a strike that was illegal under state law. The applicable state law provided that a teacher who is found to have participated in a strike will have withheld from her pay an amount equal to twice the teacher's daily pay for each day (or part thereof) that the teacher was absent from school in violation of the state law. Had the taxpayer not been on strike, she would have received $1,509 pay for the days that she was absent. The school district did not pay the taxpayer the $1,509 wages for those days, and the district withheld an additional $1,509 from her subsequent salary payments for work performed after the strike was discontinued. The Tax Court held in *Tucker v. Commissioner*, 69 T.C. 675 (1978), that the $1,509 that was withheld from the taxpayer because she did not work on those days was not included in her gross income; but the additional $1,509 which was withheld as a penalty for her illegal strike constitutes gross income to the taxpayer and because of IRC § 162(f) is not deductible by her. See Rev. Rul. 76–130. The taxpayer is deemed to have received the $1,509 for work performed subsequent to the strike and then to have paid that amount to the state as a fine for her illegal activity.

§ 10.1822. Deductible Civil Penalty. For a civil penalty to fall within the IRC § 162(f) bar against deductibility, it must be one which punishes or deters the taxpayer who pays the penalty. If the "penalty" is remedial in nature (e.g., if it constitutes a provision for liquidated damages), the payment will not be subject to IRC § 162(f) and will be deductible if it otherwise qualifies as a business expense or some other deductible expense. *Middle Atlantic Distributors, Inc. v. Commissioner*, 72 T.C. 1136 (1979). In *Middle Atlantic*, the federal government sued the taxpayer to recover, under 19 U.S.C. § 1592, the value of liquor fraudulently withdrawn from the taxpayer's warehouse and, contrary to United States customs law, introduced into commerce in the United States. The suit was settled for less than 20% of the amount claimed, and the Tax Court allowed the taxpayer a deduction for the amount paid by the taxpayer in settling the suit. The court determined that 19 U.S.C. § 1592, on which the suit was brought against the taxpayer, is both remedial and punitive in its nature. Consequently, the court looked to the intention of the parties in settling the suit to characterize the payment as remedial or punitive. Since the taxpayer's offer to settle and the settlement agreement itself referred to the settlement as an amount representing liquidated damages, the court concluded that the settlement payment was remedial and, therefore, was a deductible business expense.

§ **10.1823. Purpose of Penalty.** The Commissioner will examine the purpose of requiring a payment that is characterized as a "penalty" to determine whether it is truly intended as a punitive measure. For example, in Rev. Rul. 88–46, the Commissioner allowed a deduction for the payment of a "nonconformance penalty" imposed by the Environmental Protection Agency under the Clean Air Act on a manufacturer of trucks for failing to conform to emission standards established under that Act. The Commissioner determined that the purpose of the "penalty" was to prevent nonconforming manufacturers from gaining a competitive advantage over conforming manufacturers who incurred higher costs in order to meet the emission standards.

§ **10.1824. Restitution Payments.** A taxpayer's repayment to a third party of funds improperly or unlawfully obtained from the third party usually will not be a "penalty" to the taxpayer even if the restitution was made pursuant to a court order. If the taxpayer's receipt of the funds caused him to recognize gross income, the repayment of the funds to the victim usually will be deductible by the taxpayer. However, in several Tax Court cases, restitution payments that were ordered to be made by a court as an alternative to a jail term were characterized as "penalties," and so the Tax Court found that the payments were not deductible by the taxpayer. The fact that the payments were made to private individuals did not preclude their being characterized as penalties by the Tax Court. It was deemed sufficient that the State exercised control over the disposition of the penalty; the payment need not be made directly to the State. The Tax Court and the Ninth Circuit held that the test for penalty characterization is the origin of the liability rather than the identity of the payee. *Waldman v. Commissioner*, 88 T.C. 1384, 1389 (1987), aff'd by court order, 850 F.2d 611 (9th Cir. 1988); *Stephens v. Commissioner*, 93 T.C. 108 (1989), rev'd, 905 F.2d 667 (2d Cir. 1990). The Tax Court concluded that the purpose of ordering the taxpayers in those cases to make monetary restitution to their victims was to punish the taxpayers since the restitution payments were ordered as an alternative to a prison term. In *Waldman*, the courts applied IRC § 162(f) to deny a deduction. In *Stephens*, the Tax Court applied the Congressional policy exemplified by IRC § 162(f) to deny a deduction claimed under IRC § 165(c)(2) as a loss incurred in a profit transaction. The

Second Circuit reversed the Tax Court's decision in *Stephens* and allowed a deduction. The decisions of the Tax Court and of the Second Circuit in *Stephens* are discussed at **§ 7.1000**, *supra*.

§ 10.1830. Treble Damages Under the Antitrust Laws. If a taxpayer is convicted of a criminal violation of the antitrust laws or if his plea of guilty or nolo contendere to such a charge is accepted, then the taxpayer cannot deduct two-thirds of any amount paid by him on a judgment under (or in settlement of an action brought under) Section Four of the Clayton Act on account of such violation or related violation. IRC § 162(g).

§ 10.1840. Contributions to Charitable Organizations. No deduction is allowed under IRC § 162 for a contribution or gift that would have been deductible under IRC § 170 as a charitable contribution if it were not for the percentage, dollar, or timing limitations set forth in that section. IRC § 162(b). The genesis of this limitation is described in *Marquis v. Commissioner*, 49 T.C. 695, 698–701 (1968). The limitation imposed by IRC § 162(b) applies only to a contribution or gift—i.e., to a payment for which there was no expectation of financial return commensurate with the payment. *Marquis v. Commissioner*, *supra*; Rev. Rul. 77–124; and Rev. Rul. 72–314. If a payment to a charitable organization is made with the expectation of receiving a quid pro quo therefor, the payment is not a contribution or gift and so can qualify as a business expense under IRC § 162, if the requirements of that provision are satisfied.

§ 10.2000. CREDIT FOR CHILD CARE AND HOUSEHOLD EXPENSES. The expenses of a working parent or parents for the care of a child (or other dependent) while the parent is at work are not deductible as a business (or nonbusiness) expense. While the expense of caring for children may be a necessary cost of freeing the parent from the home so that he can earn income, it also is an expense arising out of personal, family obligations. The cost of child care is analogous to commuting expenses which are not deductible even though a taxpayer is not able to earn gross income unless he travels from his residence to his place of work. The business overtones of these expenses and of related household expenses were sufficiently compelling, however, to induce Congress to provide tax relief in some circumstances. For taxable years beginning prior to 1976, IRC § 214 allowed a limited amount of deduction for such expenses, but that provision was repealed by the 1976 TRA. The 1976 Act substituted a tax credit for the deduction that had previously been allowed and altered some of the requirements for qualifying for the tax relief. IRC § 21 grants a credit equal to 35% of so-called "employment-related expenses" [defined at **§ 10.2200**] to an individual who qualifies under the statute.

The percentage of employment-related expenses that qualify for the credit is reduced by one percentage point for each $2,000 (or fraction thereof) by which the taxpayer's AGI for that year exceeds $15,000; but in no event shall the percentage be less than 20%. IRC § 21(a).

Note that dependent care assistance provided by an employer to its employees is excluded from the employee's gross income by IRC § 129. While no more than $5,000 can be excluded in a taxable year, the amount excluded is not subject to any reduction because of the size of the taxpayer's AGI. However, to qualify under IRC § 129, the employer's plan for providing such benefits cannot discriminate in favor of highly compensated employees. IRC § 129(d)(2).

§ 10.2100. Qualifying Individuals. IRC § 21 grants a credit only to an individual for which there is at least one "qualifying individual." A "qualifying individual" is a person who is either (1) a dependent of the taxpayer (as defined in IRC § 152(a)(1) who has not attained the age of 13 years, or (2) a dependent or spouse of the taxpayer who is physically or mentally incapable of caring for himself and who has the same place of abode as the taxpayer for more than one-half of the taxable year). For the meaning of the term "dependent," see **§ 4.1220.** The statute provides a special rule for treating certain children of divorced or separated parents as qualifying individuals with respect to one of the parents. IRC § 21(e)(5).

§ 10.2200. Employment–Related Expenses. A qualified taxpayer is allowed a credit equal to 20% to 35% of the amount paid for household services and for expenses for the care of a "qualifying individual" if such expenses are incurred to permit the taxpayer to be gainfully employed during a period for which there is at least one qualifying individual with respect to the taxpayer. These expenses are referred to as "employment-related expenses." Such expenses for services performed outside the taxpayer's household are taken into account only if incurred on behalf of a dependent of the taxpayer who is under the age of 13, or on behalf of a qualifying individual who spends at least eight hours each day in the taxpayer's household. If the outside care is provided by a dependent care center (as defined by IRC § 21(b)(2)(D)), expenses therefor are taken into account only if the center complies with all rules and regulations of a state or local government unit. IRC § 21(b)(2)(C).

§ 10.2300. Limitations on Credit.

§ 10.2310. Dollar Limit.
The amount of employment-related expenses incurred in a taxable year, which is taken into account under IRC § 21, cannot exceed $3,000 if the taxpayer has only one qualifying individual for that year or $6,000 if the taxpayer has two or more qualifying individuals. IRC § 21(c). Those dollar figures are reduced by the amount of dependent care assistance that the taxpayer receives from his employer that is excluded from the taxpayer's gross income by IRC § 129. *Ibid.* Thus, if a taxpayer has AGI of $15,000 or less and received no dependent care assistance from an employer, the maximum credit allowable for a taxable year is 35% x $3,000 = $1,050 for one qualifying individual and 35% x $6,000 = $2,100 if there is more than one qualifying individual. If a taxpayer had AGI of $25,000 for a taxable year, the maximum credit for one qualifying individual is 30% x $3,000 = $900; and the maximum credit for more than one qualifying individual is 30% x $6,000 = $1,800 [see § **10.2000**].

§ 10.2320. Earned Income Limitation.
The amount of a taxpayer's employment-related expenses which are taken into account under IRC § 21 cannot exceed: (1) the "earned income" of the taxpayer if the taxpayer is not married at the end of the taxable year, or (2) if the taxpayer is married at the end of the taxable year, the *lesser* of the taxpayer's earned income and the earned income of the taxpayer's spouse for that year. IRC § 21(d). However, for each month that one (and only one) of the spouses was either a full-time student at an educational institution or was physically or mentally incapable of caring for himself, the statute treats such spouse as having earned income of no less than either $250 or $500 depending upon whether there is only one qualifying individual or whether there is more than one. IRC § 21(d).

§ 10.2330. Payments to Dependents.
IRC § 21(e)(6) prohibits a credit for amounts paid by a taxpayer to a person for whom a dependent exemption under IRC § 151(c) is allowable either to the taxpayer or his spouse. No credit is allowable for payments made to a child of the taxpayer (as defined at § **4.1231**) who has not attained the age of 19 by the close of the taxable year regardless of whether the child qualifies the taxpayer for a dependent exemption.

§ 10.2340. Married Taxpayers. If a taxpayer is married at the close of a taxable year, no credit will be allowed under IRC § 21 for that year unless the taxpayer and his spouse file a joint return. IRC § 21(e)(2). An individual who is separated from his spouse under a decree of separate maintenance or divorce is considered unmarried. IRC § 21(e)(3). A married taxpayer is treated as unmarried for a taxable year if he: (1) filed a separate tax return for that year; (2) maintained as his home a household which was the principal place of abode of a qualifying individual; (3) the taxpayer's spouse was not a member of that household at any time during the last six months of such taxable year; and (4) the taxpayer furnished over one-half the cost of maintaining the household during the taxable year. IRC § 21(e)(4).

§ 10.3000. TRAVEL EXPENSES.

§ 10.3100. General. Traveling expenses (including reasonable amounts expended for meals and lodging) while away from "home" in the pursuit of a trade or business are deductible under IRC § 162(a)(2). If the taxpayer is self-employed, the deductions are nonitemized deductions. But, if the taxpayer is an employee and if the expenses are not reimbursed, the deductions will constitute miscellaneous itemized deductions that are subject to the 2% of AGI floor and also are subject to the reduction of itemized deductions imposed by IRC § 68. In addition, if an employee's expenses for meals are not reimbursed, subject to a few narrow exceptions, only 50% of the cost of those meals is allowable as an itemized deduction (the remaining 50% is disallowed). IRC § 274(n). The 50% of meals' cost that constitutes an itemized deduction is then added to other miscellaneous itemized deductions and subjected to the 2% of AGI floor and to the reduction of itemized deductions imposed by IRC § 68. If the employee's expenses are reimbursed by his employer, then the entire amount of such expenses is deductible as a nonitemized deduction. IRC § 62(a)(2)(A). In that case, the 2% of AGI floor does not apply, and the employee can deduct 100% of the cost of his meals; but the employer can deduct only 50% of the amount of cost of the employee's meals that he reimbursed.

Note that for employees engaged in the transportation industry, a higher percentage of the cost of their meals is deductible. IRC § 274(n)(3).

§ 10.3110. Conditions to be Satisfied. The Supreme Court has held [*Commissioner v. Flowers*, 326 U.S. 465 (1946)] that a taxpayer must satisfy three conditions to become entitled to deduct a travel expense under IRC § 162(a)(2):

(a) the expense must be reasonable and appropriate;

(b) the expense must be incurred while away from home; and

(c) the expense must arise out of the exigencies of the taxpayer's business (i.e., there must be a direct connection between the expenditure and the conduct of the taxpayer's business).

In addition, IRC § 274(d) requires that the taxpayer substantiate his travelling expenses by adequate records or sufficient evidence. See Notice 95–50. If the taxpayer is an employee who is reimbursed by his employer for travel expenses, the substantiation requirement will be satisfied if the employee is provided with a per diem allowance that does not exceed certain guidelines. See Rev. Proc. 97–59. See also, § **10.3500**, *infra* for an explanation of the availability of an optional standard automobile mileage allowance instead of substantiating the cost of operating an automobile.

§ 10.3120. "Transportation Costs" Distinguished. It should be noted that the cost of *transportation*, unlike meals and lodging, may be deducted either under the general language of IRC § 162(a) as an ordinary business expense or under IRC § 162(a)(2) as part of a traveling expense. The general provision of IRC § 162(a) does *not* require that the expense be incurred away from the taxpayer's home. Also note that the term "transportation" is a narrower concept than the terms "travel expense" or "traveling expense" in that the latter include both transportation costs and the expenses of meals and lodging; whereas the term "transportation costs" does not include meals and lodging costs.

§ 10.3130. Deduction of the Cost of Meals That Are Not Incurred as Travel Expenses. It is possible in certain cases for 50% of the cost of meals to be deductible under the general language of IRC § 162(a) as an ordinary business expense even when the meals are not part of a travel expense. For example, the cost of a business entertainment that is deductible can include the cost of 50% of the taxpayer's meal. See IRC § 274(a), (k). Fifty percent of the cost of meals taken during a business discussion or pursuant to a business program can be deductible. Treas. Reg. § 1.274–2(f)(2). Apart from entertainment expenses and business meetings, there are only a few circumstances when the cost of a meal that is not part of a travel expense can be deducted. In a divided decision, the Eighth Circuit permitted state troopers who were required by their employer to take their meals at public restaurants adjacent to the highways they patrolled to deduct the cost of those meals. *Christey v. United States*, 841 F.2d 809 (8th Cir. 1988). See also *Sibla v. Commissioner*, 611 F.2d 1260 (9th Cir. 1980).

§ 10.3140. Travel Expense of Individual Accompanying Taxpayer. Under IRC § 274(m)(3), the travel expenses of a spouse, dependent, or other individual accompanying the taxpayer (or accompanying an officer or employee of the taxpayer) on business travel are not deductible unless:

(1) the spouse, dependent or other individual is an employee of the taxpayer [while the statute refers to employment by the taxpayer, the Statement of Managers on the Conference Report to the 1993 Reconciliation Act describes this condition as requiring that the spouse, dependent or other individual be a bona fide employee of the person paying or reimbursing the expenses; it does not indicate that the person must be employed by the taxpayer];

(2) the travel of the spouse, dependent, or other individual must be for a bona fide business purpose; and

(3) such expenses must otherwise be deductible by the spouse, dependent, or other individual.

The denial of travel expense deductions for such persons does not apply to moving expenses that are deductible under IRC § 217. See **§§ 10.3400–10.3430**, *infra*.

§ 10.3200. Away From Home: General. Since IRC § 162(a)(2) is available only for expenses incurred by the taxpayer while away from "home," it is necessary to locate the taxpayer's "home." The Service maintains that for purposes of IRC § 162(a)(2), a taxpayer's "home" is the location of the taxpayer's regular, or principal (if more than one regular) place of business rather than the location of the taxpayer's residence. Rev. Rul. 99–7. The Tax Court and at least five Circuit Courts of Appeals concur with the government's view, but the Second Circuit has held that a taxpayer's home is his residence. Compare *Six v. United States*, 450 F.2d 66 (2d Cir. 1971); *Rosenspan v. United States*, 438 F.2d 905 (2d Cir.); and the concurring opinion of Judge Keeton in *Hantzis v. Commissioner*, 638 F.2d 248 (1st Cir.

1981) with *Coombs v. Commissioner*, 608 F.2d 1269 (9th Cir. 1979); *Michel Jr. v. Commissioner*, 629 F.2d 1071 (5th Cir. 1980); *Weiberg v. Commissioner*, 639 F.2d 434 (8th Cir. 1981); *Andrews v. Commissioner*, 931 F.2d 132 (1st Cir. 1991).

The Sixth Circuit also adopted the "principal place of business" test and held that, when the taxpayer has two business localities, the determination of the location of a taxpayer's principal place of business rests on a weighing of three factors: (a) the length of time spent in each locality; (b) the degree of taxpayer's business activity in each locality; and (c) the relative portion of income derived from each locality. *Markey v. Commissioner*, 490 F.2d 1249, 1255 (6th Cir. 1974). See also *Andrews v. Commissioner*, *supra*.

In several cases, the courts of appeals have eschewed the need to determine a taxpayer's home and instead have rested their decision on the question of whether there was a business reason for the taxpayer to maintain his home in one locality while working in another locality. If not, no deduction was allowed. *Hantzis v. Commissioner*, *supra*; *Daly v. Commissioner*, 662 F.2d 253 (4th Cir. 1981) (a divided en banc decision). Despite those cases, if the job at the other locality is temporary and if the taxpayer's residence is an abode in a real and substantial sense [see § **10.3250**], there should not be a requirement of a business reason to live in one locality and work in the other. However, if there is no business reason for the taxpayer to reside where he does, it will be difficult to establish that the taxpayer lives in an abode in a real and substantial sense.

§ 10.3210. Military Assignment. In *Commissioner v. Stidger*, 386 U.S. 287 (1967), the Supreme Court held that the "home" of a military officer who was assigned to a post in Japan was his post abroad rather than the state of California where his wife and children resided. The Court relied heavily on the special position of the military with particular emphasis on the tax-free allowance Congress has granted military personnel to provide them subsistence and quarters.

§ 10.3211. *Stidger* and Non–Military Taxpayers. In *Stidger*, the Court expressly declined to resolve the question of what constitutes the tax home of non-military taxpayers. However, there is language in *Stidger* which refers with apparent approval to the Service's position that a taxpayer's home for tax purposes is his principal place of business, and, therefore, *Stidger* has been cited in support of that position. See *Sanders* *v. Commissioner*, 439 F.2d 296 (9th Cir. 1971). But in rejecting the Service's construction of "home," the Second Circuit treated the decision in *Stidger* as *sui generis* for military personnel. *Six v. United States*, § **10.3200.**

§ **10.3220. Overnight or "Sleep or Rest" Rules.** The Service maintains that travel "away from home" refers only to travel where the taxpayer is away for a sufficient period of time to reasonably require sleep or rest. The application of this rule (sometimes referred to as the "overnight rule" and sometimes as the "sleep or rest rule") is explained in Rev. Rul. 75–168. As to the deductibility of meals, the Supreme Court sustained the government's "overnight rule" and denied a deduction for meals where the taxpayer was not away from home for a sufficient period to require sleep. *United States v. Correll*, 389 U.S. 299 (1967). You will recall that even if meals are deductible, only 50% of the cost of the meals can qualify for a deduction (a larger percentage for employees working in the transportation industry). See § **10.3100.**

Several courts have applied the overnight test to deny a deduction for transportation expenses, rather than limiting that rule to the cost of meals. E.g., *Turner v. Commissioner*, 56 T.C. 27 (1971) (reviewed by the entire court but vacated and remanded by the Second Circuit on the government's motion); and *Sanders v. Commissioner*, § **10.3211.** Note, however, that in *some* cases, notwithstanding the inapplicability of IRC § 162(a)(2), a taxpayer can deduct his cost of transportation for non-overnight trips under the general provision of IRC § 162(a) which is not subject to the overnight rule. Rev. Rul. 90–23 as modified by Rev. Rul. 99–7. See § **10.3312–4B** for a discussion of the policy considerations underlying the overnight rule.

§ **10.3221. Transportation Between Residence and Work Location (Commuting Expense).** In the absence of one of several exceptions, a taxpayer's transportation cost of travelling between his residence and a work location is a nondeductible commuting expense. Treas. Reg. §§ 1.162–2(e), 1.262–1(b)(5). While the taxpayer could not earn income if he did not travel to his place of work, the expense also has personal, nonbusiness elements in that the taxpayer chose his place of residence for personal reasons, and a commuting expense is as much a cost of getting to and from the residence as it is to get to and from the work location. Rather than to divide the expenses into business and nonbusiness portions, the tax law denies a deduction for all of the costs.

There are important exceptions to the nondeductibility of commuting expenses. These exceptions are set forth in Rev. Rul. 99–7. In examining these exceptions, keep in mind that a deduction is allowed for the taxpayer's transportation costs in travelling from one work site to another work site, regardless of whether the two work sites are part of the same employment or whether they are sites of different employments with different employers. Rev. Rul. 55–109. There is no personal element in travelling from one work location to another. However, if one of the work sites is also the taxpayer's residence, there is some personal element to the travel, and so a special set of rules have been designed for that situation.

1) If the taxpayer's principal place of business, as determined under IRC § 280A(c)(1)(A) is located in his residence, the taxpayer can deduct the daily transportation cost incurred in going between the residence and another work location in the same trade or business, regardless of whether the other work location is regular or temporary, and regardless of whether the other work location is within or outside the metropolitan area in which the taxpayer resides. Rev. Rul. 99–7. This is merely an application of the rule that the transportation costs of travelling between work locations are deductible. It would seem, although omitted from the ruling, that where the residence is the taxpayer's principal place of business, a taxpayer can deduct the daily transportation costs of travelling between his residence and a work location for a different business than the one conducted as his residence. There is no personal element in making that trip.

2) If the taxpayer has at least one *regular* work location (i.e, a regular place of business) away from his residence, the transportation cost of going between his residence and a *temporary* work location in the same trade or business is deductible, regardless of whether the temporary work location is within or outside of the metropolitan area in which the taxpayer resides. Rev. Rul. 99–7. The meaning of a "temporary job" is discussed at § **10.3312.**

3) Even if a taxpayer does not conduct any business at his residence, the taxpayer can deduct the transportation costs of

going between his residence and a temporary work location that lies *outside* the metropolitan area in which the taxpayer lives and normally works. If the temporary work location is within the metropolitan area in which the taxpayer lives, no deduction will be allowed for the transportation costs unless either of the exceptions in 1) and 2) above is applicable. Rev. Rul. 99–7. The meaning of a "temporary job" is discussed at § **10.3312.**

As to the meaning of the term "regular place of business," which term is used in Rev. Rul. 99–7, the Tax Court has held that the term is broader than the "principal place of business" standard. *Walker v. Commissioner*, 101 T.C. 537 (1993). In *Walker*, the taxpayer (a professional tree cutter) worked seven hours a week at his residence, maintained a workshop there, stored his tools there, and was contacted there for employment at temporary job sites. The court held that his residence was a "regular place of business," but not a "principal place of business." In PLR 9806007, the Service ruled that a work location at which the taxpayer spent 25% to 27% of his working days was a regular place of business. While the Service has stated it will not follow the *Walker* decision, that rejection does not refer to the portion of the *Walker* decision that determined the meaning of a "regular place of business." See Rev. Rul. 99–7.

§ **10.3230. Major and Minor Post.** When a taxpayer has a principal place of business in one location and a minor post in another location, he may deduct the round-trip expenses incurred in traveling to his minor post, including (if he complied with the overnight rule) the cost of his meals and lodging. Of course, if unreimbursed, only 50% of the cost of meals is deductible, and (unless reimbursed) the travel expenses of an employee are subject to the 2% of AGI floor and the reduction of itemized deductions imposed by IRC § 68. IRC §§ 67(b), 274(n).

The Commissioner ruled in Rev. Rul. 63–145 that a taxpayer who is residing at a temporary or minor post can deduct the cost of commuting from his lodging to his place of business at that temporary or minor post provided that such costs are reasonable in amount and incurred away from home (i.e., the area in which taxpayer's principal place of business is located) in the pursuit of his business. The Commissioner also ruled in Rev. Rul. 63–145 that the taxpayer can deduct his laundry and dry cleaning expenses while away from home on business. Other incidental expenses that can be deducted are tips for baggage handlers and for waiters. See Rev. Proc. 93–50, Sec. 3.02(3). Even if the taxpayer does not remain overnight at his minor post, he can usually deduct under IRC § 162(a) his cost of round-trip transportation between his principal and minor post [see § **10.3221**]; but since the taxpayer is not "away from home" if he fails to remain overnight, he cannot deduct any part of the cost of his meals or other living expenses. Rev. Rul. 55–109.

§ **10.3231. Illustration.** A taxpayer is employed in Detroit for nine months of the year, but he is required by his employer to work in Dallas for three months of the year. Dallas is the taxpayer's minor post, and the taxpayer can deduct his cost of transportation from Detroit to Dallas and return. Since the taxpayer satisfied the overnight rule, he can also deduct his reasonable costs of meals (subject to the 50% limitation described at § **10.3100**) and lodging while living and working in Dallas, and he can deduct the cost of commuting from his lodging in Dallas to his Dallas office. These deductions are allowable even though the taxpayer is required to work for three months of each year in Dallas (i.e., the trip to the minor post is a recurring one). Rev. Rul. 75–432. Unless reimbursed by his employer, the travel expenses of an employee constitute miscellaneous itemized deductions that are subject to the 2% of AGI floor imposed by IRC § 67.

§ **10.3232. Travel Among Multiple Jobs.** When a taxpayer works at several jobs in the same day, his transportation cost of traveling from one job site to the other is a deductible business expense. Rev. Rul. 55–109. While the taxpayer may not be away from home and so IRC § 162(a)(2) is inapplicable, the expenses are deductible under the general provision of IRC § 162(a). In PLR 8023052, the taxpayer held three jobs. There was no indication in the ruling that the taxpayer's residence could qualify as a principal place of business. The Commissioner ruled that no deduction is allowed for the cost of the taxpayer's transporting himself to the first job of the day, but the costs of transporting himself from the first job to the second and from the second job to the third are deductible. The letter ruling suggests that the transportation costs incurred in going from the third job to the taxpayer's home at the end of work may be deductible if the third job lies outside the general locality of the taxpayer's customary employment; otherwise, those costs are not deductible. In light of Rev. Rul. 99–7, it would seem that regardless of the distance between the third job's work location and the taxpayer's residence, no deduction will be allowed for the cost of returning to the residence unless the third job was temporary.

§ 10.3233. Office in Residence as Minor Post. When a taxpayer maintains an office in his residence so that he may work there in the evening or on the weekends and the home office does not qualify as the principal place of business, the taxpayer *can not* deduct the cost of going between his home and the downtown office at which he works during the day. *Green, Jr. v. Commissioner*, 59 T.C. 456 (1972); *Mazzotta v. Commissioner*, 57 T.C. 427 (1971), aff'd per curiam, 465 F.2d 1399 (2d Cir. 1972); and *Matteson v. Commissioner*, 514 F.2d 43 (8th Cir. 1975). See **§ 10.3221.** The downtown office is not a temporary job site. The primary purpose of such transportation costs is personal rather than business-oriented, and therefore no deduction is allowed. In effect, such expenses do not satisfy the "exigencies of the business" requisite. See **§ 10.3110.** However, the Commissioner and the Tax Court have held that if the taxpayer's home office is his *principal* place of business, the taxpayer's round-trip expenses of going from his home office to other work locations may be deductible. Rev. Rul. 94–47; *Wisconsin Psychiatric Services, Ltd. v. Commissioner*, 76 T.C. 839, 849–850 (1981); *Curphey v. Commissioner*, 73 T.C. 766 (1980).

§ 10.3240. Boundaries of a Taxpayer's "Home." The Service has held that a taxpayer's home includes the general geographic area in which his principal place of business is located and is not restricted to city limits or to other political divisions. Rev. Rul. 55–109. Presumably, if a taxpayer's home is deemed to be his place of residence, it would include the general geographical area in which he resides.

§ 10.3250. No Principal or Regular Place of Business but a Regular Place of Abode. If a taxpayer who is in a trade or business has no principal or regular place of business, but does have a regular place of abode in a real and substantial sense, then his residence may qualify as his tax home, and he may be "away from home" when he is at work on a temporary job *in a different vicinity.* Rev. Rul. 73–529. However, if the temporary job is located within the metropolitan area in which the taxpayer's regular place of abode is located, then no deduction is allowable for the transportation costs of going to and returning from the temporary job. Rev. Rul. 99–7. The significance of classifying an abode as the taxpayer's home is that the taxpayer might then be able to qualify travel expenses away from home for the § 162(a)(2) deduction.

The Commissioner has listed three criteria which the Service will employ in determining whether an abode is sufficiently substantial to constitute a home: (1) whether the taxpayer performs a portion of his business in the vicinity of the abode and resides at the abode on such occasions; (2) whether the taxpayer incurs double living expenses when away from the abode on business; and (3) whether the taxpayer either (a) has not abandoned the vicinity of his historical place of lodging, (b) has a spouse or lineal descendant residing at the abode, or (c) uses the abode frequently for his lodging. Rev. Rul. 73–529. If a taxpayer satisfies all three criteria and has no principal or regular place of business, the Service will treat the abode as his home. If he satisfies only two of the criteria, the Service *may* treat the abode as his home but will not necessarily do so; if he fails to satisfy two of the criteria, the Service will treat him as an itinerant. See § **10.3260.**

Even if a taxpayer's abode is treated as his tax home, the taxpayer may founder on the exigencies of the business requisite [see *Hantzis v. Commissioner*, 638 F.2d 248 (1st Cir. 1981); *Tucker v. Commissioner*, 55 T.C. 783 (1971)], or on the overnight rule [see *Turner v. Commissioner*, 56 T.C. 27 (1971)] and thus lose his claim for a deduction under IRC § 162(a)(2). See also *Daly v. Commissioner*, 662 F.2d 253 (4th Cir. 1981) (en banc). Transportation costs to a temporary job sometimes can be deducted under the general provision of IRC § 162(a). See § **10.3220.**

It is not clear whether the Service will still be willing to treat an abode, however substantial, as a taxpayer's home. That is, the Service may no longer apply that approach. However, it seems that there should be some principle that allows a deduction for travelling to a distant location for a temporary job. when the taxpayer has no principal or regular place of employment.

§ 10.3260. No Principal or Regular Place of Business and No Permanent Residence. If a taxpayer has no principal or regular place of business and also has no regular place of abode in

a real and substantial sense, he has *no tax home* and, therefore, can have no traveling expenses under IRC § 162(a)(2) for expenses incurred away from home. Rev. Rul. 75–432; *James v. United States*, 308 F.2d 204 (9th Cir. 1962); *Brandl v. Commissioner*, 513 F.2d 697 (6th Cir. 1975); *Deamer v. Commissioner*, 752 F.2d 337, 339 (8th Cir. 1985); and *Rosenspan v. United States*, 438 F.2d 905 (2d Cir. 1971) (denying deductions to a traveling salesman who had no permanent residence and who traveled throughout the year). See also *Barone v. Commissioner*, 85 T.C. 462 (1985). However, in certain cases, a taxpayer's costs of transporting himself (but not his family and not his food and lodging expenses) may be deductible under IRC § 162(a) as an ordinary business expense. For example, the costs of the taxpayer's going from one work location to another are deductible. Since such a taxpayer has no permanent residence, his food and lodging expenses do not constitute extraordinary expenses caused by the exigencies of his trade or business.

§ 10.3270. Temporary Jobs. Even if the Commissioner's interpretation of "home" is adopted, a taxpayer who leaves the location of his principal place of business in order to travel to a temporary job for a sufficient time to require sleep or rest is deemed to be away from home. See *Six v. United States*, 450 F.2d 66 (2d Cir. 1971); Rev. Rul. 75–432. Of course, if the Commissioner's interpretation of "home" is rejected, as one Circuit Court has done, a taxpayer who travels to a temporary job is away from home if he is away from his place of residence. To obtain a deduction, the taxpayer must also satisfy the requirement that his travel expenses are within the exigencies of his business. The application of the temporary job exception to the "exigencies" requirement is discussed at **§ 10.3312**. The distinction between a temporary job and a job of indefinite duration is discussed at **§ 10.3312–1**.

§ 10.3271. Summer Employment of a Student. In *Hantzis v. Commissioner* at **§ 10.3270**, the First Circuit denied a deduction for transportation costs between Boston and New York City and living expenses in New York City for a Harvard law student who worked as a legal assistant in a New York law firm for her summer employment. The taxpayer's husband remained in Boston because his work as a university professor required him to teach in Boston that summer The taxpayer claimed that she was away from her home in Boston when she lived in New York at a temporary job. The First Circuit, in reversing the Tax Court's determination that a deduction was allowable, held that a taxpayer is not away from home unless the taxpayer can demonstrate a business reason both for having a location in the place she claims as home as well as in the place where she is working. The taxpayer had no *business* reason for maintaining a home in Boston. While the court did not rest its decision on the taxpayer's failure to satisfy the exigencies of the business requirement, its construction of the "away from home" requirement resembles the exigencies of the business requirement. In general, the courts and the Service have resisted claims for deductions for temporary summer jobs of students.

§ 10.3300. Exigencies of the Business.

§ 10.3310. **Commuting Expenses.** The cost of a taxpayer's transportation from his residence to his business office and the cost of returning to his residence is normally a nondeductible expense. Treas. Reg. §§ 1.162–2(e), 1.262–1(b)(5). While the taxpayer could not earn gross income if he did not make the trip from his residence, the expense also has overtones of personal, nonbusiness considerations in that the taxpayer chose his place of residence for personal reasons. There are a few instances where commuting-type expenses are deductible (e.g., the cost of commuting to a place of business while the taxpayer is living at a temporary or minor post). Other examples are set forth in § 10.3221.

§ 10.3311. **Transportation of Tools.** If a taxpayer drives from his residence to his place of work and if he carries tools or heavy objects with him in his car, the question arises as to whether he will be allowed to deduct his transportation expense under IRC § 162(a) as an ordinary business expense of transporting the tools even though the expense is not deductible as a traveling expense under IRC § 162(a)(2).

§ 10.3311–1. **Requisites for Deduction.** The Commissioner initially adopted the position in Rev. Rul. 63–100, which was later revoked, that a taxpayer will be permitted a deduction in such cases only if: (1) the tools or other objects are too heavy or too bulky to be carried with the taxpayer by an alternate method of transportation; and (2) the taxpayer would not have driven to work *but for* the need to transport his tools or other objects.

§ 10.3311–2. The *Fausner* Decision. Two Circuit
Courts of Appeals (the Second and the Seventh Circuits)
rejected the reasoning of Rev. Rul. 63–100 and allowed a
taxpayer, who would have driven to work even if there
were no need to transport his tools, nevertheless to deduct
a portion of his commuting costs. In *Fausner v. Commissioner*, 472 F.2d 561 (5th Cir. 1973), the Fifth Circuit
declined to follow the lead of those two Circuits Courts.
The taxpayer in *Fausner* was a commercial airline pilot
who drove his automobile 84 miles round trip from home to
his place of employment, and the taxpayer claimed a deduction for the expenses of driving that distance because he
carried a flight-kit bag and an overnight bag in his automobile. The taxpayer admitted that he would have driven to
work even if it were not necessary to carry the bags since
no public transportation was available. In a per curiam
opinion, the Fifth Circuit denied the taxpayer a deduction.
The court stated: "Since the record shows that Fausner
would have driven his car to and from his place of employment anyway, we cannot find that he is entitled to what
would amount to special relief which would distinguish him
from other taxpayers because of the mere fortuity that he
placed the bags he was required to carry in the trunk of his
commuting vehicle." The court also stressed that there was
no evidence that the taxpayer incurred any additional
expenses in carrying the bags over his nondeductible commuting expenses (which he would have incurred in any
event).

§ 10.3311–3. The Supreme Court's Decision. The Supreme Court granted certiorari in *Fausner* and summarily
(without oral argument or briefs) affirmed the Fifth Circuit's decision. *Fausner v. Commissioner*, 413 U.S. 838
(1973). In a brief per curiam opinion, the Court noted that
the taxpayer would have driven to work in any event, and
the Court stated: "Additional expenses may at any time be
incurred for transporting job-required tools and materials
to and from work. [The Court here cited Rev. Rul. 63–100
which had propounded the *but for* text described at
§ 10.3311–1.] Then an allocation of costs between 'personal' and 'business' expenses may be feasible. But no such
allocation can be made here."

§ 10.3311–4. The Commissioner's Revised Position. In Rev. Rul. 75–380, the Commissioner revoked Rev. Rul. 63–100, rejected the *but for* test, and adopted an entirely new standard. The Commissioner's current position, as expressed in that ruling, is that a taxpayer cannot deduct the cost of commuting to work even if he would not have driven but for the need to transport bulky or heavy tools. A taxpayer will be allowed a deduction for any additional expense he incurs in transporting the tools over his commuting expense. Thus, if the taxpayer rented a trailer in which to carry the tools, the additional cost of renting the trailer will be deductible, but the cost of driving to work in his car (to which the trailer is attached) will not be deductible. Rev. Rul. 75–380. The Commissioner contends in Rev. Rul. 75–380 that this "additional expense" standard was the one adopted by the Supreme Court and by the Fifth Circuit in *Fausner*. Despite making this contention in Rev. Rul. 75–380, in litigating subsequent cases, the Commissioner has applied the *but for* test. See *Fausner v. Commissioner*, 38 T.C.M. 1365 (1979); and see § **10.3311–5.** For an interesting controversy concerning the operation of the *but for* test, see *McCabe v. Commissioner*, 76 T.C. 876 (1981), aff'd by a divided court, 688 F.2d 102 (2d Cir. 1982).

§ 10.3311–5. Litigation Position of the Commissioner. In *Grayson v. Commissioner*, 36 T.C.M. 1201 (1977), and in *Randazzo v. Commissioner*, 36 T.C.M. 1199 (1977), the Tax Court stated that the Commissioner conceded in his briefs in those cases that a taxpayer can deduct his expenses of driving his car from his home to work and back where the taxpayer would have used public transportation had it not been for the need of transporting his tools, which he kept in the trunk of his car. The concession of the Commissioner is inconsistent with Rev. Rul. 75–380, and instead follows the *but for* test. The Commissioner's concession apparently was made also in *Radocy v. Commissioner*, 36 T.C.M. 1129 (1977). Notwithstanding the Commissioner's concession, the Tax Court denied the taxpayer's claims for a deduction in *Randazzo* and in *Radocy* because the court believed that the taxpayers in those cases would have driven their cars to work even if they did not have to transport their tools. However, in the *Grayson* case, the court allowed the taxpayer to deduct the transportation costs. The court accepted the taxpayer's contention that he would not have used his car but for the need to transport his tools even though the taxpayer would have had to "hitchhike" part of the distance to and from work if he did not use his own car.

§ 10.3311–6. Future Treatment. It is by no means certain that Rev. Rul. 75–380 will be followed by courts in future litigation. But see *Coker v. Commissioner*, 487 F.2d 593 (2d Cir. 1973). There is language in the *Fausner* opinions to support the Commissioner's position, but the opinions could even more readily be construed to support the *but for* test, especially since both the Fifth Circuit and the Supreme Court took pains to point out that Fausner would have driven to work in any event and since the Supreme Court cited with apparent approval Rev. Rul. 63–100 (which promulgated the *but for* test). Moreover, the fact that the Supreme Court's decision was a summary affirmance and that the opinions of both courts were merely brief per curiam opinions makes it less plausible that either of those courts intended to promulgate an entirely new standard for deductibility. The revised position of the Commissioner [Rev. Rul. 75–380] may not have great practical significance because few taxpayers (if any) will be able to meet the *but for* standard if it were made applicable; if so, there is not likely to be much future litigation of this issue.

§ 10.3312. Temporary Job Exception. When a taxpayer travels from his residence to a temporary post of duty or to a place of employment where his job is temporary, there is an administratively created exception to the requirement that traveling expenses under IRC § 162(a)(2) be incurred for the exigencies of business. In such cases, if the requirements laid down in Rev. Rul. 99–7 are satisfied [see **§ 10.3221**], or possibly if the taxpayer has a regular place of abode in a real and substantial sense [§ **10.3250**], the taxpayer's cost of transportation to the job location and back are deductible under IRC § 162(a)(2). *Peurifoy v. Commissioner*, 358 U.S. 59 (1958); *Six v. United States*, 450 F.2d 66 (2d Cir. 1971). The taxpayer's costs of meals and lodging while living at the temporary post also are deductible if the "sleep or rest" requirement is satisfied. See *Six v. United States, supra*. The rationale for this rule is that where a taxpayer accepts a job in a different location, it is reasonable to expect him to move his residence to that location. If he fails to do so, that is a personal decision the cost of which is not a business expense. However, if the job is of short duration, it is not reasonable to expect him to move his family and belongings there. Consequently, in such cases, the additional costs borne by the taxpayer should be treated as business expenses. Note that when a taxpayer is away from home in the pursuit of a trade or business, the fact that the taxpayer rents out his residence for all or part of the period that he is away will not preclude the taxpayer from deducting his travel expenses under IRC § 162(a)(2). IRC § 280A(f)(4).

§ 10.3312–1. Meaning of Temporary. If a taxpayer realistically anticipates that he will be away from his abode for less than one year and if, in fact, he is away for less than one year, the job will qualify as temporary. As a consequence of a 1992 amendment to IRC § 162(a), the literal terms of the statute would seem to require that if a taxpayer's period of employment away from home lasts for more than one year, regardless of how short a time the taxpayer had anticipated that the away-from-home employment would last, the employment will not qualify as "temporary," and therefore the taxpayer's travel expenses will not be deductible. IRC § 162(a) (last sentence). However, in several rulings that were promulgated in 1993 and 1999, the statutory amendment has been construed more liberally than the explicit language would suggest.

First, the Commissioner discussed the operation of the 1992 amendment in Notice 93–29. While the statutory language bars temporary job treatment when the period of employment away from home exceeds one year, the Commissioner described the rule in Notice 93–29 as barring temporary job treatment when "the taxpayer's period of employment away from home *in a single location* lasts for more than one year." [Emphasis added.] The limiting language "in a single location" is consistent with the Conference Report to the amending Act. One question that needs to be resolved is whether the rule will apply when the taxpayer is employed away from home for more than one year at two or more different jobs for different employers but at the same location. In Notice 93–29, the Commissioner stated that the Service intends to publish further guidance on the 1–year rule and requested comments from the public on that rule.

In a subsequent ruling, Rev. Rul. 93–86, which was essentially repeated in Rev. Rul 99–7, the Commissioner again addressed the meaning of the 1992 amendment. According to those rulings:

(1) If employment away from home in a single location is expected to last for more than one year, or if there is no realistic expectation that the employment will last for one year or less, the employment will be treated as indefinite (and so does not qualify for the travel expense deduction) even if the employment actually lasts for less than one year.

(2) If employment away from home in a single location is realistically expected to last for one year or less, but at some later date it becomes realistic to expect the employment to last for more than one year, the employment will be treated as temporary (in the absence of facts and circumstances indicating otherwise) until the date that the taxpayer's realistic expectation changed, and it will be treated as not temporary from that date forward.

§ 10.3312–2. **Travel to Nearest Habitable Community.** If the general area of a taxpayer's permanent employment is not a habitable community for the taxpayer (e.g., where a civilian employee works at a large military base which prohibits civilians from living on the base), the question has arisen as to whether the taxpayer can claim a deduction for the expense of the round-trip transportation between the nearest habitable community and the place of employment.

§ 10.3312–2A. **Illustration.** Jones is employed at an AEC plant in Neutron, Arizona. The nearest habitable community is Proton, Arizona, which is 50 miles from Neutron. Jones resides in Electron, Arizona, which is 60 miles from Neutron and 10 miles from Proton. Jones seeks to deduct the transportation cost of traveling the 100 mile round-trip distance between Neutron and Proton each work day. Jones contends that while the cost of the 20 miles he travels round-trip between Electron and Proton is incurred as a consequence of his personal decision to live in Electron and therefore is not deductible, the transportation cost of the 100 miles he travels round-trip between Proton and Neutron is incurred as a consequence of the exigencies of his business and therefore is deductible.

§ 10.3312–2B. Justification for the Deduction. There is considerable justification for granting a deduction to taxpayers in the position of Jones in the Illustration above. The transportation cost of traveling round-trip from Proton to Neutron is little different from the cost of transportation to different offices of an employment after first reporting to work at one such office, which costs are clearly deductible. The Ninth Circuit initially allowed a taxpayer a deduction for transportation costs between his work post and the nearest habitable community [*Wright v. Hartsell*, 305 F.2d 221 (9th Cir. 1962)]; but the court subsequently overruled *Wright v. Hartsell*, and held that such costs are not deductible. *Sanders v. Commissioner*, 439 F.2d 296 (9th Cir. 1971). The decision in *Sanders* rests heavily on the Supreme Court's decision in *Correll* that for purposes of claiming a deduction for meals, a taxpayer is not away from home under IRC § 162(a)(2) unless his trip extends overnight (i.e., the Court extended *Correll* to bar a deduction for transportation costs).

§ 10.3313. Commuting Combined With Tour of Duty. In *Pollei v. Commissioner*, 877 F.2d 838 (10th Cir. 1989), rev'g 87 T.C. 869 (1986), the Tenth Circuit allowed a deduction to city police captains for the cost of driving from their residence to police headquarters and return because the captains were required by the police department to be on duty during such commuting trips as part of a cost-cutting program. The court determined that the tour of duty requirement was imposed upon the taxpayers and was bona fide. The Service noted its fear that a decision for the taxpayers in *Pollei* might open the floodgates in that many employers would adopt a tour of duty requirement. The Tenth Circuit suggested in dictum that there would not be many cases in which commuting expenses would qualify for a deduction because most taxpayers would not be able to demonstrate that their tour of duty requirement was imposed on them involuntarily and that their work requirement was of sufficient amount to warrant a deduction.

§ 10.3400. Moving Expenses. A taxpayer's unreimbursed expenses in moving from his former residence to the location of a new place of work which is at least 50 miles further from his former residence than was his former place of work (or if none, at least 50 miles from his former residence), is a deductible expense if the conditions established in IRC § 217 are satisfied. In general, these conditions are that the taxpayer must either: (a) be a full-time employee in the new location for at least 39 weeks during the 12–month period following his arrival; or (b) during the 24–month period following his arrival, be a full-time employee or perform services as a self-employed individual on a full-time basis for at least 78 weeks, of which not less than 39 weeks were performed during the 12–month period described above. IRC § 217(c)(2). If the taxpayer fails to satisfy either of the above conditions because of his death, disability, discharge (other than for willful misconduct), or transfer by his employer, he will nevertheless be permitted the deduction. However, the premature discharge or transfer of a taxpayer will not excuse the taxpayer's failure to satisfy the work period requirements unless his employment was one in which he could reasonably have been expected to comply with those requirements. IRC § 217(d)(1).

§ 10.3410. Deductible Items. The expenses deductible under IRC § 217 include: (a) the cost of traveling, including lodging, incurred by the taxpayer and members of his household in moving from the former location to the new one; and (b) the cost of moving the household goods and personal effects of the taxpayer and the members of his household. IRC § 217(b)(1). The moving expenses of a person other than the taxpayer will be deductible only if such person has both the old residence and the new residence as his principal place of abode and is a member of the taxpayer's household. IRC § 217(b)(2). No deduction will be allowed for the cost of meals (including meals taken while travelling from the old to the new location). IRC § 217(b)(1).

§ 10.3411. Deductions For Relocation Expenses. Prior to 1994, deductions were allowed, subject to a dollar limitation, for the cost of traveling to the new job location to search for a new residence and for the cost of meals and lodging incurred while occupying temporary quarters at the new job location for any 30 consecutive day period after the taxpayer obtained employment. Also, prior to 1994, the taxpayer could deduct certain expenditures, subject to a dollar limitation, incurred in connection with the sale of the taxpayer's former residence, the purchase of a new residence, the settlement of a lease on the taxpayer's prior residence, or the acquisition of a lease for the taxpayer's new residence. None of those expenses are now deductible. The provision for deducting those items was deleted from the Code by the Omnibus Budget Reconciliation Act of 1993.

§ 10.3412. Nonitemized Deduction. Unreimbursed moving expenses that are deductible under IRC § 217 are nonitemized deductions. IRC § 62(a)(15).

§ 10.3420. Reimbursement by Employer. A reimbursement of an employee's moving expenses by his employer is excluded from the employee's gross income to the extent that the reimbursed expense would have been deductible by the employee under IRC § 217 if he had not been reimbursed. IRC § 132(a)(6),(g). **§ 2.1628** and **§ 2.1720.**

§ 10.3430. Members of the Armed Forces. IRC § 217(g) provides special (and liberal) rules for the treatment of the expenses of a member of the Armed Forces on active duty who moves pursuant to a military order and incident to a permanent change of station.

§ 10.3500. Substantiation and Records. IRC § 274(d) imposes requirements as to record keeping and substantiation that a taxpayer must maintain to qualify for a deduction for travel expenses which are otherwise deductible under IRC §§ 162 or 212. If the taxpayer is an employee and if his travel expenses are reimbursed by his employer by providing a per diem allowance that does not exceed certain limits, no substantiation will be required. See **§ 10.3100.**

Instead of maintaining records for the use of an automobile for business travel, the Service permits the use of a standard mileage allowance. This allowance represents operating costs (e.g., depreciation of the car, gasoline, oil, maintenance and tires). Parking fees, tolls, interest and taxes can be deducted separately. The current mileage allowance for business use is 40.5¢ a mile, and the mileage allowance for moving expenses under IRC § 217 is 15¢ a mile. Rev. Proc. 2004–64. The amount of the mileage allowance is revised periodically.

§ 10.4000. EDUCATION EXPENSES.

§ 10.4100. Deductible Expenses. Except as noted otherwise in **§ 10.4200**, educational expenses are deductible business expenses, even though the education may lead to a degree, if the education either: (1) maintains or improves skills required of the taxpayer in his employment or other trade or business, or (2) satisfies a requirement imposed by the taxpayer's employer, or by some law or regulation, as a condition of the taxpayer's retention of an established employment relationship, status, or rate of compensation. Treas. Reg. § 1.162–5(a).

§ 10.4200. Nondeductible Education Expenses. Even though an education expense complies with one of the requirements established in **§ 10.4100**, it will not be deductible: (1) if the education in question is essential to satisfy the minimum requirements for qualification in the taxpayer's chosen employment or other trade or business, or (2) if the education will lead to qualifying the taxpayer for a new trade or business regardless of whether the taxpayer intends to enter the new trade or business. Treas. Reg. § 1.162–5(b).

§ 10.4210. Illustration 1: Continuing Professional Education Courses. *X*, a licensed attorney practicing in Washington, D.C., attends a two-week course on federal taxation in New York City. *X* is maintaining and improving his skills as an attorney. Consequently, *X*'s costs of attending the course, including the cost of his transportation and of his lodging and 50% of his meals while living in New York City are deductible.

§ 10.4220. Illustration 2: Law School Course. *Y*, a licensed CPA, attends night law school and acquires a law degree. *Y* took the law courses to improve his skills as an accountant, and he has no intention of leaving his profession to practice law. Since the law degree satisfies the minimum requirement for becoming an attorney, *Y* cannot deduct his educational expenses regardless of the fact that he does not intend to enter the legal profession. *O'Donnell v. Commissioner*, 62 T.C. 781 (1974).

§ 10.4230. Illustration 3: University Courses. *Z* became an ordained minister at the age of 19. *Z* subsequently entered college and earned a bachelor's degree. The Tax Court and the Ninth Circuit permitted *Z* to deduct the expenses of his attending college because *Z*'s college education aided him in serving his congregation and did not qualify him for a new profession. *Glasgow v. Commissioner*, 486 F.2d 1045 (10th Cir. 1973); aff'g 31 T.C.M. 310 (1972); see also *Ford v. Commissioner*, 487 F.2d 1025 (9th Cir. 1973), aff'g 56 T.C. 1300 (1971), allowing a high school teacher to deduct the expenses of obtaining a Ph.D. degree; and *Toner v. Commissioner*, 623 F.2d 315 (3d Cir. 1980), allowing a parochial school teacher to deduct the cost of taking college courses towards earning a bachelor's degree where the requirements for teaching at the parochial school were satisfied by a high school education. While in *Toner,* a bachelor's degree was a minimum requirement for qualifying to teach in public schools, the Third Circuit deemed that that did not qualify taxpayer for a new trade or business because, under the special regulatory treatment accorded to teachers, all types of teaching are considered to involve the same general kind of work. These cases are atypical; in most cases, the expenses of obtaining a college or advanced degree will not be deductible. See, e.g., *Davis v. Commissioner,* 65 T.C. 1014 (1976) (expenses of a Ph.D. program were nondeductible); *Browne v. Commissioner,* 73 T.C. 723 (1980) (expenses of obtaining a bachelor's degree were nondeductible); *Link v. Commissioner,* 90 T.C. 460 (1988), aff'd 869 F.2d 1491 (6th Cir 1989) (summer employment was not sufficient to establish taxpayer in a trade or business, and so cost of obtaining MBA degree was not deductible); and *Robinson v. Commissioner,* 78 T.C. 550 (1982) (no deduction for cost of 4–year degree program at a university nursing school).

§ 10.4240. Bar Review Courses. In *Sharon v. Commissioner,* 66 T.C. 515 (1976), a majority of the Tax Court allowed the taxpayer to amortize over his life expectancy the cost of obtaining a license to practice law in New York, the subsequent cost of his obtaining admission to the bar of the state of California, and the subsequent cost of obtaining admission to the bar of the Supreme Court of the United States. The Court included the cost of the taxpayer's traveling from California to Washington to be present for his admission to the Supreme Court's bar (as required by the Court's rules) in the taxpayer's amortizable cost of obtaining admission to the bar. However, the Tax Court held that the taxpayer's cost of his college and law school education and the cost of a New York bar review course and a California bar review course were nondeductible educational expenses and could not be deducted or added to the amortizable cost of the taxpayer's obtaining a license to practice law in either of those states. A majority of the Tax Court deemed the taxpayer's admission to the California bar as acquiring a new trade or business even though the taxpayer was already an attorney licensed in New York. Consequently, the majority held that the California bar review expenses were incurred to meet the minimum educational requirements of that trade or business. See Treas. Reg. § 1.162–

5(b)(2)(iii), Ex. (3). On appeal, the Ninth Circuit affirmed the Tax Court's decision to deny a deduction for the expenses of taxpayer's college and law school education and of his two bar review courses. The court said that the "allocation of those expenses between the nondeductible personal component and any deductible capital component would not be feasible." *Sharon v. Commissioner*, 591 F.2d 1273 (9th Cir. 1978).

§ 10.4250. Common Sense. The Tax Court stated that it will apply a common sense test for resolving education expense cases where the taxpayer obtains a degree (i.e., it will make a factual comparison of the type of activities performed by persons with such a degree with the type of activities performed without such a degree). *Glenn v. Commissioner*, 62 T.C. 270 (1974). For example, in *Robinson v. Commissioner*, 78 T.C. 550 (1982), a licensed practical nurse was denied a deduction for the costs of a 4–year university degree program at the University of Minnesota School of Nursing, which degree allowed taxpayer to take an examination to qualify as a registered nurse.

§ 10.4260. Teachers. The Commissioner and the courts are more liberal in permitting a deduction for educational expenses of teachers than for other professions or trades. For example, Treas. Reg. § 1.162–5(b)(3)(i) states that "'all teaching and related duties shall be considered to involve the same general type of work." Thus, courses taken by a classroom teacher to qualify as a principal are not courses to qualify for a new trade or business and so typically are deductible. The Commissioner ruled in Rev. Rul. 71–58 that a taxpayer who held a permanent teaching certificate in State *A* and who had been employed as a secondary teacher in that state could deduct the cost of courses that she took in order to satisfy the teaching certificate requirements of State *B* to which she had moved. The Commissioner ruled that the change of employers and location was merely a change of duties in the same general type of work as a classroom teacher and did not constitute a change to a new trade or business. Similarly, in *Laurano v. Commissioner*, 69 T.C. 723 (1978), Acq., the Tax Court allowed a Canadian citizen, who was certified to teach in Toronto, Canada and who had moved to New Jersey, to deduct the cost of several courses that she took in order to obtain certification to teach in New Jersey. The court distinguished its treatment of lawyers in *Sharon v. Commissioner*, **§ 10.4240**, on the ground that Treas. Reg. § 1.162–5(b)(3)(i) expressly adopted a liberal construction of the trade or business requirement for teachers. See also *Toner v. Commissioner* at § **10.4230.**

§ **10.4270. Previously Engaged in a Trade or Business.** An educational deduction will not be deductible unless it is in furtherance of a trade or business in which the taxpayer is already engaged. The Tax Court's decision in *Wassenaar v. Commissioner*, 72 T.C. 1195 (1979) provides an interesting application of that requirement. In *Wassenaar*, the taxpayer graduated from Wayne State University Law School in Detroit, Michigan, and, without first obtaining a job in the legal profession, he went to New York City and enrolled in the LL.M. program in taxation at New York University (NYU). The taxpayer received the LL.M. degree after one academic year and then returned to Detroit to join a law firm. In the summer before his graduation from Wayne State, the taxpayer had clerked for a law firm for which he was compensated. In addition, the taxpayer had served as a member of the board of editors of the Wayne State Law Review for two years for which he received compensation. The taxpayer passed the Michigan bar examination before enrolling at NYU, but he was not formally admitted to the bar until after he graduated from NYU. The Tax Court held that although the taxpayer was qualified to practice law when he enrolled at NYU, he had not yet engaged in the practice of law. The court acknowledged that the taxpayer had performed work of a legal nature before attending NYU, but the court held that it did not constitute the practice of law. The court noted that since the taxpayer was not formally admitted to the bar until after receiving his LL.M., he was not authorized to practice law before that date. The court also noted that the taxpayer's attendance at NYU constituted an essentially uninterrupted continuation of his legal education. Accordingly, the court denied the taxpayer's claim for a business expense deduction for the expenses incurred in attending NYU. See also *Kohen v. Commissioner*, 44 T.C.M. 1518 (1982). If the taxpayer had first practiced law (even for a brief period) before enrolling at NYU, he likely would have qualified for a deduction. PLR 9112003. But cf., *Link v. Commissioner*, 90 T.C. 460 (1988) (§ **10.4230**); *Johnson v. United States*, 332 F.Supp. 906 (E.D.La. 1971).

§ **10.4300. Travel As Education.** Travel itself may educate a taxpayer by improving his skills in his profession or trade. For example, travel to France would improve the skills of a French teacher. An amendment to the Code made by the 1986 TRA denies a deduction for travel *as a form of education*. IRC § 274(m)(2). The cost of travel that is not itself educational but is merely the means of reaching a place where the taxpayer will receive a business-related education continues to be deductible subject to the limitations on the deductibility of employee expenses and on the deductibility of meals.

§ **10.5000.   FRUSTRATION OF PUBLIC POLICY.** Prior to 1970, an expense would not qualify as "necessary" under IRC § 162 if allowance of the deduction would frustrate a sharply defined national or state policy (i.e., such an expenditure would not be "appropriate and helpful"). *Tank Truck Rentals, Inc. v. Commissioner*, 356 U.S. 30 (1958). The national or state policies involved had to be evidenced by some governmental declaration and not merely by the mores of the community. *Lilly v. Commissioner*, 343 U.S. 90 (1952). However, the regulations state that an expense paid or incurred after December 30, 1969, which would otherwise be allowable as a business deduction, will *not* be disallowed as a deduction solely because it violated "a sharply defined public policy." Treas. Reg. § 1.162–1(a). Thus, such an expense will be disallowed only if deduction is barred by a specific statutory provision. See Rev. Rul. 74–323 discussed at § **10.1731.** For the treatment of fines and penalties, see § **10.1820.** In *Conley v. Commissioner*, at § **10.1521**, the Tax Court used public policy as a reason for disallowing a deduction. See also § **16.1200.**

§ **10.5100.   Illegal Under State Law.** In *Tank Truck Rentals*, the Supreme Court noted that if the expenditure in question is illegal under state law, "the frustration of state policy is most complete and direct." However, in *Commissioner v. Sullivan*, 356 U.S. 27 (1958), decided the same day as *Tank Truck Rentals*, the Court allowed a deduction for salaries and rent paid by an Illinois bookmaker even though the payment of rent for the use of a bookmaking establishment was itself illegal under Illinois law. As noted in § **10.1730**, the *Sullivan* case apparently was overturned by the 1971 Congressional amendment to IRC § 162(c)(2).

§ **10.5200.   Reconciliation.** The *Sullivan* case might be reconciled with *Tank Truck Rentals* on the basis that the payment of rent for premises is a normal expense of most legal businesses and therefore to disallow the deduction in *Sullivan* would in effect constitute imposing a discriminatorily higher tax on the taxpayer merely because he was engaged in an illegal business. Since the Government taxes illegally obtained income, it would ill behoove it to deny deductions for expenses that are so comparable to deductible expenses of legitimate business enterprises. Nevertheless, such expenses are disallowed as deductions by IRC § 162(c)(2) which renders the *Sullivan* case a virtual nullity.

§ 10.5300. Expenses to Defend Criminal Action. If a taxpayer has a criminal action brought against him because of activities connected with his business (e.g., an antitrust violation), his legal expenses in defending that criminal action are deductible under IRC § 162, regardless of whether he is convicted or acquitted. *Commissioner v. Tellier*, 383 U.S. 687 (1966). The rationale for allowing a deduction for such expenses is that the origin of the expense arose in a business setting. See Rev. Rul. 68–662.

§ 10.5310. Illustration 1: Defending Tax Fraud Charges. In Rev. Rul. 68–662, a taxpayer who was an officer of a corporation with the responsibility of filing the corporation's tax returns, embezzled corporate funds and did not report the amounts on either the corporation's tax return or on his own. The taxpayer was indicted on two criminal counts—one for filing a false corporate tax return and one for filing a false return of his own. The taxpayer was convicted on both counts. The Commissioner allowed the taxpayer to deduct his legal fees for litigating count one under IRC § 162 because the charge of filing a false corporate return arose out of his duty as an employee to file that return. The fees for litigating the second count were held to be deductible under IRC § 212(3).

§ 10.5320. Illustration 2: Resisting Forfeiture of an Asset. Taxpayer, a corporation, incurred legal fees in an unsuccessful effort to resist the government's forfeiture of its car when taxpayer's president and sole shareholder had been caught carrying marijuana in the car. The Tax Court held that the taxpayer's legal fees were nondeductible capital expenditures to defend the taxpayer's title to the car, and so the amount of the fees were added to taxpayer's basis in the car. *Holmes Enterprises, Inc. v. Commissioner*, 69 T.C. 114 (1977). The deductibility of the fees therefore depends upon whether the taxpayer is allowed a deduction for the loss it suffered on the forfeiture of its car; and that issue is discussed at **§ 10.5500.**

§ 10.5400. Theft Loss from Illegal Transaction. In many instances, a "confidence" scheme is designed to steal from a victim by inducing the victim to engage in an illegal transaction. For example, in *Mazzei v. Commissioner*, 61 T.C. 497 (1974), the taxpayer was induced to give $20,000 cash to several persons who were to put the bills through a little black box that they represented would create identical bills. Instead, they stole taxpayer's money. The majority of the Tax Court denied the taxpayer's claim for a theft loss deduction on the ground that it is against public policy to permit a deduction for a loss suffered by one who was engaged in a counterfeiting scheme, albeit the taxpayer was a somewhat naive participant. See also *Richey v. Commissioner*, 33 T.C. 272 (1959). Five judges dissented in the *Mazzei* case because they felt that the deduction would not frustrate public policy as the frustration doctrine was defined in the *Tank Truck Rentals* and *Sullivan* cases. Moreover, the dissenters pointed out that while the exclusivity of the exclusions from deductibility of illegal expenses stated in IRC § 162(c) operates directly only as to IRC § 162 business expense deductions, the legislative history of that provision "does seem to call for judicial restraint in other areas where Congress has not specifically limited deductions." 61 T.C. at 506. In Rev. Rul. 81–24 the Commissioner ruled that the frustration of public policy doctrine continues to be applicable to deny a claim for a deduction for a loss under IRC § 165. See **§ 10.5500.** See also *Stephens v. Commissioner*, at **§ 7.1000**; and GCM 36963 (1976).

§ 10.5500.   Loss Deductions That Contravene Public Policy. As noted at **§ 10.5000**, an expense that would otherwise be deductible under IRC § 162 (or under IRC § 212) will not be disallowed as a deduction solely because it contravenes "a sharply defined public policy." Treas. Reg. § 1.162–1(a). The question arises as to whether a deduction otherwise allowable under IRC § 165 for a loss can be disallowed because the grant of a deduction would contravene public policy—that is, are only IRC §§ 162 and 212 deductions immune from the public policy exception? As noted in **§ 10.5400**, the Tax Court has disallowed a theft loss deduction for reasons of public policy, and the Commissioner maintains that the frustration of public policy doctrine is applicable to IRC § 165. In *Blackman v. Commissioner*, 88 T.C. 677 (1987), the Tax Court disallowed a claim for a casualty loss deduction for the destruction of taxpayer's home by a fire that the taxpayer started when he put his wife's clothes on the stove, set them on fire and left the house. The Court held that the taxpayer was grossly negligent at least and that it would contravene public policy to allow him a deduction. In *Holmes Enterprises, Inc. v. Commissioner*, 69 T.C. 114 (1977), the sole shareholder and president of the taxpayer (a corporation) was caught carrying marijuana in an automobile owned by the taxpayer. The automobile was seized by the United States and forfeited to it. Although the car was used by the taxpayer for business purposes, the Tax Court denied the taxpayer a loss deduction for the forfeiture under IRC § 165 because the deduction would frustrate a sharply defined national policy against the possession and sale of marijuana. Accord, *Holt v. Commissioner*, 69 T.C. 75 (1977), aff'd per curiam, 611 F.2d 1160 (5th Cir. 1980). The forfeiture of an automobile to a government because the automobile was used to transport contraband might be characterized as a fine or penalty for which no deduction is allowable under IRC § 162(f). Although that issue was one of several urged by the government in *Holmes Enterprises*, the court chose to rely on the frustration of public policy for its decision. See also *Stephens v. Commissioner*, discussed at § **7.1000**, in which both the Tax Court and the Second Circuit agreed that the public policy limitation does apply to deductions claimed under IRC § 165, although they disagreed as to how the public policy limitation is to be construed.

§ **10.6000.   BAD DEBTS.** A deduction is allowed to a creditor for a bona fide debt which becomes worthless. If a debt was created in connection with a taxpayer's trade or business, the taxpayer can deduct part of the debt when it becomes partially worthless, but a nonbusiness debt can be deducted only when it becomes wholly worthless. IRC § 166. The 1986 TRA repealed the provision that previously existed that allowed most businesses to use a bad debt reserve method (i.e., a method in which a current deduction is taken for the amount of receivables that are expected to become uncollectible at some future date). Bad debt reserves now are available only to certain financial institutions. See IRC §§ 585 and 593; § **10.6400.** However, if an accrual-method taxpayer who is engaged in one of a list of specified trades or professions, or who satisfies a gross receipts test, obtains accounts receivable for *services* performed by him, the taxpayer need not accrue as income that portion of the accounts receivable that experience indicates will not be collected; but this provision does not apply if interest is payable on the receivable or if there is a penalty for late payment. IRC § 448(d)(5).

§ **10.6100.   Nature of Deduction.** A business bad debt deduction is deducted from the taxpayer's ordinary income. A nonbusiness bad debt is treated as a short-term capital loss. IRC § 166(d)(1)(B).

§ **10.6200.   Business versus Nonbusiness Debts.** A nonbusiness debt is a debt other than a business debt, and consequently the definition of business debt is crucial.

§ **10.6210.   Definition.** A business debt is a debt created or acquired in connection with the taxpayer's "trade or business," or a debt the worthlessness of which was incurred in connection with the taxpayer's "trade or business." IRC § 166(d)(2).

§ 10.6220. Debt of Corporation to Its Shareholder. When a taxpayer makes a bona fide loan to a corporation in which he or a member of his family owns shares, the debt is treated as a nonbusiness debt unless: (a) the taxpayer is in the business of making loans; (b) the taxpayer made the loan to protect some income-producing interest of the taxpayer other than his owner-ship of the corporation's stock (for example, the loan will create a business debt if the taxpayer made it to protect his employment relationship with the corporation); or (c) the taxpayer is engaged in the business of promoting corporations for a fee or for a profit on their sale to customers. *Whipple v. Commissioner*, 373 U.S. 193 (1963). A taxpayer's investment interest in a corporation as a shareholder does not constitute a "trade or business" and conse-quently the corporation's debts to him will usually be treated as nonbusiness debts unless the taxpayer can establish that he fits within one of the preceding exceptions or that some similar exception should be applied.

§ **10.6221. Primary Purpose.** Until 1972, an issue fre-quently raised by a taxpayer who was both an employee and a shareholder of a corporation in seeking a business bad debt deduction for a loan made to the corporation was that the loan was made to protect the taxpayer's position as an employee of the corporation. The Courts of Appeals divided on the question of whether the characterization of such loans as business debts rested on a finding that the dominant motive of the taxpayer in making a loan to the corporation was for the purpose of protecting his job or whether it was sufficient if that were a significant factor. Compare *Niblock v. Commissioner*, 417 F.2d 1185 (7th Cir. 1969), adopting the dominant purpose test, with *Weddle v. Commissioner*, 325 F.2d 849 (2d Cir. 1963), adopting the significant purpose test. The problem arises because the taxpayer has a dual status (i.e., a business status as an employee and a nonbusiness status as an investor) and the characterization of the debt turns upon whether the loan was made in connection with his business or his nonbusiness relationship to the corporation. The Supreme Court resolved this issue by holding that such bad debts will not be treated as business bad debts unless the *dominant* motive of the taxpayer in making the loan was to protect his employee status. *United States v. Generes*, 405 U.S. 93 (1972).

§ **10.6221–1. Extension of *Generes*.** The Supreme Court's holding in *Generes* appears applicable to all dual status questions (e.g., a taxpayer who is both a landlord of property leased to a corporation and a shareholder of the corporation). Business bad debt deductions will be allowed in such cases only if the dominant purpose of the loan is connected with the taxpayer's business relationship with the debtor.

§ 10.6222. Guarantee of a Corporate Debt. If a taxpayer is required to make a payment on the obligation of a corporation whose debt the taxpayer guaranteed, the payment is treated as a loan to the corporation and consequently its tax treatment will depend upon whether the taxpayer's "loan" to the corporation is a business or a nonbusiness bad debt. *Putnam v. Commissioner*, 352 U.S. 82 (1956). Thus, the guarantee is equivalent to a direct loan to the corporation, and such loans are usually characterized as nonbusiness bad debts.

§ 10.6223. Guarantee of a Noncorporate Debt. As a consequence of the 1976 TRA, a loss incurred by a taxpayer in making payment on his guarantee of a noncorporate debt is treated as a loan to the debtor and characterized accordingly. The House Report to section 605 of the 1976 Act, repealing IRC § 166(g) which had provided special tax treatment for certain losses of this type, contains a helpful discussion of the current treatment of such losses.

§ 10.6224. Guarantee Creating Deductible Bad Debt. A taxpayer's payment on a guaranty cannot qualify for a bad debt deduction unless the taxpayer had received reasonable consideration for agreeing to act as a guarantor, endorser or indemnitor. Reasonable consideration is not limited to the receipt of cash or property; it is sufficient if the guaranty was in accordance with normal business practice or for a good faith business purpose. However, if the consideration is provided by taxpayer's spouse or by certain persons related to taxpayer, then the consideration must be in the form of cash or property. Treas. Reg. § 1.166–9(e)(1). See *Lair v. Commissioner*, 95 T.C. 484 (1990).

§ 10.6300. Amount Deductible. The amount deductible as a bad debt is determined by the taxpayer's adjusted basis in the debt. IRC § 166(b). Thus, when a cash-basis taxpayer has no basis in an account receivable because it is not includable in his gross income until collected, the taxpayer cannot deduct his loss when the receivable becomes worthless.

§ 10.6400. Disallowance of Bad Debt Reserve. A taxpayer who reports his business income on the accrual method will report income on credit sales by taking the accounts receivable at face value. But see **§ 10.6000** for an exception for receivables obtained for services. This is followed even though the taxpayer's experience with such receivables is that a percentage of them will never be collected (i.e., the taxpayer reasonably expects some of his receivables to prove uncollectible but he does not know which of his customers will default). This method of reporting will distort the taxpayer's income picture since the income he will report in the year of sale will be unrealistically large and the income he will report in the year in which an account becomes worthless and thus deductible as a bad debt will be unrealistically small. Prior to the adoption of the 1986 TRA, to permit a taxpayer to match the deduction for uncollectible debts with the income from the sales in which the debts arose, a taxpayer was permitted to elect the reserve method of deducting bad debts in lieu of deducting individual accounts when they become worthless. Congress concluded that the allowance of a bad debt reserve deduction results in a tax windfall to the taxpayer because of the time value of money (i.e., the tax reduction obtained from a deduction has a greater value when obtained in an earlier year). Consequently, in the 1986 Act, Congress repealed the provision allowing the use of a bad debt reserve (except for certain financial institutions). Except for such financial institutions and for the comparable treatment of accounts receivable obtained for the services of certain accrual-method taxpayers [**§ 10.6000**], taxpayers can only deduct bad debts when they become wholly or partially worthless.

§ 10.6500. Collection of Previously Deducted Debt. When a taxpayer claimed a bad debt deduction for a debt which appeared worthless at the time, enjoyed a tax benefit from the deduction, and subsequently was able to collect all or part of the debt, the amount so collected will be included in the taxpayer's gross income for the year in which collection was made. If the taxpayer enjoyed a tax benefit for only part of a bad debt deduction claimed in a prior year, the amount subsequently collected by him on that debt will not be included in his gross income to the extent that the prior deduction did not provide an actual tax benefit to him. IRC § 111. The "tax benefit rule" is discussed at **§ 2.3000.**

§ 10.6510. Illustration: Operation of Tax Benefit Rule. In connection with his business, in Year One, X loaned Y $10,000. In Year Four, X claimed that Y's debt was worthless, and, therefore, X claimed a $10,000 business bad debt deduction on his Year Four tax return. X was unmarried and had no dependents. On his Year Four return, X reported gross income of $12,000, and he reported the following deductions:

$2,000—personal exemptions
$1,400—interest on home mortgage
$2,000—state income taxes
$2,200—alimony
$10,000—bad debt
$17,600—Total

Thus, X reported a net loss of $5,600 for Year Four and none of his loss qualified as a "net operating loss." X deducted his interest expense and state income taxes as itemized deductions because the amount of deduction for those two items was greater than his standard deduction. If X had not deducted the $10,000 business bad debt, he would have reported a net income of $4,400 for Year Four. Thus, of the $10,000 deduction X claimed, he received a tax benefit from $4,400 of that deduction, and he received no tax benefit from the remaining $5,600 of the deduction. In Year Nine, Y inherited property, and X collected $5,000 on Y's debt. Since X got no tax benefit from $5,600 of the bad deduction he took in Year Four, his subsequent collection of $5,000 of that debt does not cause X to recognize any gross income. In Year Ten, X collected $3,000 on the unpaid balance of Y's debt. $600 of that collection is not included in Y's gross income because he received no tax benefit for that amount of his Year Four deduction (i.e., X got no tax benefit from $5,600 of his Year Four deduction, but he recovered $5,000 of that amount in Year Nine and so only $600 of that amount had not yet been recovered). However, the remaining $2,400 is included in his gross income for Year Ten. Any additional amounts collected on Y's debt will be included in X's gross income.

§ **10.6600. Worthless Securities.** When a taxpayer holds a security of a corporation (e.g., stocks or bonds) that becomes worthless during a tax year, the taxpayer is treated as having sold the security for zero at the end of the year and thus recognizes a loss equal to his basis in the security. IRC § 165(g). Typically, this will result in a long-term capital loss to the taxpayer unless the taxpayer is a corporation that is affiliated with the debtor. IRC § 165(g)(3). Thus, where a shareholder loans money to his corporation and as evidence of the debt receives a note that does not qualify as a security, the debt will usually be treated as a nonbusiness bad debt so that the shareholder will recognize a short-term capital loss if it becomes worthless. However, if the debt instrument constitutes a security, the shareholder will usually recognize a long-term capital loss if it becomes worthless.

§ 10.7000. AT RISK LIMITATION. IRC § 465 limits the amount of deductions that certain taxpayers can take in connection with a trade or business activity or with an activity for the production of income. The provision applies to individuals and to certain closely held corporations. IRC § 465(a). Note that the § 465 at risk limitation applies only to deductions; it does not limit credits. However, comparable at risk rules are applied by other Code provisions to certain credits. See, e.g., IRC § 49 and § 42(k). Even as to deductions, the § 465 at risk provision limits them only to the extent that they produce a loss. **§ 10.7200.**

§ 10.7100. Separately Identified Activities. If IRC § 465 is applicable to a taxpayer, the taxpayer's various business interests and investments (including the taxpayer's share of such interests held by a partnership or an S corporation) must be divided so that each activity is separately identified. For example, each oil and gas property of a taxpayer will be treated as a single activity. Similarly, each film or video tape that the taxpayer holds for the purpose of exploitation constitutes a separate activity. IRC § 465(c)(2); Prop. Reg. § 1.465–42. In a small number of cases, all the activities in a specific category can be aggregated and treated as a single activity. IRC § 465(c)(2)(B), (3)(B), (C). A few categories of activities that cannot be aggregated are set forth in IRC § 465(c)(2)(A), but the categorization of most activities has been left to the Commissioner to accomplish by way of regulation. IRC § 465(c)(3)(C). See Temp. Reg. § 1.465–1T for the aggregation of certain (but not all) activities of a partnership or an S corporation.

§ 10.7110. Safe Harbors. Except for those activities that the Treasury singles out in regulations to be treated as separate activities, the Code provides that all of the taxpayer's activities which constitute a trade or business and in which the taxpayer actively participates in the management are aggregated and treated as a single activity. IRC § 465(c)(3)(B). As we shall see, the significance of aggregating several actively conducted trades or businesses into a single activity is that losses incurred in one such trade or business can then be deducted against income earned in another such trade or business without regard to the amount that the taxpayer has at risk.

§ 10.7120. Partnerships and S Corporations. Trades or businesses conducted by a partnership or by an S corporation will be aggregated and treated as a single activity if at least 65% of the losses for the taxable year of such a partnership or S corporation are allocable to persons who actively participate in the management of the business. IRC § 465(c)(3)(B)(ii). Also, certain designated activities of a partnership or S corporation can be aggregated and treated as a single activity. See Temp. Reg. § 1.465–1T.

§ 10.7200. Limitation on Deductions. IRC § 465 limits the extent to which deductions incurred in one activity can be offset against income earned from a different activity. This provision imposes no restrictions on the extent to which deductions incurred in an activity can be utilized to reduce income earned from that same activity. See IRC § 465(d). Thus, the taxpayer's income from the activity is determined as of the end of the taxpayer's taxable year (unless the income is earned by a separate entity, such as an S corporation, in which event it is the end of the taxable year of the entity that is the point of reference), and the taxpayer's deductions that arise from that activity for that taxable year are allowable to the extent that they do not exceed such income. When the deductions (otherwise allowable) for one taxable year from one activity exceed the income for that year from the same activity, the excess is termed a "loss." IRC § 465(d). Note that as used in IRC § 465, the term "loss" has a different meaning than the same term has in IRC § 165 [see Chapter Seven]. Such losses are often referred to as a "section 465(d) loss." Prop. Reg. § 1.465–11(a)(1). Since a taxpayer is denied a deduction only for "losses," a deduction is allowed to the extent that deductions (including carryover losses) from an activity do not exceed the income received or accrued from that activity. The amount of section 465(d) loss from an activity is deductible by the taxpayer for that taxable year only to the extent that the taxpayer is "at risk" for such activity at the end of the taxable year. IRC § 465(a).

§ 10.7210. Carryover of Nondeductible Losses. When a taxpayer is precluded by IRC § 465 from deducting all or a portion of a loss from an activity for a taxable year, the section 465(d) loss is carried over to the next taxable year and treated as if it were a deductible item incurred in that year. IRC § 465(a)(2). Thus, to the extent that the taxpayer has net income from that activity (regardless of the character of that income (i.e., ordinary, capital gain etc.)) in the next year, the carryover loss can then be deducted. See Prop. Reg. § **1.465–12(a).** Similarly, the carryover can be deducted in the next year to the extent of the amount that the taxpayer is at risk with regard to that activity at the end of such year. The amount of loss (including deductions from a carryover of section 465(d) losses) that is not deductible in the next year because of IRC § 465 will be carried forward and treated as a deduction incurred in the next succeeding year. So, a loss that is nondeductible because of IRC § 465 can be carried forward to future years until fully deducted or until the taxpayer ceases to exist. A carryforward section 465(d) loss can be deducted in a subsequent year to the extent that the taxpayer has a positive amount at risk in such year.

The section 465(d) loss that is carried over is sometimes referred to as a "suspended section 465(d) loss."

§ 10.7220.   Gain Recognized on the Disposition of an Activity. The income received or accrued from an activity includes gain recognized on the disposition of that activity or of an interest in that activity. Prop. Regs. §§ 1.465–12, 1.465–66. Consequently, any deductions incurred in any activity in the year of its disposition and any suspended section 465(d) losses from that activity carried over to that year can be deducted to the extent that the taxpayer recognized a gain on the disposition. See Prop. Regs. § 1.465–12(b), Ex.

§ 10.7230.   Real Property. The holding of real property pursuant to a trade or business or profit-seeking activity is a separate activity to which the at risk limitations of IRC § 465 apply. Prior to the adoption of the 1986 TRA, the holding of real property was excluded from the at risk rules. While the 1986 Act expanded the at risk rules of IRC § 465 to apply to the holding of real estate, Congress provided a more generous scheme for real estate holdings for determining what constitutes being at risk than is provided for other types of activities. §§ **10.7231–10.7234.** For purposes of determining whether the special rules for calculating the extent to which a taxpayer is at risk with regard to the holding of real property apply, the activity of holding real property includes the holding of personal property and the providing of services that are incidental to making real property available as living accommodations. IRC § 465(b)(6)(E)(i). For this purpose, the activity of holding real property does not include the holding of mineral property. IRC § 465(b)(6)(E)(ii).

§ 10.7231. Liberal Definition of "At Risk." The special treatment accorded to the activity of holding real property is that the amount at which a taxpayer is at risk includes certain nonrecourse debts which are secured by real property used in that activity. The nonrecourse debts which qualify for inclusion in the amount for which the taxpayer is at risk are referred to as "qualified nonrecourse financing." IRC § 465(b)(6)(A).

§ 10.7232. Qualified Nonrecourse Financing. "Qualified nonrecourse financing" is financing:

(a) which is secured by real property used in the holding of a real property activity;

(b) which is borrowed by the taxpayer with respect to the activity of holding real property;

(c) which is borrowed from a "qualified person" [see § 10.7233], or from a federal, state or local government, or is guaranteed by a federal, state or local government;

(d) except when regulations provide otherwise, for which no person is personally liable for repayment [of course, to the extent that the taxpayer himself is personally liable, the debt is a recourse debt which is included in the amount for which the taxpayer is at risk];

(e) which is not a convertible debt. IRC § 465(b)(6)(B).

§ 10.7233. Qualified Person. A nonrecourse debt will qualify for at risk treatment only if the amount was borrowed from (or guaranteed by) a federal, state or local government or if the amount was borrowed from a "qualified person." A qualified person is any person who is actively and regularly engaged in the business of lending money and who is not:

(a) a person related to the taxpayer,

(b) a person from whom the taxpayer acquired the property (or a person related to such person); or

(c) a person who receives a fee with respect to such property (or a person related to such person). IRC §§ 465(b)(6)(D)(i), 49(a)(1)(D)(iv).

Financing from a person related to the taxpayer is permitted if the lender is actively and regularly engaged in the business of

lending money and if the terms of the financing are commercially reasonable and are on substantially the same terms as
those involving unrelated parties. IRC § 465(b)(6)(D)(ii). As
used in the Code, the term "person" includes corporations,
partnerships, associations, and trusts as well as individuals.
IRC § 7701(a)(1).

§ 10.7234. Related Person. For purposes of IRC § 465(b),
a person is related to another person (and is therefore referred
to as a "related person") if the related person bears a relationship to the other that is specified in IRC §§ 267(b) or
707(b)(1), except that in applying those two provisions "10
percent" is substituted for "50 percent" wherever the latter
appears. IRC § 465(b)(3)(C). In addition, a person is related to
another if both are engaged in trades or business under
common control. IRC § 465(b)(3)(C)(iii).

§ 10.7240. Basis. If a deductible item would otherwise have
reduced a taxpayer's basis, the fact that the at risk limitation
prevents the deduction of that item will not prevent the reduction
of the taxpayer's basis. Prop. Reg. § 1.465–1(e). The at risk
limitation rules have no effect on the determination of basis.

§ 10.7300. Computation of At Risk Amount. The amounts for
which the taxpayer is deemed to be at risk for an activity are
described in IRC § 465(b). A number of the adjustments that are
made in computing the taxpayer's at risk amount are described in
§§ 10.7310–10.7320.

§ 10.7310. Additions to the At Risk Amount.

(a) the amount of money and the adjusted basis of property in
kind that are contributed by the taxpayer to the activity will
increase the taxpayer's at risk amount. If the contributed funds
were borrowed by the taxpayer, the adjustment is determined as
described below in (c). If property that the taxpayer contributed
in kind is encumbered, the increase to taxpayer's at risk amount
will nevertheless equal the adjusted basis of the property if the
taxpayer is personally liable for repayment of the debt; but if the
taxpayer is not personally liable, *no more* than the excess of
taxpayer's basis over the encumbrance will increase that at risk
amount (and in certain circumstances the amount of increase will
be less than that figure). Prop. Regs. §§ 1.465–22(a), 1.465–23(a).
A subsequent reduction of the encumbrance will increase the at

risk amount if taxpayer was not personally liable on the debt but will not increase the at risk amount if the taxpayer was personally liable. Prop. Regs. §§ 1.465–23(a)(2)(ii), 1.465–24(b)(1), 1.465–25(b)(2)(i).

(b) The taxpayer's share of income from the activity (including tax-exempt income) in excess of the taxpayer's share of allowable deductions from the activity for the taxable year will increase the taxpayer's at risk amount. Prop. Reg. § 1.465–22(c).

(c) Amounts borrowed by the taxpayer for use in or contribution to the activity will increase the taxpayer's at risk amount to the extent that the taxpayer either is personally liable for the repayment of the debt or has pledged property (other than property which is used in such activity) as security for the repayment of the debt. Such pledged property will permit the inclusion of borrowed funds in the taxpayer's at risk computation only to the extent of the fair market value of the taxpayer's interest in the pledged property. Certain borrowed funds are excluded from the at risk computation; for example, funds borrowed by the taxpayer from a person who has an interest (other than an interest as a creditor) in the activity, or from a person related to someone (other than the taxpayer) who has an interest in the activity, are disregarded. IRC § 465(b)(3). The exception for funds borrowed from a person who has an interest in the activity does not apply to a loan made by a shareholder to a corporation. IRC § 465(b)(3)(B)(ii).

(d) Repayment of loans by the taxpayer will increase the taxpayer's at risk amount to the extent that the debt had previously prevented an increase in the taxpayer's at risk amount for contributions that he had made to the activity. Prop. Reg. § 1.465–25(b)(2).

(e) Notwithstanding the above, transactions which are designed to avoid the reach of IRC § 465 and which do not normally occur in commercial practice will be disregarded. Prop. Regs. §§ 1.465–1(b), 1.465–4. Similarly, where a taxpayer who appears to be at risk for an amount is insulated through guarantees, nonrecourse financing and the like, the amount purportedly at risk is not taken into account. IRC § 465(b)(4).

§ 10.7320. Reduction of At Risk Amount.

(a) To the extent that the taxpayer's share of a section 465(d) loss from an activity (i.e., a section 465(d) loss is the excess of deductions from the activity over its income) is allowable as a deduction because of the amount at which the taxpayer is at risk for such activity, the amount at which the taxpayer is at risk will be reduced by the amount of such deduction that is thereby allowable. IRC § 465(b)(5). A taxpayer's at risk amount is also reduced by the taxpayer's share of nondeductible expenses that relate to the production of tax exempt receipts for the activity. Prop. Reg. § 1.465–22(c)(2).

(b) Money withdrawn by a taxpayer from an activity will reduce the at risk amount of the taxpayer. Prop. Reg. § 1.465–22(b). The taxpayer's at risk amount will be reduced by the excess of the adjusted basis of property in kind which is withdrawn from the activity by or on behalf of the taxpayer over any liabilities to which the property is subject and for the payment of which the taxpayer is not liable. Prop. Reg. § 1.465–23(c).

§ 10.7400.   Recapture of Loss Deduction. When a taxpayer deducted a section 465(d) loss from an activity by virtue of the taxpayer's at risk position in that activity, the taxpayer should not be permitted, without tax consequences, to reduce his risk in the activity in a subsequent year to the extent that the reduction in risk would have prevented the deduction of past section 465(d) losses had the loss and the risk reduction occurred in the same year. IRC § 465(e) deals with that problem by requiring the taxpayer to recapture such prior deductions by including a like amount in his gross income for the taxable year in which the reduction of his at risk amount occurred. For carryover purposes, the amount so included in the taxpayer's gross income is treated as a deduction incurred in that activity in the next succeeding taxable year. IRC § 465(e)(1)(B). Thus, if the taxpayer subsequently earns sufficient income from the activity or obtains an increase in his at risk position, the recaptured loss can be deducted at that time. The operation of this recaptured rule is described and illustrated in §§ **10.7410** and **10.7420.**

§ 10.7410.   Computation of Amount of Recapture Section 465(d) Losses. The recapture of previously deducted section 465(d) losses is accomplished in the manner described below after making an annual determination of the amount that a taxpayer is at risk in an activity; this determination (you may recall) reflects a reduction for the deductible losses from that activity and the money and property withdrawn from that activity. See §§ **10.7310** and **10.7320.** If at the end of a taxable year, the amount that the taxpayer has at risk is a negative amount (i.e., the net amount deducted from the taxpayer's at risk amount for the year exceeds the amount at which the taxpayer was at risk at the beginning of the year), the taxpayer shall include in his gross income an amount equal to the negative figure. IRC § 465(e)(1). However, the amount so included in the taxpayer's gross income shall not exceed the amount of section 465(d) losses from that activity that were allowable as deductions in prior years reduced by the amounts previously included in the taxpayer's gross income as a recapture of previously deducted losses from that activity. IRC § 465(e)(2).

§ 10.7420. Illustration: Operation of Recapture Rule. *B* invests $5,000 in a business activity in Year One. The activity incurs a section 465(d) loss in Year One of which *B*'s share is $2,400. *B* is allowed a deduction for the loss, and *B* then has $2,600 at risk at the beginning of Year Two. In Year Two, the activity earns a profit of which *B*'s share is $300. In July of Year Two, *B* receives a cash distribution of $3,500 from the activity. *B*'s at risk position at the end of Year Two is $2,600 + $300 − $3,500 = − $600. *B* is required to include the negative at risk amount of − $600 in his gross income for Year Two. *B*'s aggregate loss deductions for prior years ($2,400) less the amount of loss previously recaptured ($0) is greater than the $600 negative figure, and thus that amount of income is recognized. At the beginning of Year Three, *B*'s at risk amount will be zero since the $600 negative figure is increased by the $600 of income recognized by *B* in Year Two. *B* will carry forward a $600 deduction to Year Three (i.e., the $600 of income recognized as a recapture of previously taken deductions is treated as a deduction incurred in that activity in the next year). In Year Three, without regard to the $600 carryover deduction, the activity earns a profit of which *B*'s share is $200. *B* will deduct $200 of his carryforward deduction in Year Three and carry forward the remaining $400 deduction to Year Four.

§ 10.7500. Interaction With Passive Activity Losses and Credits. The "at risk" limitations of IRC § 465 are applied first without regard to the limitations on passive activity losses ("PAL") imposed by IRC § 469. See §§ **7.9000–7.9620.** The PAL rules apply only to losses that would be deductible after applying the IRC § 465 limitations. If a section 465(d) loss is allowable under the at risk rules but is disallowed under the PAL rules of IRC § 469, the amount at which the taxpayer is at risk is nevertheless reduced by the loss for which a deduction was denied by the PAL rules.

§ 10.7600. Donative Transfer of Entire Interest in Activity With Suspended Section 465(d) Loss.

Prop. Reg. § 1.465–67 deals with the treatment of a transfer of a transferor's entire interest in an activity with suspended section 465(d) losses if the basis of the transferee in the transferred interest is determined in whole or in part by the basis of the transferor. This covers gifts as well as some nonrecognition exchanges. If the transferor recognizes any gain on such transfer, see § 10.7220.

A suspended section 465(d) loss that is not deductible prior to the transfer cannot be deducted thereafter. However, the amount of suspended section 465(d) loss is added to the transferee's basis in the transferred interest.

§ 10.7700. Donative Transfer of Entire Interest in Activity in Which Transferor Has a Positive Amount at Risk.

Prop. Reg. § 1.465–68 deals with the treatment of a transfer of the transferor's entire interest in an activity in which the transferor has a positive amount at risk if the basis of the transferee in the transferred interest is determined in whole or in part by the basis of the transferor. In that case, the transferee will include in his amount at risk the sum of: (1) the amount at which the transferor was at risk, plus (2) the amount of gift tax (if any) paid on the transfer that increased the transferee's basis under IRC § 1015(d). In other words, the transferee inherits the transferor's at risk account and adds the amount of increase in basis allowed by IRC § 1015(d) for gift tax payment. There is a limitation on the at risk amount that the transferee can obtain by this provision. The at risk that the transferee obtains from this provision cannot exceed the difference between the transferee's basis and the amount that the transferee paid the transferor (including in the payment the acceptance of any liabilities encumbering the transferred property). Prop. Reg. § 1.465–68(c).

§ 10.7800. Transfer of an Interest in an Activity by Reason of Death.

Prop. Reg. § 1.465–69 deals with the treatment of the passing of an interest in an activity by death. If, at the close of a taxable year in which the decedent died, the decedent's amount at risk in an activity in which he held an interest is a positive figure, that amount is added to the successor's amount at risk. In addition, a successor will increase his amount at risk in the activity by the amount of increase in basis that the successor has in the interest over the decedent's basis because of IRC § 1014. In other words, any step-up in basis caused by IRC § 1014 is added to the successor's amount at risk.

CHAPTER ELEVEN

DEPRECIATION AND AMORTIZATION

§ 11.0000. COST RECOVERY.

§ 11.1000. GENERAL. This chapter and the following chapter deal with the manner in which deductions for capital expenditures are determined. When a taxpayer incurs a current expense in connection with his trade or business, he usually will be allowed to deduct that expense during the tax year in which he pays or accrues it. For example, the cost that a retail business incurs in advertising for the sale of its goods is a current deduction. However, as previously explained, the cost of purchasing an asset to be used for more than 12 months is usually not currently deductible. The taxpayer has not actually spent the dollars he paid for such an asset, but rather has converted them into a different type of property. For example, if *A* buys a typewriter at a cost of $800 in Year One and if *A* expects to use the typewriter in his business for five years, he cannot deduct the $800 cost of the typewriter in Year One since he acquired an asset of like value. But see **§ 12.2000.**

Nonetheless, *A*'s typewriter will not last forever. Each year, a portion of the useful life of the typewriter will be exhausted until, after five years, the typewriter is no longer useful. In effect, each year that *A* uses the typewriter, *A* uses up a portion of the $800 purchase price. An accurate measurement of *A*'s net income for any one of those years will include a deduction of some amount to represent the portion of the $800 cost that is properly allocable to that year. The allocation of the cost of an asset over the years in which the asset is employed in a profit-seeking activity can be accomplished by a depreciation allowance or by some other method of amortizing the cost of the asset. Depreciation and amortization, therefore, are methods for deducting (and thereby "recovering") a capital expenditure over the period of time (the "recovery period") to which the expenditure relates.

§ 11.1100. Meaning of Depreciation. Depreciation is an allocation of the cost or basis of property (tangible or intangible) among the years of its use in a trade or business or for the production of income. To qualify for a depreciation deduction, the property must be used in a trade or business or for the production of income. This requires the taxpayer to demonstrate that he had "an actual and honest objective of making a profit" from the activity in which the property is used. The test is subjective. The taxpayer's expectation of a profit need not be reasonable on an objective standard, but it must be bona fide. *Beck v. Commissioner*, 85 T.C. 557 (1985).

While business expenses must be "ordinary and necessary" to be deductible under IRC § 162 (see **§ 10.1500**), a majority of the Tax Court held that there is no such requirement for allowing depreciation deductions under IRC § 168 (and so also under IRC § 167). *Noyce v. Commissioner*, 97 T.C. 670, 689–691 (1991) (reviewed by the court). The depreciable item need only be used in the taxpayer's trade or business or for production of income. The use need not meet the "ordinary and necessary" standard; nor need the amount of the depreciation deduction be reasonable when considered in light of the income to be produced. *Ibid.*

A deduction is allowed under IRC § 167 (and IRC § 168) for the exhaustion, wear and tear, and obsolescence of qualified property that was placed in service by the taxpayer. The deduction is determined by reference to the asset's basis. The deduction is distributed over a recovery period. Unless the depreciation is taken under IRC § 168, the "recovery period" is equal to the "useful life" of the asset. Useful life is described in **§ 11.3100.** No depreciation deduction is allowable for inventory or for property held for sale to the taxpayer's customers in the ordinary course of business. Treas. Reg. § 1.167(a)–2, and Rev. Rul. 89–25.

For tax purposes, "depreciation" refers to the deduction allowable under IRC §§ 167 or § 168 for the amortization of the taxpayer's basis. Depreciation is merely a special type of amortization; it is an amortization deduction that is authorized by either of those two sections of the Code—IRC §§ 167 or 168. A deduction taken under either of those two Code sections is referred to as "depreciation." An amortization deduction allowable under any other section of the Code (for example, IRC §§ 169, 197, and 248) is referred to as "amortization." The operation of the amortization deduction provisions requires that the allocation of basis be spread evenly over the recovery period, but depreciation deductions are not always so restricted.

§ 11.1110. Accelerated Cost Recovery System (ACRS).
The depreciation of most (but not all) tangible property, real or personal, is determined by IRC § 168. The depreciation methods established by IRC § 168 are referred to as the accelerated cost

recovery system or "ACRS." ACRS is merely a type of depreciation that a taxpayer is required to use for most tangible property. IRC § 168(a). The methods of depreciation that are employed by the current modified version of ACRS are described in Chapter Twelve.

§ 11.1111. **Modified Accelerated Cost Recovery System (MACRS).** The original version of ACRS applies to tangible property that was placed in service between 1981 and 1986. Substantial modifications were made to ACRS in 1986, and the modified version of that system is referred to as the "Modified Accelerated Cost Recovery System" or simply as "MACRS." MACRS applies to tangible property that was placed in service after 1986. In this text, the author discusses only the modified version of ACRS (i.e., the current version), and so all references hereafter to the system will be to "MACRS."

§ 11.1112. **Continuing Significance of IRC § 167.** IRC § 167 applies to intangible property and to tangible property that was placed in service by the taxpayer prior to 1981. There are a few circumstances in which the depreciation of tangible property that is placed in service after 1980 is determined by IRC § 167 [see § 12.3100], but most such properties will be depreciated under MACRS or amortized under a specific statutory provision. MACRS is discussed in the next chapter. Properties for which depreciation is precluded (such as undeveloped land and inventory) are not depreciable under MACRS.

Note that IRC § 168(a) states that the depreciation of tangible property provided by IRC § 167 is to be determined by using IRC § 168. In other words, the MACRS system is itself a system of depreciation that is incorporated into IRC § 167. For convenience of distinction, in this work a reference to MACRS refers to depreciation under IRC § 168, and a reference to depreciation under IRC § 167 usually refers to depreciation allowable under a method other than the MACRS system.

§ 11.1120. **Sufficiency of Interest.** A question may arise as to whether the nominal owner of property has a substantial enough interest in the property to entitle him to a depreciation deduction. In *Frank Lyon Co. v. United States*, 435 U.S. 561 (1978), the Court sustained a taxpayer's claim for depreciation deductions for a building that the taxpayer owned under a sale and leaseback arrangement (i.e., the taxpayer purchased the building from the tenant while the building was under construction and then, after the building was completed, rented the building to the tenant on a net lease basis so that the tenant thereafter occupied and used the building). It is arguable that the substantive role of the nominal owner in this type of transaction is merely that of a mortgagee and that the nominal tenant is actually the owner of the property. The Court held that the sale and leaseback arrangement was not a sham and that, in substance, the taxpayer was the owner of the building.

§ 11.1200. Depreciation as a Capital Expenditure. Typically a depreciation or amortization allowance is deductible in the year to which the allowance is attributable. However, if depreciable equipment is used to construct a capital asset, the depreciation allowance for the equipment is treated as a capital expenditure and, thus, is added to the taxpayer's basis in the constructed asset; the amount so added to the taxpayer's basis in the constructed asset may be depreciated over that asset's recovery period. *Commissioner v. Idaho Power Co.*, 418 U.S. 1 (1974); see IRC § 263A.

§ 11.1210. Starting Date for Depreciation. Depreciation of an asset first becomes allowable when the asset is placed in service; this occurs when the asset is placed "in a condition or state of readiness and availability." Rev. Rul. 76–238. See Rev. Rul. 76–428; and *Cooper v. Commissioner*, 542 F.2d 599 (2d Cir. 1976).

§ 11.1300. DEPRECIABLE PROPERTY.

§ 11.1310. Tangible Property. Prior to the adoption of ACRS in 1981, tangible property used in a trade or business or held for the production of income which had a *determinable useful life* could be depreciated. The requirements for depreciating tangible property under ACRS or MACRS are the same except that, according to a majority of the Tax Court and two Circuit Courts of Appeals, there is no requirement that the property have a determinable useful life. **§ 12.3110.** Instead, tangible property that is used in a trade or business or held for the production of income can be depreciated under ACRS or MACRS if the property can be shown to be subject to wear and tear, exhaustion or obsolescence. For example, while land is tangible property, it is not subject to exhaustion, wear and tear, or obsolescence; so it cannot be depreciated. Treas. Reg. § 1.167(a)–2.

§ 11.1320. Intangible Property. Intangible property used in a trade or business or held for the production of income which has a *determinable useful life* may be depreciated on a straight-line basis. Treas. Reg. § 1.167(a)–3. Intangible property is not covered by MACRS. IRC § 168(a). Instead of utilizing straight-line depreciation, certain types of intangible property (e.g., movies and television films) can be depreciated on an income-forecast method. IRC § 167(g); *Schneider v. Commissioner*, 65 T.C. 18, 32 (1975); Rev. Rul. 60–358. See § **11.3370.** Certain intangible properties can be amortized under specific Code provisions. For example, IRC § 197 permits the amortization of goodwill, going concern value, and similar intangibles over a 15–year period. See § **11.1321.**

§ 11.1321. Goodwill and Similar Intangible Properties. Prior to the adoption of the Omnibus Budget Reconciliation Act of 1993, the general rule was that goodwill and some similar intangible properties could not be depreciated or amortized because there was no ascertainable limit to their useful life. However, when a taxpayer was able to segregate an intangible item from goodwill and demonstrate that the item had an ascertainable useful life, the cost of the item could be depreciated on a straight-line basis. The most prominent example of this was the Supreme Court's decision in *Newark Morning Ledger Co. v. United States*, 507 U.S. 546 (1993) to allow the amortization of the paid subscription lists of several newspapers that the taxpayer had purchased. The uncertainty of the application of the doctrine permitting the amortization of some (but not all) intangibles that were similar to, if not part of, goodwill generated friction between taxpayers and the Service and had an adverse effect on negotiations for the purchase of a going business. There were many related areas that generated disputes and led to somewhat artificial distinctions. For example, the payment made by a purchaser of a business for the seller's covenant not to compete could be amortized, but a similar payment to protect the goodwill that the purchaser sought to acquire could not be amortized. In an effort to bring certainty and predictability to this area, Congress added IRC § 197 to the Code.

As a consequence of that amendment, a taxpayer is permitted to amortize a purchased "amortizable section 197 intangible" over a 15–year period, beginning with the month in which the intangible was acquired. When this provision is applicable to an intangible item, it is the exclusive source of amortization of that item; no depreciation or amortization of such an intangible will be permitted other than that provided by IRC § 197. IRC § 197(b). Subject to a number of specifically described exceptions, the following items are an incomplete list of section 197 intangibles:

(1) goodwill[1],

(2) going concern value[2],

(3) the labor force of the acquired business,

(4) business books and records, operating systems, and any other information base,

(5) patents, copyrights, computer software, formulas, processes, knowhow and similar items,

(6) licenses, permits, and other rights granted by a governmental unit or agency,

(7) a covenant not to compete obtained in connection with the acquisition of an interest in a trade or business or a substantial portion thereof, and

(8) a franchise, trademark, or trade name. IRC § 197(d).

There are a number of items that are excluded from section 197 intangibles notwithstanding their inclusion in the above list. IRC § 197(e). For example, a sports franchise is excluded, and so the cost of such a franchise cannot be amortized or depreciated. IRC § 197(e)(6). Certain computer software is excluded as is an interest in land or in a lease of tangible property. Certain properties that were not acquired in connection with the acquisition of a trade or business (or a substantial portion thereof) are excluded from section 197; such properties include: patents and copyrights, and an interest in a film, video tape, book or similar property. IRC § 197(e)(4). So, if an interest in a patent or copyright is acquired separately and not as part of an acquisition of a trade or business, IRC § 197 will not apply. Section 197 does not apply to any property acquired by reason of someone's death so that the property's basis is determined under IRC § 1014. IRC

---

1.   Goodwill is the value of a trade or business that is attributable to the expectancy of continued customer patronage, whether due to the name or reputation of a trade or business or any other factor.

2.   Going concern value is the additional element of value of a trade or business that attaches to property by reason of its existence as an integral part of a going concern.

§ 197(f)(9)(D). Also, any interest in a partnership, trust or estate, or corporation cannot be amortized under IRC § 197. IRC § 197(e)(1).

In some cases, as in the case of a patent or copyright, the cost of an excluded item can be depreciated or amortized under IRC § 167 or under some other Code provision. Treas. Reg. § 1.167(a)–14(c)(4). In some cases, as in the case of a sports franchise, the exclusion from IRC § 197 means that no deduction for depreciation or amortization will be allowed.

A section 197 intangible is amortizable under that provision if: (1) it is held in connection with a trade or business or a profit-seeking activity, and (2) either was acquired after August 10, 1993, or (if the taxpayer so elects) was acquired after July 25, 1991. If an intangible is self-created by a taxpayer, there are additional limitations on whether it can qualify for amortization. IRC § 197(c)(2). A self-created intangible is not excluded from IRC § 197 if it is one of the following properties: (1) a franchise, trademark or trade name, (2) a license, permit or other right obtained from a governmental unit or agency, or (3) a covenant not to compete. Other self-created properties will be excluded unless they were created in connection with a transaction involving the acquisition of assets constituting a trade or business or substantial portion thereof.

In general, if an amortizable section 197 intangible that was acquired in a transaction (or series of related transactions) is sold for a loss or becomes worthless, and if one or more other amortizable section 197 intangibles that were acquired in the same transaction (or series of transactions) are retained, no loss will be recognized, and the taxpayer's adjusted basis in the retained amortizable section 197 intangibles will be increased by the amount of loss that was disallowed. IRC § 197(f)(1).

§ 11.1330. Inventory or Stock in Trade. Inventory, stock in trade, and property held for sale to customers in the ordinary course of business cannot be depreciated. Treas. Reg. § 1.167(a)–2, Rev. Rul. 89–25.

§ 11.2000. IMPORTANCE OF DISTINCTION BETWEEN DEPRECIATION AND AMORTIZATION. The distinction between amortization and depreciation [see **§ 11.1100**] is important principally because amortization deductions must be spread evenly over the useful life of the property; on the other hand, some tangible property may be

depreciated under methods which concentrate the deductions in the
earlier years of the property's life. Amortization is similar to the
straight-line method of depreciation.

§ **11.2100. Shortened Amortization Period.** In certain circumstances defined by statute, an asset or an expenditure may be
amortized over a specific period of time that typically is far shorter
than the asset's useful life. For example, the expenses of organizing a
corporation may be amortized by the corporation over a 180–month
period. IRC § 248. In some cases, up to $5,000 of the organizational
expenses can be deducted immediately (i.e., expensed). Id. However,
some, items that are required to be amortized under IRC § 197 will
be amortized over a longer period by that provision than would have
been the case if IRC § 197 did not apply.

§ **11.3000. ELEMENTS OF A DEPRECIATION DEDUCTION.**
Since depreciation is a method of allocating the adjusted basis of an
asset to the years in which it is used, the first element to be determined
is the adjusted basis of the depreciable asset. Unless MACRS is applicable, once the adjusted basis of the depreciable asset is known, the
taxpayer must determine the expected useful life of the asset, the
salvage value of the asset, and the method of depreciation to be employed. As we will see, when MACRS is applicable, the determination of
depreciation is simpler.

§ **11.3100. Useful Life.** The estimated useful life of an asset is the
length of time, determined at the date of acquisition, that the
taxpayer expects to use the asset. For example, if a taxpayer buys a
new business car and sells his old car every two years, the new car
has an estimated useful life of two years. It is the estimated "useful
life" to the taxpayer in his business that controls, not the estimated
physical life of the property. *Massey Motors, Inc. v. United States*, 364
U.S. 92 (1960). To adopt a life that is shorter than the asset's
physical life, the taxpayer had to show the actual experience with
such assets in his trade or business or the experience with similar
assets in the type of trade or business that the taxpayer conducts.
Honodel v. Commissioner, 722 F.2d 1462 (9th Cir. 1984).

§ **11.3110. No Exhaustible Life.** Some assets, such as unimproved land, have no exhaustible "useful life" and, therefore,
cannot be amortized or depreciated in the absence of a specific
statutory provision. Some such assets, for example, goodwill, are
permitted in certain circumstances to be amortized over a specified period of time by an explicit Code provision. See § **11.1321.**

§ 11.3120. General Asset Accounts or Multiple Asset Accounts. At their election, many businesses do not compute depreciation separately for each business asset. The depreciation of a single asset is sometimes referred to as depreciation under a "single asset account method." Instead, the assets acquired in a taxable year are divided into broad categories; the assets in each category are lumped together into one account; and the cumulative total of the bases of the assets in each account is depreciated at a single rate and method over a single recovery period This method of depreciating assets is sometimes referred to as a "general asset account method" or as a "multiple asset account method." All of the assets that comprise a general asset account will have been acquired in the same taxable year. Treas. Reg. § 1.168(i)–1(c)(2)(i)(E). General asset accounts can be used for properties that are depreciated under MACRS. IRC § 168(i)(4). Under MACRS, the types of properties that qualify for general asset treatment are more extensive than was permitted under the pre–1981 version of depreciation. Under MACRS, the manner in which depreciation is determined in a general asset account and the treatment of dispositions of property held in such an account are described in Treas. Reg. § 1.168(i)–1.

§ 11.3130. Conclusive Guidelines. In order to reduce conflict over the useful life of an asset, the Treasury adopted a regulation that established a range of "useful lives" within which a taxpayer could select the life he preferred. The taxpayer's selection was conclusive. This method, called "asset depreciation range" or "ADR," was elective. The mid-point of the range of recovery periods that applied to a class of assets under ADR was referred to as the "class life" of those assets.

The ADR plan stirred considerable controversy, but it was codified by Congress in the Revenue Act of 1971. The ADR system was replaced by ACRS (and later by MACRS) when § 168 was adopted in 1981. As will be seen in Chapter Twelve, an updated version of the class lives that were adopted under the ADR plan are utilized in IRC § 168 to determine the MACRS recovery period of many assets. The MACRS recovery period is not necessarily equal to the ADR class life, but it often is determined by reference to that class life.

§ 11.3140. Depreciation or Amortization of a Term Interest. Section 167(e) denies a depreciation or amortization deduc-

tion for a term interest in property if the remainder interest is
held by a person who is related to the person who holds the term
interest. A related person is a person bearing a relationship to the
taxpayer that is described in IRC § 267(b) or (e). IRC
§ 167(e)(5)(B). The basis in the term interest of the person
holding that interest is reduced by the amount of depreciation
disallowed as a deduction by that provision, and (with two exceptions) the remainderman's basis in the remainder interest is
increased by a like amount (adjusted for depreciation allowable to
the holder of the term interest because of the depreciation for the
underlying property). IRC § 167(e)(3), 4(A).

Section 167(e) does not apply to a term interest that was acquired
by gift, bequest, or inheritance. IRC § 167(e)(2)(A). In such a
case, IRC § 273 precludes any deduction for depreciation or
amortization of such a term interest regardless of the identity of
the remainderman; and when IRC § 273 applies, no adjustment
to basis is made because of the disallowed depreciation.

IRC §§ 167(e) and 273 deny a deduction only for the depreciation
or amortization of a taxpayer's basis in a term interest; those
provisions do not prevent the taxpayer from deducting depreciation or amortization of underlying property to which the term
interest relates to the extent that such depreciation or amortization is allocated to the taxpayer under IRC § 167(d). See
§ 16.1410.

> **§ 11.3141. Illustration.** The *Y* trust held a commercial
> building. On January 1, Year One, *A* sold his 10–year term
> income interest in the trust to *B* for $40,000, *B* is the brother
> of *S*, and so they are related persons for purposes of IRC
> § 167(e). *S* holds the remainder interest in the *Y* trust. The
> trust is entitled to $2,000 of depreciation for the use of the
> building in Year One. That $2,000 of depreciation is allocated
> between *B* (the income beneficiary) and the trust according to
> IRC § 163(d); but, in this case, all of the $2,000 of depreciation
> will be allocated to *B*. IRC § 163(e) does not deny *B* a
> deduction for the depreciation of the building that is allocated
> to him.
>
> *B* has a $40,000 basis in his term interest which interest is
> being exhausted every year. If there were no IRC § 163(e), *B*
> would be allowed to amortize his basis over the 10–year term
> and deduct $4,000 in Year One. IRC § 163(e) prevents *B* from

deducting any depreciation for his $40,000 basis. *B*'s basis is reduced by the disallowed depreciation,. The $4,000 of depreciation that reduced *B*'s basis in his term interest, apparently reduced by the $2,000 of depreciation on the building that was allocated to *B*, is added to *S*'s basis in her remainder interest in the trust. IRC § 163(e)(3).

§ 11.3200. Salvage Value. The salvage value of an asset is an estimate (made at the time of acquisition) of what the resale value of the asset will be at the end of its estimated useful life. It should be emphasized that salvage value is an *estimate*; it is not recomputed each year that the market value of the asset fluctuates. As noted in Chapter Twelve, salvage value is ignored in determining depreciation under MACRS.

§ 11.3300. Methods of Depreciation. The *method* selected by the taxpayer determines the rates at which the asset will be depreciated. For certain kinds of property, but not all kinds, any method which provided a "reasonable allowance" of depreciation was acceptable if the total depreciation taken during the first two-thirds of the useful life of the property would not exceed the amount that would have been taken had the double declining balance method been used. **§ 11.3360.** Three methods of depreciation that were specifically permitted by the Code, and were the most commonly used, are straight-line, declining balance, and sum of the years-digits. IRC § 167(b). The sum of the years digits method is no longer permitted, and is discussed here to provide background information as to the development of the depreciation rules. However, there are other reasonable methods of depreciation that are still allowed (e.g., the units of production method, and the "income forecast" method). IRC § 167(g). When the latter two methods (units of production and income forecast) are permitted, they can be utilized in lieu of MACRS. IRC § 168(f)(1). The declining balance and straight-line methods are employed by MACRS.

§ 11.3310. Units of Production Method. The units of production method measures the life of the asset in terms of its production capacity and allocates depreciation according to the units produced.

§ 11.3311. Illustration. *X* purchased a machine for $10,000 which is estimated to be capable of producing 1,000,000 widgets during its *economic* life. During Year One, the machine produces 220,000 widgets. Assuming no salvage value, the depreciation deduction for Year One under the units of production method is $2,200 (220,000 × $10,000 ÷ 1,000,000).

§ 11.3320.   Straight–Line Method. The straight-line method measures the annual depreciation deduction for an asset by deducting the asset's salvage value from the original basis of the asset and dividing the difference by the estimated useful life of the property.

§ 11.3321.   Illustration. On January 1, 1970, X purchased a desk for his office for $5,000. Its estimated "useful life" is ten years at the end of which its value is expected to be $500. X can deduct $450 depreciation each year for ten years ($5,000 − $500 ÷ 10). Dividing the number of years (ten) into 100% produces the straight-line rate (10%). The straight-line rate times the difference between the asset's original basis and its salvage value equals the depreciation to be taken each year. Note that salvage value is ignored when depreciation is taken under MACRS.

§ 11.3330.   Declining Balance Method. The declining balance method measures depreciation by applying a fixed percentage to the property's adjusted basis as of the beginning of the tax year for which the depreciation is claimed. Since the adjusted basis will be lower each year, this method is called "declining balance." Salvage value is disregarded in making this computation.

§ 11.3331.   Salvage Value Disregarded. Even before MACRS was adopted, salvage value was not taken into account in computing declining balance depreciation because the application of a fixed percentage to a declining amount leaves a residue of undepreciated basis, usually equal to between ten and thirteen percent of the original basis, when the asset's "useful life" has expired. Thus, the method of depreciation itself has a salvage value built into the annual computations.

§ 11.3332.   Minimum Useful Life. With very *few* exceptions, the declining balance method could be employed only if the depreciable asset had a useful life of at least three years. Rev. Rul. 67–248; and see *Holder Driv–Ur–Self, Inc. v. Commissioner*, 43 T.C. 202 (1964).

§ 11.3333.   New Property. Prior to MACRS, declining balance, other than 150 percent declining balance, could be used only if the taxpayer was the first person to use the depreciable asset or if the taxpayer built or constructed the asset. One hundred fifty percent declining balance depreciation could be deducted for used *personal* property having a useful life of at least three years. In determining the depreciation of personal properties under MACRS, it is irrelevant whether the property is new or used. The declining balance method was available only to a limited extent for realty acquired between 1969 and 1986; for realty acquired after 1986, the declining balance method is not available.

§ **11.3333–1. Illustration.** In 1970 (a pre-MACRS year), *X* purchased a second-hand desk with a useful life of six years for use in his business office. *X* could elect to use either the straight-line or the 150 percent declining balance method of depreciation, but *X* could not use the double declining balance method or the sum of the years-digits method, which were limited to new property. As we will see in Chapter 12, if the desk had been purchased in a year to which MACRS applies, the TP could have depreciated it on the double declining balance method.

§ **11.3334. Rate of Depreciation.** The percentage to be applied against the declining balance is a multiple of the straight-line rate. For example, 150 percent declining balance on a ten-year life asset is one and one-half times the straight-line rate of 10% or a 15% rate, and double declining balance is twice the straight-line rate or a 20% rate.

§ **11.3334–1. Illustration.** On January 1, 1971, a taxpayer purchased new office furniture for $20,000 which had an estimated life of eight years and a salvage value of $3,500. The taxpayer elected to use the double declining balance method.

1. The taxpayer's depreciation for 1971 is computed as follows:

$100/8 = 12\frac{1}{2}\%$—straight-line rate

$2 \times 12\frac{1}{2}\% = 25\%$—double declining balance rate

25% of $20,000 = $5,000 depreciation in 1971.

(Note that salvage value is ignored in computing the deduction.)

2. The depreciation for 1972 is calculated as follows:

25%—double declining balance rate (the percentage remains fixed)

25% × $15,000 (i.e., $20,000 original basis minus $5,000 depreciation taken) = $3,750 depreciation for 1972

3.   The depreciation for 1973 is calculated as follows:

25%—double declining balance rate

25% × $11,250 (i.e., $20,000 − $5,000 − $3,750) = $2,812.50 depreciation for 1973.

§ 11.3340.   Sum of the Years–Digits Method. The sum of the years-digits method measures depreciation by applying a fraction with a constant denominator but a declining numerator to the original basis of the asset less salvage value. The numerator of this fraction is the number of remaining years of the asset's "useful life" and the denominator is the sum of the digits representing each year of the asset's "useful life." Note that this method is not available for property placed in service after 1980.

§ 11.3341.   Illustration. On January 1, 1971, X purchased a new machine for use in her business. X paid $11,000 for the machine which has a "useful life" of ten years and a salvage value of $1,000. Thus, X will use $11,000 − $1,000 salvage = $10,000 as her depreciable basis.

1.   In 1971, the first year, the rate of depreciation will be 10 (remaining useful life) ÷ (10 + 9 + 8 + 7 + 6 + 5 + 4 + 3 + 2 + 1) = 10/55, and the amount of deductions allowed X will be 10/55 × $10,000 = $1,818.

2.   In 1972, X will deduct 9 ÷ (10 + 9 + 8 + 7 + 6 + 5 + 4 + 3 + 2 + 1) = 9/55 × $10,000 = $1,633.

3.   In each subsequent year, the rate will be 8/55, 7/55, 6/55, 5/55, etc.

§ 11.3342.   Shorthand Technique. A shorthand method of computing the denominator is to multiply the "useful life" of an asset times the "useful life" plus one year and then divide by two. Thus, for example, the denominator for an asset having a useful life of ten years would be 10 × (10 + 1)/2 = 110/2 = 55. So in Year One, the fraction is 10/55; in Year Two 9/55, etc. The denominator for an asset having an eight-year "useful life" would be (8 × 9)/2 = 36, and the denominator for an asset having a five-year useful life would be $(5 \times 6)/2 = 15$.

§ 11.3343. Required Useful Life. The sum of the years-digits method was available only for depreciating assets having a "useful life" of at least three years. It is not available for real property acquired after 1969, and it is not available for any property acquired after 1980.

§ 11.3344. New Property. The sum of the years-digits method was available only for new property (i.e., property first put to use by the taxpayer or property built or constructed by the taxpayer).

§ 11.3350. Accelerated Methods. Both declining balance and sum of the years-digits are accelerated methods of depreciation (i.e., a greater amount of the asset's basis is depreciated in the earlier years of the asset's life than in its later years).

§ 11.3360. Other Methods of Depreciation. In addition to declining balance and sum of the years-digits, prior to 1981, a taxpayer could elect to use any other consistent method of depreciation which would provide aggregate depreciation deductions during the first two-thirds of the asset's full life that did not exceed the amount of depreciation that would have been allowed to the taxpayer during that period under the double declining balance method. IRC § 167(b)(4). This provision applied only to personalty with a "useful life" of at least three years and which the taxpayer either built or purchased new, and to some, but not to all, realty. This flexibility is not available for property placed in service after 1980.

§ 11.3370. Income Forecast Method. The rights that a taxpayer has in motion picture films, video tapes, and certain other properties have a limited useful life and can be depreciated as intangible property. As with many intangible properties, the rights in such properties would be depreciated on the straight-line method. Because the flow of income from such properties is greatly uneven (for some films, virtually all of the income will be produced in the first one or two years of the film's exploitation, whereas some films will continue to produce income for many years), straight-line depreciation does not provide an accurate allocation of the cost of acquiring or creating the film to the years of its exploitation. Consequently, the Commissioner permits a taxpayer to utilize an income forecast method for depreciating such properties, and that method was codified by Congress when it added IRC § 167(g) to the Code in 1996. See Rev. Rul. 95–52; Rev. Rul. 60–358, as amplified by Rev. Rul. 64–273, and Rev. Rul. 79–285. *Citizens & Southern Corp. v. Commissioner*, 91 T.C. 463, 512–513 (1988), aff'd without opinion, 900 F.2d 266 (11th Cir. 1990). The types of properties which can be depreciated on the income forecast method are listed in IRC § 167(g)(6) and include (in addition to films and video tapes) books, copyrights, sound recordings, theatrical productions, and patents. Prop. Reg. § 1.167(n)–5(a). This method cannot be used for an asset which is amortizable under IRC § 197. IRC § 167(g)(6) Prop. Reg. § 1.167(n)–5(b).

The income forecast method permits a taxpayer to depreciate certain assets over an 11–year period in a manner that conforms each year's deduction to the proportion of income that is derived from the asset that year. The income forecast method requires the taxpayer to make an estimate (i.e., a forecast) of the amount of income that his interest in the property will produce over the first 11 years of its exploitation. Each year, the taxpayer can take a depreciation deduction equal to a fraction of his original basis in the property; the fraction for a year's depreciation is determined by making the actual income from the property for that year the numerator and by making the denominator equal to the total amount of income that is estimated will be derived from the property over the first 11 years of its exploitation. The estimate of the total amount of income that constitutes the denominator of the fraction is redetermined in a year in which information becomes available indicating that the forecasted income is inaccurate. Prop. Reg. § 1.167(n)–3(c). The basis of the property, against which the fraction is applied, remains the same without reduction for depreciation, but the basis can be redetermined to reflect additions to basis for amounts expended after the property was put into service. Prop. Reg. § 1.167(n)–2(b).

If a TP has any basis remaining in the asset at the beginning of the 11th taxable year of its exploitation, the TP can deduct all of the remaining basis in that taxable year. IRC § 167(g)(1)(C). So-called "look-back" rules can cause a TP to receive or pay interest if the depreciation taken under the income forecast method proves excessive or inadequate in some years. IRC § 167(g)(2)–(4).

§ 11.4000. LAND. Undeveloped land cannot be depreciated or amortized because it has no ascertainable useful life. Treas. Reg. § 1.167(a)–

2. If improved realty is acquired, only the improvements can be depreciated. It is therefore necessary to allocate the taxpayer's basis between the land and the improvements, and no depreciation is allowed for the land.

§ 11.4100. **Illustration.** A taxpayer paid $400,000 for improved real estate. The purchase price must be allocated according to fair market values at the time of taxpayer's acquisition between the land, which is not depreciable, and the improvement, which is depreciable. Thus, if at the time that the taxpayer purchase the property, the fair market value of the building on the land was $350,000 and the fair market value of the land was $50,000, the taxpayer can depreciate only his $350,000 basis in the building.

§ 11.5000. **DEPRECIATION OF IMPROVED REAL ESTATE.** While land is not depreciable, having no exhaustible life, real estate improvements are depreciable. Prior to the Tax Reform Act of 1969, the rules for depreciating personalty also applied to realty, but subsequent to the 1969 Act, real estate had to be considered separately and depreciated under a different set of rules. Subject to certain exceptions, those special depreciation rules apply to realty improvements purchased or constructed after July 24, 1969 [Treas. Reg. § 1.167(j)–1] and placed into service before 1981. Since realty placed in service after 1980 is depreciated under ACRS or MACRS, the current provisions of which are described in Chapter Twelve, the text will omit any discussion of the special rules that apply to realty placed in service between 1969 and 1981.

§ 11.6000. **ADJUSTMENT TO BASIS.** The basis of depreciable property is reduced by the amount of depreciation claimed by a taxpayer on his tax return (the amount "allowed") that actually provided the taxpayer with a tax benefit. IRC § 1016(a)(2). The depreciation so claimed is called the depreciation "allowed" to the taxpayer, and the amount allowed reduces basis only to the extent that it provided the taxpayer with a tax benefit. In no event will basis be reduced by less than the amount of depreciation deduction that is "allowable" under the method of depreciation elected by the taxpayer. IRC § 1016(a)(2). The amount of *allowable* deduction reduces the taxpayer's basis without regard to whether the *allowable* deduction would have provided a tax benefit to the taxpayer.

As to personal property that is depreciable under MACRS but for which the taxpayer failed to claim any depreciation deduction, prior to 1990 the allowable depreciation that reduced the taxpayer's basis *usually* would be determined under IRC § 168(b)(1), which establishes a more rapid rate of depreciation than the taxpayer might have elected under IRC §§ 168(b)(5) or (g)(7). Prop. Reg. § 1.1016–3(a)(3). As a consequence of the amendment of IRC § 1016(a)(2) by Section 11812(b)(10) of the Omnibus Budget Reconciliation Act of 1990, it appears that the allowable depreciation will be determined by employing the straight line method of depreciation. The 1990 amendment changed the second sentence of IRC § 1016(a)(2) to require the use of the "straight line method" when the taxpayer failed to adopt a method of depreciation, and the amendment is made applicable to property placed in service after November 5, 1990.

§ 11.7000. RECAPTURE OF DEPRECIATION. The extent to which depreciation deductions may be "recaptured" when the taxpayer disposes of the depreciable property is discussed later in this work. See IRC §§ 1245 and 1250 discussed in Chapter Nineteen.

§ 11.8000. DEPRECIATION IN THE YEAR OF SALE. When a depreciable asset that was not depreciated under MACRS is sold or otherwise disposed of during a tax year, depreciation may be deducted for the portion of the tax year prior to the sale or other disposition. Such depreciation may be deducted regardless of whether the taxpayer's adjusted basis in the asset, after adjusting for depreciation deducted in the year of sale, is lower than the price for which the taxpayer sold the asset. *Fribourg Navigation Co., Inc. v. Commissioner*, 383 U.S. 272 (1966). Depreciation is also allowed for part of the year in which an asset that was depreciated under MACRS is sold or otherwise disposed of; the manner in which such depreciation is determined is explained in Chapter Twelve.

§ 11.9000. RETIREMENT OR ABANDONMENT OF A DEPRECIABLE ASSET. If a TP ceases to use a depreciable asset in the TP's trade or business, whether by retirement of the asset or by its abandonment, and if the TP does not sell or exchange the asset, the TP usually will be allowed a loss deduction for the difference between the asset's adjusted basis and its salvage value. Salvage will be ignored in the case of an abandonment. Treas. Reg. § 1.167(a)–8.

CHAPTER TWELVE

MODIFIED ACCELERATED COST RECOVERY SYSTEM (MACRS)

§ 12.0000. COST RECOVERY.

§ 12.1000. GENERAL. As noted in **§ 11.1110**, for most tangible property placed in service after 1980, depreciation is determined under a method set forth in IRC § 168 and referred to as the accelerated cost recovery system (ACRS) or, for years after 1986, as the modified accelerated cost recovery system (MACRS). MACRS is merely one type of a depreciation system. The manner in which MACRS operates and the types of properties to which it applies are discussed in this chapter. As noted at **§ 11.1111**, IRC § 168(a) states that the depreciation of tangible property that is provided by IRC § 167(a) is to be determined by using IRC § 168 (i.e., by using MACRS). Temp. Reg. § 1.168(a)–1T states, "The allowance for depreciation under section 168 constitutes the amount allowable under section 167(a)." Thus, a deduction allowable under MACRS is properly referred to as depreciation. For example, the reference in the title to IRC § 179 to "depreciable" business assets includes assets the cost of which is recoverable under MACRS. Properties which are precluded from depreciation (such as undeveloped land) cannot be depreciated under MACRS.

When the cost of an item can be deducted in full in the year paid or incurred, as contrasted to amortizing the cost over a period of time, that treatment of the cost is called "expensing." In other words, if a cost is "expensed," it is deducted when paid or incurred and is not depreciated or otherwise amortized.

§ 12.2000. EXPENSING THE COST OF CERTAIN BUSINESS ASSETS. Before examining MACRS, it is useful to consider the special deduction allowable under IRC § 179 for the cost of purchasing certain tangible property that is used in a trade or business. IRC § 179 permits a taxpayer who purchases so-called "section 179 property" to elect to deduct all or part of the cost of purchasing the asset as a current expense in the taxable year in which the asset is placed in service. IRC § 179(a). This deduction is sometimes referred to as "bonus depreciation," even though it is a misnomer to refer to an expensed item as a kind of depreciation. Any amount of the cost that is deducted under IRC § 179 will not be included in the taxpayer's basis in that asset. IRC § 179(a), Treas. Reg. § 1.179–1(f)(1). The TP's remaining basis is depreciable under the normal rules of depreciation. So, in the year of acquisition of the property, the TP gets both bonus depreciation and regular depreciation for the asset.

The maximum amount that can be deducted under IRC § 179 in a taxable year beginning in the period 2003 to 2007 is $100,000, but that amount is reduced (not below zero) by the amount by which the cost of section 179 property that was placed in service in that year exceeds $400,000. IRC § 179(b)(1), (2). For a taxable year beginning in the period 2004 to 2007, those dollar amounts are increased by cost-of-living adjustments. IRC § 179(b)(5). For example, the maximum amount that can be deducted under IRC § 179 for the year 2005 is $105,000, which is reduced if the cost of section 179 property for that year exceeds $420,000. Rev. Proc. 2004–71. Those dollar amounts currently are scheduled to become $25,000 and $200,000 respectively in taxable years beginning in 2008 and thereafter; but it is likely that Congress will change those amounts before that date arrives. The amount deductible for the cost of a sport utility vehicle is subject to a special dollar limitation. IRC § 179(b)(6).

If a taxpayer is married and files a separate return, the maximum cost of section 179 properties that can be deducted is determined by treating the taxpayer and his spouse as one person except that the "taxable income" limitation described below is applied separately to each party; and the maximum amount of section 179 cost that is then determined to be deductible is allocated between the taxpayer and the spouse equally unless they elect otherwise. IRC § 179(b)(4).

The maximum amount that can be deducted under IRC § 179 by a taxpayer in a taxable year cannot exceed the aggregate taxable income that the taxpayer derived that year from the active conduct of trades or businesses. IRC § 179(b)(3). For this purpose, taxable income is determined by aggregating the net incomes or losses for that year of all trades or businesses that are actively conducted by the taxpayer. Treas. Reg. § 1.179–2(c)(1). The taxable income from a trade or business is computed by excluding deductions allowable under IRC § 179 and certain other deductions listed in Treas. Reg. § 1.179–2(c)(1). IRC § 179(b)(3)(C).

In general, the active conduct of a trade or business means "meaningful" participation in the management or operations of the trade or business. Treas. Reg. § 1.179–2(c)(6)(ii). Any amount that is disallowed as a deduction because of this taxable income limitation is carried forward and treated as a cost of section 179 property in the next year (and so may be deductible in that year or, if not, can be carried forward again). IRC § 179(b)(3). If section 179 property is sold or if it is transferred in a transaction in which some or all of the gain or loss is not recognized, immediately prior to that sale or transfer, the adjusted basis of the asset is increased by any outstanding carryover of unused deduction with respect to the property. This provision also applies to transfers at death (Treas. Reg. § 1.179–3(f)(1)); but under current law, in which basis will usually be changed to date of death value by IRC § 1014, an increase in decedent's basis does not appear to have much significance. However, if the carryover basis rule of IRC § 1022, which is scheduled to apply to property of decedents who die after 2009, is allowed to become effective, an addition to the decedent's basis would then be significant.

The taxpayer's election to take a deduction under IRC § 179 must specify the items whose cost is to be expensed and must specify the amount of cost of each such item that is to be deducted. Once made, the election can be revoked only with the permission of the Commissioner, which will be granted only in extraordinary circumstances. IRC § 179(c)(2), and Treas. Reg. § 1.179–5(b). However, an election made with respect to a taxable year beginning in the period 2003 to 2007 can be revoked by the TP unilaterally; but, once made, that election cannot be revoked. IRC § 179(c)(2). The meaning of "cost" is specially defined in IRC § 179(d)(3).

The type of property to which IRC § 179 applies (section 179 property) is tangible property to which MACRS applies and which is section 1245 property (as defined in IRC § 1245(a)(3)), and which is "purchased" for use in the active conduct of a trade or a business. IRC § 179(d)(1). The meaning of "purchase" is specially defined in IRC § 179(d)(2), which employs a narrower definition than is customarily applied to that term. IRC § 179 does not apply to buildings or to their structural components.

If "at any time" an item of section 179 property is not used predominantly in the taxpayer's trade or business, part of the deduction that the taxpayer obtained under IRC § 179 for that item is recaptured by requiring the taxpayer to include that amount in his gross income. IRC § 179(d)(10). The Blue Book for the 1986 TRA states that the reference in IRC § 179(d)(10) to "any time" is limited to any time prior to the expiration of the recovery period for the depreciation of that asset. General Explanation of the Tax Reform Act of 1986, prepared by the Staff of the Joint Committee on Taxation (1986) at p. 110. The regulations have adopted that construction and so limit recapture to the recovery period. Treas. Reg. § 1.179–1(e)(1). The "recovery period" of an asset is explained at § **12.3430.**

The amount recaptured is the excess of the amount expensed under IRC § 179 (regardless of whether that deduction provided taxpayer with a tax benefit) over the amount of additional depreciation that would have been allowable under IRC § 168 for the period preceding the event causing the recapture if IRC § 179 had not been elected and thereby reduced the depreciable basis of the section 179 property. Treas. Reg. § 1.179–1(e)(1). In most circumstances where section 179 property is sold or transferred, IRC § 1245 will apply to the disposition and cause recapture of all or some of the expensed deduction. IRC § 1245(a)(1)–(3). See § **19.3000** *et seq.* The recapture provision of IRC § 179(d)(10) does not apply when IRC § 1245(a) applies to the disposition. Treas. Reg. § 1.179–1(e)(3).

If IRC § 179(d)(10) recapture applies, the amount that is recaptured under that provision is added to the adjusted basis of the section 179 property immediately before the event that caused the recapture. Treas. Reg. § 1.179–1(e)(3). This prevents double taxation of the recaptured amount.

If an IRC § 179 deduction is taken for a luxury automobile (or for certain "listed property"), special limitations on the amount of deduction that is allowable will apply. IRC § 280F(d)(1). In that case, for purposes of applying the limitation, the IRC § 179 deduction for that year is treated as an IRC § 168 deduction, and so the total of the IRC §§ 168 and 179 deductions for that year are subject to the IRC § 280F limitations. Treas. Reg. § 1.280F–2T(b)(4), (e), Exs (4)–(7).

The Omnibus Budget Reconciliation Act of 1993 amended the Code to provide for certain geographic areas to be designated as "empowerment zones" and "enterprise communities." IRC §§ 1391–1397(F). One of the benefits granted to businesses that operate in an empowerment zone is that the amount that can be expensed under IRC § 179 for qualified businesses in such a zone is substantially increased. IRC § 1397A.

§ **12.2100.   Estates and Trusts.** The bonus depreciation deduction is not available to a taxpayer that is an estate or trust. IRC § 179(d)(4).

§ 12.2200. Illustration. *B*, an unmarried individual, reports his income on a calendar year basis. In 2005 (when the maximum amount of IRC § 179 deduction that can be allowed is $105,000), *B* purchased both a machine (at a cost of $112,000) and a truck (at a cost of $20,000) for use in his business. *B* made no other purchases in 2005. *B* had taxable income of $240,000 from the active conduct of his business in 2005. Both the truck and the machine were placed in service in 2005. *B* can make any one of the following elections under IRC § 179. *B* can elect to deduct:

(a) $20,000 of the cost of purchasing the truck, and no expense deduction for the cost of purchasing the machine; or

(b) $20,000 of the cost of purchasing the truck, and $85,000 of the cost of the machine; or

(c) $105,000 of the cost of purchasing the machine, and no expense deduction for the cost of the truck; or

(d) $92,500 of the cost of the machine and $12,500 of the cost of the truck; or

(e) $91,500 of the cost of the machine and $13,500 of the cost of the truck; or

(f) some other combination of the costs of the two items so long as the total cost taken as a deduction does not exceed $105,000.

B's election must specify each item selected and the amount of cost of that item to be deducted under IRC § 179. This specification is required so that the adjusted basis of the assets can be determined and so *B*'s regular depreciation deductions of the asset can be determined. Note that B is not required to utilize the bonus depreciation deduction and can elect to use only part of it or none.

§ 12.3000. MACRS (THE MODIFIED ACCELERATED COST RECOVERY SYSTEM). MACRS is a system of depreciation that utilizes straight-line and declining balance methods of depreciation. The straight-line and declining balance methods of depreciation are described at §§ **11.3320–11.3330** and §§ **11.3334–11.3334–1.** The initial system that was adopted in 1981 was known as ACRS, but after it was modified in 1986, it came to be referred to as MACRS to distinguish the amended version from the original system. ACRS was adopted by Congress in 1981 and has been modified several times since then; the modifications adopted as part of the 1986 Tax Reform Act are especially significant, and since that modification was made the system has been referred to as MACRS. The current operation of MACRS is explained in

§ 12.3400. Some of the salient distinctions between MACRS and prior systems of depreciation are that MACRS:

- does not take salvage value into account for any purpose;

- adopts a statutorily specified period of time over which the adjusted basis of property is recovered (in contrast to prior systems of depreciation which typically used a recovery period that was based on the property's useful life);

- makes no distinction between new and used property (the depreciation of used property under MACRS is not subject to special restrictions and is determined the same as it is for new property);

- utilizes the half-year or mid-quarter convention for personalty and the mid-month convention for buildings;

- and generally (for personalty) provides a greater acceleration of recovery of cost than was provided by the depreciation systems that were used prior to 1981.

For guidelines to the application of MACRS, see Rev. Proc. 87–57.

§ 12.3100. MACRS Property. The only property that is depreciable under MACRS is tangible property, real or personal, of a character subject to the allowance for depreciation that either is used in a trade or business or otherwise is held for the production of income. IRC §§ 167(a), 168(a). Neither MACRS nor ACRS applies to any property that was placed in service by the taxpayer prior to 1981. MACRS does not apply to intangible property. Even some tangible properties that are placed in service after 1980 are excluded from MACRS—for example, certain public utility property, sound recordings, films and video tapes are excluded. IRC § 168(f). MACRS also does not apply to tangible property that the taxpayer elects to exclude from MACRS if the property is properly depreciated by the taxpayer on the units of production method of depreciation [see §§ 11.3310–11.3311] or (subject to one exception) on some other method of depreciation that is not determined by reference to a term of years. IRC § 168(f)(1). One example of a method available in lieu of MACRS is the standard mileage rate that is permitted for determining the deduction for the business use of an automobile. See Rev. Proc. 2004–64.

§ 12.3110. Determinable Useful Life. Prior to the adoption of ACRS in 1981, the period over which depreciation could be taken was the useful life of the asset. See §§ **11.3000–11.3100.** Because of that requirement, an asset could not be depreciated unless the taxpayer could show that it had a determinable useful life. See Rev. Rul. 68–232. When Congress adopted ACRS, it eliminated useful life as the measure of an asset's recovery period. § **12.3000.** Instead, the recovery period for depreciation under ACRS or MACRS is a statutorily established period, and it does not depend upon the actual life of the asset.

The Service maintains that, notwithstanding the elimination of useful life in determining the amount of depreciation for a given year, there remains a requirement that a tangible asset cannot be depreciated under ACRS or MACRS unless the taxpayer can show that the asset has a determinable useful life. The Service maintains that the statement in IRC § 168(a) that that section is a special application of IRC § 167(a) depreciation of tangible property means that the requirement of IRC § 167 that the asset have a determinable useful life applies also to MACRS.

The Service litigated this issue in two separate cases, and lost both. A majority of the Tax Court and the Second and Third Circuit Courts of Appeals held that there is no requirement that an asset have a determinable useful life to be depreciated under ACRS or MACRS. *Simon v. Commissioner*, 103 T.C. 247 (1994) (reviewed by the court), Nonacq., aff'd 68 F.3d 41 (2d Cir. 1995); *Liddle v. Commissioner*, 103 T.C. 285 (1994) (reviewed by the court), Nonacq., aff'd 65 F.3d 329 (3d Cir. 1995). The courts held that it is sufficient that the asset be subject to exhaustion, wear and tear, or obsolescence.

In *Simon*, the items in question were 19th Century violin bows. The taxpayers were highly skilled professional musicians that used the bows in their performances. The taxpayers produced evidence that the use of the bows did cause wear and tear to the bows and that the bows would lose their capacity to produce excellent sound after much use. However, the bows were also collectible items that were valuable without regard to their capacity to produce outstanding music. Consequently, the value of the bows rose while the taxpayers used them because of their value as collectibles. The Tax Court and the Second Circuit Court of Appeals held that the bows could be depreciated under ACRS (because of the years involved in the suit, ACRS was the applicable statutory system). Since the bows suffered wear and tear and exhaustion in the use to which the taxpayers put them, they qualified for depreciation as 5–year property. See § **12.3410.** On a similar set of facts, the Tax Court and the Third Circuit Court of Appeals reached the same result in *Liddle*.

The Commissioner nonacquiesced in both the *Simon* and the *Liddle* decisions. The Commissioner has stated that the Service will litigate this issue in other circuits when the opportunity arises. AOD 1996–009.

> **§ 12.3111. Works of Art.** A valuable painting by a master does not have a determinable useful life. Rev. Rul. 68–232. In *Clinger v. Commissioner*, 60 T.C.M. 598 (1990), the Tax Court held that a painting, which was hung in the taxpayer's place of business for a business purpose, was not depreciable under ACRS (IRC § 168) because it does not have a determinable useful life. The court also denied taxpayer's claim for an expense deduction under IRC § 179.

As noted above, in several subsequent decisions that were reviewed by the entire court and affirmed by two Circuit Courts of Appeals, the Tax Court held that there is no requirement in ACRS or MACRS that an asset must have a determinable useful life. See **§ 12.3110.** However, taxpayer still must show that the asset to be depreciated under MACRS is subject to exhaustion, wear and tear, or obsolescence. *Simon* and *Liddle*, **§ 12.3110.** In *Simon* and *Liddle*, there was evidence that the musical instruments in those cases were suffering wear and year and exhaustion. That may not be true when dealing with a fine painting. Who has the burden of proof on that issue? See **§ 1.4400.**

It should be noted that not every painting constitutes a fine work of art. If a painting does not qualify as an artistic achievement, it may be no more than a wall decoration; and, as such, can be depreciated if used in a business office (the same as any office furnishing).

§ 12.3200. Adjusted Basis. Since MACRS utilizes the straight-line and declining balance methods of depreciation, deductions are determined by reference to the adjusted basis of the property. See IRC § 167(c).

§ 12.3300. Salvage Value. Salvage value is not taken into account in determining depreciation under MACRS regardless of whether depreciation is determined under the straight-line or declining balance method. IRC §§ 168(b)(4), (g)(2)(A). The elimination of salvage value as a factor in determining depreciation is one of the important changes that was made by the Congressional adoption of ACRS and of MACRS.

§ 12.3400. Determination of the Amount of Depreciation. To determine the amount of depreciation that is allowable for an item of MACRS property, it is necessary first to determine the classification of the property in question and then to determine three factors: "the applicable depreciation method," "the applicable recovery period," and "the applicable convention." IRC § 168(a).

§ 12.3410. Classification of Property. The current version of MACRS divides MACRS properties into nine classifications: three-year property, five-year property, seven-year property, ten-year property, fifteen-year property, twenty-year property, water utility property, residential rental property, and nonresidential real property. IRC § 168(e)(1), (2). In addition to the nine classifications, note that a special classification is provided for a railroad grading or tunnel bore. IRC § 168(c)(1), (e)(4).

§ 12.3411. Use of ADR Class Lives. With some exceptions, the MACRS classification of an asset is determined by reference to its class life under a method for determining the recovery period for depreciating properties that was available prior to 1981; this method was called "asset depreciation range" or "ADR." ADR is described at **§ 11.3130.** Under ADR, a taxpayer could elect to use a recovery period that fell within a range of years that was provided for broad categories of properties. The mid-point of the range of years for each class of property is referred to as the "class life" for that property. Thus, properties that had a depreciation range under ADR of from four to six years are said to have a class life of five years.

The class life of an asset under ADR is established by the Commissioner's publication of a Revenue Procedure that sets class lives for broad categories of properties. For example, the class life for office furniture, fixtures and equipment is ten years. While ADR is not available for assets placed into service after 1980, an updated version of the ADR class lives is used to determine the classification of many categories of assets under MACRS. For that reason, the Commissioner continues to update the lists of ADR class lives. See IRC § 168(i)(1) which provides that for MACRS purposes "class life" means the class life of an asset under ADR as that system was established by statute as of January 1, 1986. The current list of ADR class lives is set forth in Rev. Proc. 87–56 (as modified by Rev. Proc. 88–22).

Rev. Proc. 87–56 (as modified) not only sets forth the current ADR class lives of categories of assets, the Revenue Procedure also sets forth the recovery period for each category for general MACRS depreciation purposes and the recovery period for each category for purposes of the MACRS alternative depreciation system. See § **12.3460.** For example, office furniture, fixtures and equipment are listed in the Revenue Procedure as having a recovery period of seven years for the purpose of the general depreciation allowance provided by MACRS, and such assets have a recovery period of ten years for the purpose of the alternative MACRS depreciation allowance set forth at IRC § 168(g). Rev. Proc. 87–56.

Since the Revenue Procedure provides the recovery periods of assets for both regular MACRS depreciation and alternative MACRS depreciation purposes, a taxpayer can use those tables to compute the proper depreciation allowance, and the taxpayer does not need to know the asset's class life (albeit the Revenue Procedure also sets forth the asset's class life). However, the reader should be alert to the possibility that Congress will change the recovery period for an item by amending the statute and that change will not be reflected in the Revenue Procedure. For example, late in 1988, Congress changed the recovery period for nonresidential buildings from 31.5 to its current period of 39 years. Both Rev. Proc. 87–56 and its modification in Rev. Proc. 88–22 were promulgated prior to that statutory change, and therefore do not reflect it.

§ **12.3412. Classification by Class Life.** Many types of property are classified into MACRS categories by reference to their class lives. IRC § 168(e)(1). As noted in § **12.3413,** a number of items of property are classified by specific provisions in IRC § 168 itself, but, in the absence of a specific provision, the class life of the asset will control its classification. For example, unless specifically provided for in IRC § 168, an asset that has a class life of four years or less is classified as three-year property, and an asset that has a class life of more than four years but less than ten years is classified as five-year property. IRC § 168(e)(1). Most personal properties that do not have a class life (i.e., they are not included in the ADR list) are classified as seven-year property. IRC § 168(e)(3)(C).

§ 12.3413.   Classification by Specific Provision in IRC § 168. A number of items of property are classified by a specific provision in IRC § 168 itself without regard to the item's class life. IRC § 168(e)(3). For example, a race horse that is more than two years old when placed in service and any horse (other than a race horse) that is more than twelve years old when placed in service is treated as three-year property. IRC § 168(e)(3)(A). In addition, if a dealer holds consumer property that the dealer will lease to individuals under a "rent-to-own contract," the property is three-year property. IRC § 168(e)(3)(A)(3). A rent-to-own contract is a lease with an option to purchase that meets the requirements of IRC § 168(i)(14), and there are numerous requirements. Several of the requirements are (1) that the tenant is not obligated to make all of the serial payments under the lease, but if he does so, the property passes to the tenant; (2) that the tenant can terminate its rental obligation at anytime by returning the property in good working order to the dealer; and (3) that a substantial portion of the contracts that the dealer makes are terminated by the tenant's returning the property to the dealer.

The five-year property category includes any automobile or light purpose truck, any property used in connection with research and experimentation, and any "qualified technological equipment." IRC § 168(e)(3)(B). The term "qualified technological equipment" is defined in IRC § 168(i)(2) to include *inter alia* computers and peripheral equipment, but the term does not include typewriters, calculators, adding machines, copiers, and several other items listed in IRC § 168(i)(2)(B)(iv). The treatment of buildings is described later in this chapter.

Note that the tables in Rev. Proc. 87–56 [see **§ 12.3411**] that set forth the recovery period of categories of assets for the purpose of applying the MACRS general and alternative depreciation systems incorporates the recovery periods established for certain assets by IRC § 168 itself. For example, the Revenue Procedure lists that the recovery period of automobiles and taxis for general depreciation purposes is five years even though the class life of such assets is listed as three years.

§ 12.3414. Monitoring of MACRS Categories. Congress instructed the Treasury to monitor and analyze the actual experience of taxpayers in using depreciable assets. IRC § 168(i)(1). Initially, Congress also authorized Treasury to modify class lives or assigned recovery periods when Treasury's study of the experience that taxpayers have had with such assets warranted a change in the recovery period, but this authority was withdrawn by Congress in its amendment of IRC § 168(i)(1) in the Technical and Miscellaneous Revenue Act (TAMRA) of 1988. Perhaps, if the studies of experience that Treasury reports to Congress indicate that a class life or a recovery period is unrealistic, Congress will alter it.

§ 12.3415. Buildings. Most depreciable buildings will be classified either as residential rental property or as nonresidential real property. "Residential rental property" is a building or structure 80% or more of the gross rental income from which for the taxable year is rental income from dwelling units; but the term does not include hotels, motels or any other establishments more than 50% of whose units are used on a transient basis. IRC § 168(e)(2)(A). "Nonresidential real property" refers to buildings (and certain other real properties) that are not residential rental property and that have a class life of 27.5 years or more. IRC § 168(e)(2)(B), (i)(12).

§ 12.3416. Change in Use. Congress authorized Treasury to promulgate regulations for the determination of depreciation deductions of an asset whose property status is changed even though the asset continues to be held by the same taxpayer. IRC § 168(i)(5). For the depreciation of an asset that is converted from personal use to business or income-producing use or vice versa, see **§§ 12.3500–12.3600.** For the determination of depreciation when the recovery period or depreciation method of a MACRS asset changes, see Treas. Reg. § 1.168(i)–4(d).

§ 12.3417. Short Taxable Year. A short taxable year is a taxable year of less than 12 months. The manner in which depreciation is determined for a taxpayer's short taxable year is described in Rev. Proc. 89–15.

§ 12.3420. Applicable Method of Depreciation. While the declining balance method of depreciation provides a more accelerated rate of recovery than does the straight-line method, there is a point in time during the recovery period of an asset being depreciated on the declining balance method when the recovery for the remaining years of that period will be decelerated if the taxpayer continues to use the declining balance method. The maximum acceleration of recovery is obtained by using the declining balance method to depreciate the asset in the early years of its recovery period and then, at some point, to switch to the straight-line method to depreciate the remaining adjusted basis of the asset. The change to the straight-line method is made by amortizing the adjusted basis of the property at the beginning of the year over the remaining time of the asset's recovery period. Where declining balance is used under MACRS, the statute provides that the depreciation will switch to straight-line at the beginning of the first taxable year that the straight-line method will produce a larger allowance than would the continued use of the declining balance method. IRC § 168(b)(1).

§ 12.3421. Straight–Line Method Required for Certain Properties. Buildings and their structural components placed in service after 1986 must be depreciated on the straight-line method. IRC § 168(b)(3). Any addition to or improvement of a building also will be depreciated on the straight-line method. IRC § 168(i)(6). Other properties that are requried to be depreciated on the straight-line method are: (1) railroad grading or tunnel bore, (2) tree or vine bearing fruit or nuts, (3) water utility property, (4) qualified leasehold improvement property (described in IRC § 168(e)(6)), and (5) qualified restaurant property (as described in IRC § 168(e)(7)). IRC § 168(b)(3). As noted in **§ 12.3460**, property depreciated under the Alternative Depreciation System is depreciated on the straight-line method.

§ 12.3422. Method for Depreciating 15–Year and 20–Year Property. The 150 percent declining balance method is used to depreciate 15–year and 20–year property and property used in a farming business. IRC § 168(b)(2). As stated in **§ 12.3420**, the depreciation method for such properties will change to straight-line in the first year that straight-line will produce a larger allowance than does the 150 percent declining balance.

§ 12.3423. Method for Depreciating Other Properties.
All other classifications of properties (e.g., three-year and five-year properties) are depreciated on the 200 percent declining balance method (i.e., the double declining balance method), switching to the straight-line method in the optimum year. IRC § 168(b)(1).

§ 12.3424. Election to Use the Straight–Line or 150 Percent Declining Balance Method. When a taxpayer otherwise would have depreciated an asset on the declining balance method, the taxpayer can elect instead to depreciate that asset on the straight-line method. IRC § 168(b)(3), (5). Similarly, when a taxpayer otherwise would have depreciated an asset on the 200 percent declining balance method, the taxpayer can elect to depreciate that asset on the 150 percent declining balance method (or, as noted above, on the straight-line method). IRC § 168(b)(2)(C), (5). The election can be made for one or more classes of property, but, once made, it is irrevocable and applies to all items of property in the selected class that are placed in service in the taxable year for which the election is made. IRC § 168(b)(5). An election is made for one taxable year at a time and need not be made again in the next taxable year. When an election is made under IRC § 168(b)(5) to employ either the straight-line or the 150 percent declining balance method of depreciation, the recovery period for the assets that are subject to that election is the same as it would have been if no election had been made.

§ 12.3424–1. Illustration. In Year One, X purchased and placed into service in his business: three items of seven-year property, two items of three-year property, six items of five-year property, and an apartment house that constitutes residential rental property. The apartment house is depreciated by X on the straight-line method over a 27.5–year recovery period. IRC § 168(b)(3), (c). The other items of property that X acquired in that year can be depreciated on the double declining balance method. Instead, X elected to depreciate the items of property that are classified as seven-year property on the straight-line method. Because of that election, all three items of seven-year property will be depreciated on the straight-line method; the election cannot be made on an asset by asset basis. However, since X made no election for the other two classifications of properties, the three-year and five-year properties will be depreciated on the double declining balance method. In Year Two, X purchased and placed in service two items of seven-year property. Unless X makes another election, those items of seven-year property will be depreciated on the double declining balance method.

§ 12.3425. Straight–Line Under the Alternative System. As shown in **§ 12.3460**, an alternative system of depreciation is required to be used for certain properties. This alternative system can be elected by the taxpayer for assets that are not required to be depreciated under that system. **§ 12.3462.** If applicable, the alternative system requires that the assets subject to that system be depreciated on the straight-line method over a recovery period that often (but not always) is longer than that employed by MACRS for assets that are not subject to the alternative system.

If the taxpayer elects the alternative system for a building, the election can be made on an asset by asset basis. For other assets, the election must be made for all assets in the same classification. IRC § 168(g)(7). Once made, the election to use the alternative system of depreciation is irrevocable for that classification of assets for that taxable year. IRC § 168(g)(7). The difference between making an election under the alternative system and making it under IRC § 168(b)(5) is that the former may require the use of a longer recovery period than does the latter; both elections require the use of the straight-line method.

§ 12.3430. Applicable Recovery Period. The recovery period is the period over which the asset is to be depreciated. The recovery period of an asset is determined by the MACRS classification of the asset. IRC § 168(c). Except for buildings, water utility property, railroad gradings and tunnel bores, the recovery period for an item of property is the same as the years used in classifying the property. For example, the recovery period for three-year property is three years; the recovery period for five-year property is five years; and so forth. The recovery period for residential rental property is 27.5 years, and the recovery period for nonresidential real property that is placed in service after 1993 is 39 years. IRC § 168(c). The recovery period for railroad gradings and tunnel bores is 50 years. Certain qualified property that is used predominantly in the active conduct of a trade or business within an Indian reservation is given a substantially shorter recovery period than otherwise would apply. IRC § 168(j). The reader should be alert to the fact that Congress tends to change these recovery periods from time to time—especially as to buildings.

§ 12.3431. **Alternative System.** As noted in § 12.3460, certain assets are required to be depreciated under an alternative system of depreciation that is set forth in IRC § 168(g). The alternative system also can be elected by the taxpayer for classifications of property or for individual buildings. § 12.3462. Typically, the recovery period for assets depreciated under the alternative system is longer than the periods provided under the normal method. For example, buildings will be depreciated over a 40–year recovery period under the alternative method, as contrasted to the 27.5–year period and 39–year period that are used in IRC § 168(c). The recovery period under the alternative system sometimes is the same as the period under the normal method, but it is never less.

§ 12.3440. **Applicable Convention.** Depreciable property can be purchased or disposed of at various times throughout a taxable year. The question can arise as to the amount of depreciation that can be deducted for an asset in the year that it is placed into service or sold. See Rev. Proc. 89–15. MACRS adopts several conventions which are used to determine the percentage of the year for which depreciation is allowable for such an asset. For buildings (and structural components), the "mid-month convention" is used. IRC § 168(d)(2). For other MACRS properties, the "half-year convention" is used unless the aggregate bases of such properties (other than buildings, railroad gradings, tunnel bores, and property which is placed in service and disposed of in the same taxable year) that were placed in service in the last quarter of the taxable year is greater than 40% of the aggregate bases of all such properties that were placed in service in that taxable year. IRC § 168(d)(1), (3). In the latter case, "the mid-quarter convention" is used for all such properties that were placed in service in that taxable year. The mid-quarter convention does not apply to: nonresidential real property, residential rental property, railroad gradings, tunnel bores, and property placed in service and disposed of in the same taxable year; and such properties are not taken into account in applying the more than 40% of aggregate bases computation to determine whether the mid-quarter convention applies to other properties.

§ 12.3441. Mid–Month Convention. The mid-month convention applies to buildings. When a building is placed in service in a calendar month, it is treated as having been placed in service in the middle of that month. When a building that is subject to the mid-month convention is disposed of in a calendar month, it is treated as having been disposed of in the middle of that month. IRC § 168(d)(4)(B).

§ 12.3442. Half–Year Convention. When property that is subject to the half-year convention is placed in service during a taxable year, it is treated as having been placed in service on the mid-point of such taxable year. When such property is disposed of in a taxable year, it is treated as having been disposed of on the mid-point of such taxable year. IRC § 168(d)(4)(A). If the half-year convention applied to the property when it was first placed into service, it will also apply to the property in the year of its disposition. Treas. Reg. § 1.168(d)–1(c).

§ 12.3443. Mid–Quarter Convention. When property that is subject to the mid-quarter convention is placed in service in a quarter of a taxable year, it is treated as having been placed in service on the mid-point of such quarter. When such property is disposed of in a quarter of a subsequent taxable year, it is treated as having been disposed of on the mid-point of such quarter. IRC § 168(d)(4)(C). If the mid-quarter convention applied to the property when it was first placed into service, it will also apply to the property in the year of its disposition. Treas. Reg. § 1.168(d)–1(c).

§ 12.3450. Illustrations. All of the properties in the following examples are tangible properties that are used by the taxpayer in his business, are subject to wear and tear and exhaustion, and so are depreciable under MACRS. All of the properties were purchased and placed into service after the year 1986. All of the parties in the following examples report their income on a calendar year basis and are unmarried.

§ 12.3451. Illustration 1. On January 5, Year One, X purchased and placed into service a light general use truck. X made no other purchases that year. X paid $25,000 for the truck. X elected to expense $10,000 of that cost under IRC § 179. The $10,000 of cost that X expensed is not charged to capital account [IRC § 179(a)] and so is not part of X's basis in the truck. X, therefore, has an adjusted basis of $15,000 to depreciate under MACRS. Since the truck is five-year property [IRC § 168(e)(3)(B)(i)], and since taxpayer did not elect otherwise, it is to be depreciated on the double declining balance method over a five-year recovery period, using a half-year convention. Accordingly, the depreciation deduction for Year One is $3,000—i.e., 40% of $15,000 for one-half a year. The straight-line rate for a five-year recovery period is 20%, and so the double declining balance rate is 40%. Because of the half-year convention, the property is treated as having been placed in service in the middle of Year One (notwithstanding that it was actually placed in service in the first month of the year), and so depreciation is allowable for only one-half of that year. The total amount of deductions allowable to X for Year One because of the truck is $13,000 − $10,000 deduction under IRC § 179 and $3,000 of depreciation deduction.

§ 12.3452. Illustration 2. The same facts as those stated in **§ 12.3451.** On April 24, Year Two, X sold the truck to an unrelated party for its fair market value. Since the half-year convention applied to the truck when it was first put into service, the half-year convention will also apply to the truck in the year in which is sold. Under the half-year convention, X is treated as having sold the truck at the mid-point of Year Two. Accordingly, X is allowed a depreciation deduction of $2,400 for Year Two—i.e., 40% of the truck's $12,000 adjusted basis for a half of a year.

Since under IRC § 1245(a) the sale of the truck will be subject to recapture of previously deducted depreciation and amortization, (and a previously deducted expense under IRC § 179 is treated as an amortization deduction that can be recaptured by IRC § 1245), the recapture provision of IRC § 179(d)(10) is preempted and does not apply. Treas. Reg. § 1.179–1(e)(3).

§ 12.3453. Illustration 3. On February 8, Year One, Y purchased and placed into service a computer. Y paid $40,000 for the computer. On April 10, Year One, Y purchased and placed into service a factory building that qualified as nonresidential real property. Y paid $100,000 for the building. Y leases the land on which the factory is situated on a 50–year lease. On September 16, Year One, Y purchased and placed into service an automobile. Y paid $10,000 for that automobile. On October 3, Year One, Y purchased and placed into service a light general purpose truck. *Y* paid $35,000 for the truck. *Y* elected not to expense under IRC § 179 any of the cost of the properties that he purchased in that year. Consequently, *Y* obtained no deduction under IRC § 179. *Y* made no other purchases in that year, and *Y* did not dispose of any property in that year.

The building is depreciated over a period of 39 years on the straight-line method so the depreciation for the building for an entire year would be $100,000/39 = $2,564. Under the mid-month convention, *Y* is treated as having placed the building in service in the mid-point of April; thus, *Y* is allowed depreciation for only 8.5 months. The depreciation for Year One, therefore, is 8.5/12 × $2,564 = $1,816.

The depreciation of the other assets placed in service in Year One (the personalty) will be determined under the double declining balance method over a five-year recovery period. Usually, the half-year convention would be used for such properties, but, in this case, the mid-quarter convention must be used. Exclusive of the building, *Y*'s aggregate bases for properties placed in service in Year One is $85,000. Two of those properties—the computer and the automobile—were purchased in the first and third quarters of the year respectively. The truck was purchased in the fourth quarter of that year. Since *Y*'s basis in the truck ($35,000) represents more than 40% of *Y*'s aggregate bases ($85,000) in all the depreciable assets (other than the building) that he placed in service that year, the mid-quarter convention must be used for all those assets. Note that if Y were to dispose of one of those three items in a subsequent year during the recovery period of that item, the mid-quarter convention would apply to the item in the year of its disposition since the mid-quarter convention applied to it when it was first placed in service.

The computer was placed in service in the first quarter, and so it is deemed to have been placed into service in the mid-point of that quarter. *Y*'s depreciation for the computer for Year One is 40% × $40,000 × 10.5/12 = $14,000. The depreciation for the automobile is 40% × $10,000 × 4.5/12 = $1,500. The depreciation for the truck is 40% × $35,000 × 1.5/12 = $1750. Note that the limitation on the amount of depreciation deduction allowable for a passenger automobile that is imposed by IRC § 280F(a)(1) does not apply in the instant case because the amount of depreciation for the automobile is lower than the statutory ceiling.

§ 12.3454.   Illustration 4. The same facts as those stated in § **12.3453.** On July 3, Year Two, Y sold the computer that he had acquired in Year One. Y purchased a new computer and placed it in service in September of Year Two. Y made no other purchases or dispositions in that year. The depreciation for the new computer that Y purchased is determined under the half-year convention. However, since the depreciation for Y's old computer was determined under the mid-quarter convention in the year that it was placed in service, the depreciation for the year that Y disposes of that computer also will be determined under the mid-quarter convention. IRC § 168(d)(3)(A), (4)(C). The computer was sold in the third quarter, and Y had an adjusted basis of $26,000 in the computer at the beginning of the year. Y's depreciation for that computer for Year Two is 40% × $26,000 × 7.5/12 = $6,500.

§ 12.3460.   Alternative Depreciation System. Certain properties that are subject to MACRS are required to be depreciated on an alternative system that is set forth in IRC § 168(g). The alternative system utilizes only the straight-line method of depreciation and provides recovery periods that often are longer (and never are shorter) than those provided by IRC § 168(c). The recovery period for buildings is 40 years and the recovery period for property which has no class life (i.e., it is not listed in the ADR lists) is 12 years. All other properties have a recovery period equal to their class life, which typically is determined by the ADR lists (see Rev. Proc. 87–56, at § **12.3411**). IRC § 168(g)(2)(C). However, the statute provides a special class life for a number of specified properties, and that class life then becomes the recovery period for such properties. IRC § 168(g)(3). For example, the class life for municipal sewers is 50 years. IRC § 168(g)(3)(B). Some of these special class lives provide the same recovery period as is provided by the ordinary version of MACRS. For example, the recovery period for automobiles, light general purpose trucks, and qualified technological equipment is five years under both ordinary MACRS and under the alternative system. IRC §§ 168(e)(3)(B), 168(g)(3)(C), (D). The recovery periods for categories of assets for the purpose of the alternative depreciation system are set forth in Rev. Proc. 87–56.

§ 12.3461. Properties for Which the Alternative System is Required. The properties for which the alternative depreciation system must be used are listed in IRC § 168(g)(1)(A)–(D). They include among others: tangible property used predominantly outside the United States in that taxable year, property which was financed by tax-exempt bonds, and certain properties that are leased to a tax-exempt entity.

In addition, if certain specified properties (referred to as "listed properties") are used only partly for a business purpose and if the business use constitutes 50% or less of the taxpayer's use, the depreciation for the portion of the property that is employed in the business is determined under the alternative depreciation system. IRC § 280F(b)(1), (3). The "listed properties" are described in IRC § 280F(d)(4). Subject to certain exceptions, they include passenger automobiles, other transportation means, and computers. An employee's use of listed property in connection with his employment is not treated as a business use of that property unless such use is for the convenience of the employer and is required as a condition of employment. IRC § 280F(d)(3).

§ 12.3462. Election. When an item of property is not required to be depreciated on the alternative system, the taxpayer can elect to use that system. IRC § 168(g)(7). For buildings, this election can be made on a building by building basis; for other properties, the election must be made for an entire MACRS classification of property. The election is made for a single taxable year. If another election is desired for the next year, it must be made anew. Once made, the election is irrevocable.

§ 12.3463. Corporations' Earnings and Profits. The alternative depreciation system serves an important function in measuring the amount of corporate distributions to shareholders that are treated as dividend income to the shareholders. A "dividend" from a corporation is a distribution made by the corporation on account of its outstanding stock to the extent that the distribution is made out of the corporation's "earnings and profits." IRC §§ 301(c)(1), 316(a). "Earnings and profits" is a term of art that refers to the accumulated earnings of the corporation as measured in a special manner so as to more accurately represent economic reality. The depreciation deductions for computing a corporation's earnings and profits is determined by using the alternative system of depreciation regardless of whether the corporation's depreciation was determined for taxable income purposes under either the ordinary MACRS or the alternative system. IRC § 312(k)(3).

§ **12.3464. Minimum Tax.** As noted in Chapter Fifteen, the alternative minimum tax that is imposed by IRC § 55 uses the alternative depreciation system (but uses the 150 percent declining balance method for many properties) to determine the alternative tax. IRC § 56(a)(1).

§ **12.3470. Optional Tables.** In Rev. Proc. 87–57, the Commissioner has provided tables that set forth the amount of depreciation deduction allowable in each year of an item's recovery period under various depreciation methods, recovery periods, and conventions. The depreciation for a year is determined by multiplying the appropriate percentage listed in the table times the *unadjusted* basis of the asset. The taxpayer is given the option to use these tables. The tables include depreciation schedules for the alternative depreciation system and for the alternative minimum tax as well as for the ordinary MACRS depreciation system. Note that the tables in the Revenue Procedure for the ordinary MACRS depreciation of a nonresidential building are no longer applicable because they do not reflect the 1988 expansion of the recover period for such properties to 39 years.

§ **12.3480. Luxury Automobiles.** IRC § 280F imposes dollar ceilings on the amount of annual depreciation deductions and rental deductions that are allowable for the business use of passenger automobiles. For this purpose, the expense deduction allowed by IRC § 179 is treated as depreciation and so is subject (along with actual depreciation) to those ceilings. IRC § 280F(d)(1).

§ **12.3490. Disposition of MACRS Property.** When MACRS property is sold in a taxable transaction, the depreciation allowable to the seller in the year of disposition turns on the convention that is applicable to that property (i.e., half-year, mid-quarter, or mid-month). See § **12.3440.** The convention that applies to the property is the same as the convention that was applied to the property when it was first placed into service or use. Treas. Reg. § 1.168(d)–1(c). However, it appears that if

MACRS property is disposed of in the same taxable year that it was acquired, no depreciation is allowable to the TP. See Treas. Reg. § 1.168(i)–4(c). The buyer will commence depreciating the purchased property by referring to his basis in the property and by using his applicable method, convention, and recovery period.

§ 12.3491. Disposition of MACRS Property in a Nonrecognition Transaction.

When MACRS property is disposed o f in a nonrecognition transaction *of a type listed in IRC § 168(i)(7)(B)*, the transferee steps into the shoes of the transferor and continues to depreciate the property as if he were the transferor. Prop. Reg. § 1.168–5(b). The types of transactions to which this provision applies include certain transfers between a partnership and a partner, and between a corporation and a shareholder. This provision applies only to so much of the transferee's basis in the MACRS asset as does not exceed the transferor's basis. Prop. Reg. § 1.168–5(b)(1). To the extent that the transferee's basis in the MACRS asset exceeds the transferor's, the transferee can depreciate that excess amount of the basis as if it were newly purchased property. Prop. Reg. § 1.168–5(b)(7). To the extent that the transferee's basis does not exceed the transferor's basis, and if the transferor and transferee use the same taxable year, the depreciation allowance for the year of disposition is allocated between the transferor and the transferee in proportion to their holding period in that year (utilizing only whole months). See Prop. Reg. § 1.168–5(b)(4).

If a TP makes a gift of MACRS property to a donee who holds the property for a business or income-producing use, the Proposed Regulations apply the same treatment for determining the donee's depreciation of the property, and the allocation of depreciation for the year in which the gift was made, as the one described above for certain nonrecognition transactions between partnerships and partners and between corporations and shareholders. Prop. Reg. § 1.168–5(f)(3).

If a taxpayer acquires MACRS property in exchange for MACRS property that the taxpayer held, and if the exchange is a like-kind transaction to which IRC § 1031 applies, the method for depreciating the newly acquired property is set forth in Notice 2000–4, 2000–1 C.B. 313. See **§ 17.3000** *et seq.* for a discussion of the operation of IRC § 1031. For so much of the basis of the acquired MACRS property as does not exceed the basis of the MACRS property transferred by the TP, the TP will be allowed the same depreciation deductions as would have been allowable for the transferred property if the exchange had not taken place. If the TP's basis in the acquired MACRS property exceeds the basis that the TP had in the transferred property, that excess amount of TP's basis is depreciable as newly purchased MACRS property under whatever method TP chooses that is permitted by the MACRS rules. See also, Prop. Reg. § 1.168–5(f)(2).

If MACRS property of a TP is involuntarily converted, and if the TP reinvests some or all of the proceeds of the conversion in MACRS property that qualifies some or all of the TP's gain from the conversion for nonrecognition under IRC § 1033, the method for depreciating the newly acquired property is set forth in Notice 2000–4, 2000–1 C.B. 313. See § **17.4000** *et seq.* for a discussion of the operation of IRC § 1033. For so much of the basis of the acquired MACRS property as does not exceed the basis of the converted MACRS property, the TP will be allowed the same depreciation deductions as would have been allowable for the converted property if the conversion had not taken place. If the TP's basis in the acquired MACRS property exceeds the basis that the TP had in the converted property, that excess amount of TP's basis is depreciable as newly purchased MACRS property under whatever method TP chooses that is permitted by the MACRS rules. It would seem that the depreciation for the converted property in the year of conversion and for the replacement property in the year of replacement will apply only to the portion of those years in which the property is in the service or use of the TP. See, Prop. Reg. § 1.168–5(f)(1).

§ **12.3500. Conversion of Property From Personal To Business or Income–Producing Use.** If property that was held for personal use is converted to business or income-producing use in a taxable year, the property will be depreciable as if it were first placed in service on the date of the conversion. Treas. Reg. § 1.168(i)–4(b). The basis to be used in beginning to depreciate the property is the *lesser* of its adjusted basis or its fair market value at the time of conversion. Id. Note that if the TP's personal use of certain properties comprises 50% or more of a taxable year, the limitations on depreciation deductions imposed by IRC § 280F may apply to that year. See § **12.3461.**

§ 12.3510.   Illustration. In Year One, G purchased an automobile for $20,000 for her personal use. On March 12, Year Three, G began to use the automobile exclusively in her business which is conducted by her as a self-employed person. The conversion of the automobile from personal to business use makes the automobile depreciable under MACRS. G's basis in the automobile at the time of conversion was still $20,000, but the fair market value of the automobile at that date was $12,000. G can depreciate the automobile under MACRS in Year Three and thereafter, but she must use the lower fair market value of $12,000 as the basis to be depreciated. Unless G purchased other MACRS property for her business that required use of the mid-quarter convention, G will use the half-year convention for the Year Three's depreciation for the automobile. G can use whatever method of depreciation and recovery period that MACRS would permit for newly acquired property.

§ 12.3600.   Conversion of Property From Business or Income–Producing Use To Personal Use. If MACRS property that was used in a business or income-producing activity is converted to personal use, it will be treated as a disposition of the property. Treas. Reg. § 1.168(i)–4(c). A fraction of the depreciation that would have been allowable for use of the property in the year of conversion if no conversion had occurred is allowable to the TP. The fraction is equal to the percentage of the whole months in that year that the TP is deemed to have used the MACRS property for business or income-producing purposes, utilizing the applicable convention to determine the number of months that the property was so used. Id. The conversion of the property does not cause the TP to recognize gain or loss; nor is there any recapture of depreciation under IRC §§ 1245 or 1250. Id. However, IRC §§ 1245 or 1250 will apply to a subsequent disposition of the converted property. Id. No depreciation is allowed for MACRS property that is placed in service and then disposed of in the same taxable year. Id. Note that if the TP's personal use of certain properties comprises 50% or more of a taxable year, the limitations on depreciation deductions imposed by IRC § 280F may apply to that year. See **§ 12.3461.**

*

CHAPTER THIRTEEN

MISCELLANEOUS CREDITS AND DEDUCTIONS

§ 13.0000. MISCELLANEOUS CREDITS AND DEDUCTIONS.

§ 13.1000. CREDITS AND DEDUCTIONS IN GENERAL.

A tax credit is deducted from a taxpayer's tax liability in contrast to a tax deduction which is deducted from either the taxpayer's gross income or his adjusted gross income (AGI). Thus, each dollar of tax credit allowed a taxpayer is a full dollar of benefit to him, while the dollar of benefit of a deduction depends upon the taxpayer's marginal tax bracket. Note, however, not all tax credits are refundable. Some tax credits provide a refund for a taxpayer whose tax liability is less than the amount of his credit while others do not. For some credits, an unused credit can be carried back or forward to other taxable years and utilized in those years. See, e.g., IRC § 39.

§ 13.1100. Examples of Tax Credits and Deductions.

Several examples of tax credits include the nonrefundable dependent care credit, the refundable earned income credit, and the refundable credit for a return of income held under a claim of right. Among the miscellaneous deductions noted in this chapter are net operating losses, depletion, alimony, and income in respect of a decedent.

§ 13.2000. INVESTMENT TAX CREDIT.

The regular investment credit, which was repealed by the Tax Reform Act of 1986, allowed a taxpayer a credit for an investment in certain qualified tangible personal property used in the taxpayer's trade or business. The amount of investment credit allowed for such purposes was a percentage, generally ten percent, of the *basis* of *new* property or of the *cost* of *used* property placed in service in the taxpayer's business during the taxable year. While the former regular investment credit has been eliminated, an investment credit is still permitted for a few specified expenses. IRC § 38(a)(2), (b)(1). The current investment credit is comprised of two separate credits: the rehabilitation credit and the energy credit. IRC § 46. See IRC §§ 47 (the rehabilitation credit) and 48 (the energy credit). The basis of the property with respect to which an investment credit was allowed will be reduced by all or a portion of the amount of that credit. IRC § 50(c). Subject to several exceptions (e.g., for death), if within five years after investment credit property is placed in service, the property is disposed of, or ceases to be investment credit property with respect to the taxpayer, all or a portion of the investment credit allowed with respect to such property will be recaptured. IRC § 50(a).

§ 13.3000. EARNED INCOME CREDIT. A refundable credit, referred to as the "earned income credit" is provided for the purpose of reducing the tax burden of certain low income individuals who earn income from providing services. IRC § 32. An individual who is eligible to receive the credit is referred to as an "eligible individual." See **§ 13.3140** for the requirements to qualify as an eligible individual. The credit is available only to those eligible individuals who have "earned income" and whose total income for that year is below stated boundaries. To that end, if the amount of an eligible individual's adjusted gross income (or the amount of the individual's earned income if that is greater) for a taxable year exceeds a specified figure, the credit is phased out by a specified percentage of that excess. IRC § 32(a). In general, an individual's "earned income" refers to income produced by the individual's services or work as contrasted to income produced from investments or otherwise from capital. See **§ 13.3120.**

The credit is disallowed if the taxpayer's aggregate amount of "disqualified income" for a taxable year exceeds a specified figure, which figure is adjusted annually for cost-of-living increases. IRC § 32(i), (j). For the year 2005, the specified figure is $2,700. Rev. Proc. 2004–71. "Disqualified income" refers to certain types of investment income including dividends, interest (both taxable and tax-exempt), and net capital gains. IRC § 32(i)(2).

§ 13.3100. Determination of Credit. An "eligible individual" [see **§ 13.3130**] who is in a low income bracket is allowed a refundable credit for a percentage of his "earned income." See **§ 13.3120** for a definition of "earned income." The percentage that is applied to the eligible individual's earned income to determine the amount of credit is referred to as the "credit percentage." The amount of the credit percentage depends upon the number of "qualifying children" [see **§ 13.3140** for a definition of that term] that the eligible individual has in that year. Currently, the credit percentage that is applicable for an eligible individual is: 34% if the individual has one qualifying child, 40% if the individual has more than one qualifying child, and 7.65% if the individual has no qualifying child. IRC § 32(b)(1)(A). See **§ 13.3150.**

The statute imposes a ceiling on the amount of an eligible individual's earned income that can be used to establish the amount of the individual's earned income credit. IRC § 32(a)(1). In other words, the amount of an individual's earned income that can be multiplied times the credit percentage is limited to a maximum figure. This maximum figure is referred to as the "earned income amount." The earned income amount depends upon the number of qualifying children that the individual has in that year. The earned income amounts for different categories of individuals are set forth in § **13.3110.**

The amount of an individual's credit is reduced by a percentage (referred to as the "phaseout percentage") of the excess of the individual's adjusted gross income (or earned income if that is greater) over a specified amount. IRC § 32(a). The specified amount is referred to as the "phaseout amount." The amount of the phaseout percentage and of the phaseout amount depends upon the number of qualifying children that the individual has in that taxable year. The schedule of the amounts of the phaseout percentages and the phaseout amounts for different categories of individuals are set forth in § **13.3160.** Note that the dollar figure of the phaseout amount for each such year will be increased to reflect changes in the cost of living (i.e., the figures will be indexed to reflect inflation). IRC § 32(j).

Since there is a ceiling on the amount of earned income that can be used to establish an earned income credit (the earned income amount), that results in there being a ceiling on the amount of credit that an eligible individual can obtain in a taxable year. For example, for the year 2005, the *maximum* amount of earned income credit that an eligible individual with one qualifying child can obtain is $2,662— i.e., the product of multiplying 34% (the credit percentage for that category) times $7,830 (the earned income amount for that category).

§ **13.3110. Earned Income Amount.** As noted above, the "earned income amount" is the maximum amount of earned income that can be used to determine an individual's earned income credit. For a taxable year beginning in 2005, the earned income amounts for the three categories of eligible individuals are as follows (Rev. Proc. 2004–71):

Eligible individual with	Earned income amount
1 qualifying child	$ 7,830
2 or more qualifying children	$11,000
No qualifying children	$ 5,220

The scheduled dollar figures for the earned income amount is indexed for inflation. IRC § 32(j).

§ 13.3120. Earned Income. The term "earned income" means wages, salaries, tips, other employee compensation, and a taxpayer's net earnings from self-employment (as defined in IRC § 1402). IRC § 32(c)(2). A number of items are excluded from earned income. For example, earned income is determined without regard to community property laws, and no amount received as a pension or annuity is taken into account. IRC § 32(c)(2)(B). For years ending after October 4, 2004, and before January 1, 2006, a taxpayer can elect to treat as earned income combat zone pay, which otherwise is excluded from income by IRC § 112. IRC § 32(c)(2)(vi).

§ 13.3130. Eligible Individual. An individual who has at least one qualifying child [see **§ 13.3140**] is an "eligible individual" for that taxable year. IRC § 32(c)(1)(A). An individual who does not have a qualifying child for the taxable year will nevertheless qualify as an eligible individual if the following three requirements are satisfied:

(1) the individual's principal place of abode was in the United States for more than one-half of the taxable year,

(2) before the close of the taxable year, the individual (or the individual's spouse) attained his or her 25th birthday but did not attain 65 years of age, and

(3) the individual does not qualify under IRC § 151 as a dependent exemption deduction [see **§ 4.1220** for the meaning of that term] for another taxpayer. IRC § 32(c)(1).

Note that in the third requirement listed above, it is the individual's *qualification* for a dependent exemption deduction that precludes that individual, who has no qualified children, from being an eligible individual; it does not matter for this purpose whether the other taxpayer claimed such a deduction on account of the individual.

Certain persons are precluded from qualifying as an eligible individual. See IRC § 32(c)(1)(B), (C), and (D). For example, an individual who is a qualifying child of another taxpayer for a calendar year that begins within the individual's taxable year cannot qualify as an eligible individual for his taxable year.

§ 13.3140. Qualifying Child—New Standards. Prior to 2005, IRC § 32 established the requirements for a person to be a qualifying child with respect to a taxpayer. For years beginning after 2004, Those requirements were changed by the Working Families Tax Relief Act of 2004 which adopted a new uniform definition of the term "qualifying child" for several Code provisions including the earned income credit. A qualifying child is now defined in IRC § 152(c), but the earned income credit provision makes several modifications to that uniform definition. IRC § 32(c)(3). See **§ 4.1232** for a description of the uniform definition. For purposes of the earned income credit, the uniform definition is modified as follows:

(1) there is no requirement that the individual not have provided over one-half of his support (i.e., the "support test" of IRC § 152(c)(1)(D) does not apply).

(2) the special rules for children of divorced parents (IRC § 152(e)) do not apply,

(3) the requirement in IRC § 152(c)(1)(B) that the individual occupy the same principal place of abode as the taxpayer for one-half of the year is satisfied only if that abode is in the United States (however, the principal place of abode of a member of the Armed Forces is treated as being in the United States for any period during which that person is stationed outside of the United States while serving on extended duty),

(4) an individual who is married at the end of a taxable year cannot be a qualifying child of the taxpayer unless the taxpayer is entitled to a dependent exemption deduction for that individual under IRC § 151 (or would be entitled to a deduction if it were not for IRC § 152(e)),

(5) an individual will not be taken into account as a qualifying child unless the taxpayer includes certain required information on his tax return or by some other method that the Service prescribes for providing that information.

§ 13.3150. Credit Percentage. As previously stated, the percentage that is multiplied times an individual's earned income in order to arrive at the earned income credit is referred to as the "credit percentage." The amount of the credit percentage depends upon the number of qualifying children that the eligible individual has in that taxable year, and it depends upon the year for which the credit is utilized. The following schedule sets forth the credit percentages for the years beginning after 1995 for the three categories of eligible individuals.

Eligible individual with	Credit percentage
1 qualifying child	34%
2 or more qualifying children	40%
No qualifying children	7.65%

§ 13.3160. Phaseout of Credit. As noted in **§ 13.3100**, an individual's earned income credit is phased out when the individual's adjusted gross income (or earned income if greater) for that taxable year exceeds a threshold figure. The threshold figure is referred to as the "phaseout amount." IRC § 32(a)(2)(B). The phaseout of the credit is accomplished by reducing the earned income credit by the product of multiplying a specified percentage (referred to as the "phaseout percentage") times the excess of the individual's adjusted gross income (or earned income if greater) over the phaseout amount. The amounts of the phaseout percentage are determined by a statutory schedule that establishes those figures according to the number of qualified children that the individual has and according to the year in question. IRC § 32(b)(1). The following schedule sets forth the phaseout percentages for the three categories of eligible individuals for the years after 1995.

Eligible individual with	Phaseout percentage
1 qualifying child	15.98%
2 or more qualifying children	21.06%
No qualifying children	7.65%

For the year 2005, the phaseout amounts (set out in Rev. Proc. 2004–71) are:

Eligible individual with:	Married, Filing Jointly	Single
1 or more qualifying children	$16,370	$14,370
No qualifying children	$ 8,530	$ 6,530

The phaseout amounts for a taxpayer filing as a Head of Household or as a Surviving Spouse are the same as those for a single taxpayer. The phaseout amount figures are indexed for inflation. IRC § 32(j). Currently, the phaseout amount for a married taxpayer is $2,000 greater than the phaseout amount for a single taxpayer. The difference between the married and single taxpayers is scheduled to grow to $3,000 for years beginning after 2007, but the additional amounts for married taxpayers is scheduled to expire in the year 2011 unless Congress extends it. IRC § 32(b)(2)(B). Unless the provision for additional amounts for married taxpayers is extended, the phaseout amounts for married and single taxpayers will be the same in years beginning after 2010.

§ 13.3170. Illustration. In order to demonstrate how the credit operates, the determinations in this illustration are made without using tables provided by the Service for that purpose. IRC § 32(f). The calculations can be made much more easily by using the tables.

In 2005, *B*, a widow, had two children—a five-year old daughter and a two-year old son, both of whom live in *B*'s home in the United States. Since *B* has qualified children, she is an eligible individual. In 2005, *B* had earned income of $12,000, and she had adjusted gross income of $15,000. Let us first calculate the credit (we will refer to as the "tentative credit") without taking into account the phaseout provisions. Before taking the phaseout into account, *B* has a tentative earned income credit of $4,400. The tentative credit is determined by multiplying 40% (the applicable percentage credit) times $11,000 (the earned income amount). Although *B* had earned income of $12,000, the maximum amount that can be used in determining her credit is the earned income amount, which in this case is set at $11,000. The $4,400 tentative credit is then reduced by the product of multiplying 21.06% (the phaseout percentage) times $630 (i.e., the excess of $15,000 (the greater of *B*'s adjusted gross income and her earned income) over the statutory phaseout amount of $14,370). Since 21.06% times $630 = $132.67, *B*'s earned income credit for the year 2005 is $4,267.33 (the difference between her tentative credit of $4,400 and the $132.67 phaseout reduction). If the Service's tables were used, the actual figure for the credit will be slightly different than the one calculated here since the tables employ income brackets and round off their figures.

§ 13.3200. Refundable Credit. Since the earned income credit is refundable, if the amount of an individual's credit exceeds the amount of that individual's tax liability, the excess will be refunded to the individual. IRC § 6401(b)(1).

§ 13.3300. Married Individual. If an eligible individual is married, the individual will not be allowed an earned income credit for a taxable year unless the individual files a joint income tax return for that taxable year. IRC § 32(d). In certain circumstances described in IRC § 7703(b), an individual who actually is married nevertheless is treated for tax purposes as an unmarried individual. See § **14.1220.**

§ 13.3400. Alternative Minimum Tax. The alternative minimum tax (IRC § 55) is described in Chapter 15. Prior to 2002, an individual's earned income credit was reduced by the amount of alternative minimum tax that was imposed on the individual for that taxable year, but that provision was repealed by a 2001 Act. However, the 2001 Act has a sunset provision, and so the reduction for the alternative minimum tax is scheduled to return to the Code in years beginning after 2010.

§ 13.3500. Tables Provided by the Service. To facilitate the computation of the earned income credit, IRC § 32(f) requires the Service to provide tables which are to be used in determining the amount of an eligible individual's credit.

§ 13.3600. Advance Receipt of A Portion of an Individual's Credit. An employee who has at least one qualifying child can require his employer to make an advance payment to him of a specified part of the earned income credit for which the employee likely will qualify at the end of the year. Such payments are not treated as additional compensation to the employee; instead, they are treated as if they were made out of withholding or FICA taxes that otherwise would be payable by the employer on behalf of the employee. IRC § 3507.

§ 13.4000. RETURN OF INCOME HELD UNDER A CLAIM OF RIGHT. When income is received because of a mistake of fact or law, the income is nevertheless included in the gross income of the recipient under the so-called "claim of right" doctrine. See § **2.2300.** Similarly, income obtained illegally is included in the recipient's gross income. *United States v. Sullivan*, 274 U.S. 259 (1927), and *James v. United States*, 366 U.S. 213 (1961); see Treas. Reg. § 1.61–14(a). When the mistake or illegality is discovered and the taxpayer returns the income to its rightful owner, the taxpayer is granted a deduction. Rev. Rul. 65–254. See *Healy v. Commissioner*, 345 U.S. 278 (1953). The statutory basis for the deduction typically is IRC § 165(c)(2). See *Stephens v. Commissioner*, § **7.1000.** This deduction often will be an itemized deduction (it will be a nonitemized deduction in certain circumstances such as when the income was received in connection with the taxpayer's self-employed business), but it is not subject to the 2% of AGI floor that applies to certain itemized deductions. IRC § 67(b)(9). While IRC

§ 67(b)(9) excludes from the 2% of AGI floor a deduction allowed under IRC § 1341 for a return of an amount held under a claim of right, it appears likely to the authors that the exclusion will be construed as applying also to a deduction allowed under IRC § 165 or common law tax rules (and not under IRC § 1341) for the return of such amounts. **See § 13.4100.** When it is an itemized deduction, however, this item is subject to the reduction of itemized deductions that is imposed by IRC § 68 when a taxpayer's AGI exceeds a specified amount.

For an interesting case involving the deductibility of a taxpayer's return to his victims of fraudulently obtained funds, see *Stephens v. Commissioner*, § **7.1000.**

> **§ 13.4100. Illustration.** *X* embezzled $2,000 from his employer *Y* in Year One. In Year Three, the theft was discovered, and in Year Four, *X* returned the $2,000 to *Y*. *X* must include the $2,000 of embezzled funds in his gross income for Year One, and *X* may deduct the $2,000 he returned to *Y* from *X*'s AGI for Year Four. This is an itemized deduction. While this deduction is not derived from IRC § 1341, it nevertheless is likely that it will be excluded from the 2% of AGI floor by IRC § 67(b)(9).
>
> **§ 13.4200. Tax Bracket Differential.** If a taxpayer who received income under the claim of right doctrine was in a higher marginal tax bracket when he received the gross income than when he returned it, the differential in tax rates will constitute a tax cost to the recipient. This cost is harsh when the income was received through an innocent error, particularly when the error was not made by the taxpayer himself. Consequently, Congress has provided statutory relief. Note that if the taxpayer was in a lower marginal tax bracket when he received the gross income item than when he returned it, the deduction allowable to the taxpayer will provide him with a windfall. The amount of that windfall is mitigated by the fact that the taxpayer lost the use of the money that he paid to the government as the tax on the claim of right income, and the taxpayer earns no interest on that amount from the government. But, taxpayer did have the use of the funds that were received under a claim of right until those funds were returned to the payor.
>
> **§ 13.4300. Statutory Relief.** Under IRC § 1341, when an item was included in a taxpayer's gross income in a prior year because "it appeared that the taxpayer had an unrestricted right to such item" and when the taxpayer is entitled to a deduction of more than $3,000 in a later tax year because of the repayment of that item, the

taxpayer's income tax bill for the year of repayment will be computed by whichever of the following methods produces a smaller tax bill for the taxpayer:

(1) the taxpayer computes his tax in the normal manner by taking the repayment as a deduction (typically as an itemized deduction from his AGI) for that year; or

(2) the taxpayer computes the tax without deducting any part of the repayment made in that year, and then the taxpayer reduces his tax liability by the amount of tax he paid in prior years because of the inclusion of the mistaken amount in his gross income at that time. In other words, the taxpayer is granted a benefit equal to the value of the deduction at the marginal tax rates applicable to the taxpayer when the item was included in his gross income. If the amount of such tax reduction exceeds the taxpayer's current tax bill, the difference is refunded to the taxpayer. IRC § 1341(b)(1). In other words, the tax reduction is a refundable tax credit.

§ 13.4310. **Limitations.** The benefits of IRC § 1341 are expressly withheld from certain items. For example, the amount of the allowable deduction must exceed $3,000. Also, the statutory relief does not apply to an item which was included in gross income by reason of the sale or other disposition of a taxpayer's inventory or other items held for sale to customers in the ordinary course of his business. IRC § 1341(b)(2). Perhaps the reason for this latter exclusion from IRC § 1341 is that the deduction arises because of the taxpayer's guarantee or because the customer returned the item. Those are common occurrences that likely take place repeatedly during each year, and it would be an administrative nuisance to make the calculations for each such occurrence.

§ 13.4320. **Unrestricted Right.** The Commissioner has strictly construed the requirement in IRC § 1341 that the item in question was included in the taxpayer's gross income "because it appeared that the taxpayer had an unrestricted right to such item." The Commissioner contends that the above language establishes a narrower test for IRC § 1341 than the "claim of right" doctrine. Consequently, even though an item is included in a taxpayer's gross income under the "claim of right" doctrine, if, from all the facts known at the time, it did not appear that the taxpayer had an unrestricted right to the item, IRC § 1341 will not apply.

§ 13.4321. Embezzled Funds and Other Funds Obtained By Intentional Wrongdoing. Rev. Rul. 65–254 holds that the return of embezzled funds does not qualify for the relief granted by IRC § 1341. See also Rev. Rul. 68–153. The embezzler is entitled to a deduction under IRC § 165(c)(2), but under the Commissioner's view, the taxpayer cannot enjoy the special relief afforded by IRC § 1341 since in the year that he acquired the money he did not appear to have an unrestricted right to it. The Commissioner's position was sustained by the Tax Court in *Yerkie v. Commissioner*, 67 T.C. 388 (1976), by a district court in *Hankins v. United States*, 403 F.Supp. 257 (N.D.Miss. 1975), aff'd by court order (5th Cir. 1975) and by the Sixth Circuit in *Kraft v. United States*, 991 F.2d 292 (6th Cir. 1993), *cert. denied*, 510 U.S. 976 (1993). Those courts also held that the repayment of the embezzled funds (which exceeded taxpayer's income for that year) could not qualify as a net operating loss carryover or carryback because embezzlement was not the taxpayer's trade or business. See **§ 13.6200.** The Commissioner's position was also sustained by the Fifth Circuit in *McKinney v. United States*, 574 F.2d 1240 (5th Cir. 1978). In *McKinney*, the district court in Texas treated the rule requiring an embezzler to recognize income as separate and distinct from the claim of right doctrine, and so the court did not deal with the question of whether IRC § 1341 covers all claim of right income. In affirming the district court, the Fifth Circuit said that it was not necessary to reach that question because the embezzler did not have an unrestricted right to the money and so IRC § 1341 clearly did not apply. See also *Kraft v. United States*, *supra*. In a 1986 decision involving a taxpayer who had received illegal kickbacks and salary while acting in a manner disloyal to his employer, a district court held that the taxpayer's return of those funds did not qualify for IRC § 1341 treatment because the taxpayer had no bona fide claim of right to the funds. *Zadoff v. United States*, 638 F.Supp. 1240 (S.D.N.Y. 1986). See also, *Parks v. United States*, 945 F.Supp. 865 (W.D. Pa. 1996); and *Culley v. United States*, 222 F.3d 1331 (Fed. Cir. 2000).

§ 13.4322. Obligation to Repay. Similarly, the Commissioner maintains that IRC § 1341 applies only if the taxpayer *did not actually have an unrestricted right* to the item in the year of receipt, even though he appeared to have it. Therefore, if the taxpayer's obligation to repay arises only because of an

event that occurred *after* the year in which the taxpayer
received the item, the Commissioner contends that IRC § 1341
is inapplicable because the taxpayer did have an unrestricted
right to the item in the year he received it. Rev. Rul. 67–437.
This argument was rejected by the Sixth Circuit in *Van Cleave
v. United States*, 718 F.2d 193 (6th Cir. 1983), where the
taxpayer received a salary which he was contractually required
to return to his corporate employer to the extent that it was
subsequently determined to be excessively large and, therefore, partly nondeductible by the employer. The taxpayer was
a majority shareholder and president of the corporate employer. In holding that IRC § 1341 applied to taxpayer's repayment of part of the salary, the court indicated its belief that
the taxpayer did not have an unrestricted right to the excessive portion of the salary payment in the year of receipt. Thus,
the subsequent determination was not an independent event,
but was merely evidence establishing that the taxpayer's salary was excessive. See also, Rev. Rul. 68–153 (Situation 3).

§ **13.4322–1. Validity.** The validity of Rev. Rul. 67–437 is
very much in doubt. The *Van Cleave* decision (discussed in
§ **13.4322**) rejected the Commissioner's position, and the
Commissioner himself sometimes ignores or overlooks that
issue in his rulings. For example, in Rev. Rul. 78–25, the *X*
corporation sold its assets to *Y* and then liquidated. The
shareholder, *A*, reported a gain of more than $3,000 as a
consequence of receiving liquidating distributions in excess
of his basis in the *X* corporation's stock. Under the terms of
X's sale of its assets to *Y*, *X* and its shareholder, *A*, were
required to fulfill certain subsequent conditions, and they
failed to do so. *Y* sued *A* for the latter's failure to fulfill the
required conditions. As a result, *A* paid *Y* an amount in
excess of $3,000. The Commissioner ruled that the provi-
sions of IRC § 1341 are applicable to the payment that *A*
made to *Y*.

§ **13.4323. Mathematical or Clerical Error.** The Commissioner has ruled that IRC § 1341 does not apply to the
return of an overpayment received as a consequence of a
clerical error or an error of computation. Rev. Rul. 68–153.
The rationale for this ruling is that on the basis of all facts
known at the end of the year (at least when the facts are
viewed correctly), it would not appear "that the taxpayer had
an unrestricted right to such an item." The validity of this

ruling has not been established. Indeed, if all of the Commissioner's rulings on IRC § 1341 were valid [see § **13.4321** and § **13.4322**], there would be precious few transactions to which IRC § 1341 would apply.

§ **13.4330.   Net Operating Loss.** The computation under IRC § 1341 is made somewhat more complicated when either the deduction of the returned item from the taxpayer's gross income for the year of return, or the exclusion of the returned item from the taxpayer's gross income for the year in which the item was received (or accrued), results in a net operating loss for such year. The method of computation is described in Treas. Reg. § 1.1341–1(d)(4)(iii), Ex. (5).

§ **13.4340.   Prompt Refund.** When a taxpayer claims a refund based on IRC § 1341, the Code provides that the claim will be examined and a refund paid within 90 days after the claim was filed. IRC § 6411(d). The prompt refund made thereby is tentative and can be revised by the Commissioner at a later date after he has had more time to study the claim.

§ **13.4350.   Significance of IRC § 1341.** The 1986 TRA reduced both income tax rates and the number of income tax brackets. While those rate and bracket changes reduced the significance of IRC § 1341, much of the tax bracket significance was restored when Congress raised tax rates in 1993. However, the tax rates have been reduced in recent years thereby reducing the importance again. In any event, even apart from tax bracket considerations, IRC § 1341 retains considerable vitality. For example, if capital gain income is returned in a later year, IRC § 1341 could be extremely helpful in avoiding the limitations on the deductibility of capital losses which might otherwise deny the taxpayer a deduction. If IRC § 1341 does not apply to such a repayment, the deduction may be classified as a capital loss in order to correlate the deduction with the type of income to which it relates. See § **18.4420.**

§ **13.5000.   OTHER CREDITS.** The Code provides credits for a variety of expenses (e.g., a credit for household and dependent care expenses [IRC § 21, see § **10.2000**]; an adoption credit [IRC § 23]; a child tax credit [IRC § 24]; a credit for increasing research activities [IRC § 41]; a credit for the acquisition, rehabilitation, or construction of low-income housing [IRC § 42]; and a credit for the elderly and for the permanently and totally disabled [IRC § 22].)

§ 13.5010. Higher Education. The Code provides two separate credits for qualified higher education costs. The Hope Scholarship Credit provides a maximum credit of $1,500 per student for the first two years of postsecondary education. IRC § 25A(b). The Lifetime Learning Credit provides a maximum credit of $2,000 per taxpayer (i.e., it does not depend on the number of eligible students in the taxpayer's family). IRC § 25A(c). Both credits are phased out for taxpayers with a AGI above a specified amount. IRC § 25A(d). Both the amounts of each credit and the income limitations applicable the each credit are subject to inflation adjustments. IRC § 25A(h).

§ 13.6000. NET OPERATING LOSS CARRYOVER AND CARRYBACK. Because income and deductions are reported annually, in the absence of a statutory exception, a taxpayer cannot use a deduction allowable in one tax year to offset income reportable in another tax year. *Burnet v. Sanford & Brooks Co.*, 282 U.S. 359 (1931). This principle falls under the so-called "annual accounting" rule. To mitigate the harshness of the annual accounting rule, Congress permits a carryover and a carryback of a "net operating loss" to other tax years when the loss can be deducted. IRC § 172. This puts the tax treatment of businesses that have fluctuating income on a par with businesses that have stable income. In general, subject to a few exceptions, a net operating loss (NOL) can be carried back for two years prior to the year of loss and carried forward for twenty years after the loss was incurred. Thus, the loss is deductible over a span of twenty-three years.

§ 13.6100. Computation. A net operating loss for a taxable year is computed by determining the taxpayer's taxable income for that year with certain modifications described in IRC § 172(d). For example, applying IRC § 172(d), the deduction for exemptions under IRC § 151 is disallowed, and, with certain exceptions, nonbusiness deductions can be used to reduce only nonbusiness income. The net operating loss will usually be less than the loss a taxpayer shows on his return in computing his taxable income because of the modifications required by IRC § 172(d).

§ 13.6200. Types of Losses Deductible. Generally, a net operating loss, which may be carried over to offset income of other years, includes:

(a) losses from the operation of a business;

(b) losses from sales, exchanges or involuntary conversions of assets used in a trade or business;

(c) casualty and theft losses on property *not* used in a trade or business allowed under IRC § 165(c)(3).

§ 13.6300. Chronology of Carryover. Subject to a few exceptions, a net operating loss is carried back two years and forward twenty years from the year that the loss was incurred. IRC § 172(b)(1)(A), (B). It must be carried first to the second preceding year, and any loss not offset against income is applied to reduce income of the subsequent years in chronological order. However, a taxpayer can elect not to carry back a net operating loss, and if the taxpayer so elects, the taxpayer will only carry forward such loss for twenty years. IRC § 172(b)(3).

§ 13.7000. DEPLETION. The owner of a natural deposit or other wasting asset (e.g., oil, gas, minerals, gravel, timber) is entitled to a depletion deduction to offset his capital investment against the income from the sale or use of the asset. IRC § 611.

§ 13.7100. Depletable Property. Most natural deposits and certain other wasting assets, such as timber, are depletable.

§ 13.7200. Economic Interest. A taxpayer must have an "economic interest" in a depletable asset to be permitted a depletion deduction. Treas. Reg. § 1.611–1(b). "Economic interest" is a term of art defined in Treas. Reg. § 1.611–1(b). Generally, one has an economic interest if he must look to the extraction of the mineral or severance of the timber to recover his capital investment. *Commissioner v. Southwest Exploration Co.*, 350 U.S. 308 (1956).

§ 13.7300. Methods of Depletion. There are two methods of determining the deduction for depletion; the cost depletion method, and the percentage depletion method. The bulk of the political controversy over depletion allowances focuses on percentage depletion.

§ 13.7310. Cost Depletion. The cost depletion method is similar to the units of production method of depreciation [described at §§ 11.3310–11.3311]. The cost depletion method allocates a portion of the taxpayer's cost or other basis for a wasting asset to the units of that asset sold or consumed during a tax year. The allocation is made by dividing the taxpayer's adjusted basis in the asset at the beginning of the tax year by the estimated number of recoverable units (tons of ore, barrels of oil, board feet of timber, etc.) remaining as of the beginning of the tax year. The cost of each unit sold or consumed during the tax year is deducted from the income from the deposit or extract. Treas. Reg. § 1.611–2(a). The estimated number of recoverable units includes units that have been extracted from the property but which were not sold prior to the beginning of the tax year. Under the cost depletion method, the aggregate depletion deducted by a taxpayer cannot exceed the taxpayer's investment in the asset (i.e., his cost or other basis).

§ 13.7311. Illustration 1. In Year One, X purchased a deposit for $1,000,000 and determined that the number of recoverable units was 100,000 tons. X mined 30,000 tons in Year One, but X sold only 20,000 tons and stored the remaining 10,000 tons. X's cost depletion for Year One is:

$$\frac{\$1,000,000 \text{ basis}}{100,000 \text{ recoverable units}} \quad x \quad 20,000 \text{ units sold} = \$200,000 \text{ depletion deduction.}$$

§ 13.7312. Illustration 2. In Year Two, X discovered that the number of remaining recoverable units in the deposit was 200,000 tons, including the 10,000 tons mined but unsold but excluding the 20,000 tons sold in Year One. X sold the 10,000 remaining units from its Year One activity, but X did not mine or sell any additional units in Year Two. X's depletion allowance for Year Two is:

$$\frac{\$800,000 \text{ adjusted basis (as of 1/1/02)}}{200,000 \text{ recoverable units}} \quad x \quad 10,000 \text{ units sold} = \$40,000 \text{ depletion deduction.}$$

§ 13.7320. Percentage Depletion. Percentage depletion provides a deduction equal to a specified percentage of the taxpayer's *gross* income from the depletable property during the tax year, but the deduction cannot exceed 50% of the taxable income from the property computed without the depletion allowance. The percentage of taxable income limitation is 100% for oil and gas properties. If the percentage depletion allowance in any year is less than the cost depletion allowance, the taxpayer may use the cost depletion method for that year. IRC § 613(a).

§ 13.7321. Percentage Based on Type of Deposit. The percentage of gross income that may be deducted as a percentage depletion allowance depends upon the kind of deposit (e.g., the depletion percentage for sulphur and uranium is 22% of gross income; for gold and silver, 15%; and for gravel, peat and sand, only 5%). IRC § 613(b). Percentage depletion is available only for those natural deposits listed in IRC §§ 613(b) and 613A. Timber is not subject to percentage depletion. With certain exceptions (particularly for small producers), there is no percentage depletion for oil and gas. IRC § 613A(a), (c). Even for small producers, the percentage allowed for oil and gas depletion was scaled down to 15% for 1984 and subsequent years. IRC § 613A(c). However, percentage depletion at 22% is allowed for regulated natural gas and natural gas sold under fixed contract. IRC § 613A(b)(1).

§ 13.7330. Cumulative Depletion Deduction Allowed in Excess of Taxpayer's Basis. Since percentage depletion is a percentage of gross income from the property, it is not limited to recovery of actual basis. The cumulative depletion deductions taken by a taxpayer under the percentage depletion method may exceed the taxpayer's capital investment in the asset. In this very important respect, percentage depletion is quite unlike depreciation, amortization, or even cost depletion.

§ 13.8000. ALIMONY. Under IRC § 215, alimony (or a separate maintenance payment) is deductible by the payor spouse to the extent that it is included in the recipient's gross income under IRC § 71. A taxpayer's gross income is reduced by the taxpayer's alimony deduction in determining the taxpayer's AGI. IRC § 62(a)(10) and see **§ 2.1400.** Thus, alimony is a nonitemized deduction. Note that in certain circumstances described in **§ 2.1430**, a taxpayer who properly took an alimony deduction may be required to "recapture" part of that deduction in a later year by including an amount equal to a part of that deduction in the taxpayer's gross income for the later year.

§ 13.9000. INCOME IN RESPECT OF A DECEDENT (IRD). If a person dies possessing the right to income which he had earned but correctly had not reported for income tax purposes, the income will be included either in the gross income of the decedent's estate, or in the gross income of the beneficiary who collects it, as "income in respect of a decedent." IRC § 691. In addition, the value of the decedent's accrued rights to such income will be included in the decedent's gross estate for federal estate tax purposes. Thus, the same property may be subjected to both an estate tax and an income tax. In mitigation of this "double" tax, IRC § 691(c) grants an income tax deduction to the recipients of "income in respect of a decedent" for the amount of federal estate tax paid by the decedent's estate on the value of the right to income included in the decedent's gross estate. The method for computing this deduction is established in IRC § 691(c). See Chapter 21. While the deduction under IRC § 691(c) is an itemized deduction, it is not a miscellaneous itemized deduction and so is not subject to the 2% of AGI floor imposed by IRC § 67(a). However, as an itemized deduction, it is subject to the overall limitation imposed by IRC § 68. The authors believe that this deduction is misclassified and should be listed as a nonitemized deduction. See Jeffrey H. Kahn, *Beyond the Little Dutch Boy: An Argument for Structural Change in Tax Deduction Classification*, 80 Washington Law Review 1 (2005).

§ 13.9100. Deductions in Respect of a Decedent. Congress adopted a provision in IRC § 691(b) in which obligations incurred by a decedent before his death which were not properly allowable as deductions on the final or any prior income tax return of the decedent, but which otherwise would have qualified as deductions under IRC §§ 162, 163, 164, or 611, are allowed as deductions subject to various limitations. See **§ 21.4200.**

CHAPTER FOURTEEN

Joint Returns, Head of Household, and Surviving Spouse

§ 14.0000. JOINT RETURNS, HEAD OF HOUSEHOLD, AND SURVIVING SPOUSE.

§ 14.1000. JOINT RETURN.

§ 14.1100. Qualifications. A joint return may be filed by a husband and a wife even if one of them has no gross income. IRC § 6013. A joint return is not permitted:

(a) unless a valid election is made [described in **§ 14.1110**] if, at any time during the taxable year, either spouse is a nonresident alien [for the definition of "nonresident alien" see Treas. Reg. §§ 1.871–2 to 1.871–5]; or

(b) if the spouses have different tax years, with the exception that a joint return can be filed if the spouses' tax years begin on the same day but end on different days because of the death of one or both spouses and if the surviving spouse does not remarry before the close of the tax year.

§ 14.1110. Election for Nonresident Alien. A joint return can be filed even though one spouse is a nonresident alien if the other spouse is a citizen or resident of the United States and if a proper election is made by both spouses under IRC § 6013(g) or (h) to have the nonresident alien spouse treated as a resident of the United States for income tax purposes.

§ 14.1120. Marital Status. The determination of whether a taxpayer is married is made as of the last day of the taxpayer's taxable year. However if a spouse dies before the close of the tax year, the status is determined as of the date of death. IRC § 7703(a). A taxpayer who is legally separated from his spouse under a decree of divorce or separate maintenance is not considered to be married for purposes of filing a joint return. IRC § 7703(a)(2). In certain circumstances, a married individual who maintains a household in which the individual and a dependent child reside and whose spouse did not reside there during the last six months of the taxable year is treated as unmarried. IRC § 7703(b). For further discussion of marital status, see §§ **2.1490–2.1493.**

§ **14.1130. Change of Election.** In most (but not all) circumstances, a husband and wife may file a joint return for a tax year for which they had previously filed separate returns if they do so within three years after the last day for timely filing of the return for such year (without regard to extensions of time). IRC § 6013(b). The situations when this election is not permitted are set forth in IRC § 6013(b)(2). No election to change from a joint return to separate returns may be made after the due date of the return. Treas. Reg. § 1.6013–1(a)(1).

§ **14.1140. Joint Return with a Deceased Spouse.** In the case of the death of one or both spouses during the tax year, a joint return may be filed for the year of death. The decedent's executor or administrator makes the election except that the surviving spouse can file the joint return for the decedent if: (a) no return has previously been made for that year for the decedent; and (b) no executor or administrator has been appointed and none is appointed before the last day permitted for the timely filing of the return of the surviving spouse. If an executor or administrator is appointed subsequently, he may disaffirm the joint return at any time within one year after the last day for timely filing the return of the surviving spouse. IRC § 6013(a)(3). When a joint return is filed for a deceased spouse, the taxable years of both spouses shall be treated as having ended on the closing date of the surviving spouse's tax year. IRC § 6013(c).

§ **14.1200. Tax Computation for Joint Returns.**

§ **14.1210. Marriage Bonus and Marriage Penalty.** In some circumstances, a man and woman who marry and file a joint return will incur a lower tax than the combined tax that they would have paid if they were unmarried. This tax reduction obtained through marriage is sometimes referred to as a "marriage bonus." However, in some circumstances, a man and woman who marry will incur a greater tax than would have been incurred if they had remained unmarried. The added tax cost that arises because of their married state is sometimes referred to as a "marriage penalty." See § **14.1400.** The focus of the critics of the marriage penalty has been on the manner in which the tax rate schedules can increase the aggregate tax burden of a married couple. The tax effect of a marriage (as a bonus or as a penalty) depends upon the amount of income that the man and woman have and upon how evenly or disproportionately their combined income is divided between them. Congress has mitigated some aspects of the marriage penalty. See § **14.1400**.

§ **14.1220.   Combining Deductions.** One of the advantages of a joint return is that one spouse's excess of deductions over gross income can be used to reduce the gross income of the other spouse.

§ **14.1230.   Increase of Limitations on Deductions.** Some limitations on the amount that a taxpayer can deduct for certain items are increased for married taxpayers who file a joint return. A number of dollar limitations on specified deductions are more restrictive for a married taxpayer who files a separate return than for other taxpayers. For example, the limitation on the amount of a taxpayer's net capital loss that can be deducted from ordinary income for a married taxpayer who files a separate tax return is one-half the amount allowable for an unmarried individual. IRC § 1211(b). Regardless of whether they file joint or separate returns, a husband and wife are treated as one person for purposes of applying some of the limitations on the amount of aggregate cost of business property that can be expensed under IRC § 179. IRC § 179(b)(4).

§ **14.1240.   Qualification for Tax Advantage.** Some tax advantages can be enjoyed by either married taxpayer only if they file a joint return. For example, subject to the exception provided by IRC § 21(e)(4), married taxpayers must file a joint return to obtain a credit for dependent care and household expenses; and a married individual must file a joint return to qualify for the earned income credit. IRC §§ 21(e)(2), 32(d).

§ **14.1300.   Disadvantages of Joint Returns.**

§ **14.1310.   Joint and Several Liability.** Unless one of several exceptions applies, when a joint return is filed, each spouse is liable for the entire tax liability on their joint income, including any tax deficiency subsequently determined to be owing for that tax year. IRC § 6013(d)(3). Prior to 1998, there were only limited exceptions to this joint and several liability of joint filers. In 1998, Congress added IRC § 6015 to the Code and greatly liberalized the extent to which a spouse can escape liability for a deficiency that is attributable to actions of the other spouse.

§ 14.1320.   Relief From Joint Liability. There are three provisions (all of which are set forth in IRC § 6015) which allow relief to a spouse who filed a joint return and later finds that a deficiency is owing to the Service because of an item attributable to the other spouse. First, in general, all joint filers have the option of electing to be liable for tax deficiencies for that return only to the extent that the deficiency would have been allocable to that filer if the filer had filed a separate return. IRC § 6015(b). The conditions under which this election can be made and the limitations on the relief given are described in **§ 14.1321.** This election is referred to as the "innocent spouse election." Second, when joint filers subsequently cease to be married, are legally separated, or have not lived together for at least 12 months, either can elect to limit that filer's liability for a deficiency on the joint return to the portion of the deficiency properly attributable to the electing filer. IRC § 6015(c). The conditions for this election and the limitations on its application are set forth at **§ 14.1322.** This election is sometimes referred to as the "separate liability election." Thirdly, the Service is authorized to grant relief from liability to a joint filer, who does not qualify for either of the two elections noted above, if it would be inequitable to hold that person liable for any unpaid tax, deficiency, or a portion thereof. IRC § 6015(f). The Service has provided guidance for taxpayers seeking equitable relief under IRC § 6015(f) in Revenue Procedure 2003–61.

§ 14.1321.   Innocent Spouse Election. The election must be filed with the Service no later than the date two years after the day on which the Service began collection activities with respect to the electing filer. IRC § 6015(b)(1)(E). The following conditions must be satisfied:

1.   There must be an understatement of tax on a joint return on which the electing party was a joint filer.

2.   The understatement must be attributable to erroneous items of the other joint filer.

3.   The electing individual establishes that, in signing the joint return, he "did not know, and had no reason to know," that there was an understatement.

4. Taking into account all facts and circumstances, it would be inequitable to hold the electing filer liable for the deficiency attributable to the understatement.

In some circumstances, an electing party who does not qualify for full relief from such liability may be relieved of a portion of the liability. IRC § 6015(b)(2).

§ 14.1322. Separate Liability Election. An election for immunity from liability for a joint return deficiency that is attributable to the other filer can be made by a joint filer who is no longer married to the other filer, or who is legally separated from the other filer, or who had not lived as a member of the same household as the other filer for the entire 12–month period ending on the date on which the election was made. IRC § 6015(c)(3). Some of the conditions on this election are:

1. The election must be made no later than 2 years after the Service has begun collection activities with respect to the electing filer.

2. The election will not be effective to any part of the deficiency that is attributable to an item of which the electing filer had *actual knowledge* at the time of signing the return. Note that the absence of "actual knowledge" is a more lenient standard than the "did not know and had no reason to know" requirement that is employed in the innocent spouse election. The Service has the burden of proof on the question of whether the electing filer had actual knowledge of the item that is the source of the deficiency. Even if the electing filer had such actual knowledge, he can make the election if he can establish that he signed the return under duress. IRC § 6015(c)(3)(C).

3. The electing filer has the burden of proof on the issue of what portion of the deficiency is attributable to the other filer.

4. If the nonelecting filer transferred property to the electing filer for the principal purpose of avoiding tax or the payment of tax, the amount of joint return deficiency for which the electing filer will be liable is increased by the value of such transferred property. IRC § 6015(c)(4).

5. If the Service can establish that property was transferred between the joint filers as part of a fraudulent scheme of both

parties, the separate liability election is void. IRC § 6015(c)(3)(A)(ii).

§ 14.1330. Loss of Dependency Deduction. If one spouse is a dependent of a taxpayer (who is not the other spouse), the dependent's filing of a joint return will deny the dependency exemption to the taxpayer. IRC § 151(c)(2).

§ 14.1340. Medical Deduction. If both H and W have gross income and H has paid all of the medical expenses of the family, H will have a lower AGI if he files a separate return. Therefore, the limitation on allowable medical deductions will be reduced (only the excess over 7½% of AGI is deductible). However, if H itemizes his deductions, W must do so also (i.e., W will not be allowed to use the standard deduction). IRC § 63(c)(6)(A). Consequently, in most circumstances, the reduction of the medical expense limitation will not constitute a sufficient reason to file separate returns, but it can be a factor when other reasons exist.

§ 14.1400. Marriage Penalty. As noted in **§ 14.1210**, while some couples enjoy a marriage bonus from their marriage, others incur a marriage penalty. The critics of the marriage penalty focus on the rate schedules, but another form of penalty is that the marriage may reduce the aggregate amount of certain deductions that would have been available to the couple if they did not marry. For example, the aggregate amount of cost of business property that can be expensed by a couple is halved if they are married. IRC § 179(b)(4). Similarly, the aggregate amount of net capital loss that can be deducted from a couple's ordinary income is halved if they are married. IRC § 1211(b).

Recent tax legislation has made two specific changes aimed at reducing the marriage penalty. First, the standard deduction for joint returns has been increased and is now twice the size of the standard deduction for single filers. See **§ 3.2200.** Second, the maximum taxable income in the 15% income tax bracket is statutorily required to be a specified percentage (ranging from 180% to 200%) above the maximum taxable income in the 15% bracket for a single filer. IRC § 1(f)(8).

§ 14.2000. SURVIVING SPOUSE. A surviving spouse may use joint return rates to compute his or her tax liability for the two tax years following the year of death of the decedent spouse. This is in addition to the privilege of filing a joint return for the year of death. IRC § 1(a).

§ 14.2100.   Definition. A surviving spouse is a taxpayer:

(a) whose spouse died during either of the two tax years immediately preceding the taxable year;

(b) who maintains as his or her home a household which constitutes for the taxable year the principal place of abode of a dependent son, daughter, stepson or stepdaughter of the taxpayer for whom the taxpayer is entitled to an exemption; and

(c) who does not remarry before the close of the taxable year. IRC § 2(a).

In addition, a taxpayer will not qualify as a surviving spouse unless a joint return could have been filed with the deceased spouse for the tax year of the taxpayer in which the spouse died. IRC § 2(a)(2)(B).

§ 14.2200.   Limited to Two Years. The effect of the surviving spouse provision is to extend the use of joint return rates for two years after the year of the decedent's death if the surviving spouse maintains an abode for a dependent child. The year of the decedent's death is not included in the surviving spouse provision because in that year the taxpayer can elect to file a joint return with the deceased spouse. After the two-year period has expired, the taxpayer may become eligible for head of household rates.

§ 14.3000.   HEAD OF HOUSEHOLD. A "head of household" pays taxes at rates that are lower than those imposed on single taxpayers but higher than those imposed on married taxpayers filing a joint return. IRC § 1(b).

§ 14.3100.   Definition. A "head of household" is an individual who is neither married nor a surviving spouse entitled to joint return rates at the end of his tax year, and who either:

(a) maintains as his or her home a household which for more than one-half of the tax year is the principal place of abode, as a member of the household, of either:

   (i) a "qualifying child" of the taxpayer as defined in IRC § 152(c) [see **§ 4.1232**] with several modifications including that the child must not be married at the end of the taxpayer's taxable year, and, unless adopted, must be either a citizen of the United States or a resident of the United States or a contiguous country, or

   (ii) any other person who is a dependent of the taxpayer for whom the taxpayer is entitled to an exemption for the tax year; or

(b) maintains a household (not necessarily the taxpayer's home) which for the tax year constitutes the principal place of abode of the father or mother of the taxpayer for whom the taxpayer is entitled to a dependency exemption. IRC § 2(b).

Note that except for a taxpayer's father or mother, the other person must have his principal abode in the taxpayer's home for the taxpayer to qualify as a head of household. Also, except for a "qualifying child" of the taxpayer, only dependents of a taxpayer can qualify the taxpayer for head of household treatment.

CHAPTER FIFTEEN

ALTERNATIVE MINIMUM TAX

§ 15.0000. ALTERNATIVE MINIMUM TAX.

§ 15.1000. ESTABLISHMENT OF THE MINIMUM TAX.

Many of the deductions authorized by the Code do not relate to an accurate determination of the amount of net income earned from an income-producing activity as much as they establish tax incentives to encourage or reward a taxpayer for investing in certain areas deemed desirable by Congress. However, Congress felt that virtually all citizens should share the burdensome cost of taxation to some extent; and, therefore, a taxpayer should not be permitted to enjoy an amount of such tax advantages that is out of proportion to the taxpayer's economic income. Accordingly, Congress imposed special taxes on those taxpayers with an excessive amount of such tax advantages.

Congress originally designed the minimum tax to reach only a relatively small number of taxpayers. However, the scope of the system has been greatly expanded since its original enactment in 1969. It has been predicted that, if no changes to the Code are made, thirty-five million taxpayers (33% of the total number of taxpayers) will be subject to the alternative system by 2010.

§ 15.1100. Alternative versus Add–On Minimum Tax.

An "add-on minimum tax" is one which imposes an additional tax (i.e., a surtax) on a taxpayer who has an excessive amount of statutorily specified tax advantages. An "alternative minimum tax" is determined by recomputing the taxpayer's taxable income by making certain specified adjustments and additions to that taxable income and by applying a specified tax rate to the adjusted income figure. The resulting figure (the taxpayer's "tentative minimum tax") is then reduced by the taxpayer's regular tax, and only the difference (if any) is payable by the taxpayer as an alternative minimum tax. See § 15.3000. In effect, a taxpayer pays either his normal tax liability or his tentative minimum tax, whichever is higher.

§ 15.1200. Exclusivity of the Alternative Minimum Tax.

Immediately prior to the adoption of the Tax Reform Act of 1986, individuals and other noncorporate taxpayers were subject to an alternative minimum tax, and corporations were subject to an add-on minimum tax. However, Congress felt that the pre–1986 structure was not achieving its remedial purpose. The Tax Reform Act of 1986 repealed the corporate add-on minimum tax, created a new alternative minimum tax on corporations, and expanded the scope of the alternative minimum tax on individuals and noncorporate entities. The rules regarding alternative minimum tax are contained primarily in IRC §§ 55–59.

§ 15.1300. Alternative Minimum Taxable Income (AMTI). The computation of the alternative minimum tax begins by recomputing a taxpayer's taxable income by making certain adjustments and additions to the figures that are used in determining a taxpayer's taxable income for normal income tax purposes. The recomputed figure is referred to as the "alternative minimum taxable income." IRC § 55(b)(2). For convenience, the alternative minimum taxable income is sometimes referred to hereafter as "AMTI."

§ 15.1400. "Adjustments" and "Tax Preferences." A taxpayer's alternative minimum taxable income (AMTI) is determined: (a) by adjusting the amount of certain items that are taken into account in determining taxable income (such adjustments are made by substituting a specially computed item for the figure that is used in computing the taxpayer's taxable income), and (b) by adding the amount of certain tax benefits referred to as "items of tax preference" or TPI. IRC § 55(b)(2). A "tax preference" item will be a positive figure—that is, it will always increase the amount of a taxpayer's AMTI. On the other hand, while an "adjustment" to a taxpayer's income often is positive, some adjustments are negative (i.e., they reduce the amount of a taxpayer's AMTI). It, therefore, is possible for a taxpayer to have taxable income that is greater than his AMTI, but that will not be typical. The adjustments utilized in determining AMTI are set forth in IRC §§ 56 and 58. Tax preference items are set forth in IRC § 57.

§ 15.1500. Determination of Alternative Minimum Tax (AMT). In general, the next step in determining a taxpayer's alternative minimum tax is to apply a specified rate to as much of the taxpayer's AMTI for the taxable year as exceeds an exemption amount. IRC § 55(b)(1). The amount of a taxpayer's exemption amount depends upon the filing status of the taxpayer. See **§§ 15.3300–15.3330.** If the taxpayer's AMTI exceeds a specified figure, the taxpayer's exemption amount is phased out. IRC

§ 55(d)(3). See § **15.3310**–§ **15.3330** for the determination of exemption amounts for different classes of taxpayers and for the manner in which the exemption amounts are phased out.

§ 15.1510. Noncorporate Taxpayers—Taxable Excess, Tentative Minimum Tax, and AMT.

For a noncorporate taxpayer, the excess of AMTI over the taxpayer's exemption amount is referred to as the "taxable excess." IRC § 55(b)(1)(A)(ii). The alternative minimum tax rate to be applied to the taxable excess is 26% for so much of the taxpayer's taxable excess as does not exceed $175,000 ($87,500 for a married taxpayer filing a separate return) and is 28% for so much of the taxpayer's taxable excess as does exceed $175,000 (or $87,500). IRC § 55(b)(1)(A)(i). The total amount of tax as so computed is then reduced by the taxpayer's "alternative minimum tax foreign tax credit" (§ **15.3510**), if any, and the resulting figure is referred to as the "tentative minimum tax" for that taxable year. IRC § 55(b)(1)(A). The difference (if any) between the tentative minimum tax and the taxpayer's "regular tax" constitutes the alternative minimum tax (AMT). § 55(a). The manner in which a taxpayer's "regular tax" is computed for this purpose is described at § **15.4000.**

If a noncorporate taxpayer has net capital gains or qualified dividends, the preferential rates that apply to such gains for regular tax purposes (IRC § 1(h)) will also be applied in determining the taxpayer's tentative minimum tax (and therefore in determining taxpayer's AMT). IRC § 55(b)(3).

§ 15.2000. MINIMUM TAX INCOME ALTERATIONS (MTIA).

IRC § 55(b)(2) requires that certain "adjustments" and items of "tax preferences" must be considered in computing AMTI. "Adjustments" involve a substitution of a special alternative minimum tax treatment of an item for the regular tax treatment. A tax preference requires that the difference between the special alternative minimum tax treatment and the regular tax treatment be added to AMTI. In the following discussion, both adjustments and tax preferences are sometimes referred to as Minimum Tax Income Alterations or MTIA.

§ 15.2100. Tax Preference Items (TPI).

IRC § 57 lists the items of tax preference (TPI) that are included in the determination of a taxpayer's AMTI. Currently, there are five items listed in IRC § 57. Those items are described in §§ **15.2110–15.2150.**

§ 15.2110. Percentage Depletion.

The extent to which a taxpayer's deduction for the percentage depletion of a property exceeds the taxpayer's adjusted basis in that property constitutes a TPI. IRC § 57(a)(1). However, this provision does not apply to the depletion deduction allowed by IRC § 613A(c) for certain amounts of domestic crude oil and domestic natural gas. *Ibid.*

§ 15.2120. **Intangible Drilling Costs.** The cost of drilling for oil, gas and geothermal property typically is deductible in determining a taxpayer's taxable income. Absent this special treatment, such costs would have to be capitalized and amortized on a straight-line method. If the additional deduction allowable because of the special treatment accorded to such intangible costs constitutes an excessively large percentage (i.e., more than 65%) of the taxpayer's net income from that activity, a portion of the cost will constitute a TPI. The computation of this item is described in IRC § 57(a)(2).

§ 15.2130. **Accelerated Depreciation or Amortization of Certain Properties Placed in Service Prior to 1987.** Depreciation or amortization for property placed in service by the taxpayer after 1986 is not included in tax preference items, but a portion of such deductions may be included in MTIA as an "adjustment" required by IRC § 56(a)(1). Since the adjustment required by IRC § 56 does not apply to property placed in service prior to 1987, part of the accelerated depreciation or amortization deductions for such properties is included in TPI under IRC § 57(a)(6) to the same extent that such deductions would have been included in TPI under pre–1986 law. IRC § 57(a)(6). In other words, the pre–1987 treatment of accelerated depreciation and amortization continues to apply to property placed in service prior to 1987.

§ 15.2140. **Tax–Exempt Interest.** Interest on "specified private activity bonds," which is exempt from taxable income, is included in AMTI. This provision does not apply if the bond was issued prior to August 8, 1986. IRC § 57(a)(5)(C)(i). The amount of such tax exempt interest is reduced by the deductions that are not allowable in determining taxable income but which would have been allowable if such interest were included in taxable income. IRC § 57(a)(5)(A). The term "specified private activity bonds" is defined in IRC § 57(a)(5)(C). Tax-exempt interest on state or local bonds other than "specified private activity bonds" is not included in AMTI.

§ 15.2150. **Small Business Stock.** In general, IRC § 1202 excludes from gross income 50% of the gain from the sale or exchange of "qualified small business stock" (defined in IRC § 1202(c)) that was held for more than five years. Seven percent of the amount so excluded by IRC § 1202 from gross income is a TPI and so is added in determining AMTI. IRC § 57(a)(7). The percentage of the excluded amount that constitutes TPI is scheduled to be increased beginning in 2009.

§ 15.2200. AMTI Adjustments. In addition to the additions required by IRC § 57 for TPI, IRC §§ 56 and 58 require that certain items be determined differently for purposes of computing a taxpayer's AMTI than they are determined for purposes of computing a taxpayer's taxable income. The differently computed items are substituted for the figures used for such items in determining taxable income. The recomputed items are sometimes referred to as "adjustments." IRC § 55(b)(2)(A). The adjustments are not all the same for corporate and noncorporate taxpayers. We will discuss only adjustments that apply to noncorporate taxpayers regardless of whether those provisions also apply to corporate taxpayers.

§ 15.2210. Depreciation. As previously noted, there is no "adjustment" for depreciation or amortization deductions allowable for property placed in service prior to 1987, but a portion of such deductions may be included in TPI (and therefore added to the Minimum Tax Income Alterations) to the extent that those deductions would have constituted TPI under pre–1986 law. See **§ 15.2130.** A 1997 amendment changed the alternative minimum tax treatment of depreciation deductions for years beginning after 1998. The alternative minimum tax treatment of depreciation deductions for tangible property placed in service after 1986 and before 1999 is described in **§ 15.2211.** The alternative minimum tax treatment for tangible property placed in service after 1998 is described in **§ 15.2212.**

§ 15.2211. Tangible Property Placed in Service after 1986 and before 1999. The following rules determine the amount of AMTI adjustments arising from property placed in service after 1986 and before 1999. For most real property (i.e., buildings and their structural components) and for property which is being depreciated for regular tax purposes under the straight-line method, the depreciation deduction for alternative minimum tax purposes must be computed in accordance with the alternative depreciation system set forth in IRC § 168(g). IRC § 56(a)(1). In general, under the alternative depreciation system, buildings and their structural components are depreciated on a straight-line basis over a 40–year period and personal property is depreciated over a recovery period that usually will be longer than the normal MACRS recovery period. For all other property (i.e., personal property that for purposes of determining taxable income is being depreciated on an accelerated method under MACRS), the alternative minimum tax depreciation deduction is computed by using the 150 percent declining balance method (switching to the straight-line method in the year that that method yields a higher deduction than the 150 percent declining balance method) and by using the recovery period set forth in IRC § 168(g), the alternative depreciation system.

The several properties listed in IRC § 168(f)(1)–(4) [for example, films, video tapes and sound recordings are included in that list] are excluded from this AMTI provision, and so no adjustment is made to the depreciation allowed for regular tax purposes for those items. IRC § 56(a)(1)(B). Accordingly, no adjustments are made to property that is depreciated on a method other than MACRS. For example, property which is depreciated on the units of production method is not subject to AMTI adjustments.

In determining AMTI, the depreciation deduction, as determined by the method described above, is substituted for the depreciation deduction used in determining taxable income. The substituted figure may be higher or lower than the regular depreciation amount; in the later years of the recovery period of a depreciable asset, the AMTI depreciation often will be greater than the regular depreciation amount. This can result in a taxpayer's having higher taxable income than he has AMTI in a taxable year.

§ 15.2212. Tangible Property Placed in Service After 1998. The AMTI rules for depreciating tangible property placed in service after 1998 are much simpler. IRC § 56(a)(1)(A). The recovery periods used for AMTI purposes are the same as those used by the taxpayer for regular MACRS purposes, so no adjustments are made for recovery period. If the property is depreciated on the straight line method for regular tax purposes, no adjustment is made for AMTI purposes. Consequently, no adjustments are made for the depreciation of buildings or of any property that the taxpayer elected to depreciate on the straight line method. Also, no AMTI adjustment is made for property that is depreciated for regular tax purposes on the 150% declining balance method. The only tangible property for which AMTI adjustments must be made are those depreciated for regular tax purposes on the 200% (or double) declining balance method. The depreciation of such properties for AMTI purposes must be determined by utilizing the 150% declining balance method (switching to straight line at the optimum year), but using the same recovery period as is applied for regular tax purposes. IRC § 56(a)(1)(A)(ii). The tangible properties excluded from AMTI adjustments described in § **15.2211** also are excluded for years subsequent to 1998.

§ **15.2213. No Adjustments for Deductions Allowed as Expenses under IRC § 179.** For all properties, whenever placed in service, a deduction allowed the taxpayer under IRC § 179 for the cost of acquiring certain business assets [§ **12.2000**] does not cause any adjustment to be made for AMTI purposes. Subject to a dollar limitation, § 179 permits a taxpayer to expense the cost of certain tangible personalty that is acquired for business use; the § 179 deduction is sometimes referred to as "bonus depreciation."

§ **15.2314. Basis Adjustment.** Since the depreciation deduction allowable for AMTI can be different from the depreciation allowable for taxable income, in determining a taxpayer's gain or loss on the sale of a depreciable item, the taxpayer's adjusted basis may be different for AMTI purposes than the basis used for taxable income purposes. IRC § 56(a)(6). See § **15.3400.**

§ **15.2220. Use of the Completed Contract Method.** Taxpayers who use the completed contract method of accounting for long-term contracts in computing regular tax liability must substitute the percentage of completion method in determining AMTI. IRC § 56(a)(3). This provision does not apply to a contract entered into prior to March 1, 1986.

§ **15.2230. Mining Exploration and Development Costs.** In computing deductions for alternative minimum tax purposes, mining exploration and development costs incurred after 1986 must be capitalized and amortized on a straight-line basis over ten years. IRC § 56(a)(2). This provision does not apply to costs incurred in connection with an oil, gas, or geothermal well.

§ 15.2240. Certified Pollution Control Facilities. Amortization deductions on certified pollution control facilities [IRC § 169] placed into service after 1986 and before 1999 must be computed by using the alternative depreciation system [described in **§ 12.3460**] set forth in IRC § 168(g). IRC § 56(a)(5). For facilities placed into service prior to 1987, the pre–1986 rules for determining tax preference items continue to apply—e.g., the excess of the amortization deduction allowable for a taxable year over the depreciation deduction which otherwise would have been allowable for such tax year under IRC § 167 is a TPI. See **§ 15.2130.** Facilities placed in service after 1998 are depreciated under IRC § 168 using the straight line method.

§ 15.2250. Alternative Tax Net Operating Loss Deduction (ATNOL). A taxpayer with a net operating loss must recompute the net operating loss for AMTI purposes by taking into account the taxpayer's alternative minimum tax adjustments and TPIs. The recomputed amount is the taxpayer's "alternative tax net operating loss" [ATNOL] and may offset future income that would otherwise be subject to the alternative minimum tax. Also, special rules specify the amount of ATNOL carryover allowed for that year. IRC § 56(a)(4), (d).

§ 15.2260. Alcohol Fuel Credit. Sections 40(a) and 38(b)(3) allow a tax credit for the use of alcohol as a fuel. Section 87 requires that the amount of a taxpayer's alcohol fuel credit be included in the taxpayer's gross income. Since no such credit is allowed for alternative minimum tax purposes, it would be inappropriate to include the credit in a taxpayer's AMTI. Accordingly, the § 87 inclusion of that credit in income does not apply in determining AMTI. § 56(a)(7).

§ 15.2270. Denial of Tax Shelter Farm Losses. In computing AMTI, no deduction is allowed for losses attributable to tax shelter farming activities. IRC § 58(a). In general, this provision does not apply to the loss incurred by a taxpayer on the disposition of his entire interest in a tax shelter farm activity. IRC § 58(c)(2). Also, in general, the amount of tax shelter farm loss that is disallowed by this provision is reduced by the amount (if any) by which the taxpayer is insolvent at the end of the taxable year. IRC § 58(c)(1).

§ 15.2280. Disallowance of Passive Activity Losses (PAL). In general, the regular tax provisions regarding limitations on the deductibility of passive activity losses [IRC § 469] also apply for alternative minimum tax purposes. The passive activity loss (PAL) provisions are discussed at §§ **7.9000–7.9620.** However, for alternative minimum tax purposes, the amount of PAL that is subject to disallowance is determined after taking into account AMTI adjustments under IRC § 56 and TPI listed in IRC § 57. IRC § 58(b). Also, in general, the PAL that is disallowed by this provision is reduced by the amount (if any) by which the taxpayer is insolvent at the end of the taxable year. IRC § 58(c)(1).

§ 15.2290.   Itemized Deductions. Not all of an individual taxpayer's itemized deductions [IRC § 63(d)] that are allowable for regular tax purposes can be deducted in computing AMTI. However, for those itemized deductions that are allowed, the overall limitation of § 68 does not apply. IRC § 56(b)(1)(F).

§ 15.2291.   Medical Expenses. Medical expenses may be deducted for alternative minimum tax purposes only to the extent they exceed 10% of the taxpayer's adjusted gross income (AGI). IRC § 56(b)(1)(B).

§ 15.2292.   Taxes. No deduction is allowed for alternative minimum tax purposes for state, local and foreign taxes on income or on real or personal property. IRC § 56(b)(1)(A)(ii). Such taxes are deductible for alternative minimum tax purposes, however, to the extent that they are deductible by the taxpayer under IRC § 62 in computing the taxpayer's AGI. IRC § 56(b)(1)(A). Thus, such *property* taxes are deductible for alternative minimum tax purposes only if they are incurred in connection with a trade or business in which the taxpayer is self-employed, and *no such income taxes* can be deducted. See **§ 6.4000.** If a tax that is disallowed as a deduction by this provision is subsequently recovered by the taxpayer, the recovery is excluded from the taxpayer's AMTI. IRC § 56(b)(1)(D).

§ 15.2293.   Interest. A taxpayer may deduct "qualified housing interest" in computing AMTI. IRC § 56(b)(1)(C). Qualified housing interest is qualified residence interest (as defined in IRC § 163(h)(3)) which is paid or accrued on a debt incurred to acquire, construct or substantially rehabilitate a taxpayer's principal residence and one other personal use dwelling; and the term also includes interest resulting from refinancing such debt. IRC § 56(e). Additionally, most other interest that is deductible for regular tax purposes is deductible for alternative minimum tax purposes. IRC § 56(b)(1)(C).

§ 15.2294. Miscellaneous Itemized Deductions. Miscellaneous itemized deductions [defined in IRC § 67(b)] are not deductible in computing AMTI. IRC § 56(b)(1)(A)(i).

§ 15.2295. Standard Deduction and Personal Exemption Deduction. The standard deduction and the personal exemption deduction [IRC §§ 63(c), 151] are not deductible in computing the alternative minimum tax. IRC § 56(b)(1)(E).

§ 15.2296. Other Itemized Deductions. All other itemized deductions may be deducted for alternative minimum tax purposes. Such itemized deductions include gambling losses, casualty and theft losses, and charitable contributions. The overall limitation on the deduction of itemized deductions that is imposed by IRC § 68 does not apply in determining AMTI. IRC § 56(b)(1)(F).

§ 15.2310. Circulation, Research, and Experimental Expenditures. In computing the deduction for alternative minimum tax purposes for expenditures incurred after 1986 in circulating a newspaper or other periodical, such expenditures must be amortized on a straight-line basis over a three-year period. Research and experimental expenditures incurred after 1986 must be amortized on a straight-line basis over a ten-year period. IRC § 56(b)(2). This provision does not apply to research and development expenses incurred in connection with an activity in which the taxpayer materially participates. IRC § 56(b)(2)(D).

§ 15.2320. Incentive Stock Options. The special tax treatment accorded by IRC § 421 to an individual's purchase of stock at a bargain price pursuant to an incentive stock option does not apply in determining the individual's AMTI. IRC § 56(b)(3). However, no AMT adjustment is required if the exercise of the option and disposition of the stock occur in the same year. Id.

§ 15.2330. Nonresident Aliens. IRC § 897(a)(2) provides that the taxable excess [see **§ 15.1510**] of a nonresident alien shall not be less than the lesser of (1) the individual's AMTI or (2) the individual's net gain from sales of United States real property (as defined in IRC § 897).

§ 15.3000. COMPUTATION OF ALTERNATIVE MINIMUM TAX. The first step in computing a taxpayer's alternative minimum tax is to apply the appropriate alternative minimum tax rate [**§ 15.3200**] to the excess of the taxpayer's AMTI over the taxpayer's exemption amount [see §§ **15.3300–15.3320**]. The resulting figure is then reduced by the taxpayer's foreign tax credit as specially computed for alternative minimum tax purposes; this specially computed credit is referred to as the alternative minimum tax foreign tax credit (AMTFTC). The amount of difference between the resulting figure and taxpayer's AMTFTC is referred to as the taxpayer's "tentative minimum tax." IRC § 55(b)(1). The taxpayer's alternative minimum tax is the amount by which his tentative minimum tax exceeds his regular tax for the taxable year. IRC § 55(a). The manner in which the taxpayer's "regular tax" is determined is described at § **15.4000**. In effect, a taxpayer pays an amount of tax equal either to his regular tax liability or to his tentative minimum tax, whichever is greater. However, apart from the AMTFTC, nonrefundable tax credits otherwise available in determining a taxpayer's normal tax liability are not allowed to reduce the taxpayer's alternative minimum tax. IRC §§ 26(a), 29(b)(6), 30(b)(3), and 38(c).

§ 15.3100. Alternative Minimum Taxable Income (AMTI).

The alternative minimum tax applies to the taxpayer's "alternative minimum taxable income" (AMTI) which equals the taxable income of the taxpayer adjusted by the applicable AMTI adjustments and TPI. IRC § 55(b)(2). The adjustments and additions that are applied to determine AMTI are collectively referred to herein as Minimum Tax Income Alterations. § **15.2000.**

§ 15.3200. Alternative Minimum Tax Rates.

As previously noted, the alternative minimum tax rate for noncorporate taxpayers is 26% of so much of the taxpayer's "taxable excess" (i.e., the excess of the taxpayer's AMTI over his exemption amount) as does not exceed $175,000, and 28% of so much of his taxable excess as exceeds $175,000. IRC § 55(b)(1)(A).

§ 15.3300. Exemption Amounts.

The alternative minimum tax rate is imposed on the taxpayer's AMTI that exceeds specified exemption amounts. However, a taxpayer's exemption amount will be phased-out, but not below zero, to the extent that taxpayer's AMTI exceeds a specified amount. IRC § 55(d).

§ 15.3310. Married Individual Filing Jointly and Surviving Spouses.

The exemption amount is $45,000 less 25% of the amount by which AMTI exceeds $150,000. IRC § 55(d)(1)(A), (3)(A).

§ 15.3320. Single Individual Other Than a Surviving Spouse.

The exemption amount is $33,750 less 25% of the

amount by which AMTI exceeds $112,500. IRC § 55(d)(1)(B), (3)(B).

§ 15.3330. Married Individual Filing Separately, Estate, or Trusts. The exemption amount is $22,500 less 25% of the amount by which AMTI exceeds $75,000. IRC § 55(d)(1)(C), (3)(C). However, the AMTI of a married individual who files a separate return is increased by the lesser of: (i) 25% of the excess of AMTI (determined without regard to this sentence) over $165,000, or (ii) $22,500. IRC § 55(d)(3).

§ 15.3340. Expiration of Temporary Increase in Exemption Amounts. In 2001 through 2004, the exemption amounts were temporarily increased. However, beginning in 2005, the exemption amounts reverted back to their original pre–2001 amounts (described in **§§ 15.3310–15.3330**).

§ 15.3400. Adjusted Basis of Certain Properties for Adjusted Minimum Tax Purposes. To reflect that the aggregate deductions for expenditures connected with certain properties can be less for AMTI purposes than for taxable income purposes, the taxpayer can have a greater adjusted basis in those properties for AMTI purposes than for taxable income computation purposes. IRC § 56(a)(6), (b)(3). Accordingly, on the sale of such properties, the taxpayer could have a larger gain or a smaller loss for taxable income purposes than the taxpayer will have for AMTI purposes. Some properties for which this can occur are: (a) depreciable property, (b) property with respect to which circulation or research and experimental expenditures were paid by an individual, (c) property with respect to which mine exploration or development expenditures were paid, (d) pollution control facilities, and (e) stock acquired pursuant to the exercise of an incentive stock option.

§ 15.3500. Credits. Except for the AMTFTC, a taxpayer whose tax is determined by the alternative minimum tax (i.e., taxpayer's tentative minimum tax is greater than his regular tax liability) is not allowed the benefits of nonrefundable credits that are available for regular tax purposes. **§ 15.3000.** The AMTFTC is described at **§ 15.3510.**

§ 15.3510. Alternative Minimum Tax Foreign Tax Credit (AMTFTC). A taxpayer may offset his alternative minimum tax (computed without regard to this credit or the ATNOL deduction) by his alternative minimum tax foreign tax credit (AMTFTC). In general, the AMTFTC is computed in a manner that is similar to the computation of the regular tax foreign tax credit under IRC § 27. IRC § 59(a). Some of the differences are that in computing the AMTFTC, the AMTI of the taxpayer is used instead of the taxpayer's taxable income, and the tentative minimum tax (before deducting the AMTFTC) is the tax against which the credit is taken.

§ 15.4000. REGULAR TAX. A taxpayer's alternative minimum tax is the difference between his tentative minimum tax and his regular tax. A taxpayer's "regular tax" for a taxable year is his tax liability for that year without regard to any alternative minimum tax that may apply and with several adjustments. For example, the "regular tax" is not reduced by any nonrefundable credits other than the foreign tax credit provided by IRC § 27. IRC § 55(c).

§ 15.5000. MINIMUM TAX CREDIT. Many of the adjustments and TPI taken into account in determining AMTI deal with deferrals of income rather than exclusions. Congress wished to permit taxpayers to offset the alternative minimum tax paid on such deferrals against the greater regular tax incurred when the deferral expires. Accordingly, Congress provides that the alternative minimum tax paid in any year may be carried forward indefinitely as a credit against a taxpayer's regular tax liability for a taxable year to the extent that the taxpayer's regular tax exceeds his tentative minimum tax for that year. IRC § 53. This credit is referred to as the "minimum tax credit." The alternative minimum tax that can create a minimum tax credit is only that amount of the taxpayer's alternative minimum tax that arises because of adjustments or TPI attributable to deferral items (such as depreciation deductions). IRC § 55(d). The deferral amount of a year's alternative minimum tax is computed by subtracting from the taxpayer's alternative minimum tax for that year the amount of alternative minimum tax the taxpayer would have had in that year if the only applicable adjustments and TPI were non-deferral items (i.e., items listed in IRC §§ 56(b)(1), 57(a)(1), (5), (6)). The difference is called the "adjusted net minimum tax." The minimum tax credit for a taxable year is the excess of adjusted net minimum taxes for prior years beginning after 1986 over the amount of minimum tax credits allowable for such prior years. IRC § 53(b).

§ 15.6000. SPECIAL ELECTION FOR PROLONGED WRITEOFFS OF CERTAIN EXPENDITURES. A taxpayer can prevent certain expenditures (including research and experimental expenditures, circulation expenditures, intangible drilling costs, and mine development and exploration expenditures) from being treated as tax preference items (TPIs) or as adjustments by electing to amortize the expenditures (for all tax purposes) on a straight-line basis over a ten-year period (a three-year period in the case of circulation expenditures, and a 60–month period in the case of intangible drilling and development expenditures). IRC § 59(e).

§ 15.7000.   TAX BENEFIT REQUIREMENT. IRC § 59(g) permits the Treasury to prescribe regulations under which items of tax preference will be properly adjusted when the tax treatment giving rise to such items will not result in a reduction of the taxpayer's income tax liability.

CHAPTER SIXTEEN

REALIZATION OF GAIN OR LOSS ON THE DISPOSITION OF PROPERTY

§ 16.0000. REALIZATION OF GAIN OR LOSS ON THE DISPOSITION OF PROPERTY. A basic principle of tax law is that gain or loss is not included in or deducted from the gross income of a taxpayer until it is "realized." While there are a few special circumstances in which unrealized income is included in gross income, realization typically is required, and the realization principle is a basic tenet of the tax law. The word *realized* is a term of art that refers to a significant event that represents the severance of gain from the property that produced the gain. See §§ **1.7200–1.7220.** The gain realized from the sale or other disposition of property is the excess of the amount realized over the taxpayer's adjusted basis [the term "basis" is explained at §§ **1.7300–1.7336–3**] in the property sold or otherwise transferred by him. If the taxpayer's adjusted basis in the property exceeds the amount realized by him, then the difference is the amount of loss realized by the taxpayer on the sale or other disposition. IRC § 1001(a). A realized gain or loss will be "recognized" by the taxpayer for tax purposes unless a section of the Code (e.g., IRC § 1031 for exchanges of certain kinds of property) provides that gain or loss will not be recognized. IRC § 1001(c). Several such nonrecognition provisions are discussed in **§ 17.0000** and following. It should be noted also that a recognized loss is not deductible from gross income unless some section of the Code authorizes a deduction (e.g., IRC § 165 authorizes a deduction of many types of losses).

> **§ 16.1100. Recovery of Cost.** When a taxpayer has an investment (or "basis") in property, only the amount realized in excess of his investment can constitute a gain. While there is no dispositive authority on the question, there is a view that the Constitution prohibits the taxation of a taxpayer's recovery of his capital because such a tax would be a direct tax on his property and, therefore, invalid unless apportioned among the states by population. In effect, this view construes the term "income" in the Sixteenth Amendment as referring to gross income as contrasted to gross receipts. The Supreme Court's decision in *Stanton v. Baltic Mining Co.*, 240 U.S.

103 (1916) (a case dealing with the depletion deduction allowable to a mining corporation) raises questions concerning the viability of that construction. In *Baltic Mining*, the applicable income tax law permitted only a 5% depletion allowance on the sale of the ore in question, and the taxpayer's actual cost for the ore was greater than the amount of deduction it obtained from the 5% depletion allowance. The taxpayer objected that it should be permitted to deduct its actual cost of the ore since the application of the inadequate depletion allowance resulted in its being taxed on receipts that were merely a return of its capital investment and such a tax is an unconstitutional direct tax on its property. The Court sustained the application of the income tax to the taxpayer's receipts less the depletion allowance even though that allowance was inadequate to provide the taxpayer a recovery of its capital. The language of the Court's opinion is less than illuminating—the Court even suggested that the tax is an excise tax (and therefore an indirect tax) on the privilege of conducting a mining operation—but the decision does not repudiate the view that a taxpayer normally must be permitted to recover his cost. *Baltic Mining* can be explained on the ground that the allocation of the cost of a mine to the tons of ores mined and sold requires an estimate of the number of tons in the mine and this estimate is often too speculative to be reliable. When the determination of the cost of a ton of ore is so speculative, it is permissible for Congress to establish a specific depletion rate which is a reasonable rate on the basis of industry-wide experience even though a predetermined rate will produce hardships in some cases and windfalls in others. The interests of administrative convenience can preclude individual determinations of cost where the established rate is reasonable for the industry as a whole. *Penn Mutual Indemnity v. Commissioner*, 32 T.C. 653 (1959), aff'd, 277 F.2d 16 (3d Cir. 1960).

§ 16.1110. Gain Attributable to Inflation. In many cases, much or all of the gain that is recognized by a taxpayer on the sale of an asset is attributable to inflation and does not reflect an increase in true economic value. In other words, on the sale of an asset, a taxpayer's receipt of more dollars than that initially expended for the asset some years earlier may be attributable to the declining value of a dollar during that period; that is, the purchasing power of a dollar decreased so that the larger number of dollars that the taxpayer received does not represent any greater purchasing power than the smaller number of dollars that the taxpayer had initially invested in the asset. In *Hellerman v. Commissioner*, 77 T.C. 1361 (1981), the Tax Court held that gain due solely to inflation nevertheless constitutes income within the meaning of the Sixteenth Amendment; thus, the federal tax on such income is constitutional. Congress can establish the dollar as a unit of legal value independent of the purchasing power that a dollar might possess.

From time to time, proposals have been made to adjust a taxpayer's basis in property to reflect changes in the cost of living. If adopted, such a proposal would preclude the imposition of an income tax on appreciation that is attributable to inflation. To date, no such proposal has been adopted.

§ 16.1200.   Cost Reflecting Unlawful Expenditure. Prior to the Tax Reform Act of 1969, business expenses were sometimes held to be nondeductible on the ground that the allowance of a deduction would frustrate public policy. In 1969, Congress expressly disallowed deductions for certain business expenses (e.g., illegal expenses). That statutory disallowance was intended to be exclusive; hence, the public policy exception no longer applies to business expenses (or profit-oriented expenses under IRC § 212) that are not expressly barred by statute. See Treas. Reg. § 1.162–1(a) and **§ 10.5000.** It is possible that the public policy exception continues to apply to deductions allowed for losses and for nonbusiness and non-profit oriented expenses. *Mazzei v. Commissioner*, 61 T.C. 497 (1974); *Conley v. Commissioner*, 36 T.C.M. 1644 (1977); *Lincoln v. Commissioner*, 50 T.C.M. 185 (1985); see **§§ 7.1000, 10.5400** and **10.5500.** In any event, in the absence of a statutory provision, the public policy exception generally will not apply to bar a taxpayer from recovering his cost of an item on its disposition even though the cost represents an unlawful expenditure. *Sullenger v. Commissioner*, 11 T.C. 1076 (1948). However, the availability of such costs as an offset to an amount realized may be barred by statute. In this regard, note that Treas. Reg. § 1.471–3(d) provides that the "cost" of an item "shall not include an amount which is of a type for which a deduction would be disallowed under section 162(c), (f) or (g) and the regulations thereunder in the case of a business expense."

§ 16.1300.   Part Gift, Part Sale. When a taxpayer sells property for less than its value and the difference constitutes a gift to the purchaser (and not merely an arm's length bargain), the taxpayer cannot realize a loss on the sale. Treas. Reg. § 1.1001–1(e). If the amount paid exceeds the taxpayer's basis in the transferred property, the taxpayer will recognize a gain in the amount of such excess.

Treas. Reg. § 1.1001–1(e). Unless the part gift, part sale is made to a qualified charity, the taxpayer's entire basis is allocated to the amount realized in determining his gain. If the part gift, part sale is made to a qualified charity, the taxpayer's basis must be allocated between the portion that was sold and the portion that was given away. IRC § 1011(b); see §§ **9.3000–9.3100.**

§ 16.1310.   Illustration. *X* sold Blackacre to his son, *S*, for $10,000. *X* had a basis of $30,000 in Blackacre, and the value of Blackacre at the time of sale was $25,000. The $15,000 difference between the value of Blackacre and the amount paid by *S* constitutes a gift to *S*. Even though *X* received an amount which was $20,000 less than his basis in Blackacre, *X* did not realize a loss on the sale.

§ 16.1320.   Disguised Sales. In appropriate circumstances, a transfer for which no direct consideration is paid by the transferee nevertheless may be treated as part gift, part sale. For example, consider the transfer of encumbered property [discussed at §§ **16.1510–16.1520**], and consider a transfer made subject to the transferee's payment of the gift tax [discussed at § **16.1550**].

§ 16.1400.   Sale of a Term Interest.

§ 16.1410.   Disregard of Basis. When a taxpayer sells or otherwise disposes of a "term interest in property" that the taxpayer had acquired from a spouse or by gift or inheritance, then the taxpayer's gain (or loss) is determined without allocating to the taxpayer any part of the uniform basis of the property as determined under IRC §§ 1014 (inheritance), 1015 (gifts), or 1041 (transfer from a spouse or former spouse). In determining the gain from such a sale, the taxpayer's basis in the term interest will be zero. IRC § 1001(e). The effect of this provision is to treat the entire proceeds received from the sale of certain term interests as income to the vendor. The significance of this provision is noted in an illustration at § **20.3500.**

Note that IRC § 273 prohibits a depreciation or amortization deduction for a term interest that was acquired by gift, bequest or inheritance. Also, IRC § 167(e) precludes a depreciation or amortization deduction for a taxpayer's term interest for any period during which the remainder interest in such property is held (directly or indirectly) by a person related to the taxpayer (i.e., a person bearing a relationship to the taxpayer described in IRC § 267(b) or (e)). When § 167(e) applies, the disallowed depreciation or amortization deduction nevertheless reduces the taxpayer's basis in his term interest. IRC § 167(e)(3)(A). With a few exceptions, the amount of the disallowed deduction that reduces the taxpayer's basis in the term interest will be added to the remainderman's basis in his interest. IRC § 167(e)(3)(B), (4)(A). The overlap of IRC §§ 167 and 273 is cured by granting priority to § 273; hence, IRC § 167(e) does not apply to a term interest if IRC § 273 is applicable. IRC § 167(e)(2)(A). Note also that IRC §§ 273 and 167(e) prevent only the depreciation of the taxpayer's term interest; if the underlying property to which the term interest relates is depreciable, part (or all) of that depreciation deduction may be allocated to the taxpayer under IRC § 167(d) and deducted by the taxpayer. Any such allocated deduction will reduce the taxpayer's basis.

§ 16.1420. Definition of "Term Interest." A "term interest in property" means: (a) a life interest in property; (b) an interest in property for a term of years; or (c) an income interest in a trust. IRC § 1001(e)(2).

§ 16.1430. Exception. The taxpayer is entitled to use his basis in a term interest in property if the sale or disposition of the term interest is part of a transaction in which the entire interest in the property is transferred (e.g., both the income and remainder interests are transferred). IRC § 1001(e)(3).

§ 16.1440. Illustration 1. *X* died on January 1, Year One, and bequeathed 1,000 shares of Win All, Inc. stock in trust, the income from which is to be paid to *X*'s 48–year-old widow, *W*, for her life, and upon *W*'s death, the trust corpus is to be distributed to *X*'s daughter, *D*. The value of the 1,000 shares of Win All, Inc. stock at *X*'s death was $500,000, and *X*'s executor did not elect the alternate valuation date. The basis of the stock is $500,000 (its value at the time of *X*'s death). *W*'s basis in her income interest in the trust under IRC § 1014 is determined by utilizing tables provided by the Service that allocate the $500,000 basis of the stock between the life income beneficiary (*W*) and the remainderman (*D*). Assume that the tables initially allocate $430,000 of the stocks basis to *W* and $70,000 to *D*. Although *W*'s life interest (a term interest) has an exhaustible life, *W* is not permitted any deduction for depreciation or amortization of her basis. IRC § 273. On February 1, Year One, *W* sold her income interest in the trust to her nephew, *N*, for its fair market value of $400,000. *W*'s basis in the income interest is disregarded, and *W* recognized a gain of $400,000 on the sale. Treas. Reg. § 1.1014–5(c), Ex. (1). *N* has a basis of $400,000 in the income interest that he purchased, and *N* can amortize and deduct that basis over the period of *W*'s life expectancy.

§ 16.1450. Illustration 2. The same facts apply as in § 16.1440 except that on February 1, Year One, *D* sold her remainder interest in the trust to *N* for $75,000. Thus, in effect, *W* and *D* joined together to transfer the entire interest in the trust to *N*. Consequently, assuming that the sales made by *W* and *D* were integrated parts of a unified transaction, *W*'s basis is not disregarded, and she recognized a loss of $30,000 ($430,000 basis minus $400,000 amount realized). IRC § 1001(e)(3); see *McAllister v. Commissioner*, 157 F.2d 235 (2d Cir. 1946). *D* recognized a gain of $5,000.

§ 16.1500. Amount Realized. The amount realized from a sale or other disposition of property is the sum of the money received plus the fair market value of any property (other than money) received. Treas. Reg. § 1.1001–1(a).

§ 16.1510. Encumbered Property. When encumbered property is transferred, the amount realized by the transferor includes the amount of the encumbrances on the property plus any personal obligation of the transferor that is assumed by the transferee. *Crane v. Commissioner*, 331 U.S. 1 (1947). This rule is part of the so-called "*Crane* doctrine," which doctrine is sometimes referred to as the "*Tufts* doctrine" instead of *Crane*. The *Crane* doctrine applies when the debt that constitutes the encumbrance on the property is a nonrecourse debt. In the case of a nonrecourse debt, the fair market value of the encumbered property is not relevant to a determination of the tax consequences of a transfer, including a transfer to the creditor. The treatment of a transfer subject to a nonrecourse debt when the fair market value of the encumbered property is less than the outstanding debt is described at § 16.1511. The treatment of a transfer of encumbered property when the debt is a recourse debt is described at §§ 16.1511–1–16.1511–3.

§ 16.1511. Nonrecourse Debt in Excess of Value. A nonrecourse debt is one for which the debtor has no personal liability to repay and for which, upon default, the creditor can collect only by foreclosing on the property securing the debt. When encumbered property is transferred and the amount of nonrecourse debt secured by the encumbrance is greater than the fair market value of the property, the question arises as to whether the amount realized by the transferor under the *Crane* doctrine includes the excess of the debt over the property's value. In an often cited footnote in the *Crane* case (fn. 37), the Supreme Court suggested *in dictum* that the excess of nonrecourse debt over the fair market value will not be included in the amount realized by the transferor. In a case decided a few years after *Crane*, this suggestion was rejected by the Tax Court. The Commissioner also rejected it in Rev. Rul. 76–111. Treas. Reg. § 1.1001–2(b), promulgated in 1980, repudiates fn. 37 and treats the amount realized by the taxpayer as including the entire debt even if the fair market value of the transferred property is less than the debt. See also Treas. Reg. § 1.1001–2(c), Ex. (7). The Supreme Court laid this issue to rest in 1983 when the Court repudiated fn. 37 and held that the entire amount of the debt is included in the transferor's gross income regardless of the value of the transferred property. *Commissioner v. Tufts*, 461 U.S. 300 (1983). For this purpose, it makes no difference whether the encumbered property is transferred to the creditor or to a third party. The *Tufts* application of the *Crane* doctrine principle has been codified in several recent statutory provisions; e.g., IRC §§ 311(b)(2), 336(b), 7701(g). But see § 752(c).

§ 16.1511–1. Recourse Debt in Excess of Value— Transfer to Creditor Who Cancels Debt.

A recourse debt is a debt which the debtor is personally liable to repay. If a taxpayer holds property that is encumbered by a recourse debt of a greater amount than the value of the property, and if the taxpayer transfers the property to the creditor, the tax consequence of that transfer depends upon whether it is made in partial or in full satisfaction of the debt. If the creditor agrees to cancel the debt in exchange for receiving the property even though the property's value is less than the amount of the debt, then the transaction is divided into two parts for purposes of applying the tax rules. First, the difference between the amount of the recourse debt and the value of the property is treated as a cancellation of indebtedness, which will be included in the taxpayer's gross income under IRC § 108 as ordinary income unless one of the exceptions to IRC § 108 is applicable. Treas. Reg. § 1.1001–2(a)(2), (c), Ex. (8). The balance of the recourse debt is treated as the amount realized on the disposition of the encumbered property; the difference between the amount realized and the taxpayer's adjusted basis in the property will constitute a gain or loss, which typically will be either a capital gain or loss or a section 1231 gain or loss. *Ibid.*

§ 16.1511–1A. **Illustration.** *F*, who is solvent, holds Blackacre (unimproved land). *F*'s basis in Blackacre is $25,000. Blackacre is encumbered by a $45,000 mortgage for which *F* has a personal liability (i.e., the mortgage debt is a recourse debt). The fair market value of Blackacre is $40,000. *F* transfers Blackacre to the mortgagee who agrees to cancel the mortgage. The mortgagee, who is a bank, was not the person who had sold Blackacre to *F*. *F* has $5,000 of cancellation of indebtedness income. The exception to income treatment provided by IRC § 108(e)(5) is inapplicable since the mortgagee was not the person who sold the property to *F*, and the insolvency exception is inapposite.

In addition, *F* received $40,000 as the amount realized on the disposition of Blackacre, and so *F* recognized a gain of $15,000 on that disposition. Treas. Reg. § 1.1001–2(c), Ex. (8). The gain likely is a capital gain.

§ 16.1511–1B. **Rationale for Different Treatment of Recourse and Nonrecourse Debts.** As noted above, when property that is encumbered by a nonrecourse debt is transferred to the creditor, the entire amount of the debt is treated as an amount realized by the transferor even when the amount of the debt is greater than the value of the transferred property. However, if the debt is a recourse debt and if the debt is greater than the value of the property, then if the creditor cancels the debt, the difference between the amount of the debt and the value of the property constitutes a cancellation of indebtedness. What justification is there for this difference in treatment?

If a loan is made to a taxpayer on a nonrecourse basis, the lender implicitly agrees to accept the encumbered property as full payment for the outstanding balance of the debt if the debtor does not satisfy the debt in cash or other property. In effect, the parties agree at arms' length that the property will be treated by them as never having a value that is less than the amount of the outstanding debt. So, if the property is acquired by the creditor as the final payment on the debt, there is reason to treat the property as having been valued by the creditor and the debtor at a figure that is equal to the outstanding debt. The treatment of the entire debt as consideration for the transferred property in such cases is warranted by the usual rule that a value set at an arms' length bargain will not be disturbed by the tax authorities.

On the other hand, when the debt is a recourse debt, the creditor has not consented at the time of the loan to treat the underlying property as never having a value that is less than the outstanding debt. To the contrary, the creditor has retained the right to collect from the debtor any deficiency in the payment received that results from an inadequacy in the value of the encumbered property. So, if the creditor agrees to forego his right to collect the deficiency from the debtor, that constitutes a forgiveness by the creditor of that portion of the debt. The regulation reflects the reality that the creditor does forgive a portion of the debt when he chooses not to enforce his right to require the debtor to make-up the unpaid portion of the debt.

§ 16.1511–2. Recourse Debt in Excess of Value of Property—Transfer to Creditor Who Does Not Cancel Debt. If the creditor who acquires the encumbered property does not cancel the recourse debt, the excess of that debt over the value of the property is not satisfied by the transfer. The debtor continues to be personally liable to the creditor for the repayment of the unsatisfied amount. There is no reason to assume that the debtor will not repay that amount. While the authors know of no authoritative resolution of this issue, it appears to the authors that there is no cancellation of indebtedness in that circumstance. The amount of the debt equal to the property's fair market value should be treated as the amount realized on the disposition of the property, and the balance of the debt remains outstanding, albeit no longer secured by any property.

§ 16.1511–3. Recourse Debt in Excess of Value of Property—Transfer to Third Party Who Assumes the Debt. If the debtor transfers the encumbered property to a third party who assumes personal liability for the recourse debt, the debtor remains secondarily liable for the debt if there is a default and the property is inadequate to satisfy the debt. One possible treatment of this transaction, which however was rejected by the regulations, would be to limit the amount realized by the debtor to the fair market value of the property. Instead, Treas. Reg. § 1.1001–2(a)(4)(ii) treats the debtor as having been discharged of the entire recourse debt in such cases. The treatment mandated by the regulation avoids administrative difficulties that would be encountered if there were no immediate tax consequence for the excess debt since the matter would then have to be kept open until it could be determined whether the third party, the debtor or neither will actually pay the excess amount of the debt. It is much simpler administratively to assume that the third party will pay the entire debt since he assumed personal liability to do so. Consequently, it appears that the entire amount of the recourse debt will be included in the amount realized by the debtor on the disposition of the property. The debtor and the third party are dealing at arms' length, and they have arrived at an agreement under which the purchaser is willing to undertake personal liability for the entire debt as payment for the property, and so the parties should be deemed to have treated the property as having a value equal to the debt.

§ 16.1512. Transfer Subject to a Liability That Was Incurred on Taxpayer's Acquisition of the Transferred Property. If a taxpayer incurs a liability by reason of the acquisition of property, the taxpayer's basis in the property typically will reflect that liability; that is, the likelihood that the taxpayer will satisfy the liability is deemed sufficient to treat the taxpayer as having paid the amount as part of the cost of the property. Where the liability is included in the taxpayer's basis, the taxpayer's transfer of the property, subject to the unpaid balance of that liability, presents a situation where it is clear that the taxpayer will not satisfy that amount of the liability which will be paid by the transferee or by some other party. The inclusion of the balance of the liability in the amount realized by the taxpayer is required by the fact that the taxpayer previously enjoyed a tax benefit from that liability in having obtained an increased basis in the property on the assumption that the taxpayer would eventually pay that amount to the creditor. The failure of the taxpayer to make that payment (as evidenced by the transfer of the property) causes the liability to be included in the amount realized under an approach that is similar to the tax benefit rule. See § **2.3000.** If a liability incurred on the acquisition of property is not to be taken into account in determining the taxpayer's basis in that property, the unpaid balance of the liability will not be included in the amount realized by the taxpayer on transferring the property. Treas. Reg. § 1.1001–2(a)(3).

§ **16.1512–1. Illustration 1.** *M* died owning Blackacre having a fair market value of $100,000 and subject to a mortgage of $115,000. *M*'s executor did not elect the alternate valuation date. *M* devised Blackacre to *D* who took the property subject to the mortgage. While it is not settled, it is likely that *D*'s basis in Blackacre will be $100,000 (the fair market value at *M*'s death). Cf., Treas. Reg. § 1.1001–2(c), Ex. (8); Rev. Rul. 80–42. Two years later, *D* transfers Blackacre to *X* (an unrelated party) for $5,000 cash, and *X* took the property subject to the mortgage, the outstanding balance of which was still $115,000. Assuming that the author correctly determined that *D*'s initial basis in Blackacre was $100,000, only $100,000 of the outstanding debt will be included in the amount realized by *D* (plus, of course, the $5,000 cash that *D* received).

§ **16.1512–2. Illustration 2.** The same facts apply as in § **16.1512–1** except that *D* made payments on the principal of the mortgage before transferring it to *X* so that, at the time of transfer, the unpaid balance was $105,000. In this circumstance, the result is unclear. Should the amount excluded from the amount that *D* realized be $15,000, or $5,000, or should it be 15,000/115,000 x $105,000? Should the $10,000 that *D* previously paid on the principal of the mortgage be added to her basis so that only $5,000 of the debt taken over by *X* will be excluded from the amount realized by *D*?

§ **16.1512–3. Illustration 3.** HUD, a government agency, insured a mortgage on realty purchased by the taxpayer. After taxpayer's default, HUD acquired the mortgage.

HUD then paid the real estate taxes when they became due, and HUD charged taxpayer for interest payments on the mortgage debt. Taxpayer did not make any payments to HUD, and the latter added to the principal of taxpayer's mortgage debt the taxes that HUD had paid and the interest that was owing to HUD. These additions amounted to advances of funds by HUD to taxpayer. The mortgage debt was a nonrecourse debt. Taxpayer accrued the property tax and interest obligations and deducted the accrued items from its gross income. Subsequently, taxpayer defaulted on the debt, and HUD took title to the encumbered realty. At that time, the value of the realty was less than the amount of the nonrecourse debt. The entire amount of the debt, including the amounts representing advancements made by HUD to taxpayer, constitute an amount realized by taxpayer. Even though the advancements were not included in taxpayer's basis, they are included in his amount realized. See *Allan v. Commissioner*, 856 F.2d 1169 (8th Cir. 1988); § **16.2220.**

§ **16.1513.** **Insolvent Transferor.** The solvency or insolvency of a transferor does not affect the amount realized by the transferor under the *Crane* doctrine. In *Estate of Delman v. Commissioner*, 73 T.C. 15 (1979), property acquired through a nonrecourse debt was repossessed by the seller, and the purchaser was insolvent both before and after the repossession. The Tax Court held that the repossession constituted a sale or exchange under the *Crane* doctrine; thus, the forgiveness of indebtedness rules of IRC § 108 and of the common law doctrine enunciated by the Supreme Court in *Kirby Lumber* [see § **2.1210**] are inapplicable. The unpaid balance of the nonrecourse debt constituted an amount realized by the purchaser and caused the recognition of gain to the extent that the balance of the debt exceeded the purchaser's basis in the repossessed property.

§ **16.1514.** **Gift of Property Subject to Nonrecourse Debt.** A question has arisen as to whether a transfer of property subject to a nonrecourse debt will cause the debt to be an amount realized by the transferor if no other consideration was paid. In other words, for a sale or exchange to occur under the *Crane* doctrine, is it sufficient that the taxpayer is treated as having realized an amount under *Crane* or must the taxpayer have intended to sell or exchange the property as contrasted to making a gift? While this issue usually will arise only when the liability in question exceeds the taxpayer's basis, when such a transfer is made to a qualified charity, the allocation of basis required by IRC § 1011(b) may cause the recognition of gain by the taxpayer in some circumstances (even in some circumstances where the transferor's basis in the transferred property is greater than the outstanding liability) regardless of the fact that the transfer was intended to be a gift. See *Estate of Levine v. Commissioner*, 634 F.2d 12 (2d Cir. 1980), aff'g 72 T.C. 780 (1979). The treatment of such donative transfers to a charitable donee is discussed in Rev. Rul. 81–163. See §§ **9.3000—9.3100.**

A somewhat similar type of problem arises when a gift is made on condition that the donee pay any gift taxes imposed on the donor for making the gift (the so-called "net gift" transaction). The nature of this problem and the Supreme Court's resolution of it are discussed at § **16.1550.**

§ **16.1515. Transfer in Trust for Spouse or Former Spouse.** In general, no gain or loss is recognized on a transfer of property, outright or in trust, to or for a spouse (or a former spouse if incident to a divorce). IRC § 1041; §§ **2.1461– 2.1462–2.** This nonrecognition provision applies to such transfers regardless of whether made gratuitously or as part of a sale or exchange. One exception to this provision is that gain will be recognized on a transferor of property in trust for a spouse (or former spouse) to the extent that the sum of the liabilities assumed or accepted by the trust exceed the transferor's basis in the transferred property. IRC § 1041(e). A second exception arises when the transfer is made in trust and the transferred property is an installment obligation. IRC § 453B(g).

§ **16.1520. Illustration.** *X* sold Blackacre to *Y*. At the time of sale, Blackacre was subject to a mortgage, the outstanding balance of which was $30,000. *X* had no personal obligation to satisfy that $30,000 mortgage. *X*'s adjusted basis in Blackacre at the time of sale was $38,000. In payment for Blackacre, *Y* paid *X* $15,000 cash, and *Y* took Blackacre subject to the outstanding $30,000 mortgage. The amount realized by *X* on the sale was $45,000 ($15,000 cash plus the $30,000 mortgage), and, consequently, *X* realized a gain of $7,000 ($45,000 amount realized minus $38,000 basis). It should be noted that Y's basis in Blackacre immediately after purchasing it is $45,000 ($15,000 cash paid plus the $30,000 mortgage).

§ 16.1530.   Expenses of Sale. Certain expenses of selling property (such as commissions and brokerage fees) are not deductible expenses but instead reduce the amount realized on the sale and thereby reduce the gain realized (or increase the loss realized) on the sale. Treas. Reg. § 1.263(a)–2(e). But see **§ 1.7110.**

§ 16.1540.   Selling Commissions. Selling commissions, such as brokerage fees on the sale of stock, constitute a selling expense and, thus, typically reduce the amount realized on the sale; except for "dealers" in securities, such commissions are not treated as a deductible expense. Treas. Reg. § 1.263(a)–2(e).

§ 16.1550.   Transfer Subject to Gift Tax (Net Gifts). If a donor makes a gift on which a gift tax is payable, the donor is primarily liable for the payment of the gift tax. If the donor fails to pay the gift tax, the donee is obligated to make that payment. If a donor makes a gift subject to a condition that the donee pay the gift tax on that transfer, the payment of the gift tax by the donee satisfies a legal obligation of the donor and so is treated as consideration paid by the donee to the donor. Such transactions are sometimes referred to as "net gift" transactions—i.e., the amount of the gift is the "net" of the value of the transferred property reduced by the amount of gift tax paid by the donee. While the initial court decisions were contrary, it is now settled that the gift tax paid by a donee in a net gift transaction constitutes consideration received by the donor for income tax purposes. *Diedrich v. Commissioner*, 457 U.S. 191 (1982). Consequently, the donor will recognize income to the extent (if any) that the gift tax paid by the donee exceeds the donor's adjusted basis in the transferred property.

§ 16.1551.   Illustration. R transferred Blackacre (unimproved land) to her daughter, L. At that time, the fair market value of Blackacre was $100,000, and R had an adjusted basis of $12,000 in Blackacre. The transfer was made subject to the condition that L pay any gift tax imposed on the transfer. The gift tax was $20,000, and L paid the tax. R recognized a gain of $8,000 on this transaction.

§ 16.1552.   Computation of Donor's Gain. The amount of a donor's gain from a net gift transaction is equal to the difference between the gift tax on the transaction and the donor's basis in the transferred property. In a net gift transaction, the gift tax on the transaction is determined by applying the applicable gift tax rate to the amount of the gift—i.e., the difference between the fair market value of the transferred property and the amount of the gift tax imposed on the transaction. The difficulty is that the amount of the donor's gift and the amount of the gift tax imposed on the transaction are mutually dependent figures. There is an algebraic formula for determining those two figures, and so it is possible to ascertain the amount of the gift tax on the transaction and accordingly to determine the amount of gain realized by the donor.

§ 16.1553.   Donee's Basis. A net gift transaction is one type of a part-sale, part-gift transaction. A transferee's basis in property acquired in a part-sale, part-gift transaction is equal to the greater of: (1) the amount of consideration paid by the transferee or (2) the adjusted basis of the transferor in the transferred property. Treas. Reg. § 1.1015–4(a); **§ 2.4243.** In the circumstance where the gift tax on the transaction is greater than the donor's adjusted basis in the transferred property (and so, the donor recognized a gain), the donee's basis in the transferred property is at least equal to the amount of consideration paid by the donee (i.e., the donee's payment of the gift tax is the consideration paid by the donee). In addition, the amount of gift tax paid on the appreciated element of the transferred property is added to the basis that the donee otherwise would have in the transferred property, and the sum is the amount of the donee's basis. IRC § 1015(d)(6); Treas. Reg. § 1.1015–4(a); §§ **2.4230, 2.4244.** While the increase to a donee's basis cannot raise it to an amount in excess of the fair market value of the transferred property, the addition to a donee's basis of the gift tax paid on a net gift will never cause the donee's basis to exceed the fair market value of the transferred property; and so that limitation has no effect on a net gift transaction. In the situation where the gift tax is greater than the donor's basis, then the entire amount of the gift to the donee is a gift of appreciated property, and so the entire amount of the gift tax payment is an adjustment to the donee's basis. Thus, when the gift tax is greater than the donor's basis, the donee's basis in the transferred property will be an amount equal to double the gift tax imposed on the transaction.

§ 16.1554.   Illustration. *X* made a gift of unimproved Blackacre to *Y*, subject to *Y*'s payment of any gift tax imposed on the transaction. The fair market value of Blackacre was $450,000, and *X* had a basis of $50,000 in that property. The gift tax on the transaction was $120,000, and *Y* paid that amount. *X* recognized a gain of $70,000 on the part-sale, part-gift transaction. *Y*'s basis in Blackacre is equal to the sum of the consideration paid by *Y* ($120,000) and the gift tax imposed on the gift portion of the transaction (i.e., $120,000). Thus, *Y*'s basis in Blackacre is $240,000.

§ 16.1560.   Receipt of Property with Unascertainable Value. The amount realized by a transferor on an exchange of property is measured by the fair market value of the property received by the transferor in exchange. If the property received is of a type that is not traded on a market, it may be necessary to value it by estimating what a hypothetical buyer would pay for the item and what a hypothetical seller would charge for the item if both the buyer and the seller were in possession of all relevant facts and were under no compulsion to buy or to sell. However, if the property received is one which cannot be readily valued and is one on which self-liquidating payments will be made over a period of time (for example, a second mortgage on realty when the amount that will actually be collected from the debtor is uncertain), it may not be necessary to close the transaction when the transferor receives the right to such payments. If so, in such cases, rather than close the transaction when the transferor receives the instrument representing the right to the liquidating payments and so to value the instrument that the transferor received on the basis of speculation as to the amount that will actually be collected by the transferor, the transaction will instead be left open so that no gain will be recognized by the transferor until the amount collected by him under the instrument exceeds his unrecaptured basis in the property transferred by him. In such cases, after recovering his basis, all subsequent payments received by the transferor will be included in the transferor's gross income. This method of reporting gain is sometimes called the "cost recovery method." *Burnet v. Logan*, 283 U.S. 404 (1931) is the landmark case on keeping a transaction open when the value of the property received is not ascertainable because there is no market for it. See also *McShain v. Commissioner*, 71 T.C. 998

(1979); but see *Warren Jones Co. v. Commissioner*, 524 F.2d 788 (9th Cir. 1975).

§ 16.1561. Installment Sale Treatment. The Installment Sales Revision Act of 1980 amended IRC § 453 to permit installment reporting of gain from sales when the amount payable is subject to contingencies. IRC § 453(j)(2). The Senate Finance Committee's report on the 1980 Act states that as a consequence of so extending installment reporting treatment, the cost recovery method should be allowed only in "extraordinary cases involving sales for a contingent price when the purchaser's obligation cannot reasonably be ascertained." For a detailed discussion of the installment method of reporting gain, see §§ **20.5000–20.5540.**

§ 16.1562. Illustration. *L* owned 6¼% of the stock of the A & H Iron Co. (A & H), a publicly held corporation. A & H owned a 12% interest in a 97–year lease to mine iron ore from the *M* mine. The lease agreement to mine *M* did not establish any maximum or minimum tonnage to be mined per year, and the actual tons of iron ore that were allocated to A & H varied from year to year. *L* had a basis of $250,000 in her shares of A & H stock. In Year One, the shareholders of A & H sold their shares to the *Y* Corporation for a cash payment plus the right to 60 cents for every ton of ore thereafter acquired either by *Y* or by A & H under the lease agreement to mine *M*. For her shares, *L* received $140,000 cash and the right to 6¼% of the 60 cents per ton payments to be paid by *Y* for each ton of ore it or A & H acquires under the lease. The government treated the sale by the shareholders as a closed transaction. The government estimated the amount of iron ore in the *M* mine, and it calculated the present value of *L*'s right to 6¼% of 60 cents times A & H's 12% share of the iron ore contained in the *M* mine. The government treated the sum of the cash paid to *L* plus the present value of her right to a share of the iron ore payments as the amount realized by her on the sale. However, in *Burnet v. Logan*, § **16.1560**, on similar facts, the Supreme Court held that "it was impossible to determine with fair certainty the market value" of the agreement by *Y* to pay 60 cents per ton, and, consequently, the Court held that the transaction was to remain open until the payments were completed. The Court held that *L* did not recognize any gain until the cash payments to her (including the initial cash payment) exceeded her basis. Once the payments to *L* exceed her basis, every dollar received by her thereafter will constitute a gain to *L* from the sale of her A & H stock. Note, however, that a portion of *all* payments received more than six months after the sale *may* be treated as interest on the deferred amount and so taxable as ordinary income. See IRC § 483.

§ 16.1563. Extraordinary Circumstances. In an exchange of property, the property received typically will have an ascertainable fair market value, and it is only in extraordinary circumstances that the property cannot be valued so that the cost recovery rule is employed. Treas. Reg. § 1.1001–1(a). See also Rev. Rul. 58–402 (but compare *Dorsey v. Commissioner*, 49 T.C. 606 (1968) where the Tax Court rejected the general thrust of the Revenue Ruling). This is especially true in light of the expansion of IRC § 453 by the 1980 Act as indicated in **§ 16.1561.** In *Tribune Publishing Co. v. United States*, 836 F.2d 1176 (9th Cir., 1988) the Ninth Circuit held that the cost recovery method of *Burnet v. Logan* does not apply when it is clear that the taxpayer realized a gain on the exchange even though the amount of that gain is uncertain. According to the Ninth Circuit, it is only where it is uncertain that the taxpayer had any gain that the cost recovery method can apply. However, apart from the applicability of the cost recovery method, a difficult question remains as to whether a purchaser's bare unsecured nonnegotiable promise to pay money to the seller is the equivalent of cash as required by the cash receipts and disbursements method for reporting the seller's gain. See *Warren Jones Co. v. Commissioner* in **§ 16.1560.**

§ 16.1600. Material Differences in Exchanged Properties. Treas. Reg. § 1.1001–1(a) states that an exchange of one item of property for another that differs *materially*, either in kind or in extent, will trigger realization of gain or loss. In *Cottage Savings Assoc. v. Commissioner*, 499 U.S. 554 (1991), the Supreme Court sustained the validity of that regulatory provision and adopted a very broad construction as to what constitutes a *material* difference in exchanged properties. In *Cottage Savings*, a taxpayer was permitted to realize and recognize a loss on what amounted to an exchange of participating interests in 252 residential mortgages for participating interests in 305 different residential mortgages. While the mortgages were secured by different properties and had different obligors, they were economically equivalent interests. The Supreme Court held that to constitute materially different properties, it was necessary only that the exchanged properties "embody legally distinct entitlements." The Court held that the differences in obligors and security for the two sets of mortgages were sufficient to satisfy that requirement.

§ 16.1700. The Treatment of the Modification of A Debt Instrument as an Exchange of Properties. As noted in § **16.1600**, an exchange of debt instruments will trigger a realization and recognition of gain or loss if the exchanged instruments differ materially either in kind or in extent. The Supreme Court's decision in *Cottage Savings*, § **16.1600**, gave a very broad construction to what constitutes a "material" difference. So, if *A* who holds a debt instrument of *B* transfers that instrument to *B* in exchange for a new debt instrument of *B* with materially different terms, the exchange will cause *A* to realize gain or loss on the exchange. That realized gain or loss will be recognized unless the exchange qualifies for nonrecognition under some statutory provision.

Instead of a holder and debtor's exchanging one debt instrument for another, the parties can simply modify the terms of the debt instrument that the holder possesses. Of course, if the modification of a debt results in reducing the amount of the debtor's obligation, that *may* trigger cancellation of indebtedness income to the debtor under IRC § 108. See § **2.1200** *et seq.* Regardless of whether the debtor recognized cancellation of indebtedness income, there is a question as to whether the modification of the terms of a debt instrument will be treated as the exchange of one debt instrument for a new debt instrument so as to trigger realization of gain or loss by the holder of the debt instrument.

§ 16.1710. Significant Modification. According to the regulations, a "significant modification" of a debt instrument is treated as an exchange of the original instrument for a new instrument that differs materially either in kind or in extent. Treas. Reg. § 1.1001–3(b). In other words, a significant modification of a debt will cause the holder of the debt to realize gain or loss. The regulation provides guidance for determining what constitutes a modification and whether a modification is significant for this purpose.

Modification. In general, a modification means any change of a legal right or obligation of the holder or issuer of a debt instrument regardless of whether the alteration is evidenced by an amendment of the instrument, or by the conduct of the parties, or otherwise. Treas. Reg. § 1.1001–3(c)(1). Certain changes in a debt instrument that are described in Treas. Reg. § 1.1001–3(c)(2) are not treated as a modification. For example, an alteration of rights or obligations that occurs pursuant to the original terms of the debt instrument does not constitute a modification; but if the alteration occurs because of one party's exercise or waiver of a right pursuant to a power granted by the terms of the original instrument, the alteration will be treated as a modification unless that party had the *unilateral* power to exercise or waive the right.

Significant. The proposed regulation lists a number of changes to a debt instrument some of which constitute a substantial modification and some of which do not. Treas. Reg. § 1.1001–3(e)(1)–(4). If a modification of a debt instrument is not one of the types included within that regulatory list, the test of whether that modification is "significant" turns upon the facts and circumstances of each such instance. Treas. Reg. § 1.1001–3(e)(1). A few of the items that the proposed regulation specifically categorizes as either significant or not are noted below.

(1) Yield. A change in the yield that a debt instrument provides (i.e., its effective interest rate) will be significant only if the resulting yield varies from the prior rate by more than a specified percentage. Treas. Reg. § 1.1001–3(e)(2).

(2) Timing or amount of payments. Some changes in the timing or amount of payments are significant and some are not. For example, the regulation provides a safe harbor if the deferred payments are payable no later than the lesser of five years or 50% of the original term of the instrument. Treas. Reg. § 1.1001–3(e)(3)(ii). Also, deferrals of de minimis payments are ignored. *Id.*

(3) Change of obligor. A change of the obligor of a debt instrument will usually be a significant modification, but in some circumstances it will not be. Treas. Reg. § 1.1001–3(e)(4). For example, a change in the obligor of a nonrecourse debt is not significant. The addition of a co-obligor on a debt instrument is not significant unless its purpose is to circumvent other rules concerning a change of obligors. *Id.*

(4) Change of security. A change in the collateral securing a recourse debt is a significant modification if it results in a "change in payment expectations" [defined below]. A change in the collateral securing a nonrecourse debt usually will be significant; however, a change of collateral will not be significant if the items of collateral are either fungible or of a type where the particular units pledged do not alter the nature of the secured

interest (e.g., government securities or securities of the same type and rating). Treas. Reg. § 1.1001–3(e)(4)(iv)(B). The subordination of a debt instrument to other debt of the issuer is a significant modification if it results in a change of payment expectations. Treas. Reg. § 1.1001–3(e)(4)(v). For this purpose, a "change in payment expectations" occurs if there is either a substantial enhancement or impairment of the obligor's capacity to meet the payment obligation of the debt instrument. Treas. Reg. § 1.1001–3(e)(4)(vi).

(5) Changes in the nature of the instrument. A change of a debt instrument to property that is not debt for federal tax purposes is significant. Also, with some exceptions, a modification is significant if a it changes a recourse debt instrument to a nonrecourse debt instrument or vice versa. Treas. Reg. § 1.1001–3(e)(5).

(6) Multiple changes. If a number of changes are made simultaneously to a debt instrument, no one of which would have constituted a significant modification, the cumulative effect of the several changes will not constitute a significant modification. Each change is examined separately, and only if one of them is significant will the modification cause a deemed exchange of debt instruments. But. when a number of changes to a debt instrument are made over a period of time and when, while no one of those changes was significant, they would have constituted a significant modification if they had taken place at the same time, the cumulative effect will be taken into account and the changes will be treated as a significant modification. For example, if several changes were made over a period of a few years to the maturity date of a debt instrument and if the final maturity date would have been a significant modification if all of the changes had been made at one time, the changes will constitute a significant modification. Treas. Reg. § 1.1001–3(f)(3).

§ 16.1720. Installment Instruments. The regulation does not apply to an installment debt instrument and does not affect the issue of whether modifications to such an instrument cause there to be a taxable disposition of it. At this writing, the cases and rulings indicate that changes in the terms of an installment obligation do not cause a disposition of that instrument. See **§ 20.5540.**

§ 16.2000. BASIS.

§ 16.2100. General. The adjusted basis of purchased property generally is determined under IRC § 1012. When a taxpayer acquires encumbered property, the basis problems are somewhat more difficult.

§ 16.2200. Encumbered Property. When a taxpayer purchases property subject to an encumbrance, the encumbrance is treated as part of the taxpayer's purchase price and accordingly is included in the taxpayer's basis. For this purpose, it does *not* matter whether the taxpayer has a personal obligation to pay the debt underlying the encumbrance on the property. Similarly, a taxpayer's basis in property includes the amount of debt undertaken by the taxpayer as part of the taxpayer's payment for the property. Thus, the amount of a nonrecourse promissory note issued by the taxpayer to the seller is included in the taxpayer's basis if the transaction is bona fide. *Siegel v. Commissioner*, 78 T.C. 659 (1982). A nonrecourse debt or note is a debt which the debtor has no personal liability to repay; thus, the creditor can enforce the debt only by foreclosing on the property securing the debt.

In their casebook on federal income taxation, Professors Gunn and Ward state that there are two exceptions to the general rule that includes an encumbrance in the purchaser's basis: (1) a mortgage so greatly in excess of the property's value that the purchaser is unlikely to pay it off usually will not be included in the purchaser's basis (the "reasonable security" approach), and (2) "contingent and indefinite" obligations of the purchaser are not included in basis. Gunn and Ward, *Federal Income Taxation* (West Pub. Co., 4th ed. 1998), p. 495 (and cases cited therein).

§ 16.2210. Illustration 1. *X* purchased Blackacre from *Y*. Blackacre was subject to a mortgage of $35,000. *X* paid *Y* $25,000 cash, and *X* took Blackacre subject to the mortgage. *X* did not *assume* the mortgage or otherwise undertake a personal obligation to pay the $35,000 debt. *X* is treated as having paid *Y* $60,000 ($25,000 cash plus the $35,000 mortgage), and, thus, *X* has a basis of $60,000 in Blackacre.

§ 16.2220. Illustration 2. *Z* owns Blackacre which has a value of $70,000, and a basis to *Z* of $15,000. *Z* acquired Blackacre in Year One. In Year Thirty, *Z* borrowed $30,000 from the Friendly National Bank and secured the loan by a mortgage on Blackacre. *Z* has no personal obligation to repay the loan, and the Bank's sole recourse on default is to foreclose on its mortgage. *Z* does not recognize a gain by borrowing the $30,000 even though the amount of the loan exceeds his basis, and *Z*'s basis in Blackacre is not affected by the mortgage since it is not a purchase-money mortgage. See *Woodsam Assoc., Inc. v. Commissioner*, 198 F.2d 357 (2d Cir. 1952). In Year Thirty–Two, Z sold Blackacre to D for $40,000 cash, and D took Blackacre subject to the $30,000 mortgage. Z's amount realized on the sale is $70,000 ($40,000 cash plus $30,000 mortgage), and since Z's basis in Blackacre was $15,000, Z realized a gain of $55,000.

§ 16.2300. Allocation of Basis.

§ 16.2310.   General. When a part of a larger property is sold, an equitable portion of the taxpayer's basis in the larger property is allocated to the part that was sold, and the taxpayer's gain or loss is computed accordingly. Treas. Reg. § 1.61–6(a). The equitable apportionment of basis is made according to the respective values of the several parts of the property, usually determined as of the date that the taxpayer acquired the property. See *Fairfield Plaza, Inc. v. Commissioner*, 39 T.C. 706 (1963), Acq.

§ 16.2311.   Illustration. X purchased unimproved Blackacre, a 20 acre tract, in Year One at a cost of $80,000. In Year One, the front ten acres of the tract were three times as valuable as the rear ten acres, but X purchased the entire 20 acres as a single tract. In Year Thirty–One, X divided Blackacre into two tracts of ten acres each, and X sold the rear ten acres to Y for $50,000. By Year Thirty–One, the front ten acres of the tract were only twice as valuable as the rear ten acres. X's basis in Blackacre ($80,000) must be allocated equitably between the front ten acres and the rear ten acres according to their respective values at the date that X purchased Blackacre (i.e., in Year One). Thus, one-fourth of the $80,000 basis ($20,000) is allocated to the rear ten acres, and X realized a gain of $30,000 ($50,000 amount realized minus $20,000 basis) on the sale in Year Thirty–One.

§ 16.2320.   Sale of Stocks. When a taxpayer acquired stock in a corporation on different dates or at different prices, the taxpayer's sale of some of the shares of the stock will be treated as the sale of the earliest stock acquired by him unless the actual shares sold are identified. Treas. Reg. § 1.1012–1(c)(1). In other words, unless the shares of stock sold by the taxpayer are identified, the stock is deemed to have been sold on a first-in, first-out (FIFO) basis. Identification of shares of stock can be accomplished by delivering to the transferee the actual certificates of the stock sold or, if the stock is held in the custody of a broker, by instructing the broker to sell specific shares. A written confirmation of that instruction from the broker within a reasonable time will be an acceptable identification. Treas. Reg. § 1.1012–1(c)(3). Other means of identification are discussed in Treas. Reg. § 1.1012–1(c).

§ 16.2330.   No Means of Allocations. If a taxpayer sells a part of property and no reasonable allocation of the taxpayer's basis in the property can be determined, the amount realized will reduce the basis of the property and no gain will be recognized if the taxpayer has sufficient basis. If the taxpayer's basis is reduced to zero, any excess received will be gain. *Inaja Land Co. v. Commissioner*, 9 T.C. 727 (1947), Acq. However, it will be a rare case where no allocation of basis can be determined. See *Gladden v. Commissioner*, 262 F.3d 851 (9th Cir. 2001) (for purpose of allocating basis to expected water rights on land, Ninth Circuit remanded case to determine whether comparisons could be made to purchases without expectation of water rights, in which case the premium attributable to the expectation of water rights would be its basis). The holding in *Inaja* rests on the analogous doctrine established in *Burnet v. Logan* [see §§ **16.1560–16.1562**] that in an exchange, the receipt of self-liquidating property that cannot be valued may cause the transaction to be kept open until the transferor collects the payments to be made on such property.

§ 16.2331.   Illustration. Taxpayer operated a private fishing club on the bank of a river. The taxpayer had a basis of $61,000 in the land on which the club was operated. The city of Los Angeles diverted polluted waters into the river abutting the fishing club and, thereby, greatly harmed the taxpayer's use of its property as a fishing preserve. The taxpayer collected a net of $49,000 from the city in release of all claims the taxpayer had against the city. In *Inaja*, § **16.2330**, the Tax Court held that the payment was received for a right of way or easement and for damage to the taxpayer's riparian rights, and that a portion of the taxpayer's $61,000 basis in the land should be allocated to the interests in the land for which the payment was received and only that portion constitutes the taxpayer's basis. However, the Court found that no apportionment could be made with reasonable accuracy, and, therefore, for purposes of determining the taxpayer's gain, the Court permitted the taxpayer to use his entire $61,000 basis in the land to offset the payment received. Thus, the taxpayer realized no gain or loss from the payment made by the city.

Thereafter, the taxpayer's adjusted basis in the land was $12,000 ($61,000 minus $49,000).

§ 16.3000.   SETTLEMENT OF OBLIGATION. The transfer of property in full or partial settlement of a pecuniary obligation is treated as a sale or exchange of the property. *United States v. Davis*, 370 U.S. 65 (1962). Cf., *Commissioner v. Keystone Consolidated Indus.*, 508 U.S. 152 (1993). This principle has been extended to cover the transfer of property by a decedent's executor to satisfy a pecuniary bequest made in the decedent's will and to cover a transfer of property by a trustee to satisfy a pecuniary gift. Treas. Reg. § 1.661(a)–2(f)(1); *Kenan v. Commissioner*, 114 F.2d 217 (2d Cir. 1940); see also Rev. Rul. 82–4. The satisfaction of pecuniary bequests with appreciated property will cause the estate to recognize a gain to the extent that the value of the property exceeds its estate tax value (i.e., its value at the date of the decedent's death or alternate valuation date). Similarly, the satisfaction of a pecuniary bequest with depreciated property (I.e., property whose basis exceeds its fair market value) will cause the estate to recognize a loss.

§ 16.3100.   Illustration 1. *D* died owning stock which had a value of $75,000 at *D*'s death, and *D*'s executor did not elect to use the alternate valuation date. Consequently, under IRC § 1014, the estate's basis in the stock is $75,000. *D*'s will bequeathed $100,000 to *X*. A year later, the value of the stock had increased to $100,000. *D*'s executor distributed the stock to *X* in satisfaction of the $100,000 pecuniary bequest. The distribution is treated as a taxable exchange of stock for *X*'s claim to $100,000, and *D*'s estate will recognize a gain of $25,000.

§ 16.3200.   Illustration 2. *D*'s will bequeathed to *B* properties from *D*'s probate estate, to be chosen by *D*'s executor, having an aggregate fair market value of a specified amount. The distribution of such assets from *D*'s estate to *B* is the satisfaction of a pecuniary bequest that causes the estate to recognize a gain or loss. Rev. Rul. 86–105.

§ 16.4000.   MARITAL TRANSFERS. Prior to 1984, when one spouse transferred property to the other in consideration of the release of marital rights (e.g., dower and the right to a forced share), the transfer was treated as a taxable exchange to the transferor spouse who realized a gain or loss in an amount equal to the difference between the value of the transferred property and its basis. *United States v. Davis*, 370 U.S. 65 (1962). Since 1984, no gain or loss is recognized on a transfer of property (other than an installment obligation transferred in trust) outright or in trust to or for the benefit of a spouse. IRC § 1041. This

provision applies to sales or exchanges of property as well as to gratuitous transfers. This provision also applies to transfers made to a former
spouse incident to a divorce. The operation of IRC § 1041 is described at
§ **2.1461.** However, when property is transferred to a trust for a spouse
(or former spouse) and when the amount of liabilities assumed or
accepted by the trust exceeds the transferor's basis in the property, the
transferor will recognize a gain in the amount of that excess. § **16.1515.**

§ **16.5000.   GIFTS OF APPRECIATED PROPERTY TO A POLIT-
ICAL ORGANIZATION.** If a person transfers appreciated property
(i.e., property whose value is greater than the transferor's basis therein)
to a political organization, the transferor will recognize a gain to the
extent that the property's value exceeds his basis therein. IRC § 84.

§ **16.5100.   Item by Item Determination.** The language of IRC
§ 84 suggests that it applies separately to each item of property
transferred by a donor to a political organization. If so, a donor who
transfers one appreciated asset and one depreciated asset to a political organization will be required to recognize a gain on the appreciated asset but will not be permitted to recognize a loss on the
depreciated asset (i.e., a depreciated asset is an asset whose value is
less than the transferor's basis therein). Cf., *Morris Investment Corp.
v. Commissioner*, 156 F.2d 748 (3d Cir, 1946); and Rev. Rul. 76–377.

CHAPTER SEVENTEEN

RECOGNITION OF GAIN OR LOSS ON THE DISPOSITION OF PROPERTY

§ 17.0000. RECOGNITION OF GAIN OR LOSS ON THE DISPOSITION OF PROPERTY.

§ 17.1000. GENERAL.

Any gain or loss that is *realized* on the disposition of property will also be *recognized* (i.e., taken into account for tax purposes) unless a statutory provision establishes that the gain or loss will not be recognized. IRC § 1001(c). It should be emphasized, however, that a recognized *loss* is not deductible unless some section of the Code grants a deduction for it.

§ 17.1100. Illustration.

X sold his personal home to Y for $40,000. X had a basis of $50,000 in his home. X recognized a loss of $10,000, but the loss is not deductible, because it will not qualify under IRC § 165(c) or any provision of the Code that authorizes a deduction. A deduction for a loss that is recognized from the sale of a personal residence likely is explicitly disallowed by IRC § 262 (denying a deduction for "personal, living, or family expenses"), but no deduction would be allowable even if IRC § 262 were deemed to be inapplicable.

§ 17.2000. NONRECOGNITION OF GAIN OR LOSS ON CERTAIN EXCHANGES OF PROPERTY.

§ 17.2100. General.

In the absence of a statutory provision of nonrecognition, the exchange of one property for another that differs materially from the one transferred will constitute a taxable exchange in which gain or loss will be both realized and recognized. There are a number of statutory provisions either requiring or permitting nonrecognition of gain or loss for certain kinds of exchanges. Several of those provisions are described in this chapter.

§ 17.2110. Illustration.

A owns 100 shares of stock of World Wide, Inc. having a fair market value of $10,000 and a basis of $6,000. B owns 200 shares of stock of Planet, Inc. having a value of $10,000 and a basis of $12,000. *A* and *B* exchange their stock holdings so that *A* acquires *B*'s 200 shares of Planet, Inc., and *B* acquires *A*'s 100 shares of World Wide, Inc. Since the stocks of separate corporations are materially different, *A* realized and recognized a gain of $4,000 on the exchange and *B* realized and recognized a loss of $2,000.

§ 17.3000. EXCHANGES OF LIKE–KIND PROPERTY. IRC § 1031 precludes recognition of gain or loss when property held for productive use in a trade or business or for investment is exchanged solely for property "of a like kind" to be held either for productive use in a trade or business or for investment. The requirement that the exchanged properties be held either for productive use in a trade or business or as an investment is satisfied when property held for productive use in a trade or business is exchanged for property to be held as an investment and vice versa. Treas. Reg. § 1.1031(a)–1(a). An exchange of property on which neither gain nor loss is recognized is sometimes referred to as a "tax-free exchange."

In connection with deferred exchanges that qualify for IRC § 1031 treatment (see **§ 17.3150–17.3155**), the property that a TP transfers in a like kind exchange is referred to as the "relinquished property," and the property that the TP acquired in the transaction is referred to as the "replacement property." See Treas. Reg. § 1.1031(k)–1(a). That same terminology is useful to describe the property in any type of § 1031 exchange.

§ 17.3100. Like Kind. The term "like kind" refers to the nature or character of the property; it does not refer to its grade or quality. Treas. Reg. § 1.1031(a)–1(b). Thus, an exchange of improved real property for unimproved realty constitutes an exchange of like kind. *Ibid.* Realty located outside the United States is not of like kind to realty located in the United States. IRC § 1031(h)(1). Also, personal property "used predominantly within the United States and personal property used predominantly outside the United States are not property of like kind." IRC § 1031(h)(2). The standards for determining the location of predominant use are set forth in IRC 1031(h)(2).

The regulations treat a leasehold interest in realty for a term of 30 years or more as property that is of like kind to a fee interest in realty. Treas. Reg. § 1.1031(a)–1(c). In *Jordan Marsh Co. v. Commissioner*, 269 F.2d 453 (2d Cir. 1959), a taxpayer had realized a loss on a sale of realty that it owned. As part of the plan of the transaction, the taxpayer immediately had leased back from the buyer the realty that it had sold. The taxpayer's lease was for a term of a little more than 30 years, and the taxpayer had an option to renew the lease for an additional 30 years if the taxpayer constructed buildings on the property. The price at which the property was sold equalled the fair market value of the property, and the rental payments under the lease were fair rents for the property. The Commissioner contended that the purported sale and leaseback was actually a like-kind exchange to which IRC § 1031 applied so that no loss was recognized by the taxpayer on the purported sale. The court held that IRC § 1031 did not apply and allowed the taxpayer to recognize its loss from the sale. If the purchase price of the property had been significantly less than its value and if the rental payments had not been a fair rate, there is a possibility that the transaction might have been treated as a disguised loan to the purported seller; in which event, the taxpayer would have been denied a loss deduction.

Certain types of properties that are listed in IRC § 1031(a)(2) are excluded from the nonrecognition that is otherwise mandated by that section of the Code. Thus, IRC § 1031 is *not* applicable to exchanges of stock in trade, property held primarily for sale, stocks, bonds, notes, other securities or evidences of debt or interest, partnership interests, certificates of trust, or choses in action. IRC § 1031(a)(2).

Prior to the Tax Reform Act of 1984, exchanges of partnership interests were not specifically excluded from IRC § 1031 nonrecognition. The exclusion was adopted because of the belief that partnership interests typically represent investments similar to other items already excluded from like-kind treatment. Court decisions prior to 1984 had limited IRC § 1031 treatment to exchanges of interests in partnerships holding similar underlying assets, but there was concern that this limitation might prove inadequate to deal with potential tax shelter abuse and administrative burdens.

The application of the § 1031(a)(2) exclusion from § 1031 nonrecognition treatment turns upon the substance of the taxpayer's interest as contrasted to the formal designation provided for that interest. For example in Rev. Rul. 92–105, the Commissioner treated a taxpayer's interest in an Illinois land trust as an interest in the realty that was held in the trust. The taxpayer had created the land trust and transferred to it Blackacre (real property that the taxpayer held as an investment). Under Illinois law, the taxpayer (as the beneficiary of the trust) had the exclusive control over and power to manage the realty, and the taxpayer had the exclusive right to receive rents or other earnings or proceeds from the property. The taxpayer (as beneficiary) was required to file all tax returns, pay all taxes and other liabilities with respect to the realty. The trustee's only responsibility was to hold the title to the property and to transfer the title at the direction of the taxpayer. Taxpayer transferred his interest in the Illinois land trust to a third party in exchange for Whiteacre, which taxpayer then held as an investment. The Commissioner determined in Rev. Rul. 92–105 that the nominal "trustee" of the land trust was merely an agent of the taxpayer, and so taxpayer's purported transfer of his interest in the land trust was actually a transfer of Blackacre itself. The Commissioner held that the exchange qualified for nonrecognition as a § 1031 like-kind exchange.

§ 17.3110. Personal Properties. Treas. Reg. § 1.1031(a)–2, provides a detailed statement of the manner in which the like-kind standard is to be applied to exchanges of personal property. As noted above, the like-kind standard for exchanges of realty is quite liberal—realties constitute like-kind properties regardless of whether they are improved or unimproved and regardless of the functional use to which the different items of realty are put. The only exception is an exchange of realty located in the United States for foreign realty. The standard for personal properties is more restricted. Personal properties are divided into three broad categories—(1) depreciable tangible personal property, (2) intangible personal property, and (3) nondepreciable tangible personal property. A like-kind exchange of personal properties must be of properties that fit within the same broad category, but that alone is not sufficient. The types of exchanges within each of those three categories that qualify as like-kind exchanges for purposes of IRC § 1031 are discussed below. Note that personal property predominantly used in the United States is *not* of like kind to personal property predominantly used outside the United States. IRC § 1031(h)(2).

§ 17.3111. Depreciable Tangible Personal Property. Many types of depreciable tangible personal properties are classified into so-called "General Asset Classes" for the purpose of determining the recovery period to be used in depreciating those assets under the Modified Accelerated Cost Recovery System (MACRS) that is applied by IRC § 168. The Asset Class into which a type of property is catalogued determines the item's "class life," which in turn controls the recovery period for depreciating that asset. See **§ 12.3411.** Currently, the classification of assets into General Asset Classes is established b y Rev. Proc. 87–56. These classifications may be modified from time to time in the future.

Treas. Reg. § 1.1031(a)–2(b)(1) states that depreciable tangible personal properties that are listed in the same General Asset Class are treated as like-kind property for purposes of IRC § 1031. The General Asset Classes to which this provision applies are the asset classes 00.11 through 00.28 and 00.4 of Rev. Proc. 87–56. For example, asset class 00.11 includes office furniture, fixtures, and equipment that is not a structural component of a building. This class includes such items as desks, files, safes, and communications equipment (other than communications equipment that is listed in another asset class). Asset class 00.21 includes certain airplanes and all helicopters. Asset class 00.22 includes automobiles and taxis. Asset class 00.23 lists only buses. Asset class 00.241 includes light general purpose trucks (i.e., the unloaded weight of the truck is less than 13,000 pounds). Asset class 00.242 includes heavy general-purpose trucks.

So, if an office desk were exchanged for an office safe, that would b e a like-kind exchange since the two items are included in the same asset class in Rev. Proc. 87–56. However, if a helicopter were exchanged for a heavy general purpose truck, that exchange will not be one of like-kind property because the two assets are listed in different asset classes and are not otherwise of like kind.

The same-class provision is merely a safe harbor for like-kind treatment. It is not a requirement. So, an exchange of tangible personal properties that are listed in different asset classes may nevertheless qualify for IRC § 1031 treatment if the assets are of like kind. Treas. Reg. § 1.1031(a)–2 states that, "In determining whether exchanged properties are of like kind, no inference is to be drawn from the fact that the properties are not of like class."

Certain tangible personal property assets are classified into "Product Classes" in the *Standard Industrial Classification Manual* sometimes referred to as the "SIC Manual," which is provided by the Executive Office of the President, Office of the Management and Budget. The assets listed in the SIC Manual are classified into one of the Product Classes that are listed in that Manual. Some types of assets that are classified in the Asset Classes of Rev. Proc. 87–56 also are included within one of the Product Classes listed in the SIC Manual. In such cases, for purposes of applying this safe harbor provision to IRC § 1031, the item's Product Class is ignored; only the Asset Class of the item is taken into account. Some types of assets that are omitted from Rev. Proc. 87–56's list of Asset Classes are included in the list of Product Classes in the SIC Manual. For those items, the Product Class category is used in the same manner as the Asset Class categories are used. In other words, if the assets that are exchanged are not included in an Asset Class but are included in the same Product Class, the exchange will be treated as a like-kind exchange. Treas. Reg. § 1.1031(a)–2(b).

The Asset Classes list of Rev. Proc. 87–56 and the Product Classes list of the SIC Manual may be modified from time to time in the future. Unless otherwise provided, the Service will follow the modified versions of those documents once they become effective, but a taxpayer is permitted to use the unmodified version for exchanges that occur within one year after a modification becomes effective. The Commissioner is authorized not to accept a modification in whole or in part. Treas. Reg. § 1.1031(a)–2(b)(4), (5).

§ 17.3112. Intangible Personal Property. The standard employed for applying IRC § 1031 to exchanges of intangible personal property rests solely on whether the properties are of like kind. No safe harbor standard (such as a like-class standard) is provided for those properties. The like-kind standard is applied to such properties by examining the nature or character of the rights involved (e.g., patents or copyrights) and by examining the nature or character of the underlying property to which the intangible property relates. Treas. Reg. § 1.1031(a)–2(c)(1).

> **§ 17.3112–1. Illustration 1. Copyrights on Novels.** *B* exchanges a copyright on a novel for a copyright on a different novel. This is a like-kind exchange. Treas. Reg. § 1.1031(a)–2(c)(3), Ex. (1).
>
> **§ 17.3112–2. Illustration 2. Copyrights on Novels and Songs.** *C* exchanges a copyright on a novel for a copyright on a song. The regulation states that this is not a like-kind exchange. Treas. Reg. § 1.1031(a)–2(c)(3), Ex. (2).
>
> **§ 17.3112–3. Goodwill or Going Concern Value.** The regulation states that the goodwill or going concern value

of one business is not of like kind to the goodwill or going concern value of another business. Treas. Reg. § 1.1031(a)–2(c)(2).

§ 17.3112–4. FCC Licenses to Broadcast. H exchanged an FCC radio license for an FCC television license. The nature of the licenses (rather than the nature of the business in which they are used) controls whether the properties are of like kind. The Commissioner ruled that this is a like kind exchange and qualifies for IRC § 1031 treatment. TAM 200035005.

§ 17.3113. Nondepreciable Tangible Personal Property. The standard employed for the exchange of such properties is the like-kind standard. No safe harbor standard (such as a like-class standard) is provided for those properties. Treas. Reg. § 1.1031(a)–2(c)(1).

§ 17.3120. Mandatory Nonrecognition. The nonrecognition established in IRC § 1031 is mandatory (i.e., the taxpayer *can not elect* to recognize a gain or loss realized in an exchange described in that section), but the strict requirements for qualifying for IRC § 1031 treatment make it possible to plan an exchange so that IRC § 1031 does not apply. For example, if property is received by a taxpayer more than 180 days after the date the taxpayer transfers his property (or after the due date of the taxpayer's return for that year), it will not qualify as like-kind property. IRC § 1031(a)(3)(B). Also, the property to be received by the taxpayer in the transfer must be identified on or before the date 45 days after the taxpayer transfers the property he relinquished in the exchange. IRC § 1031(a)(3)(A). The operation of these time limit requirements is discussed at **§ 17.3153.** A taxpayer who wishes to recognize a gain or loss could deliberately violate one of the requisites of IRC § 1031. In most cases, however, the deliberate violation of the time limits will not be a practical means of avoiding the nonrecognition rules because the transferor will be unwilling to defer the identification or receipt of the acquired property.

§ 17.3130. Property Acquired for Purpose of Exchanging It for Other Property. If *X* acquired property for the sole purpose of exchanging it with *Y* for property of a like kind, the Commissioner contends that the transaction will not qualify for nonrecognition as to *X* since, arguably, he did not hold the property either for investment or for productive use in a trade or business. Rev. Rul. 77–297; Rev. Rul. 75–291; but see § **17.3170.** Although IRC § 1031 may not apply to *X* in such cases, *Y* can enjoy nonrecognition under IRC § 1031 even though *Y* participated in the plan for *X* to acquire the property he subsequently exchanged with *Y* (*Y* held the property that he transferred for investment purposes). E.g., *Biggs v. Commissioner*, 632 F.2d 1171 (5th Cir. 1980), aff'g 69 T.C. 905 (1978); Rev. Rul. 77–297; Rev. Rul. 90–34. Indeed, *Y* will qualify for IRC § 1031 treatment even if the property that *Y* received in the exchange was not acquired by *X* until after the date that *Y* had transferred his property to *X*, provided that the time restrictions discussed in § **17.3153** are satisfied.

§ **17.3140. Multiple Party Exchanges.** A swap of properties can qualify under IRC § 1031 even though more than two parties are involved and a pre-arrangement is made for the purchase of some of the property to be exchanged. E.g., *Biggs v. Commissioner*, in § **17.3130**; *Barker v. Commissioner*, 74 T.C. 555 (1980); *Starker v. United States*, 602 F.2d 1341 (9th Cir. 1979); Rev. Rul. 90–34; Rev. Proc. 2000–37; Treas. Reg. § 1.1031(k)–1(g)(4). See *Garcia v. Commissioner*, 80 T.C. 491 (1983), Acq., for a liberal application of IRC § 1031 in a multi-party exchange. The transaction in *Garcia* involved three properties, four parties, and various escrow agreements. Taxpayer's property was sold as a part of the transaction, but taxpayer received only like kind property in the exchange, and so the transaction, which took place over some time, was treated as an IRC § 1031 exchange as to the taxpayer. The facts of the *Garcia* case arose prior to the 1984 amendments to IRC § 1031 that established time limits for the identification and receipt of property acquired in an exchange for the exchange to qualify for nonrecognition under IRC § 1031. See § **17.3153** for a discussion of the conditions that must be satisfied when there is a deferred exchange.

§ **17.3141.   Illustration.** *X*, who owned Blackacre, wished to exchange Blackacre for Whiteacre, which was owned by *M*. *M* was not interested in exchanging Whiteacre for other property, but she was willing to sell it for cash. *Z* wanted to purchase Blackacre from *X*, but *X* preferred a swap in order to preclude the recognition of gain. *X* informed *Z* that he would sell Blackacre to *Z* through a multiple step transaction using a fourth party, *Y*, and escrow arrangements. Under the agreement that was reached, *Y* would purchase Whiteacre from *M*, transfer it to *X* in exchange for Blackacre and some cash, and then sell Blackacre to Z for cash. All of the transfers took place simultaneously, and all o f the cash was paid into escrow and then distributed. The consideration paid by Y for Whiteacre came partly from the cash Y received from Z for Blackacre, partly from the proceeds of a new mortgage taken out on Whiteacre by X, and the rest from part of the cash paid by X in connection with his exchange of Blackacre for Whiteacre. In a similar situation, the Tax Court held in *Barker v. Commissioner*, in § **17.3140**, that IRC § 1031 prevents X from recognizing any gain on the transaction. The Court applied IRC § 1031 to a four-party transaction although the purchases and exchanges were prearranged. See also Rev. Rul. 90–34; and Treas. Reg. § 1.1031(k)–1.

§ **17.3150.   Deferred Exchanges—The *Starker* Principle.** A deferred exchange is one where the relinquished property is transferred before the replacement property is acquired, or vice versa. In the mid 1980s, two cases (the *Starker* cases), involving the same set of facts, permitted a deferred exchange to qualify for § 1031 nonrecognition even though the replacement property was identified and acquired some years after the relinquished property was transferred. Perhaps the several *Starker* decisions provide the most liberal construction of IRC § 1031 to date. While the holding of the *Starker* cases has been restricted by the time limitations adopted as part of the 1984 amendments to IRC § 1031 (described at § **17.3153**) and perhaps by the conditions laid down in Treas. Reg. § 1.1031(k)–1, the principles established by the *Starker* cases continue to be viable (subject to the time restrictions adopted in 1984), and so those cases are worth exploring.

In *Starker*, the taxpayers transferred land, having a value in excess of $1,500,000, to a corporation. In consideration of the transfer, the corporation agreed to acquire realty selected by the taxpayers and to deed it to them. The corporation established a "credit account" of over $1,500,000 for the taxpayers; as each parcel that was selected by the taxpayers was purchased by the corporation and deeded over, the balance of the credit account was to be reduced accordingly. The unused balance of the credit account was to be increased by 6% each year. After five years had elapsed, any credit balance remaining was to be paid to the taxpayers in cash.

§ **17.3151.   *Starker I.*** In the first of two cases (*Starker I*), a district court held that the two Starkers involved in that suit did not recognize gain on the transaction because the realty selected by them and transferred to them from the corporation (the replacement property) was covered by IRC § 1031. *Starker v. United States*, 35 AFTR2d 75–1550 (D.Or. 1975). Those two Starkers had only a small portion of the land that was transferred; hence, relatively small amounts were involved. The Service voluntarily caused its appeal in that case to be dismissed.

§ 17.3152.   *Starker II* and *Starker III*. The Service then contended that T.J. Starker, who had owned the major share of the transferred land, recognized gain on the transaction because IRC § 1031 is inapplicable. In the second district court case (*Starker II*), the same judge who had decided *Starker I* changed his mind and held for the Service. *Starker v. United States*, 432 F.Supp. 864 (D.Or. 1977). On appeal, the Ninth Circuit reversed the lower court decision in what is referred to as *Starker III*. *Starker v. United States*, 602 F.2d 1341 (9th Cir. 1979). *Starker II* and *Starker III* involved the receipt of twelve parcels of property by the taxpayer from the corporation: nine of the parcels were deeded directly to the taxpayer (T.J. Starker); two of the parcels (at the taxpayer's direction) were deeded directly to the taxpayer's daughter (one of these parcels was used by the daughter as her residence); and title to the last parcel was not acquired by the corporation which, instead, acquired contract rights to purchase the property and transferred those contract rights to the taxpayer. In *Starker III*, the Ninth Circuit held that the decision in *Starker I* controlled the disposition of the issue in *Starker III* as to the treatment of the nine parcels deeded to the taxpayer. The court applied collateral estoppel and held that IRC § 1031 covered the taxpayer's receipt of those parcels. However, the court held that collateral estoppel did not apply to the remaining three parcels.

As to the two parcels that were deeded directly to the taxpayer's daughter, the court held that IRC § 1031 was inapplicable because title was not acquired by the taxpayer himself. However, regarding the contract rights that the taxpayer received from the corporation to purchase the twelfth parcel, the Ninth Circuit, approving of the reasoning in *Starker I*, held that IRC § 1031 provided nonrecognition. The Ninth Circuit required the taxpayer to recognize interest income for the 6% growth factor. The increase in the taxpayer's account was treated as interest income by the court.

§ 17.3153. Deferred Exchanges—Time Limitations. Congress believed that the decisions of *Starker* and similar cases, suggesting that there was no limit to the time that like-kind exchanges can be kept open, were too liberal. See General Explanation of the Revenue Provisions of the Tax Reform Act of 1984, prepared by the staff of the Joint Committee on Taxation, pp. 244–245. To remedy this, Congress amended IRC § 1031 to bar like-kind treatment for the receipt of property that the taxpayer received more than 180 days after the taxpayer transferred his property or that the taxpayer received after the due date (including extensions) for filing a return for the year in which the taxpayer transferred his property. IRC § 1031(a)(3)(B). The 1984 amendments also barred like-kind treatment for property that the taxpayer received in exchange if the replacement property was not identified as property to be transferred to the taxpayer within 45 days of the date that the taxpayer relinquished his property. IRC § 1031(a)(3)(A). While the 1984 amendments expressly bar IRC § 1031 treatment when an exchange fails to comply with the time limit requirements for identification and receipt of property, a deferred exchange can qualify for IRC § 1031 treatment when the time limitations of IRC § 1031(a)(3) are satisfied.

The conditions under which a deferred exchange will qualify for IRC § 1031 nonrecognition treatment are set forth in Treas. Reg. § 1.1031(k)–1. One of the conditions imposed by that regulation (in addition to the time limitations) is that either: (1) no more than three properties be acquired in the exchange (the three-property rule), or (2) any number of properties can be acquired provided that their aggregate fair market value at the end of the identification period does not exceed 200% of the aggregate fair market value of the properties that the taxpayer relinquished (which value is to be determined at the date that they were transferred by the taxpayer)—the 200% rule. Treas. Reg. § 1.1031(k)–1(c)(4)(i). See Handler, *Final Regs on Deferred Like–Kind Exchanges Provide Additional Clarification*, 75 J.Tax. 10 (1991). The treatment of exchanges of multiple properties is described at **§ 17.3400.**

Apart from the time restrictions, a taxpayer who utilizes a deferred exchange arrangement must take care not to have constructive or actual receipt of cash or other property that would be treated as boot. See § **17.3200** for the meaning of "boot." The regulations provide a safe harbor for taxpayers to follow and be assured that they will not be deemed to have received cash or other boot. Treas. Reg. § 1.1031(k)–1(g).

§ 17.3154. Acquisition Directly from Third Party. In Rev. Rul. 90–34, the taxpayer transferred unencumbered Blackacre directly to Y who thereby became obligated to purchase property to be identified by the taxpayer within the permitted time period and then transfer the property to the taxpayer within the required period. The taxpayer made a timely identification of Whiteacre held by Z, and Y dutifully purchased Whiteacre and had Z transfer title to Whiteacre directly to the taxpayer. Thus, Y never held title to Whiteacre. The Commissioner ruled that there is no requirement in IRC § 1031 that Y obtain title to the property that the taxpayer acquired; it is only required that the taxpayer acquire like-kind property in exchange for the property he transferred. The Commissioner held that IRC § 1031 applied to the taxpayer's exchange so that he recognized no gain or loss.

§ 17.3155. Reverse-Starker Transactions. A reverse-Starker transaction is where the replacement property is acquired before the relinquished property is transferred. One method for accomplishing this is to "park" the replacement property with an accommodation party who holds the replacement property until the ultimate transferee of the relinquished property is determined. Once that is determined, the taxpayer transfers the relinquished property to the accommodation party in exchange for the replacement property; and the accommodation party transfers the relinquished property to the ultimate transferee in exchange for cash. The accommodation party receives a fee for the service. Other methods have been adopted, including other "parking" methods. For example, the accommodation party can promptly exchange the replacement property for the relinquished property, and then hold the relinquished property (as parked property) until it is purchased from the accommodation party by the ultimate transferee. These parking arrangement will not qualify for a § 1031 exchange treatment unless certain conditions are satisfied, including that the accommodation party, even though acting as an agent of the taxpayer, will be treated as the beneficial owner of the parked property for federal income tax purposes; and so income from the parked property will be treated as income of the accommodation party. In Rev. Proc. 2000–37, the Service set forth a set of conditions, the satisfaction of which provide a safe harbor for taxpayers who wish their reverse-Starker transaction to qualify for IRC § 1031 treatment.

§ 17.3160. Momentary Ownership of Acquired Property. If a taxpayer, who acquired property in a like-kind exchange, promptly transfers the acquired property to a corporation controlled by the taxpayer, the Commissioner maintains that the taxpayer will not qualify for nonrecognition under IRC § 1031 on the like-kind exchange since the taxpayer did not hold the acquired property for investment or for productive use in his trade or business. Rev. Rul. 75–292. See also *Regals Realty Co. v. Commissioner*, 43 B.T.A. 194 (1940), aff'd 127 F.2d 931 (2d Cir. 1942). However, in *Magneson v. Commissioner*, 753 F.2d 1490 (9th Cir. 1985), aff'g 81 T.C. 767 (1983), the courts allowed nonrecognition of gain where a taxpayer acquired property in a like-kind exchange and immediately transferred the acquired property to a partnership in exchange for a partnership interest. The Ninth Circuit held that the taxpayer did not discontinue his holding of the acquired property but merely changed the form of his holding. While the position of the Commissioner in Rev. Rul. 75–292 has not yet been repudiated by the courts, its validity has been placed in doubt by the *Magneson*, *Bolker*, and *Maloney v. Commissioner* decisions, discussed at § **17.3170.**

§ 17.3170. Momentary Ownership of Property Prior to the Exchange. In Rev. Rul. 77–297, the Commissioner ruled that if *A* purchased property for the purpose of transferring it to *B* in a like-kind exchange, the exchange will not qualify for IRC § 1031 treatment as to *A* because he did not hold the transferred property as an investment for use in his business (the Commissioner further held that IRC § 1031 could apply to *B* in that transaction). See § **17.3130.** The Commissioner's view was adopted by the District Court for the Central District of Illinois. *Barker v. United States*, 668 F.Supp. 1199 (C.D.Ill. 1987). Nevertheless, several decisions of the Tax Court and the Ninth Circuit on analogous issues cast serious doubts on the validity of the Commissioner's view.

In Rev. Rul. 77–337, the Commissioner denied IRC § 1031 treatment to a taxpayer who promptly transferred property that he had acquired on the liquidation of a corporation in exchange for property of a like kind. In *Bolker v. Commissioner*, 760 F.2d 1039 (9th Cir. 1985), the Ninth Circuit allowed IRC § 1031 nonrecognition for a like-kind exchange by a taxpayer who transferred property that he had received three months earlier from the liquidation of a corporation. While the court distinguished Rev. Rul. 77–337 on the ground that the intent to transfer the liquidated property in that ruling was formed before the liquidation took place, the court was critical of that ruling (and similar rulings) and apparently rejected the Commissioner's view. The rationale for the court's allowing IRC § 1031 treatment to the taxpayer is expressed in the following quotation from the Ninth Circuit's *Bolker* decision:

> [W]e hold that if a taxpayer owns property which he does not intend to liquidate or to hold for personal pursuits, he is "holding" that property "for productive use in trade or business or for investment" within the meaning of section 1031(a). Under this formulation, the intent to exchange property for like-kind property satisfies the holding requirement, because it is *not* an intent to liquidate the investment or to use it for personal pursuits.

The corporate liquidation that took place in *Bolker* was accomplished pursuant to a special tax provision (IRC § 333) that provided partial or full nonrecognition of gain to the corporation's shareholders, and this tax provision was repealed in 1986. It is unclear whether the special tax nature of the liquidation was a factor in the court's decision in *Bolker*.

In a subsequent Tax Court case, the court allowed IRC § 1031 treatment for a like-kind exchange made by a corporation less than one month prior to liquidating pursuant to the now-repealed IRC § 333. *Maloney v. Commissioner*, 93 T.C. 89 (1989). In *Maloney*, the Tax Court emphasized the special nature of the now defunct IRC § 333 liquidation. While the disposition in *Maloney* was made of property shortly after it was acquired in a like-kind exchange, the policy for allowing momentary ownership applies equally to the question of whether it is permissible under IRC § 1031 for a taxpayer to exchange property that was obtained by the taxpayer just before making the exchange.

In *Magneson v. Commission*, § **17.3160**, the Ninth Circuit and the Tax Court allowed nonrecognition of gain for a like-kind exchange where the taxpayer promptly transferred the acquired property to a partnership in exchange for a partnership interest. While that case involved the momentary holding of property acquired in a § 1031 exchange, it does provide support for the position that the momentary holding of property before exchanging it for like-kind property does not disqualify the exchange for § 1031 treatment.

In light of the *Bolker*, *Maloney*, and *Magneson* decisions, and notwithstanding the District Court's decision in *Barker*, the Commissioner's position is very much in doubt. It appears to be an overly restrictive reading of a provision that has otherwise been liberally construed.

§ **17.3180.   Exchanges With a Related Person.** If a like-kind nonrecognition exchange takes place between "related persons," and if within two years after the date of the last transfer that was incident to that exchange either party disposes of like-kind property that that person acquired in the exchange, then gain or loss realized by both parties from the exchange will be recognized—i.e., the nonrecognition treatment of IRC § 1031 becomes inapplicable. IRC § 1031(f). There are three types of disposition of acquired like-kind property that do *not* cause the loss of IRC § 1031 nonrecognition treatment for the original exchange—i.e., a disposition of such acquired property within the proscribed two-year period will not cause recognition of gain or loss if the disposition takes place: (1) after the death of either of the parties, (2) as a consequence of a compulsory or involuntary conversion if the like-kind exchange occurred before the threat or imminence of the conversion arose, or (3) it is established that neither the exchange nor the disposition had as one of its principal purposes the avoidance of Federal income tax. IRC § 1031(f). In certain circumstances described below, the two-year period of IRC § 1031(f) will be extended. Persons are related for this purpose if they have a relationship described in either IRC § 267(b) or IRC § 707(b)(1). IRC § 1031(f)(3).

The proscribed two-year period of IRC § 1031(f) for the disposition of acquired like-kind property is extended as to any such property for the period that the holder of that property did not bear a risk of loss or whose risk of loss with respect to that property was substantially diminished because of a contractual arrangement such as a put, a short sale, or the holding of another party of a right to acquire the property. IRC § 1031(g).

The evil at which this provision is aimed can occur when a high income tax bracket taxpayer transfers appreciated property to a relative who is in a low income tax bracket pursuant to a § 1031 exchange in which the low bracket relative promptly sells the appreciated property. The § 1031 exchange could be a device to allow the shifting of the gain from a sale of the property to a low bracket taxpayer and thereby reduce the tax burden on that sale. This provision is aimed at blocking that device.

§ 17.3200.   Boot. In tax parlance, when persons exchange property, the gain or loss from the exchange of which is not recognized (e.g., exchanges of like-kind property under IRC § 1031) and, in addition to the property that is permitted to be exchanged tax-free, one or more of the transferors also transfers cash or other property that is not permitted to be exchanged tax-free, the cash or other property is referred to as "boot." Thus, a taxpayer may receive property which is permitted to be exchanged for the property he transferred under the nonrecognition statute, and he may also receive cash or other property to boot. Some commentators and courts use the term "boot" to refer exclusively to *cash* received in a nonrecognition-type transaction and refer to other nonqualified property as "other property."

§ 17.3210.   Effect of Boot on Recognition of Gain. A very few nonrecognition statutes provide that the receipt of boot by a taxpayer will cause him to recognize all realized gain from the exchange. The more typical nonrecognition statute, as exemplified by IRC § 1031, provides that a taxpayer's receipt of boot causes him to recognize gain on the exchange only to the extent of the boot received. IRC § 1031(b).

§ 17.3211.   Illustration. *X* owned unimproved Blackacre which had a value of $50,000 and a basis of $10,000. *Y* owned unimproved Whiteacre which had a value of $40,000 and a basis of $20,000. *X* transferred Blackacre to *Y* in exchange for Whiteacre plus $10,000 cash. The $10,000 cash that *X* received constituted boot to him. *X realized* a gain of $40,000 on the exchange, but he *recognized* a gain of only $10,000 (i.e., *X recognized* his realized gain up to the extent of the boot he received). *Y realized* a gain of $20,000; but since *Y* did not receive any boot, *Y* did not *recognize* any gain at all.

X's transfer of Blackacre for like-kind property plus cash constitutes an exchange of multiple properties. While Treas. Reg. § 1.1031(j)–1 sets forth the manner in which a multiple-properties exchange is to be treated under IRC § 1031, that regulation is aimed primarily at the circumstance where both parties to the exchange transferred multiple properties. However, the regulation also can apply to the less complex circumstance in which one party transfers only one asset and receives in exchange two or more assets, some of which are of like kind and some of which are not. In that less complex situation (which is presented by this illustration), the application of IRC § 1031 can readily be determined without resorting to Treas. Reg. § 1.1031(j)–1.

The operation of that regulation (Treas. Reg. § 1.1031(j)–1) is complex. The basic scheme is that in multiple asset exchanges those properties that are of like kind are matched to the extent of their equal values, and the amount that is matched does not cause the recognition of gain or loss. Any excess value is treated as boot. Because the authors believe that students will not need to know exactly how that regulation operates, it is not discussed in detail in this work

§ 17.3220. Liabilities as Boot. When property which is subject to a mortgage or other encumbrance is transferred in a § 1031 exchange (i.e., the encumbrance represents a nonrecourse debt), the amount of the encumbrance is treated as boot received by the transferor. Treas. Reg. § 1.1031(b)–1(c). This rule conforms with the *Crane* doctrine [discussed in **§§ 16.1510– 16.1550**]. If the transferor received in exchange property which was subject to a mortgage, the mortgages are offset for purposes of determining his boot. Treas. Reg. § 1.1031(b)–1(c). As a result of a 1999 amendment, a nonrecourse liability will be taken into account only if it is "assumed" by the transferee as that term is specially (and unusually) defined in IRC § 357(d). IRC § 1031(d). With one minor exception, a nonrecourse liability (a debt for which there is no personal liability to repay) that secures property is deemed to have been assumed by the transferee who took the property subject to that liability. IRC § 357(d)(1)(B). In the illustrations that follow, when property is transferred subject to a liability, the transferee is deemed to have assumed that liability for purposes of IRC § 1031.

§ 17.3221. Illustration 1. *X* owned unimproved Blackacre having a value of $100,000 and subject to a mortgage of

$60,000. *X* had a basis of $70,000 in Blackacre. *Y* owned unimproved Whiteacre having a value of $120,000 and subject to a mortgage of $80,000. *Y* had a basis of $85,000 in Whiteacre. *X* and *Y* exchanged Blackacre for Whiteacre and each took subject to the existing mortgages on the properties. *X* *realized* a gain of $30,000, but under IRC § 1031, *X* did not *recognize* any gain at all since the mortgage on Whiteacre which he accepted ($80,000) was greater than the mortgage on Blackacre ($60,000) which he disposed of and, thus, *X* did not receive any boot. *Y* *realized* a gain of $35,000 on the exchange, but *Y* *recognized* a gain of only $20,000—i.e., the mortgage on Whiteacre ($80,000) transferred by *Y* was $20,000 greater than the mortgage on Blackacre ($60,000) which *Y* received and that difference constitutes boot to *Y*.

The gain *realized* by *X* and *Y* is computed as follows:

(a) Gain realized by *X*:

Amount *realized* by *X*

Value of Whiteacre	120,000
Release of Mortgage on Blackacre	60,000
	180,000

Less

Basis of Blackacre	70,000
Mortgage on Whiteacre (assumed)	80,000
	150,000
Gain *realized*	30,000

(b) Gain *realized* by *Y*:

Amount *realized* by *Y*

Value of Blackacre	100,000
Release of Mortgage on Whiteacre	80,000
	180,000

Less

Basis of Whiteacre	85,000
Mortgage on Blackacre (assumed)	60,000
	145,000
Gain *realized*:	35,000

§ **17.3222.   Illustration 2.** The same facts as in § **17.3221**, except that the value of Whiteacre was only $110,000, and, therefore, in addition to exchanging the real properties, Y paid X $10,000 cash. X *realized* a gain of $30,000, and he *recognized* a gain of $10,000 (i.e., the $10,000 cash paid to X is boot to him and, according to Treas. Reg. § 1.1031(d)–2, Ex. (2), the $20,000 excess of mortgage accepted by X cannot be used to offset the cash he received in determining his boot). [Note that Treas. Reg. § 1.1031(j)–1 will provide the same result if the procedures established in that regulation are applied.] Y realized a gain of $25,000:

Amount *realized* by X

Value of Blackacre	100,000
Release of Mortgage on Whiteacre	80,000
	180,000
Less	
Basis of Whiteacre	85,000
Mortgage on Blackacre (assumed)	60,000
Cash paid	10,000
	155,000
Gain *realized* by Y	25,000

Y *recognized* a gain of only $10,000 since the mortgage on Whiteacre transferred by Y is reduced by both the mortgage on Blackacre and the $10,000 cash paid by Y, and therefore Y received boot of only $10,000.

§ **17.3230.   Effect of Boot on Recognition of Loss.** No loss can be recognized in an exchange of property of like kind under IRC § 1031 even if the taxpayer also receives boot in the exchange. IRC § 1031(c).

§ **17.3300.   Basis of Property Received in a Section 1031 Exchange.** The basis of property acquired by a taxpayer in a tax-free exchange under IRC § 1031 is the same as the taxpayer's basis in the property transferred by him reduced by any *money* received by the taxpayer on the exchange and increased or decreased by any gain or loss *recognized* by the taxpayer on the exchange. IRC § 1031(d). In addition, the taxpayer's basis in the property acquired by him is increased by the amount of money given by the taxpayer to the transferee as partial payment for the acquired property, and the taxpayer's basis in the acquired property is also increased by the amount of any mortgage to which such acquired property is subject. If the taxpayer transferred property to the transferee subject to a mortgage, the amount of that mortgage is treated as money received by the taxpayer and accordingly reduces the taxpayer's basis in the property acquired by him. [See § **17.3220** where it is stated that a transferee's taking property subject to a nonrecourse liability is treated as an assumption of that liability.] If the taxpayer received boot other than money, then a portion of the basis so determined in an amount equal to the value of the boot is allocated to the boot property, and the balance of the basis is allocated to the like-kind property.

§ **17.3310. Illustration 1.** *X* owned unimproved Blackacre having a value of $80,000 and a basis to *X* of $55,000. *X* transferred Blackacre to *Y* in exchange for unimproved Whiteacre which had a value of $80,000. There were no encumbrances on either Blackacre or Whiteacre. *X* realized a gain of $25,000 on the exchange, but he did not recognize any gain because of IRC § 1031. *X*'s basis in Whiteacre is equal to the basis he had in Blackacre since *X* received no boot and recognized no gain on the exchange. Thus, *X* has a basis of $55,000 in Whiteacre.

§ **17.3320. Illustration 2.** *X* owned unimproved Blackacre having a value of $100,000, and subject to a mortgage of $40,000. *X* had a basis of $55,000 in Blackacre. *Y* owned unimproved Whiteacre having a value of $90,000 and subject to a mortgage of $34,000. *Y* had a basis of $40,000 in Whiteacre. *Y* also owned 100 shares of Win All stock having a value of $4,000, and *Y* had a basis of $8,000 therein. *X* transferred Blackacre to *Y* in exchange for Whiteacre and the 100 shares of Win All stock. Both parties took the realty subject to existing mortgages. *X* realized a gain of $45,000, but *X* recognized a gain of only $10,000 (i.e., his boot was the $4,000 value of the Win All stock plus the $6,000 excess of the mortgage on Blackacre over the mortgage on Whiteacre). *X*'s basis is computed as follows:

$ 55,000	Basis in Blackacre
+ 10,000	Gain recognized
+ 34,000	Mortgage on Whiteacre received
- 40,000	Mortgage on Blackacre transferred
$ 59,000	Basis in Whiteacre and Win All stock.

$4,000 of this basis is allocated to the 100 shares of Win All stock, and the remaining $55,000 is allocated to Whiteacre.

As for *Y*, he did not recognize any gain or loss on his transfer of Whiteacre since he did not receive any boot in exchange—the mortgage on Whiteacre ($34,000) was offset by the $40,000 mortgage to which Blackacre was subject. However, *Y* also transferred Win All stock in exchange for a part of Blackacre and since that was not a like-kind exchange, *Y* recognized a loss of $4,000 on the stock (i.e., *Y* received $4,000 value of Blackacre in exchange for his Win All stock in which he had a basis of $8,000). *Y*'s basis in Blackacre is computed as follows:

$ 40,000	Basis in Whiteacre
+ 8,000	Basis in Win All stock
+ 40,000	Mortgage on Blackacre
- 4,000	Loss *recognized* by *Y*
- 34,000	Mortgage on Whiteacre
$ 50,000	*Y*'s basis in Blackacre.

§ 17.3330. Overview. The *modus operandi* of a nonrecognition provision is that any realized gain or loss for which nonrecognition treatment has been granted is merely deferred. See **§§ 1.7421–1.7423.** To provide for this deferral, the basis of certain properties of the taxpayer must reflect the realized but unrecognized gain or loss; and in the context of IRC § 1031, it is the taxpayer's basis in the like-kind property he acquired in the exchange that will reflect the unrecognized gain or loss (since the taxpayer's basis in boot received in kind will equal its fair market value, none of the unrecognized gain or loss will be reflected in the boot). Thus, an easy method of checking whether you have correctly computed the basis of property acquired in a nonrecognition exchange is to determine the difference between the property's basis and its fair market value and that difference should equal the amount of unrecognized gain or loss. For example, in **§ 17.3320**, *X* realized a gain of $45,000 of which only $10,000 was recognized; consequently, *X*'s basis in Whiteacre (the replacement property he acquired) should reflect the unrecognized gain of $35,000. Whiteacre's value was $90,000, so to reflect a $35,000 gain on Whiteacre's sale, *X*'s basis in Whiteacre must be $55,000; and that is the basis applied to Whiteacre by IRC § 1031(d).

§ 17.3400. Multiple Properties. Not all exchanges of like-kind properties are transacted as a simple exchange of one item of property (encumbered or not) for another item of like-kind property, perhaps with an addition of an item of boot. In some circumstances, the parties will exchange a number of different properties, some of which are of like kind to one or more of the properties received in the exchange and some of which are not. Multiple properties exchanges can occur when a going business is acquired in an exchange, but this type of transaction is not limited to circumstances when a going business is involved. In such complex exchanges (in which the overall exchange is at arms' length and of equal value on both sides), when a taxpayer receives like-kind properties that have a greater aggregate value than the properties of like kind that the taxpayer transferred, the excess value will be consideration for other properties transferred by the taxpayer. Conversely, if the aggregate value of the like-kind properties that the taxpayer transferred is greater than the aggregate value of the like-kind properties that the taxpayer received, the taxpayer will have received boot consideration to make up that difference. Of course, in making those comparisons of value, the effect of encumbrances or other liabilities must be taken into account. The regulations provide a system for dealing with these complex exchanges in Treas. Reg. § 1.1031(j)–1., but we will not describe the workings of that regulation in this text because it is not likely to be assigned in a basic tax course due to its complexity.

§ 17.4000. INVOLUNTARY CONVERSIONS. When property is involuntarily converted into money as a result of its destruction in whole or in part, theft, seizure, requisition, condemnation, or threat of imminence thereof, the taxpayer *may elect* to avoid recognition of the gain of the conversion if he acquires replacement property. IRC § 1033. A loss sustained because of an involuntary conversion is recognized; IRC § 1033 does not apply to losses. The loss may or may not be deductible; it must first qualify under IRC § 165.

§ 17.4100. Elective. When property is converted into money or dissimilar property, the taxpayer may elect whether or not to recognize a gain if IRC § 1033 applies. However, if the property is converted directly into other property similar or related in service or use to the converted property (a rare occurrence), then IRC § 1033 is mandatory and prohibits the recognition of gain. Only conversions into money are discussed because that is the more typical occurrence.

§ 17.4200. Requirements. If during the statutory period, for the purpose of replacing the converted property, the taxpayer purchases other property similar or related in service or use to the converted property (or purchases stock in the acquisition of control of a corporation owning such other property), at the election of the taxpayer, the taxpayer will recognize gain on the conversion of his property into money only to the extent that the *amount realized* by him on the conversion exceeds the cost of such replacement property or stock. Thus, if an electing taxpayer's cost of replacement property equals or exceeds the amount that the taxpayer realized from the involuntary conversion of similar or related property, none of the taxpayer's gain will be recognized; if the amount realized by the taxpayer exceeds his cost of replacement property, the electing taxpayer will recognize that amount of his realized *gain* that equals the excess of his amount realized over his replacement cost.

§ 17.4210. **Statutory Period.** The statutory period for purchasing the replacement property begins with the date of disposition of the converted property or the earliest date of threat or imminence of requisition or condemnation of the converted property and ends two years after the close of the taxpayer's first taxable year in which any part of the gain from the conversion was realized; however, this period may be extended by a district director upon application by the taxpayer. Treas. Reg. § 1.1033(a)–2(c)(3).

§ 17.4220. **Election.** The election not to recognize gain under IRC § 1033 is made on the taxpayer's tax return for the year or years in which the taxpayer realized a gain from the conversion. Treas. Reg. § 1.1033(a)–2(c)(2). A failure by the taxpayer to report the gain realized from such a conversion on the taxpayer's tax return for the year in which the gain was realized is treated as an election not to recognize gain under IRC § 1033. Treas. Reg. § 1.1033(a)–2(c)(2).

§ 17.4230. **Similar or Related in Service or Use.** The similarity required for replacements of converted property is greater than that required of "like-kind" property to qualify for a tax-free exchange under IRC § 1031. For example, improved real estate is not similar or related in service or use to unimproved real estate. Treas. Reg. § 1.1033(a)–2(c)(9). For real property held for business use or investment which is involuntarily converted as a result of its seizure, requisition, condemnation, or threat or imminence thereof, the statute employs a "like-kind" standard for replacement rather than a standard of similar or related in service or use, provided that the replacement property is to be held for business use or for investment. IRC § 1033(g). This special rule for the involuntary conversion of certain realty also grants the taxpayer an additional year's time to replace the converted realty. IRC § 1033(g)(4).

§ **17.4231. Investment in a Partnership.** In *MHS Co., Inc. v. Commissioner*, 35 T.C.M. 733 (1976), aff'd per curiam 575 F.2d 1177 (6th Cir. 1978), the taxpayer invested the cash proceeds of a condemnation sale of its realty in a joint venture which was formed to acquire and improve other realty. Under local law and Federal tax law, the joint venture constituted a partnership. The Tax Court and the Sixth Circuit held that the taxpayer's purchase of a partnership interest did not qualify as a like-kind replacement under IRC § 1033(g) because a partnership interest is characterized as personal property by the local state law and personalty is not of a like kind to realty. See also, Rev. Rul. 55–351. Note that IRC § 1033(a)(2)(A) permits a taxpayer to purchase a *controlling* interest in a corporation owning property that is similar or related in service or use to the converted property in lieu of acquiring such property directly.

§ **17.4300. Residence.** An involuntary conversion of a taxpayer's personal residence is covered by IRC § 1033. Note that the exclusion of gain from the sale of a residence that is allowed in certain circumstances by IRC § 121 can apply to gain from an involuntary conversion and can apply in addition to the nonrecognition provided by IRC § 1033. IRC § 121(d)(5). See § **17.5120** and § **17.5140.** If a taxpayer's *principal* residence or any of its contents are compulsorily or involuntarily converted as a result of a "Presidentially declared disaster," the provisions of IRC § 1033 are greatly liberalized for such properties by IRC § 1033(h).

§ **17.4400. Basis.** The basis of property purchased in replacement of converted property which caused the nonrecognition of at least part of the gain realized on the conversion is the cost of the replacement property less the amount of realized gain that was not recognized. IRC § 1033(b). If several properties are purchased in replacement of the converted property, the basis so determined is allocated among those properties according to their respective costs.

§ **17.4410. Illustration.** *X* owned a ship having a value of $140,000 and a basis of $80,000. *X*'s ship was completely destroyed by fire on October 4, Year One, and *X* collected $140,000 insurance proceeds on account of his loss. On January 4, Year Two, *X* purchased a new ship at a cost of $125,000. *X* elected nonrecognition under IRC § 1033. *X* realized a gain of $60,000 on the conversion of his ship, but he recognized a gain of only $15,000. The difference between the amount realized ($140,000) and the cost of the replacement ship ($125,000) establishes a ceiling on the amount of gain that X will recognize. X's basis in the new ship is its cost ($125,000) less the unrecognized gain on the old ship. Of the $60,000 gain realized on the old ship only $15,000 was recognized and $45,000 went unrecognized. Thus, X's basis in the new ship is $80,000 ($125,000 $-$ $45,000 $=$ $80,000).

§ 17.5000. OTHER NONRECOGNITION PROVISIONS. There are a number of nonrecognition provisions in addition to the two already discussed. A few of these provisions are noted in **§ 17.5200.**

§ 17.5100.   Sale of Residence. Prior to 1997, IRC § 1034 provided nonrecognition for gain realized on the sale of a principal residence to the extent that, within a specified time period, the proceeds of the sale were reinvested in acquiring another principal residence. Section 1034 was repealed in 1997.

Another provision of the pre–1997 version of the Code (IRC § 121) excluded from gross income a specified amount of gain recognized on the sale of a residence if the taxpayer was at least 55 years of age at the time of the sale. That exclusion applied only once in the lifetime of a taxpayer. The Taxpayer Relief Act of 1997 greatly liberalized § 121 by increasing the amount of gain from the sale of a principal residence that will be excluded from gross income, and by expanding the scope of that provision. The current terms and application of the IRC § 121 exclusion are described below.

The § 121 exclusion applies to gain from the sale of property if during the 5–year period preceding the sale or exchange, the taxpayer had both used and owned the property as the taxpayer's principal residence for a time or times aggregating at least 2 years. IRC § 121(a). For convenience, we will refer to those two requirements as the "2–year use requirement" and the "2–year ownership requirement" respectively. In certain specified circumstances, periods of ownership and use by other parties or of other properties are tacked onto the taxpayer's ownership and use period. See IRC § 121(d)(3), (5)(C), (g).

There is no limit on the number of times that a taxpayer can sell a principal residence and use the exclusion of IRC § 121, but the full exclusion can be taken only once every two years. IRC § 121(b)(3). In other words, if a taxpayer sells a principal residence within two years of the date on which he sold a prior principal residence for which a § 121 exclusion was allowed, the second sale will not qualify for the full amount of the § 121 exclusion. However, as described below, a taxpayer who sells a principal residence because of certain external circumstances, can qualify for an exclusion of a lesser maximum amount even though the taxpayer fails to satisfy the 2–year use and ownership requirements and even though the taxpayer had utilized § 121 for a sale of another residence within two years prior to the current sale or exchange. IRC § 121(c).

If the terms of § 121 are satisfied, the exclusion will apply unless the taxpayer elects not to have it apply. IRC § 121(f). A taxpayer might elect not to have § 121 apply to a sale in order to obtain a larger exclusion for a sale of a principal residence that the taxpayer contemplates making within two years after the first sale. It seems unlikely that this will occur often.

A transitional rule provides that the above requirements need not be satisfied if the principal residence was held by the taxpayer on August 5, 1997, and was sold or exchanged within two years after that date. Section 312(d)(3) of the Taxpayer Relief Act of 1997.

The maximum amount of *gain* that can be excluded under § 121 is $250,000. IRC § 121(b)(1). The maximum amount of gain that can be excluded is increased to $500,000 for married taxpayers who file a joint return for the year in which the sale or exchange took place, provided that the following three requirements are satisfied:

(1) either spouse meets the 2–year *ownership* requirement,

(2) both spouses meet the 2–year *use* requirement, and

(3) neither spouse had utilized § 121 for the sale or exchange of an earlier principal residence within two years of the date on which the current sale or exchange took place. Sales or exchanges that took place prior to May 7, 1997, are not taken into account for this purpose. IRC § 121(b)(2).

If the husband and wife fail to satisfy all of the requirements listed above, the terms and limitations of IRC § 121 are applied to each spouse separately as if they were not married. IRC § 121(b)(2)(B). Thus, either spouse may qualify for an exclusion of up to $250,000 if that spouse qualifies for § 121 treatment. For this purpose, each spouse is treated as owning the property during the period that the other spouse owned it. IRC § 121(b)(2)(B). This latter provision liberalizes the application of the 2–year ownership requirement, but does not affect the 2–year use requirement.

If a taxpayer or a married couple fail to satisfy the 2–year use or ownership requirement or if they sell a principal residence within two years of having applied § 121 to a prior sale, of if they fail to satisfy all or any combination of those restrictions, the taxpayer or married couple nevertheless can qualify for an exclusion of a lesser maximum amount if the current sale or exchange is due to a change in place of employment, health or (to the extent provided in regulations) unforeseen circumstances. IRC § 121(c). The maximum amount that can be excluded under § 121(c) is a fraction of the maximum amount that could have been excluded if the three requirements mentioned above had been satisfied—i.e., a fraction of either $250,000 or $500,000 depending upon whether the qualified party is one taxpayer or a married couple. The denominator of the fraction is 2 years. The numerator is the shorter of: (1) the aggregate periods during the 5–year period ending on the date of sale or exchange in which the property was owned and used by the taxpayers his principal residence, or (2) the period between the last date on which the taxpayer used § 121 and the date of the current sale or exchange. IRC § 121(c)(1).

§ 17.5110.   Interface of IRC §§ 121 and 1033. The destruction, theft, seizure, requisition, or condemnation of a principal residence is treated as a sale of that property to which IRC § 121 can apply. If a principal residence is involuntarily converted and if the taxpayer qualifies for and elects nonrecognition of gain under IRC § 1033, both the IRC § 121 exclusion of gain and the § 1033 nonrecognition can be utilized. The amount of gain excluded by IRC § 121 is taken first. Then, the amount realized on the sale is reduced by the amount of gain excluded by § 121. Only the balance remaining need be reinvested in another residence to qualify for § 1033 treatment. IRC § 121(d)(5). In other words, for purposes of applying § 1033, the amount realized on the conversion of the principal residence is the actual amount realized reduced by the amount of gain excluded by § 121.

§ 17.5120.   Basis. The difference between a nonrecognition provision and an exclusion is that in the former the unrecognized gain or loss is reflected in the taxpayer's basis and therefore in a sense is merely deferred while an exclusion permanently removes all tax consequences from the transaction. IRC § 121 grants an exclusion of a specified maximum amount of gain, but IRC § 1033 is a nonrecognition provision, and consequently the unrecognized gain from IRC § 1033 is reflected in the taxpayer's basis in the new property. IRC § 1033(b).

§ 17.5200.   Other Sales or Exchanges. Gain or loss from certain exchanges of insurance policies [IRC § 1035], United States obligations [IRC § 1037], and from certain reacquisitions of real property [IRC § 1038] is not recognized. A considerable number of nonrecognition provisions operate in the corporate tax law area (e.g., transfers to a controlled corporation [IRC § 351], certain exchanges pursuant to a reorganization [IRC §§ 354 and 361], certain exchanges (or receipt of stock) pursuant to a corporate division [IRC § 355], exchange of certain stock of the same corporation [IRC § 1036], and others). The partnership tax area also contains nonrecognition provisions (e.g., nonrecognition of gain or loss on contribution or property to a partnership in exchange for a partnership interest. IRC § 721).

§ 17.6000.   DISALLOWANCE OF LOSS DEDUCTION FOR CERTAIN SALES OR EXCHANGES.

§ 17.6100.   Sales Between Related Parties. IRC § 267 denies a loss deduction to a taxpayer where the loss resulted from a sale or exchange to a person who is deemed to be related to the taxpayer under the terms of IRC § 267(b). For example, to list a few of the parties to which § 267 applies, no deduction is allowed for a loss recognized on a sale or exchange between: (1) a taxpayer and certain members of his family (e.g., his ancestors, descendants, and brothers and sisters) listed in IRC § 267(c)(4); (2) an individual and a corporation when more than 50% of the value of the stock is owned by the individual; (3) a grantor and a fiduciary of a trust; except in the case of an exchange resulting from a distribution from an estate in satisfaction of a pecuniary bequest, a personal representative of an estate and a beneficiary of that estate. IRC § 267(b). IRC § 267 does not apply to transfers between spouses or former spouses under IRC § 1041(a); such transfers are controlled exclusively by IRC § 1041. IRC § 267(g).

§ 17.6110.   Transferee's Gain on Subsequent Sale. Where the purchaser of property from a vendor who recognized a loss on the sale but was disallowed a deduction under IRC § 267 subsequently sells or exchanges the property (or other property whose basis in his hands is determined by reference to the original property), any gain realized by the purchaser on the subsequent sale will be recognized only to the extent that it exceeds the amount of loss deduction disallowed to the original vendor under IRC § 267. IRC § 267(d). This provision applies only to realized gain; it does not serve to increase the taxpayer's loss deduction if the property is subsequently sold at a loss. Also, this exclusion of gain provision applies only to sales or exchanges made by the *original purchaser*.

§ 17.6120.   Illustrations. *X* had a basis of $10,000 in Blackacre which he held for investment purposes. *X* sold Blackacre to his brother *Y* for its value of $7,000. *X* recognized a loss of $3,000, but he was barred from taking a tax deduction for the loss by IRC § 267.

> **§ 17.6121.   Illustration 1.** *Y* subsequently sold Blackacre for $11,000. *Y* realized a gain of $4,000, but only $1,000 of the gain is recognized because IRC § 267(d) precludes recognition of *Y*'s gain to the extent that *X*'s loss was disallowed under that section.

> **§ 17.6122.   Illustration 2.** *Y* subsequently sold Blackacre for $6,000. *Y* realized a loss of $1,000, and he may deduct that amount if he held Blackacre as an investment. IRC § 267(d) has no application.

> **§ 17.6123.   Illustration 3.** *Y* gave Blackacre to his son *S*. *S* subsequently sold Blackacre for $11,000. *S* recognized a gain of $4,000 on the sale. IRC § 267(d) applies only to a sale by *Y* (the original transferee) and, therefore, has no effect on the amount of gain recognized by *S*.

§ 17.6130.   Sales Between Two Related Trusts. No deduction is allowed for a loss recognized by a trust on a sale to another trust if the same person is the grantor of both trusts. IRC § 267(b)(5). Two trusts with a common income beneficiary, but with different grantors and contingent beneficiaries, were allowed to deduct losses from sales to each other in *Joseph E. Widener Trust v. Commissioner*, 80 T.C. 304 (1983), Acq. The Tax Court said that IRC § 267 was inapplicable, and a deduction could be denied only if the sale were not bona fide.

§ 17.6200.   Denial of Certain Deductions. IRC § 267(a)(2) denies a taxpayer a deduction for certain expenses or interest owing to persons related to the taxpayer until such time as the item is included in the income of the related person. This provision applies primarily to accrual method taxpayers who accrue interest or expenses owing and unpaid to related persons who report their income on the cash receipts and disbursements method. In such cases, the accrual taxpayer's deduction is deferred until the item is paid so that it is included in the related person's income.

§ 17.6300. Wash Sales. No deduction is allowed for a loss sustained by a taxpayer on the sale or other disposition of stock or securities when, within 30 days before or 30 days after the sale, the taxpayer acquired by purchase (or a taxable exchange) or contracted to acquire substantially identical stock or securities. IRC § 1091. A contract or option to acquire or sell stock or securities will itself constitute "stock or securities" except to the extent that regulations provide otherwise. IRC § 1091(a). A sale or disposition that falls within IRC § 1091 is sometimes called a "wash sale." The denial of a deduction for such a "wash sale" does not apply: (1) to a corporation that is a dealer in stocks and securities and sustained a loss on the disposition of stocks and securities in the ordinary course of its business, or (2) to a noncorporate taxpayer if the disposition of the stocks and securities is made in connection with the taxpayer's trade or business. Treas. Reg. § 1.1091–1(a).

§ 17.6310.   Forbidden Period. The 61–day period in which the purchase of substantially identical stock or securities will deny the taxpayer a loss deduction is the period beginning 30 days prior to the sale or other disposition and ending 30 days after the sale or other disposition.

§ 17.6320.   Basis of Purchased Stocks or Securities. If a loss deduction is disallowed because the sale or disposition constituted a "wash sale," the taxpayer's basis in the purchased stocks or securities is equal to the taxpayer's basis in the stock or securities disposed of in the wash sale increased or decreased by the difference between the selling price of the loss stock or securities and the purchase price for the newly acquired stock or securities. IRC § 1091(d). Since basis is adjusted under IRC § 1091, that section is actually a nonrecognition provision (i.e., a deferral of the loss rather than a permanent disallowance).

§ 17.6330.   Matching Stocks or Securities Sold with Those Acquired. The stocks or securities sold shall be matched in accord with the order of their sale with the stocks or securities acquired during the 61–day period in the order of time or acquisition. Treas. Reg. § 1.1091–1(b), (c) and (d). This matching device is used to determine the identity of the shares of stocks or securities sold or otherwise disposed of for which no loss deduction is allowed and to determine the basis of the newly acquired shares of stocks or securities.

§ 17.6340.   Illustrations.

§ 17.6341.   Illustration 1. *X* and *Y* are not related. *X* owned 100 shares of Win All, Inc. common stock in which he had a basis of $10,000. On February 6, Year One, X sold the 100 shares of Win All stock to Y for $6,500—their fair market value. On March 2, Year One, X purchased 100 shares of Win All common stock from his broker for $6,700. X cannot deduct the $3,500 loss he sustained on the February sale because the transaction constitutes a wash sale under IRC § 1091. X's basis in the 100 shares purchased on March 2 is $10,200 (i.e., the $10,000 basis in his old stock plus the $200 difference between what he paid for his new stock and the selling price of his old stock).

§ 17.6342. Illustration 2. The same facts apply as in **§ 17.6341** except that on March 2, Year One, X paid only $6,250 for the 100 shares of Win All stock he bought on that date. IRC § 1091 bars X from taking a loss deduction for the February sale. X's basis in the 100 shares of stock purchased on March 2 is $9,750 (i.e., the $10,000 basis in his old stock minus the $250 difference in the payment he received for his old stock and the price he paid for the new stock).

§ 17.6343. Illustration 3. In Year One, X purchased 100 shares of common stock in Widget, Inc. for $5,000 (i.e., $50 per share of stock). On August 10, Year Ten, X purchased an additional 200 shares of Widget's common stock for $6,000 (i.e., $30 per share of stock). On September 2, Year Ten, X sold to an unrelated person for $3,000 (i.e., $30 per share of stock) the 100 shares of Widget's stock that he had purchased in Year One. X realized a loss of $2,000 on that sale, but X cannot deduct any of that loss because he had purchased substantially identical stock within the 61–day period and therefore the sale was a wash sale. X has a basis of $5,000 in 100 of the shares of Widget stock he acquired in Year Ten, and he will have a basis of $3,000 in the other 100 shares that he purchased in that year. Since the order of time of acquisition probably cannot be determined, it is possible that X will have a basis of $8,000 in his 200 shares of Widget stock to be allocated equally among the shares (i.e., $40 per share).

*

CHAPTER EIGHTEEN

CAPITAL GAINS AND LOSSES

§ 18.0000. CAPITAL GAINS AND LOSSES.

§ 18.1000. GENERAL. Current tax law provides preferential treatment in the form of a ceiling on the applicable tax rate that is applied to "net capital gains." The excess (if any) of a taxpayer's net long-term capital gain over his net short-term capital loss for a taxable year is characterized as a "net capital gain." § 18.2300. In 2005, the maximum marginal rate on an individual's income is 35% while the maximum rate on an individual's net capital gain typically will be 15%. IRC § 1(a)–(d), (h), (i)(2). As we will see, currently there are four different maximum rates that apply to different types of capital gains, but the maximum rate that will apply most frequently is the 15% rate.

Currently, there is no preferential tax treatment for a *corporation's* net capital gains.

Any gain or loss that is not treated as a capital gain or loss is referred to as "ordinary income" or as "ordinary loss." IRC §§ 64 and 65.

§ 18.2000. TAX TREATMENT OF CAPITAL GAINS AND LOSSES.

§ 18.2100. Groupings of Long-and Short–Term Gains and Losses. Capital gains and losses are separated into two groups: long-term gains and long-term losses are placed into one group, and short-term gains and short-term losses are placed into a different group. A capital gain or loss that is recognized on the sale or exchange of a capital asset is long-term if the taxpayer had held the asset for more than one year, and such a gain or loss is short-term if the taxpayer had held the asset for one year or less. IRC § 1222(1)–(4). A capital gain or loss generally is the gain or loss recognized on the sale or exchange of a capital asset. A "sale or exchange" is a term of art that has a specific meaning in the Code. See §§ 18.5000–18.5300. The definition of "capital asset" is set forth in IRC § 1221 and is discussed later in this chapter.

§ 18.2200. Netting of Gains and Losses. A taxpayer's long-term capital gains and *deductible* long-term capital losses are netted to determine the "net long-term capital gain" or the "net long-term capital loss." IRC § 1222(7), (8). The taxpayer's short-term capital gains and *deductible* short-term capital losses are netted to determine the "net short-term capital gain" or the "net short-term capital loss." IRC § 1222(5), (6).

§ 18.2300. Net Capital Gain. After completing the preliminary grouping and netting process described in **§ 18.2200**, the taxpayer's net long-term capital gain (if any) for the taxable year is reduced by the taxpayer's net short-term capital loss (if any) for that taxable year. This excess of net long-term capital gain over net short-term capital loss is referred to as a "net capital gain." IRC § 1222(11). It is only a noncorporate taxpayer's net capital gain that qualifies for a preferential rate.

A taxpayer is granted an election to exclude from net capital gain (and therefore treat as ordinary income) all or part of the net gain from the disposition of property held as an investment. IRC §§ 1(h)(2), 163(d)(4)(B)(iii). That election will qualify the net gain from the disposition of such property as "investment income" from which "investment interest" can be deducted. IRC § 163(d)(4)(B)(iii). See **§ 5.1220.**

§ 18.2310. Significance of Tax Rate Ceiling. Currently, the maximum marginal tax rate that can be imposed on an individual's taxable income is 35%. IRC § 1(i)(2). If an individual's income places him in the 35% marginal tax bracket, the maximum marginal tax rate that can be imposed on specified types of that individual's net capital gain is 15%. IRC § 1(h)(1)(C). Therefore, the preference granted to net capital gains can be as great as 20 percentage points. As we will see, currently there are four different maximum rates that can apply to net capital gains depending upon the nature of the long-term gains that comprise the taxpayer's net capital gain. For some of those rate brackets, there may be no benefit from the ceiling on rates or the benefit will be less.

§ 18.2320. Application of the Maximum Tax Rates. Currently, the three highest marginal tax brackets for individuals are: 28%. 33%. and 35%. An individual's net capital gain will qualify for a ceiling on the rate of tax that can be imposed. A capital gains rate can be viewed as an alternative rate to the normal tax rate structure. Instead, since none of the several capital gains rates will apply to a capital gain to the extent that the normal rate that would be applicable to that gain is smaller, a capital gains rate can be viewed as a maximum rate. In this text, the capital gains tax is described as the maximum tax rate that can be applied to certain types of net capital gains.

The maximum rates on net capital gains apply for purposes of both the regular income tax and the alternative minimum tax. IRC §§ 1(h), 55(b)(3). The alternative minimum tax is discussed in Chapter Fifteen.

The first step in applying the capital gains rates is to divide the noncorporate taxpayer's capital gains and losses into two separate categories—long-term and short-term. The long-term capital gains and losses are aggregated to arrive at the net long-term capital gain or loss, and short-term capital gains and losses are aggregated to arrive at the net short-term capital gain or loss. Only if there is a net long-term capital gain that is greater than a net short-term capital loss (if any) for that year will the maximum rate limitations for capital gains apply. The excess of net long-term capital gain over net short-term capital loss (if any) is referred to as the "net capital gain." The maximum rates apply to the net capital gain.

§ 18.2321. **Treatment of Gains.** Prior to the 1997 and 1998 amendments to the Code, the task of determining the tax on capital gains was largely completed once the net capital gain for the year was computed. As a consequence of those amendments, it is no longer sufficient to determine the net capital gain. The current version of the Code applies different maximum rates to several categories of net capital gain, and so the taxpayer's capital gains and losses must be divided into subcategories. Currently, the several maximum rates for net capital gain are (reading from top to bottom) 28%, 25%, 15%, and 5%. For years beginning after 2007, the 5% rate is scheduled to be reduced to 0%. For convenience, properties the gain from which would be taxed at one of those rates will sometimes be referred to herein as property in the 28% category, or in the 25%, 15%, or 5% category.

Keep in mind that the rates applicable to long-term capital gains are *maximum* rates. If the normal marginal rate (under the tax rate schedule) that would be applied to that income is less than the maximum capital gain rate, the lower normal rate is used.

For convenience, let us refer to a taxpayer's taxable income that is not part of the net capital gain as "ordinary income." The amount of tax on the taxpayer's ordinary income is determined by applying the rates from the regular tax schedule to that income. IRC § 1(h)(1)(A). The application of the regular tax rate schedule is applied to taxable income after excluding the net capital gain, and so applies first to the taxpayer's ordinary income. Thus, the taxpayer's net capital gain is placed in the marginal tax bracket for taxable income immediately above the taxpayer's ordinary income. This stacking maximizes the benefit of providing a ceiling on the tax rate applicable to net capital gains since a taxpayer's lower tax rates will be applied to the ordinary income.

Subject to several exceptions described below, the general rule is that the maximum tax rate that will be applied to a net capital gain is 15%. IRC § 1(h)(1)(C). If the gain, or a portion of the gain, on property in the 15% category would be taxed at less than a 28% rate by the regular tax rate schedule if no special treatment were accorded to net capital gains, then such gain, or portion of that gain, will be taxed at a 5% rate instead of the 15% rate. IRC § 1(h)(1)(B), However, there are three subcategories of net capital gain that do not qualify for either the 15% or the 5% maximum rates, and so the gains and losses from the sale or exchange of properties in those subcategories must be separately determined. The portion of the net capital gain that is not within any of those three subcategories and is not so-called "qualified dividend income" is referred to as the "adjusted net capital gain." IRC § 1(h)(3). "Qualified dividend income" is described in § **18.6300.**

There are three categories of capital gain and loss that have to be identified and separated from the rest. Two of those subcategories, collectibles and section 1202 gain, are taxed at a maximum rate of 28% and therefore comprise the 28% category property. Let us examine the collectibles and section 1202 gain subcategories separately.

The gain and loss from the sale or exchange of a "collectible" which is a capital asset that has been held for more than 1 year must be separated. IRC § 1(h)(5). Only gains that are included in gross income and losses that are taken into account in computing taxable income are included in this separate calculation. IRC § 1(h)(5)(A). A gain or loss from the sale or exchange of collectibles that qualify for this treatment (i.e., capital assets held for more than one year) is referred to as "collectibles gain" and "collectibles loss" respectively. IRC § 1(h)(5)(A). Collectibles gain also includes the gain from the sale of an interest in a partnership, S corporation, or trust that is attributable to unrealized appreciation of collectibles. IRC § 1(h)(5)(B). A "collectible" includes works of art, antiques, rugs, gems, alcoholic beverages, stamps, and coins (but certain coins are excluded). IRC §§ 1(h)(5)(A), 408(m). The gains and losses from the sale or exchange of collectibles that were capital assets which had not been held for more than 1 year are short-term capital gains and losses and are not included in the collectibles gains or the collectibles losses. The collectibles gains are combined with the "section 1202 gain" (described below), and the sum is then reduced by collectibles losses and capital losses (the manner in which capital losses are allocated among the several categories of capital gains is described in § **18.2322.**). The maximum tax rate on the net of collectibles gains and section 1202 gain reduced by collectibles losses and capital losses is 28%.

Section 1202 excludes from income 50% of the gain recognized by a noncorporate taxpayer on the sale or exchange of so-called "qualified small business stock" that had been held for more than 5 years. See § **18.8000** *et seq*. There is a ceiling on the amount of exclusion that is allowable. § 1202(b)(1). See § **18.8200.** The amount of gain from the sale or exchange of qualified small business stock that is included in TP's income (usually 50% of the gain) is included with the gain from collectibles in the 28% category and so is taxed at a maximum rate of 28%. IRC § 1(h)(4), (7). The gain from the sale or exchange of qualified small business stock that is excluded from § 1202 treatment by § 1202(b) is excluded from the 28% category. See §§ **18.8200–18.8240.** The amount of § 1202 income that is included in the 28% category is referred to as "section 1202 gain." IRC § 1(h)(7). Thus, if the ceiling on the § 1202 exclusion does not apply, only 1/2 of the gain from the sale of such qualified small business stock is taxed, and the rate of tax on that amount cannot exceed 28%. The net effect is that, unless the § 1202(b)(1) ceiling applies, the gain from such qualified small business stock is taxed at a maximum rate of 14%. Compared to the typical 15% maximum rate on net capital gains, the effective 14% rate is of small value.

The collectibles gain and the section 1202 gain are added together and comprise the gains in the 28% category. The accumulated gain is then reduced by the sum of: collectibles loss, net short-term capital loss, and long-term capital loss carried over to that year. IRC § 1(h)(4). In addition, if the aggregate losses in the 15% category exceed the aggregate gains in the 15% category, the excess loss is allocated to the 28% category and included with the deductions in that category. Notice 97–59. For convenience, the sum of the losses in the 28% category is sometimes referred to herein as the "28% category losses." After deducting the 28% category losses, if the net figure is a gain, it is taxed at a maximum rate of 28%. As explained in § **18.2322**, if (after deducting the 28% category losses) the net figure is a loss, that loss is deducted from lower rate categories of net capital gains in descending order of the rate category. See Notice 97–59.

The third subcategory is gain from the disposition or involuntary conversion of section 1250 property (primarily buildings and their structural components) that has been held for more than 1 year, but only to the extent that such gain is treated as a long-term capital gain. The extent to which the gain from the sale or exchange or involuntary conversion of depreciable property will be treated as a long-term capital gain is set forth primarily in IRC § 1231 and is explained in Chapter Nineteen. To the extent that such gain that qualifies for treatment as long-term capital gain is attributable to depreciation adjustments that were made to the property's basis, the gain is taxed at a maximum rate of 25%. IRC § 1(h)(1)(D), (6). This is the only type of gain that is subject to the 25% rate, and therefore is the only gain included in the 25% category. This type of gain is referred to as "unrecaptured section 1250 gain." IRC § 1(h)(6). If the 28% category losses exceed the 28% category gains, the excess losses will reduce the unrecaptured section 1250 gain that is subject to the 25% maximum tax rate. IRC § 1(h)(6)(A)(ii). If the losses allocated to the 25% category exceed gains in that category, the excess is allocated first to the 15% category, and any excess remaining from that category is then allocated to the 5% category. See Notice 97–59.

As explained in Chapter Nineteen, the gains and losses from the disposition or conversion of certain properties (sometimes called section "1231 property," which includes real property used in a trade or business) are aggregated. A gain or loss from such a disposition or conversion is referred to as a "section 1231 gain" or a "section 1231 loss." IRC § 1231(a)(3). If, after aggregating the sections 1231 gains and losses for a taxable year, there is a net gain, it is referred to as a "net section 1231 gain;" and if there is a net loss, it is referred to as a "net section 1231 loss." IRC § 1231(c)(3), (4). A taxpayer's unrecaptured section 1250 gain, which qualifies for the 25% maximum rate, cannot exceed the taxpayer's net section 1231 gain for that year. IRC § 1(h)(6)(B).

If there is a net section 1231 gain, all of the section 1231 gains and losses are treated as long-term capital gains and losses; but if there is a net section 1231 loss, all of the section 1231 gains and losses are treated as ordinary income and ordinary loss. See **§ 19.2200.** However, if a taxpayer has a net section 1231 gain within five years of having had a net section 1231 loss, the ordinary loss treatment accorded to that prior year's net section 1231 loss is "recaptured" by treating a comparable amount of the current year's net section 1231 gain as ordinary income. IRC § 1231(c). See **§ 19.2220.** If part of the net section 1231 gain in the current year is comprised of unrecaptured section 1250 gain, and if there is a recapture under IRC § 1231(c) of part of the net section 1231 gain because of a prior year's net section 1231 loss, the question is how the recapture (which constitutes ordinary income treatment) is to be allocated among the several section 1231 gain items. The amount of such recapture that is allocated to the unrecaptured section 1250 gain will cause it to be treated as ordinary income to that extent, and so that amount will no longer qualify as unrecaptured section 1250 gain and will not qualify for the 25% maximum rate. The 1998 amendment to the Code states that the manner in which the recaptured net section 1231 gain is to be allocated among the section 1231 gain items can be determined by Treasury in the promulgation of either forms or regulations. IRC § 1(h)(8). In Notice 97–59, which was promulgated prior to the adoption of the 1998 amendments, the IRS provided that any recaptured ordinary income under IRC § 1231(c) is to be allocated first to section 1231 gain in the 28% category, second any remaining ordinary income is allocated to section 1231 gain in the 25% category, and finally any remaining ordinary income is allocated to section 1231 gain in the 15% category. It seems likely that the Service will retain that approach for the post–1997 years.

§ 18.2322. Allocation of Capital Losses. Let us now look at how capital losses are allocated among the four capital gain categories. The first step is to divide into separate computational baskets long-term and short-term capital gains and losses and to compute the net gain or loss for each separate basket. If there is no "net capital gain" (i.e, there is no excess of net long-term capital gain over net short-term capital loss), then no preferential tax rates are applicable. However, if there is a "net capital gain," certain items must be carved out of that figure and the tax thereon is limited by specified maximum rates. See **§ 18.2321.** For example, "unrecaptured section 1250 gain" is separated and taxed at no greater than a 25% rate.

Short-term capital losses for a taxable year (including short-term losses carried to that year under IRC § 1212) are deducted first from short-term capital gains. If the aggregate short-term capital losses exceed the aggregate short-term capital gains (which means that there is a net short-term capital loss for that year), the net short-term capital loss is applied first to reduce any net long-term capital gain in the 28% category. If there is a net loss in the 28% category, that loss is then allocated to the 25% category, and then any unused loss is allocated to the lower categories in descending order.

The operating principle is that gains and losses in each category are netted. If there is a net loss in any category, that loss is applied to the highest rate category that has a net gain; and any excess loss in that category is applied to lower rate categories in descending order. As noted above, short-term capital losses are deducted first from short-term capital gains, and any resulting net short-term capital loss is allocated first to the 28% category. The operation of this approach is described more specifically below.

The long-term capital gains in the 28% category (i.e., collectibles gain and section 1202 gain) are reduced by the sum of: (1) collectibles loss, (2) net short-term capital loss, (3) long-term capital losses carried to that year under IRC § 1212, and (4) net losses from the 15% category. IRC § 1(h)(4), and Notice 97–59. If there is a net loss in the 28% category, it is applied in descending order to the next highest categories that have a net gain—i.e., first to gains in the 25% category, and then to gains in the 15% category. If there is a net loss in any of the other categories, that excess loss is applied first to the highest rate category (the 28% category) and then in descending order to the next highest rate categories. Notice 97–59. Any long-term capital loss remaining after applying it to the four categories is deducted from the taxpayer's net short-term capital gain (if any).

If there is a net loss remaining after applying the losses to all four categories and to the net short-term capital gain, that loss is treated as described in § **18.2400** *et seq.*

§ **18.2323.** **Illustration 1.** For the year 2005, *F*, an unmarried individual who is neither a head of household nor a surviving spouse, had taxable income of $140,000, of which $30,000 is a net capital gain. None of *F*'s capital gains or losses were derived from 28% or 25% category items. F had no carryover losses to that year.

To determine *F*'s tax, first reduce his taxable income by his $30,000 net capital gain, and then compute the tax on the resulting figure of $110,000. The entire amount of *F*'s net capital gain is taken out because the resulting figure of $110,000 is greater than the amount of *F*'s taxable income that, under the 2005 normal rate schedule, is taxed at a rate below 28% (i.e., $29,700 of *F*'s 2005 taxable income is taxed at a rate below 28%). The first partial tax is the tax at normal rates on $110,000; the tax on that amount is $25,307. The second partial tax is equal to 15% of $30,000 (the amount of *F*'s net capital gain which was excluded from the first computation), which provides a partial tax of $4,500. All of *F*'s net capital gain qualified for the maximum 15% rate since *F* had no 28% or 25% category gain. The total tax due then is the sum of the two partial taxes. The tax due is $29,807 ($25,307 + $4,500).

If no preference had been provided for net capital gains, the tax on *F*'s $140,000 of taxable income would have been $33,706. The preference reduced *F*'s tax bill by $3,899 (the difference between the $33,706 tax that he would have incurred and the $29,807 tax that he actually incurred).

§ **18.2324.** **Illustration 2.** For the year 2005, *G*, an unmarried individual who is neither a head of household nor a surviving spouse, had taxable income of $55,000, of which

$35,000 was a net capital gain. *G*'s net capital gain included a $5,000 gain from the sale of a collectible that was a capital asset and had been held for more than one year. None of *G*'s other capital gains or losses were derived from 28% or 25% category items. In 2005, *G* had no short-term capital losses and had no carryover capital losses. The $30,000 difference between *G*'s net capital gain ($35,000) and the sum of her 28% and 25% category gains ($5,000) constitutes her adjusted net capital gain. Accordingly, *G*'s adjusted net capital gain is $30,000.

To determine *G*'s tax, it will be necessary to compute four partial taxes, and then add all four partial taxes together to arrive at *G*'s total tax liability.

The first partial tax requires a calculation of several figures to determine which is greater. First determine the difference between *G*'s taxable income ($55,000) and her net capital gain ($35,000). The difference is $20,000. For convenience, let us call that $20,000 figure the "ordinary income figure." The ordinary income figure will be used to calculate the first partial tax unless the lesser of the two following calculations provides a larger figure. The next figure to be determined is the *lesser* of: (1) the maximum amount of *G*'s taxable income that is taxed under normal rates at a rate below 28% (i.e.,$29,-700); or (2) taxable income ($55,000) reduced by *G* adjusted net capital gain ($30,000) = $25,000. For convenience let us call the difference between taxable income and adjusted net capital gain the "adjusted taxable income." Since the $25,000 adjusted taxable income figure is the smaller of those two amounts, it is compared with *G*'s ordinary income figure ($20,000) to determine which is greater. Since the $25,000 figure is the greater of those two amounts, it is used to determine the first partial tax. IRC § 1(h)(1)(A).

The first partial tax is the tax at normal rates on $25,000 (the figure computed above). The normal tax on $25,000 is $3,385. The first partial tax then is $3,385.

To determine the second partial tax, first determine the maximum amount of taxable income which at normal rates is taxed at less than 28%; for *G* in 2005, that amount is $29,700. Then subtract from that $29,700 figure *G*'s adjusted taxable income of $25,000 (as used herein, "adjusted taxable income" is the difference between *G*'s taxable income and her adjusted net capital gain). The difference of $4,700 is taxed at a 5% rate. IRC § 1(h)(1)(B). The second partial tax then is $235.

The third partial tax is 15% of the difference between G's adjusted net capital gain ($30,000) and the amount to which a 5% rate was applied to determine the second partial tax ($4,700 in this illustration). The difference is $25,300. So, the third partial tax is $3,795 (15% X $25,300).

The fourth partial tax is 28% of the difference between G's taxable income ($55,000) and the sum of the three amounts on which a partial tax was computed above (i.e., $25,000 + $4,700 + $25,300 = $55,000). The difference is zero; and, accordingly, the fourth partial tax is $0 (28% X $0 = $0).

G's tax liability for 2005 is the sum of the four partial taxes. Her tax liability then is $7,415 ($3,385 + $235 + $3,795 + $0).

If no preference had been provided for net capital gains, the tax on G's taxable income would have been $10,415. The preferential treatment accorded to net capital gains reduced G's tax liability by $3,000 ($10,415—$7,415).

§ 18.2325. Additional Tax Rate. A taxpayer's net capital gains are included in his adjusted gross income. Therefore, those tax deductions and credits that are reduced when a taxpayer's adjusted gross income (AGI) exceeds a specified figure are affected by a taxpayer's net capital gains. A few examples of tax benefits that are so reduced are: the 2% of AGI floor on miscellaneous itemized deductions, the 7.5% floor on medical expense deductions, the reduction of itemized deductions under IRC § 68 when a taxpayer's AGI exceeds a specified figure, the phaseout of the personal exemptions under IRC § 151(d), the 10% of AGI floor on the deduction of net personal casualty losses under IRC § 165(h)(2), and the reduction of the credit available for dependent care services that is mandated by IRC § 21(a)(2). The *effective* rate on a net capital gain can therefore exceed the nominal rate listed in the Code when the gain causes a reduction of deductions or credits.

§ 18.2330. Significance of Groupings. The existence of any preference for net capital gains makes it necessary to group long-term and short-term capital gains and losses separately so that the amount of net capital gain can be determined. Apart from the preferential treatment of net capital gains of noncorporate taxpayers, there are independent reasons to group long-term and short-term capital gains separately. One reason is that there are some provisions in the Code that treat long-term capital gain differently from other income. For example, in general, a gift of appreciated property to a qualified charity is treated more favorably if the sale of that property would have produced a long-term capital gain than would be the case if the sale would have produced short-term capital gain or ordinary income. See IRC §§ 170(b)(1)(C), (D), 170(e)(1)(A). Also, in determining the "distributable net income" of a trust or estate for the purpose of allocating the income and deductions of that trust or estate among the entity itself and its beneficiaries, capital gain income and losses are given special treatment. IRC § 643(a)(3).

In addition to the difference in the treatment of capital gains, it is necessary to distinguish capital gains and losses from ordinary income and losses because of the limitations that Congress imposes on the deductibility of capital losses. See §§ **18.2400–18.2420.**

§ 18.2400.   Limitation on Capital Loss Deductions: General. Capital losses are deductible only if a provision of the Code specifically authorizes the deduction. Typically, if deductible, the statutory authorization is under IRC § 165, but that section is not exclusive. For example, IRC § 166(d) allows a deduction for a nonbusiness bad debt as a short-term capital loss. If permitted under a Code provision, the capital loss is also subject to the limitation on deductibility of capital losses imposed by IRC § 1211. The following discussion describes the limitations contained in IRC § 1211 upon capital losses otherwise deductible under IRC § 165 or under some other Code provision.

§ 18.2410.   Deductible from Capital Gains. A taxpayer's capital losses which are otherwise deductible may be deducted from his capital gains. IRC § 1211. For this purpose, it is irrelevant whether the losses or gains are short-term or long-term; as previously noted in describing the groupings procedure, a capital loss is first deducted from the capital gains of like term (long-term or short-term) and only the excess loss (if any) is deducted from the net gain of the other term. The allocation of capital losses among the four rate categories of net capital gains is described in **§ 18.2322.** If, after allocating the capital losses to all of the capital gains, there is an excess of capital loss remaining, a noncorporate taxpayer may deduct his excess capital loss against up to $3,000 of his ordinary income. IRC § 1211(b). See § **18.2420.** The excess capital loss, which is not deductible because of the limitations of IRC § 1211, may be carried over to other years under the provisions of IRC § 1212 described later in this chapter. See §§ **18.2430–18.2443.**

§ 18.2411. Illustration 1. In Year One, X, an individual, had a long-term capital gain of $20,000, a long-term capital loss of $5,000 and a short-term capital loss of $10,000. X had ordinary income of $100,000. All of X's capital gains and losses were recognized from the sale of corporate stock so that, apart from IRC § 1211 limitations, the losses are deductible under IRC § 165(c)(2). X may offset both his $5,000 long-term capital loss and his $10,000 short-term capital loss against his capital gains. He has a net capital gain of $5,000. Since X had no 25% or 28% category income, his net capital gain qualifies for the 15% maximum rate.

§ 18.2412. Illustration 2. In Year One, Win All, a corporation, had the following gains and losses from the sale of corporate stock: $20,000 short-term capital gain; $8,000 short-term capital loss; $10,000 long-term capital loss. All of Win All's gains and losses are from the sale of corporate stock. Win All may offset its $18,000 of capital losses against its $20,000 of short-term capital gain. Win All first deducts its $8,000 short-term capital loss from its $20,000 of short-term capital gain, and that provides Win All with a net short-term capital gain of $12,000. Win All then deducts its $10,000 long-term capital loss from its $12,000 net short-term capital gain, leaving a remaining short-term capital gain of $2,000. Note that since Win All had no long-term capital gains, its $10,000 long-term capital loss constituted a net long-term capital loss of that same amount. Win All has a net short-term capital gain of $2,000 in excess of its net long-term capital loss.

§ 18.2420. Deductible from Ordinary Income. Where the capital losses of a noncorporate taxpayer exceed his capital gains for that year, the taxpayer can deduct the excess against up to $3,000 of his ordinary income. IRC § 1211(b). A corporate taxpayer is not permitted to deduct its excess capital losses against any of its ordinary income. In the case of a married taxpayer who files a separate tax return, such an excess loss can be deducted from no more than $1,500 of ordinary income. The deductibility of such excess capital losses is the same whether the excess is attributable to a short-term loss or a long-term loss. To the extent that a capital loss is not deductible because of the limitations of IRC § 1211 (e.g., the amount of an individual's capital losses that exceeds the sum of his capital gains plus $3,000 of his ordinary income is not deductible because of IRC § 1211), that amount can be carried forward to subsequent years under the provisions of IRC § 1212, which is described at § **18.2440.**

§ **18.2421.   Illustration.** In Year One, X, an unmarried individual, had taxable income of $38,000 before taking into account her capital gains and losses. In that year, X had a short-term capital gain of $8,000, and X had a long-term capital loss of $17,000. All of X's capital gains and losses were from the sale of corporate stock, and so, subject to the IRC § 1211 limitations, her losses were deductible under IRC § 165(c)(2). Under IRC § 1211(b), X can deduct $8,000 of her long-term capital loss since that is the amount of her short-term capital gain for that year. X can also deduct an additional $3,000 of her net loss. So, X is permitted to deduct a total of $11,000 of her long-term capital loss, and the remaining $6,000 of that loss cannot be deducted from her Year One income. The nondeductible $6,000 of X's loss can be carried over and deducted in subsequent years.

§ **18.2430.   Carryover of Capital Loss: Corporations.** If the capital losses of a corporate taxpayer exceed the capital gains for a tax year (the excess is referred to as the "net capital loss"), IRC § 1211 denies a deduction in that taxable year for the net capital loss. The net capital loss is carried to other taxable years and treated as a short-term capital loss in each carryover or carryback year. IRC § 1212(a). In essence, corporate capital losses may be deducted only to the extent of capital gains in any given tax year. Except for certain special corporations (e.g., an "S corporation," sometimes referred to as a "tax option corporation"), a corporation's net capital loss can be carried back three years to offset capital gains of those years and carried forward for five years to offset future capital gains. However, a corporation's net capital loss cannot be carried back to a prior year to the extent that the carryback would increase or produce a "net operating loss." IRC § 1212(a)(1)(A)(ii). For the meaning of the term "net operating loss," see §§ **13.6100–13.6200.**

§ **18.2431.   Limitations.** Certain capital losses called "foreign expropriation capital losses" cannot be carried back but can be carried forward for ten years. The capital losses of an electing S corporation cannot be carried forward or back to any other year, and the capital losses of a non-electing corporation cannot be deducted in a tax year in which the corporate taxpayer is an electing S corporation. IRC § 1371(b). The net capital loss of a regulated investment company (as defined in IRC § 851) can be carried forward for eight years. IRC § 1212(a)(1)(C)(i). However, a capital loss cannot be carried back to a year in which the corporation was a regulated investment company or a real estate investment trust (REIT). IRC § 1212(a)(3).

§ 18.2432. Loss Not Absorbed by Carryback. If a corporate taxpayer's excess net loss is not fully absorbed under the three-year carryback, the amount of net capital loss that was not offset against the prior years' capital gains is carried forward as a short-term capital loss. This loss is carried forward to each of the five tax years subsequent to the tax year in which the loss was recognized until the loss is fully offset by capital gains or until the five-year period is exhausted.

§ 18.2440. Carryover of Capital Loss: Noncorporate Taxpayers. A noncorporate taxpayer's excess capital loss for a tax year (i.e., capital losses that are not used to reduce the taxpayer's income for that year because of the limitations of IRC § 1211) is carried forward to the taxpayer's succeeding tax year and is treated as if it were actually recognized in that succeeding year. IRC § 1212(b). Thus, if any of the carryover loss cannot be deducted in the next taxable year because of IRC § 1211 limitations, it will be carried forward to the next year and so on. A carry forward capital loss has the same character (long-term or short-term) as it had when the loss was incurred. IRC § 1212(b)(1). A carry forward long-term capital loss is applied to the taxpayer's 28% category in the carryover year. IRC § 1(h)(4)(B). If there is a net loss in the 28% category, the excess loss is treated as described in **§ 18.2322.** A carry forward short-term capital loss is first applied to the taxpayer's short-term capital gains of the carryover year, and any excess of short-term capital loss for that year is deducted from long-term capital gains in the same manner that long-term capital losses are allocated.

§ 18.2441. Contrasted with Corporate Taxpayers. The effect of the carryover is to permit a noncorporate taxpayer to carry forward capital losses for an indefinite number of years until the loss is absorbed or until the taxpayer dies. With one minor exception (IRC § 1212(c)), a capital loss of a noncorporate taxpayer can only be carried forward; it cannot be carried back to prior years. In contrast, most corporate taxpayers can carry forward their capital losses for only five years, but can carry back a capital loss for three years. The capital loss carryforward of a noncorporate taxpayer retains the same characteristic (long-term or short-term) that it had when the loss was incurred. IRC § 1212(b). This is in contrast to the carryover (and carryback) of a capital loss of a corporate taxpayer which is treated as a short-term capital loss. The principal significance of the determination that a capital loss is long-term or short-term is the effect that that characterization can have on the amount of a taxpayer's net capital gain.

§ 18.2442. **Priority of Allocation.** If a noncorporate taxpayer has both a net short-term capital loss and a net long-term capital loss in the same year, a question can arise as to the order in which those two net losses should be used as a deduction against $3,000 of the taxpayer's ordinary income. This question arises only for the purpose of determining the characterization of the taxpayer's losses that are carried forward to subsequent years. In these circumstances, the taxpayer's net short-term capital loss will be deducted first. Only to the extent that the amount of the net short-term capital loss is inadequate to obtain the full $3,000 deduction will the net long-term loss be deductible from ordinary income. IRC § 1212(b)(2).

§ 18.2443. **Unclaimed Carryover Loss Deduction.** In Rev. Rul. 76–177, the Commissioner ruled that a carryover capital loss that could have been deducted in a subsequent year was used up in that year even though the taxpayer failed to claim a deduction for the carryover loss.

§ 18.3000. **DEFINITION OF "CAPITAL ASSET."** IRC § 1222 defines capital gains or losses as the gain or loss from the "sale or exchange of a capital asset."

§ 18.3100. **Statutory Definition.** IRC § 1221 defines a capital asset as "property held by the taxpayer (whether or not connected with his trade or business)," excluding an enumerated list of items which are not treated as capital assets. Four of the exceptions are discussed below. Despite the broad statutory definition of a capital asset as all property other than a list of enumerated exceptions, the Supreme Court initially determined that the statute encompasses only those kinds of properties that the Court believed Congress intended to qualify for the special capital gains tax treatment, but the Court subsequently retreated from that view. Compare *Corn Products Refining Co. v. Commissioner*, 350 U.S. 46 (1955) with *Arkansas Best Corp. v. Commissioner*, 485 U.S. 212 (1988). See §§ **18.4200–18.4210.**

§ **18.3200. Meaning of the Term "Property."** While the term "property" in IRC § 1221 would appear on its face to cover most rights that a taxpayer might sell, the courts have excluded some interests from the scope of that term—perhaps as a means of excluding a transaction from capital gains treatment which may have appeared unwarranted to the court.

§ **18.3210. Compensatory Payments.** Where the taxpayer, a motor carrier, received compensation from the government for the temporary requisition of the taxpayer's facilities during World War II, the Supreme Court held that although an interest of the taxpayer was taken by the government within the meaning of the compensatory requirements of the Fifth Amendment, the taken interest did not constitute property within the meaning of IRC § 1221. *Commissioner v. Gillette Motor Transport, Inc.*, 364 U.S. 130 (1960). In effect, the Court treated the compensatory payments to the taxpayer as rent for the use of property. Similarly, a taxpayer's collection of insurance for the loss of the use of a production facility may constitute ordinary income to the taxpayer. Rev. Rul. 74–444.

§ **18.3220. Relinquishment of Personal Rights.** Any right that a taxpayer might have in her deceased husband's life story was held not to be property within the meaning of IRC § 1221, and, consequently, the payment received by the taxpayer from a moving picture company for the relinquishment of those rights was ordinary income to the taxpayer. *Miller v. Commissioner*, 299 F.2d 706 (2d Cir. 1962); see also Rev. Rul. 65–261.

§ **18.3230. Validity of Narrow Construction of the Term "Property."** As the paragraphs above reflect, the courts have adopted the view that certain items, which in other settings are considered to be "property," are denied capital asset characterization because they do not qualify as "property" for purposes of IRC § 1221. The Supreme Court's decision in the *Arkansas Best* case (at § **18.4220**) rejected the view that the term "capital

asset" could be construed by courts to exclude property that is
not excluded by one of the statutory exceptions set forth in IRC
§ 1221. However, the Court expressly approved of the view that
the term "property" has a narrower meaning in IRC § 1221 than
it has in other contexts, and the Court expressed its approval of
several such cases including the *Gillette Motor* decision (at
§ **18.3210**). 485 U.S. at 217. n.5.

§ **18.3300.   Statutory Exclusions.** IRC § 1221 lists eight categories of property which are excluded from the term "capital asset."
Four of those categories are discussed below.

> § **18.3310.   Property Held Primarily for Sale to Customers
> in the Ordinary Course of the Taxpayer's Trade or Busi-
> ness.** The most litigated statutory exclusion is IRC § 1221(a)(1),
> which excludes a taxpayer's stock in trade, inventory, or property
> held by the taxpayer primarily for sale to customers in the
> ordinary course of his trade or business. Most of the litigation on
> IRC § 1221 deals with the construction of the phrase "property
> held . . . primarily for sale. . . ."

>> § **18.3311.   Taxpayer's Purpose.** The term "primarily" re-
>> fers to the purpose of the taxpayer for holding the property *at
>> the time of sale*. The term "primarily" does not refer to the
>> taxpayer's purpose for the entire period he held the property.
>> For example, if a taxpayer held land for ten years as an
>> investment and then held it for sale to customers for one
>> month prior to selling it, the purpose at the time of sale
>> controls. The taxpayer's prior dealings are significant only as
>> evidence of his purpose at the time of sale. Most taxpayers
>> hold property primarily for sale at the time of the sale. But
>> see, §§ **18.3314–18.3314–3A.** Thus, the majority of cases in
>> this area focus on the question of whether the property was
>> held primarily for sale *to customers in the ordinary course of
>> the taxpayer's trade or business*.

>> § **18.3312.   Customers.** A taxpayer who buys and sells large
>> numbers of stocks and securities but who deals through a
>> stock broker does not hold such stocks and securities for sale
>> to customers—i.e., the taxpayer makes no sales to a "custom-
>> er." *Van Suetendael v. Commissioner*, 3 T.C.M. 987 (1944),
>> aff'd 152 F.2d 654 (2d Cir. 1945). Indeed, the term "custom-
>> ers" was incorporated into IRC § 1221 to preclude ordinary
>> loss treatment for the sale of most stocks and securities.
>> Congress feared that if an ordinary loss were recognized on

the sale of stock, the federal revenue might be reduced severely in a year in which stock prices dipped. Consequently, except for a few statutory exceptions for certain specially defined types of stock [e.g., IRC §§ 306 and 1244], gain or loss from the sale of stock usually constitutes capital gain or loss.

§ 18.3313. Ordinary Course of Trade or Business. Property is not within the "primarily for sale" exception unless the property is held for sale to customers in the ordinary course of the taxpayer's trade or business.

§ 18.3313–1. Illustration 1. *X* purchased Blackacre as an investment in 1958. In 1990, *X* decided to sell Blackacre. *X* listed Blackacre for sale and after a few months sold it to *Y* for a gain of $30,000. *X* does not trade in real property as a business. While at the time of sale *X* was holding Blackacre for sale, he was not holding it for sale to customers in the ordinary course of his trade or business. Consequently, he recognized a long-term capital gain of $30,000 on the sale. If *X* had subdivided Blackacre into 100 lots and sold the lots to separate purchasers, his activity in selling the lots may constitute a trade or business so that IRC § 1221(a)(1) would apply to exclude the land from the definition of capital asset. That is, *X*'s multiple sales of lots may cause purchasers to be "customers," and *X*'s activity in subdividing lots and selling them may place *X* in the trade or business of selling realty. *Mauldin v. Commissioner*, 195 F.2d 714 (10th Cir. 1952). See **§ 18.3314–21.** Even in that latter circumstance, *X* may qualify for relief affording capital gains treatment for much of the gain recognized from the sale of lots under IRC § 1237. See **§ 18.3350.**

§ 18.3313–2. Illustration 2. *X* regularly buys and sells real estate in the course of her business. *X* purchased Blackacre as an investment. After five years, *X* sold Blackacre to *Y*. Blackacre will be treated as a capital asset if *X* can satisfy her heavy burden of proving that she did not hold it for sale to customers even though she held other realty for sale to customers in her business.

§ 18.3314. Definition of "Primarily." The meaning of the term "primarily" is important if a taxpayer holds property both for sale to customers in the ordinary course of business and for another purpose or purposes. To exclude the property under IRC § 1221(a)(1), is it sufficient that the taxpayer's intent to sell was a significant but not the dominant purpose for holding the property? After several courts of appeals divided on that question, the Supreme Court held that the exclusion applies only if the taxpayer's purpose to sell the property to customers in the ordinary course of his business was his dominant purpose. So, the word "primarily" means "of first importance" or "principally." *Malat v. Riddell*, 383 U.S. 569 (1966).

§ **18.3314–1. Dual Purpose.** The *Malat* rule is most significant in a dual purpose case (e.g., a situation where a taxpayer held property either for sale or for rent at the option of the customer). As noted below, this situation will arise more frequently in connection with depreciable or real property which is not a capital asset but *may* be an IRC § 1231 asset. See § **19.2000.**

§ **18.3314–1A. Illustration.** For the past five years, *R* has held a number of unimproved lots, which she offers either for lease or for sale at the option of the buyer or lessee, whichever the case may be. During that period, *R* has leased 14 lots, and she has sold 28 lots. *R* has no preference as to whether a lot is sold or leased. In February of this year, *K* (an unrelated party) elected to purchase one of the lots (Blackacre) from *R* pursuant to her continuing offer either to rent or to sell. *R* recognized a profit on that sale. *R*'s gain will be a capital gain unless the property is deemed to have been held primarily for sale to customers in the ordinary course of *R*'s business or unless the property is excluded from capital asset treatment by IRC § 1221(a)(2) as real property used in a trade or business. While the property likely is excluded by IRC § 1221(a)(2), for the sake of examining the dual purpose doctrine, let us assume that IRC § 1221(a)(2) is inapplicable. Let us also assume that the number of *R*'s sales of realty over the five-year period and the manner in which she has conducted her real estate activities would be sufficient to place her in the business of selling realty to customers in the ordinary course of a trade or business. Finally, let us assume that Blackacre was an isolated lot in *R*'s holdings; and so, its sale will not qualify for relief under IRC § 1237 because it is not part of a subdivided tract. The question then is whether, under the *Malat* rule, *R*'s dual purpose for holding Blackacre will preclude the taxation of her gain as ordinary income on the ground that she did not hold the property *primarily* for sale. While it appears that *Malat* does grant capital gain treatment to *R* (again, assuming unrealistically that IRC § 1221(a)(2) is inapplicable), it is difficult to see why someone who regularly sells property to customers should enjoy capital gains treatment merely because that person also regularly rents such property to customers and is indifferent as to which takes place. The answer may be that dual purpose property will not qualify for capital asset characterization because it will always be depreciable or real property used in a trade or business, which is excluded from capital asset treatment by IRC § 1221(a)(2). If so, while such property may then appear to qualify for treatment under IRC § 1231, which treatment is similar to capital gain treatment, the gain from the sale of such property likely will be denied IRC § 1231 treatment for the reasons described at §§ **19.2141–19.2152.**

§ 18.3314–2. Change of Purpose. A taxpayer may purchase property for one purpose and subsequently change his purpose for holding the property. The crucial issue is the taxpayer's purpose *at the time of sale.*

> **§ 18.3314–2A. Illustration 1.** *X* purchased a large tract of land for the purpose of going into the cattle business. *X* intended to use the land to graze cattle that he planned to purchase. However, because of adverse influences on the cattle business, *X* never purchased cattle and, consequently, never entered the cattle business. *X* held the land for 18 years, and then he subdivided it into lots and promoted the sale of the lots. While *X*'s original purpose was to use the land in a business or to hold it for investment, he changed his purpose before he sold the lots, and his dominant purpose at the time of sale was to sell to customers. *X*'s activities in subdividing the land into salable units, clearing the lots, preparing them for sale, advertising the lots, soliciting sales, and the number of his sales were deemed sufficient to make the sale of lots a business activity of *X* so that his gain was not capital gain by virtue of IRC § 1221(a)(1). *Mauldin v. Commissioner*, 195 F.2d 714 (10th Cir. 1952); see also *Biedenharn Realty Co., Inc. v. United States*, 526 F.2d 409 (5th Cir. 1976). As noted

previously, IRC § 1237 may provide some relief for a taxpayer in this circumstance.

§ 18.3314–2B. Illustration 2. A taxpayer is in the business of selling television sets. He decides to liquidate his business, and so he sells his entire inventory of television sets to another dealer. The inventory is excluded from capital assets under IRC § 1221(a)(1). The courts have not been receptive to a contention that the taxpayer changed his purpose for holding the television sets before the liquidating sale and that he was not holding them for sale *to customers* at that time. Since "inventory" is expressly excluded by IRC § 1221(a)(1), the courts apparently are unwilling to regard the television sets as having lost their characteristic as inventory even though the taxpayer is liquidating his business. See *Williams v. McGowan*, 152 F.2d 570 (2d Cir. 1945); and *Grace Bros., Inc. v. Commissioner*, 173 F.2d 170 (9th Cir. 1949).

Surprisingly, the prospects of establishing a change of purpose for holding land are better than is the case for inventory. Land held for sale to customers in the ordinary course of a trade or business is not "inventory" and that formalistic distinction may well enhance the prospects of establishing that a taxpayer changed his purpose so that he held the land for investment immediately prior to the sale. In this regard, compare *Ridgewood Land Co., Inc. v. Commissioner*, 477 F.2d 135 (5th Cir. 1973), granting capital gains treatment to land sold under a condemnation order even though prior to condemnation the land had been held for sale to customers, with *Juleo, Inc. v. Commissioner*, 483 F.2d 47 (3d Cir.), and *McManus v. Commissioner*, 583 F.2d 443 (9th Cir. 1978) holding that land sold under a condemnation order in similar circumstances retained its characteristic of property held for sale to customers and accordingly that the gain therefrom was ordinary income. The Third and Ninth Circuits held that the condemnation sale was merely the means by which the sale was effected, but the Fifth Circuit held that the condemnation of the land converted it to investment property because the taxpayer could no longer hold it for sale to customers. The Sixth Circuit, in *Case v. United States*,

633 F.2d 1240 (6th Cir. 1980), held that a condemnation of land is one of the factors to be weighed in determining capital asset characterization, but it is only one factor and not conclusive.

§ 18.3314–3. Undecided Purpose. A taxpayer may purchase property for the purpose of either renting it, developing it, or selling it, depending upon the market circumstances. For example, a taxpayer may purchase land for the purpose of either subdividing it into lots and selling the lots or developing apartment units on the land and leasing the units, depending upon which appears more profitable at the time that the taxpayer makes his election. This is a different situation from that described as a "dual purpose." In the dual purpose situation, the taxpayer leaves the decision to buy or to rent to the "purchaser," but in the instant circumstances, the taxpayer himself will decide subsequently how he will use the property. This type of situation might better be described as an "undecided purpose," and it is more closely analogous to a change of purpose than to a dual purpose. Thus, it would appear that the proper test in an undecided purpose case should be the purpose of the taxpayer at the time of sale. Since the taxpayer will likely be holding the property for sale at that time, capital asset classification should turn on whether the taxpayer is holding the property for sale *to customers in the ordinary course of a trade or business*.

§ 18.3314–3A. Treatment in the Courts. However, in *Malat v. Riddell* [**§ 18.3314**], the taxpayer had an undecided purpose, and the Supreme Court characterized it as a dual purpose and treated it accordingly. As Professor Bernstein observed in his excellent article *Primarily for Sale: A Semantic Snare*, 20 Stan.L.Rev. 1093 (1965), the Court was probably led astray by the error of counsel and the lower courts in characterizing the issue as a dual purpose case, and it is possible that *Malat* will not be applied to subsequent, undecided purpose cases. This, however, is speculative, and the *Malat* decision has not yet been so restricted. See *Hollywood Baseball Ass'n v. Commissioner*, 423 F.2d 494 (9th Cir. 1970); and *Gamble v. Commissioner*, 68 T.C. 800 (1977). In *Gamble*, the Tax Court applied *Malat* to an undecided purpose case and held that a sale qualified for IRC § 1231 treatment.

§ **18.3315. Appellate Review.** What is the correct standard for appellate review of a trial court's determination that property was or was not held by a taxpayer primarily for sale to customers in the ordinary course of the taxpayer's trade or business? If the trial court employed proper legal principles, is its determination a finding of fact to be sustained unless clearly erroneous? The Circuit Courts of Appeal are divided as to whether such determinations are a resolution of an issue of law and reviewable as such, or whether such determinations are factual findings which are subject to the clearly erroneous standard of review. Compare *Biedenharn Realty Co., Inc. v. United States*, 526 F.2d 409, n. 25 (5th Cir. 1976), treating this as an issue of law, with *Gartrell v. United States*, 619 F.2d 1150 (6th Cir. 1980) which treats this as a factual issue. The Fifth Circuit subsequently rejected its prior position on this issue; and, basing its decision on a non-tax Supreme Court decision, held that the trial court's determination is one of fact and reviewable under the clearly erroneous standard. *Byram v. United States*, 705 F.2d 1418 (5th Cir. 1983). See also *Jersey Land & Development Corp. v. United States*, 539 F.2d 311 (3d Cir. 1976) which rejects the clearly erroneous standard.

§ **18.3320. Real Property Used in a Trade or Business and Depreciable Property Used in a Trade or Business.** IRC § 1221(a)(2) excludes from the category of "capital assets": (a) real property used in a trade or business; and (b) property used in a trade or business of a character which is subject to the allowance for depreciation under IRC § 167. While such properties will not qualify as capital assets, the gain or loss on the sale or exchange of such properties may qualify for the special tax treatment afforded by IRC § 1231 [discussed at § **19.0000**]. Note that except for a holding period requirement, the language of IRC § 1231 includes within its rules the exact properties excluded from the definition of capital assets by IRC § 1221(a)(2).

§ **18.3321. Illustration 1.** *X* operated an insurance brokerage business at a building which *X* owned. *X* depreciated the building on the straight-line method. *X* subsequently sold the building and the land on which it is situated to *Y*. Since the realty was used in *X*'s business, it does not qualify as a capital asset, but any gain or loss recognized by *X* on the sale will be granted special treatment under IRC § 1231 if X had held the realty for more than one year. If IRC § 1231 characterizes the gain from the sale of the realty as a long-term capital gain, the amount of such gain that is attributable to adjustments made to taxpayer's basis in the building because of depreciation deductions will be "unrecaptured section 1250 gain" for which the maximum tax rate is 25% § **18.2321.**

§ **18.3322.** **Illustration 2.** X used an automobile exclusively for business purposes. The automobile, therefore, was a depreciable asset. X sold the automobile and recognized a loss on the sale. The automobile is not a capital asset, but will be treated as an IRC § 1231 asset if held for more than one year.

§ **18.3323.** **Illustration 3. Goodwill.** X sold his hardware business to Y, and Y paid $10,000 for the goodwill of the business. At the time of the sale, X had owned its goodwill for more than one year.

For many years, goodwill and going concern value were treated as capital assets. While they were used in a trade or business, they were not of a character that is subject to depreciation. However, when Congress added IRC § 197 to the Code in 1993, goodwill, going concern value and similar intangibles that are purchased as part of the acquisition of a going business became amortizable and are treated by IRC § 197(f)(7) as property which is of a character subject to the allowance for depreciation. The characterization of goodwill as property subject to the allowance for depreciation applies only to goodwill that is amortizable under IRC § 197. Goodwill that is self-created by the efforts of a taxpayer is not amortizable and so continues to be a capital asset. Only goodwill that is purchased can be amortized. So, while the gain or loss recognized on the sale of goodwill purchased before August 11, 1993 will still be treated as capital gain or loss, the gain or loss recognized on the sale of goodwill that was purchased after August 10, 1993, as part of the acquisition of a going business will be treated as IRC § 1231 income or loss except to the extent that the IRC § 1245 recapture of depreciation rule causes the recognition of ordinary income. Prop. Reg. § 1.197–2(g)(8). See Chapter Nineteen.

§ **18,3324.** **Illustration 4. Rental Real Property.** A sold to B realty which A had rented at a fair rental for use by the tenant as a single family residence. A recognized a gain on the sale. A had bought the property five years earlier for the purpose of renting it, and she held it for rent until she sold it to B. A never occupied the premises herself, and continuously rented it to unrelated tenants except for two short periods of vacancy between tenants. The question is whether A is deemed to have held the property in a trade or business or did she hold it as an investment? If A's rental activity constitutes the conduct of a trade or business, the property is not a capital asset since it will be realty that is held in a trade or business. The gain on the sale will constitute IRC § 1231 gain. See § **19.1100.** However, if A's rental activity does not constitute the conduct of a trade or business, the realty will be a capital asset, and A's gain on the sale will be a long-term capital gain. The criteria for resolving that issue are discussed at § **10.1122.** It is likely that A managed the property, maintained it, advertised for tenants when there was a vacancy, and collected the rent herself or through an agent; and that activity likely will be sufficient to classify A as having been in the trade or business of renting the property.

§ **18.3330.   Copyrights, Literary or Musical Compositions, and Similar Properties.** IRC § 1221(a)(3) excludes from capital assets a copyright; a literary, musical, or artistic composition; a letter or memorandum; or similar property held by a taxpayer:

(a) whose personal efforts created the property; or

(b) in the case of a letter, memorandum, or similar property, if the property was prepared or produced for the taxpayer; or

(c) if the taxpayer acquired the property in such a manner that his basis in the property is determined in whole or in part by reference to the basis that a person described in (a) or (b) above had in the property.

§ **18.3331.   Patents.** While the Code excludes a copyright held by its creator from the definition of capital assets, no exclusion is made for a patent held by an inventor. This omission is deliberate, and the gain or loss from the sale of a patent will be a capital gain or loss unless the patent is excluded from capital assets under some other specific exception (e.g., if the taxpayer is a professional inventor who is in the business of selling patents to customers). Even a professional inventor can enjoy capital gains treatment if the specific conditions of IRC § 1235 (dealing with the sale of patents) are satisfied. Care should be taken that the patent will be treated as sold and not merely licensed since income from a license is ordinary income. However, for income tax purposes, an *exclusive* license to exploit an invention (possibly including an exclusive license to exploit it only within a specified geographic area or for a specified field of use) is treated as a sale and thus may qualify for capital gains treatment. If a taxpayer wishes to qualify for the special relief accorded by IRC § 1235 to the sale of a patent, the taxpayer must transfer *all substantial rights* to the patent; a restriction as to geographic use will preclude the application of that special relief provision. Treas. Reg. § 1.1235–2(b). A writer, composer, or artist (professional or amateur) receives no comparable relief to that provided for inventors by IRC § 1235.

§ 18.3340. Accounts Receivable. Accounts or notes receivable acquired in the ordinary course of business from services rendered or from the sale of inventory or of property held for sale to customers in the ordinary course of business are not capital assets. IRC § 1221(a)(4). Thus, gain recognized from the sale of such receivables will be ordinary income rather than capital gain.

§ 18.3350. Real Property Subdivided for Sale. As previously noted, if a taxpayer who otherwise is not in the business of selling realty to customers subdivides a tract of land into a number of lots or parcels and then sells the lots or parcels in a series of individual transactions, the number of such sales and the extent of the taxpayer's commercial activity in marketing the lots (or parcels) may cause the taxpayer to be treated as engaged in the business of selling realty to customers. If no statutory relief were afforded, the taxpayer's profits from those sales would be treated as ordinary income. However, Congress has provided relief in IRC § 1237.

If the requirements of § 1237 are satisfied, all or part of a taxpayer's gain from the sale of such a lot (or parcel) will qualify for capital gain treatment. The requirements are as follows:

(1) The tract (or any part thereof) was not previously held by the taxpayer primarily for sale to customers in the ordinary course of a trade or business (determined after applying IRC § 1237),

(2) In the taxable year in which the sale of the lot or parcel occurred, the taxpayer did not hold any other realty (i.e., realty

other than the tract) primarily for sale to customers in the ordinary course of a trade or business,

(3) No substantial improvements that would enhance the value of the sold lot (or parcel) were made by the taxpayer (or by certain other persons described in the statute) on the tract either while the taxpayer held the property or pursuant to a contract of sale of the property.

(4) Unless acquired by the taxpayer by inheritance or devise, the lot (or parcel) was held by the taxpayer for at least 5 years before the sale.

If the total number of lots (or parcels) of the same tract that were sold by a taxpayer within the coverage of IRC § 1237 is five or fewer, then all of the taxpayer's gain from such sales will be a capital gain. If a taxpayer sells more than five lots (or parcels) of the same tract, then a portion of the taxpayer's gain will be treated as ordinary income. IRC § 1237(b)(1). The imposition of ordinary income treatment for a portion of the taxpayer's gain applies only to gain recognized from the sale of such lots (or parcels) in and after the first taxable year in which the taxpayer sold the sixth lot (or parcel). The amount of gain from the sale of any such lot (or parcel) that is treated as ordinary income is equal to 5% of the selling price of that lot (or parcel).

The provisions of IRC § 1237 do not apply to the sale of a lot or parcel unless the gain that a taxpayer recognizes from that sale would be treated as gain from property held primarily for sale to customers in the ordinary course of business, and the exclusive reason for that treatment must be because of the taxpayer's activity in subdividing the tract and selling the lots or parcels. If the gain would be treated as ordinary income for some other reason, then IRC § 1237 is inapplicable.

Of course, IRC § 1237 is merely a safe harbor. If the gain from the sale of a lot or parcel would be treated as a capital gain in the absence of IRC § 1237, then the latter section will not apply and the gain will be so treated. Thus, the 5% of selling price exception to capital gain treatment will be inapplicable.

§ 18.4000. JUDICIAL EXCEPTIONS TO CAPITAL GAINS TREATMENT.

§ 18.4100. **Anticipation of Ordinary Income.** When a taxpayer receives an amount from the sale of a property interest which amount represents an anticipation of ordinary income to be earned by the property (i.e., the amount realized is received in lieu of ordinary income), the amount realized by the taxpayer is characterized as ordinary income. Thus, where a landlord receives a payment from his tenant to terminate the tenant's lease, the amount received by the landlord is a substitute for rent and is treated as ordinary income. *Hort v. Commissioner*, 313 U.S. 28 (1941); see also Treas. Reg. § 1.61–8(b). The doctrine of anticipation of income is similar to the principle of "anticipatory assignment of income." Consequently, those two principles are discussed together in § **20.0000** *et seq.* In general, the anticipation of income doctrine applies when a taxpayer retains a residual interest (as contrasted to a fractional share of the entire property) in the property part of which was sold to the purchaser. *Commissioner v. Lake*, 356 U.S. 260 (1958). See § **20.3000** *et seq.*

§ 18.4200. *Corn Products* **Doctrine.** In *Corn Products Refining Co. v. Commissioner*, 350 U.S. 46 (1955), the Supreme Court denied capital gain and loss treatment for gains and losses recognized by the taxpayer from the sale of corn futures which the taxpayer had purchased to insure that its cost of acquiring corn to be used in the manufacture of starch, syrup and other products would not exceed a specified amount (i.e., the amount payable for the delivery of corn under the futures contract). The corn futures were purchased by the taxpayer as a "hedge" against a rise in the price of corn. As we shall see, there is very little viability left to the *Corn Products* doctrine, and it appears likely that the doctrine is completely defunct. But, compare § **18.4220** with § **18.4230.** Note that, as a consequence of a subsequent amendment, gain or loss from a hedging transaction that is identified as such within a specified time period will be ordinary income or loss. IRC § 1221(a)(7), treas. Reg. § 1.1221–2.

> **§ 18.4210. Rationale.** While the Court conceded that the corn futures were not excluded from capital assets by any of the statutory exclusions, it determined that Congress did not intend to provide capital gain and loss treatment to profits and losses arising from the everyday operations of a taxpayer's business. Since the purchase and sale of corn futures was integrally related to the taxpayer's business, the gains and losses were treated as ordinary gain and loss. This doctrine is frequently referred to as the *"Corn Products* doctrine." While the reasoning of the Court in *Corn Products* has been repudiated, hedging transactions may nevertheless result in ordinary income or loss. The treatment of hedging transaction is set forth in Treas. Reg. § 1.1221–2.

§ 18.4220. Repudiation of the Doctrine. The significance and scope of the *Corn Products* doctrine was substantially reduced by the Supreme Court's decision in *Arkansas Best Corp. v. Commissioner*, 485 U.S. 212 (1988). But see **§ 18.4230.** In *Arkansas Best*, the Supreme Court did not purport to overrule the *Corn Products* case, but the Court so narrowed the holding of *Corn Products* as to repudiate much of the doctrine (the *Corn Products* doctrine) that had previously been thought to have been established. In *Arkansas Best*, the Supreme Court rejected the notion that there are exceptions to the capital asset characterization of IRC § 1221 apart from those statutory exceptions expressly stated in IRC § 1221 itself (or in another Code provision). After *Arkansas Best*, the general rule is that the motive of the taxpayer when acquiring an asset is not relevant in determining the character of gain or loss recognized on the disposition of the asset. See *First Chicago Corporation and Affiliated Corporations v. Commissioner*, 69 T.C.M. 2089 (1995). The Supreme Court limited the *Corn Products* holding to a determination that the "inventory" exception set forth in IRC § 1221(a)(1) applies to gain or loss incurred on a "hedging" transaction that was designed for limiting the cost of inventory that the taxpayer would acquire for its business. As noted below (**§ 18.4230**), the Tax Court and the Court of Federal Claims have construed *Arkansas Best* as authorizing an expansive construction of the explicit statutory exceptions in IRC § 1221 to the term "capital assets."

§ 18.4230. Corporate Stock. Corporate stock usually constitutes a capital asset so that the sale or exchange of that stock will produce capital gain or loss. There are several statutory exceptions that mandate ordinary gain or loss treatment in special circumstances. See IRC §§ 306, 1244. In a number of cases that were decided prior to the *Arkansas Best* decision (at **§ 18.4220**), the courts held that the gain or loss recognized from the sale of corporate stock which had been purchased for a business purpose, as contrasted to an investment purpose, was ordinary gain or loss (actually, only cases involving a loss would arise because a taxpayer who had a gain on such sales was not likely to point out that it had acquired the stock for a business purpose). See, e.g., *Campbell Taggart v. United States*, 744 F.2d 442 (5th Cir. 1984). While the business or investment motive of the taxpayer is no longer a factor in determining capital or ordinary treatment, one aspect of that pre-*Arkansas Best* doctrine (the "source of supply" principle) may still be valid. One of the more common circumstances in which ordinary loss treatment was allowed was where stock of a corporation was purchased in order to give the purchaser access to assets of the target corporation which the purchaser needed for its inventory (the so-called "source of supply" context). See *Booth Newspapers, Inc. v. United States*, 303 F.2d 916 (Ct. Cl. 1962). The Supreme Court's decision in *Arkansas Best may* have vitiated the doctrines laid down in those decisions, but the Claims Court has held that the "source of supply" principle continues to be viable in the post-*Arkansas Best* period. *Circle K Corporation v. United States*, 68 AFTR 2d 91–5462 (Cl. Ct. 1991).

In a 1991 decision that relied on *Corn Products*, the Claims Court held that the loss recognized on the sale of corporate stock which had been purchased to protect the taxpayer's inventory source was an ordinary loss. *Circle K Corp. v. United States*, 68 AFTR2d 91–5458 (Cl. Ct. 1991) and 68 AFTR 2d 91–5462 (Cl. Ct. 1991). The Claims Court held that the *Corn Products* doctrine required ordinary loss treatment and that *Arkansas Best* had not overruled that aspect of *Corn Products*. The court agreed that *Arkansas Best* had repudiated the construction of the *Corn Products* doctrine that looked to the motive of the taxpayer in having acquired an asset, but the court maintained that the Supreme Court did not repudiate the doctrine that a loss should be ordinary when there was a substantially close connection between the taxpayer's acquisition of the stock and the conduct of taxpayer's business so that it fairly can be characterized as an integral part of taxpayer's inventory-purchase system. For a criticism of the *Circle K* decision as being irreconcilable with *Arkansas Best*, see Sheppard, *Circle K: How Taxpayer Choice Survives Arkansas Best*, 51 Tax Notes 1359 (March 17, 1991). Note that the name of the Claims Court has been changed to the "Court of Federal Claims."

The position of the Claims Court was adopted by the Tax Court in a 1993 decision that was reviewed by the court. *Federal Nat'l Mortgage Ass'n v. Commissioner*, 100 T.C. 541 (1993) (reviewed by the court). In that case, the taxpayer acquired certain properties as a hedge against its risk of loss both on securities it held and on securities that it issued where the loss could arise because of changes in interest rates. The court held that losses that the taxpayer recognized on the disposition of the hedge properties constituted an ordinary loss. The court held that *Arkansas Best* authorized a broad, non-literal construction of *all* of the statutory exceptions in IRC § 1221 to the term "capital asset"; the authorization is not limited to the inventory exception. The court further

held that the hedge properties in question fit within IRC
§ 1221(a)(4), the exception for certain accounts and notes receivable. While the court conceded that the literal terms of IRC
§ 1221(a)(4) do not apply to the hedging property in that case, the
court held that a non-literal expansive reading of that provision is
permissible and appropriate. The court also held that the hedging
property need only be a surrogate for the property for which a
risk of loss is hedged; it need not be the same type of property.

§ 18.4300.   Sale of Right to Personal Services or Contract Rights.

§ 18.4310.   **Personal Services.** When a taxpayer has a right to
future income as consideration for services performed, the taxpayer's gain from the sale of his right to such income will usually be
treated as ordinary income. See *Bellamy v. Commissioner*, 43 T.C.
487 (1965). This is particularly true if the taxpayer's services
were to have been performed after the sale. *Holt v. Commissioner*,
303 F.2d 687 (9th Cir. 1962). The cases on this issue usually rely
on the "in lieu of" test; the payment was received as a substitute
for, or in lieu of, ordinary income payments such as wages.

§ 18.4320.   **Contract Rights.** While there is a division of authority, a taxpayer's gain from the sale of contract rights, other
than a tenant's sale of his leasehold interest, will often be treated
as ordinary income. See *Commissioner v. Pittston Co.*, 252 F.2d
344 (2d Cir., 1958). The courts rest their characterization of the
gain as ordinary income either on the "in lieu of" test or on the
ground that there was no "sale or exchange" as required by IRC
§ 1222. The "sale or exchange" requirement is discussed at
§ 18.5000. The decisions in this area cannot be harmonized
under any general principles. A better view would not preclude
capital gain treatment for the sale of all contract rights, but
instead would rest upon the nature of the contract rights involved
in the sale.

§ 18.4321.   **Illustration.** In *Commissioner v. Ferrer*, 304
F.2d 125 (2d Cir. 1962), the taxpayer had executed a contract
with an author for the taxpayer to produce the author's play.
The contract granted the taxpayer the exclusive right to produce the play, the right to prevent the disposition of motion
picture rights before a certain date, and, if a motion picture
was produced, the taxpayer was entitled to a percentage of the
proceeds from the picture. The taxpayer made advance pay-

ments to the author in consideration of this agreement, and, consequently, the taxpayer had an investment in his contract rights. The taxpayer released the author from this contract in consideration of specified payments from a company that wished to produce the work as a motion picture. The court treated the "release" as a sale and held that the taxpayer was entitled to capital gains on the sale of a capital asset, with the exception that the portion of the payment attributable to the release of the taxpayer's right to a percentage of the movie proceeds was treated as ordinary income because it was received "in lieu of" license fees.

§ 18.4322. Characterizing Payment. Thus, *Ferrer* suggests that capital gain treatment should not rest on the artificial distinction between a release and a sale. The payment received by the taxpayer should be characterized according to what was actually sold, and, where appropriate, the gain should be treated in part as capital gain and in part as ordinary income.

§ 18.4323. Illustration. *X* leased premises to a tenant, *Y*, who wished to modify the premises for its own special uses as a TV studio. *Y* was obliged under the lease to restore the premises to their original condition upon the termination of the lease. *Y* became concerned, after several years of rising costs, about the cost of making such restorations at a future date. To protect itself against rising future costs, *Y* paid *X* $125,000 in consideration of *X*'s releasing *Y* from its obligation to restore the premises. The Tax Court held that the payment constituted ordinary income to *X* [*Sirbo Holdings, Inc. v. Commissioner*, 61 T.C. 723 (1974)], and, after expressing some doubts in an earlier appeal, the Second Circuit affirmed the Tax Court's decision. 509 F.2d 1220 (2d Cir. 1975).

§ 18.4330. Leasehold Interest. A tenant's sale of his leasehold interest in property will usually be treated as a capital transaction. *Metropolitan Bldg. Co. v. Commissioner*, 282 F.2d 592 (9th Cir. 1960). Indeed, IRC § 1241 eliminates any "sale or exchange" problems from such cases by providing that any amount received by a lessee for cancellation of a lease is considered as an amount received "in exchange" for such lease.

§ 18.4400. Correlation with Prior Transactions. A gain or loss (or an expenditure) may be characterized as ordinary or capital, whichever is appropriate, in order to correlate the current year's tax consequences with the tax consequences imposed on prior transactions that are related to the current year's gain, loss, or expenditure.

§ 18.4410.   Illustration 1. *X*, a bank, deducted overdue notes as business bad debts, which are fully deductible from ordinary income. Subsequently, the debtors became able to make payments on the overdue notes, and *X* then sold the notes to a third party for about 40% of the unpaid balance of the notes. The payment received by *X* on the sale of the notes was treated as ordinary income. Since the substance of the transaction was to reduce the amount of the debts that was actually uncollectible and since *X* had deducted the full amount against ordinary income, the payment received in the subsequent year should be treated as ordinary income. *Merchants National Bank v. Commissioner*, 199 F.2d 657 (5th Cir. 1952).

§ 18.4420.   Illustration 2. On the liquidation of a corporation, a shareholder (the taxpayer) recognized a long-term capital gain on the difference between the amount he received in liquidation of his corporate stock and his basis in his stock. IRC § 331. In a subsequent year, a judgment was obtained against the corporation. The taxpayer and other shareholders were required to pay the judgment as transferees of the corporation's assets. The taxpayer claimed an ordinary deduction for the payment, but the Supreme Court held that the tax consequence of the payment must be correlated with the treatment of the liquidating distributions that the taxpayer had received in the earlier year. The Court held that the net effect of the taxpayer's payment was to reduce the amount that he received from the corporation as a liquidating distribution, and, since those distributions had been treated as long-term capital gain to the taxpayer, his payback must be treated as a capital loss. *Arrowsmith v. Commissioner*, 344 U.S. 6 (1952). Note that IRC § 1341 may provide relief for a taxpayer in this circumstance. Rev. Rul. 78–25. See **§ 13.4300.**

§ 18.4430.   Insider Stock Profits. As a result of a settlement or of a judgment, an officer or director of a corporation is required to return to the corporation the "profits" the officer or director recognized on the sale of stock because there either was or may have been a violation of Section 16(b) of the Securities Exchange Act of 1934. As used in this context, the term "profits" has a special meaning; namely, it refers to the difference between the price at which the taxpayer sold stock and the price that he subsequently paid when he purchased stock of the same corporation. The question is whether the taxpayer's payment to the corporation, pursuant to the settlement or judgment, should be treated as a capital loss in order to correlate the payment with the treatment of the gain which the taxpayer recognized when he sold the stock subject to the Section 16(b) violation. The Tax Court has held that the payment to the corporation is not integrally related to the gain earned by the taxpayer on the sale of his stock; thus, the payment should be treated as an ordinary business expense deduction. However, four circuit courts of appeal have rejected the Tax Court's view and have held that the payment is a capital loss to the taxpayer. *Anderson v. Commissioner*, 480 F.2d 1304 (7th Cir. 1973), rev'g 56 T.C. 1370 (1971); *Mitchell v. Commissioner*, 428 F.2d 259 (6th Cir. 1970), rev'g 52 T.C. 170 (1969); *Cummings v. Commissioner*, 506 F.2d 449 (2d Cir. 1974); and *Brown v. Commissioner*, 529 F.2d 609 (10th Cir. 1976).

§ 18.4440. Application. In Year One, a taxpayer recognized losses on the sale of depreciable properties used in his business. Since the taxpayer had no gain under IRC § 1231 that year, the taxpayer deducted the losses as ordinary losses under IRC § 1231 [see **§ 19.1100**]. In Year Seven, the taxpayer was reimbursed by *X* for the losses the taxpayer had recognized in Year One; the reimbursement was paid to the taxpayer as part of the settlement of the taxpayer's claim against *X* for an antitrust offense. The reimbursement constitutes gross income to the taxpayer under the tax benefit rule. The question is: should the reimbursement be treated as a gain under IRC § 1231 (which *may* be treated as a long-term capital gain) or should the reimbursement be treated as ordinary income since the losses recognized in Year One were allowed as ordinary losses? In *Bresler v. Commissioner*, 65 T.C. 182 (1975), a similar reimbursement was treated as ordinary income. What would be the tax treatment of the reimbursement if part of the Year One loss had been "recaptured" under IRC § 1231(c) by characterizing a subsequent net section 1231 gain as ordinary income? If the *Bresler* position is adopted, it would seem that the amount of Year One loss that was recaptured should be treated as if it had been a capital loss.

§ 18.5000. SALE OR EXCHANGE. IRC § 1222 defines long-term and short-term capital gains and losses as gain or loss "from the sale or exchange of a capital asset" held for a specified period (more than one year for a long-term gain or loss, and one year or less for a short-term gain or loss). The term "sale or exchange" has been construed as a term of art establishing an additional requirement for obtaining capital gain or loss treatment. A "sale or exchange" of an asset is a narrower concept than a "disposition" of an asset. There are statutory provisions characterizing certain specific transactions as a "sale or exchange" so that the capital gain or IRC § 1231 provisions may apply to those situations. E.g., IRC §§ 1234A, 1241 (cancellation of a lease), and 1271(a)(1) (retirement of a debt instrument).

§ 18.5100. Involuntary Conversion. The amount received by a taxpayer on a forced sale of his property under a foreclosure proceeding or under a condemnation proceeding is held to be received from an actual sale of the property which meets the requirements of IRC § 1222. See *Helvering v. Hammel*, 311 U.S. 504 (1941). However, an amount received by a taxpayer as insurance proceeds for damage to his property is not received pursuant to a sale or exchange. The gain or loss from most involuntary conversions, whether or not treated as a sale or exchange, will be determined either under IRC § 1231 [discussed in **§ 19.2100**] or under IRC § 165(h).

§ 18.5110. Abandonment. When a taxpayer abandons property, the loss does not result from a sale or exchange. This creates an artificial distinction between abandoning property for an ordinary loss and selling it in a foreclosure proceeding which may result in a capital loss.

§ 18.5200. Bootstrap Sales. When a taxpayer sells income-producing property for a set price and when the buyer makes no down payment on the purchase and has no *personal obligation* to pay the purchase price but is obligated to pay the purchase price only out of his earnings (if any) from the purchased property, the transaction is sometimes referred to as a "bootstrap sale." In one case involving a bootstrap sale to a charity, the government contended that the transaction was not a sale or exchange under IRC § 1222, but rather was akin to a joint venture in which the seller continued to share in the profits of the property. The Supreme Court, however, rejected that contention in *Commissioner v. Clay B. Brown*, 380 U.S. 563 (1965) where the lower court had found that the price for which the stock was sold was a reasonable price. But see *Kraut v. Commissioner*, 62 T.C. 420 (1974), holding that *in fact* a transaction which was similar in form to *Clay Brown* was not a sale but rather was a fee paid to the charity for the use of its tax exempt status.

§ 18.5300. Cancellation of Lease or Distributor's Agreement. Amounts received by a lessee for his agreement to cancel the lease are treated as amounts received for the lessee's exchange of the lease and so comply with the "sale or exchange" requirement. IRC § 1241.

The gain recognized by the lessee *may* therefore qualify for capital gain treatment or for IRC § 1231 treatment if other requirements are satisfied. The same provision also applies to a distributor of goods who receives payment for the cancellation of the distributor's agreement (but only if the distributor has a substantial capital investment in the distributorship). *Ibid.*

§ 18.6000. STATUTORY CHARACTERIZATION OF CERTAIN TRANSACTIONS.
Certain transactions are characterized as capital or ordinary by specific statutory provisions. Two of those provisions are listed below. Other provisions include the rules on recapture of previously claimed deductions in IRC §§ 1245, 1250, and 1252, and the recognition of ordinary loss on the sale of certain stock covered by IRC § 1244. Some other statutory provisions are IRC § 1235 (sale or exchange of patents), IRC § 1237 (real property subdivided for sale), IRC § 1256 (Section 1256 contracts), and IRC § 1258 (conversion transactions).

§ 18.6100. Bad Debt Deduction.
A nonbusiness bad debt deduction is treated as a short-term capital loss by IRC § 166(d).

§ 18.6200. Worthless Security.
A worthless security is treated as if it were sold for zero at the end of the tax year in which it becomes worthless and, thus, will usually be treated as a long-term capital loss. IRC § 165(g).

§ 18.6300. Qualified Dividend Income.
Most dividends from domestic corporations (and from certain foreign corporations) will be taxed at capital gain rates. IRC § 1(h)(11). Such dividends will qualify for a maximum tax rate of 15%, or even 5% if the taxpayer is in a low tax bracket. While the dividend is taxed at capital gain rates, it is not treated as a capital gain. Consequently, capital losses cannot be deducted from dividend income except to the extent of the $3,000 of excess capital losses that can be deducted from non-capital gain income. See § 18.2410. While most dividends from domestic corporations will qualify for the capital gain tax treatment, there are some exceptions. For example, the capital gain tax treatment will not apply if the stock on which the dividend was paid was not held by the shareholder for a specified period of time. IRC § 1(h)(11)(B)(iii).

§ 18.7000. HOLDING PERIOD.
A taxpayer's holding period of a capital asset determines whether a gain or loss on the sale or exchange of the asset will be long-term or short-term. A long-term gain or loss is recognized on the sale or exchange of an asset held for more than one year. A short-term gain or loss is recognized on the sale or exchange of an asset held for one year or less. IRC § 1222. The taxpayer's holding

period is also important in determining whether a gain or loss recognized on the sale or exchange or involuntary conversion of an asset will be included in the IRC § 1231 hotchpot [discussed in **§ 19.2200**].

§ 18.7100. Tacking. A taxpayer's holding period for an asset is determined under IRC § 1223. In some circumstances, the previous holding period of one person in property may be "tacked" on to the period of a taxpayer who subsequently holds the same property. If a transferee's basis in transferred property is determined in whole or in part by reference to the transferor's basis, the transferor's holding period is tacked on to the transferor's holding period. IRC § 1223(2).

§ 18.7110. Illustration. *X* held Blackacre for twelve months then gave Blackacre to *Y* as a gift, and *Y* sold Blackacre one month later. *Y*'s basis in Blackacre is determined by reference to the basis that *X* had in the property. IRC § 1015. *X*'s twelve-month holding period is tacked on to *Y*'s holding period so that *Y* is deemed to have held Blackacre for thirteen months when he sold it. IRC § 1223(2).

§ 18.7120. Tacking in Tax–Free Exchanges. In some circumstances, a taxpayer's holding period for one property may be tacked to the holding period of another property acquired in a tax-free exchange. To qualify for tacking, the property transferred by taxpayer in the exchange must have been either a capital asset or property described in IRC § 1231 in the hands of the taxpayer. IRC § 1223(1).

§ 18.7121. Illustration 1. *X* held Blackacre (unimproved land) as an investment for ten years and then exchanged Blackacre for Whiteacre (unimproved land) which *X* also held as an investment. *X* realized a substantial gain on the exchange, but under IRC § 1031 no gain is recognized. *X* sold Whiteacre three months later. Presumably, Blackacre was either a capital asset or an IRC § 1231 asset in *X*'s hands. *X*'s ten-year holding period for Blackacre is tacked on to this period of holding Whiteacre. IRC § 1223(1).

§ 18.7122. Illustration 2. *X* held Blackacre as an investment for eight years and then exchanged it for Whiteacre (unimproved land) plus $5,000 cash. *X* also held Whiteacre as an investment. Blackacre qualified as a capital asset of *X*'s. *X* realized a substantial gain on the exchange, but under IRC § 1031 *X* recognized only $5,000 of that gain (the amount of "boot" received by *X*). *X* sold Whiteacre three months later.

X's basis in Whiteacre is determined in part by his basis in Blackacre. Consequently, *X*'s eight-year holding period for Blackacre is tacked on to his holding period of Whiteacre. IRC § 1223(1).

§ 18.8000. GAIN FROM QUALIFIED SMALL BUSINESS STOCK.

§ 18.8100. Exclusion from Gross Income. In 1993, Congress adopted a provision to provide tax relief for gains recognized from the sale or exchange of stock of certain small corporations referred to as "qualified small businesses." When this provision is applicable, 50% of the gain from the sale or exchange of such stock will be excluded from the taxpayer's gross income. IRC § 1202(a). The purpose of this relief provision is to facilitate the raising of capital by small, newly incorporated businesses by reducing the tax burden on a shareholder's disposition of original issue stock in certain circumstances described below. The availability of tax relief on the disposition of such stock will provide an inducement to invest in new ventures. In order to qualify for the 50% exclusion from gross income, the stock must have been held by the shareholder for more than 5 years, it must have been acquired as part of an original issue after August 10, 1993, and only noncorporate shareholders can obtain the exclusion (i.e., a sale of such stock by a corporate shareholder will not qualify for the 50% exclusion). IRC § 1202(a), (c).

§ 18.8200. Limitation on Amount of Exclusion. The gain that qualifies for application of the 50% exclusion is called "eligible gain." The maximum amount of "eligible gain" from a disposition of qualified stock that a noncorporate shareholder can take into account in applying the 50% exclusion is the *greater* of: (1) $10,000,000 ($5,000,000 for a married taxpayer filing a separate return) reduced by the aggregate amount of eligible gain that the shareholder had taken into account in prior years because of dispositions of qualified stock of the same corporation, or (2) 10 times the shareholder's aggregate adjusted basis in the qualified stock of that corporation that the shareholder disposed of in that taxable year. IRC § 1202(b)(1).

§ 18.8210. Eligible Gain. "Eligible gain" means gain from the sale or exchange of "qualified small business stock" (**§ 18.8400**) that had been held for more than five years. IRC § 1202(b)(2).

§ 18.8220. Treatment of Non–Excluded Eligible Gain. Any eligible gain recognized by the taxpayer in excess of the limitation described above typically will be treated as a long-term capital gain. Such gain typically will qualify for the maximum 15% rate for net capital gain.

§ 18.8230. Minimum Tax. Seven percent of the amount that is excluded from gross income by IRC § 1202(a) is treated as an alternative minimum tax preference item and so may cause the taxpayer to be subject to the alternative minimum tax. IRC § 57(a)(7); see Chapter Fifteen.

§ 18.8240. Section 1202 Gain. The amount that is not excluded from income by the percentage limitation imposed by IRC § 1202(a) is classified as "section 1202 gain" and is included in the group of long-term capital gains that receive a 28% maximum tax rate. See **§ 18.2321.** In effect, this means that the portion of eligible gain that is not excluded from gross income by IRC § 1202(a) is taxed at a 28% maximum rate rather than the more typical 15% maximum rate.

§ 18.8300. Qualified Small Business. A "qualified small business" is a domestic corporation (certain types of corporations are precluded from qualifying—e.g., an S corporation (sometimes called a tax-option corporation) cannot qualify) whose aggregate gross assets did not exceed $50,000,000 at any time during the period between August 10, 1993, and the time immediately after the issuance of the qualified stock. In addition, the corporation must agree to make such reports to the Service and to its shareholders as the Service may require. IRC § 1202(d). For this purpose, the corporations comprising a parent-subsidiary chain as defined in § 1202(d)(3) are treated as a single corporation. The "aggregate gross assets" of a corporation (or of a parent-subsidiary chain) refers to the cash and aggregate basis of its other assets, except that for this purpose the basis of a contributed asset is deemed to be equal to the value that that asset had at the time of contribution. IRC § 1202(d)(2).

§ 18.8400. Qualified Small Business Stock. "Qualified small business stock" is defined in IRC § 1202(c). To be qualified small business stock:

(1) the stock must be acquired by the shareholder after August 10, 1993, and at its original issuance (directly or through an underwriter) in exchange for money, other property (other than stock) or as compensation for services (other than services as an underwriter);

(2) the issuing corporation must be a qualified small business (**§ 18.8300**) at the date of issuance and during the period that the shareholder holds the stock;

(3) during substantially all of the shareholder's holding period for such stock, the corporation either (i) meets the "active business" requirements of IRC § 1202(e), or (ii) was a "specialized small business investment company" as defined in IRC § 1202(c)(2)(B).

*

CHAPTER NINETEEN

Quasi-Capital Assets and Recapture of Depreciation

§ 19.0000. QUASI–CAPITAL ASSETS AND RECAPTURE OF DEPRECIATION.

§ 19.1000. BACKGROUND: PROPERTY USED IN TRADE OR BUSINESS.

As noted in § **18.3320**, real property or depreciable property used in a trade or business is excluded from the definition of capital assets by IRC § 1221(a)(2). During World War II, many such properties were involuntarily converted by government requisition, condemnation, or, in the case of some ship owners, by the destruction of the ships by foreign powers. In addition, plants and equipment were sold to the federal government. From 1938 to 1942, any gain recognized by the taxpayer from such conversions or sales was ordinary income. In the case of an involuntary conversion, the taxpayer could defer the gain under the antecedent to IRC § 1033 by reinvesting the proceeds in property similar or related in service or use. During the war, however, there frequently were no replacement properties available.

§ 19.1100. Congressional Relief.

To relieve the taxpayer's plight, Congress adopted the antecedent to IRC § 1231 in 1942. Under IRC § 1231, the recognized gains and losses from sales or exchanges of property used in a trade or business and the recognized gains and losses from involuntary conversions of certain capital assets and property used in a trade or business are netted. Each such gain or loss is referred to as a "section 1231 gain" or a "section 1231 loss." IRC § 1231(a)(3). Subject to several exceptions described later in this chapter, if the netting computation results in a net gain (referred to as a "net section 1231 gain"), all such gains and losses are treated as long-term capital gains and long-term capital losses. But see § **19.2220**. If the net figure is a loss (referred to as a "net section 1231 loss") or if the net is zero, all such gains and losses are treated as ordinary income and loss. The effect of this netting procedure (referred to as a "hotchpot") is that section 1231 gains and losses are offset against each other, and if there is a net loss, the net figure is given ordinary loss treatment, but if there is a net gain, the net figure is given long-term capital gain treatment except to the extent that the recapture provision of IRC § 1231(c) [§ **19.2220**] applies. In making this comparison of recognized gains and losses (the "hotchpot"), only gains that are included in gross income and losses that are deductible (without regard to the limitation in IRC § 1211 on the deductibility of capital losses) are taken into account. IRC § 1231(a)(4).

If a net section 1231 loss did not qualify as an ordinary deduction, a businessman would have a disincentive against selling a depreciable asset for a loss since he could retain it and continue to claim ordinary deductions for the asset's depreciation. Because of the "hotchpot" formula that is utilized in IRC § 1231 and because a net section 1231 gain may be treated as ordinary income to the extent that the taxpayer had net section 1231 losses in any of the preceding five taxable years [§ **19.2220**], it is a mistake to refer to a gain from the sale of depreciable property as a long-term capital gain. Such a gain should be thought of as a section 1231 gain which may or may not be treated as a long-term capital gain depending upon the taxpayer's other section 1231 gains and losses during the tax year and during the preceding five years. The operation of IRC § 1231 and the recapture of depreciation provisions are discussed in this chapter.

As a consequence of statutory amendments made in 1997 and 1998, even when a net section 1231 gain qualifies for long-term capital gain treatment, the extent to which such gain is attributable to depreciation adjustments to the basis of depreciable realty (primarily buildings and their structural components) that was converted or disposed of, that amount of the gain must be segregated. Such gain is referred to as the "unrecaptured section 1250 gain," and the maximum tax rate applicable to such gain is 25% instead of the more typical 15% rate. See § **18.2321**.

§ 19.2000.   IRC § 1231.

§ 19.2100.   Transactions Included in IRC § 1231. IRC § 1231 applies to the gain or loss recognized on the sale or exchange of "property used in the trade or business" and to the gain or loss recognized from the involuntary conversion (as a result of destruction in whole or in part, theft or seizure, or an exercise of the power of requisition or condemnation, or the threat or imminence thereof) of "property used in the trade or business" and of capital assets held by the taxpayer for more than one year and held in connection either with a trade or business or with a transaction entered into for profit. Note that gains and losses from the involuntary conversion by casualty or theft of capital assets that are not held in connection with a trade or business or with a transaction entered into for profit are dealt with in IRC § 165(h). See §§ **7.2531–7.2537.** One important consequence of including the involuntary conversion of certain capital assets in IRC § 1231 is that the gains from such conversions may thereby qualify for long-term capital gain treatment even if the conversion did not constitute a sale and exchange. Note that if the aggregate of gains and losses from involuntary conversions by casualty and theft that are otherwise included in IRC § 1231 is a net loss, then the gains and losses from such conversions are excluded from IRC § 1231 treatment. See § **19.2213.**

The term "property used in the trade or business" is a term of art that is explained in §§ **19.2140–19.2152.** As you can see from that explanation, a capital asset that is used in connection with a trade or business is separate and distinct from "property used in the trade or business" since the latter phrase refers only to real property and property of a character that is subject to depreciation, neither of which can be a capital asset because of IRC § 1221(a)(2).

§ 19.2110. Involuntary Conversion Qualified. An involuntary conversion includes a loss from a casualty or theft even though no compensation is received. Note that the gain or loss on a *capital asset* falls under IRC § 1231 only if it results from an involuntary conversion and only if the asset is held in connection with a trade or business or profit-seeking transaction for more than one year. In certain circumstances, even the gains and losses from the involuntary conversions of such capital assets are excluded from IRC § 1231. See § **19.2213.**

§ 19.2120. Illustration 1. *X*'s personal residence is destroyed by fire and *X* collects $40,000 insurance proceeds. *X* does not reinvest the proceeds in realty. *X* had owned her home for ten years and had a basis of $30,000 in it. From the receipt of the proceeds, *X* recognized a gain of $10,000 which will not be characterized as a section 1231 gain because the residence was not held in connection with a trade or business or a profit-seeking transaction. The treatment of the gain is dealt with in IRC § 165(h). See §§ **7.2531–7.2537.**

§ 19.2130. Illustration 2. *X* owned land which he used in his business for two years. *X* sold the land for a $4,000 gain. *X*'s gain is a section 1231 gain.

§ 19.2140. Definition of "Property Used in the Trade or Business." "Property used in the trade or business" is a term of art in tax law meaning real property and depreciable property held by the taxpayer for more than one year and used in the taxpayer's trade or business; however, this definition is subject to some statutory qualifications. IRC § 1231(b). In this context, "depreciable property" is property of a character which is subject to the allowance of depreciation. Id.

§ 19.2141. Property Excluded. IRC § 1231(b)(1) expressly *excludes* from "property used in the trade or business": (a) the taxpayer's inventory; (b) property held by the taxpayer primarily for sale to customers in the ordinary course of his trade or business; (c) a copyright, a literary, musical, or artistic composition, a letter or memorandum, or similar property that is held by a taxpayer who created that property or who is described in IRC § 1221(a)(3) [this section of the Code establishes an identical exclusion from capital assets and is discussed in **§ 18.3330**]; and (d) a United States government publication received from the government without charge or for a price less than that at which the publication is sold to the general public.

§ 19.2142. Compared with Exclusion from Capital Assets. The exclusion of property held by the taxpayer primarily for sale to customers in the ordinary course of his trade or business is identical to the exclusion from capital assets established in IRC § 1221(a)(1), and should be construed in the same manner. The Supreme Court's decision in *Malat v. Riddell* [discussed in **§ 18.3314**] that the word "primarily" refers to the taxpayer's dominant purpose is also applicable to IRC § 1231(b)(1)(B). *Hollywood Baseball Ass'n v. Commissioner*, 423 F.2d 494 (9th Cir. 1970); *Gamble v. Commissioner*, 68 T.C. 800 (1977). The First Circuit has held that the function of the word "primarily" in IRC § 1231 is to distinguish sales in liquidation of an asset which is of no further use to the taxpayer in his business (which sales may come within IRC § 1231) from sales, made in the ordinary course of business, of an asset that (if not sold) would still be useful in the taxpayer's business. The latter sales are excluded from IRC § 1231 treatment by the "primarily for sale" exception even though such sales are made infrequently and even though the taxpayer preferred to rent the asset rather than to sell it. *International Shoe Machine Corp. v. United States*, 491 F.2d 157 (1st Cir. 1974). See also *Honeywell Inc. v. Commissioner*, 87 T.C. 624, 633 (1986). The "primarily for sale" condition is satisfied in such cases because: (1) the sale is made in the ordinary course of taxpayer's business, and (2) at the time of the sale, the taxpayer holds the property primarily for sale (regardless of what purpose the taxpayer had prior to that time). In essence, this construction of the word "primarily" was adopted by the Commissioner in Rev. Rul. 80–37. See also, PLR 8621003.

§ 19.2150.   *Corn Products* Doctrine. There was a question whether, in addition to the statutory exclusions listed in IRC § 1231(b), sales which are integrally related to the normal conduct of a taxpayer's business should be excluded under the judicial exception established by the Supreme Court in *Corn Products Refining Co. v. Commissioner*, 350 U.S. 46 (1955). The virtual demise of the *Corn Products* doctrine makes that question moot. The *Corn Products* doctrine [discussed at **§§ 18.4200– 18.4230**] was established in denying capital gain and loss treatment under IRC § 1222. The Ninth Circuit held that the *Corn Products* doctrine also applied to IRC § 1231. *Hollywood Baseball Ass'n v. Commissioner*, 423 F.2d 494 (9th Cir. 1970). The application of *Corn Products* to IRC § 1231 would be one means of preventing gain from the sale of property held for a dual purpose from being treated as a long-term capital gain. An alternative ground for denying IRC § 1231 treatment to such sales was stated in the *International Shoe Machine* case, *supra*, and was adopted by the Commissioner in Rev. Rul. 80–37. See **§ 19.2142.** In view of the Supreme Court's repudiation in *Arkansas Best Corp. v. Commissioner*, 485 U.S. 212 (1988) of much of the *Corn Products* doctrine (or at least of the doctrine that the *Corn Products* case previously had been thought to have established) [see **§§ 18.4200–18.4230**], the tax treatment of such sales likely will be controlled exclusively by the *International Shoe Machine* approach.

§ 19.2151.   Illustration 1. *X* offered typewriters for sale or for rent. *X* actually preferred to rent the typewriters because his profit margin was greater on rentals than on sales, but *X* was required by his distributor to offer the typewriters for sale as well. *X* sold relatively few typewriters, and only 8% of his annual profit is attributable to sales, while 92% is attributable to rental income. *X* holds the typewriters for a dual purpose; but even if his dominant purpose is to rent rather than to sell, *X*'s sales are an integral part of his business. In view of the Supreme Court's decision in the *Arkansas Best* case [§ **19.2150**], the *Corn Products* doctrine either no longer exists or has been so substantially narrowed that it will not affect the characterization of *X*'s gain. Under similar facts, the First Circuit held, in the *International Shoe Machine* case, *supra*, that the gain from such sales constituted ordinary income for the reasons stated in § **19.2142**. But see § **19.2152**. The Commissioner adopted the *International Shoe Machine* approach in Rev. Rul. 80–37. See also, PLR 8621003

§ **19.2152.   Illustration 2.** *Y* manufactured and sold steel cable. *Y* delivered the cable to its customers on steel reels which *Y* owned. *Y* took depreciation deductions for the steel reels. *Y*'s customers were required to pay a deposit on the steel reels. If a customer did not return the reel within one year, title to the reel passed to the customer, and *Y* retained the deposit. Most customers did return the reels. The question was whether *Y*'s gain on the reels which were not returned was ordinary income or a section 1231 gain. In Rev. Rul. 75–34, the Commissioner ruled that *Y*'s gain on the sale of the reels which were not returned was section 1231 gain except to the extent that the recapture of depreciation rules (IRC § 1245) applied. It is difficult to reconcile this 1975 ruling with the *International Shoe Machine* case and with Rev. Rul. 80–37. See § **19.2142**. It seems likely that the Commissioner will not adhere to the view taken in Rev. Rul. 75–34.

§ **19.2200.   How IRC § 1231 Applies to Gain and Losses.** The recognized section 1231 gains and the recognized section 1231 losses are netted. If the result is a net gain, both gains and losses are treated as long-term capital gains and losses (subject to the "recapture" rules described at § **19.2220**); if the result is a net loss, both gains and losses are treated as ordinary gains and losses. The practical effect of this "hotchpot" procedure is that a net section 1231 gain is treated as a long-term capital gain and a net section 1231 loss is an ordinary loss deduction. However, because of the recapture rules described at § **19.2220**, all or part of a net section 1231 gain may be treated as ordinary income.

§ 19.2210. Computation of the Hotchpot.

§ 19.2211. **Gains and Losses Included.** Gains are included only to the extent they are included in the taxpayer's gross income. Losses are included only to the extent they are otherwise deductible. IRC § 1231(a)(4)(A). For this purpose, the limitation on deducting capital losses established in IRC § 1211 is ignored.

§ 19.2212. **Gains Excluded.** Gains are excluded from IRC § 1231 to the extent that such gains are treated as ordinary income because they represent recapture of deductions under, for example, IRC §§ 1245, 1250, 1252, or 291(a)(1).

§ 19.2213. **Gains and Losses from Certain Involuntary Conversions.** Recognized gains and losses from involuntary conversions arising from fire, storm, shipwreck, or other casualty, or from theft of property used in the trade or business or of a capital asset held for more than one year in connection with a trade or business or profit-seeking transaction are excluded from IRC § 1231 *if,* for the taxable year, the losses from such involuntary conversions exceed the gains therefrom. IRC § 1231(a)(4)(C). However, if such gains exceed such losses for the taxable year, then both are included in IRC § 1231. Thus, there is a second "hotchpot" of gains and losses from such involuntary conversions of such properties. This rule is designed to give a taxpayer an ordinary deduction for casualty and theft losses (in excess of gains from such sources) under IRC § 165 rather than offsetting the loss against other section 1231 gains that might otherwise be treated as a long-term capital gain.

§ 19.2214. **Unrecaptured Section 1250 Gain.** The gain from the disposition or conversion of certain depreciated realty (primarily buildings and their structural components) that is attributable to depreciation adjustments to basis and that qualifies as a long-term capital gain is referred to as "unrecaptured section 1250 gain." The maximum tax rate on such gain is 25% instead of the more typical 15% rate. IRC § 1(h)(1)(D), (7). See § **18.2321.**

§ 19.2220. **Recapture of Net Section 1231 Losses.** If in a taxable year a taxpayer has a greater amount of section 1231 losses than he has section 1231 gains, the gains and losses are treated as ordinary. The effect of this hotchpot treatment is to characterize the net section 1231 loss (i.e., the excess of the aggregate of section 1231 losses for that year over the aggregate of section 1231 gains for that year) as an ordinary loss. This ordinary loss treatment for a net section 1231 loss is recaptured to the extent that the taxpayer has a net section 1231 gain in any of the succeeding five years. IRC § 1231(c). The recapture is accomplished by treating a net section 1231 gain for a taxable year as ordinary income to the extent that the taxpayer had net section 1231 losses in any of the preceding five years that had not previously been recaptured (a so-called "non-recaptured net section 1231 loss").

§ 19.2221. Allocation of Recapture. Currently, there are at least four different maximum tax rates that apply to net capital gains (28%, 25%, 15% and 5%). When a taxpayer has a net section 1231 gain, part of which will be treated as ordinary income because of the IRC § 1231(c) recapture rule, the question arises as to which of the underlying section 1231 gains is to be treated as ordinary income. Some section 1231 gains may qualify for a 15% maximum tax rate, some (the unrecaptured section 1250 gain) for a 25% rate, and perhaps some for a 28% maximum rate. The amount that is recharacterized as ordinary income under the IRC § 1231(c) recapture rule will not qualify for the maximum rate limitation. Treasury has been authorized by IRC § 1(h)(8) to determine by forms or regulation the manner in which such recaptured income is to be allocated. In Notice 97–59, which was promulgated prior to the 1998 amendment of the capital gains rates, the Commissioner stated that the recaptured ordinary income is to be allocated first to 28% category section 1231 gain, then any remaining recapture ordinary income to 25% category section 1231 gain, and any remaining recapture ordinary income to 15% category gain. See **§ 18.2321.** It is likely that this same approach will be applied to section 1231 gains under the 1998 amended version of the Code as well.

§ 19.2230. Illustrations: Operation of IRC § 1231. All properties referred to in the following examples were held by the taxpayer for more than one year. All years referred to in the following examples are taxable years that began after the year 1984. In the following examples, there were no events having significance for IRC § 1231 purposes other than the events mentioned in the examples.

§ 19.2231. Illustration 1. In Year One, X recognized a gain of $10,000 from the sale of land that he used in his business, and X recognized a loss of $4,000 from the sale of depreciable property used in his business. X had no net section 1231 loss in any of the five years preceding Year One. Since X's section 1231 gains for Year One exceed his section 1231 losses for that year, the gain from the sale of the land is treated as a long-term capital gain and the loss from the sale of the depreciable property is treated as a long-term capital loss. The effect of this characterization is to net the section 1231 gains and losses and to treat the net gain (referred to as the "net section 1231 gain") as a long-term capital gain. For the significance of qualifying as long-term capital gain, see **§ 18.2321.**

§ 19.2232. Illustration 2. The same facts apply as those stated in **§ 19.2231** except that in Year One X had a valuable sculpture stolen from his office and an automobile that X owned and used in his business was destroyed by fire. As a work of art, the sculpture had not been a depreciable asset. The sculpture was a capital asset that was used in connection with X's business, and the automobile was "property used in the trade or business." X had a basis of $4,000 in the sculpture which had a value of $10,000 and was uninsured. X's basis in the automobile was $2,000. X collected $3,000 on his insurance coverage for the car. X is entitled to a $4,000 theft deduction for the sculpture [IRC § 165(c)(1)], and he recognized a $1,000 gain from the insurance proceeds that he received for his car. X did not elect under IRC § 1033 not to recognize the gain from the conversion of his car. While the theft loss and the gain on the involuntary conversion of the car otherwise would have been included in IRC § 1231, they will be excluded by IRC § 1231(a)(4)(C) because X's losses from such conversions are greater than his gains from such conversions. X is allowed an ordinary deduction of $4,000 for the theft of the sculpture, and he recognizes ordinary income of $1,000 from the receipt of the insurance proceeds. [The gain that X recognized by receiving insurance proceeds for the conversion of his car does not arise from a "sale or exchange" and so does not qualify for capital gain characterization under IRC § 1222.] X's $10,000 gain from the sale of land will be a long-term capital gain, and X's $4,000 loss from the sale of depreciable property will be a long-term capital loss.

§ **19.2233.** **Illustration 3.** The same facts as those stated in § **19.2232** except that in Year One a painting that X held for personal purposes and kept in his residence was destroyed by fire. X had a basis of $30,000 in that painting, and he collected $38,000 insurance proceeds to compensate for that loss. X recognized a gain of $8,000 from the conversion of that painting, and he did not elect under IRC §§ 1033 not to recognize that gain. The $8,000 gain is not included in IRC § 1231. X's painting is a capital asset, but it is not held in connection with a trade or business or a profit-seeking transaction. The $8,000 gain is treated as long-term capital gain by IRC § 165(h)(2)(B). The tax consequences of the other events that occurred to X in Year One are the same as was described in § **19.2232.**

§ **19.2234.** **Illustration 4.** In Year One, Y recognized a $30,000 loss on the sale of an apartment building that Y had owned and operated as a business. In that same year, Y received $3,000 insurance proceeds because of the loss of a valuable painting that was destroyed by a fire in Y's office. The painting was a capital asset that was used in connection with Y's business since it had been hung on Y's office wall as a decoration and was a nondepreciable work of art. Y had a basis of $1,000 in the painting, and so he recognized a gain of $2,000 from his collection of the insurance proceeds. Since Y had no losses from involuntary conversions in Year One, his gain from the conversion of his painting is included in IRC § 1231. Y's section 1231 loss for Year One ($30,000) exceeds his section 1231 gain for that year ($2,000), and so both gain and loss will be treated as ordinary. The effect of this characterization is to net the gain from the painting against the loss from the sale of the apartment building and to treat the excess loss, referred to as the net section 1231 loss, as an ordinary loss. Thus, Y had a net section 1231 loss of $28,000 in Year One.

§ **19.2235.** **Illustration 5.** The same facts as those stated in § **19.2234.** In Year Two, Y had no section 1231 gains or losses. In Year Three, Y had a $10,000 section 1231 gain and a $6,000 section 1231 loss. If there were no recapture rule, that gain and loss would be treated as long-term capital gain and long-term capital loss. IRC § 1231(a)(1). Y has a net section 1231 gain of $4,000. The recapture rule causes that $4,000 of net section 1231 gain to be characterized as ordinary income. IRC § 1231(c). The net section 1231 gain for Year Three is treated as ordinary income to the extent that Y has an unrecaptured net section 1231 loss (referred to in the statute as a "non-recaptured net section 1231 loss") from the five years prior to Year Three. In Year One, two years prior to Year Three, Y had a net section 1231 loss of $28,000, and none of that loss was recaptured in the intervening year between Years One and Three. Therefore, all of Y's $4,000 net section 1231 gain for Year Three is treated as ordinary income. That constitutes a recapture of $4,000 of the net section 1231 loss that Y had in Year One. After Year Three, Y has a non-recaptured net section 1231 loss from Year One of $24,000. Because of the treatment of the $4,000 of net section 1231 gain as ordinary income, Y's remaining section 1231 gain of $6,000 exactly equals Y's section 1231 loss for that year. Since Y's section 1231 gains do not exceed Y's section 1231 losses, the remaining $6,000 section 1231 gain and the $6,000 section 1231 loss will be treated as ordinary gain and ordinary loss. IRC § 1231(a)(2).

§ 19.2236.   Illustration 6. The same facts as those stated in **§ 19.2235.** Y had no section 1231 gains or losses in Years Four and Five. In Year Six, Y had a net section 1231 gain of $42,000. In that year, Y had a non-recaptured net section 1231 loss of $24,000 from Year One which is within the five-year period preceding Year Six. Therefore, $24,000 of Y's net section 1231 gain for Year Six is treated as ordinary income, and the remaining $18,000 of his net section 1231 gain is treated as a long-term capital gain.

§ 19.3000.   RECAPTURE OF DEPRECIATION: GENERAL. The statutory scheme which allowed a deduction against ordinary income for depreciation of business property, yet permitted the gain from the sale of such property to be treated as a section 1231 gain, was regarded by some as a system that effectively authorized the conversion of an ordinary income deduction into a long-term capital gain. The availability of accelerated depreciation methods (including MACRS) and of the expense deduction (so-called "bonus depreciation") under IRC § 179 aggravates this problem.

§ 19.3100.   Illustration of Purported Abuse of Trading a Capital Gain for Ordinary Deductions. On January 1, 1960, X purchased a new truck to be used in his business at a cost of $5,000. The truck had a useful life of five years. X elected to use the double declining balance method of depreciation and accordingly took a depreciation deduction of $2,000 on his 1960 tax return (the half-year convention does not apply since the year involved precedes the adoption of ACRS). On January 1, 1961, X sold the truck to Y for $4,000. Since X's adjusted basis in the truck was $3,000 ($5,000 cost minus $2,000 depreciation), X recognized a section 1231 gain of $1,000 on the sale. X had no section 1231 losses in 1961, so the $1,000 gain recognized on the sale of the truck would be treated as a long-term capital gain. But X realized a $1,000 gain only because he had taken a $2,000 depreciation deduction. The net effect of this rule is that X deducted $1,000 from ordinary income at the cost of a $1,000 long-term capital gain only $500 of which was subject to tax under the tax treatment of long-term capital gain at that time.

§ 19.3110. Statutory Imposition of Recapture. The Treasury characterized the $1,000 gain in **§ 19.3100** as a "recapture" of the depreciation that the taxpayer had previously deducted and urged Congress to tax such gain as ordinary income. The government sought a statutory rule that would correlate the tax characterization of the taxpayer's gain with the tax characterization of the depreciation deductions that were effectively recouped when the property was sold. For a criticism of the Treasury's characterization of such gain as a "recapture" of depreciation, see Douglas Kahn, *Accelerated Depreciation—Tax Expenditure or Proper Allowance for Measuring Net Income?*, 78 Mich. L.Rev. 1, 43–53 (1979). Beginning with the year 1962, Congress added several sections to the Code that recapture some or all of the ordinary deductions that would otherwise have created section 1231 gains. The recapture provisions have been expanded and modified by Congress since the first provision was adopted in 1962.

In addition to the recapture provisions, gain from sale or exchange of certain types of non-capital assets between persons of specified relationship is treated as ordinary income. For example, any gain recognized on the sale or exchange of depreciable property between certain related parties is treated as ordinary income by IRC § 1239. The characterization as ordinary income is not restricted to depreciation recapture; *all* of the gain is treated as ordinary income. Similarly, IRC § 707(b)(2) treats as ordinary income any gain recognized on the *sale or exchange* of property that is not a capital asset in the hands of the transferee if the gain is from a sale or exchange between a partnership and either (1) persons owning more than 50% interest in the partnership, or (2) another partnership a majority of whose ownership is held by the same persons as hold the ownership of the transferor partnership.

§ 19.3200.   IRC § 1245: In General. IRC § 1245 provides that gain realized from the disposition of depreciable personal property and a very narrow category of certain depreciable tangible realty will be treated as ordinary income to the extent that the gain is attributable to adjustments to basis caused by deductions previously allowed for depreciation or amortization of the property. Gain will be treated as ordinary income to the extent that the gain arises because of adjustments for depreciation or amortization reflected in the taxpayer's adjusted basis. Note that this recapture rule will apply to the amortization deductions allowable under IRC § 197 for goodwill, going concern value and other intangible properties. Certain other adjustments to basis (i.e., an adjustment caused by an IRC § 179 expense deduction and an adjustment caused by IRC §§ 108 and 1017 because of the nonrecognition of income realized from a discharge of indebtedness) can cause ordinary income recognition under IRC § 1245 on the disposition of the asset. IRC §§ 1017(d), 1245(a)(2)(C).

§ 19.3210.   Priority of Recapture of Depreciation Deductions. While IRC § 1245 causes the recapture of certain kinds of amortization deductions as well as depreciation deductions, hereafter reference will be made primarily to depreciation deductions. However, the reader should keep in mind that amortization deductions are included in the discussion.

IRC § 1245 recaptures depreciation not only on sales and exchanges but also on other dispositions of depreciable property unless exempted by an express provision in IRC § 1245 itself. IRC § 1245 takes priority over any other section of the Code. Consequently, a disposition of property may cause a taxpayer to recognize ordinary income under IRC § 1245 even though another section of the Code provides that no gain will be recognized. A disposition of IRC § 1245 property can cause the recognition of income unless it is a type of disposition that is excluded from income recognition by IRC § 1245(b); an exclusion is available only to the extent that that provision so provides. See **§ 19.3240.**

§ 19.3220.   Section 1245 Property. Property, the disposition of which is subject to so-called recapture of depreciation under IRC § 1245, is referred to as section 1245 property. The types of property that are so characterized, and therefore are subject to IRC § 1245, are properties of a character subject to the allowance for depreciation under IRC § 167 that are either:

(a) personal property (tangible or intangible);

(b) certain real property (other than a building or its structural components) which is either depreciable property or for which certain amortization deductions are allowed; or

(c) any property which otherwise is not section 1245 property or section 1250 property will be treated as section 1245 property if the basis of such property was reduced under IRC § 1017 because of the taxpayer's nonrecognition of income caused by a discharge of indebtedness. IRC § 1017(d)(1).

Several types of properties (e.g., a single-purpose agricultural or horticultural structure) are subject to IRC § 1245 by specific provisions in that section. IRC § 1245(a)(3)(D), (E), and (F).

Thus, section 1245 property applies to all depreciable or amortizable personalty. Section 1245 property does not include buildings or their structural components. Section 1245 property does include certain depreciable or amortizable realty (other than a building or its structural components). Note that the disposition of a building that was placed in service between 1981 and 1986, and that was depreciated on some method other than the straight-line method, may be subjected to recapture of depreciation under IRC § 1245. **§ 19.3310.** Also note that a *corporation* will recapture a percentage (usually 20%) of the amount of depreciation or amortization that the corporation would have been required to recapture under IRC § 1245 upon its disposition of a building if IRC § 1245 had been applicable to the disposition of the building. IRC § 291(a)(1). See **§ 19.3330.**

§ 19.3230. Computation of Ordinary Income. On the disposition of section 1245 property, the amount recaptured is either the depreciation claimed or the gain, whichever is the lesser amount. For this purpose, "gain" refers to the amount of appreciation of the asset (the excess of its value over the taxpayer's basis). The technical terms of the statute state that the taxpayer will recognize ordinary income in the amount by which the taxpayer's adjusted basis is exceeded by the lower of either: (a) the taxpayer's "recomputed basis" (defined below); or (b) either (1) the amount realized by the taxpayer in the case of a sale or exchange, or (2) the fair market value of the property in the case of other dispositions.

§ 19.3231. Recomputed Basis. A taxpayer's recomputed basis equals the taxpayer's adjusted basis plus any deductions, allowed or allowable to the taxpayer or to any other person (e.g., a donor), for depreciation or amortization to the extent that such deductions are reflected in the taxpayer's adjusted basis. The adjustments to the basis of an asset that are taken into account include: depreciation allowable under IRC §§ 167 or 168 (MACRS), the amount of expense deduction taken under IRC § 179 [see § **12.2000**], and the amount of reduction of basis of the asset caused by IRC §§ 108 and 1017 because of the nonrecognition of income realized from a discharge of indebtedness. IRC §§ 1245(a)(2) and 1017(d)(1)(B). If the taxpayer can prove that the amount of such deductions that was *allowed* (i.e., the amount claimed as deductions on a federal tax return and permitted to be deducted) is less than the amount of such deductions that was allowable, then only the amount allowed is used in determining recomputed basis. IRC § 1245(a)(2)(B). Note that there are special rules for determining the recomputed basis of player contracts on the sale or exchange of a franchise to conduct a sports enterprise. IRC § 1245(a)(4).

> **§ 19.3231–1. Illustration 1.** On January 14, Year One, X purchased a truck for use in his business at a cost of $5,000. The truck was five-year property, and X used the half-year convention. X did not expense any of the cost of the truck under IRC § 179. X properly claimed a depreciation deduction of $1,000 for the truck for Year One. On February 5, Year Two, X sold the truck for $4,100. X properly claimed a depreciation deduction of $800 for the truck for Year Two. X's adjusted basis in the truck was $3,200, and X's recomputed basis was $5,000 ($3,200 of adjusted basis plus $1,800 of adjustment to basis attributable to depreciation). Since the amount realized by X ($4,100) is less than his recomputed basis ($5,000), the difference ($900) between the amount realized and the adjusted basis constitutes ordinary income to X. Thus, X recognized a gain of $900, all of which is treated as ordinary income.

> **§ 19.3231–2. Illustration 2.** The same facts apply as in § **19.3231–1**, except that X sold the truck for $2,500. The amount realized by X is less than his recomputed basis and is also less than X's adjusted basis ($3,200). Consequently, X has no IRC § 1245 gain from the sale. X recognized a section 1231 loss of $700.

§ **19.3231–3. Illustration 3.** The same facts apply as in § **19.3231–1**, except that X sold the truck for $6,000. X's recomputed basis ($5,000) is less than the amount realized ($6,000). The difference between X's recomputed basis ($5,000) and his adjusted basis ($3,200) constitutes ordinary income under IRC § 1245. Thus, X recognized a gain of $2,800 on the sale—$1,800 of which constitutes ordinary income and the remaining $1,000 of which constitutes a section 1231 gain. Stating it differently, if X had not been entitled to any depreciation deductions for the truck (and if none had been allowed), X would have had a $5,000 basis in the truck when he sold it, and so X would have recognized a gain of only $1,000—the appreciation in value which took place after he acquired the truck. Yet, because of the depreciation allowable to X, he had a basis of only $3,200 when he sold the truck, and, therefore, he recognized a gain of $2,800 on the sale—$1,800 of which gain would not have been recognized but for the depreciation adjustments to his basis and $1,000 of which would have been recognized in any event. The $1,800 of X's gain which is attributable to his depreciation allowance is treated as ordinary income and the remaining $1,000 of X's gain is treated as section 1231 gain.

§ **19.3231–4. Illustration 4.** The same facts apply as in § **19.3231–1**, except that on January 1, Year Two, X gave the truck to his son, S, who then used the truck in his business. X did not recognize any gain under IRC § 1245 when he disposed of the truck because gifts are specifically excluded from recapture treatment by IRC § 1245(b)(1). Assume that X is not entitled to any depreciation deduction for Year Two, and all of the depreciation deductions for the use of the truck in Year Two is allocable to S. Prop. Reg. § 1.168–5(f)(3). S properly deducted $1,600 depreciation for the truck in Year Two. On January 15, Year Three, S sold the truck for $5,500. Under IRC § 1015, S's adjusted basis when he received the truck in Year Two was equal to his father's adjusted basis of $4,000. S properly took a depreciation deduction of $480 for Year Three. After taking depreciation deductions for Years Two and Three that totaled $2,080, S's adjusted basis was $1,920 at the time of the sale. S's recomputed basis was $5,000 (i.e., $1,920 adjusted basis plus $2,080 depreciation allowed to S plus $1,000 depreciation allowed to X since X's depreciation deduction is reflected in S's adjusted basis). The amount of IRC § 1245 recapture is determined by the recomputed basis ($5,000) since that is a lesser figure than the amount realized on the sale ($5,500). Thus, the difference between S's recomputed basis ($5,000) and his adjusted basis ($1,920) is ordinary income. Accordingly, S recognized $3,080 ordinary income and $500 section 1231 gain from the sale.

§ 19.3240. Exceptions to IRC § 1245. You will recall that IRC § 1245 overrides other provisions of the Code and can cause the recognition of income on a disposition that otherwise is covered by a nonrecognition provision of the Code. IRC § 1245(a)(1), (d). However, certain dispositions are excluded (in whole or in part) from IRC § 1245 by the provisions of IRC § 1245(b). Unless a transfer or disposition is listed in IRC § 1245(b), recapture will occur. Some of the transactions to which IRC § 1245(a) does not apply are: (a) gifts; (b) transfers at death (other than income in respect of a decedent); (c) certain tax-free transactions (i.e., certain transactions upon which gain or loss is not recognized because of a statutory provision), but only those tax-free exchanges that are listed in IRC § 1245(b)(3) are excluded; (d) "like-kind" exchanges and involuntary conversions, to the extent that gain is not recognized under IRC § 1031 or IRC § 1033, ordinarily are not dispositions that require recapture, but if property to which IRC § 1245 does not apply is received in exchange for or in replacement of IRC § 1245 property, then IRC § 1245 will apply to the extent of the value of such non-IRC § 1245 property; and (e) transactions described in IRC §§ 1071 and 1081.

§ 19.3300. Recapture of Depreciation Taken on Buildings. As noted above, IRC § 1245 does not apply to a disposition of a building, its structural components, or to many other types of realty. In 1964, two years after IRC § 1245 was adopted, Congress enacted IRC § 1250 to recapture a portion of the depreciation that was allowed on real property (other than the limited types of realty that were covered by IRC § 1245). IRC § 1250 applies to "section 1250 property" which is defined as real property that is of a character subject to depreciation and is not included within the terms of IRC § 1245. As originally adopted, IRC § 1250 was far gentler on real property than IRC § 1245 is on personalty. The recapture rules of IRC § 1250 were broadened by Congress in the years following its adoption. Since those changes were prospective, it is necessary to determine the status of IRC § 1250 at the time that an item of section 1250 property was first placed into service by the taxpayer to determine the consequences of disposing of that item. In most of the years of its applicability, for realty held longer than one year, IRC § 1250 required a recapture of no more depreciation than the excess of the depreciation deductions allowed to the taxpayer over the amount of depreciation that was allowable under the straight-line method over the same period of use. This excess amount of depreciation is referred to as the "additional depreciation." In certain circumstances only a portion of the additional depreciation would be recaptured. This limitation of recapture to all or part of the additional depreciation applies only if the taxpayer's holding period of the section 1250 property is greater than one year. IRC § 1250(b)(1).

§ 19.3310. Recapture for the Disposition of Buildings That Were Placed into Service Between 1981 and 1986. Most buildings other than residential rental property that were placed into service after 1980 and before 1987 and that were depreciated on a method other than the straight-line method, are subjected to the recapture rules of IRC § 1245 rather than those of IRC § 1250. Thus, on the disposition of such a building that was depreciated on an accelerated method, all of the allowed depreciation (and not just the additional amount of depreciation) is subject to recapture.

§ 19.3320. Current Treatment. The current rules for IRC § 1250 recapture only the additional depreciation that was reflected in the asset's basis and was allowed as a deduction provided that the taxpayer's holding period for the asset is greater than one year. IRC §§ 1250(a)(1), 1250(b)(1). For certain types of low-income housing, only a percentage of the property's additional depreciation is subject to recapture. As far as virtually all buildings and their structural components are concerned, for noncorporate taxpayers there will be no recapture on their disposition if the property was acquired after 1986 and if the taxpayer's holding period is greater than one year. This is because virtually all buildings placed in service after 1986 cannot be depreciated on an accelerated method; they must be depreciated on the straight-line method. IRC § 168(b)(3). Since by definition there can be no additional depreciation for a building that is depreciated on the straight-line method, the recapture rules will apply only to the disposition of buildings that were placed into service prior to 1987 unless the taxpayer's holding period for a building that was placed in service after 1986 does not exceed one year. As noted below, a corporation can have recapture of depreciation when it disposes of a building or other section 1250 property.

If a taxpayer's holding period for a building used in his business does not exceed one year, the building does not qualify as "property used in the trade or business" as that term is defined in IRC § 1231(b)(1), and so the gain from the sale of that property is not section 1231 gain. Since the building is excluded from being a capital asset by IRC § 1221(a)(2), gain from the sale of the building is ordinary income. In addition, but not in duplication, IRC § 1250 will recapture any depreciation deductions that were allowed, but that will not affect the result in a sale or exchange since the taxpayer will recognize ordinary income on all of his gain without regard to the application of § 1250. IRC § 1250(a)(1)(A), (b)(1).

§ 19.3330. Corporate Disposition. When a corporation disposes of section 1250 property, it will have recapture income equal to 20% of the excess of: (1) the amount of depreciation that would be recaptured under IRC § 1245 if that provision applied to the disposition over (2) the amount treated as ordinary recapture income under IRC § 1250. IRC § 291(a)(1). This provision applies only to corporations.

§ 19.4000. SALE OF A BUSINESS. Where a taxpayer (individual, corporation, or partnership) sells the assets of a business (as contrasted to the sale of the stock of a corporation which owns and conducts a business), the purchase price must be allocated among all the assets of the business that were sold according to their respective fair market values. *Williams v. McGowan*, 152 F.2d 570 (2d Cir. 1945). Prior to 1986, when a buyer and seller dealt at arm's length, any reasonable allocation made by them in their sales agreement would usually be accepted by the Commissioner. As a consequence of the adoption of IRC § 1060 in the Tax Reform Act of 1986, the purchase price is allocated among the assets of the business according to a formula that allocates to goodwill or going concern value any premium that the purchaser paid.

§ 19.4100. Gain and Loss. Once the price is allocated to each asset, the taxpayer can determine the gain or loss on each asset and the character of that gain or loss. For example, the gain or loss on accounts receivable is ordinary income or loss; the gain on depreciable property will be ordinary income to the extent that IRC §§ 1245, 1250 or 1239 (or § 291(a)(1) if the taxpayer is a corporation) cause a recapture of depreciation, and the balance of such gain (if any) usually will be section 1231 gain.

§ 19.4110. Goodwill. Prior to the adoption in 1993 of IRC § 197, the basis of goodwill could not be amortized, and gain recognized on the sale of goodwill was treated as capital gain. Where a taxpayer who is engaged in a personal service business (such as a doctor, an accountant or a lawyer) sells his practice to another or where such a taxpayer accepts a payment from another to become the taxpayer's partner, the Commissioner was reluctant to permit any amount of the payment to be attributed to the purchase of the taxpayer's goodwill (which previously would have constituted capital gain to the taxpayer). However, the Commissioner was unsuccessful in contending that no goodwill can be sold in such circumstances. Accordingly, the Commissioner has narrowed the area in which he makes this contention, but, to date, the Commissioner has not prevailed even on this less ambitious proposal.

Since goodwill acquired after August 10, 1993, in connection with the acquisition of assets constituting a trade or business (or a substantial portion thereof) can be amortized under IRC § 197, the gain recognized on the disposition of such goodwill will be section 1231 gain (subject to the recapture of amortization rule of IRC § 1245). Prop. Reg. § 1.197–2(g)(8). Perhaps, the change will induce the Commissioner to abandon entirely the effort to preclude the allocation of purchase price to goodwill.

§ 19.4111. Going Concern Value. Going concern value is the increase in value of a group of assets due to their existence as integral parts of an ongoing business. While this might appear to be no more than an aspect of the goodwill of the business, the Sixth Circuit held that going concern value is an intangible asset that is separate and distinct from goodwill. *Concord Control v. Commissioner*, 615 F.2d 1153 (6th Cir. 1980). Accordingly, the Sixth Circuit held that the Tax Court's decision that a business had no goodwill but had going concern value was not inconsistent. The Sixth Circuit remanded the case to the Tax Court to explain the method that the Tax Court employed in calculating the going concern value. On remand, the Tax Court described the capitalization of earnings method that it employed. *Concord Control v. Commissioner*, 78 T.C. 742 (1982), Acq.

§ 19.4120. Covenant Not to Compete. In connection with a sale of a closely held business, the vendor often will give a covenant not to compete to the purchaser; and in many cases, a specific amount of the consideration paid for the business will be allocated to the covenant not to compete. The payment received for giving the purchaser such a covenant constitutes ordinary income to the vendor. On the other hand, the amount paid by a purchaser for the vendor's covenant not to compete is amortizable over a 15–year period. IRC § 197. In many cases, the granting of a covenant not to compete is merely an incident of the sale of the goodwill of the business, and the payment ostensibly given for the covenant should be treated as part of the payment for goodwill (which constitutes capital gain to the vendor and also is amortizable by the purchaser over a 15–year period). However, in many cases, the covenant not to compete has been bargained for separately and has independent significance to the parties; in such cases, the payment is ordinary income to the vendor. The designation given to the transaction by the parties is entitled to great weight, but the courts may apply a "substance over form" rule in appropriate cases and thereby find that the reality of the transaction was different from the parties' description of it. See *Schulz v. Commissioner*, 294 F.2d 52 (9th Cir. 1961); and *O'Dell & Co. v. Commissioner*, 61 T.C. 461 (1974).

Prior to the adoption of IRC § 197, the issue of distinguishing the purchase of goodwill from a payment for a covenant not to compete often arose because the cost of the latter could be amortized while the former could not. Now that both can be amortized over a 15–year period, the issue is more likely to arise with the seller in determining whether the seller has ordinary income or capital gain.

§ 19.4121. Substance over Form Doctrine—Availability to Taxpayer. While the government is free to challenge the form that the parties adopted for a transaction, a taxpayer who was a party to the agreement that established the form of the transaction may encounter greater difficulty in seeking to have a court disregard the form that the taxpayer himself chose even if it differs from the substance. See *Bolger v. Commissioner*, 59 T.C. 760 (1973); *Coleman v. Commissioner*, 87 T.C. 178 (1986); *Bradley v. United States*, 730 F.2d 718, 720 (11th Cir. 1984); *Estate of Leavitt v. Commissioner*, 875 F.2d 420 (4th Cir. 1989); *Harris v. United States*, 902 F.2d 439, 443

(5th Cir. 1990). In *Proulx v. United States*, 594 F.2d 832 (Ct. Cls. 1979), the Court of Claims adopted the *Danielson* approach and held that a taxpayer cannot have the form of his transaction disregarded unless the taxpayer can prove facts that would be admissible in an action between the parties to the agreement to alter the terms of the agreement or to show that the agreement is unenforceable because of fraud, duress, threats, mistake or undue influence. See also *Commissioner v. Danielson*, 378 F.2d 771 (3d Cir. 1967) (en banc); *Plante v. Commissioner*, 168 F.3d 1279 (11th Cir. 1999). This strong restriction on the taxpayer's ability to repudiate the form of a transaction is sometimes referred to as the *Danielson* rule or approach. See also *Spector v. Commissioner*, 641 F.2d 376 (5th Cir. 1981), where the Fifth Circuit adopted the *Danielson* approach that was used in *Proulx*. *Spector* involved a partnership taxation issue.

In *Grojean v. Commissioner*, 248 F.3d 572 (7th Cir. 2001), Judge Posner, writing for the court, said that a taxpayer cannot use the substance over form doctrine to change the nature of a transaction from the form that the taxpayer had adopted. Judge Posner said that only the government can do that. The Seventh Circuit's position appears to be even stricter than the *Danielson* rule.

The restriction on the circumstances in which a taxpayer can repudiate the express terms of an agreement that the taxpayer executed sometimes has been said to rest on the parol evidence rule. In *Molasky v. Commissioner*, 897 F.2d 334 (8th Cir. 1990), the court applied the parol evidence rule to preclude a taxpayer from successfully contending that a payment earmarked for a covenant not to compete was in substance paid for goodwill.

The Tax Court has imposed a "strong proof" requirement on taxpayers seeking to repudiate the substance of the allocation made in their agreement; this "strong proof" test is less demanding than the *Danielson* and *Proulx* rule. *Major v. Commissioner*, 76 T.C. 239 (1981); *Coleman v. Commissioner*, 87 T.C. 178 (1986). The "strong proof" test requires a showing that the requested reallocation is based on the intent of the parties at the time that the contract was executed *and* that the requested reallocation has independent economic significance. *Major v. Commissioner*, *supra*, 76 T.C. at pp. 247–249. This test does not rest on an application of the parol evidence rule.

The "strong proof" test applies only where a taxpayer seeks to repudiate or alter the terms of his agreement; the test does not apply to a taxpayer who urges a particular construction of ambiguous terms of an agreement. *Peterson Machine Tool v. Commissioner*, 79 T.C. 72 (1982). In *Peterson*, a contract for the sale of all of the stock of a corporation stated that the purchase price was paid for the stock and for the sellers' covenants not to compete. Further, the agreement stated that the covenants were "materially significant and essential to the closing" and "are a material portion of the purchase price." The agreement made no dollar allocation of the purchase price to the covenants. The Tax Court allocated 25% of the purchase price to the covenants.

In *Uri v. Commissioner*, 949 F.2d 371 (10th Cir. 1991), the Tenth Circuit stated this principle in very broad terms. The court (quoting from *Harris v. United States, supra*) stated that for tax purposes "[o]rdinarily, taxpayers are bound by the form of the transaction they have chosen...." 949 F.2d at 374–375, n. 4. While the court did use the word "ordinarily," the context of the court's opinion suggests that there will be few circumstances in which the court would permit a taxpayer to repudiate the form in which he had previously cast a transaction.

§ 19.4122.   Duty of Consistency. The Tax Court and several courts of appeals have applied a duty of consistency rule (sometimes called "quasi-estoppel") under which a taxpayer who reports a transaction to the government in one form will not be allowed to prevail on a contention that the transaction had a different substance from the form it took. E.g., *Estate of Ashman v. Commissioner*, 231 F.3d 541 (9th Cir. 2000). The purpose of the rule is to prevent a taxpayer from benefitting in a later year from an error or omission he made in an earlier year because the time to assess a tax for the earlier year has expired. See *Estate of Posner v. Commissioner*, RIA Memo TC ¶ 2004–112. The Sixth Circuit's application of this rule is much narrower than the Tax Court's approach and imposes additional requirements for the rule to apply, including the requirement that the taxpayer have knowingly made a representation to the government or concealed a material fact. *Banks v. Commissioner*, 345 F.3d 373 (6th Cir. 2003), rev'd on another issue, ___ U.S. ___ (2004).

The rule of consistency has been applied only to factual issues (or to issues of mixed fact and law) and does not apply to a situation where all relevant facts were disclosed, but the report of the transaction made an error in law. See *Estate of Posner v. Commissioner*, supra. See also, Raby and Raby, *Duty of Consistency: Facts versus Law*, 103 Tax Notes 1131 (2004).

CHAPTER TWENTY

ASSIGNMENT AND ANTICIPATION OF INCOME, "KIDDIE TAX," AND INSTALLMENT SALES

§ 20.0000. ASSIGNMENT AND ANTICIPATION OF INCOME, "KIDDIE TAX," AND INSTALLMENT SALES.

§ 20.1000. SPLITTING OF INCOME. Since the federal income tax has a progressive rate structure, the tax burden will be lighter if the same amount of income is taxed to several taxpayers than if it is taxed to one taxpayer.

§ 20.1100. Illustration. X earns an annual salary of $100,000 and has three minor children. If X could divide his salary equally among himself and his three children, there would be four taxpayers each reporting $25,000 income, rather than one taxpayer with $100,000. While non-tax considerations may make such an arrangement undesirable, the tax advantages of splitting X's income into four parts are obvious.

§ 20.1200. Devices. A number of income splitting devices have been tried by taxpayers with varying degrees of success. While generally Congress and the Service have sought to prevent the successful splitting of income, Congress has expressly authorized income splitting in certain circumstances. For example, the alimony deduction [IRC § 215] is a congressionally blessed income splitting arrangement, and the special treatment provided for a husband and wife filing a joint return is another. The use of trusts, partnerships, or corporations as income spreading devices is not discussed in this work.

§ 20.1300. Citizens of Community Property States. When a married couple is domiciled in a state that has a community property system and when the spouses have not contracted out of that system, the income earned from the services of either spouse is divided equally between both spouses for income tax purposes. *Poe v. Seaborn*, 282 U.S. 101 (1930). Similarly, income produced by community property is divided equally between the two spouses. Eight states have adopted a community property system: Arizona, California, Idaho, Louisiana, Nevada, New Mexico, Texas, and Washington.

§ 20.1400. Citizens of States Having a Marital Property Act. The Uniform Marital Property Act creates a new system of property rights that are similar to the rights granted by community property systems. The Commissioner ruled in Rev. Rul. 87–13, that income from services performed by either spouse of a married couple who are domiciled in Wisconsin (a state that has adopted a version of the Uniform Marital Property Act) is divided equally between the two spouses unless they had previously altered their property rights through a marital property agreement. Income earned by the spouses' property also is divided equally between the spouses except that gain realized on the appreciation of a spouse's *individual* property is the income of that spouse alone.

§ 20.2000. ANTICIPATORY ASSIGNMENT OF INCOME.

§ 20.2100. Assignment of Income from Services. If a taxpayer executes a valid contract assigning to another person all or a portion of the income the taxpayer may earn at a future date from services previously performed by the taxpayer or from services to be performed by the taxpayer at a future date, the income is nevertheless taxed to the taxpayer when earned. *Lucas v. Earl*, 281 U.S. 111 (1930); *Helvering v. Eubank*, 311 U.S. 122 (1940).

§ 20.2110. Illustration of Attempted Income Splitting. In Year One, X contracted with Y that each of them was entitled to one-half of the income earned by the other. In Year Three, X earned a salary of $20,000, and, pursuant to his contract, X turned $10,000 over to Y. X must include the entire $20,000 salary in his gross income.

§ 20.2120. Illustration: Assignment of Renewal Commissions. Z was employed as an agent of a life insurance company. When Z sells a life insurance policy to a customer, Z receives a portion of the initial premium paid by that customer as a commission. Moreover, Z is entitled to a percentage of each subsequent premium paid by that customer; this right of Z to a percentage of future premiums is referred to as "renewal commissions." Z's right to renewal commissions can be assigned by Z to others or can be bequeathed by Z at her death. In Year One, Z retired and assigned to D, her daughter, all of her renewal commissions. In Years Two, Three and Four, while Z was still living, D collected the renewal commissions for premiums paid on policies that Z had sold before her retirement. All of the commissions received by D are included in Z's gross income. *Helvering v. Eubank*, 311 U.S. 122 (1940). Z died on January 1, Year Five. The renewal commissions collected by D after that date are included in D's gross income. The anticipatory assignment of income doctrine ceases to apply when the assignor dies.

§ 20.2130. Services in Consideration of Payment to Third Parties. When a taxpayer agrees to perform services in consideration of a payment being made to a third party such as a charity, the taxpayer must include the payment in his gross income. Treas. Reg. § 1.61–2(c). However, if the payment is made to a qualified charity, the taxpayer may be entitled to a charitable deduction subject to the limitations of IRC § 170. However, if the services are provided directly to a party (including a charity) under an arrangement in which no compensation is to be paid the taxpayer, then the taxpayer is merely providing his services without charge, and the taxpayer does not recognize income. Treas. Reg. § 1.61–2(c); GCM 27026; Rev. Rul. 68–503.

§ 20.2131. Illustration 1. Michael, a prominent comedian, participates in a television special sponsored by a breakfast cereal manufacturer. Michael agreed to perform in consideration of the sponsor's paying $100,000 to the American Red Cross. Michael must include the $100,000 in his gross income. Michael will be treated as having donated $100,000 to the Red Cross and will be allowed a charitable deduction for that donation to the extent that a deduction is allowable under IRC § 170. If Michael could demonstrate that he participated in the television special in his capacity as an agent or employee of the Red Cross, the $100,000 would not be taxed to him, but the burden of proof on that question is formidable. See **§ 20.2226.**

§ 20.2132. Illustration 2. The American Red Cross sponsored a play in New York City, and H, a prominent actress, agreed to perform in the play without compensation. The Red Cross earned a substantial income from the play largely because of the drawing attraction of H as an actress. H's normal income for her performance would be $30,000. H has no income from donating her services to the Red Cross enterprise.

§ 20.2133. Illustration 3. In one interesting case, a majority of the Tax Court held that a taxpayer who won an essay contest, the prize for which was an annuity of $1,500 payable to some person under the age of 17 to be named by the winner, did not have income in the value of the prize. The taxpayer was older than 17 and therefore did not qualify as a potential recipient of the annuity. The court reasoned that under the terms of the contest the taxpayer could not receive the prize and, therefore, did not make an anticipatory assignment to his seven-year-old daughter whom he named as the beneficiary of the prize. *Teschner v. Commissioner*, 38 T.C. 1003 (1962). The Commissioner has issued a nonacquiescence in that decision. The decision of the Supreme Court in *United States v. Basye*, 410 U.S. 441 (1973) may well overrule *Teschner*. While *Bayse* can be distinguished from *Teschner*, the thrust of the Court's opinion in *Bayse* runs counter to the Tax Court decision. In *Armantrout v. Commissioner*, 570 F.2d 210 (7th Cir. 1978), aff'g 67 T.C. 996 (1977), amounts were paid by an employer into a trust fund to provide for the college education expenses of children of certain key employees. When distributions were made from the trust to defray the college expenses of a child of an employee, the courts held that the amounts distributed constituted gross income to the employee-parent. The courts distinguished *Teschner* because the term of an employee's employment theoretically is determined by arm's-length negotiations between the employer and the employee, but the taxpayer in *Teschner* had no opportunity to negotiate. The distinction is tenuous at best.

§ 20.2200. Assignment of Income from Property. Since most property is capable of producing income, the transfer of property necessarily includes an assignment of the property's income potential. In such cases, the transferor is not taxed on the income subsequently earned by the property.

§ 20.2210. Illustration. *X* owned an apartment development which produces an annual rental income of $90,000. *X* transferred the apartment development to his son, *S*, as an irrevocable gift. The rental income from the property earned after the gift will be taxed to *S* and not to *X*. However, when a taxpayer transfers a property interest shortly before income was distributed on that property, the taxpayer will be taxed on that income if the taxpayer had a legal right to the income at the time that he transferred the underlying property. For example, if *X* transferred stocks the day before a previously declared dividend of $20,000 was payable, and where state law gave a stockholder a legal right to a dividend at the time that the dividend was declared, X will be taxed on the $20,000. See *Smith's Estate v. Commissioner*, 292 F.2d 478 (3d Cir. 1961). However, if state law did not give X a legal right to the dividend when it was declared, and if X gifted the stock after the dividend was declared but before he obtained a legal right to the dividend, X will not be taxed on the $20,000 dividend. *Caruth Corp. v. United States*, 865 F.2d 644 (5th Cir. 1989) (not taxing a dividend in a similar circumstance).

In some circumstances, the steps towards producing income from the donated property may have reached such an advanced state by the time of the gift as to make the realization of that income a virtual certainty. Examples of this have arisen where stock was gifted after the corporation had adopted a plan of liquidation or after a firm offer was made to acquire that stock. In some such cases, applying the anticipatory assignment of income doctrine, the transferor has been taxed on the gain recognized subsequently when the liquidation or purchase took place. E.g., *Ferguson v. Commissioner*, 108 T.C. 244 (1997); *Hudspeth v. United States*, 471 F.2d 275 (8th Cir. 1972); *Kinsey v. Commissioner*, 477 F.2d 1058 (2d Cir. 1973).

§ 20.2220. Assignment of Income Interest. A difficult tax issue previously arose when a taxpayer retained an underlying interest in property the income from which was assigned by the taxpayer to a third party. The question was whether the interest transferred by the taxpayer has sufficient significance to warrant taxing the assigned income to someone other than the taxpayer. It seems likely that changes to the rules concerning the taxation of trust income that were adopted as part of the Tax Reform Act of 1986 have simplified the application of the anticipatory assignment doctrine in this area.

§ 20.2221. Illustration 1: Transfer of Interest from Bonds. In 1981, X owned a corporate bond with coupons attached. The coupons represented interest to be paid on the bond at future dates, and the interest coupons could be transferred to third parties who could collect the interest when the coupons mature. In that year, X gave several unmatured coupons to Y, but X retained the bond and the remaining coupons. X's attempt to divert the interest income, represented by coupons, from himself to Y will be unsuccessful for tax purposes. The interest paid to Y will be included in X's gross income. *Helvering v. Horst*, 311 U.S. 112 (1940).

The separation of all or part of the interest element of a bond from the right to the principal of the debt is referred to as stripping the bond. Such a bond is referred to as a "stripped bond," and such a coupon is referred to as a "stripped coupon." IRC § 1286(e). If a bondholder disposes of a stripped coupon after July 1, 1982, a number of tax consequences may be imposed by IRC § 1286. There is a question whether § 1286 is invoked by making a gift of a stripped coupon (as contrasted to a sale), but the language of IRC § 1286(b) applies to any disposition of a stripped coupon or bond. Among other tax consequences, IRC § 1286 will require the donor of the stripped coupon to (1) recognize income for any accrued interest on the bond and for any "accrued market discount" on the bond ["accrued market discount" applies to a bond that is purchased after its original issue and constitutes the difference between the bond's stated redemption price at maturity and the purchase price]; (2) increase the donor' basis by the accrued income and discount; (3) allocated the basis (as adjusted) between the items retained by the donor and the items that were transferred to the donee; and (4) the donor will be treated as having purchased the retained items and will thereby become subject to recognizing original issue discount income pursuant to IRC § 1286(a). IRC § 1286(b).

§ 20.2222. Illustration 2: Transfer of Term Interest for a Period of Less Than Ten Years. X is the income beneficiary of a trust, the annual income from which is approximately $10,000. The income is payable to X for life. In Year One, X assigned to Y the right to receive the income from the trust for a period of three years. X's attempt to assign several years' income to Y while retaining his underlying interest in the trust (his right to income after the three-year period) will be unsuccessful for tax purposes. The income distributed to Y will be included in X's gross income. See *Harrison v. Schaffner*, 312 U.S. 579 (1941).

§ 20.2223. Illustration 3: Transfer of Entirety of Transferor's Interest. The same facts apply as in **§ 20.2222** except that in Year One X assigned to Y the right to income from the trust for the rest of X's life. Thus, X assigned all of his interest in the trust and retained nothing. This assignment is successful for tax purposes and the income earned after the assignment is not taxed to X. See *Blair v. Commissioner*, 300 U.S. 5 (1937).

§ 20.2224. Illustration 4: Transfer of Fraction of Transferor's Interest or Transfer of an Annuity for the Period of the Transferor's Interest. The same facts apply as in **§ 20.2222** except that X assigned to Y the right to one-fourth of the income from the trust for the remainder of X's life. While X retained a continuing interest in three-fourths of the trust, X has no residual interest in the one-fourth interest assigned to Y (i.e., X will have no interest in the one-fourth portion of the trust assigned to Y upon the expiration of Y's interest), and, consequently, the income subsequently paid to Y is not taxed to X. This assignment is distinguishable from an assignment of income for a period of three years since in the latter case, the assignor retains an interest in the future income of the entire trust. In *Blair v. Commissioner*, in **§ 20.2223**, a life income beneficiary's assignment of a fixed annual dollar amount for the life of the income beneficiary (i.e., an annuity for the life of the life income beneficiary) was held to be a successful assignment for tax purposes.

§ 20.2225. Illustration 5: Transfer of Term Interest for a Period of More Than Ten Years. The same facts as in **§ 20.2222** except that X assigned to Y the right to all the income from the trust for a period of 11 years, and X retained no power over the trust or to affect Y's income interest during that period. While X retained a reversionary interest in the trust upon the expiration of the 11–year period, prior to the adoption of the Tax Reform Act of 1986 it was likely that the assigned interest would be deemed sufficiently significant that X would not be taxed on the income paid to Y during that 11–year period. Prior to the amendment of Subchapter J that was made by the Tax Reform Act of 1986, a transfer to a trust to pay income to a third party for more than ten years would ordinarily result in the trust's income being taxed to the third party even though the trust corpus reverts to the grantor when the ten-year or longer period expires. Under the pre–1986 tax law, it, therefore, would be reasonable to allow a taxpayer to assign successfully an income interest if the assignment is for a period of at least ten years. Under Rev. Rul. 55–38, a pre–1986 ruling, X would not recognize income during the 11–year period if the assignment of that 11–year interest were made by X prior to March 2, 1986. The Tax Reform Act of 1986 amended IRC § 673 to provide that, for transfers made in trust after March 1, 1986 (subject to two minor exceptions), the income from the transferred property will be included in the grantor's gross income if the grantor retained a reversionary interest in either the corpus or income of the trust. Consequently, if X assigned the 11–year interest to Y after March 1, 1986, the income paid to Y should be included in X's gross income. The common law anticipatory assignment of income rule should be modified to track the statutory provision for trust income.

§ 20.2226. Illustration 6: Income Earned by an Agent.

A member of the faculty of a law school receives fees under the Criminal Justice Act for serving as the supervisory attorney for cases handled by the faculty member and by law students pursuant to a course in clinical law conducted by the faculty member. Pursuant to the faculty member's agreement with the law school, he endorses all such fees given to him over to the law school. The Commissioner has ruled that the faculty member's endorsement of the fees (and his agreement to endorse the fees) does not constitute an assignment of income, and the faculty member, therefore, is not required to include the fees in his gross income. Rev. Rul. 74–581. The faculty member was deemed to have acted as an agent of the law school in earning the fee. The Commissioner is not always so liberal in his treatment of persons performing services for others on behalf of a charitable organization; strong evidence of an agency relationship will be required. E.g., *Schuster v. Commissioner*, 800 F.2d 672 (7th Cir. 1986).

If instead the fees were included in the faculty member's gross income, and if he could then treat the fees as contributions to a qualified charity, his deductions would be subject to the limitations (including the limitation on the maximum amount deductible) imposed on charitable deductions. See Chapter Nine. If the fees were included in the faculty member's income and if the payment to the law school were deductible as a business expense, the deduction would be for an employee business expense and so would be an itemized deduction that is subject to the 2% of AGI floor of IRC § 67 and to the overall limitation of IRC § 68.

§ 20.2230. Conversion of Services to Property. As noted in § 20.2100 and § 20.2200, the assignment of future income that is derived from the assignor's services is an anticipatory assign-

ment of income, but the transfer of the donor's entire interest in an item of property does not cause the donor to be taxed on the income subsequently produced by the donated property. The question arises as to what extent a person can convert his services into property and successfully give away the property without being taxed on income produced by that property or from the sale of that property. In the case of renewal commissions, an insurance agent's right to receive a percentage of premiums paid in the future is treated as a kind of deferred compensation for the agent's services in selling the policy, and so the renewal commissions are taxed to the agent even when he has assigned the right to them to another. § **20.2120.** However, when an artist paints a painting and then gives it to another, the income recognized on the donee's sale of that painting will be included in the donee's gross income and not in the gross income of the artist who painted it. The painter is deemed to have converted his effort into property which can be given away without triggering anticipatory assignment problems. Similarly, when an author gives away his copyright interest in a work he wrote, the author will not be taxed on the royalty income that the donee receives on the exploitation of that written work. See PLR 8444073.

§ **20.2240. Taxation of Plaintiff on Portion of Taxable Award Paid to Taxpayer's Attorney Pursuant to Contingent Fee Arrangement.** A taxpayer seeks to enforce a claim for damages which will be taxable income to the taxpayer if the taxpayer prevails. See § **2.1332** for a discussion of when tort damages are taxable or excludable from income. The taxpayer employs an attorney to enforce the claim and to collect on it. The taxpayer and the attorney agree to a contingent fee arrangement under which the attorney is entitled to a specified percentage of any amount collected on the claim. The claim is settled for $1,000,000 of which $400,000 is paid to the attorney pursuant to the contingent fee arrangement. The Supreme Court held that the entire amount of the award ($1,000,000), including the $400,000 that was paid to the attorney, is taxable to the taxpayer under the anticipatory assignment of income doctrine. *Commissioner v. Banks*, ___ U.S. ___ (2005). The *Banks* decision dealt with two cases that were consolidated in the Supreme Court. While the payment made to the attorney was deductible as an expense of collecting income (IRC § 212), it was treated as a miscellaneous itemized deduction at the time that the facts of the *Banks* case arose. See § **3.1110.** Consequently, the taxpayer's deduction of the fees is subject to limitations imposed on miscellaneous item-ized deductions, and is not deductible at all if the taxpayer's tax liability is determined under the Alternative Minimum Tax sys-tem. The obvious inequity of this result led Congress to amend the Code while the cases were pending in the Supreme Court to make attorney fees and court costs nonitemized deductions when incurred in cases involving discrimination and a few comparable causes of action. IRC § 62(a)(19), (e). That 2004 amendment cured the problem for those taxpayers who litigate actions covered by the amendment, but it left the problem undisturbed for those not covered by the new provision. The nature and extent of those problems are discussed in Jeffery H. Kahn, *Beyond the Little Dutch Boy: An Argument for Structural Change in Tax Deduction Classification*, 80 Wash. L. Rev. 1 (2005). See **§ 10.1231.**

In *Banks*, the taxpayers contended that the contingent fee agree-ment with the attorney effected an assignment of a portion of the taxpayer's claim to the attorney who therefore should be taxed on that portion of the award instead of the taxpayer. Rejecting that contention, the Supreme Court held that the assignment of the claim was covered by the anticipatory assignment of income doctrine because of the control that the taxpayers maintained over their claims (i.e., each taxpayer had control as to whether to accept a settlement and over other major decisions concerning the prosecution of the claim). The taxpayer's control over the asset that produced the income in question caused the taxpayer to be taxed on that income. The Court also rejected a contention that the agreement between the taxpayer and the attorney created a partnership or joint venture to enforce and collect the claim.

While the Supreme Court in *Banks* declined to pass upon several issues raised for the first time in that Court, the decision in *Banks* likely is dispositive of the question of whether a taxpayer is taxed on the portion of a taxable award that is payable to the attorney. The remedy for that harsh consequence lies with Con-gress to change the treatment accorded to deductions for expenses incurred in collecting income (as Congress did in 2004 for a limited list of cases).

While the authors agree that the result reached by the Supreme Court in *Banks* is correct, notwithstanding the patent inequity of the result (the inequity is a product of faults in the Code's classification and treatment of certain deductions), we believe that the Court's analysis is questionable. The taxpayer's assign-ment of a portion of the claim should have been characterized as an "anticipation of future income" event rather than as an anticipatory assignment of income. The anticipation of future income rule is discussed at § **20.3000** et seq. In effect, the taxpayer sold a portion of the claim to the attorney in exchange for the attorney's services. The taxation of that "sale" would then be deferred under IRC § 83 until the attorney's interest vested which occurred when the case was finally settled. The result, however, under that approach would be approximately the same as the result that the court's approach reached. For a thorough discussion of this alternative approach, see Gregg D. Polsky, *A Correct Analysis of the Tax Treatment of Contingent Attorney's Fee Arrangements: Enough With the Fruit and Trees*, 37 Ga. L. Rev. 57 (2002).

§ **20.2300.   Discharge of Debt.** When a creditor forgives a debt the collection of which would have caused the creditor to recognize gross income, the forgiveness *may* constitute an assignment of income to the debtor which is treated as if the creditor had collected the debt and had subsequently turned over the cash proceeds to the debtor. In *Commissioner v. Fender Sales, Inc.*, 338 F.2d 924 (9th Cir. 1964), the court held in a two to one decision that a corporation's distribution of equal shares of its own stock to its two equal shareholders in satisfaction of accrued but unpaid salary owed to the shareholders for services rendered was gross income to the shareholders. While the court's reasoning is not entirely clear, it appears that the source of the shareholders' income was not the corporation's distribution of its stock (which in substance merely constituted a non-taxable stock dividend to the shareholders), but rather was the shareholders' forgiveness of the debt that the corporation owed them for accrued salary, which constituted an anticipatory assignment of income from the shareholders to the corporation. But see Rev. Rul. 67–402, for a construction of the *Fender Sales* case that treats the distribution of stock to the shareholder as compensation rather than treating the shareholders' cancellation of the corporate debt as an assignment of income; see also *Putoma Corp. v. Commissioner*, 66 T.C. 652 (1976), aff'd, 601 F.2d 734 (5th Cir. 1979) for a similarly narrow reading of *Fender Sales* and see §§ **2.1270** and **2.1272.** The specific problem that arises when a shareholder forgives a debt owed to the shareholder from the corporation was resolved by Congress in 1980 when it adopted IRC § 108(e)(6). See §§ **2.1271–2.1272.** See also *Dwyer v. United States*, 622 F.2d 460 (9th Cir. 1980) where the court held that a shareholder recognized income under the anticipatory assignment doctrine when the shareholder canceled the interest that his corporation owed him on a debt; the cancellation occurred simultaneously with the liquidation of the corporation.

For the treatment of stock issued in satisfaction of a debt, see IRC § 108(e)(8) (as amended by the Omnibus Budget Reconciliation Act of 1993). The author questions whether that provision will apply when the corporation's stock is distributed pro rata among its shareholders as was the case in *Fender Sales*. Instead, in such a case, the author believes the transaction should be treated as a stock dividend coupled with a cancellation of debt. For a discussion of this issue, see **§ 2.1272.**

> **§ 20.2310. Waiver of Statutory Fee.** When a fiduciary (such as a personal representative of a decedent's estate) becomes entitled to a fee set by statute for services performed, the Commissioner has ruled that the fiduciary's waiver of his right to that fee constitutes a gift to the debtor for gift tax purposes and constitutes an anticipatory assignment of income so that the fiduciary is taxed on the amount of the waived fee. Rev. Rul. 64–225. If the fiduciary waives the fee before performing any services or in certain cases within a reasonable time after commencing his fiduciary duties, the waiver will not constitute a gift or an anticipatory assignment of income. Rev. Rul. 56–472; and Rev. Rul. 66–167. The Commissioner's position has not been litigated.

§ 20.3000. ANTICIPATION OF FUTURE INCOME. Instead of assigning income to a third party in the hope that the income will be taxed to the assignee, a taxpayer may sell the right to the income to a third party in an attempt to convert ordinary income to capital gains and to utilize his basis in the underlying property to offset income. If a taxpayer sells his entire property interest to a third party and if the property is a capital asset, the taxpayer will usually recognize a capital gain on the gain from the sale; but if a taxpayer sells the right to income from property and retains a reversionary interest in the property, the sale's proceeds are likely to be treated as an anticipation of future income, all of which may be taxed to the taxpayer as ordinary income.

> **§ 20.3100. Illustration 1.** On July 10, *X* sold shares of stock of the *M* corporation to *Y*, who collects the dividends thereafter. Since *X* sold his entire property interest, the amount realized by *X* on the sale less *X*'s basis in the stock will be a capital gain.

> **§ 20.3200. Illustration 2.** The same facts apply as in **§ 20.3100** except that on June 14, *M* declared a cash dividend to shareholders of

record on July 8; the dividend was to be distributed on July 15. Since X sold the shares after the July 8 record date, X was entitled to receive the dividend that had been declared on June 14. Ordinarily, then, X would be taxed on that dividend. Treas. Reg. § 1.61–9(c). However, the rules of the stock exchange on which the stock was sold required that when X sells the stock on a date between the record date and the date of payment, X is required t o execute an agreement assigning X's right to such dividend to Y (the purchaser). X did execute such an agreement; thus, Y collected the dividend from M when it was distributed on July 15. On similar facts, the Commissioner ruled in Rev. Rul. 82–11 that the price paid by Y to X must be allocated between payment for the dividend and a payment for the stock. The portion of the payment that is allocated to the sale of the dividend was treated by the Commissioner, under the anticipation of income doctrine, as dividend income to X. To the extent of the amount of Y's payment to X that is allocated to the purchase of a right to the dividend, the dividend collected by Y on July 15 constitutes a return of Y's capital and is not included in Y's income.

If X had sold the stock on July 1, which date is after the declaration date but before the July 8 record date, the dividend would be payable to the purchaser (who would be the holder on the July 8 record date); the purchaser ordinarily will be taxed on the dividend. Treas. Reg. § 1.61–9(c).

§ 20.3300. Illustration 3. X owns an office building. Y is the principal tenant under a lease expiring in ten years. Y desires to cancel the lease. X agrees to release Y from the lease in consideration of Y's payment to X of $50,000. The entire $50,000 is ordinary income to X—it was received by X "in lieu of" the rent Y otherwise would have had to pay. See *Hort v. Commissioner*, 313 U.S. 28 (1941). The "in lieu of" approach has been used by some courts in a few cases, but it is not a useful tool. The outright sale of property (for example, corporate stock) can be seen as the sale of the income stream that that property will produce. Obviously, the fact that the payment represents a substitute for the future income the property will produce does not prevent the seller from qualifying for capital gain treatment. The better reason for taxing X on the $50,000 receipt is that X still owns the building and thus continues to own the residual interest that will produce the future income. For example, if a life income beneficiary sells her entire life income interest to an unrelated party, any gain or loss she recognizes will be a capital gain or loss. See **§ 20.3500.**

§ 20.3400. Illustration 4. *X* owned an apartment building which was leased to *Y* for 15 years. *X* sold to *Z* for $30,000 his rights to receive annual rents from *Y*, but *X* retained his reversion in the building. *X* recognized $30,000 ordinary income on the "sale." The retention of any reversionary interest by a seller will usually be sufficient to prevent the seller from enjoying capital gains treatment. *Commissioner v. Lake*, 356 U.S. 260 (1958).

§ 20.3500. Illustration 5. *M* is the life income beneficiary of a trust which was established by her deceased husband's will. *M* sells her entire interest in the trust to *S* for $30,000. It was held in *McAllister v. Commissioner*, 157 F.2d 235 (2d Cir. 1946), cert. denied, 330 U.S. 826 (1947), acq. that *M* could utilize her basis in the trust (as determined under IRC § 1014) in determining her gain or loss on the sale. The difference between the amount realized and her basis would then constitute a capital gain or loss to *M*. While the holding in *McAllister* that *M*'s gain or loss will constitute a capital gain or loss is still valid, IRC § 1001(e) will prevent a taxpayer from using a basis acquired under IRC §§ 1014, 1015, or 1041 in such sales unless all of the interests in the property are sold as part of the same transaction. See §§ **16.1400–16.1450.** Thus, under current law, if *M* sold her trust interest, the entire $30,000 would be capital gain to her. Note, the Commissioner has ruled that he will follow the *McAllister* decision that such transactions are treated as the sale of a capital asset. Rev. Rul. 72–243.

§ 20.3600. Change of Timing of Recognition. A taxpayer might sell a right to income from his property for the purpose of manipulating the timing of when the income is recognized. For example, in *Estate of Stranahan v. Commissioner*, 30 T.C.M. 1070 (1971), the taxpayer had a large interest deduction in one year. In order to utilize those interest deductions, the taxpayer "sold" to his son the right to a dollar amount of future dividends from certain publicly held stock owned by the taxpayer, and the son paid the taxpayer $115,000 for that right. The taxpayer claimed that the $115,000 was ordinary income to him in the year of sale and that the dividends purchased by the son were not taxable to taxpayer when paid to the son. The Tax Court held that the purported sale was a sham and, thus, treated the dividends as income to the taxpayer when paid. The Tax Court's decision was reversed in *Estate of Stranahan v. Commissioner*, 472 F.2d 867 (6th Cir. 1973). On facts somewhat similar to those in *Stranahan*, other courts have rejected the anticipation of income contention of the taxpayer on the ground that the taxpayer's purported sale of his right to income was a sham, and that the substance of the "sale" was a loan to the taxpayer that was disguised as a sale. E.g., *Mapco Inc. v. United States*, 556 F.2d 1107 (Ct. Cls. 1977); *Martin v. Commissioner*, 56 T.C. 1255, aff'd without opinion, 469 F.2d 1406 (5th Cir. 1972); *Hydrometals, Inc. v. Commissioner*, 31 T.C.M. 1260 (1972), aff'd per curiam, 485 F.2d 1236 (5th Cir. 1973).

§ 20.3700. Family Partnerships.

§ 20.3710. **General.** A partnership pays no federal income tax. Instead, all of the tax items of the partnership (its income, deductions, credits, etc.) are allocated among the partners. Each partner treats his allocated share of a partnership tax item as if he personally had received the income or had incurred the expenditure for which the deduction or credit is allowed. IRC § 702(b). In many cases, the tax items of a partnership are allocated among the partners according to the terms of the partnership agreement. IRC § 704.

§ 20.3711. **Income Splitting.** The conduit attributes of a partnership make it a tempting device to split income among family members. A taxpayer could form a partnership in a trade or business with his spouse and children, seeking thereby to divide the partnership income among members of his family. This device became an alternative to the irrevocable trust as an income splitting arrangement. Just as the judiciary and then Congress responded to such use of the trust device, so did they respond to the family partnership device.

§ 20.3712. **Judicially Imposed Restriction.** Prior to 1951, the judicial decisions concerning family partnerships were somewhat checkered. In its landmark decision of *Commissioner v. Culbertson*, 337 U.S. 733 (1949), the Supreme Court held that the test of the validity of income splitting by a family partnership was whether the parties formed and conducted the partnership in good faith—that is, whether they joined together with a business purpose for the present conduct of an enterprise. If a partner contributed no services to the enterprise, did not participate in management control, and did not contribute "original capital" to the enterprise, there was a strong (but not conclusive) presumption against his qualifying for partnership treatment. The judicial trend was to hold invalid for tax purposes a family partnership interest where the partner performed no vital services for the partnership and where the partner received his capital interest as a gift from a member of his family.

§ 20.3720.   Statutory Resolution. In 1951, Congress adopted the antecedent to IRC § 704(e) in order to resolve the tax treatment of family partnerships and to reconcile the treatment of partnerships with general assignment of income principles. Under IRC § 704(e), a person may successfully give a capital interest in a partnership to another (regardless of whether the donee performs services for the partnership) provided that capital is a material income-producing factor of the partnership's business. In that event, partnership income may be allocated to the donee partner, but a reasonable allocation of income must be made to the donor for any services that he performs for the partnership. Thus, a taxpayer can use a family partnership to split income but only to the extent that the income is attributable to capital, and the taxpayer must give that capital interest to the donee in order to qualify the allocation of the income from that capital for taxation to the donee. A capital interest in a partnership means an interest in its assets as contrasted to a mere right to participate in the earnings and profits of the partnership. Treas. Reg. § 1.704–1(e)(1)(v). These rules are similar to those adopted generally for the assignment of income (i.e., income from property that was earned subsequent to the donation of the property will be taxed to the donee, and income from the services of a taxpayer that was gratuitously assigned to another in anticipation of the donor's earning the income nevertheless is taxed to the donor). The family partnership rules cannot be avoided by having a family member "purchase" a partnership interest from another, and such purchased interests are treated as gifts for purposes of the family partnership statute if the terms of a purported purchase indicate that it has the characteristics of a gift. IRC § 704(e)(3); Treas. Reg. § 1.702–1(e)(4).

§ 20.3721.   Bona Fides. A purported gift of a capital interest to a donee will not qualify the donee as a partner unless he is the real owner of such capital interest. The criteria for determining whether a donee is a bona fide partner are discussed in Treas. Reg. § 1.704–1(e)(2).

§ 20.3722.   Corporate Tax Parallel. For a statutory provision applicable to Subchapter S corporations that parallels the treatment of family partnerships, see IRC § 1366(e).

§ 20.4000.   TAXATION OF CHILD'S UNEARNED INCOME— KIDDIE TAX.

§ 20.4100.   Income Splitting with Minor Children. Prior to the adoption of the Tax Reform Act of 1986, children (especially minor children) were a favored beneficiary of income splitting. A minor child typically has little or no earned income, and so the child will usually be in a low-income tax bracket. By transferring income-producing property to a child, the income thereafter produced by that property would generate much lower taxes than would be the case if the donor retained the property so that the property's income would be taxed at the donor's marginal tax rate. The tax benefits were maximized if the child could utilize a personal exemption deduction and a standard deduction in determining his taxable income. While some tax benefit is still obtainable by transferring income-producing property to a child, the 1986 Act has substantially reduced those benefits, especially for transfers to young children.

§ 20.4110. Dependent's Deduction for Personal Exemption. Typically, an individual taxpayer is granted a deduction for a personal exemption (for the year 2005, the exemption amount is $3,200). However, as noted in **§ 4.1210**, an individual who qualifies as a dependent exemption deduction for another person is not allowed a personal exemption deduction for himself. IRC § 151(d)(2). Most young children will be supported by a living parent or parents and will qualify as a dependent exemption for that parent. Therefore, most young children will not be allowed a deduction for a personal exemption. So, if income is effectively shifted to such a young child, the child cannot use an exemption deduction to reduce the amount of that income that is taxable. In some cases with older children (even with older children who are still minors), the child may not be a dependent of anyone and so can deduct a personal exemption for himself.

§ 20.4120. Dependent's Use of Standard Deduction. If an individual qualifies as a dependent exemption deduction for another person, the standard deduction allowable to that individual cannot *exceed* the greater of: (1) $250 plus the individual's earned income, or (2) a specified dollar amount (for the year 2005, the specified dollar amount is $800). IRC § 63(c)(5). In general, "earned income" refers to income earned by a person from his services (e.g., wages and fees) as contrasted to income earned from investments. In effect then, a dependent's standard deduction is available to reduce income earned by that dependent from his employment, but the standard deduction will reduce *no more* than $800 of the dependent's passive income. See the illustrations at **§§ 3.2120–3.2124.** From year to year, the $800 figure mentioned above is increased to reflect changes in the cost of living. IRC § 63(c)(4).

§ 20.4200.   Kiddie Tax on Passive Income. Some of the passive income of a child who is under the age of 14 may be subjected to special tax treatment by IRC § 1(g). For convenience, this special tax treatment of some of a child's passive income is sometimes referred to as a "kiddie tax." Note that the so-called "kiddie tax" is merely a special method for computing the tax on some of a child's passive income that provides a higher tax than does the normal method; it is not a surtax.

§ 20.4210.   Children Who Are Subject to the Kiddie Tax. The kiddie tax can apply to a child for a taxable year only if the child does not attain age 14 before the close of the taxable year and the child has at least one parent who is alive at the close of the taxable year. IRC § 1(g)(2). Thus, the tax has no application to a child who is 14 years of age or older or to a child who is an orphan.

§ 20.4220.   Operation of the Kiddie Tax. Where applicable, the kiddie tax isolates a child's "net unearned income" from the child's other income and then computes the tax on the net unearned income at the same marginal rates as would have been applied if that amount had been included in the gross income of the child's parent or parents. The statute accomplishes this by defining the child's tax liability as the sum of the child's share of the "allocable parental tax" and the tax (at an unmarried taxpayer's normal rates) on an amount equal to the difference between the child's taxable income and his net unearned income. IRC § 1(g)(1). If the application of a separate kiddie tax causes a smaller tax liability on all of the child's income than would be imposed if all of the child's income were taxed at normal rates, then the kiddie tax will not apply and the child's tax liability will be determined in the normal manner without any special treatment of unearned income. IRC § 1(g)(1). In other words, if the normal application of the tax schedule yields a higher tax than the tax determined by using the kiddie tax, the higher tax is imposed. The definition of "net unearned income" and "allocable parental tax" and the operation of the kiddie tax are explained below.

§ 20.4221.   "Earned Income." The "earned income" of a child is the income that the child earned as wages, salaries or professional fees, and other amounts received as compensation for personal services actually rendered by the child. IRC §§ 1(g)(4)(A)(i), 911(d)(2). If the child is engaged as a self-employed person in the active conduct of a trade or business in which both capital and services are material income-producing factors, that portion of the child's self-employed income from the trade or business that represents reasonable compensation for the child's services (not to exceed 30% of the child's share of the net profits from the business) constitutes earned income. IRC § 911(d)(2)(B).

§ 20.4222. Net Unearned Income. The adjusted gross income of a child that is not "earned income," as defined in **§ 20.4221**, is "unearned income." In general, unearned income refers to passive income produced by capital as contrasted to income derived from the child's services. As used herein, the unearned income of a child will reflect that income's proportionate share of the child's allowed nonitemized deductions (if any).

The "net unearned income" of a child is the excess of the child's unearned income over the greater of: (1) $1,600, or (2) the sum of $800 and the child's itemized deductions that are directly related to the production of the unearned income. The meaning of the terms "itemized deductions" and "nonitemized deductions" is explained at **§ 3.1200.** The $1,600 and $800 figures mentioned above are the figures for the year 2005. Rev. Proc. 2004–71 (Sec. 3.02). For subsequent years, those figures will be changed to reflect changes in the cost of living. IRC § § 1(g)(4)(A), 63(c)(4), (5)(A). A child's net unearned income cannot exceed the child's taxable income. IRC 1(g)(4)(B).

§ 20.4223. Amount of Child's Income That Is Subject to Kiddie Tax. The kiddie tax operates only on a child's net unearned income. Thus, all of a child's earned income and some of his unearned income is excluded from the kiddie tax treatment. As stated in **§ 20.4222**, for the year 2005, a *minimum* of $1,600 of a child's unearned income is excluded from the kiddie tax.

§ 20.4224. Application of the Kiddie Tax. When the kiddie tax applies, the tax on the net unearned income of a child is determined by reference to the marginal income tax brackets of the child's parent. If only one parent is alive, reference is made to that parent's tax bracket. If both parents of the child are alive and file a joint tax return, reference is made to the parents' tax bracket for their joint return. If the parents are not married, reference is made to the tax bracket of the custodial parent of the child; if the parents are married but file separate returns, reference is made to the tax bracket of the parent with the highest amount of income. IRC § 1(g)(5). According to the legislative history of the Tax Reform Act of 1986, in the case of a foster child, it is the income of the foster parent that determines the tax on the child's net unearned income. S.Rept. 99–313, 99th Cong., 2d Sess. at p. 863 (1986).

§ 20.4225. Computation of the Child's Tax. When the kiddie tax applies, the total amount of the child's tax liability for a taxable year is the sum of two partial taxes. The first partial tax is the amount of tax that is imposed by the normal tax schedule on an amount equal to the difference between the child's taxable income and the child's net unearned income for the year. Thus, this partial tax is the normal tax on all of the child's taxable income other than the child's net unearned income, which is isolated and subjected to a special partial tax computation referred to as the "child's share of the allocable parental tax" described in § **20.4225–1.**

§ 20.4225–1. Partial Tax on Net Unearned Income— The "Allocable Parental Tax." The second partial tax imposed on a child is the specially computed tax on the child's net unearned income; this partial tax constitutes the "kiddie tax." The first step in computing this partial tax is to determine the parent or parents of the child whose income tax bracket will be employed. The criteria for selecting that parent are described in § **20.4224.** Once the relevant parent has been determined, the next step is to add to that parent's taxable income for that year the net unearned incomes of all of the children of that parent whose incomes are subject to the kiddie tax. Using normal tax schedules, the amount of tax that would be imposed on the parent's reconstituted taxable income is then reduced by the amount of tax that is imposed on the parent's actual taxable income. The purpose of this computation is to determine the amount of additional tax that the parent would incur if the net unearned incomes of his children were included in the parent's income. This additional tax is referred to as the "allocable parental tax." The allocable parental tax is then allocated among the parent's children according to the proportion that each child's net unearned income bears to the total amount of net unearned incomes that went into the computation of the allocable parental tax. IRC § 1(g)(3).

§ **20.4225–2. Total Tax Liability.** The amount of the allocable parental tax that is attributed to a child constitutes that child's second partial tax. This second partial tax is referred to as the "child's share of the allocable parental tax" or is sometimes colloquially referred to as the "kiddie tax." The child's total tax liability, then, is the sum of the two partial taxes—the partial tax on the child's taxable income other than his net unearned income (described at § **20.4225**) plus the child's share of the allocable parental tax.

§ **20.4300. Illustrations.** All of the income that is mentioned in the following illustrations is recognized in the calendar year 1994. Since the year in these illustrations is 1994, the dollar figures and rates that are used are different from the figures and rates that are currently used. All of the taxpayers mentioned in the illustrations report their income on a calendar year basis.

§ **20.4310. Illustration 1.** D is the only child of F, a widower who files a return as an unmarried individual. D is eleven years old. In 1994, D had no earned income, and D had $2,700 of dividend income from stocks that D's grandmother had given to D on her birth. D's only deductible expense (other than the standard deduction) is a $100 state income tax payment that qualifies as an itemized deduction. F is entitled to a dependent exemption deduction for D since he provides her support. Regardless of whether F chooses to claim the dependent exemption deduction, the fact that he is entitled to take it is sufficient to disqualify D from using a personal exemption deduction for herself. For the year 1994, D is allowed a standard deduction of $600. Since the standard deduction is greater than D's itemized deductions ($100), D will use the standard deduction. F's taxable income for that year is $61,000.

D has taxable income of $2,100 after deducting her standard deduction. All of D's income is unearned. After deducting from her $2,700 of gross unearned income the $1,200 of unearned income that is excluded from the kiddie tax by IRC § 1(g)(4), D has $1,500 of net unearned income, which is the amount that is subject to the kiddie tax. *D*'s tax liability is comprised of two partial taxes. First, the partial tax on the $600 difference between *D*'s taxable income ($2,100) and *D*'s net unearned income ($1,500) is determined by applying the rates provided by the tax schedule for an unmarried individual, which is *D*'s filing status. This $600 of income is taxed at a 15% rate, which yields a partial tax of $90. The tax on the $1,500 of net unearned income that is subject to the kiddie tax is determined by adding $1,500 to *F*'s taxable income and computing the additional tax that would be incurred by that addition. The additional tax is $465, and that amount constitutes the second partial tax on *D*'s income. Note that the tax rates that apply to 1994 tax an additional $1,500 of taxable income to *F* at a 31% marginal rate. *D*'s total tax liability for that year is $555 (the sum of the two partial taxes—$465 + $90). Note that if *D*'s stocks were owned by her father, *F*, the $2,700 of dividend income produced by those stocks would have been taxed to *F* at a 31% rate, causing an increased tax liability of $837. The tax reduction obtained by having the stocks owned by *D*, rather than by *F*, is $282. The tax savings from splitting income to a young child may be too small in most cases to warrant the administrative costs of dividing the income.

§ 20.4320. Illustration 2. The same facts as those stated in § 20.4310 except that in addition to her dividend income of $2,700, *D* also has earned income of $700. So, *D* has gross income of $3,400. Since *D*'s earned income is greater than $600, *D* is granted a standard deduction of $700 (i.e., the amount of her earned income). IRC § 63(c)(5). *D*, therefore, has taxable income of $2,700. *D* has $2,700 of adjusted gross unearned income of which $1,200 is excluded in determining her net unearned income. *D*'s net unearned income is $1,500. The partial tax on the $1,200 difference between *D*'s taxable income ($2,700) and her net unearned income ($1,500) is determined by applying the rates provided by the tax schedule for an unmarried individual. This $1,200 amount is taxed at a 15% rate, and so the partial tax on that figure is $180. The $1,500 of *D*'s net unearned income is taxed at *F*'s marginal rate of 31% and so yields a partial tax of $465. *D*'s total tax liability is $645 (i.e., $180 + $465).

§ 20.4330. Illustration 3. *H* and *W* are married and file a joint tax return. *H* and *W*'s taxable income for the year 1994 is $27,750. *H* and *W* have three children: *K*, a seventeen-year-old daughter; D, a twelve-year-old daughter; and S, a nine-year-old son. All three children are supported by their parents and qualify as dependent exemption deductions for H and W. None of the children has earned income and none has any nonitemized deductions. None of the children has itemized deductions in excess of that child's standard deduction. K has unearned income of $14,000. D has unearned income of $5,000. S has unearned income of $2,700.

K is not allowed a personal exemption deduction, and she is entitled to a standard deduction of only $600. K's taxable income is $13,400. Since K has already attained her fourteenth birthday, the kiddie tax does not apply to her. The tax on K's income is $2,010.

D has unearned income of $5,200 and taxable income of $4,600. D's net unearned income is $4,000. S has unearned income of $2,900 and taxable income of $2,300. S has net unearned income of $1,700.

The tax liability of D is the sum of two partial taxes. The first partial tax is the tax at normal rates on the $600 difference between D's taxable income ($4,600) and D's net unearned income ($4,000). The partial tax on that $600 of income is $90. The partial tax on D's $4,000 of net unearned income is D's share of the allocable parental tax. The allocable parental tax is determined by adding to H and W's taxable income of $27,750 the sum of S and D's net unearned income ($4,000 + $1,700 = $5,700) and computing the additional tax incurred by adding that amount. If $5,700 is added to H and W's taxable income, it would increase their taxable income to $33,450, and would cause a tax liability of $6,896. The tax liability caused by the parents' taxable income of $27,750 is $5,300. The additional tax incurred by adding the children's net unearned income to the parents' taxable income is $1,596, and that amount constitutes the allocable parental tax. The allocable parental tax is then allocated between D and S in proportion to their respective net unearned incomes. No portion is allocated to K since K is not subject to the kiddie tax provisions. So approximately 70% of the allocable parental tax is allocated to D—that is, 70% of $1,596 or a little more than $1,117 is D's share of the allocable parental tax. D's total tax liability is then $90 + $1,117 = $1,207.

The tax liability of S is the sum of two partial taxes. The partial tax on the $600 difference between S's taxable income and his net unearned income is $90. S's share of the allocable parental tax is about 30% of $1,596 or a little less than $479. So, the total tax liability of S is $569 (i.e., $90 + $479).

§ 20.5000. SALES UNDER THE INSTALLMENT METHOD. In the absence of a statutory provision, a cash method taxpayer who sells property for a profit and receives as full or partial consideration a debt instrument of the purchaser that is payable in installments over a period of time usually would have to treat the fair market value of the debt instrument as an amount realized in the year of sale. In such cases, the taxpayer would have to recognize the entire gain on the sale of the asset before the taxpayer received the cash that he might need to pay the tax thereon. IRC §§ 453–453B address this problem. IRC § 453 provides that gain realized from the sale of property under an installment sales contract may be spread over the period in which payments are made if certain conditions are met. This method of reporting is available at the election of the taxpayer on the sale of any type of property (other than properties and sales described in **§§ 20.5100–20.5150**) where at least one payment is to be made after the close of the taxable year in which the disposition occurred. IRC § 453(b)(1). In such cases, the installment method will apply unless the taxpayer affirmatively elects not to have it apply. IRC § 453(d). The election out of installment treatment must be made on or before the due date (including extensions of time) for filing the taxpayer's return for the year in which the disposition occurs. A tardy election will rarely be permitted and then only if the taxpayer can show good cause. Temp. Reg. § 15A.453–1(d)(3)(ii).

§ 20.5100. Property Disqualified from Installment Treatment. The installment method cannot be used for the sale of stocks and bonds that are traded on an established securities market, and the installment method also cannot be used for the sale of certain other properties of a kind that are regularly traded on an established market. IRC § 453(k)(2). Because of IRC § 453(b)(2), a so-called "dealer disposition" does not qualify for installment reporting under IRC § 453. A "dealer disposition" is a disposition of: (1) real property which is held by the taxpayer for sale to customers in the ordinary course of the taxpayer's trade or business, or (2) personal property by a person who regularly sells or otherwise disposes of personal property of the same type on the installment plan. IRC § 453(l)(1). A limited exception permits installment reporting for the disposition of property used or produced in the trade or business of farming and for the disposition of certain time share rights and residential lots. IRC § 453(l)(2), (3). The installment method is not available for sales of personalty that would be included in the taxpayer's inventory if on hand at the close of the taxable year. IRC § 453(b)(2)(B). The installment method is not available for sales of personalty under a revolving credit plan. IRC § 453(k)(1). A revolving credit plan is a plan under which customers of the taxpayer who purchase personalty on credit have their debts accumulated into a single account for which the customer agrees to make payments each month of a part of his balance.

§ 20.5110. Sale of Depreciable Property to or by a Controlled Entity. The installment method is not available for sales or depreciable property between a person and a controlled entity or between certain commonly controlled entities or between a taxpayer and a trust in which the taxpayer or his spouse have a beneficial interest (other than a remote contingent interest). IRC § 453(g). This exclusion does not apply if Federal income tax avoidance was not one of the principal purposes of making the disposition. IRC § 453(g)(2).

§ 20.5120. Recognition of Recapture Income. When property, all o r part of whose gain is subject to the recapture of depreciation provisions of IRC §§ 1245 or 1250, is sold on an installment basis, the installment reporting rules do not apply to so much of the seller's gain as is subject to those recapture rules. The property's section 1245 or section 1250 recapture income must be recognized by the seller in the year of sale regardless of when the seller receives cash payments. IRC § 453(i). The recapture of depreciation rules of IRC §§ 1245 and 1250 are discussed at §§ **19.3000–19.3330.**

§ 20.5130. Contingent Selling Price. Prior to the adoption of the Installment Sales Revision Act of 1980, the installment method did not apply if the selling price could not be determined with reasonable accuracy. The 1980 Act, however, permits the installment method to be used in cases where the gross profit, the total contract price, or both cannot be readily ascertained. IRC § 453(j)(2). If the aggregate selling price of a sale or other disposition cannot be determined by the close of the taxable year in which the sale or disposition occurred, the transaction is referred to as a "contingent payment sale." The manner in which contingent payment sales are to be reported under the installment method is set forth in Temp. Reg. § 15A.453–1(c).

§ 20.5140. Nondealer Dispositions. As noted in § **20.5100**, the installment method of reporting is not available for "dealer dispositions" (and dispositions of certain farm property, residential lots, and timeshares are not treated as "dealer dispositions"). Several other exclusions from installment method reporting are described above. If a disposition of property qualifies for installment reporting, and if the amount of the sales price for the property exceeds $150,000, then two special rules may apply—one requiring the taxpayer to make interest payments to the Service and one imposing special consequences if the installment obligation is pledged as security for a loan. IRC § 453A. The interest and pledging rules that are imposed by IRC § 453A are described below in §§ **20.5141** and **20.5142.** These two special rules will not apply unless: (1) the installment obligation that the taxpayer acquired in the disposition in question is outstanding at the close of the taxable year, and (2) the aggregate face amount of the installment obligations that the taxpayer acquired in dispositions of property (in which the sales price exceeded $150,000) in that taxable year and which amounts are outstanding at the close of the taxable year exceeds $5,000,000. IRC § 453A(b). These special rules do not apply to dispositions of certain farm property, residential lots, and timeshares; but other interest rules [IRC § 453(1)(3)] may apply to installment sales of residential lots and timeshares. IRC § 453A(b)(3), (4).

§ **20.5141.   Interest Payments.** If an installment obligation that is subject to IRC § 453A as described above is outstanding at the close of a taxable year, the taxpayer is required to make an interest payment to the Service for the benefit the taxpayer enjoys from having his tax liability deferred under the installment method of reporting. The rate of interest is the same rate as is imposed by IRC § 6621(a)(2) on a taxpayer for the underpayment of a tax liability. IRC § 453A(c)(2)(B). The interest rate is applied against the "applicable percentage of the deferred tax liability" with respect to such obligation. The "deferred tax liability" for an installment obligation is the product of multiplying the unrecognized gain from the obligation as of the close of the taxable year times the maximum rate of tax applied by either IRC §§ 1 or 11, whichever is appropriate, for that taxable year. IRC § 453A(c)(3). The "applicable percentage" that is applied to the "deferred tax liability" is determined by dividing (1) the amount by which the aggregate face amount of all such installment obligations that are outstanding at the close of the taxable year exceeds $5,000,000 by (2) the aggregate face amount of all such installment obligations that is outstanding at the close of the taxable year.

§ 20.5142. Pledges of Installment Obligations. If an installment obligation that is subject to IRC § 453A, as described in **§ 20.5140**, is used as security to secure a loan, the net proceeds of the secured debt will be treated as a payment that was made on the installment obligation that serves as the security for the debt. IRC § 453A(d). The amount of such constructive payment is subject to a ceiling described in IRC § 453A(d)(2). Of course, the constructive payment will cause the taxpayer to recognize all or some portion of the gain that was deferred by using the installment method of reporting. See **§ 20.5300.**

§ 20.5150. Installment Sale to Related Party. Prior to the adoption of the Installment Sales Revision Act of 1980, taxpayers were sometimes able to use the installment method as a tax avoidance device by selling an appreciated asset to a related party on an installment sale. The purchaser would acquire a basis in the asset equal to the purchase price and, thus, could promptly sell the asset to a third party for cash and recognize no income thereby. The income recognized by the original vendor (which was the source of the step-up in basis that the purchaser obtained) would be recognized in stages over a period of years. The 1980 Act closed that loophole. IRC § 453(e).

§ 20.5200. Definitions. The definition of the following terms are peculiar to the reporting of income under the installment method.

§ 20.5210. Selling Price. The selling price is the established purchase price for the property (i.e., the amount that the parties agree is to be paid for the property), but the selling price does not include interest payments. When mortgaged or encumbered property is sold and the purchaser either assumes the debt or takes the property subject to that mortgage or encumbrance, the selling price includes the amount of the mortgage or encumbering debt. Treas. Reg. § 1.453–4(c); Temp. Reg. § 15A.453–1(b)(2)(ii). If any interest is imputed to the transaction under IRC §§ 483 or 1274, the imputed interest is excluded from the selling price; that is, the nominal price must be reduced by the amount that is treated as interest. Commissions or other selling expenses of the vendor do not reduce the selling price. Temp. Reg. § 15A.453–1(b)(2)(ii).

§ 20.5220. Total Contract Price. The total contract price is equal to the selling price except that if the property sold is subject to a "qualifying indebtedness" and the purchaser either assumes that debt or takes the property subject thereto, the total contract price includes only so much of that debt as exceeds the vendor's basis in the property. Temp. Reg. § 15A.453–1(b)(2)(iii). The term "qualifying indebtedness" is defined in Temp. Reg. § 15A.453–1(b)(2)(iv).

§ 20.5230. Gross Profit. The vendor's gross profit is equal to the difference between the selling price and the vendor's adjusted basis in the property. The gross profit effectively is reduced by commissions and other selling expenses of the vendor. Temp. Reg. § 15A.453–1(b)(2)(v).

§ 20.5240. Payments. For purposes of reporting gain on the installment method, payments include: cash or other property, marketable securities, *certain* assumptions of liabilities, evidences of indebtedness of the purchaser that are payable on demand, and evidences of indebtedness of a corporation or government that are readily tradable. Temp. Reg. § 15A.453–1(b)(3). In general, the seller's receipt of the purchaser's debt instrument is *not* a payment unless the debt is payable on demand or the debt is a readily tradable instrument of a corporation or a government. IRC § 453(f)(3), (4); Temp. Reg. § 15A.453–1(e)(1). The amount (if any) by which the mortgage (or certain other encumbrances) on the property that are assumed or accepted by the purchaser exceeds the vendor's basis in the property constitutes a payment received in the year of sale. Otherwise, the purchaser's assumption or acceptance of a mortgage debt is not a payment.

§ 20.5300. Installment Reporting. Where a sale qualifies for installment reporting and the vendor does not make a timely election under IRC § 453(d) to exempt the sale from the installment method, the vendor will include in income for a taxable year only that proportion of the payments received (or deemed to have been received) in that year which equals the proportion of gross profit to the total contract price. Temp. Reg. § 15A.453–1(b)(2)(i). Interest payments are reported when received or deemed to have been received; interest is not included in the installment reporting of the vendor's profit.

§ 20.5400. Illustration. In Year One, Mrs. *S* purchased a house for $20,000 cash. Mrs. *S* used the house as a summer residence, and she never rented it to anyone. In Year Six, Mrs. *S* sold the house to

Mr. *B* for $30,000, and she incurred no commissions or other selling expenses in that sale. Mr. *B* paid a $5,000 down payment in Year Six, and he gave Mrs. *S* a mortgage to secure his debt for the remaining $25,000, which debt was to be satisfied over a 30–year period and bore adequate interest so that no interest was imputed to the transaction under IRC §§ 483 or 1274. In addition to the down payment, Mr. *B* made payments totalling $1,000 against the principal of the debt during Year Six, and he made timely payments of his interest obligation. Mrs. *S* did not elect out of the installment method; thus, IRC § 453 is applicable. Under that method, Mrs. *S*'s gross profit is $10,000 which is the difference between her basis of $20,000 (since no improvements were made on the house and no depreciation was allowable) and the $30,000 selling price. Mrs. *S*'s contract price is $30,000. In this case, the contract price and the selling price are equal because the property was not transferred subject to an existing encumbrance. The proportion of gross profit to total contract price, one-third, will be applied to the $6,000 payments made in Year Six; thus, 1/3 x $6,000 = $2,000. Mrs. *S* will report the $2,000 as gross income, and she will report one-third of all future principal payments as gross income. The character of the gross income that Mrs. *S* recognizes from her receipt of the installment payments will be determined by the property that she sold. In this case, it appears that the income will be a long-term capital gain.

§ 20.5500. Disposition of Installment Obligation. If an installment obligation is satisfied at less than its face value, if it is canceled or becomes unenforceable, or if it is distributed, transmitted, sold, or otherwise disposed of, gain or loss will be recognized in an amount equal to the difference between the basis of the obligation and: (a) the amount realized on a sale or exchange or satisfaction for less than face value; or (b) the fair market value of the installment obligation at the time of distribution, transmission, or disposition other than a sale or exchange or cancellation. IRC § 453B. Any gain or loss so recognized is treated as resulting from the sale or exchange of the property for which the installment obligation was received. If the obligor and obligee of a cancelled installment obligation (or one that becomes unenforceable) are related (within the meaning of IRC § 453(f)(1)), the fair market value of the obligation is deemed to be no less than its face amount. IRC § 453B(f)(2).

§ 20.5510. Illustration. If in the illustration at **§ 20.5400**, in Year Seven, Mrs. *S* made a gift to her son, *R*, of the debt owing to her from Mr. *B*, and if the value of Mr. *B*'s obligation at that date was $24,000 (the unpaid balance of the obligation), Mrs. *S* would recognize a gain of $8,000 because of the disposition of the installment obligation. Mrs. S had a basis of $16,000 in the obligation (the basis equals the difference between the face value of the obligation ($24,000) and the amount of income to be returned when it is paid in full ($8,000) [IRC § 453B(b)]), and, consequently, she recognized $8,000 income on the disposition.

§ 20.5520. **Exceptions.** A number of types of dispositions or transmissions of installment obligations are permitted to be made without causing the recognition of gain. For example, in general, transfers to a controlled corporation, transfers effected by death, and, in many cases, transfers in liquidation of a controlled subsidiary corporation do not cause the transferor to recognize a gain. IRC § 453B(c), (d); Treas. Reg. § 1.453–9(c)(2). A transfer of an installment obligation to a spouse or former spouse will not cause the transferor to recognize income if the transfer is one that is described in IRC § 1041, but this exception does not apply if the transfer is made in trust. IRC § 453B(g).

§ 20.5530. **Cancellation at Obligee's Death.** When the terms of an installment obligation provide that it is to be canceled at the death of the obligee, the debt instrument is sometimes referred to as a "death-terminating installment note," and the sale for which such an instrument was received as partial or full payment is sometimes referred to as a "death-terminating installment sale." The Tax Court and the Eighth Circuit treated the cancellation of a death-terminating installment note upon the obligee's death as a disposition of the note (under IRC § 453B(f)(1)) that triggers recognition of income to the obligee or to his estate (as described in **§ 20.5500**). The Tax Court held that it was the obligee himself who recognized the income, but the Eighth Circuit held that the income is recognized by the obligee's estate as "income in respect of a decedent" (IRD) under IRC § 691(a)(5)(A)(iii). *Estate of Frane v. Commissioner*, 98 T.C. 341 (1992), aff'd in part and rev'd in part, 998 F.2d 567 (8th Cir. 1993). The concept of "income in respect of a decedent" is discussed in Chapter Twenty One.

§ 20.5540. **Change of Terms of Installment Obligation.** As discussed in **§§ 16.1700–16.1720**, the proposed regulations provide that a significant modification of the terms of a debt instrument will cause there to be a constructive exchange of the "old" debt instrument for a "new" debt, and that constructive exchange will cause the holder of the instrument to realize gain or loss.

However, the preamble to those proposed regulations indicate that they do not apply to a modification of the terms of an installment obligation. See § **16.1720**. Consequently, the proposed regulations do not cause a modification of the terms of such an instrument to constitute a disposition of the instrument.

The question then is whether, apart from the proposed regulations, a modification of the terms of an installment obligation will trigger a disposition of that instrument so that any deferred gain will be recognized. The cases and rulings on this issue to date have held that a change in the rate of interest or the period for payment of such a debt or even the identity of the obligor does *not* constitute a disposition of the instrument and so does not trigger the recognition of deferred gain. *Rhombar v. Commissioner*, 47 T.C. 75, 86 (1966), Acq., aff'd on other grounds, 386 F.2d 510 (2d Cir. 1967); *Cunningham v. Commissioner*, 44 T.C. 103 (1965), Acq.; Rev. Rul. 82–122; Rev. Rul. 75–457; Rev. Rul. 74–157; Rev. Rul 68–419; LR 8932011; and LR 8710068.

The purpose of permitting installment reporting of the amounts received on an installment instrument that was acquired as part of the payment for the sale of an item is to defer the imposition of tax on the gain from the sale of the underlying item until the seller has cash in hand with which to pay the tax. If the seller disposes of the installment obligation or if his rights in that instrument are terminated, there is no longer any justification to defer his recognition of the unrecognized gain from the original sale. In such cases, the tax on the remaining gain becomes payable when the seller's right to subsequent payments on the installment instrument cease. But, a modification of the amount of interest payable, or of the schedule on which payments are to be made, or a change of the identity of the obligor who will make the payments does not change the conditions on which deferral of gain on installment sales is granted. Accordingly, such changes do not accelerate the seller's recognition of gain and consequent liability for payment of tax. Rev. Rul. 82–122.

*

CHAPTER TWENTY-ONE

INCOME IN RESPECT OF A DECEDENT (IRD)

§ 21.0000. INCOME IN RESPECT OF A DECEDENT (IRD).

§ 21.1000. DEFINITION OF "INCOME IN RESPECT OF A DECEDENT" (IRD).
There is no statutory definition of "income in respect of a decedent," hereinafter referred to as "IRD." The term refers to items of income which a decedent earned or was entitled to before his death, but which were not received (if on the cash method of accounting) or did not accrue (if on the accrual method of accounting) until at or after his death. Treas. Reg. § 1.691(a)–1(b). In other words, although earned beforehand, the income was not recognized for tax purposes until after the decedent's death.

§ 21.2000. COMMON EXAMPLES OF IRD.

(a) Income from personal services of a cash method decedent (e.g., salaries, fees, bonuses and commissions, including renewal commissions of a deceased life insurance agent) which is payable for services performed during the decedent's life but which is not paid until after his death constitutes IRD. Treas. Reg. § 1.691(a)–2(b), Exs. (1) and (2).

(b) When property is sold by the decedent prior to his death, any amount realized thereon after his death will constitute IRD. However, if a sale is not completed prior to death (i.e., when title has not passed to the purchaser), income from a sale after death will not constitute IRD irrespective of whether the decedent had executed a valid contract to sell prior to his death. Treas. Reg. § 1.691(a)–2(b), Exs. (4) and (5).

(c) When decedent was a cash method taxpayer, uncollected interest earned on United States savings bonds is taxable as IRD when collected. Treas. Reg. § 1.691(a)–2(b), Ex. (3).

(d) Payment of a postmortem bonus award is IRD if the decedent had a right or entitlement to the bonus at the time of his death. See *Rollert Residuary Trust v. Commissioner*, 80 T.C. 619 (1983), aff'd 752 F.2d 1128 (6th Cir. 1985), where the Court held the postmortem bonus to be IRD in view of the employer's established practice of awarding bonuses and its tentative decision before decedent's death to assign funds to the bonus pool. Prior to the decedent's death, the company tentatively decided to award bonuses to all executive vice presidents, including the decedent, subject to forfeiture if, during a stated period, the employee failed to continue in the employ of the company or committed acts inimical to the company's interests. Those conditions terminated on the decedent's death so that the decedent had a nonforfeitable right to the bonus at the time of his death. While the company was not committed to making the bonus at the time of decedent's death, the company's consistent practice of paying bonuses in such cases was sufficient.

(e) Items to which the decedent had a contingent claim at the time of his death to the extent that such items would have constituted gross income to the decedent had he lived to collect it are IRD. Treas. Reg. § 1.691(a)–1(b). See *Rollert Residuary Trust v. Commissioner, supra.*

(f) Dividends payable after death in accordance with decedent's ownership of stock at the record date for the dividend prior to his death are IRD.

(g) When the decedent had been reporting gain on the installment method from a sale made while he was living, the estate or beneficiary will likewise report it in the same way and such gain constitutes IRD. IRC § 691(a)(4). A transfer of an installment obligation from the decedent's estate to a legatee (other than to a legatee who is the obligor of the debt instrument) is not a disposition that accelerates the recognition of the gain. IRC § 453(c); Treas. Reg. § 1.691(a)–4(b), 5(b). A cancellation of the unpaid balance of the installment obligation on the decedent's death or a transfer of the obligation by the estate to the obligor will constitute a disposition that triggers the recognition of IRD by the estate. See § **20.5540.**

(h) All payments coming within IRC § 736(a), including a share of profits after death, made by a partnership to the estate or other beneficiary are IRD. A deceased partner's share of the income of the partnership which is attributable to the period ending with the date of death is IRD. This is true even as to amounts withdrawn from the partnership by the decedent during the taxable year of the partnership in which death occurred. IRC § 753; Treas. Reg. § 1.753–1(b).

§ **21.3000.   REPORTING OF IRD.** An item of IRD is reported as gross income in the year of collection by the decedent's estate or by the beneficiary or transferee who receives the item irrespective of whether they report their income on the cash or accrual method. IRC § 691(a)(1).

§ 21.3100. Illustrations of IRD.

§ 21.3110. Illustration 1.

A widow acquired by bequest from her deceased husband the right to receive renewal commissions on life insurance sold by him during his lifetime, which commissions were payable over a period of years. The widow died before the period expired. Those commissions paid to the widow prior to her death are IRD and are includable in her gross income. The widow's son inherited from her the right to receive the remaining commissions, and his collection of those commissions is also IRD and must be included in the son's gross income. Treas. Reg. § 1.691(a)–2(b), Ex. (2).

§ 21.3120. Illustration 2.

A decedent was entitled at the date of her death to a salary payment from her employer. Her estate collected the payment. The payment is IRD, and the estate must include it in gross income. See Treas. Reg. § 1.691(a)–2(b), Ex. (1). If the estate collected only one-third of the payments due and then distributed the balance of the claim to decedent's sister (who was her beneficiary), the amounts subsequently collected by the sister are IRD and included in the sister's gross income.

§ 21.3200. Characterization.

IRD retains the same character to the recipient that it would have had to the decedent had the decedent lived to collect it. IRC § 691(a)(3). Note that if in the same year, the estate collects IRD and distributes an amount equal to the IRD to a beneficiary of the estate (assuming that the estate had no other gross income that year and the distribution to the beneficiary constitutes a distribution of so-called "distributable net income"), the distribution to the beneficiary will have the same character as the IRD. IRC § 662(b).

§ 21.3300. Basis.

Items of IRD do not acquire a new basis at death. IRC § 1014(c). Thus, the decedent's basis (if any) carries over and no adjustments are made.

§ 21.3400. Disposition of Rights to IRD.

§ 21.3410. General.

If the recipient of a right to receive IRD sells or otherwise transfers it to someone who is not required to treat the collection of the item as IRD of the decedent, the amount of the consideration, if any, received for the right or the fair market value of the right at the time of transfer, whichever is greater, is includable in the transferor's gross income.

§ 21.3420. Illustration. At date of death, D was entitled to a $60,000 salary payment to be made in six equal annual installments. His estate collected two installments, reported those installment payments as IRD, and then distributed the right to the remaining four installments to Smith, who was the residuary legatee of the estate. Smith collected the third installment, and he must report the amount collected as IRD. Smith then sold his right to the remaining $30,000 of payments for an amount equal to the fair market value of the right to such payments. The amount paid to Smith for the sale of the right to the remaining three installments is includable in his gross income at the date of sale.

§ 21.3430. Exceptions. On the disposition of a right to IRD, the transferor does not include the item in his gross income if the transfer results from the recipient's death, or the transfer is a distribution from an estate to a beneficiary. In either of the above events, the transferee reports the IRD item as gross income when collected or transferred by him. IRC § 691(a)(2).

§ 21.4000. INCOME TAX DEDUCTIONS ALLOWED.

§ 21.4100. Deductions for Federal Estate Taxes Paid. The tax law would be unduly harsh if items of IRD were taxed both for federal estate tax purposes as part of the decedent's gross estate and also for income tax purposes as gross income of the person who collected the IRD item after receiving it from the decedent. After all, had the decedent lived to include the items in his personal income tax return, the income tax paid would have reduced, on his subsequent death, the size of his gross estate and resulted in a smaller federal estate tax liability. However, IRD is subjected to both income tax and estate tax burdens. To mitigate this double inclusion of the same item, and to approximate the total amount of taxes (both income and estate tax) that would have been paid if the income item had been received by the decedent before his death, Congress enacted IRC § 691(c) which allows an income tax deduction to the recipient of an item of IRD for that item's allocable share of the amount of the decedent's federal estate tax that is attributable to the net value, for estate tax purposes, of the decedent's total amount of IRD. This deduction is not included in the computation of a taxpayer's adjusted gross income (AGI)—i.e., it is an itemized deduction. See Rev. Rul. 78–203. The significance of classifying a deduction as "an itemized deduction" is discussed at **§ 3.2000.** The deduction is *not* subject to the 2% of AGI floor that applies to some itemized deductions. IRC

§ 67(b)(7). However, it is subject to the overall limitation on itemized deductions that is imposed by IRC § 68. While this item is an income tax deduction, it is sometimes called an "estate tax deduction" since the amount of the income tax deduction is determined by reference to the estate tax liability caused by the decedent's IRD. In determining the amount of the deduction, the decedent's estate tax is reduced by all credits allowed against that tax; the deduction is computed on the basis of the *net* estate tax. IRC § 691(c)(2)(A). A similar deduction is allowed for IRD that was subjected to a generation-skipping tax. IRC § 691(c)(3).

The reduction of the estate tax deduction that occurs when the overall limitation of IRC § 68 is triggered runs afoul of the basic purpose for allowing the deduction–to wit, to impose on IRD received after the decedent's death approximately the same amount of aggregate estate and income tax burden that would have been borne if the item had been received by the decedent during his life. There is no apparent reason for excluding high bracket taxpayers from the full benefit of that treatment. See Jeffrey H. Kahn, *Beyond the Little Dutch Boy: An Argument for Structural Change in Tax Deduction Classification*, 80 Wash. L. Rev. 1 (2005).

> **§ 21.4110.   Net Value of IRD.** The net value of IRD equals the total estate tax value of all IRC § 691 income less the total estate tax deductions allowable for all deductions in respect to a decedent under IRC § 691(b). See **§ 21.4200.**
>
> **§ 21.4120.   Computation of Estate Tax Deduction for IRD.** An income tax deduction is permitted for the estate tax attributable to the inclusion of IRD in the decedent's gross estate, and this income tax deduction is referred to as an "estate tax deduction." **§ 21.4100.** The total amount of deductions allowable for the estate tax on all IRD items is the difference between: (a) the net estate tax actually payable, and (b) the recomputed net estate tax on the taxable estate which is determined by excluding the net value of the IRD items that were included in the decedent's gross estate. The recomputation must take into account any estate tax deductions that are lost as a consequence of excluding the net value of the IRD items from the decedent's taxable estate. Thus, the estate tax that is deductible for income tax purposes is determined at the highest marginal rates on the net value of the IRD. IRC § 691(c)(2). The total estate tax that is deductible must then be allocated among the several items of IRD.

§ 21.4130.   Collection of a Portion of the Decedent's Total IRD.   A person who receives only a portion of a decedent's total IRD is allowed a proportionate part of the estate tax deduction. The amount of a taxpayer's deduction is the proportion of the death taxes attributable to the net value of all IRD items that the gross value for estate tax purposes of the IRD that is included in the taxpayer's gross income bears to the gross value for estate tax purposes of all of the decedent's IRD. See Treas. Reg. § 1.691(c)–1(d), Ex. (1). Thus, although the total deduction for death taxes is based on the *net* value of the IRD, the apportionment of the deduction among items of IRD is based on the ratio that the *gross* estate tax value of each such item bears to the *gross* estate tax value of all such items. Treas. Reg. § 1.691(c)–1(d), Ex. (1). However, if the amount included in a taxpayer's gross income because of the collection of the IRD item is less than the gross estate tax value of that item, the proportion described above is based on the lower amount included in income rather than on the gross estate tax value of the item. IRC § 691(c)(1)(A).

§ 21.4200.   Deduction in Respect of a Decedent.   Since income earned by a decedent but recognized after his death may constitute IRD, a fair corollary would permit an income tax deduction to those who pay expenses incurred by the decedent if the decedent would have been entitled to a deduction had he lived. Congress adopted such a corollary provision for certain deductions in IRC § 691(b). Obligations incurred by a decedent prior to his death which were not properly allowable on the final income tax return for the decedent (or on any prior income tax return) but which otherwise would have qualified as deductions under IRC §§ 162, 163, 164 or 212 are allowed as deductions, in the year in which paid, to the estate or beneficiary who makes the payment. Similarly, a credit for foreign death taxes on IRD is allowed to the estate or beneficiary liable for and making such payment, and a depletion allowance under IRC § 611 is allowed to the person who receives the income to which such depletion deduction relates.

§ 21.4210.   Restriction.   Note that the deduction in respect of a decedent is allowed only for business expenses (deductible under IRC § 162), nonbusiness expenses (deductible under IRC § 212), interest charges (to the extent deductible under IRC § 163), deductible taxes (IRC § 164), and depletion deductions (IRC § 611). Note that not all interest expenses are deductible. Only the recipient of the income to which a depletion deduction (under IRC § 611) relates may take that deduction.

§ 21.4220. Double Deductions Allowed. Deductions in respect of a decedent are allowed both as an income tax deduction to the one making the payment and as a federal estate tax deduction as a claim against the estate under IRC § 2053. IRC § 642(g) and Treas. Reg. § 1.642(g)–2.

*

TABLE OF INTERNAL REVENUE CODE SECTIONS

References are to section numbers.

---

*

INDEX

References are to section numbers.

---

†